The publisher gratefully acknowledges the generous contribution to this book provided by the General Endowment Fund of the Associates of the University of California Press.

William Mulholland
and the
Rise of Los Angeles

William Mulholland

and the

Rise of Los Angeles

Catherine Mulholland

UNIVERSITY OF CALIFORNIA PRESS
Berkeley · Los Angeles · London

University of California Press
Berkeley and Los Angeles, California

University of California Press, Ltd.
London, England

First paperback printing 2002

Library of Congress Cataloging-in-Publication Data

Mulholland, Catherine.

    William Mulholland and the rise of
Los Angeles / Catherine Mulholland.

      p.   cm.

    Includes bibliographical references and index.

    ISBN 978-0-520-23466-6 (pbk. : alk. paper).

    1. Water-supply—California—Los Angeles—
History. 2. Mulholland, William, 1855–1935.
3. Engineers—California—Los Angeles—
Biography. I. Title.
  HD4464.L7 M85   2000
  979.4'9404'092—dc21   99-048289
  [B]   CIP

Manufactured in the United States of America

14   13   12

10 9 8 7

The paper used in this publication meets the minimum requirements of ANSI/NISO Z39.48-1992
(R 1997) (Permanence of Paper).

Chapter 24 contains material previously published
in modified form as "Mulholland and the St.
Francis Dam," in *The St. Francis Dam Disaster
Revisited*, edited by Doyce B. Nunis, Jr. (Los
Angeles and Ventura: Historical Society of Southern
California and Ventura County Museum of History
and Art, 1995).

*To the memory of
Richard Perry Mulholland
(1925–1992), the Chief's
only grandson*

A story that was the subject of every variety of misrepresentation, not only by those who then lived but likewise in succeeding times: so true is it that all transactions of preeminent importance are wrapt in doubt and obscurity; while some hold for certain facts the most precarious hearsays, others turn facts into falsehood; and both are exaggerated by posterity.

Robert Graves, *I, Claudius*

Contents

List of Illustrations   xi

Preface   xiii

Acknowledgments   xix

1. The Long Journey from Dublin to Los Angeles, 1855–1876   3

2. The City of Angels, 1877   14

3. The Private Water Company and Its Owners, 1878–1879   23

4. Advancing in the Water Business, 1880–1886   30

5. The New Superintendent, 1887–1892   38

6. Water Plots and Politics, 1893–1895   48

7. The Years of Mayor Eaton, 1898–1900   61

8. The City's Victory over the "Grand Monopoly," 1901–1902   75

9. New Regime for a Booming Town, 1903–1904   88

10. Desperate Remedies in a Dry Season, 1904   100

11. A Plan Revealed, 1905   112

12. Preparations for an Aqueduct and a Trip to Washington, D.C., 1906   126

13. The Big Job Begins, 1907   141

14. The Chief and the General, 1908   159

15. Building the Aqueduct: The Best Year, 1909   171

16. Troubles and Interruptions, 1910   183

17. Aqueduct Progress and Political Fireworks, 1911   196

18. The Investigation, 1912   209

19. The Completion of the Aqueduct, 1913   228

20. After the Aqueduct, 1914–1919   249

21. A Stormy Decade Begins, 1920–1923   265

22. Boulder Dam and Dynamite, 1924   282

23. More Dynamite, 1925–1927   299

24. The Saint Francis Dam Disaster and After, 1928–1935   319

Afterword   333

Notes   335

Bibliography   385

Index   393

Illustrations

William Mulholland, 1916   *frontispiece*

plates follow page 136

MAPS

1. Waterworks structures, Elysian Park area   50
2. Los Angeles Aqueduct and adjacent territory
   with divisions, 1908   143
3. Profile of Los Angeles Aqueduct   155
4. Annexations to the City of Los Angeles, 1899–1944   217
5. Greater Los Angeles, 1925   267
6. Southern California water supply, 1925   269
7. Major water distribution facilities, City of Los Angeles   332

Preface

Los Angeles . . . No ordinary rules
explain its past growth or set limits
to its future expansion. It has been,
and will be, a law unto itself.

WILLIAM E. SMYTHE,
The Conquest of Arid America

A HISTORIC DISPUTE

William Mulholland presided over the creation of a water system that
changed forever the course of Southern California history, and in so doing he became the focus of a controversy that has never died. When Los
Angeles went water hunting and laid claim to the waters of the Owens
River over two hundred miles away, its actions so conflicted with competing interests that they gave rise to a struggle of mythic proportions.
Reading the varying accounts of this action reminds one of the classic
paradox *All Cretans are liars, said the man from Crete.* Who lies? Does
everyone lie or does everyone one tell the truth? Even if the dead could
be brought back, could they tell us what we want to know? Writers who
have scrutinized the same public documents, official records, and private
correspondence have arrived at contrary conclusions, so the existing literature on the story of Los Angeles's water is not only voluminous but
also often dissonant.

When I began research for this work in 1989, four books on the subject especially deserved serious consideration, each offering different yet
valuable versions of the water story. The important pioneer effort was
The Water Seekers (1950), by Remi Nadeau, a highly readable work
that subsequent scholarship has somewhat superseded. *Water and Politics: A Study of Water Policies and Administration in the Development
of Los Angeles* (1953), by Vincent Ostrom, is probably the best and most

precise single survey of the subject but tends to be impersonal in its treatment of the individuals involved in the story. *Vision or Villainy: Origins of the Owens Valley–Los Angeles Water Controversy* (1981), by Abraham Hoffman, is a fair-minded and thorough work, especially valuable for its examination of the roles J. B. Lippincott and the Reclamation Service played in the Owens Valley saga. The fourth, *Water and Power* (1982), by William Kahrl (editor of the estimable *California Water Atlas*), while containing a wealth of documentation, technical information, and a valuable bibliography, is also full of inaccuracies and, because of its unremittingly jaundiced view of Los Angeles and its water seekers, ultimately proves to be a polemic masquerading as a scholarly study. *Water and Power* has been influential, however, in subsequent works that have relied and elaborated on Kahrl's views: *Cadillac Desert* (1986), a screed by Marc Reisner on the evils of water development in the West; *Western Times and Water Wars* (1992), by John Walton, a study of Owens Valley that is somewhat in the manner of the *Annales* school of French historiography as found in LeRoy Ladurie's *Montaillou* and that describes the purported injustice inflicted by large governmental power over a small region; and *The Lost Frontier* (1994), by John Sauder, an inquiry into the agricultural losses sustained in Owens Valley because of Los Angeles's water development. Although none of the authors of this latter group is as extreme as the popular Western writer Wallace Stegner, who wrote that he considered building a dam evidence of original sin, each reflects the fin de siècle skepticism toward large water projects along with a disapproval of Los Angeles and a resolute bias favoring Owens Valley. The inclination to side with the underdog is powerful and humane but also risks committing what Bertrand Russell called "the fallacy of the superior virtue of the oppressed." Even the objective scholar-historian Norris Hundley has described Los Angeles as "the West's most notorious water hustler" in *Water and the West* (1975), and in his extensive overview of California water history, *The Great Thirst* (1992), he trivializes the building of the Owens Valley Aqueduct under a pejorative chapter heading, "The Owens Valley Caper." These works' contentions have helped create public perceptions such as a woman recently voiced at an environmental conference I attended when she fairly shouted, "Mulholland was no engineer. All he did was take a few pipes up north and run water down and help make some men rich," or such as a recent news article expressed when it described "the shadowy fiddling that sucked Owens Valley water into Los Angeles." In these versions, Mulholland emerges as an antihero rather than an admired bringer of water. As one of his nieces once ruefully remarked, "The Greeks beat the Trojans, but now, after three thousand years, it is a greater compliment to be called a Trojan."

In fact, the whole thrust of the Los Angeles enterprise looked to the future. Just as Caesar did not look back to Alexander for his model of a Roman empire but anticipated as a model a kind of city-state existing in Rome's own peripheries and provinces, so the leaders of an expanding Los Angeles looked to extend boundaries in order to create a new kind of city. What, after all, made this venture more reprehensible than those undertaken by other American cities that had gone distances to find water: New York to Croton, Boston to Lake Winnipesaukee, and San Francisco to the Tuolumne River in the Sierra Nevada mountain range? Who still rails against the New York Catskill project, which in its construction bought and drowned ten towns and villages, removed three thousand dead from thirty-two cemeteries, relocated eleven miles of rail track, and built ten highway bridges? Furthermore, the New York project was simply a water delivery system, while the Owens River project was to produce electrical energy as well, making it at the time not only a municipally owned utility but also one of the most valuable commercial enterprises in the United States.

SOURCES AND THE ROLE OF THE PRESS

Newspapers, the "diaries of history," have been a rich source for the present work. Because the *Los Angeles Times* has outlived its former competitors, files of those defunct papers must now be sought in selected libraries where, in many cases, they exist only in incomplete runs. While the chief creators of the *Times*, General Harrison Gray Otis and Harry Chandler, enjoy enormous fame in the city's history, few trails of glory follow Colonel J. J. Ayers, Major Horace Bell, Manchester Boddy, Edward Dickson, Edwin T. Earl, J. D. Lynch, and Benjamin C. Truman. Yet all once either owned, published, and/or edited successful and influential newspapers in Los Angeles with editorial slants that are sometimes today overlooked or forgotten. Especially among journalists and popular historians, this imbalance has led to an inflation of the roles of Otis and Chandler as city-makers out of all proportion to the facts. Without in any way minimizing these powerful men's impact on the city's history, I have tried to introduce other opinion-molders who played roles in building the City of Los Angeles.

One must keep alert, however, to journalist Mark Sullivan's caveat that "a newspaper, as respects its fundamental character, is one of the least permanent of institutions . . . it can change ownership overnight," and that "even though it remain in the same ownership, its character, point of view, and policy may be altered by a change in the owner's interests, by his necessity for borrowing money, or otherwise" (*Our Times*, vol. 2, pp. 228–29). A new editor, or even a change in the post of managing-editor, can switch the emphasis upon the coverage of certain subjects. Otis's *Times*, for example, considered the leading booster for building the aqueduct and creating a municipal water system, became, under the later aegis of Harry Chandler, an implacable foe of the Boulder Dam project and the expansion of municipal power. Hearst's *Examiner* also reversed itself, beginning as an editorial foe of the aqueduct and ending as its champion, as well as later supporting Boulder Dam and the municipal ownership of water and power.

Archival papers of civic leaders and engineers also proved helpful because they document many of the interconnections between business interests and the water story of Los Angeles. Mulholland's friendship with Henry O'Melveny and Charles Dwight Willard was further demonstrated in their papers and journals, while those of political leaders John R. Haynes and Meyer Lissner augment the public record of their relationships during the rise of progressivism in Los Angeles and California.

ANOTHER VOICE ON THE SUBJECT

Biographies of engineers are scarce since they must deal with technical matters often beyond the ken of historian or biographer. Because the public and administrative life of an engineer tends to overshadow the private, it becomes the biographer's duty to render that public side in vivid, yet accurate, style. Aside from memoirs written soon after his death by close associates (engineers J. B. Lippincott and Harvey Van Norman), the first attempt at a biography of William Mulholland was a monograph, *William Mulholland: A Forgotten Forefather* (1976), by Robert Matson. Written for a master's degree at the University of the Pacific, it derives mostly from secondary materials and is only a partial account of the engineer's life. *Rivers in the Desert* (1993), by Margaret Leslie Davis, purports to be a "major biography" but is not. Mulholland's first fifty years remain unexplored, while accounts of his private and domestic life rely on hearsay and public records of marriage, divorce, and probate. Marred by many minor factual errors, the work demonstrates little depth of understanding about the complexity of the water story.

For background and information to supplement personal knowledge of the years when Mulholland was an anonymous figure in Los Angeles (1878–1904), I turned to city council proceedings, Department of Water and Power records, and reminiscences of Mulholland's early employees and associates. Only scanty information remains from the years 1888 to 1902, when he headed the private water company that ran the city's system. With records either lost or destroyed, the *Times* here proved valuable, as it provided the most detailed coverage of city council meetings during those years, when the official proceedings tended to be skeletal. Family scrapbooks, papers, and reminiscences were also useful, but especially helpful were Mulholland's office files (1902–1928) from the Los Angeles Water Department, which only in recent years have been discovered, catalogued, and made available.

This work is not only a biography of William Mulholland but also an account of how a small pueblo in a semiarid basin was able to secure the water and power that allowed it to grow into a major city. It describes the many associates—some heroic, some not—who worked in this epic endeavor. Because the water story remains the founding myth of modern Los Angeles, this work also calls into question many current versions of the so-called Owens Valley controversy. Was there really rape and betrayal by the city's leaders? Was the entire building of the Owens Valley Aqueduct the result of a conspiracy among Los Angeles capitalists to acquire water in order to develop for speculation their holdings in the San Fernando Valley? Who were the chief enemies of the city's water seekers? Also discussed are the developments leading to the building of Boulder Dam and, finally, the major disaster of the Saint Francis Dam (1928), which ended Mulholland's career.

The epigraph by Tacitus from Robert Graves's *I, Claudius* underscores the problems inherent in telling this story, with which in a sense I have lived all my life and which even now may be disbelieved, so fixed in some minds is the certainty of what transpired that nothing would alter their opinion. As the subject's granddaughter, my objectivity will be questioned. To answer that, I turn again to Tacitus, who almost two thousand years ago wrote of the profoundly divided opinions of those who were "bitterly alienated" by an event and those who were "deeply committed" to it: "But whereas the reader can easily discount the bias of the time-serving historian, detraction and spite find a ready audience.

Adulation bears the ugly taint of subservience, but malice gives the false impression of being independent." When the Chinese general Chou en Lai was asked in the 1950s what he thought had been the French Revolution's impact on western Europe, he replied that it was too soon to tell. Without insisting on Chou's long view, I would suggest that if there is to be a last word on this saga, it is yet to come. I also believe that diverse voices should continue to be heard, and I hope that mine will be among them.

Acknowledgments

Help comes from many people in a work such as this, with debts owed to librarians and archivists of special collections throughout California. Foremost of value have been materials from the Los Angeles Department of Water and Power, with special thanks to Elizabeth Wimmer, retired public affairs officer, who led me to obscure items of interest when I first began my research. Later, Paul Soifer and Tom Connors, archivists of the Records Center of the LADWP, were also most helpful, as was Linda M. Colton, former principal civil engineering drafting technician, who helped prepare the maps in this book.

Hynda L. Rudd, records management officer, and Robert B. Freeman, archivist, were generous and helpful in availing me of old city council records in the City Archives of Los Angeles.

I also extend my gratitude to the following libraries and their staffs:
Bancroft Library, University of California, Berkeley
Delmar Oviatt Library, California State University, Northridge
Huntington Library, San Marino
Los Angeles County Library, San Fernando
Los Angeles Public Library
National Library, Dublin, Ireland
Research Library, University of California, Los Angeles
Stanford University Libraries, Department of Special Collections
Water Resources Center, University of California, Berkeley

Thanks also to Thomas F. Andrews, executive director of the Historical Society of Southern California, who encouraged me to continue my work at a time when it seemed a forlorn hope, and to author, scholar, and editor Doyce B. Nunis, Jr., who heartened me with the publication of my article on Mulholland and the Saint Francis Dam in *The St. Francis Dam Disaster Revisited* (1995).

In the later stages of my work, new acquaintances took time out from their busy lives to give invaluable time and effort on my behalf. To them I give sincerest thanks:

Steven P. Erie, professor of political science at U.C., San Diego, whose own work on the rise and growth of Los Angeles has spurred me to complete my own, has been of immeasurable help with sage counsel, friendship, and as a final boon, an introduction to William Deverell for a final paving of the way to publication.

William Deverell, associate professor of history at the California Institute of Technology, performed the great service of vetting the manuscript, making significant editorial comments, and recommending it to the University of California Press.

I owe a great debt to engineer Robert V. Phillips, whose knowledge of western water matters is encyclopedic and whose friendship I prize. His father, James E. Phillips, a close associate of both Mulholland and his successor, Harvey Van Norman, was in charge of the water affairs of the Aqueduct Division of the Los Angeles Department of Water and Power from 1928 until his death in 1940. The younger Phillips, after years as an engineer of the Owens Valley Division of the Aqueduct at Independence, served as general manager and chief engineer of the Los Angeles Department of Water and Power from 1972 to 1975 and as a member of the management board of the Navajo Tribal Utility Authority (an enterprise of the Navajo Nation) from 1976 to 1993. Not only did Phillips vet my manuscript and offer advice and information on technical matters of engineering and hydrology, as a longtime dweller in Owens Valley, he provided valuable insights into aspects of the controversy there.

I am grateful to J. David Rogers, civil and geological engineer, founder of his own consulting firms (Geolith Consultants and Rogers/Pacific), and part-time faculty member of the Department of Civil Engineering at U.C., Berkeley. His research and writings on the complexities of dam construction, especially his studies of the Saint Francis Dam failure, have not only shed new light on an old engineering controversy but also illustrate the importance of maintaining a questioning mind towards problematic events. Some have chosen to attack him for what they construe as his vindication of Mulholland, but as he has written, "historical truth is much more interesting, and more complicated, than the legend."

Thanks also go to those of my family, especially cousin Lillian Sloan Macedo, who dug into their trunks, records, and memories for items that shed light on the subject, and to my former husband, Gerard T. Hurley, for his editorial advice and assistance.

A special salute goes to my sister-in-law, Katherine Powell Mulholland. Her love and generosity can never be repaid.

My godson, Frank Ditto, made such a prodigious contribution as mentor and guide into the intricacies of word processing, computer use, and manuscript preparation that a mere expression of thanks seems barely adequate.

And finally, my thanks to California history editor Monica McCormick, who has helped see this project through to completion.

William Mulholland
and the
Rise of Los Angeles

The Long Journey from Dublin to Los Angeles

1855–1876

A NOTABLE LIFE

Of those civil servants who helped develop the modern metropolis of Los Angeles in the early twentieth century, the most prominent was William Mulholland (1855–1935). For over forty years spanning the administrations of nineteen mayors, Mulholland was a central force in the creation of a municipally owned water and power system that allowed a small, otiose western outpost to swell to outsized proportions. As a self-taught and inventive engineer, he became the creator of a project that ranked in magnitude and daring with the Panama Canal.

A pen-and-ink cartoon of Mulholland drawn in 1902, about the time the City of Los Angeles had at last regained control of its domestic water supply from the private company to which it had foolishly leased its pueblo water rights thirty years earlier, portrays a sturdy man in work clothes planted in front of a pump and water trough with two buckets labeled "City Water" at his feet. By then, Mulholland had worked for that private company for twenty-four years, having advanced from anonymous ditch tender in 1878 to superintendent of the works in 1886, a position he continued to hold under the new municipal management. "When the city bought back its water, it bought me too," he later remarked. The authority of his stance and stern gaze leaves no doubt that he is indeed the keeper of the well, and at the height of his power and vigor, he was exactly that: the overseer and caretaker of water for Los Angeles. He brought fame (and some say ignominy) to the City of Los

3

Angeles when, in 1913, as chief engineer of the great Owens River Aqueduct, he delivered to the city from 233 miles away its first abundant water supply. When the University of California at Berkeley honored him with an honorary doctorate degree the following year, the inscription on the diploma read, *"Percussit saxa et duxit flumina ad terram sitientum"* (He broke the rocks and brought the river to the thirsty land). Upon the aqueduct's completion—after years of struggle and heroic labor to create this engineering marvel—Mulholland stood amidst the cheers of the crowd, and over the roar of the waters cascading down the spillway north of San Fernando, he uttered briefly and memorably, "There it is. Take it."

Not only did that moment become legendary in the city's modern history, but it also created a controversy that has never died. When *Life* magazine's fall 1990 special issue included Mulholland among the one hundred people who had most influenced American history in the twentieth century ("The engineer moved a river and made the desert bloom."), a New York journalist was quick to snipe, in an amusing instance of East Coast parochialism, that Mulholland's presence on the list seemed "a bit strained" and that it probably constituted "a sop to the hinterlands."[1]

Mulholland was to live amid political conflict and controversy into his seventies. Then while he was actively planning and campaigning for the expansion of the city's water supply from the Colorado River, a dam that he had approved failed and killed over four hundred people, thus drowning his career in the wake of the worst man-made disaster in California's history.

This saga deserves renewed scrutiny, as in recent years the popular media, relying upon old rumors and hearsay, have increasingly presented this water story as a tabloid yarn of water thievery and crooked land deals. One fictional and melodramatic movie, *Chinatown* (1979), has come to be regarded by the uninformed as a kind of documentary work on the history of Los Angeles, while others who hold the city in disdain see the film as a clever parable on the greed and ambition of an upstart town. In a May 1, 1991, article on city water systems, the *New York Times* saw fit to cite Los Angeles as a horrible example of overexploitation of resources. To substantiate its case, the *Times* egregiously cited *Chinatown* as the work "which chronicles how the city seized control" of water to which it had no right.

Three years after Mulholland's death, newspaperman John Russell McCarthy wrote of him, "He had little pity, much strength, great ambition. There is no one else in sight, past or present, whom Los Angeles is more likely to remember." And so, loved or hated, Mulholland remains important to the history of Los Angeles and Southern California, his status recalling historian Carl Becker's evaluation of Martin Luther: "The Protestant may love Luther, the Catholic may hate him, but they would agree that Luther is important for the Reformation." Whether cherished or reviled, Mulholland endures at least as a potent figure in the history of his adopted city.[2]

A NOTE ON THE PRIVATE LIFE

William Mulholland was a fine-featured, handsome man, who, although a shade under six feet, always gave the impression of being taller because of his straight-backed, commanding presence and the penetrating gaze of his blue eyes. He had enormous energy, got by on little sleep, and remained vigorous until the Saint Francis Dam disaster eroded his spirit and health. His greatest assets—and doubtless a key to his success in public life—were a ready wit and an ability to get along with men.

Mulholland's private life seldom impinged upon his public affairs. In 1890, at the age of thirty-five, he married Lillie Ferguson, then twenty-one. They remained devoted and compatible until the home-loving and retiring Lillie died of cancer in 1915. She bore seven children, five of whom survived to adulthood. The oldest, Rose Ellen (1891–1977), kept house for her father until his death, and although his domestic life amid children, relatives, and in-laws was sometimes turbulent, it rarely distracted him from work. His second daughter, Lucile (1896–1968), expressed it best when asked about her father at the time of the aqueduct's completion. "Father?" she laughed. "You mean that man who sometimes eats dinner with us."

The city's growth and change, which Mulholland had helped to create, also destroyed most of the landmarks of his private life. By the 1960s, his former family dwellings had disappeared, as had the ranch in the San Fernando Valley whose land he had purchased and which his oldest son, Perry (1892–1962), had cultivated. The Boyle Heights home at Sixth and Cummings, where the family had lived from 1894 to 1920, was bulldozed to make way for the Santa Ana Freeway, while his later home at 426 South Saint Andrews Place was razed for an apartment building. At the end of the twentieth century, the only habitation that remains is the house of his nineteenth-century childhood in Dublin, Ireland.

ORIGINS AND ANCESTORS

Mulholland was the second son of Hugh and Ellen (Deakers) Mulholland, born in Belfast, Ireland, on September 11, 1855. Although Mulholland's parents were Dubliners, his father, a mail guard, was stationed in the north when the first three children were born: Thomas (1853) and William (1855) in Belfast, Hugh Patrick (1856) in Derry. By 1860, the family had settled permanently in Dublin, five years after the end of the Great Famine, which had left Ireland a dispirited and depleted land. Mulholland later displayed little nostalgia for his native land, and when asked at the height of his career if he would not like to take a trip back to the old country, he snapped that he never wanted to see the "damned island" again.

His parents were of the newly emerging Catholic lower middle class, which had been pushed off the tenant farms of their ancestors and crowded into the cities. Since the early eighteenth century, Mulhollands had lived in northeastern Ireland, midway between Belfast and Dublin in Counties Meath and Louth, tenant farmers on the vast lands of the viscount Massarene. William's grandfather Patrick Mulholland had been born in 1798, the year of the French invasion of Ireland; his father, Hugh, born in 1827, came into the world during the first of the horrific famines that afflicted Ireland for the next forty years.[3]

Because an Irishman then was allowed to vote only if he had twenty acres, and because Patrick, a farmer in Colinbeg, had ended up through inheritance with only seven acres and a house, he and his sons were disenfranchised. Hugh, as the seventh and youngest son of a man who owned only seven acres, was at best without great expectations, and therefore had to cast about for a means of survival. Lord Massarene required his tenants to serve in the militia (Home Guard), and if a young man demonstrated ability and dependability he could advance to the position of a guard on the coaches that Massarene ran between Derry and Dublin. By this process, Hugh Mulholland worked his way into a position as a mail guard with the Royal British Mail. As there was no civil service until 1855, the only way to attain such employment was by nomination. Once nominated, one was assured of serving for the rest of one's life.

In his later public life, William Mulholland tended to couch his father's employment in general terms: "connected with the Government mail," he would say, as if he perceived something *infra dig* about his father's work. Yet in those desperate days in Ireland, a guard job with the

Royal Mail would have been a coveted post that offered a good living and some prestige, the term *royal* being not meaningless in Victorian Ireland. Long waiting lists were customary for this position, which demanded that a man be under thirty years of age and that he must pass a test on the three R's. That Hugh qualified for such a post also indicates his literacy, which was not to be assumed in his era, when 47 percent of persons ages five and up in Ireland could neither read nor write.[4]

A famous superintendent of mail coaches, Thomas Hasker, kept a voluminous record of his career and was said to have loved his guards as a great commander loves his soldiers; indeed, in the entire development of the Royal Mail service, the key men were the mail guards. "Everything depended on their integrity," Hasker wrote, "their loyalty, their tireless zeal in the discharge of their very arduous duties, their hardihood of body as well as of mind." These same admirable qualities that enabled Hugh Mulholland to survive and prosper in Victorian Ireland also produced in him a rectitude and hardness of character that ultimately drove two of his sons a world away. *Cherchez le père* may well be the watchword for the character of William Mulholland, as an interesting parallel suggests itself between a father and son who each, in different times and worlds apart, demonstrated similar abilities and behaviors as trusted employees of public agencies.[5]

In old age, Mulholland told certain questioners that he had no recollection of his mother, who had died when he was seven, but to his children he sometimes spoke of her, remembering that her wit, lively nature, and love of song had been an antidote to his father's grim seriousness. A monument to this bright-spirited young woman stands in Glasnevin, the famous Dublin Catholic cemetery built under the direction of the great emancipator, Daniel O'Connell, and immortalized by James Joyce in the Hades episode of *Ulysses*. Inscribed on the granite stele are the words "Erected by Hugh Mulholland in memory of his beloved wife—Ellen. Aged 28 years who died 18th September, 1862." Grave records further reveal that also buried in the plot with her are two infant daughters, six other members of the extended family, and later, Hugh.

Ellen Deakers had been to America as a girl before she returned to Ireland to marry Hugh Mulholland. Family lore has it that she grew so homesick for Ireland (and Hugh) that her father allowed her to return. Although no record has been found, their marriage occurred sometime between 1850 and 1852. Ellen's brother, Richard Deakers, Jr., however, remained in America and prospered in his father's draper's business in Pittsburgh during and after the Civil War. Because of Richard, two of

Ellen's sons, William and Hugh Patrick Mulholland, would one day find their way to Pittsburgh and ultimately to California.

A DUBLIN BOYHOOD

Willie Mulholland grew up in postfamine Victorian Dublin, a dispirited, shabby provincial capital, notorious for its slums, drinking, wenching, and political and religious contentions. Yet in this benighted place, within a few miles of each other, grew three little boys, all destined to become remarkable men. The most privileged, and one year older than young Mulholland, was Oscar Wilde, who lived in central Dublin on upper-class Merrion Square with parents who were both stars in the Anglo-Irish social firmament: his father, a prominent physician, and his mother, a poet and keeper of a literary salon. In a meaner part of town in a rented house on Synge Street, with a drunken father who made life seem hopeless for his stoic wife and their three small children, dwelled the youngest of the three (a year younger than Willie), George Bernard Shaw, enduring what he later called his "devil of a childhood." The coincidence of the three not only illustrates that talent can arise anywhere but also suggests that the Dublin environment, for all its shabbiness, was vibrant. Throughout the starving years, although Ireland's population declined by 20 percent, Dublin's increased by 9 percent, with 250,000 people living in the city proper and another 50,000 better-off inhabitants in the suburbs. (Dublin's growth was the result of rural depopulation as tenants of small holdings were forced off the land; farms from one to five acres declined from 182,000 in 1845 to 62,000 in 1910.)[6]

Sickness and death pervaded Willie Mulholland's childhood home. Consumption took two baby girls and then Ellen herself shortly after the birth of a sixth child, leaving Hugh, at thirty-three, a widower with four motherless boys, the youngest an infant of a few months and the oldest not yet ten. The impact of these losses upon the seven-year-old Willie is unknowable. On the evidence, he must simply have repressed much of what he felt and turned to his brothers and schoolmates for whatever companionship and warmth they could offer. His propensity for male friendships must have derived from that time when he lost the women of his family and, given the male-dominated Victorian world he lived in, perhaps concluded that it was safer to invest his time in those who did not seem to go under so easily.

At the time of their mother's death, the oldest boys, Thomas and Willie, were in their second year at the O'Connell School run by the Christian

Brothers on North Richmond Street, only a short walk from their home. Today the Christian Brothers Schools are honored for playing a leading role in the Irish Revival and are recognized for providing elite training to the urban poor of nineteenth-century Ireland. A chief justice of Ireland who attended during the same years as the Mulholland boys later wrote that "the school course contained comparatively few subjects, but they were well and efficiently taught." Willie left the O'Connell School before completing the full course of instruction, but while there he worked through three readers, four levels of grammar, four of geography, and being most advanced in arithmetic, had achieved six levels by the time he left the school.[7] The reasons for his leaving are not clear and are certainly murkier than those of James Joyce, who, a generation later, attended the same school—and was ashamed to admit it—as his devotion to the Jesuits was so powerful that he considered the Christian Brothers mere drones by comparison. "Paddy Stink and Mickey Mud," his class-conscious father, John Joyce, had dubbed two teachers there. Willie's chief memory (at least, the one he chose to tell his own children) was of the day, when almost ten, he joined his schoolmates at a special school assembly and heard the father superior tell them that a terrible tragedy had just befallen the world. In America, President Abraham Lincoln had been assassinated and they must all bow heads and pray for his soul.

Of greater immediate impact on young Willie than Lincoln's death, however, was the arrival of a stepmother. In 1865, after three years as a widower, thirty-six-year-old Hugh married Jane Smith, aged thirty, in Drogheda, where her sisters lived, wives of sea captains. By all accounts, Jane Smith tried to be a good mother to her stepsons, but as she herself was pregnant the next year with her first child (a daughter, Mary, born in 1867), followed by two sons (Joseph, 1869, and Michael, 1871), her attention never could have been fully focused upon the lively older boys, who were out of the house at school during the day and accustomed to a degree of independence. Tom, the oldest, eventually became a conforming son who followed his father into the postal service and at the time of his death from consumption at thirty-eight in 1891 was still unmarried and living at home with his widowed stepmother. Willie and Hugh Patrick, however, were another story. Only eleven months apart, they were almost like twins in their closeness, although family members who recalled them in later years always spoke of Willie as if he were much older and more dominating than Hugh. Described as "a pair of Dublin jackeens"—city kids who ran the streets with their buddies—they became the rebels of the family. At fourteen, Willie ran off to sea for the

first time after a severe beating from his father because of bad marks at
school (by then he probably was attending a national school, although
all records are lost). He returned home and after a brief period of study
entered the British Merchant Marine at fifteen. The following year, the
father enrolled Hugh Patrick, then also fifteen, into the British Navy.

FOUR YEARS BEFORE THE MAST AND WESTWARD HO!

Although much of Dublin in the 1860s was decrepit, life on the waterfront was energetic and vital, with its port being developed into one of
the best-run harbors in Europe. Between 1860 and 1914, over 38 million tons of debris were dredged from the Liffey, while docks, berths,
and the new Alexandra Basin were added to the existing facilities. Irish-
men such as John Wigham were pioneers in introducing gaslight to light-
houses and illuminating buoys. The famous Bailey light with its 9,000
candlepower, revolving lens, and gaslight that produced flashes in groups
became the model on all the world's coasts. These matters, rather than
Latin declensions or the Celtic Revival, were what excited the imagination of Willie Mulholland. Although surrounded by political tension and
unrest (the 1860s saw the rise of the Sinn Fein movement), he dreamed
of neither academic achievement nor Irish independence but rather of
going to sea at a moment in the nineteenth century when, with the su-
premacy and protection of the Royal Navy, Britain possessed the largest
merchant fleet in the world.[8]

After four years at sea, Willie would later enliven many a night circle
in California construction camps and in the high Sierras with his tales
of seafaring days on a three-masted, full-rigged merchantman, the *Gleniffer*. Those yarns have vanished with the smoke of the long-dead campfires,
and only meager accounts remain of his nineteen Atlantic crossings to
various ports in North America and the West Indies and his eventual promotion to navigating officer of the vessel.[9]

Life at sea initially must have suited the young and enthusiastic Mulholland. Freed from the strictures of family, church, and a crowded household, he did not find the cramped confines of ship life as punishing as
might a youth from a more solitary or privileged environment. By now,
he had developed a propensity for inner solitude that he would retain
for the rest of his life. Long before Joyce had articulated his youthful intention of employing "silence, exile, and cunning," Willie Mulholland,
without saying so, had pursued such a course. He retained a lifelong love
of the sea but at the end of four years concluded the sailor's life "would

get him nowhere in a material way." After sailing into New York City on June 9, 1874, Willie returned to shore with a sense of pride in having survived the nautical experience and in having deepened his understanding of life and men amid the motley crews of the fo'c'sle.

In his first summer in America, Willie found work on a vessel in the Great Lakes and later cherished the memory of its Irish captain, who noticed him on deck one night as he stood at the rail and whistled a tune. Remarking that he had not heard that air since leaving Ireland, the captain made friendly talk with his young crewman, who would always remember how the encounter had eased his loneliness in a strange land.

In the winter of 1874–75, Mulholland worked in a lumber camp in Manistee, Michigan, where a logging accident altered his life and left him permanently appalled by the reckless deforestation he had witnessed. The mishap landed him in a camp hospital with an injured leg that developed erysipelas (a streptococcal infection). From his bed, he overheard doctors mention gangrene and the probable need to amputate the limb, so he bolted and somehow made his way to Cincinnati. There, at the age of twenty, weak and barely alive from his recent illness, having only a few dollars left and too proud to let any of his family know of his plight, he reached the lowest point of his young life. "Why bother?" he wondered. Ahead he saw nothing but endless years of grinding work with no reward. As he wandered the streets in this hopeless state, he suddenly heard a choir of clear-voiced boy sopranos singing the *Gloria in Excelsis* in a nearby church and felt a surge of hope and renewed courage. He entered the church and spent an hour in prayer and meditation as the suicidal mood passed and his zest for life returned.

Willie next became attached to an itinerant mechanic with a team, who drove through the country sharpening scissors and repairing clocks. He later told his daughter, Rose, that he grew so fond of the gypsy life that he had to force himself to give it up and follow the urge to do something worthwhile with his life.

During Willie's *Wanderjahr*, Hugh Patrick, having learned that his brother had left the sea, followed suit and upon reaching American shores jumped ship. As one of the family later explained his desertion from the British Navy, "Hugh got over into some American port, and he ejected himself." Somehow the brothers found each other and made their way to the Pittsburgh home of their American uncle, Richard Deakers, who never forgot the day in the autumn of 1875 when Willie and Hugh "just showed up on the doorstep."

The Mulholland boys had landed on a prosperous threshold, for the

Deakers family in all ways qualified as "lace curtain Irish," living as they did in the Hazelwood section of Pittsburgh in a pleasant home with a cook and servants. Uncle Richard was well established as a Pittsburgh dry goods merchant and husband of Catherine Thorpe, a native of Ireland, who, by all accounts, was the abiding genius of the family business. Her few surviving letters indicate that she was a highly competent lady concerned with maintaining order, proprieties, and good appearances. Devout Catholics, she and Richard had eight children, and they now charitably welcomed their two stray nephews from Ireland.

For almost two years, cousins Willie and Hugh stayed at the Deakers home and worked at their uncle's dry goods store. Events took an ominous turn, however, when another relative remembered only as "Uncle Hobson" showed up on the Deakers doorstep carrying tuberculosis. Soon some of the Deakers children were presenting symptoms of the disease, and by 1875 two had died. As three of Catherine's brothers had been ranching in San Diego County since 1868, the family made the wrenching decision to leave the city where they were so well established and join the throng of health-seekers who had begun crowding into certain areas of California to the extent that historian Hubert Howe Bancroft worried that they had introduced a weakness into "our exceptionally youthful and hardy community by an increasing proportion of delicate women and children."[10]

The journey was a disaster. While Richard stayed behind to close business, the other Deakerses followed medical advice that the Panama or Horn routes were best during the cold months and booked passage on a large, three-decked vessel, the *Crescent City* of Liverpool, which sailed out of New York Harbor on December 9, 1876. Its passengers included not only Catherine Deakers, her six surviving children, and Uncle Hobson, but two stowaways, Willie and Hugh Mulholland. Shortly before reaching Colón, however, the pair were caught and dumped at the Isthmus of Panama. Probably because they lacked the twenty-five dollars in gold to pay for the train ride to Balboa, they were forced to hike the forty-seven miles across the isthmus. (As an old man Mulholland rather grandly glossed this over, once declaring, "I would walk that far today to make twenty-five dollars.") Once on the west side, they signed on to a Peruvian man-of-war headed for Acapulco. From there they found another ship that took them to San Francisco. Ashore, they bought two horses and made their way southward to find the Deakers family in Los Angeles.

When at last they reached the pueblo, they learned that the voyage had continued to be ill-fated for their Aunt Catherine. Two more of her children, already weak with consumption, contracted typhoid and died on shipboard. When the ship from Panama had finally made port at Santa Monica, one of the younger Deakers children, fourteen-year-old Ella, looked about, caught her first glimpse of Los Angeles, and was aghast. It was, she later said, a place "where nothing looked like anything."

CHAPTER 2

The City of Angels

1877

A PUEBLO OF 9,000 SOULS

Ella Deakers was not the first to find Los Angeles unprepossessing. "A queer little Spanish town," young author Margaret Collier Graham reported to her parents in Keokuk, Iowa, shortly after she arrived in Los Angeles in 1876 with her consumptive husband. "There is not much to say of this wonderful city of the Angels," she wrote. "We have been walking around nearly all day through the narrow streets full of strange Spanish and Chinese faces, passing long rows of low adobe houses swarming with dusky children and reeking with foreign odors." Yet beyond the "squalor and nastiness," she also saw "groves of green trees, orange, fig, walnut, and acres of grape vines."[1]

What greeted the Mulholland brothers when they rode into town in January 1877, in addition to depression, drought, and their relatives' straitened circumstances, was a settlement in the grip of a smallpox epidemic. By February 9, fifty-three cases had been reported, the majority in the "Spanish quarter," where resistance to receiving the new Jenner vaccine was high. The editor of the *Los Angeles Daily Star* called for the ouster of the city's health officer, charging incompetence, while also offering readers such health tips as the claim that because Jews did not eat pork, they were less subject to bilious attacks and, therefore, less apt to suffer from smallpox. By May, after the city had spent $21,000 to fight the disease, including funds for the Sisters of Charity to maintain one of the pest houses, the epidemic subsided.[2]

Willie and Hugh had arrived in Southern California at the end of its first thirty years of American rule, as the Anglos gained dominion over the Spanish-Mexican colonizers and landholders. Only five months earlier, in September 1876, the Southern Pacific Railroad had connected Los Angeles from the north to the rest of the world. With the arrival of the railroad, Major Horace Bell, old-time scout, soldier, and owner-editor of the caustic *Porcupine,* had anticipated a new civility after the preceding lawless years' culmination in the ghastly 1871 Chinese Massacre in Nigger Alley, during which Chinatown was sacked, many were shot, and twenty Chinese hanged. When western correspondent J. Ross Browne wrote in *Harper's Weekly* about a visit to Los Angeles in the 1860s, he had described the social tone as one in which men discussed manhunting as a sporting activity: "Why, you would sit at the breakfast table of the Queen of the Angels and hear the question of going out to shoot men as commonly discussed as would be duck shooting in any other country. At dinner the question would be, 'Well, how many did they shoot today? Who was hanged?'" As Major Bell later observed, "It was barbarism gone to seed. The decent minority—for there was such a group of nonentities—wondered when and where it would all end." He fervently believed that "the day the whistle of the first S. P. locomotive was heard in Los Angeles, civilization started on the upgrade."[3]

Even with the railroad, however, Los Angeles was not much in the 1870s. Its population was 9,000, and its biggest local excitement one January day featured a bucking bronco from the Wells Fargo office at First and Spring that, after breaking the tongue on an old rattletrap wagon parked near the courthouse steps, proceeded to kick the vehicle to smithereens. As a crowd collected to watch, a local reporter noted, "it was the most fun for the boys since Christmas." The city council was spending its best efforts on a long debate over the need to drain the frog pond at Second and Olive. Because of the current drought, the streets were being sprinkled at night, so that when the council, which sat in night sessions, complained of the noise and nuisance, one editor noted that it was because "the rumble of carts disturbs the sleep of our councilmen, who can sit longer and talk more than any municipal body in the U. S., for they do not believe that brevity is the soul of wit."[4]

With relish and colorful rhetoric newsmen chronicled the day, paying special attention to crime and punishment. Stealing a ham could earn a man thirty days on the chain gang, as could chronic public drunkenness ("afflicted with intemperance" was one description). Red-light houses abounded, and their occupants were variously described as ladies of the night, nymphs of the pavement, or when a more genteel or discreet tone seemed indicated, *nymphes du pave.*

The mention of water—or lack of it—was frequent, and fire was always a menace. A house at Twelfth and Olive burned down because no water was in reach for the fire wagon. Brush fires and smoke in the San Gabriel and Cahuenga foothills were not uncommon summer sights, and in September 1878, a fire on the Kester Ranch (part of present-day Van Nuys) in the San Fernando Valley burned between two and three thousand acres of wheat.

Los Angeles's heterogeneous nature was already apparent. A Chinese funeral—CELESTIAL FUNERAL EXTRAORDINARY—caused one reporter to muse in cross-cultural allusions, "A Chinese High Muck-a-Muck Speeded Across the River Styx—The Dead March in Saul Struggling with the Cacophony of a Chinese Band." The pueblo celebrated Mexican independence with a parade and grand ball attended by Carrillos and del Valles at about the same time that General John Charles Frémont was in town on his way to Arizona and General William Tecumseh Sherman made a station stop on the train en route to San Francisco. Dominating these picturesque groups, however, was a rising class of Anglo-Yankee settlers and entrepreneurs bent on bringing into the American mainstream this town sometimes derisively referred to as the Queen of the Cow Counties. They believed in progress, and a new technology always excited their interest, as when a leading local citizen, L. M. Holt, purchased a model of Mr. Edison's latest invention, the phonograph, and invited friends to the Odd Fellows hall for a public demonstration. There, grown men sang such ditties as "Mary Had a Little Lamb" into a mouthpiece and produced a cylinder that afterwards could be played back, reproducing the sound of their voices to the wonderment and delight of all.[5]

This jumble of types and styles, mingling visions of the future with a touch of the romantic past, appealed to young men of ambition and dreams. Mulholland was attracted to the local lore of the pueblo; the tales of the notorious *bandido* Tiburcio Vasquez, who had been captured only two years before; and the exotic intrigues of Chinatown, with its opium dens and gambling parlors presided over by the mysterious men with queues. In spite of the troubled times, Los Angeles's overall mood was optimistic, as newspapers expressed the boosterism of a small town straining for a grander destiny. In a few years that boosterism would materialize in Los Angeles's first great land boom.

FIRST DAYS IN A WESTERN OUTPOST

As an old man, Mulholland remembered the pueblo with affection. It was "so attractive to me that it at once became something about which my whole scheme of life was woven, I loved it so much." But he probably came closer to the mark years earlier, in 1907, when he told a reporter, "After a month ashore I decided I had enough, and so started for San Pedro to find a ship. On the way down there a man who was driving a well offered me a job and I took it." The man who stopped the decamping Mulholland was Manuel Dominguez, grandson of the original grantee to Rancho San Pedro, one of the great Spanish land grants. Hired to dig artesian wells with a hand drill near the recently founded town of Compton, Mulholland later claimed that "the first well I helped to drive changed the whole course of my life. When we were about six hundred feet down we struck a tree. A little further down we brought up some fossils. These things fired my curiosity. I wanted to know how they got there and so I got hold of Joseph LeConte's book on the geology of this country. Right there I decided to become an engineer."

First, however, William and his brother Hugh went gold-seeking in Arizona Territory. Ignoring all reports of Indian uprisings in 1877–78 and amid rising hostility among the southern Arizona Apaches under Victorio and Geronimo, the two Irish greenhorns traveled to Ehrenberg, northeast of Yuma, where placer finds had been reported. To raise money for purchasing outfits, they found casual employment on the steamboats along the Colorado River, thus introducing Mulholland to the river that would one day figure so large in his history. In the midst of their unrewarded efforts, United States troops rode through Ehrenberg warning that Geronimo might be on the warpath. Needing no further encouragement, the two hightailed it back to Los Angeles. Years later, Mulholland told a reporter, "I went to Arizona prospecting—a very dangerous business at the time. There were a great many hostile Indians about . . . it was one of those cases where presence of mind was best secured by absence of body."[6]

LEARNING THE WATER BUSINESS

During his apprentice years, Mulholland became familiar with the various water projects that had been undertaken in Los Angeles over the twenty years before his arrival. Today near the plaza at the north end of

Olvera Street lies a line of diagonally set brick that marks the old water course of the Zanja Madre (Mother Ditch) that made life possible in the early pueblo. Surrounded now by paved streets crowded with automobiles and draped overhead with power lines that clutter the often smoggy skyline, the original town center struggles to survive as a last vestige of the Spanish-Mexican days, and a seeker must negotiate crowded aisles of curio booths and candle shops in order to look down on the spot where precious water once flowed from the Los Angeles River. To find the source of the Zanja Madre's water, however, one must leave Olvera Street and go north past New Chinatown along North Broadway to the freight yards of the Southern Pacific Railroad Company. There, east of the rail yard, lies the Los Angeles River, today a concrete flood channel but once a stream that Mulholland called "the most valuable asset of the municipality."[7]

The Spanish crown had granted the pueblo ownership and control of its water, and one of the first tasks of the original settlers *(los pobladores)* in 1781 had been to create the Zanja Madre with communal labor for both domestic use and irrigation. Although by the end of the nineteenth century, most of the zanjas had been moved underground, in earlier times, they had been an integral part of the landscape. John S. Hittell described them in *The Resources of California* (1863): "most of them have a body of water three feet wide and a foot deep running at a speed of five miles per hour. They carry water from the river to the gardens and are absolutely necessary to secure the growth of the vines and the many fruit trees." By the time Mulholland arrived, nine tributary zanjas flowed from the Mother Ditch to provide irrigation water to various districts of the city, while a private water company controlled water for domestic use. Although both irrigation and domestic uses drew their water from a common source—the Los Angeles River—their histories are intertwined but distinct.[8]

The zanjas—a distinctive and picturesque feature of the old pueblo often rhapsodized by travel writers who hearkened back to biblical images of oases in the desert—eventually outlived their usefulness in an expanding urban scene. By the opening years of the twentieth century, when the city had over 100,000 inhabitants, the zanjas, after 121 years of service, had nearly all been covered, piped, and converted to city water mains. Thus, early in his tenure as the city's water superintendent, William Mulholland reported to the board of water commissioners in 1903 that "the *zanja* system has made its usual poor showing for the year." Citing receipts of $5,809.75 and expenditures for upkeep of $8,537.15, he recommended abandoning the system, which was done in the following year.

In the Spanish-Mexican era, water-tending had always been a municipal effort, with each family at first making a communal contribution of labor. As the settlement grew, however, local government took over its management to assure an adequate water supply for both domestic use and the irrigation of crops in the semiarid land. The *zanjero* (water steward) was to become as important a figure as the *alcalde* (mayor). Although the Americans introduced their form of municipal government with mayor and city council, they retained the Spanish-Mexican practice of appointing a zanjero just as the *ayuntamiento* had done. (*Zanjero* was officially anglicized to *water overseer* in 1881.) Americans quickly demonstrated their capitalistic tendencies with various attempts to gain ownership of the city's water supply, along with its land. Major Horace Bell, who cast a sardonic eye on life in the pueblo in those transitional years of the 1850s and 1860s, described a convenient arrangement whereby the mayor and the council, after granting a contract in currency for excavating a ditch to expand the growing town's water system, would in reality pay the contractor with municipal acreage. In his gratitude, the contractor would then kick back a fraction thereof to the mayor and each member of the council. So flagrant was this practice that at one city council hearing, George Hansen—a civil engineer and pioneer of 1850, then serving as county surveyor—hung up for study certain tract maps, across each of which he had boldly inscribed with red ink, "This tract stolen when B—was mayor"; "This tract stolen when C—was mayor"; and finally on the largest of all, encompassing thousands of acres, he named the current mayor: "This tract stolen when Joel H. Turner was mayor."[9]

In the first years of American occupation and up to 1868, several private ventures into the management and distribution of domestic water were attempted and failed. Most conspicuous and ambitious were those of Prudent Beaudry, who, along with partners Dr. John Griffin and Solomon Lazard, in March 1868 helped finance the new Canal and Reservoir Company, which was to advance his real estate dreams. Beaudry, once described as prim and Napoleonic, was a French Canadian from Quebec, reputed to have made and lost several fortunes. He had been in San Francisco during the Gold Rush and came to Los Angeles in the 1850s. After prospering with his brother, Victor, as a smelter in the silver strike at Cerro Gordo, Beaudry bought quantities of real estate to subdivide and develop, as he envisioned hillside homes on the dry empty hills north and northwest of the city. He called his arid tract Bellevue Terrace, and he prevailed upon the city to grant additional land for building a dam in the barren chaparral hills west and northwest of Figueroa on the site of today's Echo Park.

Until then the city's water systems had involved only the central district around the plaza and along the river to the south, much of which was really river bottomland. Beaudry's new dam would allow the city to grow westward, an idea that many of the old-time conservative residents found farfetched, but to which the "intrepid Beaudry," as one of his associates called him, gave his full support. Thus, Beaudry became the power behind the Los Angeles Canal and Reservoir Company, to which the city granted a portion of land on March 23, 1868.

The president of the new Canal and Reservoir Company was the engineer and former county surveyor George Hansen. His previously mentioned sarcasm notwithstanding, Hansen was considered a man of integrity as well as an able engineer. The company bought the old Feliz Ditch and the water rights of the Feliz Rancho, which took its water from the Los Angeles River about six miles northwest of the city. The company planned to improve and widen the ditch and then run the water by creating a canyon through the hill by either a cut or tunnel so that the flow would debouch onto the plain and thence into a dam of stone concrete. The course followed along what is today Glendale Boulevard, cut through where Silver Lake Reservoir now stands, and from there emptied into a dam at the site of present-day Echo Park. This dam, also called Reservoir No. 4, had an extension ditch down to approximately where the Bonaventure Hotel stands today at Fifth and Figueroa. Because the water dropped 78 feet from the dam to the ditch, the Barnard brothers, who had been brick makers, conceived the idea of building a wool mill on the site to take advantage of the power and thus created the first industrial manufacturing plant in the City of Los Angeles.

Having successfully made one water deal with the city, Beaudry, Griffin, and Lazard nearly succeeded in wresting away all rights from the municipality when they proposed to the city council a complicated fifty-year lease that in reality would have resulted in the eventual sale of the waterworks and the stripping of the city's right or authority to fix or control water rates. At that time the sentiment against municipal ownership ran strong in the city council. One member argued, "Cities and towns can never manage enterprises of that nature as economically as individuals can, and besides, it is a continual source of annoyance and is made a political hobby." After a tie vote, the president of the council broke the deadlock with his vote favoring the lease. Mayor Don Cristobal Aguilar vetoed the ordinance, however, for he was a native Californian who knew what the water would always mean to the city. Although his veto saved the city's water rights, it did not end the matter, for the trio came back with a proposition for a thirty-year lease at $1,500 a year. This new proposition still included promises to fulfill such conditions of the earlier scheme as installing hydrants at downtown street crossings, providing free water in the city's public buildings, and constructing in the plaza an ornamental fountain that was to cost not less than $1,000.[10]

Although other interested parties offered proposals, the council was stacked in favor of the trio and committed what Mulholland would later call an act of "civil idiocy" by railroading through the infamous thirty-year lease. Charges of favoritism and political pull flew as two members of the city council who voted for the lease, William H. Perry and A. J. King, soon became members of the water company's board of trustees, formed immediately after the lease was secured. Griffin, Lazard, and Beaudry now incorporated this new entity, which would control the city's domestic water supply under the name of the Los Angeles City Water Company. For this plum, they paid the bargain rent of $1,500 a year, while the politicians who had signed away their city's water rights for the next third of a century congratulated themselves on having exorcised the specter of municipal ownership. Only Mayor Aguilar mitigated the situation by insisting, before reluctantly signing the agreement, that the mayor and the council would retain the right to regulate water rates. Thus the city was not stripped entirely of its power to manage its most vital resource, although the wrangle with the company over rates became an annual council event.

The lease ultimately proved a cheat to the city, for as the private company prospered and the value of its resource grew more precious, services did not always increase accordingly and the works fell into "a woefully inefficient condition," remembered Mulholland, who also recalled the politicking that resulted as each side manipulated for an advantage. "The fat earnings also proved an attractive lure to the politicians who promptly invoked the power delegated to municipal legislative bodies by the constitution of 1879 to regulate rates. This power was freely used to extort all sorts of contributions from the Company to the last year of its existence."[11]

Within two years of obtaining the lease, the company had maneuvered the city into a rent reduction so that for the next three decades it paid $400 a year, or a little over $33 a month, for all the water it wanted from the Los Angeles River. This absurdity came about when, after waiting two years for the company to fulfill its side of the bargain and remove an abandoned reservoir from the plaza and build the long-awaited fountain, the council got up enough ginger to request that the work be done pronto, only to be unpleasantly answered by the company's attorney with a threat of lawsuit if the city persisted in its demands. Cowed, the council supinely agreed to reduce the annual rent to $400 a year if the company would deliver on its promise. Happy in its windfall, the company at last tore down the old brick reservoir, landscaped the plaza, and erected the long-promised fountain.[12]

The water company next built the Buena Vista Reservoir with a 378-foot elevation to replace an earlier one northeast of the Catholic cemetery and in 1875 set out to improve the system by laying a twenty-two-inch iron main from a point near the Buena Vista Bridge down to Main and First Streets. The partners also pursued independent projects. Griffin and his partner, John Downey, a former governor of California and now president of the Los Angeles Water Company, expanded the domestic water service on their tract in East Los Angeles (today, Lincoln Heights). Meanwhile, the tireless Prudent Beaudry continued to develop his hill lands to the west at his own expense, grading and installing streets, laying lines, pumping water and building two reservoirs, for which he was said to have spent the then staggering sum of $95,000.[13]

When Beaudry became mayor of Los Angeles in 1875, he remained determined to see his hillside developments succeed. Undaunted by drought and depression, he proclaimed with the voice of the ultimate booster, "I intend to spend money and keep on spending money in improvements and grading streets until this locality meets the attention it deserves, and it will not be long, I assure you." He then built another, even larger reservoir with a 5-million-gallon capacity on Angelino Heights. Also called Beaudry's High Reservoir, it was a basin excavated in solid rock with an elevation of 596 feet. This completed the series of reservoirs built for the various water systems in place when William Mulholland took his first job with the Los Angeles Water Company in the spring of 1878.[14]

CHAPTER 3

The Private Water
Company and Its Owners

1878–1879

THE IRISH APPRENTICE

When William Mulholland began his job with the Los Angeles Water
Company as a deputy zanjero, he tended the main supply ditch from
Crystal Springs, then the chief source of the city's domestic water supply. Paid $1.50 a day and housed in what he once described as "a shack
near the Old Sycamore Tree" (the latter then a historic landmark in early
deeds and records), he settled in for two years of work and study that
were to lead to his career as a hydraulic engineer. The locale remained
important to him. Visiting as an old man over fifty years later (after the
Saint Francis Dam disaster had ended his career), he pointed out a sturdy
oak to a young woman then writing a graduate thesis on the domestic
water system of Los Angeles. After telling her how he had rescued it as
a tiny three-inch seedling about to fall into the ditch he was digging, he
approached and, apparently moved by the memory of that life-affirming
act, reached out, "touched it lovingly and looking at it, said half to himself, 'I saved its life once. I wonder if it is conscious of my presence today?'" The old Chief's closest friends and associates later acknowledged
his affinity for the place when they chose it as the appropriate site for
the William Mulholland Memorial Fountain, erected in his honor by the
City of Los Angeles in 1940 and restored and rededicated in 1996.[1]

In that shack by the river, he had, for the first time in his life, a place
of his own. There, after a day of clearing brush and debris, removing
dead animals from the stream, and keeping the flow in proper channels,

he began the studies that ultimately led to his fame as a hydraulic engineer. Although the nearby Los Angeles River was no mighty stream such as one associates with great cities, it was, as Mulholland remembered affectionately, "a beautiful limpid little stream with willows on its banks." Originating in the western foothills of the San Fernando Valley thirty miles from the plaza and fed by the waters of the Tujunga Wash, its watershed covered about 500 square miles, and without it no city ever would have arisen.

Mulholland worked between the west bank of the river and the canal owned by the water company. The river supplied irrigation water to the zanjas and so came under the control of the city zanjero, while the channel, or main supply ditch, fed the city's domestic water system and belonged to the private company. Thus, the two groups of workers under different jurisdictions inevitably came together, sometimes in harmony but often in conflict. Although the waters of the main supply ditch flowed from Crystal Springs, contention over their source led to a great conflict between the city and the water company after the company contended that the city could not claim the springs, as they did not arise from the Los Angeles River. The controversy and legal arguments over Crystal Springs grew labyrinthine through the years and culminated in a memorable 1898 court case that concluded in the city's favor.

Crystal Springs was on the Los Feliz Rancho, six or seven miles northwest of the city's plaza. Today commemorated by Crystal Springs Drive, which runs through the golfing grounds of Griffith Park, the property had been purchased by the Los Angeles Water Company from the Feliz estate in 1868, after it had secured its thirty-year lease from the city. Formerly called the Feliz Springs, it was a marshy tract of slightly over fourteen acres south of an elbow bend where the Los Angeles River begins its southerly course through the city towards the sea. Judge Benjamin Eaton (brother-in-law of Dr. John Griffin), who earlier had superintended construction when the Canal and Reservoir Company bought the old Feliz Ditch and the water rights of the Feliz Rancho, once testified in court that the springs then "consisted of a body of water surrounded by tules" that trickled down to the river. After paying $8,000 for the property and christening it Crystal Springs, the new owners formed an auxiliary company called Crystal Springs Land and Water Company. They promptly declared it private, not city, property and proceeded to build a canal to carry water to a ravine in today's Elysian Park, where they built the Buena Vista Dam in 1868–1869.[2]

By July 1878, only months after Mulholland had been on his new job, a deputy zanjero was assigned to guard the river because parties were stealing water on the Feliz Ranch. By October, the city received a favorable judgment in the state supreme court, which ruled against the removal of water from the Los Angeles River by Leon Baldwin, the first American owner of the Feliz lands. This did not end the problem, however, for in the summer of 1879, Mulholland's second year on the river, the city council's zanja committee toured up the river and discovered three heads of water in use on the Feliz Rancho and three more on the Corralitos lands of Andrew Glassell, owner of a part of Rancho San Rafael on the river's east bank. (A head was in theory one hundred miner's inches, but because a miner's inch varies according to local agreement, Mulholland once archly described a head of water as all that the user could manage to take.) The city ran the water back into the river and placed guards on the ditches, but the guards were driven off, and the problem remained. Only years of court cases would finally settle the issue in the city's favor, but all that summer along the river where Mulholland worked and lived, the deputy zanjeros kept an alert watch for water thieves. They were authorized to arrest anyone taking water who could not produce a permit from the city.[3]

That same year, Reservoir No. 4 (Beaudry's High Dam, also called the Woolen Ditch Dam—today's Echo Park Lake) flooded part of the city when the embankment broke along the line of the exhaust tunnel. It released a flood that poured south to Agricultural Park (present campus of the University of Southern California) and east to Main and Spring Streets. No deaths occurred, and although property and crop damage was extensive, the greatest loss was the water itself, as fears arose of a possible water famine in the coming hot, dry summer. Two months after the flood, Mulholland was engaged in frantic efforts to repair and reopen a broken water line that threatened to shut off the city's supply. On June 10, a break in the canal and reservoir ditch flooded and clogged the main supply ditch. Although Buena Vista Dam was fortunately full at the time, all consumers of city water were warned to use it moderately for two or three days. These mishaps, however, were simply minor precursors of those that lay ahead as the city began to boom.

WATER BOSSES AND CITIZENS

For all its local power and ability to stir controversy, the Los Angeles Water Company was small, even for a town of only 10,000. Its owners may have been among the wealthiest in the community, but when Mulholland started work, the entire personnel consisted of fewer than a dozen people: Superintendent Fred Eaton; Assistant Superintendent Tom Burns; Burns's assistant, Thomas Brooks; a crew of four laborers; and two ditch and reservoir tenders. Eaton and Burns received salaries of $100.00 a month; the rest were paid $1.50 for a ten-hour day. The young superintendent was the son of builder Benjamin Eaton and the nephew by marriage of owner John Griffin. Being well connected to the management, he enjoyed the privilege of taking outside engineering work, so that he spent only about half his time with the company. The business office was near the plaza, and the working equipment was minimal. Brooks remembered that in the early 1880s the company had only two horses and two light one-horse spring wagons, two crude moisture-tapping "crows," some water buckets, and a few hand-operated "San Jose" pumps. The city's zanja department was equally rickety if one is to judge from a contemporary news item that reported the zanjeros failed to work one day because all the shovels were broken; in January 1882, the zanjero likewise reported to the city council that he had thirty-three broken shovels that needed to be replaced.[4]

Although Mulholland as a deputy zanjero was only a digger and tender of ditches, the city zanjero, or water overseer, ranked next in importance to the alcalde. Indeed, the zanjero's salary was larger than the mayor's, a precedent that stands to this day. When Mulholland went to work for the private water company, the city zanjero was Don Cristobal Aguilar, three-time mayor of Los Angeles (1866, 1868, and 1871), who in 1868 had vetoed the ordinance that would have handed over the city's water rights forever to private ownership.

Taking over from Aguilar in 1881 was Charles N. Jenkins, a crusty veteran who had been one of the only two men from Los Angeles to fight in the Union Army during the Civil War. After capture and a long imprisonment in Andersonville, he had returned to a Los Angeles so violently pro-Southern that he was forced to hide on San Clemente Island until some of the postwar hatreds died down. (Major Horace Bell, the other Union soldier from Los Angeles, claimed the pueblo had been so ardently pro-Confederate that "at the close of the Rebellion it was the most vindictive, uncompromising community in the United States.") Charlie Jenkins, hot-tempered and combative, was city zanjero from 1880 to 1886. Thus, during the years of his apprenticeship, Mulholland became familiar with the clashes between Jenkins and water company workers. Thomas Brooks, in charge of constructing water mains for the company, remembered that once as he had stood in a ditch inspecting the work,

Jenkins rode up and without preamble demanded that Brooks fire two men who, Jenkins felt, were interfering with city plans. When Brooks refused, Jenkins pulled a knife from his belt and demanded that Brooks come out of the ditch so that he could cut out his heart. When Brooks still refused, Jenkins simply pulled around and rode off.

Although Jenkins was of Southern California's vanishing old lawless Anglo world (his brother, William, a member of the Rangers, had been with the posse that brought down Joaquin Murrieta), and although he kept the city council anxious with his demands, he also improved and modernized the city's zanjas and wrote a city directive prescribing much more stringent duties for the deputy zanjero. Shortly after his appointment in 1881, the *Los Angeles Herald* noted that "The new Zanjero, Mr. Charles Jenkins, is giving great satisfaction . . . not only keeping the water supply of the East side up to the requisite standard, but he is actually selling water to the profit of the city. We note with pleasure any departure in the direction of swelling the city's revenues." Jenkins's reign represented the high point of the zanja system, for with the land boom of the 1880s, agricultural land was increasingly sold for commercial and residential use.[5]

Citizen complaints about water were constant, and "warm and nasty" and "so offensive to the taste and smell, as to be not only undrinkable, but positively nauseating" are only a sample. Stories one summer circulated that "a man had been drowned in the reservoir and that the water had become tainted by the putrid carcass allowed to remain there." Then variations of the story appeared: it was a cow, a horse, a sheep; two drowned "Chinamen," then a Chinaman and a horse, then two Chinamen and an Indian; finally, an Indian and a mule. Next, a leading physician of the town opined that "the offensive effluvia was nothing less than that emanating from decomposed human remains," for "he had smelled that smell on several occasions, and knew whereof he spoke." It would be good not to drink the water, he warned, lest there appear a vast amount of diarrhea and typhoid fever.[6]

Finally, William J. Broderick, the collector of the water company, explained that the water from the mains had been shut off to make necessary repairs. When the supply had been turned on again, the rush of water had stirred up the offensive slimy sediment that had been collecting in the old pipes for a long time past. With repairs completed and a steady supply of water back in the pipes, he assured, the troubles should end. Two nights later, however, the "City Water Company got a handling without gloves in the Council," and a committee of three councilmen along with the health officer were delegated to look into the matter. Investigations and debates continued for three months until October, when the board of health announced that the reservoir of the Los Angeles Water Company was "in as good condition as it can be kept."

Among the water company's owners were some of the leading capitalists in Los Angeles. (Some called them the political bosses of the city.) According to Thomas Brooks, they took a personal interest and active role in management but insisted that they receive a good return on every dollar spent for improvements. Mulholland's later opinion, however, was that because they all were men of large means and property, "the business of the water works was but a mere incident to them."[7]

The first to have a direct hand in shaping Mulholland's destiny was William Hayes Perry (1832–1906), president of the water company. Perry's life seemed to embody the wisdom of Horace Greeley's advice, "Go west, young man." The son of Michigan pioneers and a carpenter by training, in 1853 Perry joined a wagon party of about fifty, which included Colonel William Welles Hollister, of Santa Barbara, who was bringing a large band of stock to the Coast. Bedraggled and broke when he reached Los Angeles in 1854, Perry began work as a cabinetmaker but shortly advanced his affairs by opening a furniture store and factory, which in a few years, with the addition of new partners, prospered. By 1873, the firm of Perry, Woodworth & Co. was a leading dealer in lumber, hardware, and building supplies as Perry's acquisitions increased: timber lands, lumber mills, shipping vessels, and spur tracks to railroads. He became a president and director of banks and of gas and oil companies. (In 1867 he had received the first franchise to supply gas for the city after agreeing to furnish free gas for lamps to illuminate the principal crossings on Main Street.) With his endless business connections and social involvements, Perry epitomized a laissez-faire capitalist of the Gilded Age.[8]

The story has often been told how Perry, as he made his rounds of the waterworks, spied a worker vigorously clearing weeds and debris along the zanja that led to the reservoir at Elysian Park. Calling out "What are you doing?" he received a rude "None of your damn business" from the young worker, who continued shoveling. After Perry had flicked his reins and ridden on, a fellow worker informed the rude laborer, Mulholland, that the departing man was president of the water company. Prepared to be fired, Mulholland headed for the office to turn in his time but instead was advanced to foreman of the work crew. For the next twenty-four years, Perry remained Mulholland's boss, although the man who proved most significant in Mulholland's career was his immediate superior, the superintendent and engineer of the water company, Fred Eaton.

AN ENGINEERING FRIEND

Although the friendship and later discord between Frederick Eaton and William Mulholland has become notorious, perhaps the most remarkable aspect of their relationship is that they should ever have met at all. Not only were they born oceans and continents apart, their backgrounds and social standing were equally diverse. Almost exact contemporaries, they were born within days in September 1855, but whereas Mulholland was born to obscure Dubliners, Eaton came from the top drawer of pioneer Los Angeles society and was surrounded throughout his childhood by a family of strong, enterprising men and accomplished women. His father, Benjamin S. Eaton, attorney, engineer, newspaperman, and superior court judge in Los Angeles County (1865), was also one of the founders and promoters of the Indiana Colony that evolved into the City of Pasadena. His mother, Helena Hayes, was one of the sisters of Benjamin J. Hayes, the noted jurist and judge who presided over land cases during the transition from Mexican to American rule and whose writings and diaries have been invaluable in reconstructing much about that period of California history. At the time of Fred's birth, Helena's sister, Louisa Hayes, had become the first woman teacher in the Los Angeles public schools. She subsequently married the enterprising Dr. J. S. Griffin, who, in addition to his medical practice and ownership in the water company, was superintendent of schools and an associate of the senior Eaton in the development of early Pasadena.[9]

Eaton claimed that his serious interest in engineering began only after his marriage in 1875, but he had begun his apprenticeship at fifteen under Charles E. Miles, the first engineer for the Los Angeles Water Company. Miles, called Prince Charlie by his associates and later referred to as the father of the water system, was an able hydraulic engineer who, in 1868, had built the small earth dam known as the Buena Vista Reservoir for the water company in the hills of present-day Elysian Park. From that water storage site, a pipeline 7,730 feet long ran down Buena Vista Street (now North Broadway), over Short Street (now Sunset Boulevard), to First and Main Streets. As the first cast iron pipe to be laid in Los Angeles, the project was innovative in its departure from the traditional open ditch or Spanish zanja. By 1880, both Fred Eaton and Bill Mulholland would find themselves at work on expansions of Miles's projects.[10]

CHAPTER 4

Advancing in the Water Business

1880–1886

Mulholland's promotion in 1880 moved him from his shack near the river to another rude dwelling west of North Broadway in the hills of what is today Elysian Park (approximately the present site of the Buena Vista Power Station). He was to be in charge of a crew laying an extension of twenty-two-inch pipe parallel to the west bank of the river to the toe of the Buena Vista Reservoir, which, under Fred Eaton, was undergoing one of its several enlargements. Living alone and largely indifferent to creature comforts, Mulholland possessed minimal housekeeping skills and would later recall that the place "looked like the devil." His only heat was a smoky stove that his uncle, Roderick Deakers, rigged up for him. The tree-planting urges persisted, however, as out of his own pocket he paid for and planted more than a thousand saplings, as well as cultivating seedlings in salmon cans whose original contents had comprised a main staple of his diet. Around the site of the Buena Vista Reservoir he set out eucalyptus, palm, willow, and live oak, some of which still live over a century later on land now used as a park and picnic grounds.[1]

While Mulholland laid pipe during the summer of 1880, Fred Eaton went off with his father for three weeks on an expedition whose findings would one day alter the history of Southern California—and ultimately, some would say, that of the entire state. During the drought of the late 1870s, Benjamin Eaton had become concerned about water for his vineyards in Pasadena. Aware that cattlemen in the south took their herds north during the summer to Owens Valley, where water was abundant,

Eaton decided to investigate. The scouting party included his sons, Fred and the younger George, along with two friends, Ed Mosher and J. H. Campbell, the latter a lad of thirteen who as an adult would serve as both city clerk and then city treasurer of Pasadena. Almost fifty years later, Campbell spoke of the three weeks he had spent with the Eatons in the Sierras. Judge Eaton, he remembered, took "measurements of water on all the streams, even going high into the mountains." His son Fred Eaton would one day make profound use of what he observed with his father that summer.[2]

Throughout the 1880s, the increasing urbanization and anglicizing of Los Angeles dictated changes in the local water system. In 1881, the city council adopted the words *ditch* and *water overseer* to replace *zanja* and *zanjero* in the interests of easier pronunciation for English-speaking people. What did not change, however, were the continuing water complaints from the city's almost 12,000 residents. (The 1880 census reported 11,128 inhabitants.) "There exist small fish about the size of the aphis in the liquid which the City Water Company palms off for drinking water," began a typical grievance. Chronic dissatisfaction with a company perceived to be indifferent to the public interest would lead eventually to public ownership of the waterworks. That lay years ahead, but in his weekly *Porcupine,* Major Horace Bell would claim that in 1882 he had been the first to advocate "a municipal water system under the ownership and control of the people themselves." In 1884, certain members of the city council pressed for the forfeiture of the water company's franchise, but to no avail.[3]

Eaton and Mulholland in the first blush of their acquaintance must have stimulated each other's engineering passions, as their early years at the water company constituted a sort of on-the-job technical institute. Not only did these two intelligent young men of such divergent backgrounds work together in dealing with immediate problems in the field; they also discussed theoretical matters along with the latest events in hydraulic engineering. They would not have been indifferent, for example, to the announcement in the local press on January 7, 1882, that the largest aqueduct in the world—New York's 40¼-mile-long Croton Aqueduct— had just been completed at a cost of $12 million. In contrast, Eaton and Mulholland struggled with a small-town water system that seemed always to be on the brink of collapse.

When work on Buena Vista was completed four years later, Eaton was about to leave the water company and Mulholland had already left to pursue other ventures (one was a junket with his brother, Hugh, to Washington State, "to study rivers"), so that neither was present in August 1884, when a group of city fathers inspected the newly enlarged works. In its improved state the reservoir was now surrounded by a 14-foot-thick wall of cement and stone, some of the largest of which weighed 2,000 pounds. Surrounding the outside of the wall was a ditch or moat to catch any overflow from the dam, while walks planned as a scenic promenade around the dam offered panoramic views of the city and surrounding hills. Although assured for the time being of an adequate water supply, the city could never take its water for granted, as warnings soon appeared in the papers admonishing users of company water to guard against "unnecessary waste in water closets" and to sprinkle their grounds only between 6:00 A.M. and 8:00 A.M. and between 6:00 P.M. and 8:00 P.M.[4]

Mulholland's move to the Buena Vista area in 1880 not only represented an advancement (and a salary increase from $50 to $65 a month), but also brought him closer to downtown and the public library. A dedicated reader, Mulholland once pronounced, "Damn a man who doesn't read books." His granddaughter, Lillian Sloan Macedo, never forgot his rebuke when he came upon her as a child playing jacks on the sidewalk with a little friend. "Aren't there any good books in the house that you girls could be reading?" he wanted to know. Mary Foy, the city's first librarian, remembered him as "one studious young man" who had once taken out and then renewed for many months "an enormous volume on water power development which nobody else ever wanted to read."[5]

Mulholland's desire to get ahead is evident in his joining with Eaton in 1881 to become officers of Los Angeles Lodge No. 35, International Order of Odd Fellows. Such a group provided not only sociability but also access to the men who controlled civic and business affairs. For as open and free-wheeling as Los Angeles may have seemed, its prosperous new American arrivals from the East and Midwest carried with them class and caste distinctions to which a young Irish immigrant worker would have been sensitive. A visiting journalist in March 1882 artlessly revealed the increasing assumptions of Anglo superiority in this remote provincial community when he first described Los Angeles as bustling, crowded, and full of "strangely different" sights: the old Spanish town with its one-story adobes, "simply a portion of the old Aztec empire left in the centre of a progressive town of our great republic"; the Chinese quarters, "a little chip from China"; and the Frenchmen, the Germans, the Jews, and the Indians, "gathered here for health, or pleasure or profit." But, he confessed, he breathed freer as he entered on Fort Street (now Broadway), "the beautiful, new and refined Anglo-Saxon part of the town with its fine architecture, its well-kept lawns, its evergreen trees."[6]

CIVIC DISCONTENT AND COMPANY DERELICTION

Mulholland's move to the Buena Vista area in 1880 also increased his contact with the water company's staff and directors, a handful of men who not only enjoyed a camaraderie at work but also seem always to have closed ranks when embattled by the frequent public attacks and complaints aimed at their performance. In all his years with the company, Mulholland kept a discreet public silence about his employers. Only after the city took over in 1902 did he voice critical comments, for as he once told his nephew and namesake, William B. Mulholland, "When you go to work for somebody, you do *his* work for him."[7]

Tom Brooks, who came to work for the water company in 1883 during one of Mulholland's absences, found the system somewhat primitive. To lay pipes, men simply lowered them with ropes into the trenches; only as the decade came to an end did more sophisticated equipment such as cranes, tripods, power pumps, cutting or welding torches, and dry-tapping machines begin to appear. Brooks described directors reluctant to make important improvements if doing so meant incurring heavy indebtedness, while he and three laborers struggled to keep the water flowing to customers: "They insisted that every dollar spent must show a return of 100 cents." "Some job!" he once laconically remarked as he went on to explain that in those days a man had to love water and unexpected shower baths if he wished to tap into a cast iron main to insert one-inch or smaller pipe for the purpose of providing a water service. The only equipment for the job was "a rather crude affair known as a 'crow' or 'the old man' which was chained to the main about to be tapped while a special drill and reamer produced an opening with the correct taper" for the corporation cock (the part that connected the service pipe to the main). The trick was to withdraw the drill under full main pressure and drive in the corporation cock without getting oneself and everyone in the neighborhood soaked. Because one needed a hand as steady as a surgeon's to do the job well, and even then, because there could be no guarantee, nearby storekeepers and occupants of rooms in line with the water were warned to close doors and windows while pedestrians were alerted to beware of a soaking.

The water company seemed to pay little heed to public relations, as when it announced in May 1879 that it would charge extra for any household with a bathtub. The city health officer quickly protested the fee to the city council, arguing that bathing should be encouraged in the city. The company was constantly laggard in its responsibilities to install fire hydrants and supply water free of charge to public schools, city hospitals, and jails. At one point the company even balked at paying for the water that the fire company used to put out blazes. In the matter of street sprinkling, the city and the company fought a long court battle over who should pay for the water used to lay the dust in the streets. Nor was this an inconsiderable matter, as dust was the smog of that era. In 1884 a disgruntled real estate man reported to his hometown paper in Marshalltown, Iowa, that Los Angeles was the most lied about city on the Coast and that its inhabitants lived for seven months of the year in so much dust that "they can't see. . . . As to water," he wrote, "it is controlled by a few and you must pay just what they have a mind to ask." The *Evening Express,* then owned in part by members of the water company, indignantly described the critic as a failed real estate salesman who was "too honest to work and too lazy to steal."[8]

Water company representatives never failed to attend the city council's ritual of establishing new water rates at the beginning of each year, and at the least hint of a rate reduction or demand for increased services, they bleated holy poverty. In 1882, for example, the council announced reductions that the company declared unacceptable, claiming to have expended $400,000 up to this time, to have declared no dividend for the past three years, and not to have paid salaries to the president and officers. After two years of court battles, the state supreme court ruled in favor of the city, but the company promptly appealed, and the wrangling continued.[9]

While this debate proceeded in the courts and work advanced on the Buena Vista Reservoir, a landslide in 1882 destroyed a flume at the north end of Pearl Street (today, Figueroa), so that Eaton had to begin excavating a new tunnel that would connect the main supply ditch from Crystal Springs to the Buena Vista Reservoir. A *Times* editorial worried that the city "has created a good part of its debt by its water system, having spent probably $200,000 on the whole" to produce works "of an ephemeral character as yet." It concluded with the hope that something more substantial than the present trenches and wooden flumes would appear. With a promise to continue its water mains out to Washington Street, the water company began laying a four-inch cast iron main from Seventh and Main to the southern line. As the area south of Washington was then largely fruit orchards and vineyards supplied with irrigation water from the zanjas, the new line proved adequate for domestic purposes for the next few years.[10]

A BRIEF LEAVE OF ABSENCE

Because the city looked forward to a transcontinental train connection, hopes stirred in 1884 for better times, as notices of new land developments increased along with booster talk about rising values. Heavy rains and flooding in the winter and spring of 1883–1884 provided plenty of jobs repairing damages to the city. Rainfall of 38.18 inches added up to the wettest period in the history of recorded rainfall in Los Angeles, whose annual average was less than 15 inches. One old-timer remembered that every bridge except the one at Aliso Street was swept away, along with from thirty to fifty houses at the southern end of the city. Many lives were lost, and rail service between San Francisco and Los Angeles stopped for six days after the track washed out in the San Fernando Valley.[11]

When Mulholland returned from his sojourn in Washington State, he and Fred Eaton attempted unsuccessfully to contract independent jobs with the city. Next, with another associate, D. McGregor (who later worked on the Owens Valley Aqueduct), Mulholland submitted a proposal to clean the cave in the Zanja Madre Tunnel and "repair and re-timber it in a substantial manner." This time the city awarded a contract on October 14, 1884, requiring that the job be completed by December 14. With final bills handed to the city on December 2, Mulholland returned to the water company on December 20 as foreman of a large crew of laborers working on a ditch and flume connecting to the Buena Vista Reservoir. One surviving company record book indicates that the workforce varied between twenty-eight and eighty men during the six months that the job continued. For a ten-hour, six-day week, the crew received $2 a day, while Mulholland received $3, or $72 a month.[12]

Shortly thereafter, in a dispute with Perry in early 1885, Eaton walked out on his job as superintendent of the water company. The following year he became the city surveyor and engineer at a salary of $200 a month. With the boom of the 1880s under way, he and his father also began to profit from increasing sales of their holdings in Pasadena. Perry replaced Eaton with W. J. Kelley, whom Brooks later described as "more of an office man than an engineer."

ON THE SESPE

Mulholland remained on the water company payroll until September 1885, when he left for a job in Ventura County that kept him away from the city for the next eight months. Perry and associates had engaged him and another engineer, Philip (Phil) Wintz, to design and lay out a system of irrigation ditches for the Sespe Land and Water Company, which was to supply water and power to the embryonic town site of Fillmore. Wintz, a young Virginian recently employed by the water company, became a lifelong associate and would one day be in charge of building the Haiwee Dam on the Owens River Aqueduct. As the Sespe Land and Water Company's location in the Santa Clara Valley was fifty-two miles from Los Angeles with only one train running daily, the men remained there from late spring to the end of summer 1886. They grew to love the beauty of the area along the Santa Clara River with its background of rugged mountains and picturesque ranchos. Probably in payment for services, the men acquired approximately twenty acres each, on which they planted orange trees along Sespe Creek. (Mulholland would hold his Sespe land until 1903 or 1904, when he sold because of water scarcity.) Ironically, although this area would one day figure in the greatest tragedy of Mulholland's life, his original work on the Sespe has endured. As late as 1966, a Fillmore rancher reported that the routes Mulholland and Wintz laid out for irrigation lines were still in use. Perry's group also hired Mulholland to study the Sespe River's potential to provide power. He concluded that it would never be a feasible source of power because of its "fitful and unreliable" stream flow.[13]

When Mulholland returned to town in midsummer 1886, the water company was in the midst of a major overhaul of its Crystal Springs system. As the land by the river had become increasingly settled and cultivated, especially near its bend by Griffith Park, the banks had eroded and the water become progressively silted. Where the stream had once run clear, it was now clouded and often foul tasting, "a by-word of reproach" among the citizenry. At a cost of $100,000, the company was about to build a closed-conduit system 27,000 feet long and able to deliver about ten million gallons of water to the city every twenty-four hours. The three-by-four-foot conduit, beginning at the eastern edge of Griffith Park and extending to Dayton Avenue, was to be constructed of "butt-cut redwood—all carefully selected—the finest uniform quality of this kind of timber ever used in a similar undertaking on this coast," ran the company boast.[14]

Devised by local civil and hydraulic engineer J. P. Culver, the plan was not without its critics. Eaton's opposition to the use of wooden pipe may have led to his leaving the water company, for years later, in a pamphlet written for a 1905 Oakland sewer bond election, he harked back to 1886, when he had "watched the construction of a wooden conduit by the LA City Water Co., which I had formerly advised against, and observed its gradual decay thereafter, rendering the conduit entirely useless in less than ten years." Mulholland, awarded the contract to oversee the tricky flume and tunnel-building section, was to write in the same pamphlet that the timbers, lined with Portland cement and covered with earth to insure transporting the water in the cleanest possible circumstances, were giving trouble within three years of its completion and "in less than ten years had to be abandoned altogether."[15]

Shortly after beginning the project, the water company, for reasons unknown, took over Mulholland's contract and retained him as general foreman. At a time when labor organizations were struggling to break the contract system and obtain an eight-hour day, the company crews rotated on ten-hour day and night shifts so they could complete the difficult task by winter. Living in the camp with a crew of almost ninety men, Mulholland earned $5 a day while the company charged him $2.50 a day for board.

While working on this job, Mulholland became a naturalized American citizen in October 1886. When he registered to vote for the first time in November, he gave his occupation as contractor and his address as Sepulveda (then a section on the west bank of the Los Angeles River south of Mission Street). The job was also memorable because of the arrival of two tough, roistering Irish workingmen, Pat Harkins and Handsome Brady. Mulholland in aftertimes enjoyed recalling a payday when the paymaster had tossed down two silver dollars to Harkins as he completed his ten hours in the muddy ditch. As Harkins caught and flung them aloft again, he shouted to Brady, "To hell with Poverty! Tell the old lady to get out the big pot."

As work on this project wound down, fate intervened to secure Mulholland a job that, in a sense, became his for life. In November, during a recreational weekend at Santa Monica, Superintendent Kelly dropped dead of a heart attack. Perry first offered Assistant Superintendent Brooks the position, but Brooks, then twenty-four and feeling his lack of experience, suggested that Mulholland at thirty-one might be better suited. Perry offered, was accepted, and at the end of 1886, Bill Mulholland became superintendent of the waterworks.

The New Superintendent

1887–1892

BOOM TIMES AND WASHOUTS

Mulholland's advancement to superintendent of the water company co-incided with the city's first land boom, which, though brief, was dra-matic. The population of Los Angeles bounded from 11,000 to 50,000 in less than three years as large areas of heretofore unoccupied land were promoted and established as town sites and new communities. With the upheaval, the need for public services became acute, so Mulholland and Eaton, the two chiefly responsible for maintaining the city's mains and drains, must at times have felt that they were the busiest men in the ex-panding town.

Heavy rains fell during Mulholland's first months as superintendent, and although rainfall for the entire season proved normal (14.05 inches), downpours in February did almost as much damage as those that had fallen in 1883–1884. Streets flooded, bridges went out, and water from the Big Tujunga Wash roared into the Los Angeles River, destroying the railroad bridge east of San Fernando. Rumors arose that Reservoir No. 4 north of Temple Street was about to break as it had six years before. Although the reservoir held, to avert a panic, police were sent out to as-sure neighboring dwellers that they were safe. The city remained isolated for several days and suffered extensive damage. For a time, bridge washouts completely cut off Boyle Heights.[1]

Serving his second year as city surveyor, Eaton had to deal with prob-lems not only of sewage and sanitation but also those of reordering the growing city's infrastructure, such as grading and recontouring streets in the hilly downtown areas and replacing bridges that had been lost in the flood. Controversy encircled him through most of the year, beginning in March when he had to defend himself against the charge that he had made false statements to the mayor and the council as to the cost of bids to replace the destroyed Kuhrts Street Bridge, where Main Street extended east across the river. Suggestions that he had colluded with a low bidder for his own profit drew a spirited self-defense from Eaton, who denounced "ignorant men who will attempt to bring disgrace upon a man hitherto having the confidence and respect of his fellow-citizens." Ultimately, the council found no blame in the matter, or as a *Times* reporter skeptically commented, "And you are right, and we are right, and all is right as right can be."[2]

Eaton spent much of the remainder of the year making plans and surveys for an enlargement of the city sewerage that would involve expenditures of over a million dollars and that, under the name of the Eaton Plan, was presented for consideration to the city council in September. In November, a reporter caught up with Eaton on his return from an expedition to scout a route for the Salt Lake and Los Angeles Railroad, which would come into the city through the Arroyo Seco. Asked about his sewer plans, Eaton said they were still under consideration but stressed that "the situation is getting serious," for in the Vernon district surplus sewage was overflowing the land. Before leaving office at the end of the year, Eaton also revealed that his predecessor, George C. Knox, had taken thousands of dollars' worth of maps made during his term of office, along with field books containing notes of his surveys. Eaton asserted that no one who worked for a salary with the city had a right to help himself to such property. Eaton announced that he would not seek a reappointment to the post and that he already had engagements for the coming year.[3]

Meanwhile that summer, citizens once more had complained of too many fish in their water pipes and of dust and inadequate street sprinkling because the foot-dragging water company had failed again to install the hydrants that the council had ordered it to provide. The company finally did comply, so that by the end of the year, Mayor William Workman expressed satisfaction with the streets' condition. Other vexations confronted Mulholland in his first year as superintendent as several terrible fires had resulted in heavy property loss because the water company's mains had been too small to supply enough water to extinguish the conflagrations. As it became incumbent upon the company to enlarge the system, Mulholland found himself supervising the placement of increasingly large pipelines into the most heavily populated areas of the city.

At the end of 1887, most of the vineyards and orchards in the city having been subdivided so that zanjas were no longer much needed for irrigation, Mayor Workman called for a system of filtration and improved piping. He optimistically believed enough water was available "to supply a city of over a million people if it is properly handled. . . . We are blessed," he concluded, "with an abundance of water in Los Angeles, but the condition of some of it when it comes to the houses for domestic use is the reverse of tempting."[4]

EATON HAS A FAILURE

At the beginning of 1888, while Mulholland was still installing the pipeline on Buena Vista Street, Fred Eaton left the city to work on one of his engagements. During the boom years, no piece of Southern California seemed impossible to develop, so in 1887, in the remote scenic northwest corner of the San Fernando Valley on land formerly owned by Benjamin F. Porter, arose yet one more town site, this one bearing the idyllic name of Chatsworth Park. The promoters, George F. Crow and a group called the San Fernando Valley Water Company, predicted a glorious future for this beautiful but isolated area by the Santa Susana Mountains and announced grandiose plans for one of the "largest systems of waterworks in this part of the State." Eaton was to oversee building a series of reservoirs that would catch the overflow from a main dam in Brown's Canyon, through which, the promoters falsely claimed, flowed the headwaters of the Los Angeles River. A year after the completion of Eaton's first reservoir, however, the dream went a-glimmering. Not only did the boom end, but on December 24, 1889, after heavy rains, Eaton's dam washed out. Because the area was unpopulated, the damage was not catastrophic except to the builders' hopes.[5]

MULHOLLAND MOVES UP

At the beginning of 1888, during the laying of the 22-inch pipeline on Buena Vista Street, Mulholland lived nearby and alone in digs at 103 Buena Vista. When he registered to vote that year, he stated that he was superintendent of the city water company and for the first time identified himself as a civil engineer. Not all of his job demands, however, were of an engineering nature. On May 11, 1888, he was summoned to the Buena

Vista Reservoir to recover the body of a young woman whose life in California had turned bitter. Boys out hunting had seen her walk up to the reservoir, place her hat, wrap, and satchel on the ground, climb the stone wall of the dam, and jump. While the others ran off for help, one of the boys leaped in to save her, but she struggled so violently that he failed. With rope and grappling irons, Mulholland and the dam keeper retrieved the corpse from the water.[6]

The boom proved profitable to the water company, for on March 8, 1888, its directors called a meeting of stockholders to consider "the propriety of increasing the capital to $1,240,000, divided into 2,400 shares." A week later came word that the company would build new headquarters, and on Saturday, May 26, the old overcrowded office building north of the plaza was vacated as everything and everybody connected to the domestic waterworks moved to a new, two-storied brick and stone building at the corner of Alameda and Marchessault Streets.[7]

Said to have cost $11,000, the new building had a ground floor that comprised a workshop and storage area for pipes and equipment. From an entrance on Marchessault, a winding stone stairway climbed to the second floor and opened into a reception room, "well-lighted and comfortably arranged," separated from the main office by "a large carved window of pitch-pine." The main office contained desks for the clerical staff, while one wide door led off to a room for Chief Clerk S. B. Caswell's special use. All the interior fixtures were of polished pitch-pine, neat but not gaudy. In addition to a directors' boardroom upstairs, there were sleeping rooms for the superintendent and the company foreman. In effect, Mulholland and Brooks were house mates and, moreover, were never away from the job. One reporter explained, "Hitherto, when any accident occurred during the night, it was a matter of extreme difficulty to procure the company's workmen to repair the damage, but the presence of the superintendent and the foreman upon the premises at night renders it now a matter of less difficulty to attend to any damage and have it at once remedied, though it occur in the dead of night."[8]

Mulholland now lived as if back on shipboard, with round-the-clock interruptions to sleep. This may have proven no great hardship, however, as his children remembered that he never seemed to need much sleep. He was a lifelong catnapper who could doze off in a car or train for fifteen or twenty minutes and awaken fully refreshed and alert. He claimed to have acquired this ability on watches at sea, and it was to serve him in good stead during the years of aqueduct construction when he traveled constantly and arduously between Los Angeles and Owens Valley.

Out of that brief period when Mulholland and Brooks shared living quarters, they forged a lifelong friendship, for both men stayed with the water company to the end of their working days. At the time of his retirement in 1938, Brooks had been with the city's water system for fifty-five years. Associates said that Tom Brooks never took a vacation in his life, and once, as he and Mulholland watched some laborers work on a ditch, Brooks remarked that the men were growing old, to which Mulholland replied, "Yes. They got old working for you." One of the few who knew Mulholland well in his early years with the water company, Brooks later remembered that when they first met, "Bill Mulholland's library consisted chiefly of Fanning's Treatise on Hydraulics, Trautwine's Engineer's Pocket Book, Kent's Mechanical Engineer's Pocket Book, a Geometry, a Trigonometry, and Shakespeare's Works." He was also, Brooks remembered, "very fond of Grand Opera."[9]

MARRIAGE AND A GOLD WATCH

Within two years, however, Mulholland moved on to a new living arrangement, for in 1890, he married. Also that year he received a gold watch from a grateful water company for services beyond the call of duty when he had braved the torrential rains of Christmas week, 1889–1890, to save the city's water supply. During the downpours, the Los Angeles River had changed its course and broken the water connections at Crystal Springs; or as company president Perry explained, "The Los Angeles River got on a tear, cut a new channel through an alfalfa patch, and came rushing down upon the brick conduit then forming the head of the system with such force that it was knocked into a cocked hat." The water brought with it such an accumulation of sand and detritus that it filled the conduit until only a small opening "about as big as your arm" remained. If it had closed completely, no water would have flowed to the city, and so the morning before Christmas 1889, "William Mulholland, superintendent of the company, jumped out of bed when the alarm was given, . . . and he didn't get a chance to undress and go to bed like a Christian for four days; but he got the conduit open, and the city was not without its regular supply of water for a minute." Perry estimated that in two hours' time, the damage had amounted to $100,000, adding, "I did not know but that the city would have to go back to water carts for its supply."[10]

Two weeks before he was awarded his gold watch at a company din-

ner, Mulholland married Lillie Ferguson. They had met when he was overseeing a major project across the river from her father's farm in the summer of 1889. With a crew of one hundred men and several foremen, he
had begun laying percolation pipes at Crystal Springs in an effort to improve and increase the water supply for a growing population that now
consumed the equivalent of the Buena Vista Reservoir's contents every
two days in summer and every three in winter.[11] Rather than travel back
and forth to office headquarters, Mulholland had moved out to the work
camp near a new tract development called Ivanhoe. Ivanhoe was a prod-
uct of the boom, when tracts and town sites sprang up like weeds and
wildflowers in spring. Perhaps James Slauson caught the spirit of the times
best. When asked why he was laying out a town site in the Azusa district amid boulders, cactus, and dry wash, Slauson replied, "If it's not
good for a town it isn't good for anything."

Lillie Ferguson lived with her family in neighboring Kenilworth,
which, like Ivanhoe, was on Los Feliz lands, the general location today
identified by surviving street names taken from the novels of Sir Walter
Scott: Waverly, Rowena, Locksley, Kenilworth, and Ivanhoe. Rowena
Reservoir (northwest of Silver Lake Reservoir) also remains a landmark
of Ivanhoe. Kenilworth stretched to the northwest over the hills and
looked down on the banks of the Los Angeles River. Among those who
had purchased land there was Mulholland's future father-in-law, James
Ferguson, a farmer and former hotel keeper from northern Michigan.
Ferguson's ten acres lay north of present-day Griffith Park and bordered
the Crystal Springs Land and Water Company's main supply ditch, where
percolation pipes were to be laid. When the company wished to situate
a correct surveying line and needed to drill a hole slanted toward a certain point, that point proved to be on James Ferguson's land. Seeking
permission to enter the property, Mulholland one day knocked at Ferguson's front door and was met by his twenty-one-year-old daughter,
Lillie. She later told her daughters that the first time she saw Mulholland, she knew that they would marry.[12]

The courtship was brief, and the nuptials took place on a warm and
cloudless day in the Fergusons' home on Thursday, July 3, 1890. When
the job at Crystal Springs was completed, the newlyweds moved to their
first "official" home at 914 Buena Vista (today, North Broadway), where
they remained for the next three years and where their first three children
were born: Rose Ellen (1891), William Perry (1892), and Thomas Ferguson (1894).

THE AMBITIONS OF EATON

The nineties saw Fred Eaton's ascendancy in civic affairs. By the end of
the decade, while William Mulholland remained a little-noted local figure,
Eaton had become mayor of Los Angeles (1899–1900). Aside from their
shared capacity for hard work and commitment to the engineering profession, the two men differed in ways that reflected their distinct backgrounds and paternal influences: Eaton's father was a California entrepreneur and civic booster driven by the competitive urge to strive and
win, whereas Mulholland's was an Irish public servant who had suppressed his spontaneity and individuality in the service of an inimical ruling order. By the time Mulholland married at almost thirty-five, Eaton
had been a husband for fifteen years and was the father of two adoles-
cent children. He moreover maintained a full calendar of social, business, and civic activities among the leading lights of the town. On account of the lack of documentation, much about Eaton's character is
uncertain and perhaps will remain so. Existing contemporary accounts
suggest that, in addition to his outstanding engineering and business abilities, Eaton was an indefatigable go-getter and joiner. Except for the arts,
no aspect of civic life escaped his participation at one time or another.
He held city office as engineer and surveyor; he was active in real estate,
land, and water development; he served with the first volunteer fire
brigade; and he worked on committees for such events as the city's Fourth
of July celebrations and the formal opening of the Broadway Market. In
1890, he participated in the founding of the National Bank of California in Los Angeles, whose directors included associates from his water
and transportation ventures.[13]

Nor was he averse to frivolity, as a reporter once noted that "Fred
Eaton, in his trips to Santa Monica, devotes himself to showing bathers
a new trick in the waves. He has not ventured to try and instruct any of
his lady friends . . . as it is the marine equivalent of standing on your head
on horseback." Although he had been a Democrat when Mulholland first
met him, he later became an active Republican, even serving on the committee that greeted President Benjamin Harrison on his visit to the city
in April 1891. Earlier, in July 1890, he had been among the organizers
of the annual roundup and picnic of the Union League Club (a center of
Republican power), at what was then called San Juan-by-the-Sea, two
miles from Mission San Juan Capistrano on the oceanfront lands of Don
Marco Forster and Judge Richard Egan. The two-day revelry of important and wealthy Republican loyalists included such jollities as yacht

races, swimming, games, and feasts with a Mexican flavor. The menus featured barbecue, or "cabeza tatemada, hecho al gusto de Don Marco Forster," along with enchiladas, chile con carne, frijoles guisado, chiles rellenos, cerveza y vino tinto. The invitation also included the caveat, "if you expect to retire, take your blankets, and if this is your month to bathe furnish your own towels."[14]

Eaton was also involved in transportation schemes, including the promotion of an electric railway system for the city, which was rapidly outgrowing its horse-drawn car lines. He had participated earlier in a cable car company that failed and, while still city surveyor, had also played a role in gaining the Los Angeles, Salt Lake and Atlantic Railway's franchise for a right of way through the city via the Arroyo Seco. Partly impeded by economic hard times, none of these efforts succeeded until 1895, when Moses Hazeltine Sherman came to town from Arizona Territory with his partner, Eli Clark, and secured loans of $15 million dollars from Chicago capitalists to establish a successful electric rail system, the Pacific Electric Railway. When Henry Huntington later purchased the system, it evolved into the efficient interurban network of trolleys that today are happily remembered, not to say sentimentalized, as the Big Red Cars.[15]

Promotion and boosting were in Eaton's blood. A disciple of his father and uncles, between engagements of planning and building local dams, sewers, and rail lines, he planned land developments. On his wife's and mother-in-law's inherited property at Spring and Second Streets, he designed and built a commercial building, the Burdick Block, at a cost of $140,000. During the boom, he subdivided the Buena Vista Tract south of Chavez Ravine and immediately southeast of today's Dodger Stadium, and he surveyed and platted downtown tracts.[16]

A MENTOR FOR MULHOLLAND

While Fred Eaton pursued his hectic career in the 1890s, William Mulholland, apart from his newfound domestic life, could be said to have earned an advanced degree in engineering when, in August 1891, he patented a device utilizing wave force to generate power. He also acquired skills in business administration and political science, as he either witnessed or participated in the struggles and intrigues among the City of Los Angeles and rival private interests over who would control the waters of the Los Angeles River after the Los Angeles Water Company's lease expired in 1898. As he planned and oversaw the city's waterworks, he became privy to the company's business maneuvers, some of which flaunted such egregious unbridled laissez-faire capitalism that they called out for the pen of a Mark Twain, an Ambrose Bierce, or at the least, an O. Henry.

William Perry's influence was immense in the 1880s and '90s, when the notion of conflict of interest seemed a matter of indifference. At one point, he was both president of the water company and a member of the city council's water committee, the latter committee setting water rates for the very company of which he was president.

By this time most of the old Spanish-Mexican *hacendados* and rancheros were in decline, and many of the early Anglos of the pueblo were losing influence as the city filled with newcomers who were generally white, midwestern, and Protestant. During what journalist Phil Townsend Hanna called the Middle Nordic Period, old-timer Major Horace Bell, who had been a vibrant force in the legal and journalistic life of Los Angeles after the Civil War, grew increasingly disenchanted with his beloved Southern California. In the 1880s he had turned over the editorship of his lively weekly, *The Porcupine,* to his oldest son, Charles. It soon fell into decline, as Charles, a notorious boozer and womanizer, lacked his father's discipline and devotion to the job. The major himself became increasingly irrelevant in his hometown as he continued to engage in the old ways of the pueblo: drinking, roistering, challenging enemies to duels, and engaging in cantankerous litigations. Meanwhile, his sons provided scandal for the local press with their escapades of drunkenness, gambling, drug use, disorder, and in one instance, embezzlement. Although Bell was only two years older than Perry (and would outlive him by ten), he seemed to be from an earlier epoch—that of the freebooting, freethinking frontiersman—while Perry exemplified the entrepreneurial and acquisitive spirit of the Gilded Age.

Mulholland, a generation younger than either and shaped in another country, belonged to a new breed who believed that science and reason held the best hope for mankind. Though he may have shared with Bell a tart tongue and sometimes sardonic outlook on human folly, he nevertheless had cast his lot with entrepreneurs like Perry and Eaton. Eaton was Mulholland's colleague and instructor in engineering matters, but when it came to city politics and business, William H. Perry had also been a mentor.

By 1890, Perry and Mulholland had sustained a twelve-year relationship as employer and employee, but in spite of their bonhomie on the job—Tom Brooks remembered that many of the old water company's board of directors meetings consisted largely of Mulholland's entertaining the assemblage with yarns of his seafaring days—a social chasm yawned between the two. Perry, after all, was of the city's elite. His Pearl Street home was the setting for frequent soirees and musicales that featured the singing talents of his daughter, Mamie, and for lavish parties for the younger daughter, Florence, all of which were faithfully reported in the newspapers. Into this social sphere Mulholland and his wife were not to enter.[17]

CHAPTER 6

Water Plots and Politics

1893–1895

EXPANSIONIST MANEUVERS

Los Angeles's determination to grow in the 1890s led not only to the creation of a harbor through annexation of land adjoining the sea and the development of an efficient interurban transportation system but also to the laying of a groundwork for a water system that everyone hoped would provide an ample supply for a burgeoning population. Not surprisingly, the decade produced critical legal battles and decisions that arose from the city's struggle to maintain its rights to the waters of the Los Angeles River. Of one major and complicated water suit in the 1890s—*City of Los Angeles v. the Los Angeles Water Company*—a reporter once wrote, "The kaleidoscopic character of the city's water litigation becomes more pronounced with every step taken by either of the parties involved. Just when by persistent effort some faint conception of the case is formed by the ordinary intelligent layman a new turn or twist is given, and the status of the case in some of its parts or in whole affords new ground for speculation." Mulholland, who would testify in many of the cases, later wrote that the "bitterly contested" lawsuits ultimately "produced a compendium of facts that covers every phase of the subject that could possibly be gleaned either directly by observation or by theoretical inference."[1]

Much of the controversy in the 1890s concerned a crucial elbow bend of the Los Angeles River into which major feeder streams converged and flowed to the city from the San Fernando Valley, the Tujunga Wash, and the Coastal Basin. South of that bend and east of today's Crystal Springs

Drive in Griffith Park, on November 5, 1886, the water company established a new works on a few acres of marshy land and called its latest business entity the Crystal Springs Land and Water Company. The parent company then bought the new enterprise for a dollar and proceeded to assert that the underground waters of Crystal Springs did not come from the river but from springs discovered on its wetlands, thus declaring itself free from any claims the city might make upon the waters. The city had anticipated this maneuver, however, and in July 1886 had instructed Eaton, then city surveyor, to determine if the source of Crystal Springs waters were not the result of percolation from the river. Meanwhile, the water company proceeded to award Mulholland, now back from the Sespe and acting as an independent contractor, the job of building a tunnel and flume for the Crystal Springs project.[2]

Not until November 1891 did the City of Los Angeles bring suit against the Crystal Springs Company, enjoining it from making use of river water and asking damages of $225,000 for the water it had taken from the river during the past three years (1888–1891). The suit dragged through the decade until finally resolved in favor of the city in 1898 after a notable trial at which Eaton and Mulholland testified on opposing sides. This was, however, only one of many conflicts in which city and private interests struggled to gain control of water resources, especially after the boom had attracted a swarm of land speculators and fortune seekers, some quick to see the desirability of controlling the white gold of water in a semiarid land.

During the boom of the eighties, the corporate owners of the City Water Company and Crystal Springs decided to acquire some lesser systems. Shortly after they bought the Garvanza, or Arroyo Seco, works from Ralph Rogers in 1888, however, the boom died, and their expansion ceased until 1891, when they bought from Henry Hazard the East Side Springs Water Company, which delivered water east of the river and to Brooklyn Heights. Eventually they acquired the Highland Water Company servicing Highland Park; the Citizens' Water Company, headed by M. L. Wicks, which distributed water (badly!) to the hilly district northwest of Temple and Figueroa; and the Mountain Water Company, east of Brooklyn Heights. By the end of 1891, the Los Angeles City Water Company controlled almost all the city's domestic water supply.[3]

While the City Water Company—or the Grand Monopoly, as Horace Bell liked to call it in his *Porcupine*—was buying up local water plants and doing battle with the city council and the citizenry over water rates and services, local newspapers campaigned for municipal ownership of

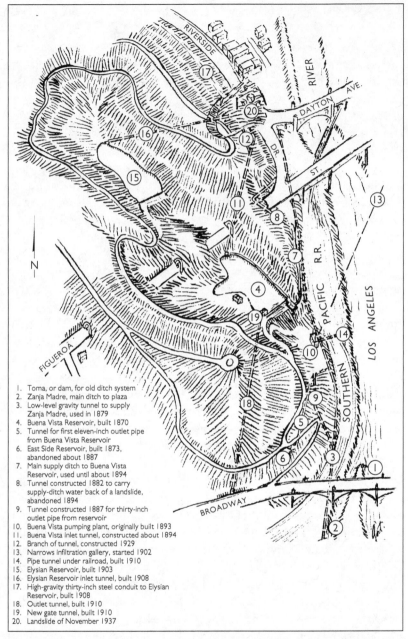

1. Toma, or dam, for old ditch system
2. Zanja Madre, main ditch to plaza
3. Low-level gravity tunnel to supply
   Zanja Madre, used in 1879
4. Buena Vista Reservoir, built 1870
5. Tunnel for first eleven-inch outlet pipe
   from Buena Vista Reservoir
6. East Side Reservoir, built 1873,
   abandoned about 1887
7. Main supply ditch to Buena Vista
   Reservoir, used until about 1894
8. Tunnel constructed 1882 to carry
   supply-ditch water back of a landslide,
   abandoned 1894
9. Tunnel constructed 1887 for thirty-inch
   outlet pipe from reservoir
10. Buena Vista pumping plant, originally built 1893
11. Buena Vista inlet tunnel, constructed about 1894
12. Branch of tunnel, constructed 1929
13. Narrows infiltration gallery, started 1902
14. Pipe tunnel under railroad, built 1910
15. Elysian Reservoir, built 1903
16. Elysian Reservoir inlet tunnel, built 1908
17. High-gravity thirty-inch steel conduit to Elysian
    Reservoir, built 1908
18. Outlet tunnel, built 1910
19. New gate tunnel, built 1910
20. Landslide of November 1937

Map 1. Waterworks structures, Elysian Park area, showing waterworks structures dating from Zanja Madre days to 1937 (from Thomas Brooks, assisted by Laurance E. Goit, *Notes on Los Angeles Water Supply*, September 1938).

water. One reported in the spring of 1890 that not only was water scarce in some of the downtown public buildings but that during afternoons and evenings the upper portions of City Hall had no water at all. By summer, crowds demonstrated to protest the bad water service, so that the city, after much debate, decided not to wait for the termination of the water company's lease in 1898 but asked at the end of 1891 for a statement of the extent of the company's plant and the price for which it would be willing to sell.[4]

This decision set off a curious episode of intrigue and apparent collusion between the water company and parties from out of town. In response to the city's proposal, President Perry promptly replied that although he would have to consult with his board of directors and other stockholders before establishing an exact amount, he himself figured the price of the properties at $2.5 million. Debate ensued, with many feeling the figure too high. But the city's desire to take control of its water grew, along with the fear that the water company might sell its property to another private company (which it had every right to do). Thus, under a new management, it might manage to delay the city's resumption of control for perhaps another fifty years.[5]

The fear proved well founded, for in January 1892, one day after a court decision had defeated the city's attempt to annul the franchise of the Citizens' Water Company, a letter in the *Los Angeles Times* attacked the water company. Singling out Fred Eaton for special opprobrium (Eaton was advocating public ownership while at the same time developing downtown commercial real estate on behalf of his father-in-law, Horace Burdick), the letter claimed the poor were overcharged "to pay for water used to put out fires in buildings owned by rich landlords and to sprinkle the broad streets in front of their business blocks and their acres of residence grounds." This apparently populist attack against Eaton (and municipal ownership) proved to be, however, not the work of a reformer but rather of a promoter and front man, J. H. "Jayhawker" Woodard, for a pair of Indianapolis investors said to be interested in buying the water company. Although ostensibly having no connection with the city's insiders, as the drama played out, it proved to be an attempted preemptive buy on behalf of the water company.[6]

With the threat of the water company's sale, the city council decided the time had come to build its own waterworks, but both a judge and a United States district attorney warned that although under its contract with the water company the city could lay pipes in the streets, it could not carry water in them for sale to the people. Judge J. A. Anderson also reiterated the doctrine of riparian rights to the council: "Now, what is it you own? Water in the river was never owned by anybody. You can't get a title to water as it flows in the river. It is like the wild animal. It has to be captured before you can get a title to the water." The city was also advised that it could take only that river water that flowed within the city limits and, moreover, that the water company owned all the percolated water it had developed, that is, Crystal Springs. The city was counseled to find a group of capitalists who would form an omnibus corporation to buy out all existing water plants, unite them into one, and then turn over all to the city for operation. Water rates would then be established that could enable the city to pay off its bonded indebtedness for such a venture.[7]

In the midst of this debate, the water company sprang its surprise by announcing that the plant was to be sold to the syndicate fronted by the Indianapolis businessmen and their advance man, Jayhawker Woodard. Negotiations had taken place in San Francisco with the president of the Wells Fargo Nevada Bank, I. W. Hellman. Although Hellman had left Los Angeles in 1890 to join the bank, he still retained his ties to the city and remained one of the major stockholders of the City Water Company. According to the announcement, the buyers had made a first payment of $500,000 on the purchase price of $2.5 million that Perry had so readily quoted to the city a year before. Assurances followed that there was to be no change in management, as "Mr. Perry, Mr. Mott and Mr. Broderick have all shown themselves so capable." Suspecting corporate jugglery, the *Los Angeles Herald* suggested that the City Water Company was using the deal as a screen in order to produce a side company similar to Crystal Springs.[8]

In the municipal election of November 1892, voters approved a bond measure for building their own water system at a cost of $526,000. Then, just as the city was about to issue and sell water bonds for its new project in the spring of 1893, another eastern syndicate announced it was ready to buy the water company. This suspected water company ploy to circumvent the city's intentions was foiled, however, by the bad economic conditions of 1893, a year of national depression that resulted in hard times and a series of disastrous bank failures in Los Angeles. (I. W. Hellman personally bailed out the recently formed Farmers' and Merchants' Bank when he arrived on the afternoon train from San Francisco with $500,000 in sacks of gold coin aboard.)[9]

The Indianapolis gentlemen arrived in September to inspect their newly purchased water company. Within a week, they told the city that they were willing to reduce their previous sale price of $3.5 million to $3.3 million. Saying they could accept nothing less, they then took the train out of town, followed by Woodard, who, once home, boasted to the *Indianapolis Journal* that he had made $15,000 by bringing off the sale of the Los Angeles waterworks while his clients stood to clear $750,000 on the deal. When this story got back to the West Coast and reached the ears of the councilmen who were studying how to place an accurate valuation on the waterworks, certain members erupted. After declaring that "the people of this city are not fools," one recommended that further parley be cut off and that the city get busy again planning its own system.[10]

Under the direction of City Engineer Henry Dockweiler, a thorough inventory was being made of the water company's holdings, especially the amount of pipeline in the streets of the city, for which there was no written record. The city reached its own estimate of the value of the waterworks at $1,490,882.50, which the Indianapolis group rejected, asserting that in the event it should acquire the property, it did not wish to sell to the city. Then, abruptly, S. H. Mott, secretary of the water company, wrote that its property was not currently on the market and, moreover, challenged the city's inventory, especially in the matter of the waters at Crystal Springs. Thus, the city lost its round with the water company, but at least had been spared the expense of buying an overpriced water system.[11]

Amid this conniving, the city also found itself in another lengthy struggle that became noted as the Hooker and Pomeroy case, important because after a six-year lawsuit, the state supreme court in 1899 found in the city's favor and granted paramount rights of the waters of the Los Angeles River to the pueblo over those of private riparian owners. The case originated in the early 1890s when the city, planning to create its own water system, had turned to lands on the Providencia Rancho Company (today Glendale) as the site for a system of filtration pipes and head works. Head works for the water company were already in place on the south bank of the river on the Los Feliz side (about where Traveltown stands today in Griffith Park). In fact, much of the city's water was already being taken from the Providencia side, for the water company had for several years paid the landowners there $5 a day for the right to use their supply ditch. Now, however, the city wanted to purchase the land in question, so, early in 1893, just as the water company seemed about to be "sold" to the Indianapolis investors, the Providencia landowners, J. D. Hooker and A. E. Pomeroy, granted the city an option to buy 400 acres for $30,000. (The final purchase was 315 acres.) The president of the council thought the price too high and said the land was not worth it, but he was told that it was not land the city was after; it was water. Then a member mentioned that he had heard that Pomeroy had told someone he would sell the 400 acres for $15,000. The president next recommended condemnation, while another member pointed out that such a lengthy proceeding would leave them for several more years at the mercy of the water company. A judicial bombshell put an end to this dickering when word came from Sacramento that the bonds they had counted on to pay for their waterworks had been declared invalid. When Hooker and Pomeroy showed up in City Hall to arrange the sale for $30,000, the officials regretfully had to reveal that they lacked the money to pay for the deed. Four city banks would shut their doors two weeks later, and feeling that the alarming financial panic left them no other choice, the council turned to condemnation proceedings that would take the rest of the decade to resolve.[12]

During the depressed mid-nineties and amid political, financial, and municipal wrangling and maneuvering, not to say chicanery, Mulholland was overseeing the installation of a new pumping plant west of the Buena Vista Street Bridge. Once the pipes were laid, the plant was to bring relief to the distressed and water-deprived hill districts, where water shortages and stoppages had been a constant source of complaint under the disgraceful management of the Citizens' Water Company. One irate citizen described the hills as dotted with the charred remains of houses that had burned down because no water was available to fight the fires. Another long-suffering soul, a laboring man as he described himself, wrote that he lived west of Bunker Hill, and for the past four years had been unable to obtain a drop of water from 6:00 A.M. to 10:00 P.M. He had been forced to collect it in tubs and barrels during the early morning for use through the day. But, he noted, the bill collector was always on hand for payment, water or no water. *The Porcupine* had also fulminated against the Citizens' Water Company, claiming that the water the city delivered to irrigators was better than the water that Citizens' gave to humans. *The Porcupine* branded the former owners as robbers of the citizens, who had to use water containing remnants of "decaying animal and vegetable matter—pieces an inch or more long of fish, bugs and half-decayed weeds!"[13]

By May 1893, with two large gangs of men laying pipe, Mulholland promised that the work would be completed in thirty days and that water delivery would then increase from half a million to two million gallons a day. Three days later, Prudent Beaudry, the man who had first looked to the hills northwest of the plaza and dreamed of building homes there, the pioneer developer and builder of water systems, died unexpectedly of a stroke at the age of seventy-four. For thirty years he had been a force in civic affairs, twice mayor and one of the organizers of the water company. The *Times* remarked, "Only those who have lived in Los Angeles many years can form an idea of how great a debt the city owes to this unobtrusive, quietly energetic man."[14]

SATISFYING THE CITY'S THIRST

In December 1892, Mulholland first appeared as an expert witness in *Vernon Irrigation Company v. City of Los Angeles,* an important suit in the court of Judge Shaw, who would hear many of the water suits of this period. Along with old-timers Antonio Coronel, J. W. Potts, and E. H. Dalton, he testified for the city in a case that, although not notable at the time, became important because it established that one must be within the city limits to enjoy the use of river water, a ruling that consequently invited annexations to the city and thereby accelerated the expansion of the Los Angeles city limits into a vast and at times unwieldy municipality.[15]

The case concerned an irrigation and water company developed in the boom settlement of Vernon by two landowners, John A. Pirtle and George Hanna. Active players in many later water deals of the era, both in Hollywood and the San Fernando Valley (where a street bears Hanna's name), both had come to Southern California in 1887. Pirtle, a bond dealer from Arkansas, owned citrus land in Vernon, while Hanna, from Aurora, Illinois, had, after a few land deals, turned to the water business. The two charged that the city violated their riparian rights, because, being downriver, they did not receive a fair amount of water; that is, the upstream defendants took more than their share.[16]

Judge Lucien Shaw rendered his opinion six months after the suit began, reaffirming the city's control of its river water: "the city has the power to acquire and own a water supply for its inhabitants; that in the exercise of this power it has acquired and owns all the water flowing in the river and also the water caused to flow by the levees; that this is not an unreasonably large supply; that even if it were, the plaintiff has no right to raise the question, and that, being the owner of the water, it has power to sell such portion of it as may, from time to time, be in excess of its present needs. It follows that the plaintiff has no right to any relief against the city." The plaintiffs appealed, but five years later, in 1895, the California Supreme Court established that the city could not sell water for irrigation to extra-municipal lands as it had done in the past, nor did the recipients of that water have any right to it either.[17]

Perhaps anticipating an adverse decision and understanding that their case did not include the question of upper riparian rights, Pirtle and Hanna next embarked on another scheme to acquire waters upstream from the city via the Tujunga Wash for a development in the Cahuenga Valley. Had they succeeded, both men would have realized fortune and power, for they planned to capture the waters of the Los Angeles River before they flowed down to the city. Calling themselves the Cahuenga Mining and Water Company and using the subterfuge of wishing to activate an old mine that never had produced much gold but did have artesian waters in its hills, they intended to build a four-foot tunnel to tap those waters, whose source was probably percolation from the Los Angeles River. Confident that this new supply was safe from the demands of the city, the company reorganized, called itself the West Los Angeles Water Company, and quietly set about creating a new and independent system to supply the arid districts of Cahuenga Pass, Hollywood, and Sawtelle, where the soldiers' home had recently located.[18]

The project escaped notice until late 1895 when the water flowing into Los Angeles was observed to be unusually muddy. A city council investigation revealed that a water project had materialized twelve miles northwest of the city, evidently carried on in great secrecy by Pirtle, who with forty men and at a cost of $8,000, had, at the end of a tunnel or ditch, built down a steep slope an inverted flume with a dirt bottom to provide a continuous flow to a holding dam below. The dam had broken and its water and dirt had flowed into the river, thus producing the telltale flow of muddy water toward the city. At first, the city council was not unduly alarmed, as the water project fell outside its municipal jurisdiction. But the council's attitude became less casual when it discovered that Pirtle's men, while constructing a pipeline for their system, had undermined the city's main water supply ditch, which provided all the irrigating water the city used in city parks, cemeteries, and East Los Angeles. Deciding that things had gone too far, the council instructed the city attorney to order the deputy water overseer in charge of the ditch to quit work. The deputy water overseer refused; the chief of police was called in; and with more than a little drama, shortly before Christmas on December 19, at eight in the evening, two mounted police officers rode ten miles up the river road to call an official halt to the proceedings. The legal action over what came to be known as the Pirtle Cut eventually reaffirmed and expanded the city's right not only to the underground waters of the Los Angeles River but also to those of the Tujunga Wash. Eventually, in 1904, Hanna sold the West Los Angeles Water Company to the city.[19]

Heightened interest in water plots sometimes led to absurd conclusions, as when, not long after the discovery of Pirtle and Hanna's project in the Cahuenga hills, a reporter thought he had uncovered another "peculiar piece of work" when he found about two hundred men boring a tunnel into the hill south of the water company's gatehouse (today, Glendale Boulevard). He noted that the tunnel was egg shaped, like the tunnels of the outfall sewer, and that the shafts were being sunk in a westerly direction. This suggested to him that the line might be headed toward the Cahuenga Valley. To add to his speculation, he reported sightings of "Mr. Mulholland, superintendent of the City Water Company, and Mr. Hawgood, engineer for the same company," and inferred that they must be connected with the work.[20]

The intrigue vanished, however, when the water company announced that because of the city's growth, especially in the southwest, it was constructing a new pipeline and reservoir to fill the need. Beginning at the Crystal Springs just north of Riverside Drive and Hyperion Avenue, workers dug a 4,785-foot-long tunnel southwesterly through the Ivanhoe hills. The water then would flow beneath a short, recently christened Reservoir Street into the new Bellevue Dam. Built in a deep ravine at what was then the western edge of the city at Lucile and Bellevue Avenues on land the company had recently purchased especially for that purpose (Lot 1, Block 33, Hancock's Survey), the new dam had a high-water elevation of 386 feet and would hold 40 million gallons of water, three times the capacity of any other in the system. Its outlet pipe of 30-inch cast iron ran down Hoover Street to Seventh Street, and on from there in 20-inch pipe to Seventh and Broadway. Completed on March 24, 1895, the system supplied the fine new homes rising on Figueroa and Adams Streets with water for their gardens and great expanses of lawn. The company hoped this new project would satisfy the city's thirst for a long time to come, but skeptics saw it as yet another of the water company's moves to create a separate project in the Crystal Springs mode, thus enabling it to continue to sell private water once its lease had expired.[21]

A PILLAR OF SOCIETY

On the morning of August 17, 1895, William Mulholland took a day off from water plots and complications to join three hundred other guests

on a special train with six coaches that pulled out of the Arcade Depot
in Los Angeles for a swift trip to Rancho La Puente. There, their host,
the popular William "Uncle Billy" Rowland, was to entertain with a bull's
head breakfast, or, as it was described on a souvenir photograph of the
occasion, *El Almuerzo de la Cabeza Tatemada* (The Lunch of the Roasted
Head). Rowland, famed as the sheriff who led the posse that ran down
the bandit Tiburcio Vasquez, was holding a traditional mortgage-burning
party in the manner of the old rancho days, when after the crops were
in and the banks paid off, the ranchero celebrated with a barbecue for
his friends. On this occasion the guests comprised the leaders of Los Angeles. Juan Bandini, Reginaldo del Valle, Juan R. Ramirez, and Ygnacio
Sepulveda mingled with H. W. Hellman, John Kenealy, William Workman, and William Llewellyn. In attendance were bankers, attorneys, merchants, manufacturers, and newspaper owners and editors, including Major Horace Bell, Colonels Harrison Gray Otis and J. J. Ayers, and old
Major Ben Truman of the recently defunct *Star*. In a memorable day of
feasting, drinking, and speechmaking, United States senator Stephen M.
White acted as toastmaster, while Major Bell and state senator Reginaldo
del Valle reminisced about the old days, and California governor Edwin
C. Markham spoke on "The New California."

Mulholland's presence signaled his successful climb in eighteen years
from obscurity to a recognized position in the community. Although not
given to saving mementos, he kept his copy of the souvenir photograph
taken that day when the assemblage had stretched out on the ground after the meal—a field of sated males caught for posterity as they stared
towards the camera. Garbed in black, with a black hat on his lap and
propped on one arm, he lounges in the front row, yet his rough-hewn
visage suggests that he was a man of many cares. With three years remaining before the water company's lease expired, he faced an uncertain future as well as a present difficulty. Only later did he publicly acknowledge some of the problems he faced at that time with the wealthy
owners of the company, who, he believed, because of their many other
holdings and interests, found the waterworks but "a mere incident." He
remembered how even the most makeshift of improvements required
"most insistent efforts" on his part as superintendent to win approval.
This proved especially exasperating, he said, in the last years before the
lease expired, when any proposals for additions or improvements were
evaded or denied because of the impending termination. Just one example was the endless bickering over hydrants used for both fire fighting
and street sprinkling, as city and company each insisted the other should

pay for water and costs. Yet Mulholland also found remarkable the tenacity with which the original stockholders held on to their investment. They had become old, he said, which had "had the disadvantage of excluding new blood which might have redeemed it from the effect of the parsimonious and timid policy of its later years."[22]

Politics also vexed Mulholland, as he heard certain "ambitious office seekers," who at that time tried to make political capital out of their views on water by proposing "all kinds of anarchistic remedies such as paralleling the pipe system or forcibly preventing the Company from taking water from the river . . . even to the act of confiscation pure and simple." Added to his list of aggravations was one of the last great fights over water rates in February 1896, when the water supply committee in the city council recommended a 33.33 percent reduction in water rates. The reporter covering the story remarked that the proposal gave the council an opportunity "for some rare 'grandstand playing,' and afforded divers and sundry City Solons occasion for an unusual display of councilmanic buffoonery." To combat that "insatiable octopus," the private water company, the city fathers unanimously adopted a 50 percent rate reduction. The water company promptly sued and, after two years of battle, won a judgment against the city in June 1898; but it was a token victory only, for a month later the company's lease expired and water revenues to the company stopped.[23]

When Mulholland joined the town leaders at Uncle Billy Rowland's gathering, he had not yet gone on record in favor of a municipally owned waterworks. As superintendent of the private works, he held his cards close to his vest and acted on his conviction that "If you go to work for somebody, you do *his* work for him." In the years of contention ahead, however, he became persuaded that the city must own its water system. For, as he once jestingly related, from his reading of history he had found that "in the progress of civilization the duty of supplying cities with water was assumed as a public work second only in importance to the defense of the country." He recalled from Scripture that Hezekiah, king of Judah from 717 to 688 B.C., had been a pioneer in constructing a system of waterworks to bring water into Jerusalem: "He made the pool and the conduit and brought the water into the city. He stopped the upper water course of Gihon and brought it straight down to the west side of the City of David, and Hezekiah prospered in all his works." Then Mulholland added that after diligent search he had failed "to find any mention of the dividends paid by this early enterprise," and so concluded that "we may infer that the works were public, for public officials are guiltless of paying dividends—except in the indirect way of good service—if it so happens that they are good servants."[24]

The road that led to Mulholland's becoming a good public servant was long and tortuous. Years later, Lincoln Steffens in his *Autobiography* described a meeting he once arranged with business and civic leaders of Los Angeles in order to argue his thesis that whatever they might otherwise believe would alleviate graft, they should "want, at the least, the public ownership of all public utilities and natural resources." (This would have been at a 1907 meeting with members of the progressive Municipal League.) In the question and answer period after his address, when someone asked "if the public operation of utilities would not put them into politics," Steffens replied:

> To answer that, I turned to William Mulholland, the popular, highly respected engineer, who was the manager of the city's water system. He had been the manager when the water company was a private corporation, and it was notorious that he was then a very active and efficient politician. Everybody in that room knew that Mr. Mulholland had said over and over again that the change from private to public operation had got him and the business out of politics. When I passed the question of politics to him he did not have to answer. The whole company burst into laughter.[25]

CHAPTER 7

The Years of Mayor Eaton

1898–1900

TROUBLES FOR THE GRAND MONOPOLY

At no time did Mulholland better demonstrate his ability to maneuver around the shoals of politics and water issues than in the closing years of the nineteenth century, when he found himself caught between private sympathy for a publicly owned system and public loyalty to his employer, the private company. Although popular sentiment seemed to favor public ownership, the community's primary desire was for "a water system which shall give pure and abundant water at fair prices." The private company defended its performance with occasional propaganda pieces claiming that it provided water at rates 50 percent less than any city on the Pacific Coast, yet critics, especially Fred Eaton, thought the company inadequate and laggard in initiating improvements. Moreover, in an era when trusts and monopolies were coming under increasing attack, the private company's links to California's major economic octopus, the Southern Pacific Railroad, influenced the public perception of "the Water Ring" as a political menace, insofar as it could influence nominations in both political parties.[1]

When no agreement emerged in the months before the expiration of the thirty-year lease, the prospect of arbitration loomed. The final resolution depended heavily, however, on the outcome of the Crystal Springs case, which would determine the source of the water-bearing lands the private company claimed as part of its improvements and for which it must receive remuneration from the city under the terms of the lease.

While the Crystal Springs Company claimed waters developed on its lands at and adjacent to Crystal Springs, the City of Los Angeles argued that the waters were legally part of the Los Angeles River, which belonged to the municipality. Of the many litigations over water rights to the Los Angeles River, none proved more troublesome than this. For Mulholland, who was often on the hot seat testifying for the company, it became a byword for any snarled, complex, and intractable situation. By the time it ended, the public had heard a veritable history of Los Angeles water projects since the American occupation.

Among the experts testifying in court were engineers who one day would work together under Mulholland's direction on the Owens River Aqueduct. Their diverse and often contradictory testimony about sometimes arcane questions of hydrology, hydrography, and engineering lingo (terms such as *plane of saturation, miner's inch, flow velocity,* and *watershed area*) sometimes led to the impression that expert opinion depended a good deal on who had hired the expert. When Mulholland conceded under questioning that the origin of the waters in the infiltration pipes he had installed at Crystal Springs remained "a mystery to him," a reporter who for weeks had been following the testimony, "replete with technicalities of verbiage and of fact," found the testimony interesting simply because it could be easily understood. When the court set May 31 as the date for final arguments to begin, the same reporter commented that he found the city's case "detailed and specific," the water company's "somewhat hazy." Yet he acknowledged that when engineers so highly regarded throughout California arrived at diametrically opposed conclusions, then the layman was indeed thrown into a state of confusion.[2]

Water issues were briefly pushed into the background when, on April 19, 1898, the United States declared war against Spain over Cuba ("Remember the Maine"). The national popularity of this conflict, with its overtones of imperialism and jingoism, infused the Far West, and when Admiral George Dewey defeated the Spanish fleet at Manila on May 1, the Los Angeles Board of Public Works promptly requested that Don Pio Street be renamed Dewey Street. On the seventeenth, the name of the last Mexican governor of Alta California, Pio Pico, was swept away for America's latest military idol. Local patriots also cheered when at the end of the month, on May 27, President McKinley elevated the founder and owner of the *Los Angeles Times,* Colonel Harrison Gray Otis, to the rank of brigadier general of the volunteers. As Otis sailed off to active service in the Philippines, he named his son-in-law, Harry Chandler, to act as the *Times*'s general manager in his absence.[3]

Amid this martial enthusiasm, the Crystal Springs trial reconvened for final arguments at the end of May. In the intervening weeks, the city council had demanded that the water company provide a detailed description of its property and its relation to the Crystal Springs Land and Water Company. The water company then indicated its willingness to sell to the city but warned that to provide a detailed description of the property would require time and labor beyond reason. Moreover, prior to 1891, records of pipe laying had simply not been kept. Just as the city seemed willing to accept a less comprehensive cataloging of the company's property, a court decision denied the city's authority to regulate water rates. Although this finding came too late to be of much benefit, the company nevertheless sued the city for over $150,000 in lost revenue from unfairly low water rates.[4]

Subsequent negotiations broke down, and when the long-awaited date arrived for the expiration of the hated lease, instead of dancing in the streets, spectators crowded council chambers before eight o'clock in the morning to learn the outcome of a transaction that had grown so crucial to the city's future. By nine o'clock, when all council members had arrived, the galleries and seats were packed as property owners, stockholders, and the curious met to see the city offer $1.3 million for the waterworks. The water company's attorneys and directors appeared in full array, along with its superintendent, mistakenly identified in the *Times* as "John Mulholland." The city made its offer, the company declined it, and the council commenced arbitration.[5]

TWO FRIENDS DIVERGE

By the end of summer, as the fall municipal election neared, Fred Eaton's name was bruited for a possible place on the Republican ticket for mayor. The *Times,* which had once attacked Eaton's engineering skills in his plans for an outfall sewer, now declared that "his personal popularity would render him a strong nominee." Moreover, with Eaton's long-standing record of support for municipal ownership of water—an important plank in the local Republican platform—he was seen as the man of the hour. At the convention, he received the sole nomination and was approved by acclamation as three or four hundred delegates rose and cheered their native son. He made a gracious acceptance speech, thanked his fellow party members for the magnificent honor they had bestowed upon him, and promised to do well for the city. "I have been among you all my life," he continued. "My occupation during the active part of my career has brought me among the people, and I have at all times been open to their criticism."[6]

The *Times* was ecstatic over Eaton's nomination and threw its full editorial weight behind his campaign. Water was to be the central issue. The Republicans painted the Democrats as tools of the water ring, and Eaton warned citizens against bondage to a company that thought nothing of spending $100,000 to bribe councilmen. Not, he quickly noted, that the entire council could be bribed; he simply wished to indicate that out of the company's great income (reckoned at about $425,000 a year), it could easily expend $100,000. After citing the dire example of San Francisco, held in thrall to the private Spring Valley Water Company, he noted his own refusal to accept positions with the Pomeroy-Hooker or West End Water Companies, saying he preferred "to stand by the people's interests." His opponents attempted a weak last-minute attack, accusing him of overcharging the city with a high professional consultation fee in the Crystal Springs case. When the sum was revealed to be a modest $50, however, that issue quickly disappeared, and Eaton soared ahead with promises of municipal water and more schools.[7]

Arbitration hearings on the water question began during the campaign. While Eaton was on the hustings attacking the water company and its corrupt political influence in the city, Mulholland sat in a city council chamber reciting to the arbitration board in painstaking detail "the size and character of the various pipes of the system, the dates on which they were laid and the character of the soil in which they were placed." (The previous June, he had been asked to draw up a complete inventory and description of the company's holdings, which included more than three hundred miles of pipe and five hundred hydrants, along with pumping stations and machinery.) The material, complained a reporter, "was composed of minutiae of little public interest," but one associate later recalled the occasion as a demonstration of Mulholland's prodigious memory. According to J. B. Lippincott, after Mulholland had presented the inventory as an oral recollection, the arbitration board asked for two hundred places to be dug up in order to verify his accuracy. When all two hundred pipes agreed in every particular with Mulholland's account, the board accepted his inventory.

During six weeks of drilling on the witness stand, Mulholland earned a reputation for probity and fair-mindedness, willing to flout even the opinions of his employer's attorneys. At one point, when a controversy broke out over whether the valuation of pipe could best be established by its age or its appearance, Mulholland disagreed with company attorney Stephen M. White's opinion that more depended on its appearance than on its age. Neither age nor appearance, countered Mulholland, was as important in fixing the pipe's value as the condition of the soil in which it had been placed. As this scrutiny of the water system dragged on, a company attorney, after an exhausting cross-examination of one witness, turned to Mulholland and whispered, "What else shall I ask him?" Mulholland replied, "Ask him where he got the red necktie he's wearing."[8]

A NEW MAYOR ATTEMPTS REFORM

On December 6, 1898, after the normal amount of political mudslinging, Fred Eaton became mayor of Los Angeles. The year ended with optimism and hope that the depressed times of the 1890s might be ending. Merchants reported record volumes of business, with shoppers in the stores until almost midnight on Christmas Eve, while attorney Henry O'Melveny noted that it was the "warmest and dryest Christmas Los Angeles has known since I have been here."[9]

Although portents had augured well for Eaton's success, he would bow out after his first term, never again to run for public office. (His popular Democratic predecessor, Meredith "Pinky" Snyder, was swept back into office, where he remained until the end of 1904.) Eaton had professed progressive ambitions for the city, and besides his strong desire for a new city charter, municipally owned water, more schools, and an improved library, he also wanted slot machines outlawed (especially the nickel slots in saloons, which he felt unfairly robbed workingmen of their hard-earned money). He was in favor of open hours for saloons, but thought women and girls should be banned from the back rooms. He proposed to accomplish this by sealing all back doors and using only the front for arrivals and departures. He was no more than a man of his time in his conviction that "the presence of women in saloons is a constant factor in promoting vice and immorality, and serves to lead astray the young." Yet he also proved gallant to the *nymphes du pave,* and at one point championed several ladies of dubious reputation against a police officer accused of maltreating them. In public works, he wanted better public access to the parks, a larger police force, and a more efficient fire department. In short, he prescribed for his city of one hundred thousand souls what many regarded as an exemplary program for its improvement. To those who saw former mayor Snyder as a tool of the saloon and gambling interests as well as a cozy buddy of the police, Eaton seemed the necessary antidote.[10]

Eaton encountered heavy sledding when he attempted to regulate the saloon business and gambling. His rows with the police and the police commission continued throughout his two years in office, although with other commissions he enjoyed more harmonious relations that were often productive and constructive. Especially congenial were his associations with the board of health, for as men with a shared faith in the scientific method, they escaped many of the political and moral disagreements inherent in the problematic fields of police, crime, and vice. Eaton moreover had the good sense to retain the health officer who, except for two years in 1895 and 1896, served from 1893 to 1911: the forceful Luther Milton Powers, M.D. A Democrat, Powers nonetheless transcended party considerations, and mayors of both parties chose him as the guardian angel of the city's health. Among those who learned valuable lessons from the esteemed Dr. Powers was William Mulholland, for Powers became his family physician and treated his children through bouts of diphtheria and typhoid. Mulholland's notions of hygiene could be rather cavalier. He told his sons on camping trips to drink the water "if you can still cut it with a knife," and they remembered how, when coming upon a stream, he would crouch down, push aside the pond scum, scoop a sample into his palm, and after a reflective sip, nod and tell them, "It's all right." In a Los Angeles that had been lax, not to say ignorant and derelict, in matters of hygiene, Powers advanced the relatively new science of public health. His years of service constituted a major contribution to the betterment of the city's sanitation and hygiene at the turn of the century.[11]

ENGINEERS DISAGREE

Drought was a specter during Eaton's two years in office. The combined rainfall for those two seasons yielded only 13½ inches. In spite of all his desire and efforts to create a municipally owned water system, he did not achieve that goal during his administration, even though he led a successful $2,090,000 bond campaign for the purchase and improvement of a city waterworks. (The water company's machinations later frustrated that hope.) His disillusionment with the interminable lawsuits and joustings with the private company probably determined his eventual withdrawal from the city as the water arbitration hearings dragged on.

Eaton and Mulholland, although ostensibly in opposing camps, had frequent occasions to parley. A few days after Eaton took office, Mulholland requested and was granted a conference that took place in the mayor's private office with the city auditor. They discussed the long-standing and unresolved question of repairs to fire hydrants, most of which had been damaged by certain careless drivers of the city's sprinkling carts. After haggling with several councilmen who joined them, they reached a compromise in which the city agreed to pay half the cost of repairs. Two weeks later, at a water arbitration hearing, they disagreed over the capacity of Buena Vista Reservoir at the time the company began to enlarge it. Mulholland thought it was 3 million gallons, while Eaton, basing his figure on a chart he remembered having seen when he was superintendent of the company, claimed it was 5 million.[12]

In the spring of 1899, Mulholland appeared almost daily before the arbitration board to testify on such matters as the value of pipe or the cost of trenching, until at last in May, the board filed its report, which placed the water company's value at $1,183,591.42. The high estimate, from company engineer Harry Hawgood, was $2,467,778.00; the low, from City Engineer J. Henry Dockweiler, was $1,071,034.00; Mulholland's was $2,182,891.00. When the third arbitrator (the water company's representative) refused to sign, the arbitration failed, and the city decided to proceed with plans to build its own system, which Mulholland later described as a folly.[13]

At this time a favorable decision from the state supreme court on the Pomeroy and Hooker case allowed the city to advance its condemnation proceedings for building its own headworks. Since spring, concerned with lack of rainfall, City Engineer Frank L. Olmstead and engineer-hydrographers Joseph B. Lippincott and O. K. Parker had been taking measurements along the river north of Crystal Springs, in part to discover if tunneling by the secretive West Side Water Company had affected the river supply below. When the city council began to complain of too many requests for payments for water measurements, especially after Olmstead proposed a trek to the Big and Little Tujunga Canyons, he strongly defended the expense. He warned that farmers in the San Fernando Valley were already "milking the river," which could run dry. Already a delegation of farmers south of the city (among them, John A. Pirtle of the Pirtle Cut) had requested permission to begin pumping underground water because too little surface water was reaching them for irrigation.[14]

The city's struggle to secure control of its water system from the private water company became its stone of Sisyphus, for with each push ahead, a setback seemed to follow. As Eaton awaited what he expected to be a happy ruling from the arbitration board, he was dashed by a supreme court decision declaring that the water company in fact had a contract with the city and not simply a lease; that the city must pay a fair valuation on the plant; and that the monies held in receivership must be released to the company. Elated, the company's attorney declared that with revenues available again, the company could begin to make improvements.[15]

In the hot dry month of July, Los Angeles hosted the annual session of the American Forestry Service, noteworthy not only because it was the national body's first meeting in the West but because among the leading authorities on forestry, hydrography, and irrigation in attendance were two men who would play important roles in the city's water history: Gifford Pinchot, then United States forester and future secretary of the interior under Theodore Roosevelt; and Frederick H. Newell, United States hydrographer. Newell lectured on "The Reclamation of Arid Public Lands," and when asked about the water prospects for Southern California, replied, "I have been surprised at what has been done in Southern California since I was here last, some two or three years ago, in the development of water from underground sources." A notable local representative, J. B. Lippincott, spoke not of his current hydrographic activities but of his experiences with the National Geological Survey in the Bitterroot Forest Reserve in 1897. He concluded with a hard-hitting attack against the timber interests and "the reckless liberality of the timber laws."[16]

During the conference, on Saturday, July 22, a series of earthquakes shook the city. A week later, apparently unconnected with the earthquakes, a washout in the city's main supply tunnel cut all flow of water to the city's reservoirs. At a point just south of Kenilworth and a quarter of a mile from the water company's gatehouse, the water flooded down the hillside, across the road, and into a disused air shaft that led to the main supply tunnel of the Crystal Springs Water Company. The force of the water with its accumulated tons of rock and earth smashed and choked the walls of the tunnel and also washed away the nearby power flume.

Mulholland rushed to the scene with a force of men. Arriving at six o'clock in the evening, they spent the night clearing debris and tons of sticky mud. As he often did in such emergencies, Mulholland was quick to assure the public that water would be available again soon, asking them only to refrain from watering their gardens. Mayor Eaton immediately announced suspension of all street sprinkling, and although the reservoirs had been full at the time of the break, Mulholland still cautioned that "Los Angeles uses 20,000,000 gallons of water a day. Of this, 2,500,000 gallons is used on the streets, and at least 5,000,000 more for sprinkling the lawns and gardens of the city." No sooner had he dismissed the damage as "a mere bagatelle" than more of the tunnel caved in.[17]

Crews worked day and night to repair the power ditch and get water running in order to turn a Pelton wheel used for pumping irrigation water into the Zanja Madre, which in the emergency was to be diverted to Buena Vista Reservoir for domestic use. In the meantime, the supply ditch was not so quickly restored because of a labor shortage. Unemployment was still high, but many jobless had fled the city in midsummer to work on the outlying ranches; one aide reported having to spend a night ransacking cheap lodging houses looking for men.[18]

In this crisis, the city and the water company laid aside their differences. The water company furnished the city with forty-inch steel pipe to repair the supply ditch so that its flow could continue into the Echo Park line. The company also helped with the pipe's installation, which involved anchoring it to the side of the hill over timber supports. As the ditch lay almost directly above the company's damaged tunnel, the men had to take care that the new installation would not interfere with repairing the tunnel. For the first time since Christmas 1889, when he had kept the channel open during a flood, Mulholland received press notice for his efforts in preserving the water supply.[19]

A week after the break, Eaton began to campaign for passage in August of the $2,090,000 bond issue to acquire a municipal water system. Although city officials were enthusiastic, they feared apathy among the general public, so on August 13, Eaton issued a general proclamation notifying the public of the election and urging them to vote. On election eve, only a disappointing few hundred turned out for a probond rally at Hazard's Pavilion, but among the speakers were Eaton and Lippincott, who paid tribute to the arbitrators' work and argued that municipalities that owned their water supplies offered rates generally 43 percent lower than those supplied by private companies. The city attorney also singled out Mulholland for his "spirit of fairness in submitting evidence" during arbitration, recalling that in some instances, when the city engineer's estimates had been too high, Mulholland had suggested their reduction. The recently organized and progressive Committee of One Hundred worked to get out the largest vote ever cast in Los Angeles at a special election. With a two-thirds vote needed for passage, it carried every precinct in the city seven to one (7,179 for and 973 against). With victory assured, Eaton left that night for San Francisco to witness the California troops' arrival from the Philippines.[20]

Jubilation was short-lived, however, for the water company filed a suit to disallow the value of the waterworks established in the arbitration hearings. Then came word from the East that a pamphlet was circulating in financial circles stating that on account of the various pending lawsuits, the city's water and school bonds would be held up on legal technicalities for several years. (Rumor had it that the pamphlet had been prepared by a "large railroad"—the Southern Pacific?) Eaton called a series of secret meetings to plan strategies for a counterattack, but so serious was the impact of these attacks that the city decided to retain the services of a leading New York bond attorney to continue the struggle. A year later when Eaton left office, the matter would still be unresolved.[21]

THE CITY RENEWS ITS WATER CLAIMS

Eaton's second year as mayor began with a disaster when on January 23, 1900, the roof at the west end of the Third Street Tunnel caved in. Of the fifteen men buried, three died and twelve survived. One of the dead was the city inspector, who had been on an inspection tour when the tunnel gave way. The coroner's inquest refused to fix responsibility for the event, but City Engineer Frank L. Olmstead later blamed what he called the vicious system of contract work, whereby public officials granted contracts solely on the basis of low bid. Eaton, who at the time of the disaster was in the midst of a clash with the police commission, had little to say on the matter, but as a veteran of the contract system probably would not have criticized it as harshly as the younger Olmstead. The council of labor moved upon the city fathers with demands for improved supervision and worker safety, and although promises and assurances were forthcoming, little of real consequence occurred.[22]

Eaton increasingly focused on the water question. In February, just a week before the deadline for setting customer water rates, he proposed that the city council begin construction of a municipal headworks and cut water rates by one-third. In a subsequent hearing before the water supply committee, a large gathering of attorneys, water company representatives, and interested parties such as members of the Lodging House Association, who were disputing the water company's method of billing, listened to the company's attorney argue for higher rates based on the prospects of a dry year. Next, Mulholland explained why the company thought its rates should be raised. Water supplies were low after two dry seasons, and because the outlook was for another dry year (which proved correct, for the season's total finally came to a meager 7.91 inches), the company would have to install a new pumping plant costing from

$35,000 to $50,000. This would include pumping stations at three different points on the river, with operating expenses at about $2,000 a month. Because the hurriedly built installations would be somewhat insubstantial, Mulholland added that they would not add notably to the company's property.[23]

As Mulholland was answering questions about the seasonal variations in water use and specifying the proposed new installations' locations, Eaton entered the room and interrupted him by asking why the water company did not put the pumping stations on city lands. That question went unanswered as Councilman Charles Toll next wondered whether the Los Angeles City Water Company or the Crystal Springs Water Company would make the improvements. Mulholland replied that he did not know and repeated that the installation would be temporary, therefore adding little to the value of either plant. Two weeks later, after Eaton and Lippincott had returned from a day up the river investigating reports that riparian owners were using more water than allowed or necessary for irrigation of their ranches, they also announced that the water company, instead of using the total flow from its water supply, was allowing millions of gallons of currently unneeded water to go to waste. Eaton then refuted Mulholland: "The Mayor does not believe the contention of the company as to the necessity for, or the cost of, pumping the water into the reservoirs during the coming summer."[24]

Eaton continued the exploratory trips up the river accompanied by Lippincott and Thomas H. Means, a soil expert from the Department of Agriculture in Washington, D.C., who had been sent out to examine soils with the aim of perfecting a system for reclaiming alkali lands. As Means's mission involved examining water supplies of various districts to establish salt contents and as the findings might provide evidence to support their fight for municipal water, Eaton and Lippincott were eager to assist him. If, for example, the samples from various parts of the San Fernando Valley agreed and it became evident that the water was all from the same watershed, they could trace the source of the city's water supply to the very head of the valley, and "mark a distinct line along which the water of the river first flowed before entering the river or coming to the surface."[25]

In April, Eaton received the heartening news that the Supreme Court of the United States had refused to consider the Crystal Springs Water Company's attempt to quiet title to what it claimed to be its waters. After three years in litigation, the highest court in the land held that the federal government had no jurisdiction over the case. Now the city could renew its claims, but another roadblock loomed in May, when the water company enjoined the city from fixing water rates. In June, Eaton announced that the Supreme Court decision freed the city from its obligation to pay the water company for water used to irrigate the parks and public lands.[26]

As the deadlock continued, the summer of 1900 advanced dry and rainless. The Democrats chose as their mayoral candidate Meredith P. Snyder, while the Republicans nominated the current president of the city council, Herman Silver. As the water rate case dragged on in circuit court, a small and curious news item appeared. The mayor was showing off a new knife to admiring friends as he explained that he had invested in it for purposes of "offense and defense in view of his approaching trip into the Sierra Nevada Mountains on a hunting expedition." The hunting party proved special, however, as Eaton's companions were United States hydrographer Frederick H. Newell, Assistant Hydrographer J. B. Lippincott, and one Dr. F. T. Hicknell. Expected to join them later in the week was William Mulholland, engineer for the Los Angeles City Water Company. The group planned to go by train to Fresno and then, by stage, to follow the Kings River Valley to the top of the divide and over into the San Joaquin Valley. As the article explained, "The party will inspect the reservoir sites in these two valleys now being surveyed by the United States Government." It described Newell and Lippincott as "personally interested in the work," while Eaton and Mulholland were interested "on scientific grounds."[27]

When Eaton returned to town at the end of August, he was greeted with the news that the city had just lost its rate fight against the water company. The judge had upheld the thirty-year contract in a sixty-page typewritten document that boiled down to the conclusion that the city's case was without merit. As September grew hotter and drier, Eaton ominously predicted that within a few years Los Angeles might have to do without the man-made lakes in its parks. In a semitropical climate, he explained, large amounts of water were needed to keep the supply sanitary. He found the daily per capita consumption of 230 gallons of water "surprising, if not alarming," and joked that "if cleanliness is next to godliness, then the City of the Angels must occupy a high place in the scale of municipal virtue." He warned, however, that if the population increased by another hundred thousand, something would have to be done. With dwindling supplies, water would be needed for domestic purposes, and it would be up to the people themselves to practice strict economies in its use. He then set about planning the headworks filtration gallery on the Pomeroy and Hooker lands.[28]

In his last month as mayor and a week after McKinley defeated Bryan for the presidency of the United States, the rains came to Los Angeles. Attorney O'Melveny, who conscientiously kept rainfall records, noted on November 21 and 22, "Magnificent rain. Streetcar service stopped. Grandest rain in ten years. Everyone happy. San Gabriel River beyond measurement." There had been nothing like it since 1891, and fortunately, because the city prudently had cleared the riverbed of brush and debris in the early fall, there was no repetition of the damaging flood of 1884 when such an accumulation had checked the flow and created havoc in the city. Even so, flooding occurred. One two-story house on South Flower collapsed after its basement filled with eleven feet of water, while over in Mulholland's Boyle Heights neighborhood, Hollenbeck Park was inundated when its lake overflowed and covered lawns and flowers with mud. Some of the exotic birds drowned in the submerged aviary, and two blocks from the Mulholland home, stinking slime pools of stagnant water filled with the overflow from a break in a zanja. Yet at year's end the rains were heralded as a harbinger of good times.[29]

AN EX-MAYOR GOES "UP THE RIVER"

In January 1900, Fred Eaton devoted his departing message to his fellow Angelenos entirely to the subject of city water, past, present, and future. He chastised his foes, chiefly the officers and stockholders of the Los Angeles City Water Company and the Crystal Springs Land and Water Company. He praised those of his fellow citizens who had demonstrated their faith in a municipal system by voting for water bonds that were now also in contention because of certain obstructionists. He remained positive in his conviction that the city ultimately would prevail in its fight to own its own waterworks. Next day, as he cleared his office of books, maps, and files, a group of deputies and officers showed up and, with a gracious speech from City Engineer Olmstead, presented their outgoing mayor with a pair of small binoculars equipped with three lenses so that they were equal in power to larger field glasses. Touched, Eaton said that when he was alone upon the desert and beneath the panoply of the heavens on some of the engineering tours he planned, the gift would remind him of the last day he spent in City Hall. Leaving, he dropped a clue to his future plans by saying that he did not intend to let his interest in the water question lapse, but that this time, it would be in his own interest and not the city's.[30]

Too little is known of Fred Eaton to draw a dogmatic conclusion about his character. His early idealism seems to have given way to acquisitiveness, yet one also senses that he was largely honorable in intent. One also feels that his undoubted intelligence and ability were accompanied by a certain hauteur, perhaps not surprising in one who was something of a princeling in this western realm. Success had come to Eaton early, and he projected a presumption of rightness that came from being well-born and assured of a secure place in life. Scarcely mentioned during his mayoralty was the fact of his drinking, about which the newspapers maintained a discreet silence. Only several years afterwards, during a time of domestic troubles, was mention made. "During his political life he was somewhat addicted to the cup that cheers . . . ," wrote a reporter at the time of Eaton's divorce in 1903. Fred Eaton should have been one of the bright stars in the history of the city. Yet in his last months in office, he seemed to recede from view, so that by the time the Republicans convened to nominate a new candidate for mayor, he had disappeared. There were few public statements of appreciation or farewell, and the *Los Angeles Times,* which had been his chief booster, said nothing either by way of praise or blame. When one reporter found the mayor's office closed at City Hall and was told he was "up the river" and was further informed that the city engineer and attorney were also "up the river," he mused that "this practice has become so prevalent that it might make a fitting subject for inquiry by the Committee of Safety that is supposed to have taken in hand all the disorders in municipal affairs."[31]

CHAPTER 8

The City's Victory
over the "Grand Monopoly"

1901–1902

LAWSUITS AND "CARPING SPIRITS"

At the beginning of 1901, the city was snarled in thirty lawsuits growing out of its struggle for municipal water control. One alone consisted of 10,000 typewritten pages. The cost of all these litigations was draining the city's coffers at a time of economic slump, and in May the council ordered a retrenchment of all city expenses. In the following months, the city and the water company engaged in a kind of high-stakes poker game that called for alertness and skill with each new deal. When a local group called the Mountain Water Company suddenly surfaced with a request for a franchise to lay pipe and supply "pure, soft mountain water" to the city from a source in the San Gabriel Forest Reserve, City Attorney William B. Mathews was at first taken aback. He knew nothing of such a development and wondered if it were not some shrewd new trick of the water company that would involve the city in further legal strife and turmoil. As this mystery remained for the moment unresolved, the city council began to debate whether it should not at last try to settle quickly with the Los Angeles City Water Company.[1]

The city at this point had a $30,000 deficit in its cash fund, and the finance committee, seeking means to cut expenses, recommended a compromise with the water company. In the ensuing debate, attorney Mathews spoke out for a continued fight: "Don't give up the ship—fight on," he exhorted. "You will never get anything out of the water company until you knock it out with a court decree." After a lively debate dur-

ing a day in executive session, the entire council emerged with its decision to attempt a compromise with the water company. The company
answered that it desired to cooperate, but when it announced its price
of $2,275,000, the city fathers' howls could be heard all the way to
Catalina Island.[2]

With its population now over 100,000, the city made increasing demands on its water sources. By April 1901, the river was lower than it
had been at the same time the year before, partly because the ground,
dried by three arid years, had absorbed a great deal of the flow, but also,
charged the city zanjero, because the water company, asserting its first
rights to the water, had now taken the lion's share into its Crystal Springs
system. If the zanjas lacked water to supply irrigators, then the city would
lose much-needed revenue from this source. (Water then sold outside the
city for $5.00 a head for a twelve-hour day run and $2.50 for a night
run; within the city, it cost $4.00 and $2.00 for the same time periods.)
The zanjero wanted the private company to insist that its customers use
water more economically, so that farmers and truck gardeners would not
suffer a water famine in the coming summer.[3]

At the end of June, with hot dry days ahead, another setback hit the
city. A court ruling declared that the water bonds passed during Mayor
Eaton's term were invalid and, therefore, could not be issued or sold.
Mathews, a determined champion of municipal control, decided, even at
a time of near penury in the treasury, to use the water-bond sinking fund
for an appeal to the state supreme court. The council, caught in a dilemma
and not even sure of the legality of using the water-bond money for a lawsuit, decided on July 12 to put out another feeler and offered the water
company $2 million for its works (a provisional offer, as the whole mat-
ter had to go before the voters and be decided by ballot). Wonderfully,
the water company answered a week later, on July 29, that if the voters
were willing, it would accept the $2 million proposal. Mulholland, who
had acted as an important mediator during these negotiations, later recalled how he had been summoned to chief stockholder I. W. Hellman's
summer home in Lake Tahoe. There, the two held lengthy conferences
during which Mulholland urged Hellman to accept the offer because he
feared the growing public discontent would harm the water company. He
would later partially defend the private water company when he remembered how, for years, "the shibboleth of every self-seeking politician was
confiscation of the works or at the very best with the more moderate ones,
gross misrepresentations as to their value and exaggerated statements of
their net earnings." In 1904, as Pasadena's civic leaders contemplated mu-

nicipal ownership, Mulholland warned them to avoid overly harsh criticism of existing private plants, explaining that "the growth of towns is generally straggling and irregular and it would require the gift of prophecy on the part of an engineer to foresee the direction in which a town may extend most; hence the oft-seeming inaptness in pipe system designs of but a few years existence in growing towns." Stressing that excessive reproaches could interfere with "a just and businesslike appraisement," he added, "I was through that mill and it ground exceeding fine in the last years of my employment with the old Los Angeles Water Co. We found that the carping spirit that prompted it served to protract the controversy for a long period to the great disadvantage of both sides. In such matters we must expect to pay for at least some bone with the meat." He echoed these sentiments a year later during a speech before the Sunset Club, declaring that when the city's progress had been "vitally jeopardized," it required "a few wise heads" to engineer "an arrangement of compromise that settled the whole matter by the city agreeing to pay this sum of Two Million Dollars for the works."[4]

A small but obdurate group opposed the deal, largely on the grounds that the water company's price was too high. Proponents of the purchase argued, however, that the eventual legal costs of pursuing their cause would ultimately outweigh the current asking price. Moreover, they pointed out that this sale would include the long-disputed Crystal Springs installation. The majority in city council approved the buy and set about to draw up a compromise stipulation for the purchase of the waterworks as well as to draft an ordinance declaring its public necessity.[5]

With a bond election set for August 28, news items calculated to sway opinion began to appear. Less than two weeks before the election the city fathers sprang their own surprise with the revelation that on August 15, for $33,250, the city had secretly purchased 310 acres of water-bearing land in the Tujunga Wash adjoining the Pomeroy and Hooker lands. Eaton, Lippincott, and the others, it turned out, had made all those trips upriver for more than water measurements. This stratagem was to be repeated on a grander scale when Los Angeles made its giant reach for water in the Owens Valley. To secure options without arousing suspicion (and thereby causing owners to raise their price), two of the city's water attorneys had used as a front one of their clients, Don Antonio Lopez, purported to be the head of a Cuban syndicate interested in founding a colony in Southern California. After the farmers had sold and the land had gone into escrow, Don Antonio Lopez signed over the deeds to the City of Los Angeles. Perhaps because the newly acquired land lay near the headworks of the West Side Water Company and thus provided leverage against that company with which the city was in litigation, those opposing the water bonds failed to object, focusing instead solely on the private water company's sale price. At the time, no one questioned the morality of this subterfuge or its possible effect upon the farmers and owners who had sold. The deal was thoroughly publicized, and the mayor and the city attorney expressed their pleasure at the plan's success.[6]

The bond contest was spirited. Proponents made much of the fact that once the city had purchased the waterworks, it not only would see an end to all litigation with the old water company but would also own the Crystal Springs system. Above all, the city would enjoy the company's revenues, which W. H. Perry had declared to be $33,000 a month. On the eve of the election, a straw vote among the Merchants and Manufacturers Association yielded 230 for the bonds, 7 against, and 3 undecided. The opposition were few but vocal and used every legal means at hand to fight the proposal. The front man for this group of propertied and professional men with mingled motives was S. A. Waldron, a former deputy city assessor and now a schoolteacher whose father, David V. Waldron, was, according to contemporary Boyle Workman, a "chronic objector" and leading opponent of municipal ownership. While some bond foes doubtless wanted to continue litigation because they were honestly indignant over the $2 million price for the water company, most, like Waldron, seem to have acted out of self-interest. One opposing owner of a large acreage in the south end of town, who had long used only zanja water for a mere $2 a month, would pay much more under the city's management. The West Side Water Company also fought the purchase, while a vicious rumor circulated that agents were at work to influence black voters against the bonds. To what end, no one could say.[7]

To convince labor to vote against the bonds, a flier, or "dodger," as they were then called, circulated on the eve of election with language that would become familiar in future Los Angeles water debates. Titled "The Water Steal," it asked such inflammatory questions as "Why should the city donate $1,000,000 to the millionaires who own the water company? Give the million dollars to the laborers and mechanics instead of to the millionaires. VOTE AGAINST THIS STEAL!" The flier was not from labor, however, which already had tepidly endorsed the purchase in its official publication, the *Union Labor News,* presenting the choice as one between two evils: either paying too much for the waterworks or being bled under the present system. As with an aching tooth, the journal declared, "the sooner it's out the better." Both the American Federation of

Labor and the Socialist Party gave full support, but the portrayal of labor as victim to a water steal that would profit only the wealthy endured beyond this first municipal water contest.[8]

Voter turnout was light, and when many of the customary layabouts proved absent from the precincts, one old hand explained, "The water company and nobody else ain't passin' out no dough. So what's the use of the boys to get out and hustle the vote?" The final, unhustled, result favored the bonds five to one (6,284 for, 1,267 against), and the city at long last had its waterworks. Mayor Snyder immediately set off on a long-delayed summer vacation, and as he left, was congratulated by a well-wisher from San Francisco, who declared that he hoped his city, in its upcoming $25 million bond election, would follow the example of Los Angeles. After the official canvass of the vote, the president of the city council called out as he bid good-bye to his colleagues for the Labor Day weekend, "Don't forget that the city begins to make $1,000 a day next Sunday."[9]

MISADVENTURES IN BOND PEDDLING

The following week President William McKinley was shot while attending the Pan American Exposition in Buffalo, New York. He lingered until mid-September, when his death was tolled in Los Angeles by "Old Tom," the two-ton fire bell at City Hall. As the hushed city listened to its familiar tones—one stroke for each of the dead president's fifty-eight years—Theodore Roosevelt entered the White House. The twentieth century in America was now to begin in earnest, especially in Los Angeles, where the new president would play a fateful role.

Before the city could savor complete ownership of its waterworks, however, it had to sell the bonds, which turned out to entail as much conflict and drama as the election and also marked the beginning of attorney William B. Mathews's lifetime dedication to the city and the cause of municipal ownership. At first the bonds did not sell, and when the city discovered that on the first day of the sale the Waldron group had issued a printed notice warning prospective bond buyers of an impending suit against the bonds, certain infuriated councilmen suggested that a lynching should be in order. A Los Angeles Times cartoon portrayed Waldron as "his satanic majesty, Waldron the dummy," while a more reasoned response came from John M. Elliott, president of the First National Bank, a director of the private water company, and soon to be among the first city water commissioners. The diplomatic Elliott suggested that business conditions in the East, "and the consequent heavy demand for money, is partly the reason why the bonds were not sold." He dismissed the Waldron litigation as little more than a nuisance.[10]

When at last word came that buyers had been found, the pair who came to be known as "the two Billies" (City Attorney "Billy" Mathews and Treasurer "Uncle Billy" Workman) embarked on their bond-selling mission, which was to keep them in the East for two troublesome months. Their hopes rose and fell as bondbuyers materialized and defaulted. When a buyer was finally secured, they became so fearful of another monkey wrench from the Waldron crowd that they went immediately to the Guaranty Trust Company of New York, where Workman, as city treasurer, set about the arduous task of signing his name two thousand times. A witness recalled that every time Workman "dipped his pen in the ink-well he absently shook it towards the universe at large, to rid it of any spare ink that might cause a blot. By the time he had finished the two thousandth signature, the office, including a brand new carpet, presented a general polka dot effect." With the transaction at last completed and the money in the bank, Workman telegraphed his son to draw a warrant for $2 million to the order of the Los Angeles City Water Company. After endorsements by W. H. Perry, president, and S. H. Mott, secretary, the money was paid. The city at last owned its waterworks.[11]

Treasurer Workman received a hero's welcome when he stepped off the train in Los Angeles and heard the music of a welcoming brass band. Mathews, who also received high praise for his adroit dealings with the eastern money men and attorneys, remained in the East consulting with lawyers about the Hooker and Pomeroy condemnation case then before the Supreme Court. Several weeks later, on a Sunday afternoon, February 25, 1902, this self-effacing man quietly slipped back into town after having made a detour to his boyhood home in Maysville, Kentucky.[12]

Two weeks earlier, on February 6, in an event as plain and down-to-earth as Mathews's return to the city, Mayor Snyder and members of the council marched from City Hall to the old water office at Marchessault and Alameda. Upon entering the building, the mayor asked for the attention of all those present and then pronounced that he now took possession of the waterworks on behalf of the City of Los Angeles. All thirty-one employees of the old water company were to be retained, and William Mulholland was officially named the new superintendent. Mulholland would later say, "When the city bought the works, they bought me along with it."[13]

THE CITY'S NEW ACQUISITION

Before the bond election, a specially appointed committee had wrestled with problems of organization and questions concerning the new city water department's management and personnel (including inquiries to fifty cities with municipal water systems in order to examine their procedures). Both the committee and city council had determined that its management would be conducted under strict civil service rules and independent of the political body; therefore, a board of elected water commissioners would control the system. Debate immediately arose over the composition of the commission, but the council finally agreed to select seven temporary commissioners until regulars could be elected the following year. Fred Eaton was considered and rejected on the grounds that "his views as an engineer might clash on technical points with those of the superintendent, who must be an experienced engineer, according to the terms of the ordinance." (Eaton was, however, retained as a consulting engineer for the first three months after the takeover.)[14]

The committee also took up the matter of a new location for the water system's headquarters. The old office on Marchessault Street where Mulholland had once lived and worked was now in the heart of the tenderloin district. Because eliminating the expense of door-to-door collectors was soon to necessitate all water customers' paying at a central office, a more convenient and desirable location had to be established. The old office would remain as a storage center and maintenance yard.

Against this backdrop of activity and confusion as the city learned how to run its own water department, William Mulholland stepped out of the shadows into the public light. His name and opinions began to appear with regularity in the newspapers. The city fathers, some of whom called him the "grand old man" of the waterworks (he was forty-seven), agreed that he should continue as superintendent, although a few were reluctant to pay the $5,000 salary that he demanded. He had received $3,000 a year from the private water company, but as he explained to the council, he had also been able to take outside work. The previous year, he had received more than $8,000 from such jobs. Standard Oil Company, for example, had retained him for a few days at $500 a day. The city ordinance, however, required the superintendent to devote his entire time to the duties of his office, so that henceforth he would be unable to take such lucrative assignments.[15]

He now met regularly with the water commissioners, who in their first meeting on February 13, 1902, requested that he prepare for them a list of all the property formerly belonging to the water company. Mulholland in turn presented a preliminary report on the system's most needed extensions, enlargements, and repairs. He later recalled how much had been needed to expand a system "at least ten years behind the actual needs of the city," which itself was about to experience "a period of growth unprecedented in the annals of any considerable city of the country." He urged giving utmost importance to two future projects: first, the building of an infiltration gallery (in effect, a "submerged dam") for water storage at the Narrows and the Buena Vista pumping station—an installation that would secure each day 6.5 million more gallons of water that were currently flowing away unused and unseen underground; second (and more controversial), the adoption of the meter system of selling water.[16]

With monthly receipts of $43,000 and operating expenses of $5,000, the department's earnings were expected to finance these projects as well as pay off its bonded indebtedness. Along with promises of lower water rates, other reforms included shortening the work day from ten to eight hours for all employees and laborers in the water department. At the urging of Commissioner Toll, the board also agreed that laborers should be paid weekly rather than monthly.[17]

After Mulholland and City Engineer Stafford indicated that the grave hydraulic engineering problems on the infiltration gallery required a consulting engineer, the board employed Fred Eaton for three months. What else he did that spring of 1902 would not be fully known for several years, but with hindsight a clue appears in an account of an April meeting of the Engineers' and Architects' Society of Southern California in the Eaton home. Described as a "delightfully unconventional social affair" and not the usual "stag" party, it was hosted by Mrs. Eaton and several other ladies, who enhanced the evening with vocal offerings, one even playing a cornet solo. "Mr. Eaton," the report read, "was unexpectedly absent, plunging around in the mountains in search of a gold mine." The treasure he sought was, in fact, water, and the date marks the renewal of his serious investigations in Owens Valley. Later he was to say that although he had informed Mulholland of his searches, he did not reveal their locations at that time.[18]

As a public official, Mulholland's activities expanded into social spheres previously unvisited. In what was apparently a combination business-social weekend in early spring, Mulholland was a guest at Henry O'Melveny's mountain retreat, the Crags, in the San Gabriel Mountains. Also present was banker John Mackay Elliott of the newly appointed water commission. Although the outing seems to have been relaxed and friendly (Elliott's family was with him), surely water matters were foremost. Soon after that weekend, Mulholland became a member of the distinguished Sunset Club, doubtless under the aegis of O'Melveny and Elliott, who were charter members.[19]

WATCHDOGS OF WATER CONSERVATION

Wasting water ranked with the seven deadly sins in Mulholland's view, and because he was passionate about water meters as a means of curtailing overuse, he began campaigning for their installation almost as soon as he became superintendent. He also began to issue warnings about Los Angeles's limited water supply. "I will call your attention," he said to the water commissioners at the beginning of 1902, "to the rather startling fact that with the exception of the 12,000,000 or 14,000,000 gallons of water daily that was delivered to irrigators last summer, the water company was delivering to its consumers every available gallon of water that could be derived by the means of supply now in use from the watershed of the Los Angeles River." Urging that the first meters be placed with the excessive users, he concluded, "I am quite confident that with the use of even 1,000 meters, to be placed at random where extravagant use is reported, a saving of from 1,000,000 to 1,500,000 gallons daily would be effected."[20]

Persuaded by his arguments and those from other authoritative sources (especially cities pioneering the meter system such as Cleveland, Detroit, Minneapolis, and St. Louis), the water commission agreed to install meters selectively. Protests were not long in coming, and as complaints arose, the public got its first taste of Mulholland's rough side. His first adversary was ironically a lawyer whose legislation, the 1887 Wright Irrigation Act, had enabled communities to form irrigation districts that challenged the dominance of California's monopolistic land moguls. Formerly a senator from Modesto, C. C. Wright had in 1901 served as a trustee of the Los Angeles Bar Association and had been a member of the citizens' committee that had supported municipalizing water. He lived in Boyle Heights not far from the Mulhollands, and here, with rising indignation, Mulholland had observed his wanton use of precious city water on an expanse of greensward. Deciding to use Wright as an example, Mulholland, water commission president Herman Silver, and several workmen descended like avenging angels on Wright's place to install a meter. (The city's water ordinance allowed department em-

ployees to enter a private property for business purposes such as repairs
and meter reading.) As work got under way, Wright appeared and threatened to kick them all into the road. At the next commission meeting,
Wright acknowledged his heavy use of water. He attempted some pla-
cating remarks to Mulholland and Silver, saying he did not object to the
idea of meters, but added, "I do object to anybody coming and digging
on my premises, without so much as saying, 'good morning, sir,' and I
will not permit it, until the courts shall have passed upon the subject."[21]

Mulholland next had his say. "For more than two years I have gone
by Mr. Wright's place many times, and I never went by, either day or
night, that sprinklers were not running. The collectors and inspectors have
constantly made the same complaints, and the water has frequently been
found running down the street from Wright's lawn, and everybody complained of the waste of water. . . . If everybody used water like he does,"
he continued, "only 3,000 consumers in the entire city would get water,
and the other 21,000 would go without. The Hazard Reservoir, from
which he is supplied, was down to two feet, and in a few hours would
have been empty, unless all waste was stopped, and as his was the most
flagrant case, I sent the men to put a meter on, and he threatened to kick
the whole outfit into the street."

The next day, Wright got a restraining order against the City of Los
Angeles, the commissioners, and Mulholland, charging that the water
meter ordinance violated the Fourteenth Amendment. The commissioners felt they should support Mulholland for fear that his authority might
subsequently be called into question, although privately some must have
wished that he could have applied a slightly more velvet glove. Tact and
diplomacy were never much in evidence when Mulholland thought he
was right, and doubtless some of the enmities that piled up against him
through the years resulted from his sometimes abrupt manner and blunt
tongue. When one man tried to sell the city a private water pipeline, Mulholland told the commissioners the city had as much use for a wooden
leg as it did for a mile of clay pipe. A year later at a water commission
meeting, a delegation from Garvanza showed up to protest the abominable water they were getting and also to complain that the young man
who was supposed to activate the pump each morning at 5:00 A.M. to
assure delivery of water was not rousing himself until 8:00 A.M., so that
Garvanzans found themselves much distressed and incommoded. Mulholland did not offer much comfort about the quality of water and told
them that lack of funds prevented any immediate action on cleaning the

system, but he did assure them something would be done about the slug-abed youth at the pumphouse. One of the committee then piped up to suggest a possible replacement: "I know a good old man . . ." Mulholland cut him short: "I'm not here to investigate the merits or demerits of old men. I'll get someone that can run that pump." One so rudely dismissed was not apt to harbor warm feelings towards Mulholland.[22]

As guardian of the domestic water supply for Los Angeles, Mulholland knew the limits of its resources. He also had a kind of rough-hewn populist social philosophy about urban water use, which is perhaps best captured in a statement he made at the time of the meter uproar. "Owing to peculiar climatic conditions we can never expect Los Angeles to rank among the cities of small water-consumption for the reason that the semi-leisure class is attracted here by the adaptability of both soil and climate for building up beautiful homes by reason of the long intervals of almost absolute cessation of rainfall." But, he concluded, that was no reason "why the privilege of using water for this purpose should be given on the present unbusiness-like basis, which compels the careful and frugal to pay for the carelessness and extravagance of others. . . . Water bills, where meters have been applied, have frequently been reduced one-half, without apparent detriment to the lawns or grounds. In my judgment, meters should be applied, and additional inspectors employed."[23]

The summer of 1902 began with Mayor Snyder's proclamation restricting water use. With the meter system under way, certain owners, especially those with lawns and large gardens, protested the limitation of six hours each day for sprinkling. The commissioners were assailed with complaints, and President Silver reported that one caller to his office had grown so abusive that he had to order him out. The beleaguered Silver said he contemplated making a requisition from the water fund for a bed and mattress in the office, as he had been called out at midnight and four o'clock in the morning "to come out to Stickety-stick Street and stop a leak." Other customers were wily in their ruses to beat the system. The hired man of oil magnate E. L. Doheny allowed the water department to put a meter on a service pipe at his employer's estate but failed to mention that there were two service pipes. After the department had installed a meter on one pipe, the hired man merely hooked up the meterless pipe and merrily continued his unlimited consumption of water. Self-styled experts began to publish figures to show that water was in fact ample and that meters were simply an unnecessary expense. When the *Evening Express* accused the commission of favoring certain big busi-

nesses with cheap rates, the board quickly rebutted, pointing out that
those establishments' low rates resulted from their use of zanja, rather
than domestic, water—a practice that was soon to stop.[24]

ENLARGING THE WORKS

Superintendent Mulholland did not only attend meetings but was often
to be found in the field, as when a reporter caught up with him in May
1902, at the Buena Vista work site. After donning rubber boots and a
sou'wester, the reporter had the thrill of riding in a tin bucket with Mulholland 112 feet down a shaft eleven and a half feet in diameter to the
site where tunnel work for the new infiltration gallery was under way.
Down this hole where lay the city's hopes for more water, the reporter
found his footing on the muddy bottom, noticed water oozing from the
tunnel walls, and observed that the sky seemed very far away. In darkness relieved only by a string of electric globes and candles in wire frames
attached to the tunnel walls, he could faintly make out a "husky fellow"
hard at it with a pick as his companion loaded the broken shale, dirt,
and mud into baskets and buckets sent to the surface by a windlass run
with a small stationary engine. The tunnel work was a hazardous
around-the-clock operation, and as only one man could work in the heading, three shifts of two men each laboriously dug and hauled with pick
and shovel. Mulholland explained that it was hard to get good experienced men to handle the pick at the bottom of the shaft, but that he was
satisfied with their progress. These toilers—the Pat Harkinses and Handsome Bradys—were never far from Mulholland's mind when he inveighed
against water-wasters. He knew the cost in human terms at which their
water was bought. Although completing the tunnel would take two years,
Mulholland hoped that by summer the water from the wells they planned
to sink and pipe to Buena Vista Reservoir by means of a new large and
modern pump would supply an additional 2 million gallons a day. When
the tunnel was completed, 6 million gallons a day could be expected. Having seen enough, the reporter climbed into the bucket and Mulholland
sent him flying to the surface with a pull of the cord. Once again in the
sunshine, the reporter concluded that one descent had been enough.[25]

In addition to proposing construction of a second reservoir near Ivanhoe on a 110-acre tract of city-owned land, Mulholland in June asked
attorney Mathews to start proceedings against the owners of two pumping plants near the Pomeroy and Hooker ranch near Burbank. The river
ran through the lands of two ranchers, and although the private water

company had left them undisturbed, now Mulholland wanted to secure the rights for Los Angeles. Mathews in the meantime created a new charter amendment (adopted by the people in the December election) by which the water commissioners alone were to administer the water plant and collect revenues, out of which operating costs would be defrayed while the surplus was applied to the interest and sinking fund on the bonds. Now officially known as the Water Department, its future commissioners (reduced from seven to five) were to be appointed by the mayor and be subject to confirmation by the council. Members would serve gratis, although the president of the commission (or board) was to receive a salary of $3,000 a year. The board was to maintain an office accessible to the public and was to meet once a week.

All in all, the first year of the new municipal waterworks went surprisingly well. Rates by the end of the year had been reduced 10 percent, and between the first of February and the end of November, water revenues amounted to $455,469.13. "Actual Gold Mine," crowed the *Los Angeles Times*. In his semiannual report, Mulholland expressed satisfaction with the tunnel work near the Buena Vista pumping station and announced that six wells had been completed, promising to add 500 inches of water to the supply. Yet beneath this optimism lay his continued worry that the dry cycle of the last decade might continue while the city's population grew. He knew he could not rely solely on admonitions to the people to conserve, and he feared having to seek water in the heavy gravel beds south of the city, a process that would be expensive. "Since the summer of 1893," he wrote, "there has not been a season that has not shown a decrease in the flow of the stream over that of the preceding year . . . until in the present year the diminution . . . amounts to considerable over 50 percent from that of 1893.[26]

New Regime for a Booming Town

1903–1904

"A SPLENDID BODY OF BUSINESSMEN"

For all the congratulatory talk about having removed the water system from politics, it never altogether escaped the controversies and power struggles centered in City Hall. Although Democrat Meredith Snyder became mayor again at the end of 1902 with a plurality of 2,700 after winning every precinct in the city, the majority of city officers and councilmen remained Republican. In selecting the new five-member board of water commissioners, Snyder reflected this balance by choosing two Republicans, one Democrat who voted Republican, and two Democrats. During this board's tenure, the Los Angeles water system would be revolutionized. All the players were assembled—heroes, villains, and simple walk-ons—for a drama that would play out in the decade ahead. The city council's reaction to the mayor's selections for membership in these new organizations reflected the growing power of white, conservative Anglo-Americans who trusted businessmen, feared labor, and equated progress with economic growth and patriotism. Their epitome became General Harrison Gray Otis, whose voice would grow louder and stronger in the decade ahead. Mayor Snyder's choices for the reorganized five-member water commission received full council approval, demonstrating its unabashed faith in capitalists and a disregard for engineer James C. Kays's suggestion that a well-paid superintendent, auditor, and engineer named by the mayor would manage the waterworks far better than a commission of businessmen. For the department now to be under the supervision of two new governmental commissions, water and civil service, the mayor named five wealthy men: two bankers, a real estate man, an electric rail magnate, and a building contractor with special ties to the Santa Fe Railroad Company. No doctors, lawyers, or representatives of labor, science, and education seem to have been considered, an indication that water affairs would be conducted with attitudes and methods not unlike those of the old water company. Indeed, within the year, such charges were being made.[1]

The first water commission apparently gave Mulholland no qualms, for he later commended its makeup ("a splendid body of business men"), especially praising the two who had served as directors with the old water company and with whom he already had congenial working relations: John M. Elliott, president of the First National Bank, and J. J. Fay, former president of Citizens Bank. Fay became the first president of the water commission, a full-time job with a salary of $3,000 a year. The others served without compensation other than a per diem of $10. A third commissioner, William Mead, had been involved in Los Angeles real estate since 1886, while the last two represented bank and rail interests. Lewis A. Grant, who served only briefly as he died the following year, was a contractor for the Santa Fe Railroad; Moses H. Sherman was vice president of the Los Angeles–Pacific Railway Company. Both were directors of the Bank of California, and Sherman was a founding stockholder. Of the five commissioners, only Sherman would become controversial and problematic in the water story.[2]

Whereas not a word arose in the city council over Snyder's choice of water commissioners, a hubbub erupted over one of his candidates for the newly formed civil service commission, Charles Dwight Willard. A civic booster and Progressive Republican who voted Democratic and had been prominent as secretary of the chamber of commerce in the fight for the harbor at San Pedro, Willard was, at the time of his appointment, secretary of the reform-minded Municipal League and also of the Jobbers' Association. He had old-guard enemies in City Hall, and his confirmation was contested because he was already a paid secretary of another organization (such fine points of conflict of interest had not disturbed the civic conscience in choosing members for the water commission). The conservative Republican councilman backed by railroad interests, Frank Nofziger (grandfather of Ronald Reagan's consultant Lynn Nofziger), branded Willard "an extremist." To avoid a showdown, Willard sent the mayor a graceful letter of withdrawal in which he said, "Like the average American citizen, I dislike to seem to retreat under fire, but if the fight is to result in endangering a reform for which thousands of the best men of the city have worked faithfully, then there is nothing for me to do but yield good-naturedly to the inevitable." Mayor Snyder, angry at the council's refusal of his candidate, unhappily accepted Willard's departure. By March, all of Snyder's appointments had been confirmed, and when as if freshly anointed he entertained his new official family with a banquet, Henry O'Melveny of the civil service sat at his right hand, J. J. Fay and J. M. Elliott of the water commission at his left. After the sumptuous feast and toasts with Mumm's Extra Dry, the mayor thanked all thirty new commissioners for their service to the municipality.[3]

HOW TO MEET WATER DEMANDS

At its first meeting, the new water commission reappointed William Mulholland as superintendent; James P. Vroman, secretary; L. M. Anderson, auditor; Niles Knickerbocker, cashier; and George D. Pessell, water overseer. Throughout the spring of 1903, water affairs advanced smoothly as the commission dealt chiefly with minor matters and began to consider bids for a new department headquarters building on city-owned property at Second and Central Avenue. Rains at the first of the year seemed to have relieved the threat of drought, but when he reported an annual rainfall of 10.26 inches in March, Mulholland was moved to tell the board, "One of the trials of my life is to make people believe we have not had a very wet year. We can't meet the demand with less than fourteen inches." A week after those words, the city was drenched with almost an inch of rain.[4]

Two large and costly projects preoccupied Mulholland in the spring of 1903: replacing the domestic water service's main conduit north of the city limits with an enlarged duct, and completing the high-gravity reservoir in Elysian Park west of the Buena Vista Reservoir. The latter, as Mulholland had explained in his annual report, was undertaken to secure greater water storage because of the growing city's increasing demands and the alarming depletion of ground supplies from agricultural use. "It may be urged that in the event of a wet winter, the river will supply all the water needed by the city for all purposes, but it is a well-known fact that the river makes no sudden response to a single year of abundant rainfall."[5]

Mulholland fretted about the expanding city he served. How would water be delivered if builders insisted on higher skyscrapers? "I don't know what we'll do if they keep on climbing skyward," he confided to a reporter. "It will not be possible to put on enough pressure to supply them, even if we were inclined to try it." He pointed out that some eastern cities had ordered a five-story limit; those who built higher had to provide their own pumping facilities. Domestic users continued to demand better water pressure, which, when provided, often resulted in bursting mains, especially among the older services. In Boyle Heights, after greater pressure had been provided, some of the old pipes, said Mulholland, "had revolted."[6]

A third major engineering project involved the manufacture and installation of two large pumps for the infiltration gallery at the Buena Vista Pumping Station. By midyear, impatient with progress on the pump ordered from the Risdon Iron and Locomotive Works in San Francisco, Mulholland traveled north several times in the spring of 1903 with his associate engineer, Fred Fischer, to consult with the company's mechanical engineer and his good friend, David Dorward. Mulholland's ten-year-old son, Perry, accompanied the men on one of their junkets and later remembered that they arrived just as the celebrations for the completion of the Pacific Cable began, a revolutionary event that meant a message now could be sent around the world in twelve minutes. Amid the sounds of gunfire and cannon salutes on the waterfront, the ten-year-old boy thought the Spanish-American War had resumed.[7]

Mulholland returned home to confront a threat to the city's water supply by an oil refinery on the banks of the Arroyo Seco. In the 1890s, oil discoveries within the city by E. L. Doheny and his partner had set off such a frenzy of drilling that, by the time Fred Eaton became mayor, Los Angeles was in danger of being permanently defaced by a landscape of rough wooden derrick towers and drilling equipment. Accusations and complaints of pollution and odors were constant, especially near the mushrooming refineries. Two weeks after Mulholland's return from San Francisco, on July 17, 1903, the department of public works ordered him and Dr. Powers of the health department to study a court ruling resulting from property owners' complaints against the Union Consolidated Refining Company on the south bank of the Arroyo Seco between Avenues 22 and 23. One hundred thirty-five feet below the sands on which the refinery was situated lay the infiltration tunnel then under construction for the city's increased water supply. After investigating the refinery, Mulholland reported that the crude oil posed no menace, as it was too heavy to percolate down into the soil, but the refined oil and liquid runoffs from the plant would endanger the water supply. He considered "the presence of the refinery in its present location as being a most decided menace to the water supply of the City," and he proposed that "all the tanks containing refined oil might be set in a concrete basin of sufficient capacity to hold all the oil in case it should escape from the tanks." Should a large fire occur, then all the oil would be caught and could not penetrate the soil. Although the manager of the plant indicated a willingness to make this correction, nearby owners continued to insist that the whole plant be removed, and so the matter went to the courts.[8]

LOCAL SCANDALS

While the first of the big pumps in the new infiltration gallery was about to be activated at the end of September, Mulholland was shocked by two scandals affecting men he knew. On September 4, the man who gave Griffith Park to the city, Colonel Griffith J. Griffith, shot and maimed his wife. Eleven days later, former mayor Fred Eaton divorced his. Mulholland later appeared as a character witness at the highly publicized Griffith trial, for which defense attorney Earl Rogers devised a new defense of "alcoholic insanity." Although Eaton's divorce may not have come as a surprise to Mulholland (the Eatons had been maintaining separate domiciles in Santa Monica), the fact that a distraught Mrs. Eaton blurted to a reporter that she could explain the breakup in one word— "whiskey"—would have struck him as an unfortunate public laundering of dirty linen. Helen Eaton now became a poignant figure living alone with her aged mother as Fred secured custody of the adult children, a curious business as by then his daughter was a married woman.[9]

Eaton listed his residence as the California Club. Apparently energized by the dramatic change in his life that included a romance with a woman twenty years his junior, he renewed his pursuit of a great water system for Los Angeles. For over ten years Eaton had been possessed of the vision that, by his own account, had come the summer of 1892 as he looked over the prospects of an irrigation project in Owens Valley, Inyo County. Finding the project economically unworkable but still intrigued with the possibility of supplying Los Angeles with the abundant water he found there, Eaton spent $10,000 "on a gamble that surveys would show it feasible." He had apparently spoken of the grandiose scheme at times to his engineering colleagues, who dismissed it as a pipe dream. Although continuing his local engineering and real estate activities, Eaton renewed his Owens Valley endeavors, especially after learning that the United States Government Reclamation Service had begun to consider the area as a possible site for an irrigation district.[10]

THE BACTERIA PROBLEM

In September, Dr. Powers announced the bacteria count was too high in tests of river water. Because of the increased number of typhoid cases in the city, he declared the supply from that source would have to be cut off. "Good drinking water should not contain more than 500 bacteria to a cubic centimeter," he said. The river was testing 6,000. Powers hastened to reassure the public that their chief source of drinking water from Crystal Springs tested less than 50. Notices listing punishable violations were now posted along the river, along with announcements that changes would have to be made along the river banks, and pigeon and livestock keepers were issued warnings.[11]

At this time a new member who would play a curious role in the coming aqueduct story joined Dr. Powers's staff. Miss Ethel L. Leonard, described as a "lady bacteriologist," was a graduate of the medical department of the University of Southern California. After advanced studies at Johns Hopkins University, she had been hired by the city to fight bubonic plague and other contagious diseases. The board of health appointed her city bacteriologist at a salary of $75 a month, jocosely announcing that the choice could not be regarded as political as she was unable to vote. Characterized as young and ambitious, she would one day become one of Mulholland's virulent enemies.[12]

"THE WATER IS YOURS. ENJOY IT BUT DON'T WASTE IT."

At the end of the rainless summer of 1903, word went out that householders were to have first claim on the domestic water supply. When asked, "How about the irrigators, Mr. Mulholland?" the superintendent shot back, "Oh, they're dead." Explaining that no water was left for irrigation after the domestic supply was taken out, he signaled his intent in the coming year to close the zanja system, which had outlived its usefulness. Would the parks suffer when the zanjas dried up? Would they receive city water? Yes, Mulholland replied with a burst of lyricism, "Make the parks blossom as the rose; make 'em fresh and green and beautiful, but—" Here the lyric mode ceased as he uttered next what was to be his essential policy and message to the city: "The water is yours. Enjoy it but don't waste it."[13]

Water commission meetings were often taken up with petitioners from outlying and sparsely settled sections leveling charges of unfair treatment. A group from the highlands northwest of the city repeatedly de-

manded that a special pump be installed to provide water on their properties. After each demand they were told that their properties were 100
feet or more above the level to which the city system could supply water
and that they must create their own water plant. Then, they were told,
when they had gained enough consumers to produce a revenue equal to
10 percent of the investment, the city would be willing to buy it. The
commission explained that because it could not comply with the demands of each small group that wanted special service, it based its policy on performing the greatest good for the greatest number. This meant
they could not supply water to the city's sparsely inhabited areas. All
this had been repeated many times, but on December 1, the group reappeared at a commission meeting led by one Mrs. Scott, who carried a
large umbrella that she used as a means of emphasizing her message.
Repeatedly whacking it on the table before the impassive faces of the
water board, she launched her tirade. "If you people were ordinary mortals and not bankers, we'd have a better chance. The trouble with you
men is that you count water like money. You show no justice nor fairness to us." Declaring that a break in the Angeleno Heights Reservoir
the week before was "a judgment" sent on them, she threatened legal
action, whacked the table one more time and departed, leaving behind
a room of silent men, with only Commissioner Elliott muttering,
"Humph." Breaking the silence, Mulholland reported that the damage
in the reservoir break would not exceed $600 or $700, and that the repair work had already begun.[14]

Although the commissioners persisted in pointing out that the city
charter strictly prohibited the delivery of water beyond the city limits,
unhappy hill dwellers continued to appear. They included former mayor
Henry T. Hazard, who insisted that he receive water on his property,
which lay outside the city limits. When denied, he left in high dudgeon,
muttering about "usurpation" and "confiscation." With the increasing
demand for water, Mulholland and the commission began to voice their
opposition to annexations to the city. In his annual report for 1903, Mulholland cited the dubious wisdom of having admitted the suburb of Garvanza, where the city had spent "not less than ten times more per capita
to properly serve that small addition than was spent for the balance of
the city, and the end is not yet." Although the Hollywood area boasted
that its supply, provided by Union Hollywood Water Company, could
provide for a city of 10,000, in fact part of its water came from a company about to be purchased by the City of Los Angeles.[15]

At year's end, complaints notwithstanding, the city's waterworks had earned general approval, improved services, and reduced rates to the consumer. Gross revenues of $614,264.92 for the fiscal year had equaled 30 percent of the purchase price; the department had laid over forty miles of mains and installed 4,002 taps; the flat rate to consumers had been reduced 10 percent, and the metered rate, 50 percent. An editorial in the *Los Angeles Herald* applauded the commission for its service and management and Mulholland "for his sound judgment and efficient supervision." It concluded, "The wisdom of taking the department out of politics is amply vindicated. The water board is composed of business and professional men who made considerable sacrifices in accepting the responsibilities thrust upon them, and the result is a credit both to their citizenship and to their ability. Nor should it be forgotten that the board attributes, in large degree, the high standard of efficiency maintained by the water force, to the fostering influence of the civil service."[16]

SEEDS OF FUTURE TROUBLE

Two events during the period from 1902 to 1903 created little stir at the time, but certain chroniclers later came to regard them as having portentous—possibly even sinister—significance in the city's water story. One was Moses H. Sherman's appointment to the water commission; the second was the formation of a syndicate that opened Whitley Heights in Hollywood and next participated in a land deal involving George K. Porter's ranch in the San Fernando Valley. In years to come, some would see the figures enmeshed in those events as conspirators in a great plot to dupe the city into paying for a costly water system devised to render their land deals profitable.[17]

Whatever qualities Mayor Snyder may have been looking for when he named Moses Hazeltine Sherman to the first water commission, idealism and devotion to municipally owned waterworks could not have counted among them. For all his undoubted intelligence, capabilities, and business acumen, a dark side lurked in Sherman, who practiced a ruthless brand of laissez-faire capitalism and had mastered the art of growing rich with other men's money. He never went to jail and he rarely lost a lawsuit, but he skirted both. A native of Vermont, he came as a young schoolteacher to Arizona Territory, where his ability and ambition soon put him in the forefront of public affairs. He shortly abandoned the classroom for a career of land acquisition, speculation, banking, and, most important, the development of transportation systems. He briefly served as Arizona's adjutant general in 1883, and afterward used the honorific "General," thus creating an interesting confusion with General William Tecumseh Sherman of Civil War fame.

Moses Sherman had early engaged in politics (Republican) and water development and in 1883 was involved in an irrigation project known as the Arizona Canal. By the time of his selection as a water commissioner in Los Angeles, he had for many years been vice president and a major shareholder in the Phoenix Water Company, which at the end of 1903 was threatened by a public that wanted to hold a bond election in order to acquire its own municipal system. Sherman announced that he would fight the attempt all the way to the Supreme Court, and in the spring of 1904 he brought suit against the municipality to stop the sale of bonds for the proposed waterworks.[18]

Accounts of the boom lured Sherman to Los Angeles in 1889, and by 1891, with his partner and brother-in-law, Eli P. Clark, he had created the first electric rail system between Los Angeles and Pasadena. After selling it to Henry E. Huntington, the brothers-in-law built lines towards Santa Monica and other ocean points. This system, sold to E. H. Harriman and expanded in 1907, was taken over by Huntington in 1910 and became property of the Southern Pacific—a network of interurban lines popularly known as the Big Red Cars that interconnected far-flung areas to central Los Angeles.[19]

In the 1890s, with their hard times and business panics, Sherman was often embroiled in legal battles that earned him enemies and a reputation for tough-minded wiliness. In the early nineties, he had figured in the case of *San Diego v. the San Diego and Los Angeles Railroad Company*. San Diego had granted 5,000 acres of pueblo land to the rail company for development of a transit system, and the suit was brought when Sherman, one of the two trustees acting for the city, proved to be a stockholder in and a director of the railroad company. Based on the general principle that no man can faithfully serve two masters, the court found that he had violated the strictures surrounding conflict of interest, even though his honesty and impartiality were unquestioned.[20]

In 1894, a San Francisco banker doing jail time after the debacle and collapse of his father's Pacific Bank accused Sherman of having helped to break that bank. Through demands, intimidation, and threats of blackmail, according to the imprisoned banker, Sherman had exacted a loan of $165,000 to convert a horse car line in Phoenix, Arizona, into an electric road. He had bullied the bank into making the loan it could ill afford by threatening to reveal its shaky financial condition to the banking commission. Then he had subsequently been unwilling to repay the loan in a timely fashion. Sherman, the banker accused, had contributed to the demise of his and his father's bank. Sherman denied everything.[21]

A year later, stockholders in the by then defunct Los Angeles Consolidated Electric Railway accused Sherman, who as founder and president had held most of its stock, of having seized control of all the assets. In the sale and reorganization, they charged, he gave them no part of the stock but instead retained it all in his own name. Four years later, in December 1899, the Pacific Bank brought an action against Sherman asking for a judgment of $250,000. Believing that Sherman had manipulated its funds so as to pay no dividends, the bank now asked for an accounting, especially in regard to 25,500 shares of stock in the Los Angeles Consolidated Electric Railway, which Sherman and the bank had held as equal owners but now had vanished into a financial maze devised by Sherman and Clark. Whatever the truth about these machinations, Sherman had earned the dislike and distrust of the *San Francisco Examiner,* and when William Randolph Hearst founded the *Los Angeles Examiner* at the end of 1903, that paper would be the first to launch an attack against Sherman in Los Angeles.[22]

By 1903, Sherman and Clark were masters of a successful and burgeoning electric railway company as well as recognized leaders in Los Angeles financial and banking circles. Their connections and business associations now included membership in land syndicates involving General Harrison Gray Otis and Harry Chandler, general manager of the *Times,* who, with various other associates, had embarked on a program of massive land acquisitions. In April, Sherman and a number of these associates participated in an event that, although apparently unconnected with Mulholland and water, did involve men who would one day be seen as having conspired in events to come. While Mulholland and the water commissioners wrestled with ways to improve the city's water system, a group of civic leaders and promoters celebrated the simultaneous opening of Whitley Heights in Hollywood and a new Los Angeles–Pacific Railway line leading there from downtown Los Angeles. Water Commissioner Sherman was one of the new road's builders. On the gala day, in his private parlor car, "Mermaid," he led a jolly crowd to the outlying district of Hollywood. As they rattled along, Sherman told amusing stories and pointed out the extensive work being done on Sunset Boulevard, the avenue that would connect Hollywood to Los Angeles. After a day of picnicking, tallyho rides, races with newfangled automobiles, visits to the grounds of the new Hollywood Hotel and to the Outpost, the nearby home of General and Mrs. Harrison Gray Otis (who also entertained with an Arbor Day tree planting on their estate), the climax arrived on Whitley Heights with a ceremony of flag raising and speeches. Amid the paeans to progress, Mayor Snyder praised new developments and loosely borrowed from John Keats's poetry when he rhapsodized that "a good road is a thing of beauty and a joy forever."[23]

While this group of self-congratulating capitalists celebrated their advancement of civilization into the Hollywood hills, back in town a strike against Sherman and Clark's rail line had just been broken up. After the labor movement's weakening in the late 1890s, an unprecedented "surge of unionism" between 1900 and 1904 had invigorated workers to take action regarding their grievances. When the strike proved of short duration, the anti-union *Los Angeles Times* jeered, "There are still laborers who call themselves strikers, but they are only men out of work." When President Theodore Roosevelt came to town a week later, local strifes were temporarily set aside, as everyone, including the Council of Labor, turned out for a great parade with brass bands and a marching group known as "Teddy's Terrors" to cheer a travel-worn president as he proceeded rumpled and unshaven from the train station to the Westminster Hotel, where he was to address a luncheon meeting.[24]

The September 1903 sale of George K. Porter's San Fernando Valley ranch land to a syndicate whose membership included General Otis was no secret; it was, in fact, trumpeted in the newspapers. The investors, including Porter himself, were E. H. Harriman, H. E. Huntington, A. B. Hammond, W. G. Kerckhoff, General H. G. Otis, J. F. Sartori, George C. Hunt, and E. T. Earl. The holding comprised one-third of the northern half of the San Fernando Valley, with the east-west Roscoe Boulevard as the approximate dividing line. The 16,450 acres sold for $575,750, or $35 an acre. During the Southern Pacific's construction of the San Fernando Tunnel in 1874 and 1875, the north half of the 175,000-acre valley had been acquired by San Francisco boot and shoe wholesalers Ben F. Porter and George K. Porter and by Senator Charles Maclay, then living in Los Angeles. Maclay's lands lay east of the Southern Pacific tracks. In 1874 he had platted lots and farmlands and had established the town site of San Fernando near the mission. The west section, owned by Ben F. Porter, began at Aliso Canyon and extended to the Santa Susana Pass. Between these two tracts (which included the west end of the town of San Fernando) lay George K. Porter's land. As earlier recounted, during the boom Fred Eaton had attempted a water project for Ben Porter near the fledgling town site of Chatsworth Park. After its dam failed, the land had remained vacant aside from a few sales and some dry farming of grain crops.

With the quarrying of rock in the Chatsworth hills for the breakwater in San Pedro and the commencement of the building of the Chatsworth Tunnel in 1898, the little settlement livened up to a degree, but during the 1890s, hard times and squatters in the valley had especially plagued George K. Porter's holding. In the spring of 1901, he began to negotiate with the syndicate through L. C. Brand, a leader in Glendale's development, who acted as agent and trustee for the parties. The sale was publicized, extravagant claims were made for the land's future development, and the usual assurances were offered that the purchase was not for speculation, "but for the purpose of holding and developing the property." Only as events unfolded did it begin to seem that some aspects of the purchase were compromised and that perhaps Sherman's presence on the water commission had made him privy to confidential information about future water plans that influenced the deal.[25]

At the end of 1903, less than half an inch of rain had fallen, and the United States Department of Agriculture warned of a grain shortage in Southern California for the coming season. Hard, dry north winds swept the land in early December, fanning brush fires in the canyons. The severest occurred along thirty miles of sea coast and into the chaparral-covered Santa Monica mountains, where the mansion of Malibu Ranch owner Frederick Rindge was reduced to ash. In the city, nine days of wind created a pestilence of dust that caused both a health problem and a transportation crisis. With the city choking, the Chamber of Commerce warned that tourists were being driven away. Health officers cautioned that the diphtheria epidemic then raging was due in part to dust-borne germs, while the street superintendent complained of the streetcars' air brakes' blowing clouds of dust onto people in the streets. When an angry city council demanded that the transit companies sprinkle the streets adjacent to the tracks, the companies protested the expense and said it was the city's job. Water users were warned to husband supplies as protection against a possible drought, while Henry O'Melveny, scrupulous in his rainfall entries, noted at the end of 1903 that aside from .46 inch in September, none had fallen since April. On Christmas Day he remarked on the dilapidated look of the plant life around him and wrote, "Driest I have ever known."[26]

CHAPTER 10

Desperate Remedies in a Dry Season

1904

A WATER CRISIS

As dry conditions continued through the winter of 1903–1904, railroad officials were announcing that they expected 10,000 colonists to arrive in California in 1904, and builders were anticipating a boom. Meanwhile, thousands of cattle were starving in the Antelope Valley for lack of rain, and returning hunters reported that Lake Elizabeth had disappeared, leaving only a mud flat. Field crop growers announced that between winter frosts and drought, shipments of vegetables from Southern California had fallen several hundred carloads below estimate. In Los Angeles, pine trees in Elysian Park were turning brown from lack of water, and on January 10, the city's clergymen called for all the churches on the coming Sabbath to pray for rain.[1]

As water demands besieged the department, Mulholland scrambled to meet the needs. Not only was the population growing but its hygienic practices were changing. When the principal of one grammar school produced estimates that only 23 percent of American homes had bathtubs, she prevailed upon the school superintendent to have a bath house built on the school grounds so the children could bathe. Although some parents were indignant at the inference that their offspring might need ablutions, the program became so successful that the superintendent began to install bathtubs and showers in other city schools. New homes with improved plumbing also increased demands for water and put a greater burden on a sewer system that was already in an alarming state of deterioration and by summer would produce a crisis.[2]

In addition to the looming water shortage, Mulholland and the water commissioners had to cut back on expenditures for improvements in order to raise funds for upcoming payments on the bonds. They had spent all of the recent revenues on improvements to the water plant, instead of putting money into the sinking fund. Now they would be forced to save incoming revenues for the rest of the year and reduce by at least half construction work for the next five months. The commissioners therefore suspended work on the main supply conduit from the headworks until August, which made Dr. Powers unhappy as he had long urged closing the tunnel in the interests of delivering a supply of pure drinking water to the city.[3]

Fred Eaton, at work on Mulholland's municipal distribution plan, added his opposition to the annexation of lands to the City of Los Angeles because of the difficulty in supplying water to them. As both Cahuenga Valley and Belvedere (about 500 acres east of the city) clamored for admission to the corporate limits of the city, Eaton argued that Los Angeles was already big enough, with its existing area of 44 square miles making it the fifth or sixth largest city in the United States. He also voiced fears that annexations could jeopardize pending court decisions regarding the city's paramount rights to the waters of the Los Angeles River. Cahuenga Valley, if annexed, would be entitled to city water at a time when the city was already arguing that it needed all available water.[4]

In June, completion of new projects promised relief as Mulholland announced that "we have relieved most of the famine today." A large new pump near Elysian Park and the new high-service Beaudry Reservoir promised to lower water anxieties, although, as the reservoir filled, warnings went out to Bunker Hill residents that the new service with its added 60 pounds of pressure might well burst some of the tired old pipes. At this juncture, the water commissioners, citing the pressure that the superintendent had been under since the first of the year, granted Mulholland a two-week vacation to be taken at his pleasure. He turned it down, saying that he felt the need of a rest but no more than did the men who worked under him. He praised their great endurance as they worked day and night for the city, and added that he could not take time off just then. A week later, he set off a debate in the city council when he announced that the city must abandon and discard the old sprinkling cars and begin to lay the dust on streets with oil. Charging that people were

still wasting water, he also announced his intention to put more inspectors on patrol to stop excessive irrigation. By the end of July, 150 viola-
tors had been caught citywide, mostly using water outside of the legal
hours (lawn-sprinkling hours were from six to nine o'clock in the morning and from five to eight o'clock in the evening).[5]

When Mulholland finally did leave town at the end of summer, it was
not for a vacation but for a trip that would alter his destiny and the city's.
His refusal to leave the city earlier had stemmed from his deep concern
over water supplies and his sense of urgency about completing current
projects. What is more, he was overseeing the installation of the second,
larger, pump for the infiltration gallery at the Buena Vista pumping station. As it was about to be activated, Mulholland was described as one
who had been "sleeplessly watching over the great system he has brought
up from its swaddling clothes . . . not the man to be satisfied with letting well enough alone." This new iron monster with its gauges staring
out like shiny eyes bore the complex description "Cross Compound Con-
densing Crank and Fly Wheel Direct Action Pumping Engine." Dwarfing
the old equipment, it had been manufactured at the Snow Steam Pump
Company in Buffalo, New York, for a contract price of $24,000 (The
figure was ridiculously low, said Mulholland, because the company had
been so anxious to beat Risdon Iron Works in San Francisco that it un-
derbid the job. The freight alone on the new pump had been $4,000.)
Now, every twenty-four hours, the new marvel promised to raise 6 million gallons of water with a lift of 240 feet to supplement the first pump
installed the year before. Brought up from the underground dam 125
feet below, the water would supply the downtown business section, with
its overflow going into the old Buena Vista Dam. One reporter felt he
had witnessed a historic occasion when he watched the great wheel begin to revolve as "Superintendent Mulholland and a corps of assistants
ran eagerly about and crawled into dangerous positions to squirt oil into
cracks or pound it with a hammer and in other ways nurse it into action. For hours this process was kept up until all the parts worked together and the monster, as the ship in Kipling's story, had 'found itself.'"[6]

Only one large city water project remained this year, and by the end
of summer, if all financial arrangements were successful, Mulholland intended to have in operation a Corliss pumping plant at Los Feliz Point
on the Griffith Ranch near Tropico. This installation promised 400
miner's inches of water to the main conduit. These additions to the city's
water system offered hope that a water famine might be averted.[7]

The celebrated new pump at the Buena Vista station soon produced a perturbing result. At the end of July, Mulholland noted that the city's water consumption for one twenty-four-hour period had been 40 million gallons, exactly the amount the water system was able to produce in the same time period. He wrote to city officials that in the week ending July 25 "the rate of water consumption had aggregated 16 million gallons in excess of supply." He also warned that should that rate be kept up, the city would be in a very serious state. Two weeks earlier, consumption had been only 33 million gallons, and Mulholland could not account for the sudden jump. More alarmingly, he also observed that one reservoir had failed to rise to its normal twelve feet during the night. Somewhere, he realized, a terrible waste was occurring, and at the present rate, the system was stretched dangerously to its limit.[8]

Seeking the cooperation of the newspapers to alert the citizens to the importance of conserving water, he set about to study the situation. A week later, on August 3, he discovered a shocking situation. NINE MILLION GALLONS OF WATER ARE WASTED read the headline in the *Los Angeles Herald*. Leaks in the outfall sewer had allowed water to flow in from the powerful new pump at the Buena Vista infiltration gallery. The water for which so much effort had been expended was simply draining out to sea in the old sewer line. "This is an outrage," Mulholland declared. With a current-meter placed on the suspected sewer line for twenty-four hours, he calculated that 5 million gallons of pure water had been lost to the leaks in the sewer line. Another 2 million gallons, he estimated, were being lost to the sewer that drained East Los Angeles and Boyle Heights. The rest he ascribed to varieties of wasteful usage such as leaky fixtures and excessive yard watering. Voicing discouragement, he spoke of the cure that must come: "The little meter that never goes to sleep will cure it; we are putting them in as fast as possible and will continue until all the water goes through meters." He then thanked the daily papers for their help in publicizing the crisis. The meter plan met with resistance. When an officer of the Los Angeles Railway Company complained that its high bill must be because the meter was not in good order, Mulholland retorted that if the meter were not in good order, it would not register at all. He then invited the officer to come to the shop where the meters were tested; there he would discover that their mechanical construction made it *"absolutely impossible* to register more than passes through them."[9]

On August 15, in a freak of nature, a wind and electric storm dumped .13 inch of rain on Los Angeles—scarcely enough to lay the dust. As the reservoirs began to resume their accustomed levels, Mulholland gave

credit not to the brief sprinkles but rather to the economies of cooperative water-users. Later, it became an article of faith among antiaqueduct
critics that water was intentionally dumped with accompanying threats
of scarcity so as to frighten and coerce citizens into voting for water and
aqueduct bonds. In view of contemporary accounts, however, that
charge lacks credence. In fact, the old sewer systems had long been neg-
lected for lack of funds and were giving way under the pressures of a
growing population. Mulholland and the city engineers had been warning of the problem and offering solutions that remained unattended until the situation blew up into a municipal scandal in 1906.[10]

The water loss had been alarming, however, and led Mulholland and
the water commissioners to act decisively to establish more completely
the paramount rights of the City of Los Angeles to the waters of the Los
Angeles River. To do this, City Attorney Mathews brought an injunction
suit restraining every owner in the San Fernando Valley from taking water
from beneath his lands. Howls of protest arose, so that Mathews quickly
had to explain that the action did not mean every landowner in the valley. In fact, he said, most of the 163 persons named in the suit were
landowners near Tropico, Glendale, and Burbank, where heavy pumping
of river water was occurring and where so many earlier dissensions had
occurred. Furious, however, the valley ranchers organized, levied themselves each a dollar, and retained two legal firms to fight their case. Mathews and Mulholland were adamant. "From our standpoint," said Mathews, "there is no equity in this case." Mulholland amplified, "To grant
this contention of the owners of the ranches in the San Fernando Valley
would be preposterous. If they can take any part of our water, they can
take all of it, and our great conduit would be a dusty run-way for squir-
rels and coyotes, and our great filtration gallery which crosses under the
river at the Buena Vista station would soon be dry enough for a railway
tunnel." Many argued against this unpopular action, however, as lacking
a moral right even though the city might have a legal right to the water.[11]

TWO FRIENDS MAKE A TREK

On September 18, an inconspicuous item in the *Los Angeles Herald* noted
that William Mulholland was to be gone on vacation for about three
weeks. It appeared two days after a spirited election in which a councilman had been voted out in the first recall ballot in the history of the United
States, a triumph for labor, the Progressives, and the recall's author, Dr.
John Randolph Haynes, a reformer who would later also play a large

role in the water story. Overshadowed by election news, the obscure item noted that in addition to taking a rest, Mulholland was also to inspect several of the large water systems in the north. He was, in fact, about to see the great water supply of which Eaton had so long boasted.[12]

The day before the water commissioners granted Mulholland his leave of absence, Fred Eaton was about to leave for New York in an effort to secure funds for purchasing the Long Valley site on the Rickey Ranch in Owens Valley. At Mulholland's request, Eaton revised his plans, and the two set out on a trek that was to alter the history of Los Angeles and Southern California. On a buckboard with a team of mules, they made their way to the Owens River along the route that Eaton had determined, while Mulholland made notes and a sketch of the plan.[13]

After exploring other water resources in the upper Owens Valley, the two "sold the team and journeyed to San Francisco by rail. From there, Eaton and his daughter, who was waiting for him, left for New York. Before parting, Mulholland asked Eaton if it would be all right to seek legal advice to see if it would be possible to acquire such a water supply." Eaton consented and, just before leaving for New York, received a telegram from Mulholland asking him to name a date when he could meet Mr. Mathews at a certain hotel in that city.[14]

This took some scrambling on Mulholland's part, as Mathews was about to leave on October 3 for Washington, D.C., where he would argue two cases before the Supreme Court concerning redistricting the gas works' operation outside the city limits. On the very eve of his departure, Mathews agreed to rendezvous with Eaton in the East. He spent a day in New York with Eaton at the law firm of Dillon and Hubbard, which had earlier helped with the bond issue for the city's purchase of the private water company. After the attorneys decided the city could go out of the county for a water supply, Mathews said that he wished to deal directly with Eaton rather than a syndicate in securing land options. Although Eaton at first demurred, he finally consented, at Dillon's urging. In short, Eaton was to act as sole agent in the Owens Valley for the City of Los Angeles.[15]

THE THIRD MAN

The third engineer in this venture, Joseph Barlow Lippincott (1864–1942), was a hydrographer-engineer with the National Geological Survey. An enthusiastic resident of Los Angeles since 1891, he was by 1903 an employee of the National Reclamation Service, whose mission was to locate and survey sites for irrigation projects and dams in the West. As supervising engineer, Lippincott worked under two highly principled officers of the service, Chief Engineer Frederick H. Newell in Washington, D.C., and Engineer Arthur Powell Davis in California. Davis had been Lippincott's partner in an earlier private water venture.[16]

A key figure in the Los Angeles–Owens Valley story, Lippincott is thought by some to have been duped by Fred Eaton, while others have accused him of duplicity on behalf of Los Angeles's municipal water interests. His role in Owens Valley began on April 29, 1903—over a year before Eaton took Mulholland there—when Newell wrote from Washington to ask if Lippincott had ever considered, with a view to a possible irrigation project, "an examination of Owens River Valley and the desirability of segregating public lands." Newell suggested that if Lippincott as supervising engineer concurred, then he should send "a suitable man . . . and have a reconnaissance quietly made, with the idea of withdrawing lands pending survey." Lippincott promptly gave the assignment to Jacob C. Clausen, a twenty-seven-year-old California native and graduate of the University of California, Berkeley. By early July, Clausen had completed his mission and wired Lippincott, "Have finished reconnaissance large reservoir site, all patents for dam site. Private parties have all water, sixty thousand public, fifty thousand private land irrigable." Lippincott in turn reported back to Newell in Washington that prospects looked good for an irrigation project but that private power interests were also checking possibilities. Still, Lippincott felt that the two groups could proceed "without mutual interference." With a continent separating them, Newell gave Lippincott the authority to make his own decision, offering the guideline that "If there is an opportunity for Government reclamation on a large scale, I think that we should not let this opportunity go by."[17]

Lippincott now made his own inspection of Owens Valley, where he found large tracts of good public land and local settlers enthusiastic over the prospect of a large irrigation project. Although concerned about possible conflicts with private irrigation and power interests, on August 6, 1903, he nonetheless recommended to Newell that "all the remaining public lands in Owens Valley should be withdrawn pending further examination."

When Fred Eaton got wind of this development, he set to laying the foundation for the project he had long dreamed of in Owens Valley and had heard promulgated by an engineer during special Senate committee hearings in 1889. In 1892, he and Frank Austin had investigated the possibilities of an irrigation project in the Owens Valley but abandoned it "as an unprofitable venture on account of the transportation facilities." (Ironically, Austin's younger brother, Stafford Austin, along with his wife, the noted author Mary Hunter Austin, would become outspoken enemies of Los Angeles and its water engineers.) Impressed by the quantities of water he had seen, Eaton had continued his investigations with a survey made by Joseph Seely, former surveyor of Inyo County, for the purpose of moving Owens River water out of its shed into Indian Wells Valley. Further research ("engineering data from Civil Engineer Brooks, war maps and Southern Pacific Railway Surveys . . . and the help of a couple of good aneroids") convinced him that conveying water to Los Angeles was feasible. Now in 1903, with the Reclamation Service showing interest in the water for an irrigation district, Eaton decided to act, and thus began the complicated drama that would one day tarnish both his and Lippincott's reputations with suspicions of conflict of interest and unprofessional conduct.[18]

Lippincott was among those whom irrigation enthusiast William E. Smythe called "Uncle Sam's Young Men"—a group of talented engineers assembled in 1902 as consultants in the newly organized United States Reclamation Service. A native of Scranton, Pennsylvania, Lippincott was the son of a distinguished minister and educator. After early training at Dickinson College, where his father taught mathematics, he earned a degree in civil engineering at the University of Kansas in either 1886 or 1887 (sources vary); worked for the Santa Fe Railway; was a topographer with the United States Geological Survey in New Mexico and California; and then worked for private irrigation companies in Arizona and California. Married in 1890 to Josephine Cook, he came to Los Angeles the following year with his wife and a baby girl, his only daughter, Rose Lippincott. As a member of the United States Geological Society, he was to serve as assistant to another of Uncle Sam's Young Men, topographer Arthur P. Davis, in mapping Southern California.[19]

At the end of a year, Lippincott left his government job and undertook several private irrigation endeavors in Southern California, but the depressed years of the early 1890s weighed against success. Drought and hard times undid various projects, including a partnership with Davis in planning a waterworks in the Antelope Valley. He returned to government service in June 1895, as state hydrographer with the U.S. Geological Survey. Because government salaries were inadequate for his family, he also secured an understanding that the survey would allow him to do some private work.[20]

Throughout the 1890s, Lippincott was active in the regional engineering fraternity: expert witness in the later phases of the Hooker-Pomeroy case and member of a panel of experts in the city's suit against the Crystal Springs Land and Water Company and the City Water Company in February 1898. Among his fellow panelists were veterans of the local water scene James D. Schuyler, A. H. Koebig, and Fred Eaton; if he had not yet met Mulholland, he would have encountered him when they testified on opposing sides regarding questions of water flows and infiltration pipes.[21]

During Eaton's mayoralty and campaign for the municipal ownership of water, Lippincott stood squarely behind him in public support of the bonds. Not only did he offer his services in preparing precinct maps, he spoke at meetings and rallies and declared that it seemed foolish "to give up this chance for municipal ownership and leave the water supply of the city in the hands of a grasping corporation." Lippincott's public utterances echoed Eaton's animus against the private water company, and certainly by the summer of 1899 the two were more than casual acquaintances.[22]

Lippincott remained active in both city and Geological Survey affairs during Eaton's administration. He reported on the progress of the survey's plans to conserve the state's water in "a period of the worst drouth ever recorded in the State." With other members of the survey, he further explored the Los Angeles River to study percolation rates through various soils. Then, with Elwood Mead (later chief engineer of Boulder Dam), City Engineer Frank Olmstead (now Lippincott's business partner), and survey member Homer Hamlin, he investigated water conditions in the San Fernando Valley. In a lengthy summary of the water situation prepared for the city engineer's annual report, he concluded, "If the comparative growth of the city during the last ten years be projected into the future for ten years more, it will indicate a population of 200,000 people at the expiration of a decade. At the rate at which we are now using our water it would appear that the natural supply would be exhausted in four and one-half years. At the termination of this period, methods will have to be devised to meet the situation. This will indicate from a physical standpoint alone, the necessity of a remedy of the situation."[23] By the autumn of 1902, as supervising engineer for California in the Reclamation Service, Lippincott was third in command under his old partner, Arthur P. Davis, and his former chief, F. H. Newell. Ten months later, he received the telegram from Newell regarding Owens Valley.[24]

BEHIND THE SCENES

After his first inspection of Owens Valley in September 1903, Lippincott proposed to Governor George C. Pardee a study for a reservoir site in Owens Valley. In December he reported that further studies were needed, especially in the matter of a storage dam. For this, he recommended a Long Valley site on property owned by a local land baron, Thomas B. Rickey. Rickey Land and Water Company was a cattle spread of 22,380 acres in Mono and Inyo Counties, and although Rickey's claim to some of the land was dubious, he was considered a tough customer who ran his fiefdom in the old ways of the roughshod West. He opposed reclamation projects, so obtaining any part of his land would require skillful negotiations.

In a disputed incident the following April, Eaton and Lippincott are said to have encountered each other in Owens Valley while Lippincott was waiting for the arrival of a drill to test the bedrock at the Long Valley dam site. Eaton by now had established his son in Independence, and the two were scouting riparian sites along the Owens River with a view to acquisition. Witnesses remembered seeing the two together frequently, but Lippincott later denied that Eaton made any mention of his interest there. For his part, Eaton denied even being in Owens Valley during April 1904.[25]

At this juncture, Newell, aware that Lippincott and his engineering partner, O. K. Parker, were involved in a number of private water projects, suggested that Lippincott's continued private practice was not acceptable for one in government service. Lippincott defended his outside work and argued that Parker had taken charge of all their private business, which was mostly with public agencies. He further agreed to avoid private work, including court appearances as an expert witness. Given this assurance, Newell approved a salary raise for Lippincott in June 1904, and plans for the Owens Valley project proceeded.[26]

In June and July 1904, Lippincott was much in the public eye in Los Angeles and keeping up an exhausting schedule. As well as being in Owens Valley in April, he had also gone on an inspection trip to Baja California and discussed irrigation problems along the Colorado River in connection with the Yuma reclamation project. In Yuma a large group of engineers had met, including Thomas H. Means, who had just returned from an inspection tour of irrigating systems in Egypt and was about to go to Owens Valley to make soil tests. In May, Lippincott appeared at the California River Convention meeting at San Francisco's Palace Hotel, where he spoke on the Geological Survey's investigations of the Sacramento Basin. Then, on June 15, he appeared before the Los Angeles Park Commission with reforestation proposals for Griffith Park. (On the eve of a trip back to Washington, D.C., the previous December, he had consulted with Henry O'Melveny over the possibility of a plant experimental station at the park and promised to bring the matter to the attention of Chief Forester Gifford Pinchot.) Lippincott was also appointed to the city's civil service commission headed by Dr. John R. Haynes, and on July 27 Mayor Snyder complimented his service to the city, citing his role in helping to purchase the properties of the West Side Water Company. Lippincott, he claimed, had worked for "a comparatively small salary" when he could have gone to the other side and earned much more. Praising his faithfulness to the city, the mayor said that Lippincott, in addition to the work at Griffith Park, was also eager to see a better road constructed through the Providencia Ranch (the Glendale area) to connect with the Cahuenga Pass road.[27]

Given this crowded life with city, state, and federal projects, a vacation seemed warranted in the late summer of 1904, but the Lippincott family's camping trip to Yosemite in August would be remembered as something more than a mere pleasant outing. The Lippincotts invited several friends to join them and their two small children (a baby boy, Joseph Reading Lippincott, had been born in 1901), and the party included Fred Eaton and artist Fernand Lungren, who was to sketch nature scenes. After camping in Yosemite, the group made its way from Tuolumne Meadows down the precipitate Tioga Pass into Bishop, where they bought supplies and met more friends, among them, Jacob Clausen and Thomas Means of the Reclamation Service. Because Clausen had done the Owens River study and was therefore the most knowledgeable about the country, he guided a tour that included the reservoir site at Long Valley.[28]

Lippincott, along with other members of the group, later claimed that none of the party suspected Eaton's interest in the place at the time, but the upshot of the camping trip was Eaton's return to Los Angeles to tell Mulholland of the Reclamation Service's intentions in Owens Valley and to express fears that the city might miss its chance. Hearing of this turn of events, Mulholland decided it was time to learn about Owens River, and so the two set out on their momentous survey.

Events now moved rapidly. Lippincott returned from his vacation and, with full knowledge of Eaton's plans, on September 17, wrote to inform Newell in Washington of the city's interest in the Owens River for domestic use. Newell agreed to come west and meet with all the parties on November 22 to discuss the matter. By now, however, he was also receiving petitions on behalf of an irrigation project from enthusiastic Owens Valley residents, as well as reports recommending the project from his department engineers, Clausen and Means. These interests were colliding at a time when the Reclamation Bureau itself faced a budget crisis. The $30 million set aside for reclamation projects had by now been largely committed to other undertakings such as those on the Yuma and Klamath Rivers, and Newell realized that his bureau could not undertake all of its desired projects in the West at this time. In the November meeting, Newell conceded the city's need for Owens River water, but insisted that the project would have to be "an exclusively municipal one." That meant Fred Eaton would have to abandon his dream of profiting in a joint venture with the city. Reluctantly Eaton agreed.[29]

For the next three months, the city conducted reconnaissance work on the Owens River project, so that by the beginning of 1905, a decision was forming. As Mulholland later wrote, "The superintendent reported favorably on the adequacy of the water supply and the feasibility of constructing a canal to bring it to the City, and the Board of Water Commissioners then asked him to make a preliminary estimate of the probable cost of such an enterprise, with a view to getting data on which to base a bond issue for the purchase of the Eaton water rights." The dry language of an engineering report scarcely conveys Mulholland's enthusiasm for the project. He had returned from Owens Valley fired with the belief that the Owens River would solve chronic water shortages in Los Angeles. Keeping silent proved difficult, however, for on October 21, when he read "The Water Supply of Southern California," his first long paper to the Sunset Club, he could not refrain from hinting at a grand solution that at present would seem only "visionary and chimerical."[30]

A Plan Revealed

1905

Some people appear to be objecting to the scheme. They say we worked in the dark. In fact, we worked in the light, while they were in the dark, for if some of the objectors had been "on" to what was happening, there would have been a migration to the Owens Valley, and we never could have obtained the water for anything like the price we are to pay.

WILLIAM MULHOLLAND, 1905

A SECRET POORLY KEPT

Months before the proposal to acquire Owens River water for Los Angeles was finally made public on July 29, 1905, hints and rumors circulated around town. In December 1904, hardly able to contain his secret or enthusiasm, Mulholland gave a statement to the city's newest morning newspaper, Hearst's year-old *Los Angeles Examiner,* which had urged the city to solve its chronic water shortage. He assured the public it had no need to panic at the present population but warned that growth beyond 225,000 would cause a problem—unless, he slyly suggested, a way were found to kill Frank Wiggins, perennial civic booster and spokesman for the Los Angeles Chamber of Commerce. Then, seemingly out of the blue, Mulholland commented that if a gigantic project were to be undertaken, it would require large expenditures. "Hence," he went on, "it would be the part of wisdom to have appointed a commission composed of good business men, together with, say, two or three hydraulic engineers of standing, whose residence and practice here have been long enough to acquaint them thoroughly with hydrographic conditions in Southern California." Mulholland also advised the city to plan ahead and not wait until it found itself short, for "it will require the work of years to guarantee against the future, and we should begin the task at once." Thus in general terms, as if preparing the public for the coming specifics, he spoke of great undertakings.[1]

COPING WITH THE PRESENT

If people in Los Angeles were largely in the dark at the beginning of 1905, those in Owens Valley had seen glimmers of some great change during 1904 as surveyors and engineers became active in their territory. While optimists foresaw a federal reclamation project for their valley, others sold their land or granted options to, among others, the apparently land-hungry Fred Eaton. By January 1905, Mulholland was corresponding with local engineer-surveyors in and around Owens Valley. As letters and money orders for work and supplies arrived there from the water department of Los Angeles, not everyone in Owens Valley could have been in the dark about the city's involvement, later disclaimers notwithstanding.[2]

Mulholland, though excited by the prospects of this magnificent and challenging project, also recognized that even if it were to materialize, the city would not enjoy the bounty of its water for years. His immediate task was to wrestle with the problems of the city's present supply, and though above-average amounts of rain fell in the winter of 1904–1905 (19.52 inches, over 3.0 inches above normal), water demands continued to threaten to exceed supply.

Discontent arose in April when fifty prominent building contractors filed a protest with the city against what they maintained were exorbitant costs for tapping mains, claiming that voters had expected these costs to go down under municipal ownership. Criticism intensified as private water promoters hatched plans to supplant the city's works. A rumor surfaced that tycoon Henry E. Huntington had a plan to supply the city with water from the Santa Clara River at a point near Newhall with a proposed aqueduct modeled on the one built to bring water to Boston, Massachusetts, from Lake Winnipesaukee one hundred miles away. Word also circulated that Frederick Rindge, owner of Malibu Ranch, had taken over the Maclay waterworks in the San Fernando Valley and intended to sell its water. (This scheme came to nothing in August, when just a week before the election that approved the Owens River water bonds, Rindge died suddenly in Yreka, California.)[3]

Lippincott was committed to aiding the City of Los Angeles with its water problem, but he also was a federal employee. At the beginning of 1905, an emergency had required him to bring a crew of reclamation workers from Owens Valley to Imperial Valley, where the Salton Sea had begun to fill and flood as the result of the Colorado River's changing its course. With rail traffic severely impeded, Lippincott's crew arrived with others to study and remedy the problem. By this time, Lippincott's in-

volvement with the City of Los Angeles was so widely recognized that
the *Imperial Valley News* even suggested that both he and his chief, Frederick H. Newell, might be under the influence of Otis and the *Los Angeles Times*.[4]

Lippincott's focus was still on the Owens River, however, as indicated
in a letter he wrote to Mulholland at the end of February. Touching upon
Reclamation Service activities in Owens Valley, he advised that in the
event "this project be turned over to the city of Los Angeles, then the
city should repay the Service for expenses incurred in surveys and
drillings for bed rock at the Long Valley dam site." Soon, however, his
juggling of city and Reclamation Service projects raised such serious ethical questions in Washington, D.C., that an investigation forced his sep-
aration from Reclamation in 1906.[5]

In March, after Mulholland and Eaton took their stand against
wooden pipe for an Oakland sewer bond election, they participated with
Lippincott in the Southern California Irrigation Congress, which was attended by most of the engineers who were to be actively involved in planning and building the Owens River project. For all the ink that has been
spilled over tales of conspiracies and devious plots in the Owens River
project, hardly a drop has been given to the large group of imaginative,
opinionated, and articulate engineers who not only knew one another
but often intermeshed at this time in a variety of water projects in the
West. A collegiality existed among them as they met at each other's
homes, exchanged ideas on outings and camping trips, and gathered at
professional conferences such as this. Mulholland's first address to this
body, "Water Waste," emphasized how the meter system had greatly reduced waste of the water supply in Los Angeles. Lippincott read a paper, "Stream Characteristics of Southern California," as well as joining
W. C. Mendenhall, also of the United States Reclamation Service, in a
discussion, "Forestry and the Supply of Water." While the veteran western engineer James D. Schuyler spoke on "The Impounding of Flood Waters," rain began to fall, pouring down a torrential 3.49 inches on the
city. The Los Angeles River went on a rampage, tore out the Seventh Street
Bridge, swept away two young men to their deaths, and caused the sewer
at Fourth Street to overflow. As if to mock the gathering of engineers and
irrigationists who had been discussing water scarcity and conservation,
local rainmaker and "Wizard of Esperanza" Charles Hatfield took credit
for causing the deluge with a secret chemical process that he claimed produced an "affinity" with rain.[6]

As the engineers concluded their conference, City Attorney Mathews hastened to Sacramento with a delegation backed by the Chamber of Commerce to fight legislation that would have threatened any possibility of an Owens River project for Los Angeles. Known as the Pendleton Eminent Domain Bill, it would have allowed a county's inhabitants to condemn for their own use any water stored or flowing therein intended for use in another county. Ironically, its author was a Los Angeles man, about whom the *Herald* said, "it would be a stretch of charity to say that he was an innocent tool of schemers who had important personal or corporate interests to subserve." Urging Governor Pardee to veto the bill, Mathews minced no words. "It means that if we are forced to go outside of Los Angeles County to develop water and bring it into the city by means of pipes and tunnels at tremendous expense that should a small town situated in the county in which the water was developed desire to use some of the water they would have the right to it."[7]

THE CAT OUT OF THE BAG

When the Owens River project was finally announced on July 29, 1905, the cat may not have been altogether out of the bag, but its nose and whiskers had certainly been visible. During the five months after Mulholland's and Eaton's first trip together to Owens Valley, both men had made many quiet returns, Eaton on a regular basis to secure land options and Mulholland five times to investigate and consult with the surveyors mapping the dam sites and route of the future aqueduct. City officials masquerading either as park developers or cattlemen (accounts differ) had inspected the area in April and consulted with Eaton regarding his proposal to sell his land options and contracts to the city. In early May, Mayor Owen McAleer was granted a ten days' leave and disappeared from the city with attorney Mathews. No one seemed to know exactly what they were up to. The *Herald* reported that they had gone to San Francisco, ostensibly to attend the hearings of a suit against Rancho Bartolo Water Company, which, rumor had it, the City of Los Angeles might buy to increase its water supply. (One old-timer who doubted the story remarked that "Johnny" Mott's scheme to sell water from Rancho Paso de Bartolo was old enough to vote.) The *Times* featured the puzzle of the missing mayor with a cartoon and headline reading, GONE A FISHING, IS IT FOR WATER?[8]

While Mulholland and his crews struggled to implement service lines and fend off citizen complaints about poor water service, voices against municipal ownership rose again. Grievances piled up at City Hall until by mid-July a group of businessmen demanded an investigation of the water commission. Local attorney Oscar Lawler, who represented private electric interests, announced that $3 million had been raised to begin construction of a huge dam across Big Tujunga Canyon. Mulholland, not unaware of this scheme, was quick to point out that the Big Tujunga Wash was part of the watershed of the San Fernando Valley, whose water rights belonged to the city. As these events threatened the municipal water system's advance, one councilman, Edward Kern, raised his voice against the various water schemes being brought to the council. "I shall fight with all my might any proposition to put it back into the hands of private corporations," he declared.[9]

This rising opposition to municipal water by citizens and private interests, along with the more urgent need to secure money by October 1 to pay for Fred Eaton's options in Owens Valley, prodded the water commissioners to spring their surprise announcement in the middle of summer. In a torrent of headlines and articles the story washed over the city: BIG DEAL IN WATER. WATER SUPPLY FOR 2,000,000 PEOPLE. A river of pure mountain water in the Sierra was to be transported to the thirsty dwellers on the plains below. At almost 240 miles, the proposed aqueduct would be second in length only to the Coolgardie in New South Wales, Australia, which ran 307. The public revelation of the Owens River plan seized everyone's attention, and then, because of journalistic rivalry, immediately provoked a controversy.

When news of the project had earlier begun to leak, city officials met with the editors of the major dailies, who agreed to remain silent and make a simultaneous announcement. The *Times,* however, in its usual bullyboy manner, jumped the gun and published a day early (July 29 instead of July 30, as agreed upon by the other papers). The scoop resulted in editorial bad feelings, especially with the rival morning newspapers, the *Examiner* and the *Herald.* (Mayor McAleer next day published a statement in the *Examiner* deploring the breach of faith by "another paper.") This furor in part reflected the circulation war between the *Times* and the *Examiner.* Published since December 12, 1903, the latter was a relative newcomer to Los Angeles, although its sister newspaper, the *San Francisco Examiner,* had long been familiar in the south. The animus between Otis and Hearst—and Henry A. Loewenthal, the editor of Hearst's *Los Angeles Examiner*—was intense but probably had less to do initially with the water question than with competition, profits, and political differences. In a personal letter to Lippincott, Mulholland blamed an engineer with the Edison Electric Company as the one "inspiring malicious communications to the *Examiner* newspaper." Despite a period of editorial opposition, the *Examiner* generally covered the water story well, and in fact, the differences among the six leading dailies on the Owens River question were minimal. Only later in the year did the *Evening News*, created specifically to oppose the water plan under the editorship of Samuel Travers Clover, grow truly scurrilous in its attacks upon the Owens River project and its architects.[10]

Alternative water proposals published in the *Examiner* came from self-interested parties such as the private owners of the water supply at Piru Creek, who reported to the city council that they could supply the city with water for $3.3 million instead of the exorbitant $23 million estimated for the Owens River project. Oscar Lawler, whose group wished to secure the water power of the Big Tujunga for lighting, warned that the Owens River plan probably would cost nearly $50 million and cautioned that the lighting companies were preparing to fight the bond election because it raised the specter of a municipal lighting plant. One Dr. Adelbert Feynes, of Pasadena, described as a physician and traveler, claimed he had personally examined the water of Owens River and found it unfit to drink; moreover, typhoid fever was endemic year-round in Owens Valley. One H. C. Morse, who claimed to pay taxes on $200,000 worth of local property, declared the plan a swindle, for in the 1870s when he had been a road master around Owens Lake, he had found its waters not fit for a dog to drink—nothing but alkali and borax—and as for the river, why, its waters moved like the hour hand on a clock. He predicted that "the city is going to get up a tree if they take that property." Mulholland laughed off the most absurd proposals and seriously answered the others. Of Piru Creek, he said, "That water would not be worth 30¢ to Los Angeles. I know all about that water shed. I owned an orange ranch on the edge of it for several years. I sold it because there was not enough water to raise a crop." He spoke of the amount of study that had gone into the proposal. "If there are any people in Los Angeles who think we have gone into this proposition like a lot of schoolboys, with a whoop and a hurrah, they should come in and look over a few of the maps we have made in this last year."[11]

Before the bond election that would decide the issue, Mulholland assessed the local scene for Lippincott, then working and vacationing at Klamath Falls, Oregon. Mulholland wanted Lippincott to return to Los Angeles to help in the bond campaign, but Lippincott in his ambiguous situation expressed considerable hesitancy about entering into a public discussion of the matter. Finding the chief opposition among engineers representing private power interests, Mulholland singled out Frederick C. Finkle, who was to become a leading adversary of the water plan. "Our worthy friend, Finkle," he wrote, "implies that he should have been employed on account of his large experience in construction work, the claim being set forth that neither you nor I have had any experience in this line."[12]

In August, when it came to a vote in City Hall to approve a $1.5 million bond election, Councilman Arthur D. "Doc" Houghton, who had replaced the councilman recalled the previous year, stood out as the lone opponent. Houghton had been hailed not only as a friend of the unions but also as a champion of free institutions and good government responsive to the will of the people. Something of a maverick (some said a "crank"), he proved pesky. The previous November he had so angered one political opponent with innuendoes of bribery that the man knocked him unconscious in an encounter at Second and Spring Streets, and he had to be hospitalized. Because of his prolabor stands, he was favored by the *Examiner* and disdained by the *Times,* which routinely referred to him as "'Spook' Howton." (He was rumored to have once conducted seances in Chicago.) The *Times* declared him a Hearst hireling (meaning prounion). The *Herald* remained content to call him simply an obstructionist, the "Honorable Misrepresentative of the Sixth Ward."[13]

OPPOSING VOICES

On August 15, before the city council's final vote to set the date for the bond election, Houghton delayed and insisted that Mulholland be summoned for questioning. Busy in a meeting with the water commissioners, Mulholland finally appeared. Although he had been patient in earlier encounters, this time he let loose when Houghton badgered him about the veracity of the chemical analysis of Owens River water. "I have been in my present position as superintendent of the water works almost thirty years and am not in the habit of deceiving the people. I have never done it yet. For five months I have examined the Owens River and valley and it looks better to me each time I go back. The mean flow of the river is 20,000 miner's inches and the water is remarkable for its purity." Undeterred, Houghton next asked if he had ever "built anything like a $23,000,000 water aqueduct, or had any personal knowledge of such an undertaking?" To this, Mulholland rounded with "Such a thing has never been done. This will be one of the greatest engineering achievements in the world."[14]

The need for haste in the matter, he explained, was his understanding that if the bonds were issued immediately and moneys paid by January 1, the city could save $45,000. Moreover, a payment of $50,000 was due on the land and water options by October 1. Houghton dismissed the $45,000 as "nothing" and next asked if a two weeks' delay would imperil the project while he personally inspected the Owens Valley area. Mulholland answered that he knew little about the time required for a bond issue and that Eaton could better answer that. Getting an admission from Mulholland that another twenty-four hours' delay while contacting Eaton would not hurt the project, Houghton moved to adjourn until the following Monday morning. Because of his gadfly performance, however, he was simply overridden, and the council approved plans for a bond election on September 7. At this point, the *Examiner*'s anti-aqueduct editor, Henry Loewenthal, blasted the city fathers. "Appearances could not have been worse had the Council been voting a $22,000,000 contract to a private corporation in which the members had an individual interest of something like $100,000 each. As it was, there could be no charges of graft."[15]

In defense of the city council, which represented a diverse group (although some critics have insisted they were all Southern Pacific hirelings), their near unanimity suggests a very real agreement about the Owens River proposal. Mulholland expressed his pleasure when he wrote to tell Lippincott (still at Klamath Falls) that the city council had approved a bond election for September 7 and that he had no doubt of its ultimate success. He renewed his opinion about most of the opposition's source. "Finkle . . . for the Edison Electric Co., is making a scurrilous and dirty fight in opposition thereto, by inspiring malicious communications to the Examiner newspaper. This, you will remember, is a pleasing occupation to him, as to my certain knowledge he has attempted to inflict his presence as an engineer on every project of importance in this country." He also cited two other disgruntled engineers, "Purcell with the Kern River project and Hawgood with the Mojave," who, on behalf of their clients "give utterance to vagrant statements that while not being particularly mendacious are at least misleading." Urging Lippincott to return soon in order to participate in the coming campaign, Mulholland closed by expressing his regret that Lippincott would not be on hand that night at the Municipal League banquet, where he was slated to speak.[16]

Although overridden, Houghton had nonetheless made telling points to which the councilmen might well have given more consideration as they pursued the enterprise through the years. When he questioned the precipitate haste of approving a project that would cost the voters at least $22 million, he made an accusation that was to have a long life. "It almost looks," he declared, "as if some of these men whose character and integrity are above reproach had been let in on this deal three or four months ago, had purchased arid lands and are in haste to have them made valuable by this water project." The San Fernando Valley lands to which he referred would in the following year become the focus of accusations and suspicions that were not to fade away.[17]

MULHOLLAND MAKES A SPEECH

The Municipal League banquet was held on August 15, after the council's approval of the Owens River plan. Sponsored by the Municipal League in order to lay before its membership a presentation of the giant undertaking the city had assumed, the affair drew one hundred and forty of Los Angeles's most prominent and influential citizens. Guests included the mayor, along with members of the city council and water department. Mulholland and Eaton spoke at length, and their combined speeches constituted a concise history of the city's water story. When Mulholland was introduced with the words "What can I say of him except that he is Will Mulholland," cheers shook the room. He demurred, "It is rather a poor return for this repast to have to ask you to swallow a few chestnuts." One reporter commented that the speech was long, but that "Mr. Mulholland has a rugged, vigorous way of putting things that is more convincing than oratory." When asked about the magnitude of the project, he replied, "The engineering project is a big one. But it is a simple one. The man who has made one brick can make two bricks. That is the bigness of this engineering problem. It is big, but it is simply big."[18]

With the aid of maps, Mulholland outlined the city's past, present, and future water needs; spoke of the Los Angeles River and its sources and its limitations; recounted his explorations of other sources with Eaton and Lippincott; and finally, detailed the investigations in Owens Valley and the reports provided by F. H. Newell and Jacob Clausen of the Reclamation Service. He referred to himself as having been "a kind of stepmother to the Los Angeles River," as for the past thirty years he had worked during storms, in gumshoes and gum coat, to keep mud out of the reservoirs so that the people would not have turbid water "such as the people of St. Louis drink the whole year round." He spoke of Lippincott's studies and explorations for water in this southern country, and of Eaton, he said, "Mr. Eaton had talked to me about Owens River for thirteen years; and would twit me with the fact that sooner or later the city of Los Angeles would go to the Owens River country to get an additional water supply. When he first broached the thing to me I thought it was so absurd that I just fairly laughed in his face." Admitting he had been a pessimist, Mulholland confessed he had thought he would never live to see the day when the city would have 100,000 people.

Eaton told of his early experiences in Owens Valley and confirmed that Mulholland was "never so enthusiastic in the future of Southern California as I was." He spoke of their trip the previous September; of Mathews's insistence that Eaton act as the sole purchasing agent for the city in the Owens Valley, along with the water commissioners' assistance; and of his success in securing the Rickey lands. He too vouched for the purity of the water and touched upon some of the engineering difficulties that would be encountered.

Water Commissioner John Elliott next explained in detail the necessity for secrecy and haste: how the water department urgently needed the funds that it had already invested in the project; how the city had to meet the payment of $50,000 on October 1 or lose its land options, which would then allow private interests to move in and take them up. "If the city votes $1,500,000 in bonds, the money can be used so that the city will absolutely own this proposition. After that, you can vote the money necessary to bring the water here. If you do not do this, the water can be sold to others. Mr. Eaton agrees to take it off your hands and pay for it." He spoke of his trust in Mulholland and said that in their thirteen years of association, he "worked within his estimates and never went over them." (This produced applause from the gathering.) After speaking of journeying to Owens Valley with a group of engineers and city officials and seeing for himself the snow-covered mountains, Elliott quoted John Muir, who, when he had drunk from the headwaters of the Owens River twenty-five years earlier, praised its taste as the best he had ever had and likened it to "unstimulating champagne."[19]

Mathews followed with his support of the plan and the need for an early bond election. He deprecated his own role, claiming that "the handling of the matter has really revolved around the prime minister of the water department—Mr. Mulholland—his practical experience and his full wisdom being consulted by every one at every step." Mathews said the city should take pride in the ownership of its waterworks, adding that when a proposal had lately been made to lease it to a private corporation, Mulholland had said, "Huh! You may as well suggest to a man that he lease his wife."

In a year crowded with events both challenging and saddening, this evening stood as a triumph for Mulholland, with his peers' recognition of his years of unswerving devotion to the city. Yet within a few days, a terrible and unsettling experience at the new filtration plant at Burbank confronted him again with the caprices of fortune. As he talked to a workman, C. F. Helsey, a rope broke on a derrick that was hoisting a heavy pipe. A falling block struck Helsey's head ("Mulholland fairly felt the wind of it") and fractured his skull. He died an hour later. Shaken by this first fatality or serious accident he had ever had on a job, Mulholland mused, "I have worked thousands of men . . . but it was the other man that was called. My time had not come."[20]

THE DARK SIDE OF THE MATTER

In the three weeks between the night of the Municipal League banquet and the bond election on September 7, several issues threatened the enterprise: questions about its undue haste; the role of Fred Eaton; and growing rumbles of anger and discontent from Owens Valley. Commissioner Elliott had been candid at the Municipal League banquet in admitting that the commission had spent money from the water fund on land options in Owens Valley without consulting anyone. He defended the action on the grounds that it had saved the city money by heading off speculators who would have driven up the land prices; therefore, the bond campaign's haste was plainly due to the urgency of raising funds to meet "a $50,000 payment which we have not got money to pay for." As events proved, few seemed to care about the action's moral niceties. Even though they had been kept in the dark about its beginnings, the citizenry, who had long put up with a water system that at its best was merely adequate, did not boggle at the means by which an improved water supply was to be secured. Any strict accounting must concede that the enterprise involved subterfuge. Had it been a military operation, it would have earned high marks for adroit stratagem, but being a civic matter, some found much that was dubious. Initially, however, the most unforgiving and censorious were those with the strongest economic motives for wishing the project to fail, those whom Mulholland called "arrant schemers."[21]

Eaton's land deals in the Owens Valley have always seemed troublesome to some and even today resonate with echoes of Mark Twain's *The Man That Corrupted Hadleyburg,* a tale of a stranger who seems to offer a possibility of riches that turn out to be quite otherwise. Eaton, the big city man, had arrived in a remote area and announced that he was going into the cattle business in a big way. Hearing of his desire to buy land, hard-pressed settlers saw a chance to bail out of their marginal existences. (Although Eaton was later accused of having misled the people, it is true that "the trickster never works alone. His audience works with him." Certainly no one was forced to sell his land. For some, the city's price was simply right.) With the revelation that the true owner of the land and water rights was to be the City of Los Angeles, the storm broke, as Eaton commented, "I used to be the best fellow in the world among those people, but now they think I am the Prince of Devils."[22]

For Owens Valleyites, the final disappointment came with the news that the Reclamation Service would not be building a dam in Long Valley, for in order to do so, it would have had to condemn land on the Rickey Ranch now held by Los Angeles (and Fred Eaton); nor did the federal government have the power to take water intended for domestic purposes. Thus, what seemed sweet to Los Angeles turned to gall in Owens Valley, whose dwellers now understood Eaton's land sales.

Eaton escaped the valley and spent a few days in a hospital in San Francisco before returning to Los Angeles on August 4, "drawn and limping with rheumatism," but ready to defend his actions. Expecting to remain in town "until things quiet down up there," he explained, "Some of those people think I sold them out in taking the water out of the valley. It will probably mean moving the county seat of Inyo County from Independence to Bishop. You know, we have practically bought Independence." On the same day Eaton spoke to the press, surveyor J. A. Killian wrote to Mulholland from Bishop, "Bishop is in a state of excitement at the present. They think Los Angeles is going to turn the place into a desert. Had a mass meeting here last night and denounced everybody connected with the scheme." Eaton tried to palliate his deeds by explaining that he had acted largely for the city rather than himself and told of an encounter in San Francisco with "old man Rickey," who chewed him out for not going in on a deal with him. They could have sold to private interests, Rickey told him, and made half a million. Nor did Eaton underestimate the rage in Owens Valley. "They say I sold them out, sold them out, and the government, too; that I shall never take the water out of the valley; that when I go back for my cattle, they will drown me in the river."[23]

Mulholland, who had not yet faced the direct fury of Owens Valley folk and was still buoyed by the euphoria of success, spoke exuberantly, if not always judiciously, of their accomplishment. "We have corralled everything upon each side of the river," he cheered, while dismissing the land around Independence as being of little value. He praised Eaton as the only one who could have pulled off the land deals without being found out; only on the last visit had "a canny old Scotch woman who owns a little piece of property south of the lake" solved the mystery. Privately, Mulholland conveyed his optimism to Lippincott:

> As I suppose you have already heard, there was a holy row raised at a meeting at Bishop in which we were all designated as scoundrels, etc. Happily this phase of the situation, while making some annoyance, tends at the same time to discount the claims a few of the knockers make, that there is no water to be had in Owens River Valley, the point being that if we take nothing, what in the world are those fellows up there making such a row about? I have no doubt that on a proper investigation by the Reclamation Department and the publication of such investigation, you will be cleared from the charge of any treacherous work to the inhabitants of that valley.[24]

The *Examiner* was not long in accusing Eaton of profiteering at the city's expense on land and cattle deals. FORMER MAYOR HAS GOLDEN KEY, blazed the headline. "Since May," the article accused, "the former mayor has been busy getting these options and at the same time getting rich." In an interview the next day, Eaton was allowed to rebut the charges. "There is no graft," he said. "I have made money but no city official gets one cent. I would rather have a moderate sum and many friends than a big sum and no friends. I'm no cattle king yet, but I have hopes of being." Eaton then gave his account of having owned land in Owens Valley since 1893, of his earlier attempts to develop water there, of his trip to New York, and of his decision finally to do business with the city after securing an option on the Rickey Ranch. According to Eaton, cattle came into the picture because owner T. B. Rickey agreed to sell only if he could "take my money and step from the ranch into a railroad train. He didn't want to be bothered with cattle, any piece of land or anything else. It must be a clean sale or nothing." The City of Los Angeles, having no desire or use for cattle, had let Eaton have them as a commission for his services. Mulholland defended his friend as one "who never made a dirty dollar in his life and never will." Attorney Mathews said Eaton's only profit was on the Rickey Ranch land; the city had paid him ten dollars a day for his services as confidential agent in securing land options along the Owens River. Thus, on the eve of a great enterprise, Eaton's character was impugned. Yet for later detractors to paint him simply as a self-seeking manipulator and exploiter is unfair, for he had demonstrated more than once in the past that he loved his native city. Ultimately he was perhaps hoist on his own petard of conflicting desires to enrich himself and to supply his homeland with abundant water.[25]

THE CITY VOTES

A week before the bond election, temperatures soared into the hundreds, and in the heat wave, city reservoirs sank with increased use. Days before the election, the Municipal League, the Chamber of Commerce, and the Merchants and Manufacturers Association, after an investigation of the project, declared their support and recommended inviting a delegation from Owens Valley to Los Angeles for a conference in an attempt to "convert antipathy into friendliness." On September 7, the public went to the polls and voted fourteen to one in favor: 10,693 for, 754 against. Even opponent Houghton's ward voted 1,879 in favor and 149 against. In an untypical outburst of "Let me tell you how I feel. I'm intoxicated, drunk with delight. I want to whoop and yell like a kid," Mulholland exulted that he would leave the next day for San Francisco to purchase equipment for six gangs of surveyors who would go into the field within fifteen days. Eaton set out for Owens Valley to attend the city's business there, and Mathews began to arrange the sale of the bonds. The great enterprise was at last under way. Four days later found Mulholland busy in San Francisco while, in the company of family and friends, he celebrated his fiftieth birthday and prepared to be drawn onto a broader canvas of history that would bring him fame and great reputation but also great calumny.[26]

CHAPTER 12

Preparations for an Aqueduct and a Trip to Washington, D.C.

1906

EARLY SKIRMISHES

Even though the overwhelming event of 1906 for California was the earthquake and fire in San Francisco, the year was pivotal for Los Angeles in that it saw not only the establishment of the city's right to import water from distant places but also marked the beginnings of the open shop's triumph over organized labor and the rise of the Progressive movement in politics. In combination, these developments produced great civic turbulence and change, beginning with a turmoil of debate on the Owens Valley question as water men continued to lay ground for the massive undertaking.

As the city pressed the federal government to turn over public lands in Owens Valley and stop all public works there, the people of Owens Valley demanded that their irrigation needs be considered. Pushed from both sides, Secretary of the Interior Ethan A. Hitchcock delayed his decision as he sought more counsel from C. E. Grunsky, city engineer of San Francisco, and also a consulting engineer and advisor on reclamation matters for Interior. Grunsky had completed a tour of western reclamation projects the year before and had already announced the previous September that Interior had no plans for a project in Owens Valley because if it proceeded with work at Klamath and Yuma no further funds would be available. Grunsky also defended Lippincott, whose work in Owens Valley, he stated, had not favored Los Angeles and whose findings were public property "accessible to all." Now Grunsky's reply to

Hitchcock on January 4, 1906, was noncommittal on the conflict between Owens Valley and Los Angeles, focusing instead on the project's
engineering feasibility. He concluded that if Los Angeles were to take
Owens River water for municipal use, then the proposed irrigation project
in Owens Valley would not be possible.[1]

Information and opinions about Owens Valley traveled among western engineers. Grunsky, for example, worked at City Hall in San Francisco, as did Mulholland's old friend and colleague J. Henry "Doc"
Dockweiler, formerly a Los Angeles city engineer but now a consulting
engineer in the San Francisco city attorney's office for the Tuolumne
River proposal. Mulholland and Dockweiler regularly shared technical
information about each other's city water systems, and shortly after
Grunsky sent his report to Hitchcock, Dockweiler asked Mulholland to
send Grunsky a copy of the last year's annual report. Then on January
5, 1906, Mulholland asked Dockweiler for a list of fifteen or twenty
names of "eminent hydraulic engineers" for the process of selecting a
board of engineers to study the plan and cost of the Owens River enterprise. (The water commissioners ultimately would be responsible for
choosing the panel but looked to experts like Mulholland for advice.)
He wanted to choose from a larger pool than those whose names he
knew, especially, he wrote, "men who have not been connected with the
booming of the cost of engineering work, as there is a very apparent effort being made on the part of local power companies here to depreciate the value of the power, and to exaggerate the probable cost of carrying through this enterprise." He was referring to recent critical articles
in the new *Evening News,* as well as to former city engineer Frank L.
Olmstead, who "had lent himself to this purpose in the fool report he
submitted a week or two ago." (Olmstead had submitted a sixty-three-
page report to the city council on how the aqueduct should be built. In
it he found all of Mulholland's estimates too low—altogether almost
$15 million too low!)[2]

An embattled Lippincott was still with Reclamation at the beginning
of 1906, still defending his assistance to the city while an employee of a
federal agency. A meeting with Newell the previous November 22 had
produced an agreement that the city could move ahead with its plans,
but by then he had come under such heavy fire for his putative unethical behavior in Owens Valley that he invited an investigation to clear his
name—only to discover that one was already under way. Notwithstanding, Mulholland, energetically laying groundwork for the aqueduct,
solicited Lippincott's help in securing power rights for the city on Cot-

tonwood Creek in Inyo County, urging him to emphasize that "the power to be derived from this stream will be of great importance to the city in the prosecution of the stupendous undertaking it is about to begin." Mathews also wired a Senate lobbyist in Washington, instructing him to take "map and letter of November 2nd to Newell, concerning City's water project" and also to inform both Hitchcock and Frank Flint, the Republican senator from Southern California who would fight for the Owens River project in Washington.[3]

By mid-February Mulholland was expecting Fred Eaton back from Owens Valley, where ditch work had begun below Charley's Butte for the aqueduct's intake. Eaton, who had spent the first six weeks of 1906 overseeing some of the preliminary survey work, now found himself balked in making further land acquisitions while a debate raged in the city council over allocating any further funds to him. Mulholland was also stalled in his plans to take the newly chosen board of public works on a tour of Owens Valley because Councilman Houghton withheld approval of the new water board on grounds that it lacked labor representation and that it had concocted a scheme whereby the aqueduct would be constructed with "alien labor." While waiting for the arrival of new machinery for a big conduit for the city works, Mulholland was asked about the wrangling in City Hall and replied with what became his well-known paradox: "If Los Angeles does not secure the Owens Valley water supply, she will never need it."[4]

THE CITY FATHERS IN OWENS VALLEY

At last, on February 20, Mulholland wrote Surveyor T. W. Young in Independence that Eaton had secured the board's approval "with regard to hasty procurement of the right of way over all the private lands in the valley" and alerted him that he would soon lead the board of public works ("when it is appointed") on an inspection of the route. They planned to go by auto as far as Haiwee, where Young was to meet them with a rig in which they would ride for the balance of the journey ("your big wagon with spring seats and four animals"). In March Mulholland alerted Young to get the spare beds ready at the Rickey Ranch and to round up enough bedding for four or five people.[5]

A trip to Owens Valley from Los Angeles was always arduous, and this one proved no exception. On a rainy Tuesday, March 20, Mayor McAleer with members of the water commission and the board of public works began their inspection tour under Mulholland's guidance. Part of the group left the city in three White steam automobiles, while three others took the night train to Mojave. They encountered flood conditions in Soledad Canyon, where the autos became mired in quicksand, washed-out roads, and torrents of water. With the three cars pulling each other out of the mud and sometimes using block and tackle snubbed to a tree, they limped into Mojave—two cars with broken springs and several of the passengers water soaked. After patching up the cars, the men proceeded the next day to Haiwee. Along the way, Mulholland pointed out the "fool plan" Olmstead had proposed, which would have taken the conduit east of Indian Wells into low-lying land, a route, he assured them, that he had never contemplated and that was "utterly impracticable." Instead, if the added cost proved acceptable, he proposed to run the line across one 400-foot depression by means of an inverted siphon.[6]

They spent the night at the Orr Ranch at Haiwee Meadows, where a number of them had to sleep out in the barn because Mrs. Orr lacked beds for the entire group. (Mira E. "Mother" Orr had sold land to the city.) As prearranged, engineer Young met them with the wagon, and the next morning they set out towards Owens Lake, where the roads became too sandy for auto travel. At Cottonwood Creek, they saw the first water that was to come to the city and were told of the barren soil at the southern end of Owens Valley, which produced little even when irrigated. Proceeding to the oasis settlement of Lone Pine and thence eighteen miles north to Independence, they were met by Fred Eaton, who had arrived by rail and was to lead them on to Big Pine, Bishop, and the Rickey Ranch.

Upon arrival in Bishop on Sunday, they dodged a conference with townspeople on the plea that they were there only to look and had no special authority to speak. The locals saw the evasion as a snub and said it was another instance of Eaton's giving them the back of his hand. The reporter covering the junket thought the delegation might have helped to allay "the apprehensions of Bishop" had they prolonged their visit. Instead the men from the big city left, still suspect and with animosities unrelieved, especially towards Eaton and Lippincott.

The return trip was equally eventful. The group traveled from Bishop to Big Pine by carriage, then by rail to Keeler on the northeastern shore of Owens Lake, and finally by wagon to Haiwee, where they picked up the automobiles and two new guests: a sheriff of Inyo and an editor from Independence, Irving Mulholland (no relation to William), who had already sold property to Los Angeles. This was the sheriff's first ride in an automobile, and he became an instant enthusiast when they accomplished

the 44-mile run from Haiwee to Coyote Wells in a dashing two hours
and twenty minutes. Luck ran out, however, when one of the cars developed engine trouble and had to be towed by Mulholland's, so that the
next stretch from Coyote Wells to Mojave—45 miles—took a tortoise-
like four hours. At Mojave they put the crippled car on a train along
with the rest of the party, while Mulholland and two board members
stayed with the two remaining automobiles. Although they were re-
warded with a spectacular spring display of desert wildflowers as they
motored back to the city through Antelope Valley, Elizabeth Lake, and
San Francisquito Canyon, the 91-mile trip from Mojave to Los Angeles
took eight hours because of rain and mud.

EARTHQUAKE WORRIES

The water board did not publish its official report on the Owens River
project until June, and in the interim, the San Francisco earthquake and
fire had pushed the Owens River affair to the back pages. Two days before the earthquake, Mulholland had been studying recent communications from engineer Young that included the sketch of a contour line for
a ditch from Haiwee Reservoir along with specifications for a portable
cookhouse. When he answered Young two days later to assure him that
the cook wagon was nearly completed and that a cook and flunky were
on their way with two pairs of mules, he also mentioned that one of the
men who had intended to work in San Francisco "will probably be able
to return to your camp by reason of failure to secure the employment he
expected, due to the frightful San Francisco catastrophe."[7]

Recalling that Inyo County had suffered a similarly severe quake in
1872, Harry Brooks, assistant editor of the *Times,* wrote Mulholland immediately after the quake to express concern about the safety of the cement pipes proposed for the Owens River project. Responding promptly
with a three-page discussion of damage to waterworks structures by
earthquakes, Mulholland declared the topic had engaged the attention
of many West Coast engineers. Noting that a full study had yet to be
made, he admitted that "possibly over fifty per cent of the property loss
due to the recent catastrophe in San Francisco is to be accounted for by
the failure of the water supply, yet it will be found that the damage to
the water works will, in all probability, prove, when full examination is
made, to be less than to any other extensive structure in the fated town."
He explained that the pipelines, being almost all substructural (buried),
could not move and shake as freely as if they had been above ground.

All of the dams, both earth and concrete, in San Francisco's Spring Valley system had held, and all had been full at the time of the earthquake and thus subject to maximum strain. Moreover, the main trunk line at Millbrae-Belmont had held; otherwise, he concluded, "the city would be entirely deprived of water."

As to the Owens Valley project, Mulholland assured Brooks that because the proposed conduit would be almost wholly buried in the ground, "little need be feared as to any irreparable destruction of it due to seismic shock." He added that he had studied "the effect of the great quake of 1872 near Lone Pine, as evidenced by the faulted condition of the ground along the crack that then occurred and the evidence of which is still as freshly apparent almost as the day it happened." Admitting that damage could occur, he contended it would be confined to local breakage here and there and probably would not be "beyond the possibility of repair in reasonable time and at moderate cost." He concluded with an upbeat statement about the brave people of Los Angeles, who would go ahead with "this great work," willing to take "their chances on earthquakes or other abnormal though seemingly inevitable happenings, rather than see the welfare of this fair country languish from lack of water."[8]

A CEMENT MAN

Shortly before the earthquake, Mulholland had been attempting without success to secure the services of engineer-geologist Edwin Duryea, Jr., to explore the possibilities of the city's manufacturing its own cement on the Owens River project. Duryea, a cement expert from San Francisco, was then in charge of the cement plant for Roosevelt Dam in Arizona. When Mulholland requested Duryea's services to examine lime deposits near the route of the aqueduct with a view to their use in cement making, Chief Engineer Newell of the Reclamation Bureau responded, "It is not legal for any regular employee of the Reclamation Service to undertake outside work." Mulholland, both aggressive and tenacious in seeking the best talents for the job, enticed Duryea with the proposal that if Duryea were to find sufficient available deposits for the project, then "we could employ you permanently under probably better conditions than the Government offers you." In response Duryea suggested taking a leave of absence from Reclamation, unofficially and without pay, to "make a recreation trip to the Owens River, say in June, and look over the ground and materials." The resulting knowledgeable report that he submitted July 1 resulted in an arrangement whereby the Department of the Interior allowed him to devote one-half of his time to the City of Los Angeles.[9]

THEODORE ROOSEVELT WRITES A LETTER

Although Mulholland was to make many trips to the nation's capital on behalf of his city's water supply, the first, in June 1906, remained memorable not only for its momentous outcome but also because he first saw Congress in action. He would later regale his children with tales of the colorful and immensely popular Republican Speaker of the House, Joseph "Uncle Joe" Cannon of Indiana. Cannon's forceful style and wit made a deep impression on Mulholland, as did the fact that he helped expedite the water bill through Congress. Then being spoken of as a possible presidential candidate, the Speaker had once ascribed his success to having been "an average man . . . one of the great army of mediocrity which constitutes the majority." The Californians arrived in Washington as Congress was scrambling to wind up its current session. In view of the impending big battles over bills for pure food, meat inspection, and railroad rates, the California water issue did not loom large on the national agenda.[10]

Shortly before the Los Angeles group left for Washington, the water commissioners released their official report, hoping to clear up public misapprehensions about the water plan. They told again the familiar story of the growing city's need for more water, of Eaton's, Lippincott's, and Mulholland's Owens River investigations and explorations, and of the decision to proceed with the project. In Washington, by mid-June the two opposing representatives from Southern and Central California, James MacLachlan of Pasadena and Sylvester C. Smith of Bakersfield and Inyo, had led the debate in the House on the Flint-McLachlan Bill, which granted right-of-way over the land of the aqueduct route: "the proposed sale of the right of way from Inyo county to the city of Los Angeles for a municipal water supply." By the time the Angelenos arrived, Smith and attorneys for the private power interests seemed about to defeat the scheme, which Smith declared to be chimerical on account of its cost. During two days of impassioned discussions that included a confrontation with a resistant secretary of the interior, Mulholland explained the project and its probable cost while Mathews addressed the legal issues. Secretary Hitchcock wanted to preclude using the water for irrigation and thus restrict the city's use to domestic purposes only. Fearful of such an outcome, MacLachlan went to President Theodore Roosevelt, who agreed to an interview with the principals.[11]

Like a god from the machine, on June 25, 1906, Roosevelt listened to all of the arguments, then retired and dictated a decisive and now famous letter to the secretary of the interior. It began, "As I think it is best that there should be a record of our attitude in the Los Angeles water supply matter, I am dictating this letter to you in your presence and that of Senator [Frank] Flint on behalf of the California delegation, of Director [Charles D.] Walcott of the Geological Survey and of Chief Forester [Gifford] Pinchot. The question is whether the city of Los Angeles should be prohibited from using the water it will obtain under this bill for irrigation purposes."

Arguing that Los Angeles sought to provide its water supply for the next half century and would have surpluses in the beginning, Roosevelt decided the city could divert those surpluses for irrigation. He further noted:

> I am also impressed by the fact that the chief opposition to this bill, aside from the opposition of a few settlers in Owens Valley (whose interest is genuine, but whose interest must unfortunately be disregarded in view of the infinitely greater interest to be served by putting the water in Los Angeles) comes from certain private power companies whose object evidently is for their own pecuniary interest to prevent the municipality from furnishing its own water.
>
> The people at the head of these power companies are doubtless respectable citizens, nevertheless, their opposition seems to me to afford one of the strongest arguments for passing the law, inasmuch as it ought not to be within the power of private individuals to control such a necessary of life as against the municipality itself.
>
> Under the circumstances I decide, in accordance with the recommendations of the director of the geological survey and the chief of the forestry service, that the bill be approved, with the prohibition against the use of water by municipality for irrigation, struck out.
>
> I request, however, that there be put in the bill a prohibition against the city of Los Angeles ever selling or letting to any corporation or individual except a municipality, the right for that corporation or that individual itself to sell or sublet the water given to it or him for irrigation purposes. [12]

After finding that everyone agreed with his statements, Roosevelt added that he submitted it "with a more satisfied heart than when I started to dictate this letter." Flush with success, MacLachlan next received Speaker Cannon's assurance that the amendment to the Flint-MacLachlan Bill would be called up quickly. Before noon of the following day, the House unanimously consented to the amended bill, which would give Los Angeles the right to take an unlimited amount of water from the Owens River for both domestic and irrigation purposes. With equal speed, Senator Flint secured Senate approval on June 28, and the bill went to the president for his signature. The victorious California delegation immediately left for New York to discuss with financiers the question of floating bonds to construct the Owens River Aqueduct.

Events moved quickly. A week later, Lippincott resigned from his Reclamation job to become Mulholland's assistant engineer on the aqueduct, and in August, Mathews became the attorney for the aqueduct's legal department. While the Los Angeles dailies applauded the victory in Washington, only the *News* warned of the project's extravagance, declaring, "The taxpayers are being bunkoed." Eaton had stayed home, but nonetheless managed to create a stir of his own just as the Flint-MacLachlan Bill triumphed in Congress by marrying Alice Slosson, whom he had known for three years. The former secretary of attorney Mathews, she was described as "a charming stenographer . . . who knew almost as much about legal forms as Mr. Mathews himself." Mulholland immediately sent good wishes to his old friend and, mindful of his bibulous propensities, added the comradely hope that "the moral restraint will be a great benefit to you and will largely make up for the many days in which you must have been somewhat unhappy."[13]

A BOUQUET AND A FEW BRICKS

Soon after returning from Washington, Mulholland set out with Lippincott in the faithful White Steamer to tour the aqueduct's route and to make an important stop to investigate the actions of George Chaffey, a prominent water and land developer whose alleged appropriations of water and power rights on Cottonwood Creek threatened to impede the project. Mathews had already sent a protest to Washington against approving Chaffey's filings, but by the end of the year a decision had gone against the city, thus launching a struggle not to be resolved until 1912. More happily for the city, however, the Department of the Interior withdrew all public lands along the surveyed line of the Owens River Aqueduct.[14]

On August 15, the Chamber of Commerce presented a formal proclamation of thanks to each of those who had been in Washington on the city's behalf. After three years of struggle, turmoil, and controversy, the City Council of Los Angeles, on August 23, 1906, confirmed the appointment of William Mulholland as chief engineer of the Owens River

Aqueduct. On the same day, the board of public works confirmed the appointment of three eastern engineers noted for their achievements in hydraulic engineering to investigate and report on the Owens River project: J. R. Freeman, F. P. Stearns, and J. D. Schuyler. The *News* lost no time in attacking the choice of Schuyler, claiming that among other shortcomings he had built a defective dam in Oregon. When Schuyler wrote Mulholland on August 31 to express his gratification at being chosen, he added that he had seen the articles and commented, "It is perhaps idle to notice such slanders, as it is well known that the reservoirs I built are all in use." He then explained that earth movement had caused the trouble with the Oregon dam.[15]

By the end of summer, the *News* had made charges against Mulholland's character that have never died. One was that Mulholland concocted water shortages to bully voters into complying with his requests for water bond issues. Changing conditions did sometimes contrive to make him appear a liar, as in June, when before going to Washington, D.C., he had assured the president of the Chamber of Commerce that Los Angeles currently enjoyed an ample water supply because of two successive years of above average rainfall. While he was in Washington, however, the Geological Survey published Walter Mendenhall's report on the groundwater resources of the coastal plain region of Southern California, and its findings put Mulholland on alert. Because of the past ten years' low rainfall and the large drafts upon the area's underground waters, the report stated that a shortage threatened in the near future. Although Mendenhall did not see an immediate crisis, he recommended prudence and restraint, especially in irrigating crops. Thus, in the annual report for 1906, Mulholland heeded Mendenhall, and after reiterating that rainfall had been abundant in the past two years, acknowledged that the Los Angeles River's flow was down 40 percent, which he attributed to pumping by San Fernando Valley ranchers.[16]

With his mandate to plan ahead for the city's needs, in early August he reluctantly invoked the city's right to shut down the pumps of certain ranchers in the San Fernando Valley (mostly those near the river in today's Burbank and Glendale areas; the western half of the valley was not involved). When he ordered a stoppage in late August, the ranchers' resistance made headlines not only at home but also in the *San Francisco Chronicle:* "THREATENED BY USERS OF WATER. Los Angeles Superintendent Says He Does Not Fear for His Life." Mulholland dismissed the anonymous threats as "the vaporings of a few crazy and disgruntled water users."[17]

THE EXPERTS INSPECT

On October 22, shortly before the formal survey of the aqueduct project was to begin, Mulholland and Lippincott made an informal survey trip to Owens Valley with Schuyler, who had just returned from Mexico. Frederick Newell, chief engineer of Reclamation, came through town on his way to Yuma from Sacramento and expressed public surprise that there should be any controversy over the project. "It doesn't seem to me to be a question of feasibility, but rather of cash and nerve," he said, adding that he had always believed the people of Los Angeles had plenty of the latter.[18]

As the city council authorized more purchases of land for the Owens River project and the *News* beat the drums for its currently favored water project on the Mojave River near Victorville, the other two eastern experts arrived with their wives on November 13. Mulholland and Lippincott escorted them from the station to the Alexandria Hotel, then considered the last word in deluxe accommodation. Both experts enjoyed outstanding reputations as hydraulic engineers. Mulholland and Lippincott had especially sought John R. Freeman because of his experience in evaluating the water systems of large cities in Massachusetts and New York. He had done a massive survey of New York City's water supply, claimed to be the most elaborate waterworks report ever made by one engineer and, according to his peers, free of any biases of local pressures or prejudices. Equally distinguished was Frederick P. Stearns, then president of the American Society of Civil Engineers and a member of the Isthmian Canal Association. He was then serving also on the water commission in charge of New York's $160 million Catskills project. Of the three experts, Schuyler had the greatest familiarity with the West. Builder of the Sweetwater Dam in Oregon (the one the *News* claimed was defective), he also had constructed the highest masonry dam in the West at Hemet, California.

All three had already studied reports of the Owens River project, and after a day's survey of the San Fernando Valley on November 14, began a trek complicated by severe winter weather: windstorms, snow, and a blizzard. From Red Rock Canyon to Haiwee, the ferocious winds continually blew out the White steam auto's fire. When it finally had to be towed, Mulholland predicted that it would prove its worth later in the trip. At Haiwee they found shelter but no warmth with Mother Orr, as the wind had blown away her chimney and she could not risk burning her house down with a fire. The weather did not abate as they strug-

Hugh Mulholland (1829–1885), Dublin.

Ellen Deakers Mulholland (1834–1862), with a daughter on lap and an unidentified relative beside her, Dublin, circa 1859.

Jane Smith Mulholland (1835–1901), with Mary Mulholland,
only daughter of Hugh and Jane, Dublin, circa 1876.

First known likeness of William Mulholland, with brother, Hugh
Patrick (*seated*), Los Angeles, circa 1878.

Mulholland (*at right*) with the Deakers family at 15 San Pedro Street, Los Angeles, 1880s. His cousin, Ella, and his uncle, Richard Deakers, are seated.

William Mulholland about the time of his marriage, 1890.

Lillie Ferguson (1868–1915)
before her marriage to
Mulholland, Los Angeles,
circa 1888.

Mulholland home from 1894 to 1921, at Sixth and Cummings Streets,
Boyle Heights, circa 1898. Children and friends are on porch. Designed by
Mulholland, the house was demolished for the construction of the Santa Ana
Freeway in the 1950s.

Family outing on Mulholland's fiftieth birthday with friends and associates, on board the moored British ship *Hyderabad* in Sausalito, California, September 10, 1905. Mulholland crouches in front, gazing at baby. His wife, Lillie, with large hat, stands at left between her niece Frances Mitchell at left and oldest daughter, Rose, to the right. His sons, Perry and Tom, sit side by side on the stairs. Because aqueduct bonds had just been approved, Mulholland was also in the Bay Area to order and procure supplies for the great undertaking.

First water supply system for Los Angeles, 1864. An early flume and water-wheel to carry water to a ditch flowing to the reservoir near the plaza of Los Angeles.

The "fathers" of the Owens River project. *Left to right:* J. B. Lippincott, Fred Eaton, William Mulholland, 1905–1906. Photograph by Andrew A. Forbes.

William B. Mathews (1865–1932), an attorney whose long, untiring efforts secured municipally owned water and power systems for Los Angeles.

ANOTHER SCARECROW TO FRIGHTEN TIMID TAXPAYERS

With water, lots of it, at hand and subject to our call,
Our rash, misguided water board won't look at it, at all,
But following in a selfish track, mapped out by selfish minds,
It says: "This is the ONLY way, all others are but blinds!"

Anti-aqueduct cartoon portraying Mulholland as a behind-the-scenes manipulator, *Los Angeles Evening News*, September 24, 1906.

Consulting engineers during inspection of aqueduct line, 1905. *Left to right:*
John R. Freeman, James D. Schuyler, J. B. Lippincott, Frederick P. Stearns,
William Mulholland. Photograph by Bledsoe. Courtesy of the Los Angeles
Department of Water and Power.

Fred Eaton on muleback during a camping trip in the Sierra
Nevada and the Kings River area, circa 1902. This photograph
and the one on the facing page are from the J. B. Lippincott
Collection (LIPP 139: 62, 63). Used with permission of the Water
Resources Center Archives, University of California, Berkeley.

J. B. Lippincott, taken on camping trip with Fred Eaton, circa 1902.

Lone Pine Lake, Owens Valley. Photograph by Andrew A. Forbes.

Snowstorm during consulting engineers' inspection tour, 1905. Photograph by Andrew A. Forbes.

City-owned freighting outfit hauling aqueduct material on the desert. Photograph by Bledsoe. Courtesy of the Los Angeles Department of Water and Power.

Building roads in the Jawbone Division. Photographs on this and facing page are by Bledsoe. Courtesy of the Los Angeles Department of Water and Power.

Dredge No. 1, working in Owens Valley.

Tunnel No. 71, Antelope Division.

Lining the aqueduct with concrete, Mojave Division.

Workers standing by one of the twenty-three inverted siphons constructed along the aqueduct line.

Owens River near the intake for the aqueduct. Photograph by Andrew A. Forbes.

Undated clipping from a scrapbook of William Mulholland's.

Opening-day ceremony for aqueduct, November 5, 1913. *Left to right:* General Harrison Gray Otis, owner-editor of the *Los Angeles Times;* Ellen "Lark Ellen" Beach Yaw, singer; and William Mulholland. His daughter Rose stands behind him.

William Mulholland with daughters, Rose and Lucile, November 5, 1913. Peering over his shoulder is Mrs. D. L. Reaburn, wife of an aqueduct engineer who would later lay out Mulholland Highway.

Last photograph of Lillie Mulholland, 1914–1915.

Mulholland's residence from 1921 until his death in 1935, 426 South Saint Andrews Place, Los Angeles. It was demolished in the 1970s to make way for apartment buildings.

Stalwarts of the Los Angeles Water Department, early 1920s. *Back row, left to right:* George Read, Roderick McKay, L. M. Anderson; *front:* Frederick J. Fischer, William Mulholland, Thomas Brooks. These men worked all their lives on behalf of city water.

A gathering of city bigwigs for a preview of Mulholland Highway, March 27, 1924. *Left to right:* William Mulholland, Moses H. Sherman, D. L. Reaburn, Harry Chandler, and three members of the water commission.

Subject—Bill Mulholland.

Trade or Occupation—Chief Engineer of the Aqueduct.

Duties—Competing with Jupiter Pluvius.

Pet Aversion—Afternoon teas.

Greatest Ambition—To meet Mayor Cryer face to face.

Favorite Fowl—Aqua Ducks.

Favorite Philosophy—Work.

Favorite Book—The family album.

Favorite Song—"Waltz Me Around Again, Willie"—as sung by Fred Eaton.

Most Famous Speech—"There it is. Take it!"—When the water first gushed through the Aqueduct.

Favorite Virtue—Brusqueness.

Favorite Vice—Receiving guests in his bathrobe.

Hobby—Collecting cuss-words.

Religion—The Golden Rule.

Favorite Maxim—"When you buy a hog you don't have to eat the bristles."

Motto—Dammit!

Remarks—Bill Mulholland wasn't born. He's a self-made man, he admits. He began life as a ditch-digger. The last ditch he dug took him five years to dig it. That ditch was the Los Angeles Aqueduct. Mr. Mulholland achieved additional fame recently by having his name tacked onto a road or a street or something up in the mountains.

Cartoon of William Mulholland, *Los Angeles Times,* February 22, 1925.

William Mulholland (*right*) and Harvey Van Norman
leaning against a boat alongside the Colorado River during
a conference on Boulder Dam, 1925.

William Mulholland and Harvey Van Norman amid the wreckage of the failed
Saint Francis Dam, March 13, 1928. Photograph courtesy of the Los Angeles
Department of Water and Power.

Mulholland with his three grandchildren at the Mulholland Ranch in the San Fernando Valley shortly after the dam disaster, Easter 1928. *To his right*: Lillian Sloan; *at left*: Richard Mulholland; *in front*: Catherine Mulholland.

William Mulholland and his son Perry on a trip to Ensenada, Mexico, 1929.

Mulholland with engineers and politicians gathered for a Metropolitan Water District project, the spreading of the upper Santa Ana River, San Bernardino County, February 17, 1932.

Last photograph of William Mulholland in the Los Angeles Water Department, March 1933. He holds a memorial vial of Owens River water from opening-day ceremonies in 1913.

gled all next day to reach Independence. When they arrived there late that night, a worried Eaton met them, fearful of what might have happened to them in such a storm.

Stearns and Mulholland must have been the least comfortable members of the group. Stearns, evidently sold on California's clement weather by Schuyler, had worn only a khaki suit and light rain coat, in which he shivered stoically. At one point, however, as the wind howled about them, he turned to Schuyler and sang a line from an old Swiss song: "You speak of sunny skies to me, of orange groves and bowers/Of winds that make soft melody through leaf and blooming flowers." Mulholland's discomfort began at Independence when he bit into a savory Inyo quail pie prepared by Eaton's daughter-in-law and wedged a pellet of shot between his teeth. Attempts to dig it out only lodged it further, so that biting was agony. To console him, the company around the table joked about dynamiting it out. Weather and personal discomforts aside, in the almost two weeks of travel and study, they visited all the necessary sites along the proposed aqueduct's route, concluding with Bishop and a visit to the proposed site of the Long Valley reservoir.[19]

Freeman, Stearns, and Schuyler returned to Los Angeles and, without comment, closeted themselves on the eleventh floor of the Union Trust Building with their mass of data, plans, and maps. "When the engineers want us, we will go to them," reported Mulholland. "I shan't go near them until they send for me. They have a pile of plans three feet high to wade through. After these are digested they will go up the Valley again. Stearns and Freeman are old campaigners—Freeman knows a great deal about that country. No engineer, with the possible exception of Lippincott, knows more about the rainfall than he does." When pressed for details about alternate routes, the Chief replied, "We want these men to figure this out themselves. I can tell you this, that we can make the route 201 miles, or 211 miles or 221 miles. The idea is not particularly to lessen the cost. The consideration of the route by the engineers would include the safety of the line."[20]

NEW WORKS AT HOME

Mulholland's immediate duties at home included supervising construction of two important and interrelated city reservoirs: the more northerly Ivanhoe, begun in 1905, and Silver Lake, begun in August 1906. Located in Ivanhoe Valley in the hills between Elysian Park and Hollywood, the first had a capacity of 50 million gallons and held all the water from the main supply conduit, which headed on the Hooker and Pomeroy tract, as well as from an area called the high gravity system. It fed a distribution point near Sixth Street and Wilshire Boulevard. The second, an impounding reservoir to be named for the old champion of municipal water, Herman Silver, anticipated a capacity of 773 million gallons. With its completion expected in February 1907, the two dams would hold the equivalent of a twenty-day supply (820 million gallons) for the entire city at its current rate of use, thus insuring against summer shortages.[21]

Because Silver Lake would be poised in the hills above the city where a break could cause a disaster not unlike the recent Johnstown flood, Mulholland did not design the usual earthen dam. Instead, its core was a concrete wall three feet thick, and at its center a continuous watertight wall of riveted steel plates extended from bedrock to water level. He also introduced an application of hydraulic sluicing that threw up the mud being dredged from the bed onto the dam that was to create the reservoir. This so-called innovation created a stir in engineering circles. At a meeting of the American Society of Civil Engineers, one member declared the method impracticable because water pressure could not force heavy material uphill through pipes, while Stearns defended the procedure, saying it was often used in hydraulic gold dredging. Mulholland added that it was all a matter of pressure. "Put on the power," he said, "and you can send anvils and flatirons through the pipe. Nothing new in it; it is done every day, and I'm surprised that any one should question so obvious a fact." The method aroused the interest of the Isthmian Canal Commission, which sent one of its engineers to observe the process. He was favorably impressed not only with the sluicing method but also with a centrifugal pump designed by Mulholland. Similar hydraulic sluicing was later used on the difficult Culebra (now Gaillard) Cut of the Panama Canal and eventually on similar projects in the Northwest.[22]

GEARING UP

All of Mulholland's organizational skills were now put to the test as he oversaw the myriad tasks necessary to put the immense project into operation. In a gigantic juggling act, he dealt with endless detail as well as matters of materiel and personnel. Shortly after his return from Washington, he told a job seeker that he was receiving an average of fifteen applications a week from engineers seeking work on the Owens River project. Fortunately, with the civil service commission recently instituted, he was spared the task of judging the applicants' qualifications. Each of them, be he engineer, surveyor, instrument man, chain man or rod-man, was told that he would have to qualify through the civil service commission.[23]

At year's end the grand jury investigating the Owens River project is-sued a terse but favorable report. "An investigation of lengthy duration was made into the matters of criticism appearing in the public press in connection with the Owens river project for Los Angeles city. Nothing was found justifying public censure by this grand jury. On the other hand, this valuable source of water supply was obtained by methods showing commendable business sense and economy on the part of those who rep-resented the city's interests in these transactions."[24]

The final good news was Freeman, Schuyler, and Stearns's fifteen-page report, which concluded:

1. The project was feasible.
2. The Owens River and its tributaries could deliver a supply of about 400 cubic feet of good quality water to the city.
3. The cost, excluding the cost of the future Long Valley Reservoir or those to be built in the San Fernando Valley or structures re-lated to the development of power, would be about $24.5 million.
4. The water conveyed through the aqueduct could develop sufficient electricity to supply 49,000 horsepower continuously, twenty-four hours per day "if portions of it are used only during ordi-nary working hours."

The report closed, "We find the project admirable in conception and out-line and full of promise for the continued prosperity of Los Angeles."[25]

Although opponents were quick to point out the experts' changes in Mulholland's original plan, Schuyler spoke to the press before he left town and said that even they had been surprised at how close their esti-mates came to those of the original. One significant difference was their recommendation for more tunneling than Mulholland planned. More-over, they altered his route somewhat and adopted different price units. Yet Schuyler concluded the overall report must be considered a thorough endorsement of "Mr. Mulholland's judgment and his natural engineer-ing insight and skill which have come from long practice." He also ex-horted the citizens of Los Angeles to realize the grandness of the project and the magnificence of the setting from which the water would come. Lastly, he urged the city to develop hydroelectric power, as the subse-quent revenues could pay for the entire project.[26]

All of the daily newspapers applauded the report. Even the *News* and *Examiner* wrote grudgingly favorable editorials, although both continued to express skepticism about the cost and amount of water that would be available while gloating that Mulholland's original plans had been "knocked into a cocked hat." Scripps's prolabor *Record* concluded that municipal power would make money for the city, pointing out that the Edison Electric Company "is paying almost as much as the estimated cost of the Owens river aqueduct for its Kern river power works, and it is bringing down electricity alone, whereas the city will have both the water and the electricity." The *Record* did warn, however, against the pitfall of politics, proclaiming in boldface type, "Mayor-elect Harper may make or ruin the Owens river project." [27]

CHAPTER 13

The Big Job Begins

1907

A NEW MAYOR AND ENGINEERING WORRIES

The year 1907 ushered in a new mayor and a political debate that did not subside until after the noisy and spirited springtime campaign for the passage of the $24 million Owens River bond issue. At the end of 1906 the mayoral campaign's four candidates had reflected the divisions within the city. Democrat Arthur G. Harper won by a slender margin after the Republicans, fearful of losing to one of the nonparty Progressive or Labor candidates, had thrown their support to him. Harper was allied to the city's old-guard political machine, with ties to Southern Pacific interests. A genial but pliant man, well connected to the town's wealthy families, Harper, along with his new administration, was feted at a banquet hosted by the reform-minded Municipal League on January 4.

With 200 of their 625 members in attendance, the municipal reformers created a formidable presence for the city's newly elected officials. One reporter likened them to the British in India "who invited the hill princes and their retinues to a grand powwow. There, ringed by troops of red coats with glittering bayonets, the guests were peaceably but forcefully made aware of the raj." After a few jocular words, Mayor Harper produced a paper from his coat and then tucked it back in, saying he had decided not to lay his plans before them at this time but promised "the best business administration I know how." When the Hon. Frank G. Tyrrell of the League next rose and grew eloquent on the need for municipal virtue, he turned directly to the mayor-elect. "Mr. Harper. It has been said that you were elected by a class of citizens that hope for and expect at last a lax administration, a wide-open town, a yielding to quasi-criminal elements. . . ." After a pause to allow a sort of mental gasp to sweep the room, he then extended the olive branch, declaring, "I don't believe it." Yet he exhorted Harper to steer the city towards a heroic age when officials would be "unpurchasable, wise, firm and true." The ovation of the evening went to Mulholland, who declared the Owens River project now beyond the talking stage and urged directing all possible energy toward its accomplishment.[1]

On January 5, Lippincott and Mathews left Los Angeles for Chicago, where they spent two days with railroad executives discussing the possibilities of building a line on the desert from Mojave to Owens Valley. Both men continued east, where Mathews was to meet with bond financiers to discover whether authorizing the entire $23 million bond issue in one election would be legal and feasible. Both men spent several days in Washington, D.C., working out right-of-way matters in the land department and seeking reassurances that the power companies would not interfere in the city's water project. In anticipation of the Owens River bond issue's passage, Lippincott next began to investigate the capacities of eastern manufacturers of steel and machines to construct and deliver material and equipment for the project. This advance work was intended to prevent unnecessary delays in orders from mills, which were then running at full capacity. While on his assignment, Lippincott received news of the death of his father, Dr. J. A. Lippincott, the former chancellor of the University of Kansas. By now the aqueduct's planning so dominated its builders' lives that after attending the funeral in Kansas City, Lippincott spoke to local reporters not to eulogize his father but to praise the Owens River project. When completed, he told them, the water supply would be sufficient for one million people as well as for irrigating 100,000 acres of suburban land. It would be, he illustrated, as if an aqueduct were to bring water from the Mississippi River to Kansas City.[2]

Mathews meanwhile had returned from the East only to become embattled in legal wrangles in Sacramento that threatened the very life of the enterprise. The first proved a minor scuffle after the state supreme court disallowed the applications for certain Owens Valley lands made by an Oregonian claiming preemptive rights. The second, however, seriously threatened the city's plans. Two years earlier the Edison Electric Company had advanced the McCartney Bill, which proposed that any city contemplating municipal ownership of heating, lighting, or water systems would first have to buy, or offer to buy, the existing private plants.

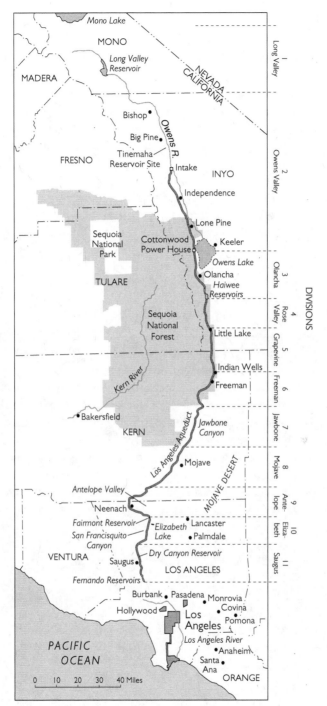

Map 2. Los Angeles Aqueduct and adjacent territory with divisions, October 1908 (Los Angeles Department of Water and Power).

Now backed by private power interests, the bill had resurfaced. As its passage would drive up costs and impede municipalization, the state's progressive forces, led by the California League of Municipalities, went into action against the measure. Mathews hastened to seek Governor Pardee's veto of the bill, while City Attorney Leslie Hewitt also traveled north to protest to the legislature. In an adroit and controversial move before leaving Los Angeles, Mathews instructed the city auditor, W. C. Mushet, to withhold from the power companies' attorney all access to contracts, records, and files pertaining to the Owens River water project. Such an outcry arose throughout the state over what was understood to be a power grab by the utility companies that the bill was withdrawn by the end of January.[3]

Mulholland meantime was absorbed in directing five parties of fifteen men each deployed along the aqueduct's route. This early phase of preliminary construction involved setting up work camps and delivering supplies. But for its larger scope, it was not unlike the many smaller projects Mulholland had supervised along the Los Angeles River. For communication with their Chief in Los Angeles, the men in the field relied on letters. At the beginning of 1907, for instance, John Gray, a veteran mining engineer who would achieve acclaim as the aqueduct's champion tunnel man, was preparing pipe for the diversion of water at Cottonwood as well as keeping Mulholland informed of George Chaffey's activities. (At this juncture Chaffey had served notice that the city had no title to any of the water rights on Cottonwood Creek and was to stop all work there.) Above all, Gray was concerned that an insufficiency of cement was delaying his work. Mulholland, always with an eagle eye on keeping expenses within bounds, ordered the hydrographer at Cottonwood, George Shuey, to avoid the expense of measuring the whole high flow of streams but simply to get a fairly correct measurement when streams were low. When R. H. Sawyer, headquartered at Mojave, needed more livestock, Mulholland answered that he was looking but found "so far nothing that can be had within reason." Learning that thieves had been busy stealing supplies at Mojave, Mulholland urged Sawyer to spare no pains seeking out the culprits, "as we are but just at the beginning of our enterprise and it stands us in hand to be strict with such pirates."[4]

NEW PERSONNEL

In the midst of these preparations for one of the world's great engineering undertakings, the chief engineer, at the age of fifty-one, received a piece of paper that must have seemed, if not tardy, somewhat superfluous. It was a diploma from the American Society of Civil Engineers certifying that he, William Mulholland, had become, as of February 6, 1907, a member in good standing. Although doubtless gratifying as a professional validation, it also would serve to rebut those who sneered at his lack of formal training.

Two engineers who were to become major players now joined the water department. The first, Ezra F. Scattergood (1871–1947), was an electrical engineer whose career and fight for municipal power will be discussed later. The second, Harvey Van Norman (1878–1954), would become not only one of Mulholland's best-loved associates but also his successor as chief of the water department. Texas-born "Van" came with his family to Los Angeles in 1882 when he was four years old. Largely self-educated in engineering like Mulholland, he began his career as a stationary engineer at a pumping plant near Yuma, Arizona. After stints as a steam engineer with the Los Angeles Railway and a construction superintendent with the Los Angeles Gas and Electric Company, he went to the Philippine Islands on a construction job during the Spanish-American War. Towering over the average man at a height of 6 feet, 5 inches, this boyish-faced giant was an affable fellow who could bend an elbow with the most roistering of men at the sometimes rowdy, always rough, construction camps. Yet when occasion demanded, he could also be sober and resolute. He had begun work for the water department in February 1907, superintending the construction of buildings and installation of equipment at the Slauson and Headworks pumping plants. By year's end, however, he was sent to Owens Valley to complete work on the Division Creek and Cottonwood hydroelectric plants that would supply power for construction work along the aqueduct from the intake to Mojave.[5]

Van Norman later recalled his excitement at the opportunity to be part of the great enterprise, even though his first trip to Owens Valley took him aback when he viewed the desolation of the country and tried to conceive of millions of gallons of water being transported through all that aridity. "For the final part of my trip," he once remembered, "the only means of transportation was a stage coach. As we crossed burning, desolate stretches of desert and laboriously crawled over bleak, forbidding mountain passes, I would close my eyes and try to visualize an aqueduct crossing that same kind of country."

Adding to his discouragement was the absence of his beautiful young wife, Bessie, whom he had married only three weeks before and had had to leave behind in Los Angeles. Bessie eventually joined him to become one of that rare number of women who not only endured the hardships of living on the aqueduct's construction areas but managed to surmount them. Our family often told the story of how she hung dotted Swiss curtains at the windows of her cabin and planted geraniums in window boxes. When the wind destroyed them, she stoically remarked, "I just started all over again." An expert seamstress in Independence remembered that Mrs. Van Norman had once asked her to help select a new hat for Easter. Taken aback as she knew of no millinery shops in Independence, the seamstress still dressed for an afternoon of shopping and knocked on the Van Normans' door. To her surprise, she was welcomed in, served tea, and then spent the afternoon with her hostess making a selection from mail order catalogs.[6]

SUSPICIONS OF SUBVERSION AT CITY HALL

Although Mayor Harper had publicly lauded the water enterprise, in late March both the *Examiner* and the *Record* revealed that he and certain councilmen had secretly inspected well sites near Long Beach, a privately owned spring in the Big Tujunga reported to have 2,000 inches of water, and a stream near Palmdale called Big Rock Creek. Moreover, after consulting an engineer whose identity they refused to reveal, this group also proposed a plan to begin work on the aqueduct at the city's end rather than at the planned intake on the Owens River. The *Examiner,* still ambivalent about the city's water plans, was quick to play up the drama of the new mayor's going around the backs of Mulholland, Lippincott, Mathews, and the board of public works. When interviewed, Mathews said he thought such projects unnecessary, but Mulholland, obviously angered by the maneuver, declared the effort a useless waste of money, and then vented his exasperation. "I want to say this. I have been working for this city since 1878, and I know I have been a faithful servant. I have worked for the Owens River scheme because I know it is the only permanent solution of the water supply. But if after all of my work the people of Los Angeles should see fit to defeat the project by voting down the bonds I would not lose one night's sleep over the matter." Assuring that water supplies would be adequate for the next few years, he silenced some of his critics a week later with the March 31 issuance of the *First Annual Report of the Los Angeles Aqueduct,* a comprehensive, clearly written account of the activities surrounding the Owens River project since its inception.[7]

Only the *News* objected to the report on the grounds that it failed to state the amounts already laid out on the project. This was a sensitive area because a few weeks before the report's release City Auditor W. G. Mushet had discovered two forged signatures on demands for payment of land in Owens Valley. Although the demands proved regular and the amounts properly due the parties to whom they were paid, the discovery set in motion a reform in the auditor's office to introduce a system already used by the aqueduct department that required strict checks on purchases and payments. By May 25, criticism was quashed when the aqueduct disbursement officer issued a statement of expenditures from the start of the Owens River project to April 1, 1907. It revealed that of the $1.5 million bond issue of 1905, $1,294,251.02 had been expended. With those funds, the city had purchased 76,581 acres of land, opened and graded 5 miles of canals in Owens Valley, built 6 miles of wagon roads, done more than 700 miles of surveys and studies of route conditions, purchased a partial right of way, and acquired necessary machinery, equipment and tools. The total of $1,035,073.77 spent on real estate and water rights included $13,014.90 in commissions to Fred Eaton and B. A. Vollmer, who had acted as land agents for the city. (Eaton had received $10,666.15.)[8]

Disturbed by indications of subversive activity at City Hall, Mulholland, Mathews, and J. A. Anderson, head of the board of public works, made an informal call on Mayor Harper the morning of April 1. They proceeded to sound out his plans regarding the Big Rock Creek scheme, his intentions to call a date for the special water bond election, and his plans for an inspection trip to Owens Valley. Harper temporized but indicated that he would travel to Owens Valley without any water officials, as he wished to spend time with ranchers and leaders of Inyo County in order to gather information that would help him to gauge the attitudes of residents there. Two days after this interview, in a night session lasting from eight until midnight, these same men, along with council members and the city attorney, agreed that the council should set a date for the Owens River bond election, which, although at first set for May 15, eventually took place June 12.[9]

Harper's plan to visit Owens Valley without water officials fell by the board. On April 12, Mulholland wrote the chief engineer of Southern Pacific, with whom he and Lippincott were conferring over the proposed railway to serve the aqueduct, that he would have to postpone their meeting in San Francisco because either he or Lippincott "has got to accompany the Mayor and Council on a contemplated trip to Owens River." As it turned out, not only Mulholland and Lippincott but J. Henry Dockweiler as well took part in a tour comprising eighteen city fathers. Mulholland stayed only long enough to ride with the mayor from Mojave to Owens Valley and point out the route of the conduit. He then returned to the city with a lone councilman, who, despite the usual quota of motor breakdowns, failed to lose his enthusiasm for what he had seen: water in such abundance, he related, that it could moisten Los Angeles for the next hundred years. When Mayor Harper and his party returned two days later under Dockweiler's guidance, they too had been converted to the cause of building the Owens River Aqueduct as rapidly as possible.[10]

THE OPPOSITION FINDS A VOICE

On May 8, the mayor gathered the council in executive session to discuss how best to rouse public interest in the upcoming bond election. On the eighteenth, less than a month before the election, a campaign committee was formed. Sam Clover's *News* had begun its fight against the aqueduct bonds a month earlier when it began publishing a series of letters over the signature "Veritas." The letters, which eventually would run from April 18 to June 8, attacked current water policies and rehashed old grievances against the city harking back to the Hooker and Pomeroy case. Veritas proved to be an old enemy of the city's water establishment, William T. Spilman. In the 1890s, while promoting his Spilman Suburban Water Company near the Hooker-Pomeroy lands in the settlement of Tropico (merged with Glendale in 1918), Spilman had almost succeeded in swindling the city of water rights along the Los Angeles River in a crafty scheme too lengthy to recount here. His subsequent bankruptcy and personal scandals had turned him into an embittered, obsessive person who held the city's water men responsible for his Tropico land scheme's failure in 1894. Now Spilman renewed his vendetta, beginning with a virulent attack on Mulholland, who, he charged, had been responsible for a water famine at a time when the city had secured an abundance of water by condemning a tract of land north of West Glendale but then failed to develop. This would have included not only the Hooker and Pomeroy land, but also Spilman's failed land and water company. He also accused Mulholland of building, for reasons not made clear, a "fake tunnel" near Elysian Park and, while doing so, depriving people of water. The supposed results were horrific. "Throughout the city the lawns were all turned brown or entirely destroyed while no proper fire protection was to be had, and the lakes in our city parks were so stagnant that the fish were drying and decaying, while the winds were carrying the death-dealing vapors and stenches from the sewers as well as from the lakes, . . . causing sickness and death especially among small children and infants—a fact that many a mother can testify to."[11]

L. M. Anderson, auditor of the water department, delivered a strong rebuttal. "You've read the truthful (?) *News* about Mulholland's 'dry tunnel,'" wrote Anderson. "The fact is this tunnel today supplies the greater part of the water used on Boyle Heights and the East Side. . . . They won't tell the truth when they know it," he continued. "They come to our office for information, which has never been refused, and though we told them, it was no use to give them the figures, as they lie about the facts." He also added that Mulholland did not care "so long as he knows he's right," but Lippincott was rather thin-skinned and had finally refused to give them anything, so that they now also considered him a rascal.[12]

Each Veritas letter piled up more charges: Mathews's injunction against the San Fernando ranchers was a meaningless exercise because Mulholland had simply been withholding water to create the impression of a water famine and deceive the people into agreeing with Eaton's and Lippincott's selfish schemes in Owens Valley. Mulholland lied about the amount of flow from the Los Angeles River. Southern California had ample water in the San Gabriel and Santa Ana Rivers, for example, without having to bring brackish and alkaline water great distances at enormous expense from Owens Valley in order to benefit the pockets of "promoter Eaton." Veritas linked Mulholland to the *Los Angeles Times* with repeated use of such phrases as "his chief organ" and "his boosting organ." The *Times* in turn called Veritas Sam Clover's "assistant Ananias" and a "sneaking coyote," asking if any sane man in Los Angeles believed that Mulholland was a liar and a thief.[13]

According to the *News,* Mulholland's alkali bond folly not only was going to bilk the good taxpayers of Los Angeles but also would end up giving them water worse than they already had. When Harry Brooks of the *Times* sent Mulholland a sample of these accusations and asked if he could provide information about the limestone content of water in eastern cities, Mulholland responded with a three-page letter, in which he commented that "the screed you enclosed is but another emanation from a source absolutely ignorant of the true conditions that obtain in the Owens River Valley." He had been unable at short notice to obtain information about eastern cities, he replied, but could say that many middle and southern states had water "more impregnated with carbonate of lime and alkaline salts than the waters of the Los Angeles River or the

Owens River at its very worst." He outlined various government labo-ratory studies that indicated water from the Owens River project would be "about twice as pure as the water we are now consuming." More-over, concluded Mulholland, "Our enemies are as conversant with these facts as we are, but persist in the reiteration of assertions to the contrary in general terms, and display in greatest eagerness the screeds of igno-rances, such as the one you mailed me."[14]

However unwelcome these attacks, the water men were fortunate that their opposition was concentrated so largely in one journal, for in the coming years other anti-aqueduct voices would diffuse and confuse the slanders. Attorney Job Harriman of the Socialist Labor Party, for ex-ample, in fighting the aqueduct bonds, claimed that the aqueduct pro-moters were robbing the workingman and that after their project had bankrupted the city they would sell out to the private power companies. Mulholland, however, enjoyed support from many workers. One, at the time of the bond campaign, said he would vote for Bill Mulholland "even if he ran for the office of town pump." When Mulholland spoke to 250 iron workers at Baker's Iron Works, a follow-up straw vote for the water bonds garnered 245 in favor and 15 against. Similar success followed him in other gatherings.[15]

Throughout the city, interest and approval greeted campaigners as they addressed political groups, women's clubs, labor organizations, and church groups. Campaign organizers feared complacency about the out-come would keep voters from the polls, so in the two weeks before the election, the water men campaigned indefatigably, sometimes speaking to several groups in one day. Lippincott made polished presentations with maps, charts, stereopticon views, and a moving picture to illustrate the project. At one gathering when a persistent fly continued to obscure the screen with its enlarged image, the chairman of the event proclaimed to great laughter and applause that it depicted "the only microbe ever found in Owens Valley water." Mulholland later remembered the public speak-ing as the least pleasant part of his job, saying he would rather skin dead dogs than make speeches. He said he was like the Irishman who got a job deep-sea diving and after one submersion in the diving suit declared that he did not like the job. "The machine works all right," he said, "but I can't spit on me hands."[16]

Boosts for the aqueduct came from what today would be unexpected places. Naturalist John Muir, visiting with friends in Pasadena, offered a testimonial to the Owens River water's purity and seemed unopposed to Los Angeles's designs. "The purest on earth," he pronounced. "The river above the basin, with its pure and sparkling flow, will be tapped for the fluid which will go into the conduit for the future water supply of Los Angeles." Two days before the election, Arthur P. Davis, Lippincott's old partner and chief engineer of Reclamation, arrived en route to Yuma to inspect a reclamation project and expressed his admiration for "the pluck of Los Angeles in going after Owens River water." He praised Lippincott "as honest and as capable as any man I ever knew." As to the project's cost, he found it cheap, certainly no more than New York spent to acquire its supply.[17]

Pamphlets on the aqueduct appeared. First, an Owens Valley primer with its catechism of questions and answers:

> *What is the proposed Los Angeles Aqueduct?*
> It is an undertaking by the city to construct, own and operate an aqueduct, two hundred and twenty-five miles long with a daily capacity of 260,000,000 gallons, to bring to Los Angeles a water supply from the high Sierras. (The present consumption of the city of 40,000,000 gallons daily.)

Elsewhere, an anti-aqueduct primer disputed every point:

> *What is the proposed Los Angeles Aqueduct?*
> It is a piece of gigantic folly that will cost the taxpayers fifty millions of dollars, or more, increasing their taxes three times the present rate.[18]

Cartoonists kept pens busy for their respective papers. One curiosity is a cartoon by George Herriman, soon to be famous as the creator of *Krazy Kat* but then a staff artist for the *Examiner*. His drawing simply showed a stern-visaged and mustachioed man with his finger pointed at the viewer over the admonishment, "It Is Your Duty to Vote Today for Owens River Bonds." The *Times* announced a contest with three hundred dollars in prizes for the closest estimate of the voting's outcome.[19]

Four days before the election, an acrimonious session took place at a rally in Simpson's Auditorium at Hope Street near Seventh. The *News* had touted the event as an occasion when Job Harriman and other aqueduct opponents would face down Mulholland and Lippincott in public debate. Mulholland and Lippincott, however, claimed they had never agreed to appear and were speaking at other gatherings. In their place were Judge R. M. Widney and political leader Meyer Lissner of the Municipal League (also president of the city's public utilities board). Harriman immediately challenged Widney's right to speak as a private citizen in favor of the bonds: "if you are not a committee representative, we don't want to hear from you." The audience began to applaud, so Widney was allowed to make his case for the city's need of water. Self-described engineer R. S. Watt, who had impugned Mulholland's and Eaton's veracity, followed. As he reiterated the now-familiar charge that the two men had once testified that 20,000 inches of water was running waste in the San Fernando Valley, Lissner challenged him from the floor to demonstrate where, in any court transcript, either Eaton or Mulholland had given such testimony. Unable to do so, a flustered Watt tried to cite Finkle. "No, no," interrupted Lissner. "Finkle does not count. Finkle is an engineer who was hired by Mr. Pomeroy and Mr. Hooker to testify in their suit against the city. This same John G. Hooker is the man who tried to sell his land to the city for $1,500,000 and was awarded by a court of condemnation only $30,000. Hooker hired Finkle, and Finkle's statements and testimony have been utterly discredited by every unbiased engineer."[20]

The final rally at Simpson's brought forth an estimated audience of 2,000 and a full complement of dignitaries: Mayor Harper, Mulholland, Lippincott, and special guest Arthur P. Davis. Three other rallies took place the eve of the election: one in the chapel at the University of Southern California where Mulholland and Lippincott gave their final speeches; the second at a midtown location where councilmen spoke; and the third, conducted in French and Spanish, outdoors at the plaza.[21]

On election morning, a light and rare June rain dampened the city. Some saw it as a fair omen. Mulholland rose early and, possessed with the calm confidence of Mark Twain's Christian holding five aces, set out for the polls, which opened at 6:00 A.M. On his way, he instructed his driver to pick up a neighbor, Erastus Root, a ninety-seven-year-old resident of the Hollenbeck Home for the Aged. At their mutual polling place they became the seventh and eighth men to vote. (Early voting proved the order of the day; half of the 24,000 voters had gone to the polls by 9:00 A.M.) Thus assured of at least two proaqueduct votes, Mulholland next drove across town to escort Fred Eaton's octogenarian father, Judge Benjamin S. Eaton, to the polls. After that, there was nothing to do but wait—and dictate a letter instructing one of the engineers at Independence to go up to the Rickey Ranch "near Division Creek and size up a locust grove . . . with a view to cutting and peeling poles for the power line that we will have to construct within a month or so."[22]

The final tally gave the bonds a 10.71 to 1 margin of victory: 21,918 for and 2,128 against. Although the *Times* had hoped for a 20 to 1 margin and the total was over 7,000 votes fewer than were cast in the previous mayoral election, the vote was still the largest ever in the city for a special election. It represented a solid validation of the city's water plans, as well as the citizens' willingness to incur a large debt to build the system. Aqueduct enemies momentarily receded from view. Old opponent Doc Houghton, who remained opposed to the end, had to endure the embarrassment of his ward's producing the heaviest pro vote of any in the city (4,315 for, 485 against). The *News* swiftly acknowledged defeat and asked that the hatchet be buried. Whatever his private thoughts about the *News* and Clover, Mulholland had no time for public grudge matches. He declared, "There is no soreness on my part. . . . It was a square fight and the people won. I was made the scapegoat and things were said about me that should not have been printed, but it is past now. If I had made the fight and got licked I would have worn the beefsteak on my eye and taken my medicine, as the *Evening News* is doing." Mathews declared Clover's statement "a manly declaration," but the *Times* granted no such absolution and published a rehash of every dubious statement the *News* (and sometimes the *Examiner*) had made during the campaign. Losing advertising revenue because of its unpopular stand on the water question, the *News* was soon to go under, but the anti-aqueduct material it had disseminated would have a long life.[23]

Nationally, the Los Angeles water story received a modicum of attention, only to be upstaged a week later by New York City, whose work on the great Peekskill Aqueduct was about to begin. To be larger than all of the Roman aqueducts combined, its cost when completed would be $161 million, and it would provide 500 million gallons of water to the city every twenty-four hours. It would become part of the Croton system, for which twenty-seven villages would eventually be condemned and lost in order to supply water to the metropolis, the entire project not to be completed until 1930.[24]

THE CHIEF RECEIVES A GO-AHEAD

On July 1, 1907, a water department purchase order authorized Mulholland "to make such trips as necessary in connection with your duties as an executive of the Los Angeles Aqueduct during the month of July." This may have been a roundabout way of granting the Chief a respite, for the bond campaign had exhausted him. Even his arch critic, Sam Clover of the *Evening News*, remarked that his face showed "the ordeal through which he has passed during the late campaign." Although Mulholland took an occasional Saturday afternoon off to watch a baseball

game with his boys and friends (especially Mathews), he seemed consti-
tutionally unable to take extended absences from his work. In mid-July,
however, he took two friends and his sons on a high Sierra camping and
hunting trip that became an annual July event during the years of aqueduct construction.[25]

To flee the city and get out on the line was always a welcome change,
especially when freed from the duties of acting as a tour guide for visiting dignitaries. The surviving photographs of that 1907 outing reveal
scenes of unspoiled forests and campsites by pure streams alive with fish.
Sons Perry and Tom, fourteen and twelve, would learn the finer points
of rod, reel, and gun from the zealous Nimrod and fisherman, George
Read, head of the city's water meter department. Also with them was
Allen Kelly of the *Times,* who had just written a profile of Mulholland
for his paper and whose account of their outing began with a memory
of his own Sierra visits years before when "there were few trails and no
maps." Remembering "the solitude of the mountains," Kelly commented
ruefully on the toll progress would take on the wilderness, as the building of a railway to Owens Valley would bring sightseers and vacation-
ers; then, "the woods shall be infested by the summer tourist, and the si-
lences and the solitude of the wilderness shall be no more." Yet, he
concluded, the Sierra forests that thousands would come to know and
enjoy could provide "a boon to the greater number that even the most
selfish seekers of solitude cannot begrudge."[26]

The group left their automobile in Round Valley, rode by mule team
to Long Valley, where they saw the bounty of water running in McGee
Creek and, further on, in the lakes of the Mammoth basin. The old mining camp of Mammoth was now "a picturesque ruin," a ghost town
where the sign on a decaying building proclaimed that it had once been
the "Windy City Hotel." North of Mammoth, they stood amid snow
banks on the crest of the Sierra, with the Owens River on one side and
the San Joaquin on the other. Across the San Joaquin gorge rose "the
sharp spires of the Minarets and the pyramid peak of Mount Lyell, clad
in snow and glacial ice." At this lonely, splendid height of 10,000 feet,
Mulholland, whose thoughts dwelt on matters other than mountain sub-
limity, turned to Kelly and said, "And there are pinheads in Los Angeles who did their measly damndest to keep that water from the city."
Musing that the city was lucky not to have paid $5 million for the water
rights, he added that they would have been worth it even at that price.[27]

Back at his desk at the end of July, Mulholland confronted a pile of
duties, problems and confusions. An engineer from the Panama Canal

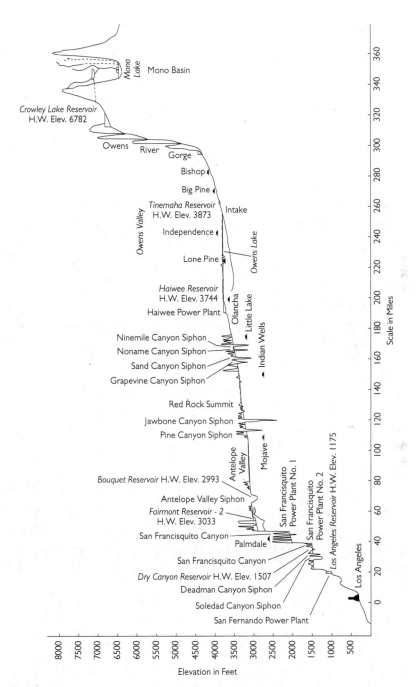

Map 3. Profile of Los Angeles Aqueduct (Los Angeles Department of Water and Power).

Commission had arrived in town to observe Silver Lake Reservoir and its hydraulic method of dam building. Less pleasantly, in Mulholland's absence, the city auditor had jeopardized aqueduct affairs by refusing to honor certain requisitions that he claimed had not been properly authorized. Hence, a grading crew about to begin work at Cottonwood had attached the equipment when it learned its payroll had not been met. More alarmingly, because the auditor had questioned its method of billing, the Southern Pacific was threatening to withdraw favorable freight rates for aqueduct materiel unless it received immediate payment.[28]

Lippincott and the field engineers kept Mulholland informed about activities and mishaps along the line: the progress on trenches and spillways; the cost of clearing up Cottonwood Ranch; the amount of pipe now at Haiwee; the eighteen sacks of cement that negligent workers left lying in the rain; the stolen lumber; and the generally poor quality of local labor in Owens Valley. Both Lippincott and Mulholland complained that the civil service board had created another vexatious labor problem by sending inexperienced "schoolboys" to work as chain men, young men who had crammed for the test but knew nothing of the nature of the work and who, after a summer out of doors, would leave and return to school. A showdown with the civil service board was about to erupt.[29]

In view of labor's turbulent history in Los Angeles during this period, the aqueduct in its first years had surprisingly little labor-management conflict, while the city itself was entering a strife-torn era as organized labor gradually lost ground to the onslaught of open shop proponents and practices. The panic of October 1907, however, created an economic slump that produced serious unemployment. Estimates of the jobless in Los Angeles by the beginning of 1908 varied from 10,000 to 20,000. While the city instituted a program to employ 400 men with families to construct a boulevard connecting Elysian to Griffith Park, the prospect of jobs on the aqueduct also promised some relief. As a municipal enterprise, the project could employ only American citizens and non-Orientals, but as labor recruitment expanded for this vast undertaking, exploiters popped up. Learning that a *Denver Post* advertisement promising aqueduct employment for 5,000 men and 1,000 teams had required applicants to pay from one to five dollars for enrollment, Mulholland shot off a letter to the editor. He explained that the city did its own hiring and had no dealings with any employment agencies. "A simple fake is being perpetrated on a class of men who can afford it least," he wrote, adding that the matter was being taken up with postal authorities "in an effort to stop the swindle," which he had learned was being worked in several cities. The *Post* promptly agreed to refuse such future advertising.[30]

Harmonious relations between Mulholland and the board of public works proved beneficial to the planning of the project, especially in dealing with the city council. In one instance, when he and Commissioner A. A. Hubbard (former owner and operator of an important brick works in Los Angeles) advertised for bids for eight hundred miles of copper wire (four hundred for the transmission of electric power on the aqueduct and the other four hundred for a municipal telephone service along the waterway) and demanded that bids be submitted within the week, certain city councilmen objected to the short notice and questioned the great quantity being purchased. The two explained that they intended to make one large purchase and had been watching and waiting for a bear market in copper. They made the interval brief to avoid being caught with a possible price rise that would raise the city's cost. The council approved the strategy.[31]

Equally cooperative were relations with the board chairman, attorney James A. Anderson (also an active member of the progressive Municipal League), who accompanied Mulholland and City Engineer Homer Hamlin for ten days along the aqueduct line in early December. The Chief had technical questions for Hamlin, a respected western geologist, regarding certain rock formations affecting the construction. Although they returned to the city on the thirteenth with the good news that 35,000 inches of water was flowing into the city's streams, for Hamlin the outing's high point had been his discovery of two fossil remains on the desert that he believed to be a new species of saurian.[32]

Before Mulholland left on the Owens Valley trip, his second annual report of the aqueduct appeared on November 30 with a reassuring account of the past year's progress along with future expectations: an arrangement secured with Southern Pacific for reduced freight rates as well as the company's assurance that it would build a railroad into Owens Valley; two reservoir sites chosen, one at Fairmount and one in the San Fernando Valley; two power plant sites selected, one at Cottonwood and one in San Francisquito Canyon; and a cement plant planned for Tehachapi. Although a group of private capitalists were touting their own plans for a cement factory at Tehachapi with claims that the city intended to purchase Portland cement from them, at the end of 1907 the board announced that the city would construct its own cement plant under Duryea's direction. He predicted they would be in operation within nine months. Work had also begun at the south portal of the tunnel near Elizabeth Lake, and twenty miles of road had been built in Division No. 2. At year's end, the report concluded, 327 men and 180 head of stock were at work on the aqueduct.[33]

Just before Christmas, Lippincott wrote from Mojave to suggest a general meeting in Los Angeles of all the aqueduct engineers and members of the general accounting office, the board of public works, and the auditor to discuss a broad array of subjects. One item on the agenda would certainly have been money; rosy reports notwithstanding, the aqueduct project was low on funds. With its banks in good shape, Los Angeles ultimately squeaked through the Panic of 1907 by declaring bank holidays and issuing scrip, but hard times were not to abate until the middle of the following year. In December, the city lacked funds to pay police and firemen's salaries until January 1908. Although the first of the water bonds had been put out for sale in August, no money had yet been realized, so that by the end of November, just at Thanksgiving, the aqueduct department found itself short. The board of public works wanted to transfer $10,000 from some other department, but the auditor objected that it could lead to vicious financial practices. After a tortuous debate, the city council finally granted permission to move funds from the water department to the aqueduct department, reasoning that the risk of losing track of the money would be less likely.

On a cheerier note, at Christmastime Van Norman wrote from Division Creek to thank Mulholland for arranging matters so that his wife could be with him over the holidays. Engineer John Gray wrote from Cottonwood that work was going well. The best holiday gift, however, came on December 27 when Mayor Harper signed the first issue of aqueduct bonds for $510,000 and Mathews delivered it to Sacramento. Now work could truly proceed.[34]

CHAPTER 14

The Chief and the General

1908

ENTER THE GENERAL

Mulholland had told Allen Kelly that he knew what building the aqueduct would entail. "I'm going into this as a man in the army goes into war, because it would be cowardly to quit. It will take the life out of me and if I stay to the end I'll come out a rickety old man, tied together with baling wire. But if you think I'm going to wear myself out for a lot of political jobbers, you can think again." This outburst was not without cause, as since the election of Mayor Harper and the passage of the water bonds, Mulholland's files had begun to fill with letters from job seekers or petitioners for friends and acquaintances of the mayor. Nor was his military analogy inapt as the organization needed to achieve this mighty task resembled a military campaign. When it began to appear that political favoritism and unwieldy red tape might subvert a clean operation, help arrived in the shape of an old army man.[1]

Although the Progressive reform group fought to retain the retiring chairman of the board of public works, J. A. Anderson, an authority on water law who had proven both able and fair handed, Mayor Harper was prevailed upon to name an aging military hero and friend of General Otis, Lieutenant General Adna Romanza Chaffee (1842–1914). General Chaffee, a great bear of a man with piercing eyes, had recently retired with his family to Los Angeles after a long, distinguished military career. He had been cited for conspicuous bravery at Gettysburg as a cavalry officer in the Civil War; he had fought Indian wars in Texas, New

Mexico, and Arizona; and he had commanded victorious troops in the Philippines during the Spanish-American War. He had also led troops into Peking to relieve the American delegation during the Boxer Rebellion in 1900, and for several years before his retirement, he had been the chief of staff of the United States Army. He enjoyed the admiration of the city and the unbounding enthusiasm of General Otis, whose esteem had more to do with his military stature than his political beliefs.[2]

As the *Times* beat the drums for his selection, a few expressed fears that the sixty-five-year-old Chaffee was too old for the job. The only serious protest, however, came from E. T. Earl's *Express,* whose Progressive editor, Edward Dickson, not only defended the departing Anderson but may have assumed the general shared Otis's anti-Progressive philosophy. That fear proved groundless after the apolitical old militarist revealed that he had never cast a vote until the presidential election of 1908. When asked then how he intended to vote, he told the reporter "to go to—Mojave!"—that even his wife did not know the answer to that.[3]

Chaffee's appointment was generally popular, and at the end of January 1908, Mulholland, Mathews, and the two other board members conferred with the general in order to acquaint him with the scope and duties of the public works board. (A new city charter effected in January 1906 had created this board, which was to consist of three men appointed by the mayor and confirmed by the council.) When Chaffee in turn told them that his greatest interest lay in the aqueduct project, they decided to name him chairman of the advisory aqueduct board rather than chairman of the board of public works. Because of his friendship with Progressives who opposed Chaffee, Mulholland initially may have harbored a certain ambivalence about the appointment, but Chaffee, with his experience supervising engineering as well as military projects, soon demonstrated his ability to improve the aqueduct operation's logistics. Within a few months, Mulholland would write Allen Kelly that "Chaffee is proving himself a very able executive." Among the few clippings saved in Mulholland's personal scrapbook is a column from the *Record* that apparently echoed the consensus of approval for General Chaffee with a cartoon of Chaffee and Mulholland sweating and breaking rock with pick and shovel as Chaffee declares, "We'll dig it, Bill."[4]

Two urgent matters confronted the board of public works: whether to accept an offer to sell water rights in Mono Lake and Owens Valley from a power company that had opposed the aqueduct; and how to deal with unexpectedly high new bids for freight rates from the Southern Pacific. The water rights offer came from Silver Lake Power and Irrigation Company, with which the city already had contended over its claimed water rights in those locations. The German-owned company's president was the son of a millionaire brewer, while its chief engineer, A. H. Koebig, was a well-known foe of the aqueduct who since 1899 had championed a Mojave River water project for Los Angeles. Koebig now proposed to convey all of Silver Lake's water rights in Mono and Inyo Counties and drop all pending lawsuits against the city for $50,000, half of the $100,000 the company claimed to have already spent on its various projects. After Mulholland inspected the site while on tour with Chaffee and Harper, and upon subsequent consultation with attorneys who felt the company's technical holdings were not of great value, the board declined the offer. It also rejected the Southern Pacific's bid for carrying freight along the aqueduct, but that was simply one move in a complicated bargaining process with the railroad.[5]

At the end of February, General Chaffee, Mayor Harper, water board member J. H. Norton, and Mulholland set out for an inspection tour of the aqueduct and Owens Valley. The entire operation consisted of eleven sections, or divisions, the first beginning at the far north in Long Valley and the eleventh in the south as it terminated near San Fernando. The group first visited the tunnel under construction at the tenth division near Elizabeth Lake. In the three months since work had begun, more than 1,000 feet of the bore had been driven at a cost of $50 a foot. Hopes rose for a completion earlier than estimated with an accompanying cost reduction of $700,000 (the original estimate had been $75 a foot) once electric power came. The city was to purchase the power from the Edison Company, and three crews were working overtime to rush lines from Castaic to the south portal of the tunnel. Then "the real work will begin," Mulholland informed them, for two mining crews would thereupon be able to excavate 600 feet of tunnel a month.[6]

As they neared the construction site, the visitors were told of the difficulties in finding horses able to haul the big freighting wagons up to the Lake Elizabeth area's 2,900-foot elevation. After viewing the camp nestled like a small village in the mountains near the mouth of the tunnel where 200 workers lived, each member of the party was handed a lighted candle and invited to enter the tunnel, 13 feet wide and 14 feet high, with little timbering for it was in solid rock. When they emerged, Mulholland picked up a piece of blue-ribbed rock from a nearby pile and said to the engineer in charge, "This is gneiss rock all right. I do not believe we shall encounter much real granite." The mayor, in an effort to be agreeable, echoed, "Very nice rock." Mulholland smiled and explained, "This nice is spelled g-n-e-i-s-s, Mayor. Striated granite and much easier to tunnel than granite." In fact, he added, if granite were found only in the ribs, it could mean a saving of at least $500,000 to the city. Very nice rock indeed.[7]

While the mayor had his geology lesson, Chaffee had spied an injured worker, his foot wrapped in towels with not a doctor in sight. An accident in the tunnel that morning had mashed the miner's toes. On the return trip, Chaffee inquired about him and was told he was recovering, but the general announced that a physician should be on the spot to take care of everyone. "If the city puts 500 men out there in the wilderness, it must send a physician along to look after them." His subsequent report to the board included the directive that "there shall be immediately organized for the Aqueduct a Medical Department; and for this purpose shall be erected at the south and north portal of the Elizabeth Tunnel, and at the cement [plant] a small hospital each sufficient to accommodate six beds, a small dispensary, and sleeping quarters for a hospital steward."[8]

By mid-May, three young doctors had received contracts to organize the medical department on the aqueduct project. To maintain it, each employee who earned forty dollars or more a month was to be assessed one dollar a month; those earning less, fifty cents. The assessments would pay the physicians, while the city was to provide field hospitals and pay for their attendants and maintenance. Patients with severe injuries and sicknesses were sent on to the California Hospital in Los Angeles. As only 400 men were employed on the aqueduct at the outset, the three physicians received a very modest recompense, but when the workforce swelled to 4,000, their financial picture improved considerably.[9]

A CIVIL SERVICE SNARL

For all his sympathy with many of the Progressive movement's aims and his approval of civil service as a means of avoiding political graft and favoritism, Mulholland was fundamentally a pragmatist, impatient with red tape, who demanded a free hand in certain decisions. He had asked the civil service commission to exempt certain workers on the aqueduct from examination because of their proven abilities. This request had included the existing staff of the city's water department, as well as Mathews and his assistant attorneys. Among others to be exempted were tunnel engineers, miners, carpenters, team bosses, blacksmiths, harriers, and certain men with specialized skills. Mulholland and Lippincott had al-

ready complained of inexperienced boys sent out to work on the line simply because they had been able to pass an examination, but neither could
have imagined that their differences with the commission in 1908 would
culminate in Lippincott's being threatened with discharge from his aqueduct post unless he himself took the civil service examination.

This absurdity came about in part because of a civil service shakeup
when one of the city's leading Progressives, Dr. John R. Haynes, was
ousted as president of the commission because he allegedly tolerated lax-
ness and misdoing by one of the examiners. Due to what it considered
dereliction under Haynes's regime, the new commission decided to institute a policy of investigating complaints in person rather than simply
relying on written evidence. Thus, in late May an examiner disguised as
a worker was sent to investigate complaints in the aqueduct camps. His
cover was blown at the first camp when he was recognized by workers
who had taken the examination under him in Los Angeles. On his return, the examiner recommended that the commission refuse to exempt
the position of tunnel engineer from civil service. As this meant dismissing
one of the two engineers in charge of the Elizabeth Lake tunnel and putting an untried man in his place, Mulholland and Lippincott, both outraged, came forth with personal appeals to retain a man who, they said,
was doing an excellent job and should not be replaced.[10]

To resolve this quasi war between civil service and the aqueduct men,
General Chaffee wrote a report proposing that the board of public works
should direct all of the aqueduct affairs and that the civil service commission should deal through the board and not, as it previously had, directly with the employee. The commission's response to General Chaffee's blunt and somewhat tactless communiqué included the stinger that
engineer Lippincott was illegally employed by the city and must take
the civil service examination. When Lippincott's case came before the
commission, Chaffee and Mulholland both argued for his exemption
on the grounds that his knowledge of hydrographic conditions in
Owens Valley was unmatched, as were his two years' experience as assistant chief engineer of the aqueduct. As to a civil service examination,
Mulholland warned, "There is always danger that he might not stand
first, . . . and his loss to the aqueduct would be a great one. He knows
what he is doing from the ground up, and if an examination were held
he would have to compete with some of the best engineers who, though
they might best him in an examination, would be vastly inferior in
knowledge of the work in hand." The board took the matter under ad-
visement, but before it reached any decision Mayor Harper had resigned

from office; his successor, George Alexander, the Good Government candidate, had renamed Haynes to the civil service commission; and Lippincott remained unscathed.[11]

A SHORTAGE OF FUNDS AND OTHER WORRIES

Of grave concern in 1908 was the growing need for money as the aqueduct project moved towards its next stage, entailing the beginning of work on the Jawbone Division. Bids had been coming in since early in the year, and Mulholland estimated the division would cost almost $2 million, most of which would pay for labor. As funds from the first bond issue were almost exhausted, new sales had to begin at once or work on the project would have to stop. Selling did not prove easy because the lingering slump from the Panic of 1907 kept investors wary, and there were no takers for the bonds at 4.0 percent. Mathews reported from New York that a sale could be arranged at 4.5 percent. As that required the city council's approval, a wrangle over whether to approve the issue arose in early July. Proponents pointed out that San Francisco and New York were paying 5.0 percent on their current public works bonds, but opponents wanted to wait until other offers materialized. Hostility against Mathews flared, but when all the dust had settled, a unanimous vote approved a contract to market $21 million of aqueduct bonds at 4.5 percent, of which $4 million was an outright purchase by the syndicate Kountze Brothers and Leach and Company of New York. The president of the council remarked that it was the greatest bond sale Los Angeles had ever made and expressed his confidence in the New York bankers while also asserting his belief that the question of financing the aqueduct was finally settled. An hour after the approval, the board of public works awarded contracts for $50,000 worth of machinery to be used on the aqueduct, while two much relieved men, Mulholland and Chaffee, predicted that Owens Valley water would be flowing into the San Fernando Valley by July 1912.[12]

Work on the formidable Jawbone Division could now proceed. Even today this section of the aqueduct stands out as the most impressive achievement of the entire undertaking with its gigantic mile-and-a-half-long siphon accomplished by the dramatic use of fifty-two-mule teams to haul the pipe up the canyon. Miners had named the canyon because its steep walls rising from the desert floor resembled a jutting lower jaw. When engineer John R. Freeman first viewed these badlands, he had told Mulholland they looked like a tough place for canal digging. Mulholland agreed that it was rough on top, explaining that he planned to take the aqueduct underground. He added, "When you buy a piece of pork, you don't have to eat the bristles." Over twelve miles of tunnel were to be bored across this desolate landscape where temperatures could soar to 120°F in the summer and drop to freezing in the winter. In a terrain without water, without trees, without any feature whatsoever to furnish sustenance and comfort to the workers or supplies for fuel or construction, a mighty work requiring an army of men, animals, and machines was about to be undertaken.[13]

Two years of preliminary study had preceded Mulholland's final approval, during which four surveys were conducted, leading the locating engineer, E. A. Bayley, to decide that the "old man" never would be satisfied. Crucial to the endeavor was a supply of potable water, for when the first surveying party began its work near Red Rock Canyon in 1906, the water there had made the men sick and Mulholland had shipped them bottled Puritas water from Los Angeles, an expense that would have been prohibitive for a large workforce. A supply of good water for the north end of the division was established twenty-two miles away in Water Canyon, where at an elevation of 4,000 feet, a water line of four-inch steel pipe was laid along trackless wilderness. To supply the south end of the division a second pipeline was run from city-owned wells in Tehachapi.[14]

The problems of transportation were no less daunting, as an estimated 350,000 tons of freight were expected to be delivered. Bids for hauling had involved months of conferences and discussions until the Southern Pacific received the contract to build eighteen miles of road that would lead almost to the mouth of Jawbone Canyon. From there northward to Red Rock Canyon the city would build a spur line of eight and a half miles. Roads for teams and trails had to be constructed; telephone lines strung; and the all-important power for the powerhouses sent from the new hydroelectric plant at Cottonwood, built under the supervision of electrical engineer Ezra F. Scattergood.

Living and sleeping quarters for 1,000 men had to be provided, as well as cook, mess, and medical facilities. Mail service for the workers was important, given their isolation, and a lively correspondence and controversy ensued over appropriate locations for post offices. When one person in the settlement of Ricardo near Red Rock Canyon applied for a station, Mulholland argued for a site at Jawbone. Ricardo, he wrote, was "only a small grocery store and a saloon," so that a post office there would serve not more than a half dozen persons. His chief objection to Ricardo, however, was that its saloon would draw workers. "As employees of the Aqueduct in this locality will be required to work under unusual climatic conditions and where free access to intoxicants will impair their efficiency it is the desire of Aqueduct officials to keep the men as far as possible from the desert saloon." He took equally strong objection to a postmaster at Haiwee who was rumored to have been run out of Oakland, California, for practicing dentistry without a license and who also stood suspected of writing bum checks. The postmaster's reputation in the community, according to Mulholland, was "decidedly unsavory." Although the dentist-postmaster was ultimately replaced, good mail service remained elusive along the aqueduct line during the construction years.[15]

A DEBATE ON THE CONTRACT SYSTEM

In early July, Mulholland retreated with his two sons into the Sierra Nevada, which, as he later wrote his friend, David Dorward, was enjoyable, although the pilgrimage through the desert heat had been rough. When he returned, a letter awaited him from Allen Kelly, now editor of the *Imperial Valley Press,* whom Harry Chandler had asked to write a progress report on the aqueduct for the *Times.* Could he join Mulholland on a trip along the aqueduct? Mulholland responded promptly on July 28 that he would be going along the line about August 10. He also confided that as the bids on the Jawbone section were coming in "somewhat over our estimates," he thought the city might do its own work. Three days later the announcement came that the city would do work on the Jawbone Division by day labor or force account, which would result in a savings of several hundred thousand dollars.[16]

Because tunneling represented the major portion of the work on the Jawbone, the board, upon the aqueduct advisory commission's recommendation, announced that it would adopt a bonus system for tunnel crews. A bonus was to be paid for completing more than an "average day's work" in twenty-four hours. The engineering department defined an average day's work in the tunnel as six feet in twenty-four hours where timbering was necessary and eight feet in twenty-four hours where it was not. Shift bosses, miners, muckers, and motormen also qualified for bonuses. Each man on a crew received forty cents for every foot in excess of the average day's work. "After paying this bonus the city will still save several dollars on each foot completed in excess of the work of the average day," Mulholland announced.

Because of high bids from private contractors, Mulholland had prevailed over Chaffee and the board, who had hoped private contracts would give the city's engineers more time for other aspects of the work. The Chief, however, maintained that the "day's work" system had been tried and always worked admirably in his experience. Dr. Taylor in his memoir remembered that Chaffee advocated letting contracts for work, while Mulholland "was confident that the city could run its own camps and do its own construction work more cheaply than by contract, and he felt they would probably get a better job." One large private contract was let, however, for construction in the Antelope Division later that year, but for the most part, the city did its own work. Chaffee prevailed in having outside contractors for food and medicine, which yielded mixed results, for although the medical crew acquitted itself well, the food contractor created a large-scale ruckus in 1910 that led to the most serious labor dispute on the aqueduct. On the other hand, Mulholland's day labor and bonus system produced prodigious results with record-breaking speeds while keeping well within—sometimes even below—both time estimates and budget.[17]

Although the relative merits of the contract and day labor systems stirred controversy among engineer-contractors at that time, neither system would have satisfied organized labor. Because of the city's high unemployment and labor's weakened organization, little argument arose over these matters, especially as the Progressive reformers were always more intent on political reform in municipal affairs than in the advancement of organized labor. Organized labor had, however, long opposed the contract system with the employers' not uncommon practice of overcharging workers for inferior accommodations at boarding camps. In 1892, the People's Party in Los Angeles had agitated for prohibition of contract work on public works and, in later years, although the labor council had taken a more aggressive stand against contracting, it had not succeeded in having it banned from public works. Another dilemma for labor and the Socialists in 1908 was their support of municipal ownership of public utilities, which the water project represented, along with their opposition to both the contract and day labor systems by which it was to be built.[18]

WORKERS AND NEW MACHINES

In the hope that aqueduct families would provide a more stable environment during construction and offset the roughhouse and vagrant ways of single men in construction camps, Mulholland announced, "Any man of family in Los Angeles who desires work at manual labor for $2 a day can secure a place." Modest homes were under construction and a one-room public school opened at the south portal of Elizabeth Lake Tunnel. Others followed at key points along the aqueduct.

New equipment and machinery appeared: a dredger invented by Mulholland that the men called "Big Bill" (both for the Chief and, depending on one's politics, presidential nominees William Howard Taft or William Jennings Bryan) proved an enormous success on a site between Black Rock Springs and the Alabama Hills. A stenographer in the aqueduct office was quoted as saying, "Mr. Mulholland thinks as much of that dredger as though it were his baby." More spectacular than Big Bill, however, was a newfangled traction engine that Benjamin Holt had developed for use in the peat bogs of Stockton, California, then being cultivated for agriculture. One amazing feature of this machine was its ability to climb hills through mud and loose gravel. Mulholland is said to have exclaimed when he first watched it maneuvering up an impossible slope, "The damn thing looks like a caterpillar," and has thus been credited with naming the Caterpillar tractor. Apocryphal or not, the new wonder did make its debut during the building of the aqueduct, where, unfortunately, it did not prove out. Other new equipment also disappointed, as in the case of an excavator whose malfunctioning sent one of the department's engineers to consult with its Chicago manufacturer in early June. As the engineer's absence extended throughout the summer, a frustrated Mulholland fumed at the delay. Not until December did the returned excavator begin to tear up ground for the conduit six miles south of Mojave.[19]

New machinery notwithstanding, certain work was entrusted to one of the great work animals of all time, the mule. When the city council received the unusual request from the board of public works to purchase 1,000 tons of hay at no more than $20 a ton, speculation broke out as to who or what would eat that mountain of hay. All became clear with the next request for the purchase of 200 mules. One councilman wondered if the mules should be subject to civil service examination. Wondering why the board wanted to make these purchases on the open market, the councilmen were told it would rather trust Mulholland's judgment on mules and hay than rely on so-called experts. After a certain amount of jocularity imagining Mulholland in the corrals inspecting animals bearing labels ("Take me home for $199.99"), the council learned that Mulholland had made a small contract on the ton-mile basis for hay, and even if the city fathers were not too clear about that, they authorized $60,000 for mules and hay. In the year to come, they would better understand the good use to which the money had been put.[20]

A QUESTION OF LAND SALES

The Eatons remained active in 1908, securing land deals both for themselves and the city. In May, Eaton's son, Harold, offered to sell the city eighty acres of riparian land near Citrus for $25 an acre. Mulholland wrote him that the board turned down the offer because it found the price unreasonable as the land had no improvements and no rights in any ditch or other means of irrigation. Then he questioned the ethics of such a deal. "Since your father was acting as Agent for the City in the purchasing of lands at the time that you contracted with the State for this land, such contract was made in view of having the City in prospect as an ultimate purchaser and that your price, in honor, should be scaled accordingly." Mulholland's increasing disenchantment with some of Eaton's real estate dealings dates from this time, especially when it appeared that Eaton was attempting to take advantage of the city in order to profit his children.

O'Melveny's journals offer another glimpse of the Eatons' activities when, on November 4, 1908, a day after Taft had defeated Bryan for the presidency and the attorney sat in his office bemoaning the election results ("hopelessly Republican"), Eaton had appeared with his son-in-law and a map. As they consulted the map, Eaton told O'Melveny that he would be selling the land to the city at actual cost and that he wanted O'Melveny to draw up the offer. The following day Eaton and his son-in-law returned to the attorney's office, looked over the offer for a sale of property in the Owens Valley to the City of Los Angeles, said it was satisfactory, and left, taking the document with them. Twelve days later, however, on November 17, O'Melveny noted that in the matter of Fred Eaton, Big Pine, and Owens River, he had met Mathews and left him the offer, but that same morning as he prepared to make a formal presentation, Mulholland informed him that "after inspection, the matter had taken a radical change and could only be settled with Eaton present." This episode was to lead to turbulent consequences in the 1920s.[21]

CONSTRUCTION "APPALLING IN ITS MAGNITUDE AND EXPENSE"

In the third annual report, released at the end of November, Mulholland explained that actual construction of the aqueduct commenced in October 1908 and that the preliminary work "necessary to enable construction to begin" had been "appalling in its magnitude and expense."

Yet it would prove justified, he continued, for engineers have long known in such projects that "Well begun is half done." He reviewed what had been accomplished: "the building of a great cement factory at Tehachapi; the laying of scores of miles of water pipe to convey water for construction and domestic purposes over the long stretches of arid desert traversed by the Aqueduct; the building of power plants and transmission lines for the development and conveyance of electrical energy to be used in construction; the building of roads, trails, and telephone lines and the erection of camps for the housing of workmen,—all these things required large expenditures of money and diligent effort." He then predicted rapid progress in the year to come, beginning in March: an acceleration in the rate of advance from the current six hundred feet per day to nine hundred. By November 1909, he forecast, an added 58 miles of aqueduct would have been constructed at a cost of $4,633,618. Nor did he see any reason why the work should not be completed well within its time schedules and cost estimates.[22]

The demands on Mulholland's time and energies were immense. The day after Christmas, Harry Brooks of the *Times* wrote to ask him about reports that polluted well water was causing unusual amounts of sickness in the Vernon area. Brooks expressed his regret that, because of the demands of putting out the annual midwinter supplement to the newspaper, he had missed the Sunset Club Christmas party. Mulholland replied, assuring Brooks that another source would have to be sought for Vernon's troubles as its district was receiving water from the same source as other parts of the city where no such incidence of illness was occurring. He added, "I too, through stress of work, found it impossible to be with fellow Sunsetters Saturday night and regretted the fact not a little."[23]

CHAPTER 15

Building the Aqueduct: The Best Year

1909

THE WICKEDEST TOWN IN THE WEST

In most ways, 1909 was the best of all the seven years of aqueduct construction. Ample funds were available, work advanced on schedule, and crews set new world records for speed in tunnel drilling. Nor did the city's uproar as it threatened to become the first in the nation to recall its mayor much affect work. In early February 1909, Mulholland wrote his friend and colleague Henry Dockweiler, who was helping San Francisco to prepare a brief in the Spring Valley water case as well as to fix rates for San Rafael, Oakland, and San Francisco. Doc had asked Bill for some specifications and plans and, not having received them, wrote again. Mulholland explained that not only was the department's auditor moving into larger quarters so that things were all torn up, but "as you can imagine, the work is keeping us all very busy these days, with a working force of over 3,000 men, 40 camps, and 230 miles of line to get over about ever so often. During the first ten days of last month we drove 2,456 feet of tunnel on the Jawbone section which brought the total up to 18,400 feet since we began in October."

When Dockweiler received the materials a week later, he wrote a note of thanks, adding that he hoped the good progress on the aqueduct would quiet those who believed a city could not do work as well as a private corporation. "I have become tired of listening," he went on, "to the objections that have been set forth, that this city [San Francisco] will never be able to accomplish anything in the way of building a water works.

The Aqueduct will be a standing refutation to that argument." As Los Angeles became a pacesetter in the municipalization and management of water, other cities looked to it as a model; Omaha and Denver sought advice in their campaigns for municipal water during 1909, while Oakland asked for help with its plans to meter its water.[1]

Even though progress on the aqueduct was excellent, hitches on a project of its magnitude were inevitable, and predictably, as the labor force increased, so did the problems. The first came when a group of aqueduct workers were involved in a fracas on the streets of Mojave and landed in jail. By now Mojave was being called "the wickedest town in the West," although in the early stages of aqueduct planning, the chief complaints against it had been climatic. In October 1905, surveying engineer T. W. Young had written to Mulholland about the Mojave wind—so strong that no work could be done and so wild that all he and his crew could do was hold onto their tents. "I braced and guyed every way, but the wind came every way also." After failing to find either a house or boxcar for shelter, they were forced to weather it out. "Prospects of cheese and crackers and sleep on the ground," wrote Young, "but I am not in the least discouraged." When the wind snapped the ridgepole of his tent the following night, he discovered the nature of the desert town, for there was "not enough lumber in the place to make a new pole, so I must send to L. A." Eventually he found an old room measuring 25 feet by 50 feet, rented it for fifty cents a day, and moved in the crew. When Mulholland wrote back, he thanked Young for the "Weather Bureau reports with regard to the climatology of Mojave," adding that "Mojave enjoys special privileges in the way of weather, for which she has reason to be proud."[2]

Pronounced *Mo-harvy* by old-time railroad men, the settlement had been a rail center since 1876 and was the jumping-off place to Owens Valley. For thousands of aqueduct workers, it also became the place where one went to blow one's pay. Surrounded by desert and edged on its west by railroad track, Mojave consisted of about a thousand feet of business frontage—a string of low, one-story wooden structures whose facades would be instantly recognizable to anyone who has ever watched a western movie. The largest building and chief reputable enterprise was Asher's general merchandise store, which drew among its respectable patrons the neighboring ranchers, and miners, along with their wives and children. Straggling off the main drag down a few side blocks stood less genteel establishments that lured men from the nearby mines and construction camps: the saloons, dance halls, fancy houses and gambling joints that earned Mojave its notorious reputation. Everyone agreed that the best and cleanest hostelry in town was the Harvey House alongside the railroad tracks. Erwin W. Widney, fresh out of high school in 1908, remembered his first impressions of Mojave when he had traveled north from Los Angeles that summer to a job with the Southern Pacific, then building along the line of the aqueduct. When he first stepped off the train just before dawn and stood on the station platform, he wrote, "I saw lights in every saloon, dance hall and gambling room, men passing in and out, some voluntarily, some propelled, some head first, some feet first. I heard a dozen different tunes being played on a dozen different pianos and phonographs; women's laughter, harsh and mirthless; men's voices expressing all sorts of emotions. It was 4:30 in the morning. I wondered at such activity, but I soon discovered that it was a pay day on the aqueduct and railroad, and hundreds, yes, thousands of men had come to town to give vent to pent-up emotions and be separated from their wages."[3] Mulholland's sons had vivid boyhood memories of Mojave— the noise and drunkenness and confusion as they left the train and walked with their father through the dirt streets to the lodging where they would spend the night. They laughingly remembered that "Dad" always first checked for bed bugs; little else of what they heard and saw was much repeated in polite company. What they managed to convey was their shock and delight at finding themselves in such an outlaw world. Once, with Harvey Van Norman, they reminisced about a gambler and pimp, who moved along the route of the aqueduct with his lady in a horse-drawn wagon tricked out as a dual-purpose brothel and gambling hall. His end came after he was suspected of cheating at faro and was later found buried head down in a canyon, with only his boot heels pointing to the sky.

The gamblers and layabouts of Los Angeles increasingly lit out for Mojave, their exodus coinciding conveniently with one of the city's periodic convulsions of civic virtue. This time the Progressives led the push to rid the city of its liquor and vice interests, along with its mayor, whom they suspected of cozy relations with these low associates. Crime began to rise along the aqueduct. Raids on cookhouses depleted supplies while holdup men lurking in the rocks and brush as paydays neared made it unsafe to walk from an aqueduct camp into town at night. Still, the men could not resist the lure of Mojave. After all, in that wilderness, what else was there? The first serious trouble occurred at a dance hall one Saturday night when a group of drinking aqueduct employees traded insults that led to blows. Some local men entered the brawl in an attempt to break it up, but they were set upon in turn. In the melee, one aqueduct foreman drew a gun but did not fire. The aqueduct men were overpowered and handcuffed by the locals who turned out to be Mojave police, although they had worn no identifying stars. Among those thrown in jail were a hospital steward and several foremen who had been attempting to stop the fighting. When Mulholland received news of this trouble, he was on the point of leaving to file the official aqueduct survey at the United States land office in Independence. While he was securing the council's approval of the survey, he and the other members of the aqueduct commission took the opportunity to request support of pending legislation that would forbid the sale of alcohol within four miles of any public work. The threat of drunkenness and brawling delaying work on the aqueduct demonstrated more than ever the need for controls over the "Mojave peril."[4]

TUNNEL DRILLERS AND MULE SKINNERS

Complaints about working conditions on the aqueduct began to drift back to the city in early 1909. In one instance, Mulholland's secretary, Burt Heinly, directly contacted an employee who had complained to the press, asking him to come in and discuss the matter with the Chief. Next, a representative from the machinists' union appeared before the board of public works to complain that not a man on the aqueduct received more than $3.50 a day, while the Southern Pacific was paying machinists $3.96 for a day of nine hours. The chairman answered that the aqueduct men worked an eight-hour day as approved by the labor council, and that the Southern Pacific's added $.44 would amount to $3.52 for an eight-hour day. The aqueduct, therefore, was $.02 behind, and the chairman told the representative to submit the complaint in writing if he wished to continue it. A more serious threat to the aqueduct budget was a measure before the legislature setting a minimum wage of $2.50 a day on all public works in California. Mulholland, who estimated that 20 percent of the aqueduct's cost was labor, grew alarmed that this bill would add $3.5 million to the aqueduct's cost and overrun his estimates. Because the state was still in a depression and unemployment remained high, the legislature, as it had already done in previous years, voted the measure down.[5]

By March 1909, 3,000 men were on the aqueduct, half the gamblers of the West had shown up to ply their trade, and 400 handpicked mules were about to appear. The city had been renting mules at $20 a head per month at a total cost of $100,000 a year, but the aqueduct men decided the city could maintain its own mules for less and would be able to recover the original cost when work ended. Mulholland, who admired the mule for its sturdiness and stability of character, had seriously considered taking time out from his busy life to choose them himself, until he learned that the law required bidding on the contract to furnish the mules. Therefore, two councilmen expert in mule matters were sent to Kansas City for the finest in the land. The 261 chosen were loaded onto fourteen stock cars, and their arrival in Los Angeles created a memorable scene as they were released into pens for a two-day rest before moving on to Mojave. Only one was lost on the journey, and an enthusiastic councilman declared that they were "the best lot of mules ever brought across the Rockies."[6]

The mules had to be good, for they faced a task that became the stuff of legend among the water men: hauling pipe for the great Jawbone Siphon. Twenty-mule teams and tractors were already in use along the aqueduct, but neither was up to this labor, which a singular use of fifty-two-mule teams was about to solve. To haul 36-foot sections of 7½-foot-diameter pipe weighing around 26 tons each from the station at Cinco 4 miles up to Jawbone Canyon, Harvey Van Norman devised an ingenious arrangement of massive wagons with flat beds on steel wheels with tires 2 feet wide. Two of these powerful wagons were then drawn in tandem by fifty-two mules controlled by three jerklines: eight rows of six animals abreast, two "wheelers" at the tongue, and a lead pair at the head.[7]

To propel this unwieldy and cumbersome arrangement of metal and beasts required the skill of a supremely gifted mule skinner, and although run-of-the-mill skinners were not hard to come by in that land of mines and desert, a gifted one was rare. Van Norman first engaged a man called Wilson, whose success on his first run from Cinco so overcame him that he picked a fight with a corral wrangler, whomped him on the head with a whip handle, and for his pains was canned and sent packing. Van Norman (a two-fisted drinker himself in those days) went down to Mojave in search of another skinner and while quenching his thirst in a local saloon overheard an old geezer at the bar bragging about how many mules he could drive. "Yeah," called Van Norman. "How many can you drive?" After a silent stare and a squirt of tobacco juice, the old man replied, "I can drive 'em as far as I can see 'em." Thus entered the legendary "Whistling Dick," who could work the jerklines as well as Itzhak Perlman can play the violin and who delivered the giant pipe from Cinco to Jawbone. At least, he did until almost at the end of the job when, for reasons unknown, he fell from his mount and was crushed beneath the wagon's steel wheels.[8]

Mules were not the only hard workers on the aqueduct. Tunnel-drilling crews began to break records for rapid hard rock tunnel excavation. They shattered two on the south portal of the Elizabeth Tunnel under the leadership of W. C. Aston, the "difficult" foreman of whom the civil service commission had earlier wished to dispose; at the north portal, John Gray, tough and capable with years of mining experience behind him, led his crew to even more record breakers. One, a run of 166 feet in thirty-one days using three shifts, bested the government's Gunnison Tunnel by 16 feet. Up on the Jawbone, where the rock was softer but the conditions severe, prodigies of speed occurred when A. C. Hansen, who had successfully built the city's latest outfall sewer, oversaw an army of one thousand men amid dust and dynamite explosions to two runs of 370 feet in record time. When Mulholland inspected the line in April, he said, "Don't think all the good men are at work on the Elizabeth Tunnel because two American records have been broken there. I don't know what the record is for two shifts, but in this contest which is going on between the tunnel men I believe the Jawbone men, with 370 feet to their credit, have surpassed anything done on the aqueduct so far. The rock in which they worked is practically the same as that encountered in the Elizabeth Tunnel, and the other conditions are about the same."[9]

Two international records fell in a contest between American and Swiss tunnel drillers. In June 1909, the men in the Saugus Division north of Newhall overtook a record established in 1903 in the Ricken Tunnel, Switzerland. Then, in August, under the direction of Tom Flanigan, a redheaded Irishman who had previously worked in the city and earned Mulholland's high regard because of his ability to handle men and get work done fast, the crew at Tunnel 17-M in a soft sandstone at the head of the Red Rock Canyon excavated from two headings a 10,596-foot-long tunnel in seven months. They then completely lined it in eight months. In other words, they drove and lined this two-mile tunnel in a year and a quarter.[10]

POLITICS AND THE AQUEDUCT: A MAYOR BOWS OUT

At the time of these exploits, journalist Allen Kelly made one of his periodic treks along the aqueduct. He noted that the Owens Valley settlers who had feared the loss of all their water seemed relieved because groundwater in the valley had risen from artesian wells since the digging of the canals. Kelly also reported that anti-aqueduct talk seemed to have died down and that the city was now leasing land to local ranchers. Impressed by the progress, he described the Chief's ability to delegate authority and his capacity for soaring above a morass of detail. Mulholland sometimes replaced elaborate notes and blueprints with mere stick scratches in the sand as he instructed an engineer to go ahead and do it "your way." Choose the right man and then give him his head, Mulholland told Kelly. Associates attested to his prodigious memory and powers of observation, recalling that although his sketches and notes on the first survey had been bare-bones by academic standards (made simply with a pocket compass and an aneroid barometer), the overarching plan and vision were clearly in his head. Remembering those earlier days, Mulholland told Kelly that the man who drove the buckboard on that occasion had thought he was "a locoed prospector hunting for a lost mine." Musing that Mulholland might have made a great general or military engineer, Kelly concluded that then he would have been responsible for "prodigies of destruction instead of construction."[11]

Accompanying this group was J. Waldo Smith, chief engineer of the Catskill aqueduct project, described as "a blown-in-the-bottle New Yorker" who "regarded everything west of the Hudson as unexplored territory peopled by semi-civilized tribes addicted to big talk." After his survey, however, Smith declared himself amazed: amazed by the courage of men who went into the desert to find water; amazed by a municipality willing to do its own work rather than contract it; and amazed that the leaders had been able to keep out the politicians and grafters. "No hint of Tammany here!" he declared.

Mulholland always credited the bonus system for the success of the tunnel work. "The men in a bonus crew themselves eliminated the drones and did not tolerate loafing." Having devised the system used on the aqueduct, he was devoted to it, but it ran into difficulties in June when the city auditor decided that the Chief's computations were too generous. Securing the board's approval of his calculations, the auditor cut bonuses 56 percent. When the payroll was delayed in order to make the changes, two hundred men walked off the job. The former system was quickly restored as General Chaffee explained that Mulholland had thought they should try the auditor's plan "to see how it would work," adding sardonically that now they had found out. With a revised system reinstated, the men returned to work, but in the following year, organized labor would raise further opposition.[12]

Los Angeles had no Tammany Hall, but its politics did impinge on aqueduct affairs, especially after Mayor Harper retired from his office in March rather than face the divisiveness and humiliation of a recall. The progressive Democratic League had backed Harper's successor, George Alexander, and almost immediately after Alexander's installation, league secretary M. G. Yoakum reintroduced the San Fernando Valley "land grab" issue in an attempt to unseat Moses Sherman from the water board. That matter had remained quiescent until Yoakum wrote letters to both the new acting mayor and the city council demanding an investigation and renewing the familiar accusations made in 1906 by the *Examiner* and *Evening News* that the funds for the aqueduct would pay for the project only as far as the head of the San Fernando Valley; that the additional land and rights-of-way needed to bring the Owens River water across the valley to the City of Los Angeles would have to be purchased from the San Fernando Mission Land Company in order to complete the work; and that Sherman was a participant in that land company.[13]

The new mayor handed this hot potato to Mulholland, admitting at the time that he did not know what the Democratic League meant by its communication. He soon found out when the water board, Mulholland, and Sherman each responded with letters dismissing the charges in the strongest terms. The board pointed out that the land company had purchased its valley holding in 1903, two years before aqueduct plans were made public. L. C. Brand, who had originated the purchase and acted as trustee for the company, also declared that he had originally feared the aqueduct project would swamp their land. When he was assured that the reservoirs would prevent such damage, he had given the city 200 acres for a reservoir and sold 155 acres more at $75 an acre. Speaking on his own behalf, Sherman acknowledged that he had once owned a one-tenth interest in the Mission Land Company as well as interests at Mojave, in the San Fernando Valley, and in Hollywood. Moreover, he regretted that he no longer held them, as they would be of greater value today than when he had bought them. This statement was somewhat disingenuous, for he omitted to say that he and some of his former associates in the Mission Land Company were now in the midst of negotiating a deal to purchase the entire southern half of the San Fernando Valley, a body of land unconnected to the Mission Land Company but which some writers have later mistakenly merged into the conspiracy theory. Mulholland, just returned from an official inspection of the aqueduct on which a group of city officials had accompanied him, wrote a sharp letter that the mayor did not make public, saying only that Mulholland's word was good enough for him and that no more was to be said on the matter.[14]

PROGRESS ACCOMPANIED BY A RUMBLE OF DISCONTENT

Between trips along the aqueduct line, Mulholland oversaw plans for the local water supply. He reported to the water commissioners in April that the old conduit at Crystal Springs should be replaced. Recalling that it had been built piecemeal between 1886 and 1891 and without a proper anticipation of how the city would grow, he now proposed a new conduit of about 9,000 feet from the Crystal Springs gatehouse in Griffith Park to the head of the Bellevue Reservoir branch line in the Ivanhoe subdivision. For the work, he recommended the purchase of a steam shovel and a gravel-loading device estimated at $65,000. By September, one hundred men and one steam shovel had completed a mile and a half of the work.[15]

Although the aqueduct was Mulholland's overwhelming concern, sometimes a lesser comedy of errors could require his attention. When the *Examiner* printed an article claiming that the city, upon the suggestion and authorization of Mulholland and Chief Forester Gifford Pinchot, was about to plant a large acreage of eucalyptus in the Owens Valley, his office was barraged with inquiries from eastern agents and investors wishing to do business with the city. Explaining to one New Yorker that "it was a story made out of the whole cloth as is so often the case these days with newspaper stories," Mulholland wrote that a eucalyptus enthusiast named Webb had appeared at the board of public works to extol the tree's virtues. The board, of course, was already familiar with the tree, as California was then in the midst of a eucalyptus boom after it had been falsely touted as a hardwood. (The boom eventually went bust, but not before the eucalyptus became almost as widespread in the Southern California landscape as the palm would later.) Once it was known that the tree could never thrive in the harsh winters and elevations of Owens Valley, the eager inquiries ceased.[16]

At midyear, Mulholland reported good progress on all aspects of the work, as did visitors returning from aqueduct tours. The once faultfinding City Auditor Mushet returned from his first visit full of enthusiasm and praise. "I wish every citizen of Los Angeles could see just what I had seen. . . . the genius of this enterprise is doing more for Los Angeles than this generation will ever dream of. . . . I take off my hat to him evermore." Dr. Luther Powers of Public Health pronounced Owens River water sweet and pure. "Any man who knocks this enterprise is a fool. He will speak without knowledge because if he saw what is being done and how it is being done, he would be ashamed of himself." Although Mulholland was encouraged to say that the aqueduct could be completed a year earlier than originally estimated, he wrote otherwise to his friend Charles Dwight Willard. Willard, former leader in the Municipal League and editor of its magazine, *Municipal Affairs,* had been sidelined by his "ancient enemy," tuberculosis. While convalescing, he had undertaken a new weekly publication, *Pacific Outlook,* in which he wanted either Mulholland or his secretary, Burt Heinly, to write a weekly account of progress on the aqueduct. When Mulholland explained that the constraints of time and work would not permit such a task, Willard then asked for a signed article about estimated times for the aqueduct's completion. Mulholland hedged with the reply that although it now looked as if it were going ahead faster than expected, he was reluctant to put that in writing, even though if "I thought that we were going to have to ask for more money and take a couple of extra years on this work, I wouldn't be able to sleep nights. As it is, my slumber is as peaceful as a baby's."[17]

Almost as he wrote those lines, trouble erupted over the food at the fifty-five camps. General Chaffee promptly left to investigate and upon return reported that he found conditions satisfactory, although he promised to seek improvement in the general sanitary conditions at the camps. Of the food, however, he warned that "one cannot expect to get things as good as at home." He had found the quality varied from camp to camp; moreover, good cooks were in short supply and providing fresh foods without refrigeration was difficult in desert areas.[18]

Until August 1908, the aqueduct had maintained its own commissary department. Each meal had cost 25¢, and the diet had been based upon what the United States Geological Survey then used. Then General Chaffee had persuaded the board that letting out the food concession to contract would simplify their burden of work and allow the enterprise to run more smoothly. The concessionaire, Daniel Joseph "Joe" Desmond, was the son and namesake of a pioneer Los Angeles hatter-haberdasher whose family Mulholland had known since his earliest times in California. Born in Los Angeles in 1875, Desmond began his career as a food contractor in his thirties when he and his partner, E. S. Shattuck, had run boardinghouses in connection with railroad construction. Their reputation grew after they set up soup kitchens in various permanent camps in San Francisco after the 1906 earthquake. Although initially praised and commended by army officers, complaints subsequently arose over the food, and five months after the disaster, Shattuck and Desmond were given notice that a local relief corporation was to replace them. As they were then serving 600 people three meals a day at 15¢ per meal, each of which cost about 7½¢ to provide, they were understandably reluctant to lose the arrangement.[19]

His partnership with Shattuck dissolved, Desmond received the aqueduct contract in July 1908, but soon discovered that some men were arranging their own private messes because of dissatisfaction with the food. In the Cinco Division, he reported that the official mess tent was almost empty. Therefore, on June 21, 1909, when an order went out along the line that all aqueduct workers were to get subsistence from the restaurants of D. J. Desmond and that they were to pay 70¢ a day whether they ate there or not, the workers' response was hostile. Chaffee acknowledged that the situation was trying, yet he also insisted that without an official subsistence organization the whole operation would degenerate.[20]

Workers reported that they moved on because of the poor food, probably only a partial truth, for many of the aqueduct laborers were men whom Mulholland called "short-stakers," those who worked from place to place, staying only long enough to collect a grubstake before moving on. A payroll for May 1909 provided 3,200 positions yet contained more than 7,000 names, indicating that over half the men remained only a few days. In October, the labor council sounded an ominous tone when it informed the city council that it had failed to secure satisfaction from either the aqueduct commission or Mayor Alexander and now requested the council to "investigate the question of wages and food conditions." Because some felt that behind this demand lay the desire to open an inquiry on "the whole question of aqueduct management," creating charges of "political trickery" at great extra expense, the council decided the whole matter must remain in the aqueduct commission's jurisdiction. Two weeks later, the commissioners traveled on the line with Mulholland and returned with a report that while the food was "not all the best in the world" and keeping fresh eatables on the desert was difficult, the bad spots were few.[21]

A YEAR OF GOOD WORK

By the end of summer, progress on the aqueduct was so well advanced that the board appointed Ezra F. Scattergood chief electrical engineer. At a salary of $5,000 a year, Scattergood was to conduct the affairs of the new power bureau, whose facilities would provide needed revenues for the enterprise. The board also voted to raise Mulholland's salary from $10,000 to $15,000 a year. More good news came in October when light broke through the mile-long Tunnel No. 35 on the Jawbone Division and jubilant crews began to celebrate its "holing." Now only a mile and a half remained to complete the twelve miles of tunnel on the Jawbone, and Mulholland commented to a friend in San Francisco that the remarkable way in which the men were "tearing up the ground" gave him cause for rejoicing. Indeed, before a meeting of city officials at year's end, he set aside the reticence he had shown with Willard and announced that the project would be completed early and under budget.[22]

As he left for his final inspection tour of 1909, Mulholland learned of the Supreme Court decision granting the City of Los Angeles the subterranean water rights of the San Fernando Valley. He and the water commissioners were quick to reassure the valley ranchers that with the coming of Owens River water they would not assert those rights. In fact, with an anticipated 20,000 miner's inches of Owens River water, they would face the problem of what to do with the excess. One municipality eager to secure some of it was Pasadena, but a great deal of discussion about consolidation and annexation would have to precede that decision.[23]

Back home a week before Christmas, the Chief described a sudden storm that had rendered Independence snowbound, with one of its canals frozen under a foot of ice. Yet, he added, only a few miles south, 2,500 men worked without interruption. The issues of labor, food, the contract system, the disposal of excess water, and San Fernando Valley land deals seemed to be receding. But as the following years would demonstrate, they had been mere forewarnings of storms to come.[24]

CHAPTER 16

Troubles and Interruptions

1910

SHAKE-UP AT CITY HALL

In an apparent attempt to keep his campaign promise of fairness and justice for all groups, incoming Mayor George Alexander shook up the city commissions with surprising additions and removals. He appointed the first union man ever to serve on a municipal commission, Ben C. Wilson of the Typographical Union, to the fire commission and restored Dr. John Randolph Haynes, a Progressive, to head the civil service commission. More controversial were his naming Lippincott to the park commission and removing Sherman from the water board. When Lippincott, with his penchant for controversial behavior, accepted the appointment, some saw a dangerous precedent in allowing one man to hold two important public offices at the same time, questioning too how he could do justice to the new post while also serving as assistant chief engineer of the aqueduct, for which he was paid a salary of $500 a month. The mayor argued that he wanted an engineer on parks, and although some wondered why some other able engineer could not be found to fill the post, Lippincott was still confirmed.[1]

Sherman's removal proved more controversial, but the Municipal League and one of its leaders, Meyer Lissner, were pressuring the mayor to force the resignation. Their charge against Sherman had been that he held stock in a downtown office building where the board of public works leased offices for the aqueduct department. As the city charter provided that no city official should have any direct or indirect interest in any contract with the city, the city attorney brought suit. Sherman's supporters were quick to point out that by that strict standard a number of other businessmen holding elective and appointive offices would also be ineligible (including two current members of the water commission who were bankers). Others, however, suggested that the chief ethical grounds for Sherman's disqualification were his ties to the Southern Pacific and the city's largest utility company. While Sherman's attorneys delayed, the Municipal League met with city council members and decided to offer him the opportunity to resign. With the same mixture of moral righteousness and defiance he had manifested regarding his conflicting interests in Arizona, San Francisco, and San Diego, he dismissed the charges as simply "technical" and refused to resign. The mayor, with council approval, then proceeded to remove him. The *Times* was predictably outraged while the Progressives savored the victory that Lissner had helped to achieve. [2]

To serve out Sherman's unexpired term and to act as president of the water commission Alexander named attorney and former mayor of Los Angeles William D. Stephens. Later in this politically volatile year that would see the election of Hiram Johnson to the governorship of California, Stephens became one of California's three successful Progressive candidates for Congress. His appointment to the $3,000 a year salaried post of water board president brought an end to J. J. Fay's eight-year tenure. The other appointment went to an old legal warrior from the days of the city's battles with the private water company, Henry T. Lee. The three remaining members included two bankers, Major John Norton and General John R. Mathews, along with Mayor Harper's last appointee, the genial and noncontroversial Democrat Reginaldo del Valle. This shakeup of the water commission also derived from Progressive opposition to the earlier commission's plans to build a four-story water department office at Fifth and Olive. Questions had been raised about the commission's power to spend water revenues on such a building, but after wrangles and accusations that the commissioners were "czars," the debate ended when the city attorney found that the city charter gave the water commission the right to build with its own funds.[3]

"THE GOOSE HANGS HIGH"

Work advanced on the aqueduct as the biggest concrete pipeline in the world (a record interior diameter of 120 inches running 955 feet) was being installed southeast of Newhall: a reinforced concrete siphon designed to operate under a head of 65 feet. In early March, the teams at the Elizabeth Tunnel under John Gray and William Aston broke yet more records amid estimates that at their present rate they would bring in the work a year early with a resultant savings of $119,000.[4]

That January, Mulholland and Mathews testified at a hearing in Independence before the United States Land Office about restoring to entry certain federal lands needed to preserve the purity of the water sent to Los Angeles. At this time Mulholland publicly addressed the local antagonisms in Owens Valley that had arisen over misunderstandings of the city's intentions and said that after all the evidence had been presented many fears had been allayed. An Inyo resident who attended all the proceedings lamented to the *Inyo Register* the absence of locals and their apparent indifference to "what is probably the most important case Inyo ever had or ever will have." He also noted that the Los Angeles men who testified presented a striking contrast to the "'tin horn' politicians and reporters who first came through the valley on earlier so-called tours of inspection." Especially impressed with Mulholland's testimony and clear recital of the history of Los Angeles's search for water in Owens Valley, he ruefully added, "If Inyo had had a Bill Mulholland to look out for her interests, in the intelligent and patriotic way he does for Los Angeles we would be in a different position today." On March 3, Senator Frank Flint wrote Mulholland that the secretaries of interior and agriculture had each agreed not to take any action without first notifying Flint. Finally, on April 27, Representative McLachlan entered a bill in the House giving the City of Los Angeles authority to a strip of land not more than 250 feet wide over public lands and forest reservations in Inyo, Kern, and Los Angeles Counties.[5]

While Mulholland spent early March on the aqueduct and in Owens Valley, the new water commissioner, William Stephens, arrived for a tour. Regardless of political affiliation, everyone who traveled the line with the Chief returned to the city a convert and enthusiast. Stephens was impressed by the quantity of water he saw, and he found the construction camps efficient, comfortable, and clean. As to the food, he allowed that a man who boarded regularly at the California Club might fault the lack of napkins and tablecloths, but compared to other construction camps, those along the aqueduct seemed clean and adequate. Another favorable report came from S. T. Henry, engineer and associate editor of *The Engineering Record of New York*. Struck by the spirit of organization and teamwork he had found along the line, he declared the food superior to any he had ever eaten at any railroad camp. Part of the current problem, he suggested, might stem from the fact that many of the men, especially those building the tunnels, were "highly paid, high class workmen who expected to be served banquets."[6]

Sanguine about affairs along the aqueduct that spring, Mulholland wrote Henry Dockweiler on March 15 that the "goose hangs high. . . . Returned from Independence Sunday night," he commented, "and have never seen things looking better than they did on this trip." He now turned his attention to the city's campaign for the passage of harbor and power bonds. A panel of experts had made a preliminary report finding that the 400-feet-per-second average flow in the aqueduct could deliver an average of 64,000 horsepower to the city and achieve a peak load of 120,000 horsepower. The proposed power bonds would finance the power plants' construction, one in San Francisquito Canyon where topographical studies by Scattergood and his assistant, Stanley Dunham, were already under way. Although not an active campaigner as he had been for the aqueduct, Mulholland issued a statement urging support for the power bonds. The project, he explained, was more of an investment than an improvement, for it would produce revenue once it was in operation. As civic sentiment seemed fairly united for passage of the bonds, the question generated little heat until almost the eve of the election when an anti-bond circular appeared. It prophesied that these bonds would cripple the city's credit and consequently hinder the aqueduct's completion. City attorneys Mathews and Hewitt assured voters that the city was well within the limits of its bonded indebtedness and retorted that the accusations smacked of a bad-faith effort that came too late in the campaign for adequate rebuttal. The voters evidently agreed, as they continued to support the city's policies for continued growth and on April 19 voted nine to one in favor of the bonds.[7]

A FORCED LAYOFF

As 3,600 men "tore up the ground" at a wonderfully rapid pace along the aqueduct, their very success—and the machinations of the eastern bond syndicate—were about to trip up the aqueduct builders. The work forged ahead until mid-May, when 2,700 men were abruptly laid off. The layoff's havoc and the emotion Mulholland must have felt were masked in the laconic engineering report he wrote months later. "This disorganization, coupled with the fact that it is naturally difficult to retain labor on the desert during the summer months, has seriously interfered with the progress schedule and the cost estimates."[8]

Because the accelerated pace of construction in 1909 had increased monthly expenditures as much as $600,000 a month, available funds by the end of May 1910 were reduced to $160,000 a month, and the work-force had to be reduced to 1,100 men. Difficulties intensified when the bond syndicate suddenly refused to make advance deliveries as it had the year before, declaring the bonds now had no buyers. The delay from its refusal to release its options on the bonds threatened to raise the cost of the project. To the argument that advancing the date of completion would bring the entire bond indebtedness to full issue in 1911 instead of 1913, Mulholland replied that an early completion would also bring equalizing benefits as the income from sales of water would also begin a year early. Faced with the necessity of raising $250,000 in additional taxes to pay the interest that would accrue a year earlier because of advancing the program one year, the city council agreed to invest $50,000 of sinking fund money in aqueduct bonds maturing from 1911 to 1918. To seek relief from the bond syndicate's hard terms and to head off a disastrous shutdown on the aqueduct, Mulholland and Mathews by the end of April prepared to go East.[9]

As this crisis mounted, attorney Henry O'Melveny persuaded Mulholland to take time out to visit the Dominguez Rancho where he had once dug artesian wells for old Manuel Dominguez. Now the heirs wished to develop the land and sought advice from Mulholland, who, after one tour over several tracts of the family's holdings, was overtaken by more urgent events so that he was not able to present a preliminary plan until the following October.[10]

A VISIT TO THE HALLS OF MAMMON

In May, Mulholland and Mathews, along with W. J. Washburn, chairman of the city council finance committee, spent three discouraging weeks in New York at the Hotel Belmont while they negotiated with the bond syndicate. Finding only a difficult market and apparently no buyers, Mulholland left Mathews to pursue the problem while he returned alone to take up aqueduct affairs. To anxious Angelenos, all he could offer was hope that things would improve. By late June, with two-thirds of the aqueduct work curtailed, Burt Heinly wrote his friend S. T. Henry, editor of *The Engineering Record*, that the cutbacks were heartbreaking. "Mr. Mulholland is wonderfully courageous," he went on. "He is the only one of the whole bunch who says nothing, but I am with him enough to know that he is thinking a great deal."[11]

While in New York, Mulholland visited his friend and associate J. Waldo Smith, chief engineer of New York City's board of water supply and of the New York Catskill Aqueduct, which would not be completed until 1917. Back in Los Angeles, he wrote to thank Smith for his hospitality and the tour of the Catskill project ("your great work"), also expressing regret that he had been unable to see him again because he had spent his last two days in the hotel with "a severe cold." It must have been a grim two days, for he wrote Smith of "your New York financiers pretty hard games." He described a moment of insight as he had stood on the steps of one of the banks. "I noticed in looking up . . . that the halls of Mammon were fully ten stories higher than the cross of Christ on the steeple of the little church across the way,—a fact which would indicate a degree of degradation that might easily exercise malign and potent influence on the habitues of that region."[12]

After a discouraged Mathews failed to find a buyer for the bonds in the East, he came home and found that civic support was about to rally. First the banker Marco H. Hellman offered to purchase $500,000 of the bonds on behalf of the New York Life Insurance Company. Hellman said he had initiated the sale after a broker came into his bank and bad-mouthed Los Angeles's credit standing. Next, the *Examiner* jumped in, boasting that it had secured a similar offer from Metropolitan Life. As lawyers and city council members huddled to see if they could legally transact a sale without first securing a release from their contract with the eastern bond company, a journal called *Spectator* sounded a sour note, wondering who had muddled affairs by making a contract with an eastern outfit that made "mutts" out of the city. The *Herald* meanwhile engaged in dark talk about the power trust that was thwarting bond sales in its determination to head off Los Angeles's plans to generate municipal electricity from Owens River water.[13]

As local offers to buy bonds came in, a July 11 message to the city council from Mayor Alexander surprised everyone by repeating the *Herald*'s accusation that the power companies were indeed holding up bond sales in the East, but that through a Los Angeles representative other eastern interests had offered to buy $5 million worth of the bonds. He then threw down the gauntlet and served notice on the syndicate that by July 31 it must either buy the bonds or terminate the option. A week later, the crisis ended when the syndicate agreed to sell to the two big insurance companies and also agreed to take up another $530,000 itself. Although this would not be the end of money woes, the aqueduct was back in business for now with $300,000 a month to draw upon. Mulholland hastened to recruit 2,000 men to get the work under way once more. Unfortunately, during the hiatus, many of the miners and mechanics had drifted off to find work in Arizona and Colorado, but as miners were to be paid $3 a day plus bonus for extra accomplishment, many returned, and the Chief remained publicly optimistic that the work could be completed by 1912.[14]

LABOR DISCONTENT

At the end of July, Mulholland and his sons took a brief vacation in the Sierras with a group of men that included Henry O'Melveny and his sons, Van Norman, and Major Henry Lee of the water board. The camping trip over, Mulholland next guided William Humphreys, latest member of the board of public works, over the project just as a dispute broke out over Joe Desmond's demand for an increase in the price of meals to twenty-five cents. Because Humphreys and Chaffee opposed the rise, the aqueduct board denied the request, but the issue was far from resolved. More disquieting to Mulholland, however, were reports of labor troubles at the south portal of the Elizabeth Tunnel, where the miners and muckers were threatening to strike unless the board met their demands for a pay raise. Then, the first week in August, the miners struck. Fifteen walked off, were paid their time, and left camp, while 250 others waited for orders from union headquarters in Denver. Two patrolmen were quickly dispatched from Los Angeles to guard the powder and dynamite stores at the site.[15]

The previous spring, when Mulholland returned from his failed New York mission reflecting on the halls of Mammon and the cross of Christ on Wall Street, the Merchants and Manufacturers' Association (M&M) in his own city had met to pass a resolution favoring the open shop. Shortly thereafter, amid growing tensions between labor and management, the city council unanimously passed a stringent antipicketing ordinance and thus created an obstacle against which previously squabbling unions could unite. The action also demonstrated that the Progressives, or Goo Goos (for good government), were not necessarily good friends of organized labor, for all had supported the ordinance. Although the stiffening attitudes and tensions surrounding labor issues inevitably affected the aqueduct, nothing during its construction equaled the infamous bombing of the Los Angeles Times building in October 1910.[16]

It is fair to say that vested private interests did more to impede the aqueduct than labor problems did. For one thing, aqueduct employees worked a union-approved eight-hour day on a public works project that promised to benefit all the dwellers of the city. In the beginning, at least, the bonus system was not unpopular with the workers; although it involved extra, speeded-up work, its reward of extra pay was a palliative. Moreover, the inaccessibility of the work camps stretched out many miles from each other hindered organizers, while the almost-military surveillance on the line tended to catch anyone suspected of agitating. Yet aqueduct construction always held the potential for labor disputes. Its skilled workers—especially the miners and tunnel men—had a strong union organization, the Western Federation of Miners, while the pipe and steel manufacturers without whose products no aqueduct could be built were notorious enemies of the closed shop and the metal-trades unions. Although General Otis may have been the dominant local voice and symbol of antiunionism, most of the city's leading capitalists and manufacturers shared his stance. Prominent among those affected by the increasing labor hostilities in 1910 were local metal manufacturers and suppliers such as Fred Baker, of Baker Iron Works; John Llewellyn, of Llewellyn Iron Works; and William Lacy, of Lacy Manufacturing Company. After strikes and walkouts in their plants, they became outspoken supporters of the antipicketing ordinance, and in the wake of the shocking *Times* explosion that killed twenty-three workers, both the Baker and Llewellyn works were subjected to less destructive dynamite attempts.

MORE TROUBLE ON THE LINE

With the city still absorbing the seismic shock of the *Times* bombing, the miners on the aqueduct struck a month later after the price of meals increased a nickel to thirty cents and the board failed to authorize a corresponding rise in wages. With dynamite dominating people's thoughts, the aqueduct strike made little news except in the pro-labor *Record,* which called it crippling and devoted a large space to the event. (The *Inyo Register* in Owens Valley also took note.) Not surprisingly, the *Times* gave it withering attention. "Preferring loafing to working, several hundred laborers, mostly miners, on the aqueduct, have quit their jobs, giving as a reason that they would not pay the increased price of mess in the camps." Mulholland, returning from a tour of the aqueduct with Mayor Alexander, made light of the business, saying it was not unusual for men to quit with the approach of cold weather and that 3,000 men were still at work along the line. The mayor said he had heard talk of a strike but had not seen much evidence of one. The *Examiner* investigated and found it "the most harmless strike that ever happened and there are no evidences of it."[17]

The *Record,* however, reported that members of the strike committee had come to Mulholland and told him they had proof that in the mad haste of construction, faulty work had been done, and that he, Mulholland, had accepted worthless work. His reply to them was direct. "All right. Prove it." Rumors of faulty construction had long circulated, especially after one section of concrete along the line had to be replaced because it had frozen before it could set. Mulholland had discussed the problem in his fifth annual report, but the sight of the discarded concrete chunks lying like boulders along several miles of the line had given rise to talk of faulty work. Perhaps to quiet the story, Mulholland challenged newspapermen, "Come on out and look it over. They say there's a lot of bum work . . . I've looked for it and I can't find it. If it's there I want to know. Come out and find it for me."[18]

The *Record* sent its City Hall reporter, Robert E. Rinehart, to cover the story. In his two informative articles on the state of aqueduct construction at that time, he had found Mulholland unduly optimistic, describing him as "persistently cheerful." While he did not deny the strike or conceal its extent, "in his heart he must regret the breaking of his wonderful working organization," wrote Rinehart. "All his division engineers do," he added. With 250 veteran miners and muckers gone, the tunnel work had dwindled, and not a single division on the aqueduct had escaped losses. At Haiwee, almost every veteran had left and been replaced with raw recruits for engineer Phil Wintz to struggle with and get back on line. Desmond's kitchens, however, were doing well, and Rinehart found the food acceptable as did most of the men he interviewed, although one workman told him that "the cook had spread himself for our coming." Finally, after days of probing and interviewing, Rinehart came away with the conclusion that only "a lynx-eyed caviller" could pick a flaw in the building of the aqueduct.[19]

A FESTIVE TREK TO OWENS VALLEY

In the month before the strike, on October 29, another junket to Owens Valley had taken place under the auspices of the *Times* and the Los Angeles Chamber of Commerce. Originally scheduled to coincide with the driving of the silver spike at Owenyo on October 18 to celebrate the almost-completed California-Nevada branch of the transcontinental Southern Pacific line that traversed Owens Valley as far as Owenyo on its way to Los Angeles, the excursion was delayed because of the *Times* bombing and Mulholland's heavy schedule. Lippincott had substituted for the Chief on the platform for dignitaries in Owenyo that day, and editor Chalfant of the *Inyo Register* later described him as a "betrayer of the reclamation project" and complained that he had been granted "a recognition to which he is not entitled."[20]

On October 29, Mulholland joined the delayed excursion, which comprised one hundred of Los Angeles's leading citizens, including at the last minute Mayor Alexander, who suddenly announced that he had never toured the aqueduct and wanted to join. Thus, on a cloudy Saturday morning, the mayor and Mulholland, with their driver, led a fleet of twenty-five automobiles out of town. One of the thrills that day was to drive through the empty aqueduct tunnels that would soon be filled with water destined for the city. After inspection stops at the south and north portals of Elizabeth Tunnel, where General Chaffee joined them, the cars pulled into Mojave by six that evening, the rapid travel time an indication of the improvements in both autos and roads since 1905. Along the rail sidings awaited sleeping cars for the night's rest. At dinner, Mulholland, now something of a cynosure, was overwhelmed by the chant of "What's the matter with Mulholland? . . . He's all right!" After a night spent listening to the clangings and crashings of train movements and shuntings in the yard, they advanced to Haiwee. Greeting them that evening were Fred Eaton, who had taken the newly completed train down from Owens Valley; Joe Desmond, in charge of their food for the weekend; and Lippincott, who assisted in explaining the engineering technicalities of the aqueduct.[21]

Earlier in the day, as they had passed Vasquez Rock, old-timers in the group were stirred to recall stories of Tiburcio Vasquez, who had used the landmark as his vantage point when ambushing miners descending from the Cerro Gordo mines with their bullion. (Among the touring group was former sheriff Uncle Billy Rowland, who had led the posse that captured Vasquez.) That night in Haiwee, after Mulholland had spoken of the challenges of building the Jawbone section and Fred Eaton had told of how he had confided his conception of the aqueduct to the Chief, a small group including Mulholland and former mayor Hazard retired to the aqueduct office and, perched on cracker barrels before bedtime, spun yarns that a captivated reporter described as the "unwritten history of Los Angeles." (Fred Eaton had slipped away on the night train to Independence to help arrange a chicken dinner for the crowd, which would arrive the following evening.) Among the tales told that night was Rowland's rambling account of how Mulholland as a young man had barely escaped being shot for a cattle thief. While riding across a stretch of dry river bed, Mulholland had come upon a well-known Los Angeles character suspected of horse and cattle rustling. The bad man and his associates were busy skinning a black cow. As Mulholland recognized both the men and the cow, he feigned indifference and simply passed by with a "Hello, boys." At nightfall, however, after leaving a lamp lighted in his window to give the appearance of being in his cabin, he struck out for Sheriff Rowland. The thieves had left by the time sheriff and posse arrived but were soon spied over towards Elysian Park, headed in the direction of the San Fernando Valley. As Mulholland followed the pursuit, a shot caused his little mare to bolt, and unable to stop her, he found himself in the cross fire. Stretching out beneath her neck, he clung to her as the bullets whizzed until finally one of the posse shot the thief dead. The reporter concluded from the yarn: "Discretion even in his younger days was part of the Mulholland."[22]

The third day, October 31, the travelers saw the steam shovels at work (still a novel sight for many) and visited the power plant at Cottonwood, where work in that section had been completed. Mulholland was constantly surrounded and barraged with questions. When asked if there were really a bug on the desert that destroyed cement walls, he replied, "Yes. I know all about that bug. Its generic name is the Crocus Knockeritis." After lunch at the hotel in Lone Pine, Mulholland and Chaffee agreed that for the best fried chicken, hot biscuits, and white gravy in town you had to go to "Mother" Green's cottage, a noted local character who had lived in Lone Pine thirty-four years. Their stayover in Independence that night so strained sleeping facilities in the town of 1,500 that several gentlemen slept in the county jail and pronounced it the best accommodations of the trip. A festive Halloween spirit developed when several wives in the party sang a concert on the hotel porch and became so enlivened that they marched to the jailhouse to serenade the sleeping men with such numbers as "Where Is My Wandering Boy Tonight?" and "Locked in the Stable with the Sheep." When they decided to find Mulholland, they entered the garden of the house where he was supposed to be and broke into the strains of "Has Anybody Here Seen Billy, Billy of the Aqueduct?" Doors suddenly opened to reveal a group of townspeople gathered for a Halloween card party. Then "Billy of the Aqueduct" revealed that he had been marching unseen behind the marauding singers, who, in a final burst of bacchanal, proceeded to march down the main street of Independence singing "Hot Time in the Old Town Tonight." Certainly in the

annals of Independence, this evening must rank as one of its odder social occasions.[23]

After a quick trip to Bishop and a visit to Eaton's ambitious chicken
ranch, Mulholland and Mayor Alexander caught a night train out of Mojave. Upon their arrival in the city next morning after a five-day, 650-mile
journey, the sunburned, enthusiastic Mayor Alexander declared he could
hardly find words to express his approval. He had seen the water with
Mulholland and been made a believer. The project was one of the biggest
things ever attempted, and "the man who laid out the line is a great genius. It is a mystery to me how human ingenuity can do such things."[24]

WORK RESUMES WITH NEW
UNDERCURRENTS OF COMPLAINT

This euphoria perhaps strengthened Alexander's resolve to reject the bond
syndicate's offer for the further sale of aqueduct bonds. The city council had been about to agree to a sale that would have cost the city $62,000
in lost premiums, but the mayor vetoed the measure. He was vindicated
in mid-December, when the bond syndicate capitulated to the terms.
Meantime, these matters did not immediately affect work on the aqueduct. Money was sufficient for the coming year; most of the hardest work
had been completed, except for fourteen miles of siphons; and Mulholland was devising new ways to cut costs. The bond strictures did, however, cause a lack of funds to purchase steel pipe for the siphons, which
had to be ordered a year in advance. All of these problems would extend
into the coming year, in addition to grave new ones. Feeling the increasing
pressures, Mulholland wrote Dockweiler in early December that he would
not be able to come north to serve in an important Contra Costa water
case. He expressed his interest in the matter but felt at present, "I would
neither do credit to myself nor be of substantial assistance to my client."
He expanded, "Now problems have arisen here which again precipitate
me into the thick of the fray; namely, the disposal of the surplus waters
of Owens River. Already, I have been charged, by innuendo and all manner of sinister hints, with a desire to favor owners of large tracts of land
in the San Fernando Valley, the instigators of these charges well knowing that inevitably large quantities of the water will be used there, and
an attempt will hence be made to imply that it was the result of undue
influence."[25]

Open sessions on the all-important question of what to do with the
surplus water from Owens River had begun in September. After the se-

crecy and closed-door planning that led to building the aqueduct, the citizens who had paid for the project would now be heard, as would those entities anxious to receive the water, such as the City of Pasadena. At the opening session the night of September 22, Mulholland presented his memorandum of proposals, which he called only "a brief treatment of a very large subject." His central principle was that the City of Los Angeles must have no thought of parting with its rights to the water. He opposed taking in other cities but suggested what he called a bonus system, by which Los Angeles would receive a premium for putting water on the land and also collect an annual rental. These ideas led to a stream of questions and objections as the sessions continued for a week, constituting only an opening exercise in a matter that had no easy solutions. Mulholland was still pondering the question on November 23, when he wrote to ask Frederic Stearns about the proceedings used in organizing Boston's metropolitan water board. Later thanking Stearns for the information he had sent, Mulholland acknowledged that Boston's conditions were very different from those of Los Angeles, which had, in addition to its domestic supply, 135,000 acres of irrigation districts where the water could be used until the domestic need increased. One point he made clear to Stearns: "It is not desired, and it is not probable that the City would ever consent to the sale of the right to a single inch of Owens River water."[26]

CHAPTER 17

Aqueduct Progress and Political Fireworks

1911

A WORK DELAYED

Having maneuvered the shoals of the previous year, Mulholland remained optimistic about the aqueduct's progress in 1911. The city demonstrated its continued faith by offering to purchase $500,000 of its own bonds in order to advance funds when the foot-dragging New York syndicate was reluctant to sell its 1911 subscription. With money available, the work could advance. Only 1,295 feet of granite separated the two Elizabeth Tunnel crews digging and blasting their way through the mountain to the anticipated meeting; the steam shovels, drillers, and concrete workers were progressing across the desert at a rate of five or six miles a month; and the Haiwee Dam was shaping up rapidly. When only the last 86 miles of the aqueduct's 235-mile stretch remained to be completed, a reporter suggested that Mulholland could turn to authorship and compose a treatise describing all the innovative machinery and engineering that the project had introduced and employed. Instead, by year's end, he found himself embroiled in the very brand of politics he had hoped to avoid.

Questions about the electric power to be developed from Owens River water now gained public attention. Was this enterprise to be completely municipal or would private companies (that is, investor-owned utilities) be allowed to coexist? The city's chief electrical engineer, Ezra Scattergood, was adamant that the project be completely municipal, but the private companies, especially California Edison, pushed to come in, and public debate grew heated. Some of the Progressives, including political leader

Meyer Lissner, who had enthusiastically supported the city's water leaders and policies since 1905, did not oppose private power; indeed, they argued that the city should entertain private offers to see if a proposition might benefit and profit the city. The Progressive and pro-labor *Record*, however, had championed publicly owned power since the earliest days of the aqueduct and now urged a straw vote on the issue in an upcoming election on charter amendments. Mayor Alexander agreed, and with the city council, called for its inclusion on the March 6 ballot. The results produced a victory for the amendments and a ten-to-one approval of municipal ownership of power (11,149 to 2,214).[1]

When Mulholland submitted his sixth annual aqueduct report in mid-July 1911, he acknowledged that the suspension of work in the past fiscal year had proven "a very expensive experience" and implicitly abandoned his dream of completion in 1912 but expressed the hope that it would be finished at the time of the original estimate, spring 1913. He could not have predicted the social turmoils that were to culminate in a nasty mayoral campaign during which his reputation was so impugned that he asked for an investigation into the building of the aqueduct.

The costly work stoppage on the aqueduct in 1910 crippled the enterprise so that even when full activity resumed, it had lost its momentum, coinciding with an increasingly unsettled economic and political climate in the city. The labor-connected bombings and deaths in 1910 had hardened lines between labor and management. Symptomatic of the strife's effect on the aqueduct was a letter that Mayor Alexander forwarded to Mulholland at the beginning of the year from a Western Federation of Mines organizer requesting a permit to visit the aqueduct camps and see if any of his members were working there. He already had been refused admittance at several camps, and he questioned their right to keep him out. He also wondered why, if the mayor approved of arbitration, he did not seek it in the "boarding-house grievance" (Desmond's food services). The mayor passed the note along to Mulholland, remarking that he "would not care to interfere in a matter of which I have no personal knowledge." A month later, after miners and other skilled laborers were denied a wage increase of fifteen cents a day to pay for the five-cent increase granted to Desmond, the steam shovel men walked off. As machinists and members of the Western Federation of Mines, they had asked for $4.00 a day and an increase in meal allowance. Mulholland argued that aqueduct workers were already better paid than private employees nearby. For a ten-hour day aqueduct laborers received $3.00 (for either wet or dry work) and $1.00 a day for board; miners received $3.50

for an eight-hour day when they worked in wet ground and $.90 a day
for board. With bonuses they could increase their wages from 10 to 40
percent. The mayor, loath to interfere in aqueduct matters, made no
protest when the aqueduct board turned down the workers' demands,
and unfortunately for the workers, the strike came too late to significantly
dent aqueduct construction. Moreover, Mulholland, anticipating trouble, had already deployed other steam shovel men to take over the work.
The ill feelings generated among certain workers, however, would feed
events later in the year.[2]

GETTING DAYLIGHT

The strike was almost obscured, however, in the jubilation over the Elizabeth Lake Tunnel's completion. Its breakthrough, or "getting daylight,"
occurred toward noon of February 27, when a candle fluttering in the
north section told the men that air was coming from the other side and
that the wall was about to be pierced. Their foreman scrambled up out
of the water in which they were standing to the top of a nearby granite
boulder and shouted, "Hey!" Suddenly the drilling on the other side
stopped, and there came an answering "Hello!" Each foreman, holding
a candle, moved forward until one said, "I can see your nose. Can you
see mine?" Amid the calls and congratulations, arguments began over
which side broke through first. With the final blast of dynamite, Superintendent John Gray said, "If it goes through, it will end the biggest thing
of its kind ever undertaken." When someone reminded him that the Gunnison Tunnel was longer, Gray returned, "Longer, but not so big and not
anywhere near as difficult."[3]

The Elizabeth Lake Tunnel's completion made national news, described in superlatives even by the deliberate *Christian Science Monitor* as "an engineering feat without parallel for low cost and the short
time employed." Begun October 1907, the work had gone on day and
night for almost four and a half years as men, drills, and dynamite tun-
neled through 5.09 miles of granite. It was a marvel of precision, as its
final alignment proved to be out only two and a quarter inches and the
grade only seven-thousandths of a foot. For finishing almost a year ahead
of schedule (the board of engineering experts had estimated five years)
and $411,800 under estimate, great credit went to its two supervisors,
John Gray and William Aston. Gray was next deployed to supervise concrete work at San Francisquito Canyon, while Aston, the man whose abilities the civil service board had once questioned, moved on with four of

his top foremen to superintend the Hilo tunnel about to be constructed across the island of Hawaii.[4]

CHANGES AT CITY HALL

Among the city charter amendments that triumphed at the polls in March was one that abolished the old water board and reorganized it into a new agency, the public service commission. Both Good Government and labor observers had questioned some of the old board's actions, such as Sherman's questionable behavior, and the *Record* had also begun to show signs of disaffection, especially when it discovered that, contrary to the provisions of the city charter, the water commission had since 1908 been allowing the Los Angeles Gas and Electric Company to place settling vats along the west bank of the Los Angeles River. Although the commission swiftly responded by ordering the gas company to vacate, the *Record* still questioned how good a job the water commission was doing in safeguarding the "interests of ALL THE PEOPLE ALL THE TIME."[5]

Members of the old board prepared a survey of its history for the new commissioners, claiming it was a record to be envied by any public agency. Since its original organization in 1902, the board had received $10,134,455.52 and had expended $9,289,402.51 for current expenses and betterments; had turned over to the aqueduct board $580,893.83; and still had $264,159.18 to its credit in the city's water revenue fund. During this same period water service had increased from 23,180 to 66,379 deliveries, and the annual income from $614,264 in 1903 to $1,102,589 in 1910. Beginning with 29 employees, including inspectors and collectors, their numbers had grown to 76 office employees. Of the original 29, 24 were still with the service; 2 had died and 3 resigned. Perhaps of greatest pride to the old-timers was that although receipts in the past year were 79 percent higher than in the administration's first year, the cost of water to consumers was now about 58 percent lower. Moreover, per capita consumption had decreased from 306 to 140 gallons a day. These changes were largely because of an increase in population and the installation of meters.[6]

A week after the new public service organization had celebrated with its first annual banquet, the mayor asked it to organize a power and light bureau headed by Scattergood. (Each of these bureaus, water and power, would operate autonomously under Scattergood's and Mulholland's leadership.) Mulholland meanwhile prepared to lead new members of both the commission and city council on yet another guided tour over the aque-

duct. Highlights on this one included a trolley ride through the five-mile
length of the Elizabeth Tunnel on which the cement work was about to
begin and one councilman's discovery of a fossil oyster more than nine
inches long amid a pile of material excavated for the aqueduct in Dry
Rock Canyon.[7]

The new public service commission began its mission by addressing
the vexing and complex question of irrigation and disposal of excess
water from Owens River. Experts chosen for the panel of consulting engineers included Homer Hamlin, city engineer; John H. Quinton, an old
hand from the United States Reclamation Service who was regarded as
the dean of American irrigation engineers; and William H. Code, new to
Los Angeles but noted as chief inspector of Indian reservation irrigation.
A leery Mulholland noted that the panel was the board's idea—not his—
but acknowledged that they were all experts and "we may learn something from them." Pointing out that more land adjacent to the city needed
water than the city could supply, he asserted, "The supply is nowhere
equal to the demand. Those who believe that we will have more water
than we know what to do with and later will get it cheaper are badly
mistaken. No one will get it any cheaper than those who have mortgaged
their homes to bring it here."[8]

Submitted in July, the consultants' report contained three major conclusions: (1) much of the excess water should be reserved in the underground San Fernando reservoir; (2) districts allotted excess water must
be annexed to the city; (3) these districts would have to pay in advance
the cost of their main distribution conduits. Those disappointed in their
hopes for the water were Pasadena, South Pasadena, and Alhambra and,
in the eastern San Gabriel Valley, Covina, Azusa, and Glendora. Mulholland argued that as they lay higher than the terminus of the aqueduct,
the added work of tunneling and piping would make the cost impracticable. This decision stirred controversy and spawned hostility towards
Mulholland in what came to be known as the high-line fight led by S. C.
Graham, a Progressive opponent of annexation and a proponent of consolidation who advocated carrying water to the east on a "high line."
His critics derided the plan with the old country joke that you can com-
pel water to run uphill—but it will cost you money to do it. Graham argued in turn for a selective system of high water rates to insure the city
a good financial return. While some areas were angered that under the
existing plan only ranchers in the San Fernando Valley could hope to irrigate with Owens River water, Mulholland was also cautioning that re-
serving water for power would make less available to outlying districts

anxious to receive it. Because the promise of water for the San Fernando Valley coincided with the opening sales promotion of the old Lankershim–Van Nuys lands and the founding of the new town of Van Nuys, earlier accusations of a capitalist conspiracy revived with added plausibility. The *Tribune,* recently acquired by Otis's enemy, E. T. Earl, was among the first to raise the issue in an editorial questioning the right of "certain rich men" to profit in land sales based on their speculations in Owens River water. Land worth $50 an acre, it charged, was selling at over $500 an acre on the assurance that it would get water.[9]

At the mayor's request, Mulholland had assembled a water department report, which, in addition to enumerating the trunk-line mains being laid in growing sections of the city, announced the building of a 40-million-gallon reservoir at Ivanhoe to store future Owens River water and also to serve the Hollywood region. Moreover, the creation of the San Fernando Dam would mark a new epoch in the city's water history, he declared, as it would form part of "a very capacious system, which will permit a sustained flow through the Aqueduct during the winter when the consumption is less and the water is not needed, thereby not only serving to perpetuate the flow through the Aqueduct for power purposes, but also providing a greater quantity of water for summer use." By summer, in his sixth annual report, he also anticipated the aqueduct's completion in the spring of 1913. Many of these matters were soon to become grist for the mill of one of Los Angeles's most notorious mayoral campaigns.[10]

FALLOUT FROM THE *TIMES* BOMBING: THE RISE OF JOB HARRIMAN

Labor remained in upheaval throughout 1911 as fresh disputes produced strikes against a candy company, a brewery, and cigar makers. Although the Progressives had achieved political victories with the election in 1910 of Hiram Johnson as governor of California and a Progressive majority in both houses of the legislature, labor found its strongest ally in the Socialist Party. Among the speakers on April 15 at a large labor rally to celebrate the passage of the eight-hour day for women workers was labor attorney Job Harriman, who by year's end, as a candidate for mayor of Los Angeles, was to launch a full-scale attack against Mulholland and his associates. Also in April came the arrest of the McNamara brothers for complicity in the *Times* bombing, and in May, carpenters, other building trades workers, and bakers had gone out on strike. Political collaboration between Socialists and labor increased as Stanley Wilson, editor of the labor newspaper, the *Citizen,* joined the Socialist Party, while Job Harriman, now a member of the McNamaras' defense team, became the Socialist candidate for mayor.[11]

The city's mayoral campaigns were animated and short, but because of increasingly splintered class attitudes in the city, this one became highly acrimonious and drew Mulholland deep into its brambles. On August 6, as the McNamara brothers' trial approached, the Socialist Party staged a kickoff rally at which Harriman laid out their objectives for the city. His major issues were the aqueduct, the harbor, and what he claimed was the unsavory record of the present administration. He intended to prevent Owens River water from being placed on San Fernando Valley lands because it would enhance their value to $1,000 an acre and enrich its owners; he would see the water taken through the city, in sewers and septic tanks if necessary, for its use on a great area that the city would buy and sell and thereby make enough to pay off the aqueduct debt. The Socialist platform promised "to abolish graft in construction of the aqueduct from the Owens River and to extend the municipally owned water system." As there had been no charges of graft from any quarter up to this point, this insinuation smacked of a straw man strategy. Yet because the complexities of the water issue rarely yielded simple or easy explanations, the tactic was effective. Was there graft on the aqueduct? No one had suspected it, but now it became a possibility. Would valley lands sell for $1,000 an acre? Though none did until almost World War II, many believed Harriman's claim. The Socialist campaign pamphlet "The Coming Victory" contained charges so scurrilous and various against the water project that the board of public works prepared a long documented rebuttal.[12]

Many believed Harriman and the Socialists simply because they were uninformed on the subject, knew little or nothing about the San Fernando Valley, and found his theme of the haves exploiting the have-nots plausible because of rising class and economic divisions in the city. Sometimes called "the era of the successful entrepreneur," this period also could have been characterized as the era of the land-grabber, for the people accused of conspiring with the city's water men to enrich their San Fernando Valley lands with Owens River water had been equally assiduous in acquiring land unrelated to the aqueduct project. Since 1901, during the first subdivision of Hollywood, these same men (who included Otis, Chandler, Sherman, Brant, and Whitley) acquired vast tracts in Kings County where they laid out the town of Corcoran; in Kern County where they purchased the 270,000-acre Rancho El Tejon; and along the California-Mexican border where they controlled the C&M Company, a spread of almost a million acres.[13]

Much of what Job Harriman charged was based upon past files of Clover's *Evening News* and the writings of W. T. Spilman. Harriman mocked Mulholland's popularity, called him "Saint Mulholland" or "the sainted Mulholland," essentially called him a liar, and pointed out that he owned 160 acres in the San Fernando Valley, which, "if supplied with water, will become worth $1000 an acre." In the same breath that he complained of graft in the present municipally owned water department he extolled municipal ownership of all public utilities as a panacea. Because he was an attractive and forceful campaigner who drew many to his cause, in September Samuel Gompers visited Los Angeles to urge support of Harriman. On October 31, a Halloween in sharp contrast to the previous year's when Mulholland had been courted and serenaded in the streets of Independence, voters went to the polls and gave Harriman a plurality. Of 45,500 votes cast, Harriman received slightly over 20,000; Alexander, 16,800; and Mushet, Republican and former auditor, 7,500. The final election on December 5 promised to be memorable, for not only would the city's women cast their first votes but a Socialist candidate might well prevail.[14]

Although some writers have dismissed Mayor Alexander as an aging nonentity, he was far from a ninny. At seventy-two, he was a sharp and vigorous administrator who had earlier served two terms on the county board of supervisors. A canny Scotsman from Iowa who referred to himself as "Uncle Aleck" (he sported a goatee for which Harriman accused him of trying to resemble Uncle Sam!), he had fought in the Civil War and settled afterwards in Los Angeles with his wife and daughter. He was a modest landholder-farmer whose subsequent actions vindicated the Progressives' faith in him. He favored women's suffrage and opposed the railroad's high freight rates, even though he was stuck with the bargain former mayor Harper had struck with the Southern Pacific. On the water and power question, he was unequivocal. He considered it the principal issue in the campaign, asserting that the city must distribute light and power at inexpensive rates. "But we are not going to succeed," he warned, "unless we are mighty sharp. The light and power corporations are not going to let us, if they can prevent it." On another hot issue, he protested, "They say I am to 'come through' for some real estate speculators in the San Fernando Valley. Come through with what?" he asked. The city charter, he pointed out, required that "the distribution of water and power must be approved of by two-thirds of the voters," so how could he give away the water?[15]

With the increased possibility of Harriman's victory in December, the *Express* worried editorially, along with most of the business community, that if he were mayor, the city might become anathema to the eastern bond market and be unable to sell its current issues. The *Citizen* rebutted with statements from New York bond dealers who declared Harriman's election would make no difference in their continued business with the city, while an anti-Alexander voice pointed out that the City of Berkeley, which had just elected the state's first Socialist mayor, did not anticipate problems with bond sales. Of the coming election, Lincoln Steffens, in town to cover the McNamara trial, claimed that Harriman's opponents were "atremble" at the possibility of his triumph.[16]

Paralleling the mayoral campaign in November and attracting national attention was the McNamara trial, with famed attorney Clarence Darrow acting for the defense. In this febrile and tense atmosphere, Steffens launched a mission that today seems quixotic: namely, he intended to defuse the labor war and class struggle by bringing together the warring factions and persuading them to be led by the Christian ethic of the Golden Rule. This meant that the General Otises and Samuel Gomperses of the world were somehow to effect a reconciliation by focusing not on blame but on the causes of the social ills that confronted and divided them. Steffens saw the situation in Los Angeles as ideal for testing his theory and, if he is to be believed, persuaded Harry Chandler, and Chandler in turn, General Otis, to consider a settlement of the McNamara case in which the bombers would escape hanging and labor would be let off the hook. On Wednesday, November 29, twenty of the city's business leaders, both conservative and progressive, met to discuss the proposition. As they seemed to find some virtue in his ideas, Steffens gathered together the next day a few other leading citizens whom he considered "insiders." Included among them were Mulholland, Lippincott, Mathews, and C. D. Willard, but as Steffens later related, although they all favored the idea, "they were too public-spirited to count big in my experiment as an experiment."[17]

THE CHIEF TILTS WITH HARRIMAN

Five days before the election, on December 1, the McNamara brothers confessed to bombing the *Times* building. Establishment figures breathed more easily, but Harriman's followers were grief-stricken and angry over the reversal of fortunes. Amid the tears and gloom of campaigners in the Labor Temple, an angry group felt that the McNamaras had betrayed their cause while the most dedicated believed them simply martyrs of the class struggle. The day after the McNamara confession, Mulholland was scheduled to defend his position against Harriman's accusations at a City Club luncheon. Instead of a somber affair, a spirited crowd of three hundred gave three cheers when Meyer Lissner made the introduction. "I want to present the biggest man in Los Angeles—Bill Mulholland." In the spirit of the occasion, the Chief had brought with him a demijohn of Owens River water left over from ceremonies the previous October when President William Howard Taft had dedicated the Buena Vista Bridge. Offering it around to those sitting at his table, he asserted its purity by declaring that it was as sweet now as then. His speech was long and repeated many of the points he had already presented to an audience of six hundred women on November 27. He said he was before them "as parliamentarians say, on a question of personal privilege." He did not intend a campaign speech but wished to elucidate "some matters that were falsely presented to the public. Not only he, but the present administration, his associates, and the work of the aqueduct had been maligned and their acts distorted."[18]

He began with Harriman's charge that Mulholland had put a valuation of $3 million on the private waterworks in 1901. Not true, he protested, going through the old valuations presented long ago at the arbitration hearings and recalling that his had been $1,732,541. He had heard that Mr. Harriman referred to him as Saint Mulholland. "Well," he mused, "I got to looking at myself in the glass and I couldn't see much semblance to a saint, a man past middle age, with a tendency to corpulence and all the other features that a man of my time of life who has lived an active life usually presents." But, he explained, after the laughter died down, "I found he is addicted to that sort of thing. I can excuse him for his representations of me being a saintly man, because he refers to himself in the placards all over the city as the modern Abraham Lincoln." This brought down the house, as Mulholland proceeded to answer more Harriman accusations. He said a famine was created "not by God all Mighty who controls the rain . . . but by the Board of Water Commissioners of the City of Los Angeles and the saintly William Mulholland." After refuting various charges with a battery of figures for rainfall and water consumption, he apologized for the length of his speech but then continued with documentation of water use, pointing out that Los Angeles goes eight or nine months each year without rain, and that because of its beautification (lawns, trees, plants, flowers) and because its streets "require constant sprinkling under the aridity of our climate and the wind that blows here in the afternoon," consumption of 300 gallons and over was not unusual.

He touched on the old canard about water being run into the outfall sewer, reviewed the history of the aqueduct's construction, and explained why it should terminate in the San Fernando Valley: "Because it is the logical geographical spot." He pretended to puzzle over the title of Harriman's campaign pamphlet, "The Coming Victory." "Oh, what was it called? 'The Coming Calamity?'" *(Laughter and applause.)*

As to releasing water in the San Fernando Valley, the chief announced that he would just "as leave think of turning a band of wild steers down Main Street here as of turning that water loose across the San Fernando. To run 20,000 inches of water to the Los Angeles River would create 'something appalling.'" Nowhere did an official document exist that even hinted of such an intent, he insisted. Yet the rumor persisted. "Why, my telephone is almost worn out by people asking me about turning the water across the San Fernando Valley." He said even his wife had taken to complaining about his speaking of it so often and wondered why he did not just publish a denial in the newspapers.

Harriman had declared he would not allow a drop of Owens River water in the San Fernando Valley, but he also chastised the city's water men for depriving the valley people of their water. Mulholland reviewed the legal struggles over the city's right to the Los Angeles River waters and then turned to the accusation that the city had colluded with the land syndicates. Now he spoke his piece on his relationship with General Harrison Gray Otis:

> It may astonish you, gentlemen, when you know that I have been in public life here for over a quarter of a century, occupying a position with a fair degree of prominence and in the public eye a great deal, and yet I have never met General Harrison Gray Otis but twice in all that time to speak to him; and if he walked into this room and I wasn't on this platform and his attention not specially called to me, I know he wouldn't know me. I pass him dozens of times on the streets without even the ignorant off-hand nod that you read of in the magazines, not a sign of recognition. I don't know him myself at all. I have spoken to him twice; once on official business and the other time on a matter of indifference. I met him in a picture store, by the way, one Christmas Eve. That is the extent of my acquaintance with Gen. Otis. He has lambasted me good and hard on the back, possibly when I deserved it, but par-

ticularly with reference to the suits against the people of the San Fernando Valley using water of the Los Angeles River.

E. T. Earl, he said, happened to be the owner of the building where the aqueduct offices were housed, but his encounters with him also had been only few and casual. They met occasionally in the elevator and Earl sometimes asked him how the aqueduct was getting along, but that was the extent of the acquaintance. With some of the land syndicate, he admitted to unfriendly relations, but named only L. C. Brand, whom Mulholland had angered in a water contest.

Then he rounded back to the question of the aqueduct's terminus. Not only was the northern point in the San Fernando Valley a logical site in the direction toward Los Angeles, but it was also at the proper elevation. At 1,450 feet above sea level, it enjoyed "a commanding position to take the water wherever we can find customers." He acknowledged that he owned land in the San Fernando Valley, "a pretty good dry land proposition. It is away up in the west end of the valley. That land has been open for years and there is lots of it there yet to be bought by anybody. It is no crime to buy it, no sedition against this city to buy a piece of land there." He pointed out that Harriman owned land in the San Gabriel Valley, that many owned land in Southern California. In fact, did anybody know of any land that somebody didn't own? They all needed water, but the city did not intend to make a present of it. The people, those "who have gone down in their jeans to pay for it, need not fear that the water would be wrested from them." For "the law is so fixed" that this could never happen.

Finally, he understood that he might be discredited if he were to say that "the aqueduct will last as long as the pyramids of Egypt or the Parthenon of Athens . . . that would sound as though I was trying to be grandiloquent or something like that. But I will tell you that the aqueduct will at least endure until Job Harriman is elected Mayor of the City of Los Angeles." (*Great applause.*)

Three days later, almost 137,000 of Los Angeles's 180,000 eligible voters went to the polls and gave Mayor Alexander a comfortable majority of slightly more than 34,000 votes. Yet with all the twists, turns, and reversals of fortune, Harriman still managed to receive 51,423 votes, a constituency that would underpin labor's continued bitter struggle. A week after the election, to counter the serious charges against himself and the aqueduct in the heat of the campaign, the Chief recommended, with the board of public works' support, that the city council create a committee

to investigate the aqueduct project. In turn, the defeated Socialists planned
to retaliate during the investigation. At their December convention, on
Harriman's suggestion, they demanded representation on the investigating committee proportional to the election results (two Socialists on a committee of five), and they listed twelve questions to be answered, covering
much the same ground as Mulholland had in his speech.[19]

CHAPTER 18

The Investigation

1912

A SEA OF TROUBLES

If 1909 can be reckoned as the year when everything went right during the building of the aqueduct, 1912 should be remembered as the one when everything went wrong: the year when Mulholland's old dream of keeping the city's water affairs out of politics was shattered in the bitter aftermath of the *Times* bombing and the deeply divisive 1911 mayoral campaign. Given the amount of sniping and insinuation aimed at the aqueduct during the campaign of 1911, Mulholland and the aqueduct advisory board probably had no choice but to request an investigation, even though the process opened a Pandora's box from which flew a cloud of spiteful and cantankerous imps. No absurdist drama by Ionesco surpasses the aqueduct investigation board's gyrations, from its preliminary skirmishes to its final conclusion that, although it found no significant fault or malfeasance on the aqueduct project, opportunities for graft did exist, and if more time (and money) had been granted, it might have unearthed something.

After the Socialists demanded that the aqueduct investigation board (hereafter, AIB) have five members, with two Socialists to reflect the party's share of the vote in the previous election, the council opted for a panel of three engineers. The angered Socialists made good their threat to submit the matter as an initiative measure in a special election at the end of May. Until May, when the voters finally approved by a margin of 867 votes an investigation along the lines the Socialists proposed, little was accomplished other than raising hackles and spreading innuendo.

The conflict reflected the shifts in city government as certain Good Government proponents allied themselves with the Socialist-labor bloc while others briefly coalesced with conservative elements to combat what they regarded as the socialist menace, the extremism of the Harriman forces, and the discontents of labor. Not surprisingly, because the aqueduct was the largest public works project the city had ever undertaken, it also became the logical focus for controversy.[1]

After a flurry of fact-finding by detectives sent to gather data along the aqueduct and look for evidence of faulty construction or other grounds for criticizing the project, an initial report yielded only picayune faults (some mismanaged warehouses and theft, but no graft) while Mulholland himself had already documented the larger problems in his 1911 annual report (poor concrete construction, not from improper engineering but from "bad fortune"; the $140,000 spent on Caterpillar tractors that had proved inadequate on the rough terrain and had been abandoned in favor of mules). Other charges proved without merit, fostered by prejudiced parties living in the vicinity: that the main dam at Haiwee did not go down to bedrock, and that the water was not fit for use. With such meager and inconclusive testimony, board member Charles E. Warner announced that the committee would have to begin to subpoena persons alleged to have important information concerning the aqueduct work.[2]

Warner, who became the leading board member in the investigation, was an electrical engineer who had come to Los Angeles in 1908 after work in Vancouver, B. C.; Nova Scotia; and San Juan, Puerto Rico. Hired to inspect metal work and wiring in the city's newly completed Hall of Records, he afterwards become a confidential advisor to Mayor Alexander in an examination of telephone and electric light rates. Although identified as a member of Good Government, he had tangled with another Good Government man, Meyer Lissner, during the phone and light rate evaluations. Before setting out on an inspection tour of the aqueduct with two fellow investigators (engineers of an older and more conservative stripe), Warner not inconspicuously signaled his departure by being photographed in the get-up he was going to wear along the aqueduct: hobnailed boots, puttees, work pants, and a red flannel shirt. "Warner to Probe Aqueduct Disguised as Laborer," proclaimed the *Times*.[3]

SHARP WORDS AND INSOMNIA

When Arthur P. Davis of the Reclamation Service returned at this time from an aqueduct tour and acknowledged that no doubt mistakes had been made but it was "the best piece of work of a big project I have ever seen," Mulholland must have appreciated the generous words, for the stress of the job and the increasing dissension on all fronts was beginning to take its toll. (At home, too, his wife had begun her struggle with the cancer that eventually took her life.) He had consulted Dr. Powers about his insomnia and had been advised, "Rest and forget the existence of the aqueduct." Mulholland's idea of a "cure," however, was to wander through City Hall visiting old and new acquaintances, to whom he would confess, "The strain and the responsibility have shattered my health." He looked forward, he said, to a long rest.[4]

Mulholland's temper had grown shorter and his tongue sharper. In a long-standing disagreement, members of the San Fernando Mission Land Company, led by L. C. Brand, contended that the site of the San Fernando Reservoir had jeopardized certain of their lands and made claims against the city for flood damages sustained after heavy spring rains. The Chief, who was frequently at the dam site overseeing work, blew up in a denial of the charges and later wrote a note of apology to the company's agent, John Wilson, for his immoderate language. At the same time, in answering those who believed that the aqueduct had been built for favored land syndicates in the San Fernando Valley, after conceding that the land had been gobbled up, that the capitalists had captured the unearned increment, and that price hikes would slow the country's growth for the next twenty years, he made a wildly exaggerated claim during the Harriman campaign, often quoted as evidence that untold millions were made in the San Fernando Valley's so-called land grab. "Arable lands," he lashed out, "which should be selling at about $100 an acre have been seized by a few capitalists who have forced the prices to $1000 an acre." In fact, no record exists that any land in the San Fernando Valley then sold for that amount. Top prices for lots in the fledgling towns of Van Nuys and Owensmouth (Canoga Park) ranged from $250 to $500.[5]

The uncertainties of financing the aqueduct also exacerbated Mulholland's insomnia as Mathews again traveled to New York in February to find bond buyers. The New York bond syndicate, having noted the many municipal projects under way in Los Angeles (harbor, municipal railway, power distribution system, and park extensions), had refused its option to buy more aqueduct bonds until the city set a debt limit. By early April, however, the untiring attorney had succeeded in selling what bonds were necessary for continued progress on harbor and aqueduct construction, as well as for the development of electrical power.[6]

THE INVESTIGATORS COMMENCE

While the AIB was on its ten-day inspection tour of the aqueduct, Mulholland submitted his plans for distributing Owens River water, a sixty-page report that outlined delivery to the City of Los Angeles from the San Fernando reservoirs. It described the trunk lines that would carry the water and named the outlying cities that would also be served—altogether an area of 195,000 acres. A week later, while the council and other officials pondered this document of charts and complexities, the investigating committee returned from its tour a day early. Despite encountering snowstorms and mud, they had learned a great deal, but they would not make any statements until they had written their report.[7]

Within the week, however, Warner, with his showboat tendencies at full throttle and much against the wishes of his two colleagues, who considered the action premature, issued his own report, which focused on bad food and the need for better wages, ground already covered by the Socialists. After indicting Desmond, the report concluded with the gratuitous suggestion that humans should at least be treated as well as mules. The mayor, who had been his chief supporter, now accused Warner of impugning Mulholland's ability and integrity. Warner replied that he had never mentioned Mulholland's name, but "Uncle Aleck" labeled that mere sophistry and answered that as chief engineer of the project Mulholland was inevitably maligned by implication in such an assault. Meyer Lissner, now thoroughly hostile to Warner, had the *Tribune* reprint a piece he had written lauding Mulholland for *The American Magazine*. A week later, the division engineer and foreman at Grapevine and Sand Canyon sent Mulholland a report denouncing Warner's criticisms, which he felt were motivated by some animus rather than a plain desire to obtain facts. Warner had been in camp for one night, he claimed, had dined with him at the private club in the canyon, and never saw the mess rooms at meal times. (Warner rebutted this, saying he did not have to eat in the mess, as he already had testimony from workingmen who had.)[8]

Mulholland reserved his opinion of Warner for a later date, although he did complain at the time that the statements were unjust and seriously reflected upon his own management and reputation. General Chaffee, however, responded swiftly. First, he criticized Warner for issuing the report without consulting either him or Mulholland; next, he peremptorily renewed Desmond's contract with the aqueduct and awarded him a new one for the power bureau construction camps in San Francisquito Canyon. With battle lines drawn for a full-scale showdown, Warner, who had taken to his bed with rheumatism after the rigors of the first Owens Valley trip, offered to resign from public service. Rallying, however, he promised to fight back with a full store of ammunition. After a spirited debate, the city council approved Desmond's contracts with only one dissenting vote from a councilman sympathetic to Warner.[9]

As the AIB prepared to leave town for its second tour in early April, Warner defended himself in an appearance before the Alembic Club, a reform-minded organization whose membership included Socialists and Progressives such as Dr. John R. Haynes. Warner declared that he had been a Good Government man and that for years he had heard nothing but good about the aqueduct, had even remained skeptical about the Socialists' bad reports in the recent political campaign. Now, however, his experiences on the investigating committee had persuaded him otherwise. His chief barbs were for Chaffee and Desmond, as he insisted that no private contracts should have been granted on the aqueduct. Yet upon his return from a second inspection tour on April 17, he moderated his stance and reported that food conditions were somewhat improved.[10]

A CONSPIRACY THEORY

In the midst of this furor, Major Henry T. Lee of the public service commission died at seventy-one after a brief illness. He and Mulholland had been fellow partisans for the city since the days of the private water company, and his death not only meant the loss of a friend and ally but created a second vacancy on the public service board, which the mayor's new appointments were about to wrench with conflict. The two new members, both Good Government men (that is, Progressives), were soon to clash with Mulholland over proposals for distributing surplus aqueduct waters. Within weeks, another member of the commission resigned in disgust over the board's disharmony, and the mayor then made the unpopular move of naming his private secretary to the board, who by voting for himself, was able to become president of the commission, thus pushing out old-timer del Valle. This loss of the old with the emergence of new, not always congenial, associates who lacked their predecessors' knowledge and background soon proved another thorn in Mulholland's side.[11]

During these springtime turmoils, a seventy-one-page pamphlet began to circulate around town, doubtless calculated to influence the voters' decision at the May election on whether to continue the aqueduct investigation. The *Municipal News* (itself a new venture in Good Government journalism) announced in April that the Alembic Club had just printed a booklet on the aqueduct controversy entitled *The Conspiracy: An Exposure of the Owens River Water and San Fernando Valley Land Frauds*. Its author was none other than that ancient adversary of the city's water establishment, W. T. Spilman. As an effective propaganda instrument, it proved durable. Beginning in the factual manner of an engineering report, it sets out to establish that Los Angeles has ample nearby water resources but then gradually heightens an attack against the power structure of Los Angeles—government, business, industry, press, and engineers—claiming a collusion against a hard-pressed tax-paying citizenry in order to profit certain capitalists and land specula-tors. It repeats old charges of an artificial water famine and the unnec-essary secrecy of the Owens River scheme from Spilman's "Veritas" letters of 1907. As the language grows increasingly melodramatic with references to "dark and vile recesses," Spilman charges that the news-papers constitute a great combine that lies to the people, suppresses in-formation, and ruins reputations so that a few wealthy gentlemen can enjoy their millions. The tract ends with a small photograph of one for-lorn billboard standing amid scrub weeds and brush against a moun-tain background. Its caption, END OF THE LOS ANGELES AQUEDUCT, is accompanied by the following text:

> Thirty miles from Los Angeles, a dismal hole in the hill, strung about with debris and wreckage, lonely, deserted and desolate, marks the end of the Owens River Aqueduct. The signboard shown above was erected by the en-gineers. This stands a living monument, a confession of the conspirators that they deceived the people of Los Angeles when they drew such glowing word pictures of the pure water coming down from the base of the snowclad Sier-ras piped into their home. . . . The end of the Aqueduct is miles away. The in-vestigation is far from its end. It has but begun. There will be no signboard marking the end of the genuine investigation until the mask shall be torn from the faces of the exploiting hypocrites who pose as public benefactors.[12]

Mulholland received an early copy of *The Conspiracy* and sent his eval-uation to the AIB on April 16. After dismissing the publication as "too frantic and hysterical to require any notice whatsoever," he addressed only one point in which Spilman, in order to demonstrate that the aque-duct was unnecessary, contended that the local water supply from win-ter rainfall in the San Fernando Valley was greater than either Mulhol-land or Lippincott had claimed; that, indeed, it amounted to "almost double the capacity of the Croton Aqueduct which supplies New York with water, the capacity of which is 300,000,000 gallons daily." Mul-holland's refutation follows:

By turning to page 10 where the document attempts to deal with the origin of the water supply of the city of Los Angeles, it will be noticed that by the method of computing the run-off, all of which the writer of the pamphlet claims to be available for use by the City of Los Angeles, he takes the total rainfall over the whole watershed and assumes it to be without waste either for evaporation, plant life or any other source of loss and resolves it into a continuous stream of even flow throughout the year. Manifestly this reasoning will deceive no one, for even if it were assumed that the whole watershed were roofed with tin or other impervious material, the resulting stream would come no where near aggregating the total volume of the rainfall.

There are very few watersheds in Southern California with our meagre rainfall that will yield ten per cent of the volume of precipitation on an average. In fact we have occasional years here—we have experienced several of them in succession—when the runoff of some of our watersheds reaches the vanishing point.

I am prepared in a single day's examination to show Your Board both by physical observation, oral testimony of men who are familiar with all the flow of the San Fernando Basin and by documentary data relating to gaugings and extending over long periods of time that the winter sources of the Basin were long since fully utilized. Also; I am prepared to show that the Narrows Tunnel, which the author of this document declares to be useless, recovers practically all of the sub-flow passing down the Valley at that point.

I present this statement, apologizing to Your Board for the implied discounting of your intelligence by even this brief reference to the document.[13]

Another longtime bugbear, Frederick Finkle, now reappeared to demand an investigation of the quality of cement produced by the city's plant at Tehachapi. His group claimed to have been retained by the American Portland Cement Company to test the city's cement, but after they charged that they had been denied test samples, Mulholland exploded, declaring that their request was made in bad faith and that they had gone along the aqueduct in "a skulking manner": "They never came near my office to ask for permission to get the samples desired," he accused, "but sneaked up there [to Monolith] and at one place represented themselves as members of the city's investigating committee, and at another as reclamation engineers." He also accused Finkle of being "a professional disturber."[14]

WHERE WILL OWENS RIVER WATER GO?

By mid-May, only twenty-six miles of aqueduct remained uncompleted and hopes were expressed for water by the beginning of 1913, yet the question of distributing surplus water remained unsettled. Of the 20,000

inches of water that the aqueduct would soon deliver, the city, presently
needed only 2,000. To decide how the overage should be distributed, three
general questions had to be settled:

1. What districts should be served? Should Los Angeles insist upon
    annexation of cities needing water?
2. Who should pay for the distributing system? Should Los Ange-
    les own all pipe lines?
3. What price should Los Angeles charge for the water?[15]

For the next two months Mulholland attended meeting after meeting addressed to these questions. He listened to groups from Pasadena, Santa
Monica, Glendale, Long Beach, and the San Fernando Valley clamor for
aqueduct water. He heard Pasadena object to annexation because Los
Angeles had saloons, heard Santa Monica conversely complain that the
city closed saloons on Sunday so that "a man had to buy a meal in order to obtain a glass of beer." He had to explain that San Pedro, in the
midst of a water famine, had tied its own hands by signing a thirty-year
franchise with the private Terminal Island Water Company, about which
he was later to quip that to buy it would be like "accepting a present of
a case of the itch." He was often attacked, sometimes treated to insults.
During one harangue, a reporter described him as keeping his eyes glued
to the ceiling throughout the diatribe.[16]

He remained adamant that any city or town that received aqueduct
water should pay for its own distribution system. "Los Angeles should
not spend one dollar on a distribution system," he declared, to which
the new water commissioner, S. C. Graham, took issue, citing a report
in April that argued the city should lay mains and pipes in order to supply maximum amounts to outlying territories, thereby insuring a steady
market, keen competition, and by maintaining water running at full capacity, the production of electric power. Graham especially wanted to
see delivery to the eastern San Gabriel Valley on what became known as
the high line. This policy drew support from none other than Mulholland's special antagonist, Frederick Finkle, who declared he had severed
his connections with Edison Company but remained a foe of the city's
power plans and leaders. Also soon to clash with Mulholland was another Graham ally on the public service commission, Good Government
appointee attorney Charles Wellborn.

Although the commission in mid-May acceded to Mulholland's plan
to create the Franklin Canyon Dam and Tunnel through the Hollywood
hills as part of the trunk line into the city, they had agreed upon nothing

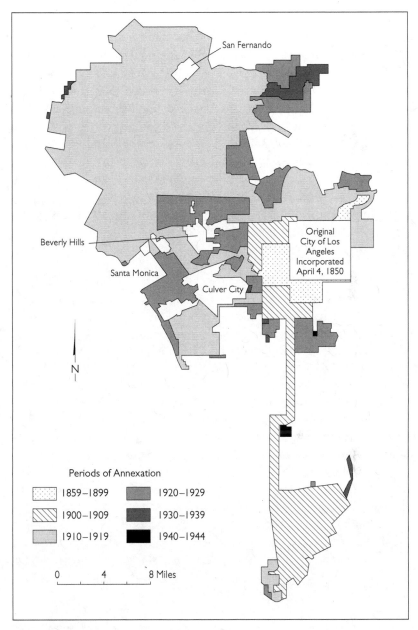

San Fernando

Original
City of Los
Angeles
Incorporated
April 4, 1850

Beverly Hills

Santa Monica

Culver City

N

Periods of Annexation

1859–1899   1920–1929

1900–1909   1930–1939

1910–1919   1940–1944

0   4   8 Miles

Map 4. Annexations to the City of Los Angeles, 1899–1944 (Bureau of
Governmental Research, University of California at Los Angeles).

else and Mulholland's patience was wearing thin. It snapped during a night session at the end of May when Wellborn remarked that after reading the reports, he doubted if Los Angeles needed Owens River water then or ever. Mulholland angrily rounded, "I am sorry that I ever had anything to do with the aqueduct. At the beginning there was a lot of you fellows pushing the aqueduct proposition along and you are now trying to delay things. We are holding these conferences night after night and getting nowhere. There are but two things to be done. Find out what territory you are going to sell the surplus water to and how much you are going to charge for it." This outburst seems to have settled down the committee to a serious policy discussion, during which Mulholland repeated his opposition to Graham's idea of demanding high prices for water. "All this talk about charging thirty, forty, and fifty dollars an acre for water is ridiculous," he insisted. "If you charge more than $10 an acre, there will be an interference with the prosperity march that is attracting so many strangers to the beautiful Southland." Commissioner Davidson voiced his belief that any municipality that wanted water should annex itself to Los Angeles, but no one seemed interested in dealing with that issue.[17]

After the stormy night session, a partial compromise was effected after attorney Mathews agreed with Wellborn and Henderson on a contract plan that combined Mulholland's insistence that each district receiving water should pay for its own distribution system and Graham's desire to put the water where it would pay the most. Fifteen-year contracts were to be issued for each inch of available surplus water (that is, 18,000 contracts) at ten dollars an acre. As one inch of water could irrigate seven and a half acres (based on a miner's inch, which was equivalent to almost 13,000 gallons of water every twenty-four hours), an owner could estimate the number of contracts he would need for his particular acreage. Tentative estimates of the proposed fees indicated that the method would be a money-maker for the city, but the city charter required a majority vote of the citizens before such a system could be put in place.[18]

Announcement of the contract plan provoked public debate, Finkle being among the first to offer opinions that bore a powerful resemblance to Graham's and Wellborn's (whom he had doubtless influenced). At a public lecture, he announced that he did not believe the city would ever use aqueduct water for general municipal service, and therefore the system of distribution (the high line) that he recommended would foil the designs of the land speculators and exploiters in the San Fernando Valley to seize the water. If the city charged high rates for the water (which Mulholland opposed), land profiteers would have to pay, and the city would profit accordingly. His argument proved to be a siren song to voters later in the year.[19]

The water commission's affairs seemed to unravel after another resignation left del Valle the solitary "old man" among a Good Government majority. In the meantime, Warner returned from yet another tour conveniently timed to coincide with the impending election, when voters would decide whether to continue the aqueduct investigation. Accompanying him was a reporter from the *Record* who published a bleak account of profiteering doctors and terrible, overpriced food managed by the careless Desmond. After voters approved continuing the investigation, the *Record* insisted upon calling the exercise the "People's Aqueduct Investigation" as it continued to denigrate the city's water establishment.[20]

SOME COMPLETIONS AND A MISHAP

At the end of May, plans began for the first stage of the aqueduct distribution system, the Franklin Tunnel between the San Fernando Valley and Franklin Canyon Reservoir, which would deliver water to Hollywood, Inglewood, Redondo Beach, and the areas west and southwest of the city. Even with the end in sight, between 2,000 and 3,000 men remained employed on the aqueduct at over forty work camps. On June 1, $2.5 million remained for the aqueduct's completion, and General Chaffee announced that if no accidents occurred the work would be finished with that amount on June 1, 1913. By now great salvage sales were disposing of equipment and material from the aqueduct, and discussions began over whether to sell the cement plant. The good news that the giant siphons at Jawbone and Soledad had been completed and were being tested came against the counterpoint of AIB charges that aqueduct mules were being improperly fed with hay containing foxtails. Although a flood at Cottonwood had destroyed an embankment, Mulholland estimated that the damage would not exceed $1,000, and in his seventh annual report (the last before the final report in 1916), he described the year along the aqueduct as one of "quiet industry." Still, the continuing attacks and accusations in the city had eroded morale, so that on June 14, as a sign of support, Mulholland and the advisory board sent letters of endorsement, praise, and approval to the engineers, officials, and workers along the aqueduct.[21]

To acknowledge the good work and to counteract some of the bad press resulting from the investigation and squabbles over water distribution, the Chamber of Commerce announced an evening smoker on June 18 to hear the latest progress reports on the aqueduct. It promised to be a grand affair in Agricultural Park, where a new art-glass ceiling portraying scenes of California's history was to be illuminated for the first time with power lights. Twelve hundred guests were expected, but the AIB struck a discordant note when, to demonstrate its independence from such doings, it issued a letter the day before the affair announcing that it was leaving on yet another tour of inspection, this one without two of the original committee members, who had refused to join them.[22]

These sparrings were suddenly pushed to the back pages when on early Sunday morning, June 16, the worst accident in the aqueduct's construction occurred. A dynamite explosion in the Clearwater Tunnel caved in the tunnel roof. Three men were killed instantly, while four others, badly injured, had to dig and claw their way to freedom. Many of the crew, largely Russian, who were timbering farther down the tunnel were also hurt by falling rock and debris. One mule survived and could be heard bawling within the dark earthen tomb from which it was rescued the following day. It was a sad ending for Superintendent John Gray after his record-breaking performance on the Elizabeth Tunnel, especially as one of the severely injured was his own son, Louis. The coroner's jury returned a verdict of "accidental powder explosion from causes unknown." A month later, more violence occurred in the same tunnel when a Russian named Boronoff and a Mexican named Morias fought a duel almost to the death with their miners' picks. Morias, the larger, had been bullying Boronoff for weeks, according to John Gray, and although savagely wounded by the enraged Russian, survived after a week in the hospital.[23]

Death and mayhem notwithstanding, the AIB continued its inspection tour while, according to which paper one read, a crowd of either 1,500 (*Examiner*), 2,500 (*Express*), or 3,000 (*Tribune*) gathered at the Exposition Building in Agricultural Park to greet Lieutenant Governor A. J. Wallace and to give a standing ovation to the man of the hour, William Mulholland. Wallace praised the city's water project and compared it to New York's, which was costing $160 million to bring water ninety miles to an already moist region, while Los Angeles's was costing only $24 million to bring half as much water 240 miles, mostly through an arid waste. He congratulated the people of Los Angeles on having a man who had accomplished this remarkable feat of engineering sagacity. Mulholland in turn revealed that when he first came to Los Angeles and was puzzling over what to do with his life, he heard a Spaniard say, "*El agua es la sangre de la tierra*" (Water is the blood of the soil). Struck by the phrase, he began his study of hydrography. Then, aided by a stereopticon, he presented views of the aqueduct, tunnels, lakes, and mountains to accompany his story. The *Record* sounded its sour note with an editorial column questioning Mulholland's candor, raising doubts about the purity of Owens River water, and marveling that men who probably considered themselves hardheaded businessmen could have sat and listened to an evening of such dubious statements.[24]

As a kind of rebuttal, Mulholland submitted a progress report to the advisory board stating that only twenty-two and a half miles of aqueduct remained to be completed. He spoke of the tunnel accident, saying that while such an occurrence was not unusual in this type of work, someone on the job doubtless had been careless or inadvertent. A rule now in place prohibited placing a cap on the fuse at the site where the powder was placed.[25]

MULHOLLAND ON THE HOT SEAT

How divided opinions about the aqueduct had become may be gauged by noting that a day after the *Record*'s attack on Mulholland, the main speaker at the Los Angeles High School commencement exercises, Colonel J. J. Steadman of the board of education, singled him out as an example of a man with a vision—not a visionary, he added—but one who was willing to see the bigness of things without losing sight of the practicalities involved in achieving the goals. The aqueduct and the Panama Canal both figured in his oration, which predicted a bright future for the city and urged those about to enter its life as young adults not to be afraid of work. Among those graduating was Mulholland's son Perry, who later sailed to San Francisco with his father, who was to consult with engineers over his and Lippincott's report earlier that year concerning the development of groundwaters in the Livermore Valley, as well as his latest report on the proposed Calaveras Creek Dam. Afterward, they took the Shasta Limited to Seattle to attend a session of the American Society of Civil Engineers, where Mulholland delivered an address on the aqueduct. After this busman's holiday, he was back at his desk on July 5, replying to a letter from former senator Frank Flint, who as a property owner in La Cañada wanted to know when the proposed high line would be built.[26]

Mulholland's answer to Flint must have reminded Mulholland of what lay ahead, as he politely explained that the board would have to make the decision on the high line. Still, he could not suppress his own opposition to the plan as he warned that the construction would be slow, expensive, and that considerable time would elapse before such a pipeline could be made ready for the water. "One single item of the survey as it now stands is a tunnel with a length a little over four miles," he explained. "This would be comparable only with the five-mile Elizabeth tunnel of the Aqueduct by which the Owens River is to be carried under the crest of the Coast Range, and which it has taken us about four years to excavate and line."[27]

Mulholland spent much of July giving evidence, beginning with the AIB on July 10. A spirit of vindictiveness pervaded the hearings from the outset, even in the manner by which Mulholland and General Chaffee were summoned to appear. While riding together in a July 9 parade to celebrate the departments of municipal government, they were accosted and slapped with subpoenas. Mulholland, who had seen the most difficult parts of his master work accomplished in good shape, who had weathered the economic crisis of 1910, and who had received the general approbation of the engineering fraternity, was now to have his competence and integrity challenged in a hearing that at times resembled a kangaroo court and at others sank into a morass of insinuations and accusations. An *Express* reporter commented that during Mulholland's first appearance "the attitude of the investigators was rather as if they were trying to show that the city had acted crookedly or ruthlessly . . . or as if the investigators were attorneys for the persons who lost to the city in the contests decided by the United States land office in those contests over water rights and water-bearing lands." He concluded that the controlling members of the board seemed more politically motivated and hostile to city government, past and present, than actually concerned with the quality of the aqueduct. Rumors circulated that the committee was acting under orders from the Socialist Party, and one disgruntled engineer claimed Warner had made a deal with the Socialists for their support in a future mayoral race, a charge that he denied.[28]

In the midst of the several days of Mulholland's testimony, two of the original committee resigned and submitted a twenty-five-page report that approved the aqueduct project and protested the manner of the investigation. This bombshell raised the question of the remaining committee's legitimacy, but the court quickly validated it, and the investigation proceeded. Mulholland soldiered on with the process he himself had set in motion. At one session he blurted that the aqueduct was worth $100 million to the city, and as if to fight fire with fire—or perhaps even to lighten the tone with the Socialist committeemen—declared it the biggest socialistic proposition in Los Angeles, as it was being built for the entire community. His inquisitors remained implacable and humorless as they interrogated him for minute details on technical water data in the San Fernando Valley. At one point, when asked what percentage of rains ran off from the surface of all portions of the watershed having an elevation of 2,500 feet, Mulholland responded, "What kind of a memory do you think I have?"

"You've been making a study of these things for years, you say, and yet you can't answer that question?" sneered his questioner.

Mulholland retorted, "You've been studying law for years but you couldn't give me a citation without going to a book and looking at it."[29]

Asked about rumors that Fred Eaton had robbed the city by obtaining land in Owens Valley, Mulholland replied, "God bless him! I'd like to see a monument a mile high in his honor when the aqueduct is done. I've known him intimately ever since he was a boy. There isn't a straighter man on God's footstool in money matters. I'd trust him with carloads of money." Only once towards the end of his time on the hot seat did Mulholland seem to inject a personal note: "I've wanted to turn over to Los Angeles a magnificent heritage. If I couldn't see ahead five or six or seven years, the reward of approbation that will surely come when the aqueduct is done and the people realize what they have, I wouldn't be here, I couldn't go on with the work. I'm worn out—worn out." Yet he continued to cooperate with the committee and fulfilled his promise to provide it with any information it desired. A few days after his last appearance, he sent written answers to eight questions that Warner had submitted, the most absurd of which was, "What is the total water delivered to consumers unmetered?" Answer: "It is of course impossible to answer this question."[30]

After his stint before the AIB, Mulholland was called on July 24 to testify in a libel suit against General Otis; Harry Chandler; and the editor of the *Times*, Harry Andrews, brought by Frank Henderson, president of the public service commission. The suit had been provoked by a *Times* editorial accusing the mayor of politicizing the public service commission by naming the "spoils hunter" Graham and enabling the mayor's "little creature, Henderson" to become the head of the board. Otis, resplendent in his familiar white flannel suit and Panama hat, arrived in court accompanied by his less conspicuous son-in-law, Harry Chandler, and the almost nondescript Andrews. On the proceedings' third day, July 25, after a jury selection complicated by the veniremen's strong opin-

ions about Otis, Mulholland was called early to the witness stand to allow him to begin a scheduled inspection trip over the aqueduct later in
the day. Testifying for the prosecution, Mulholland was asked about the
editorial statement that Graham was out "to get Mulholland's scalp."
He denied the allegation, stating he and Graham were on good terms,
but under cross-examination by the *Times*'s attorney, he admitted that
between himself and Graham "a radical and insurmountable difference
exists and always will remain because I am strenuously opposed to
spreading water over one acre more than the supply warrants. Mr. Graham's plan includes 50,000 or 60,000 acres more than can be covered
by the water which will be available."[31]

His closely reasoned criticism of the Graham plan caused one reporter
to remark that "the examination brought out a large amount of interesting aqueduct history not pertinent to the matter in hand." Under oath,
Mulholland explained that not only did the Graham plan take the water
farther east than he thought financially reasonable, but it also covered
more land with the expectation of getting higher prices and greater revenues. He amplified his objection to such a scheme. "I look farther. I have
gone through one water famine and I don't want to see a repetition of
that. This is the essential and radical difference between Mr. Graham and
myself and I always freely and forcibly express it." To take water east of
Glendora would not be good policy, he explained, because that would
supply a territory not contiguous to the city. Moreover, Graham's plan
would entail an expense of millions, and did not make clear who would
do the distribution work. Mulholland proposed that a group of incorporated cities—Pasadena, Alhambra, Monrovia, and others—band together, arrange a bond issue, and carry the water there themselves. He
also stated his belief that landowners should bear the burden of paying
for distribution works, a matter the Graham plan left unclear. In conclusion, however, he repeated that he and Graham were amicable.[32]

Throughout the *Times* libel trial and on into the dog days of August,
the AIB continued to hear a parade of witnesses: Chaffee, Lippincott,
Mathews, and Van Norman. Eaton was summoned but indicated he was
unable to come and instead sent a letter describing how he had shown
Mulholland the water supply in Owens Valley in 1904 and how he had
secured the original option on the Rickey lands. E. T. Earl was queried
about his land deals in the San Fernando Valley, and former managing
editor of the *Los Angeles Examiner* Henry Loewenthal was trotted out
to repeat all of his 1905–1906 charges against the city, Mulholland, and

the San Fernando Valley land deals. In anticipation of similar questioning, Otis printed a long article in the *Times* about his land activities in
the San Fernando Valley.[33]

By the end of August, committee funds were depleted, and the city
council refused to grant more. One opponent, Martin Betkouski, declared, "I wouldn't trust these fellows with more money if they spend it
like they have the $10,000 they have had." The council also denied a re-
quest to publish 50,000 copies of the board's eight-volume report. What
finally appeared in January 1913 was an abridged version of 163 pages
in a hard-to-read tabloid format of four columns to a page. But the committee itself had already released many of its findings and conclusions to
the press almost before the hearings were over, its most sensational being a recommendation to take legal action against Fred Eaton for recovery
of property he had retained in his land dealings with the people. To be
included as defendants in the threatened suit were those who had engaged in those deals on behalf of the city: Mathews, Mulholland, and
members of the water board. The committee also reported a long list of
deficiencies and assertions: the aqueduct project had been unnecessary
because local water supplies had not been thoroughly developed; the city
lost over $2 million in its dealing with the New York bondsmen; the dam
at Owens River gorge should be 140 instead of 100 feet; the workmen
were neither well paid nor well fed. Then, with an air of regret, the committee reported that it had been unable to find any graft on the aqueduct, although it might have, given more time. With this conflicted and
unresolved conclusion, the investigation closed, but its effect was to perpetuate the divisive opinions about Los Angeles's water story; or, as Abraham Hoffman has understated, "its dual view of the aqueduct would
prove most irritatingly enduring."[34]

The mayor lost no time condemning the report, which Warner later
accused him of not having even read. While other city officials joined in
general disapprobation, Mulholland asked for a review by unbiased citizens and engineers. He impugned Warner indirectly when he spoke of
newcomers and upstarts who had attacked men grown gray in their service to the city, to which Warner snapped back that "Boss" Tweed had
also grown gray during his years exploiting New York. Mulholland did
not respond. To have seven years of complete dedication to a project end
with one's competence and integrity thus questioned had worn him out,
or as he remarked to his sons, "I can take the shit. It's the farts that wear
me down."[35]

THE END IN SIGHT

The issue of Graham's high line was to be decided in the November election along with a new city charter and an amendment to permit horse racing. Lippincott and Mathews took to the hustings to fight the Graham plan, but Mulholland, who had spoken his mind so often on the subject, fell silent. On November 6, when Woodrow Wilson was elected president of the United States, Los Angeles voters approved the Graham plan by almost two to one and banned horse racing by the same ratio. The AIB's findings against the "old guard" in water policy may have influenced many, but probably more convincing to the electorate was the Graham plan's promise that it would be a big revenue producer for the city.[36]

Mulholland continued silent as various aqueduct matters absorbed him at the end of 1912. Tunnel construction began on the Franklin Canyon line in the Hollywood hills. A labor shortage threatened, as growing troubles in the Balkans caused workers from those countries to leave and join the fight. Serbs, Greeks, Montenegrins, and Austrians—1,500 of them—had left the aqueduct by mid-December, and Mulholland feared their departure would delay completion. "They were among the best laborers on the Aqueduct," he said, "and we found some difficulty in replacing them." There being then little unemployment in Southern California, labor was in short supply.[37]

The Graham plan was about to get under way when a hitch arose. Although landowners along the San Gabriel Valley had raised funds to finance the tunnel construction, City Attorney Shenk and water attorney Mathews reported that two weeks of legal study had established that the water board by law could not accept such advance money but must finance the project with a bond issue. That stopped everything until the city fathers gathered the day after Christmas and set a date of February 11, 1913, for a bond election that would include the Graham plan. A photograph from the *Express* shows city leaders gathered around Mayor Alexander to ponder that news, and although it is usually not wise to read much into the expressions on faces in photographs, Mulholland, his curly hair bushier than usual, stands behind a phalanx of dignitaries including Mathews and del Valle looking for all the world like the cat that ate the canary. His silence about the Graham plan during the recent bond election had not been because he had nothing to say about it.[38]

As the year came to an end and the aqueduct increasingly became a reality, human interest stories and interviews with the Chief began to crop up in the papers: his views on duck-hunting ("I like ducks . . . especially roasted, with a touch of garlic"); his escape from Dame Fortune ("What do I want with a million? I wouldn't have it. I never wanted to be wealthy. All I did want was work. A job. And I guess I have it, at last."); and on the aqueduct ("When I get through working, and it's time for me to die and give some other fellow a turn at it, I want them to put this on my monument—just this—*that I helped to build the aqueduct.*").[39]

At year's end, on December 30, 1912, the mayor and the aqueduct men gathered downtown at the Richelieu cafe to honor General Chaffee's retirement from public works. Mulholland presented the general with a hammered brass desk set. "May the ink flowing from that stand ever make as an indelible mark as your justice and good example has on our hearts," he blarneyed. Toasts and tributes went round the table, including a welcome to Chaffee's successor, newcomer Edward Johnson, the engineer who had earlier resigned from the AIB in protest after becoming convinced of its bias.[40]

CHAPTER 19

The Completion of the Aqueduct

1913

WINDING DOWN

Many old-timers of Los Angeles would long remember 1913 not as the year that saw the completion of the Owens River Aqueduct but as the year of the Big Freeze. A cold wave the first week of January produced one of the worst freezes ever in Southern California. Eighty percent of crops were destroyed and the citrus industry crippled. One land developer who surveyed the damage from Pasadena to Monrovia reported that "things are so badly frozen that it is impossible to try and clean them up." Work on the aqueduct halted when the temperature dipped to 8°F at Haiwee and water froze in the pipes to the north. Lippincott reported that in Owens Valley the winter was the most severe in memory and that work and water stoppages would delay filling Haiwee Reservoir until April or May.[1]

Although only one mile remained to complete the aqueduct, problems great and small still arose. A mule had left with an unpaid board bill of $70.50. The advisory board thought that because Desmond had sometimes worked the animal he should pay the bill, but Van Norman thought the mule had done enough work to warrant the city's paying his tab. A mule owner renting to the city demanded recompense for a twenty-year-old mule he claimed had been returned physically unfit for work. He also put in a $250 claim for a $200 mule killed in a train accident. When Mulholland heard this, along with the information that the city had been paying $10.00 a month rent and $1.50 a month pasturage, he recommended, "Don't pay it; we never guaranteed immortality to rented mules." At this same time a mysterious theft of 120,000 sacks of cement at the city's Monolith plant was reported. As the advisory board pondered this peculiar loss that had yielded no clues as to the thieves, a January 17 flare-up fire on the Jawbone Division killed three men. A cigarette or pipe was believed to have been lit while the men were painting the inside of the siphon with a coal tar preparation mixed with distillate; or perhaps one of the candles that illuminated the interior had ignited the explosive mix. The victims, burnt beyond recognition, were simply described in the newspapers as "two Mexicans and an Irishman." The accident was especially sad coming as it did so near the end of a great project and not many months after the fatal dynamite explosion at Clearwater. Even with these tragic mishaps, however, the aqueduct's safety record remained remarkably good in view of the amount of high-hazard digging, blasting, and tunneling. About five million pounds of powder had been used in driving the tunnels, yet only five fatalities had resulted from explosions.[2]

Among the various challenges and uncertainties was a threatened suit from Natural Soda Products Company, whose owners included members of a pioneer Owens Valley family, the Wattersons, leaders in subsequent battles against Los Angeles. The company had initiated a suit in Inyo County against the city to prevent it from taking any water from Owens Valley, claiming that its prior riparian rights on Owens River took precedence over the city's claims. Although some believed it to be another attempt by the "power trust" to thwart the city's plans for distributing its own power, Mathews prepared for yet another legal action. Locally, the city council reluctantly issued the AIB report, in which opponents found a new source of ammunition for a continued attack on the city's water men. Circulars began to appear with a list of questions such as, "Do you want to know how the aqueduct money was spent?" Answers included allegations that the amount of water from Owens River would be less than promised; that the cost of the project would be much greater than projected; that taxpayers would be paying for the aqueduct until 1927; and that city water was being allowed to go free to private corporations while citizens' money was spent on the aqueduct.[3]

Of greater urgency to Mulholland, however, was his participation in a campaign against Graham's high line, which Mayor Alexander had included in the upcoming February bond election. On January 9, before a joint gathering of civic bodies to discuss and debate the issue, Mulholland minced no words, declaring that he had promised the people that they would not have to bear such costs. "If I build a house in this city I must pay to have the water carried to it. That is the right principle and I contend it should apply in this instance. If the orange growers and ranchers along the high line want the water," he advised, "let them dig into their pockets and pay for their system."[4]

MULHOLLAND FOR MAYOR?

To complicate Mulholland's already crowded life, Progressive leaders E. T. Earl, Meyer Lissner, and Charles Dwight Willard proposed at the end of January that he run for mayor, as Earl's newspapers, the *Express* and *Tribune,* had begun to urge his candidacy. He answered each with a polite refusal, but Earl, in a confidential letter to Lissner, insisted that the matter be pursued, feeling that Mulholland's refusal was not unequivocal, that "there is no other man in sight to solve some of the big problems that now confront the city," and that, moreover, he was the only man around who was electable. Publicly, Mulholland declared his devotion to the city but rejected the idea of running for mayor, saying that his first loyalty to the city was with the water department, where he had worked for thirty-two years.[5]

A week earlier, however, he had also written his old friend Willard a more complete explanation of his refusal as well as a candid self-analysis more revealing than any on record. Willard, still fighting tuberculosis and rusticating in the foothills of Pasadena, had during the holiday season composed a circular Christmas letter explaining that after four years of illness and the loss of his home by fire, he was still reasonably happy but hoped that his friends out in the "step-lively" world would feel disposed to send him a word or two, which he intended to put in a scrapbook to be labeled "Christmas 1912." Mulholland, because of his crowded schedule, managed to answer only after he himself was felled by a winter illness. While convalescing, he wrote on January 24, 1913, to express his admiration for Willard's "heroic spiritual resignation" in his struggle with a disease that had taken so many of Mulholland's own family. Then he tackled the question of running for mayor:

> I feel, however, that there is but one way for me to deal with this matter and that is to recognize my temperamental unfitness for the position of Mayor. It is not generally known but it is nevertheless a fact that in the execution of my work I have tendencies that are absolutely autocratic and at times unreasonably domineering. But I am also gifted with the skill of concealing this trait from those who serve with me. This I could not do, of course, in the position

of Mayor of this City where events move so rapidly that my impetuosity under necessarily quick action would reveal my weakness.

It has always been a great pride with me that I have been able to secure
and retain the loyal devotion of my co-workers, if not to myself personally, at
least to the projects I had in hand, but I feel quite certain that in the discharge
of the multifarious duties of Mayor I would utterly fail in this particular.[6]

With that subject seemingly put to rest, two weeks later a restored Mulholland attended the ceremonial turning on of water at the aqueduct intake above Independence. With a small party of engineers and city dignitaries, he and his associates turned the wheels to open the water gates
as Van Norman's wife, Bessie, broke a bottle of champagne on the simple
concrete structure that was to divert the Owens River waters to the City
of Los Angeles. Even today one is struck by the simplicity and undra-
matic aspect of the lonely weir whose purpose would animate such an
epic struggle in the years ahead. One onlooker that day remarked that
it seemed to him that "the source, the fountain of the great waterway
should be marked with a towering arch or some other fitting monument."
Just as the long-sought water at last began to run in the pipes, a torrential rain flooded part of Los Angeles, causing a high-spirited Mulholland
to jest that it was only "evaporation from Haiwee."[7]

TURNING ON THE FIRST FLOW

Mulholland's opponents, always on the scent for some possible misdeed,
seem to have either missed or overlooked the Chief's consulting work at
the Dominguez Rancho during this time. While Scattergood was being
criticized for taking work as a private consultant, Mulholland continued serving unremarked on the Dominguez Land Company's board of
directors. Upon his return from the intake and after the heavy rains of
February, he accompanied the foreman of the estate to view flood damage and make recommendations. Pressures of public life, however, soon
brought this activity to a halt and on February 28, he met with O'Melveny to settle accounts. They agreed on $400,000 as the cost of his part
of the work, for which Mulholland would receive 2.5 percent, or
$10,000. He had already received $3,000 in cash and agreed to accept
bonds of the Dominguez Land Company for the balance. The two men
proceeded to the bank, where he received seven bonds in full payment
for services.[8]

Mulholland's preoccupation was now with overseeing the aqueduct's
completion and the orderly closing down of construction. Although crit-

icisms continued (the *South Pasadena Record* ran a letter that claimed the aqueduct line was leaking and that Owens River water was unfit to drink), Mulholland returned in mid-March after inspecting the intake to report that water flowing into Haiwee had already created a lake two miles long by a quarter of a mile wide with a maximum depth of 35 feet. He admitted that some water had leaked from an inconsequential break in the line that had been quickly repaired, but all told, he declared, there had not been "two-bits worth of damage" since the water had been turned on. A few days later, he returned to the intake and turned the full flow of the Owens River into the first sixty-five miles of the aqueduct.[9]

Engineers Lippincott and Roderick McKay were meanwhile supervising the appraisal and sale of equipment, machinery, materials and supplies from the construction of the aqueduct. Everything from chisels, hammers, and lanterns to steam shovels and mules was on the block, and offers to buy came from Canada, the Midwest, and even Honolulu. Purchases at this municipal second-hand store required cash and all sales were final. The estimated inventory was $500,000, and by June 1913, over $300,000 worth of material had been sold. Negotiations were also afoot to sell the cement mill and excess lands, evaluated at $550,000.[10]

Aqueduct engineers also began to disperse. Because the project's fame had spread over the world, calls for its veterans' services and know-how came from South America, Mexico, and the Orient. Through Mulholland's recommendations and negotiations with a major engineering company in London, John Gray, after six years on the aqueduct and with a growing reputation because of his record-breaking work on the Elizabeth Tunnel, left with two of his foremen for Barcelona, Spain, where he took over the completion of a mile-long tramway tunnel that had run into construction difficulties. Also bound for Spain was J. S. "Jack" Taney, who began as a chain man in 1906 under E. A. Bayley, had advanced through the ranks—building the Grapevine and Jawbone Division roads—and now for the next four years was to oversee a Spanish irrigation and power project. He later wrote that the first man he met on the new job in Spain had been an aqueduct laborer at Mojave. De-Witt Reaburn, of the Saugus Division, went to Argentina as a locating engineer for a railway running to Chile but returned to Los Angeles in time to participate in the aqueduct celebrations in 1913 and later became the engineer of Mulholland Highway in the Hollywood hills. William C. Aston, as earlier mentioned, went to the Hawaiian Islands after completing the Elizabeth Tunnel; T. F. "Tommie" Flanigan, who "had everything in his noodle about a tunnel that he ought to know," and who had broken a record at Red Rock Canyon, went on to the Catskill Aqueduct; and Phil Wintz, builder of the Haiwee Dam, retired to his home in the West Adams section of Los Angeles. Others found their way to Japan, the Philippines, Brazil, Bolivia, and various sites on the Pacific Coast. Not only had the aqueduct proven a training ground for beginners and a graduate school for experienced professionals, its successful completion in record time had also enhanced its builders' reputations.[11]

Mulholland was later to say of all the thousands who had worked on the great project, who dug ditches, skinned mules, and drilled tunnels, his greatest sorrow was that "the millions of dollars that were spent for labor did the men who toiled on the aqueduct so little permanent good." He praised many of them as brave, loyal, and generous and others as "a roving, happy-go-lucky lot, who, even though many earned $5 or $6 or $7 a day, spent it all." In the midst of the satisfaction surrounding the aqueduct's completion, he paid them the following tribute:

> My sympathy is alive for these men, and most of the time raw and bleeding, to think that they do so much to so little purpose. I know this type of man; in my early life as a sailor I worked with them and slept with them, and I would rather be with them, to sit around camp with them, than to be in a circle of lawyers and doctors and bankers. Professional men are trained to conceal their thoughts, but these men are frank, blunt and human and a man gets more real insight into human life and affairs with them than with the other type. They were a grand lot, they did their work and took their chances in the tunnels, dry or wet, safe or indifferent, with gas or free from it, and in other dangerous jobs, and they spent their money like sailors ashore, and that is the one thing that saddens me today.[12]

CONTENTIOUS PARTIES

Throughout the spring, Los Angeles was caught up in a series of four contentious city elections that reflected the increasing complexity of the rapidly growing city. A new charter amendment had revamped election procedures that thereby legislated the entire current administration out of office six months early. The flurry of campaigning that ensued created a rift in the Progressive Party from which it was not to recover. With Job Harriman once more a mayoral candidate and their own party deeply divided, certain Progressive leaders, anxious to thwart a Socialist victory, revived the idea of running Mulholland for mayor. Nominally a Democrat but sympathetic to many of the Progressives' aims, especially municipal ownership of water and power, he seemed an ideal coalition candidate. He was also a popular and familiar public figure.

Earl and his editor, Edward Dickson, renewed their boom for Mulholland as mayor in the *Express* and *Tribune,* while the *Times,* which represented the most conservative voice of the Republican Party, immediately opposed, saying Mulholland should remain where he was. Although Earl's papers later blamed a "reactionary alliance" for Mulholland's elimination as a prospective candidate, the truth is that Mulholland dealt himself out. Even though he is remembered for having said that he would rather give birth to a porcupine backward than be mayor of Los Angeles, he had also been momentarily beguiled by the flattery, compliments and urgings, especially when a delegation of civic leaders arrived at his home one night to persuade him to run. His two oldest children, Rose and Perry, later recalled that when he had shown signs of weakening, Lillie Mulholland entered the parlor to register her opposition. The newspapers next day reported that Mulholland had buried his own political boom, while one eyewitness commented that Mrs. Mulholland was "very much opposed to his entering the political fight."[13]

Mulholland's next effort was to defeat Graham's high line in the April bond election, which asked voters to decide on eight projects affecting the city's future. In part because of his and Lippincott's well-publicized attacks on Graham's water plan (Mulholland called it "audacious rapacity"), voters trounced the high-line bonds two to one. General Otis expressed his pleasure in a rare note to Mulholland. "The pertinence and force of your arguments and the clarity of your sentences appeal to me strongly, as one who professes to know a little about the English language," blandished the general, adding in a postscript, "It was a glorious victory, and the advocates of the 'high line' canal tumbled off their perch in so sudden and violent a manner as to inflict deserved bruises upon their impotent carcasses."[14]

Although the water bonds to complete the aqueduct trunk line overwhelmingly won approval, the power bonds to develop municipal electricity fell 5,000 votes short of a two-thirds majority. Mulholland's efforts on behalf of power, however, evoked no praise from General Otis, whose *Times,* after championing municipal water development, opposed municipal power on the grounds that private power companies were already functioning in the city. Earl's *Tribune* blamed the defeat on Hearst, Otis, and the power trust for their unremitting attack against municipal power, but also questioned if voters had understood when they originally voted for the $23 million bond issue for the aqueduct and the preliminary $1.5 million for surveys and land purchases that they had in effect pledged themselves to vote future funds necessary to develop and distribute aqueduct power. Mulholland felt voters had been confused because the issue had not been presented clearly or precisely. He believed that if the ballot had been drafted with separate votes for development and distribution, voters would have approved the plan for generating power even if they might have rejected the distribution plan.[15]

THE SAND CANYON MISFORTUNE

Of major concern at this time were construction problems on the last of the great siphons in Sand Canyon, sixty miles north of Mojave and twenty-five miles south of the Haiwee Reservoir. This was an inverted siphon, or airtight pipe, by which the water was made to drop into the canyon below the grade level of the aqueduct and rise back out. Experimental and unique to the project, it comprised two underground tunnels, one down each side of the canyon and connected across by a steel pipe. Because the canyon seemed to be massive granite, the engineering experts had thought inclined pressure tunnels could accomplish a great savings. At the end of March, however, as water began to fill the pipes and pressure tests were applied, some seepage and leakage was observed. With increased pressure, blowouts began to occur. The first, at the end of March, tore away part of the siphon's north side. As the pressure was boosted, other breaks occurred. One on Sunday, April 20, only five days after the bond election, tore out part of the south side. After inspecting the damage, a frustrated Mulholland returned to the city with the announcement that the completion of the aqueduct probably would be delayed ninety days. All testing ended a month later, between May 18 and 20, when the final blowout convinced the Chief that the project had failed and must be replaced with a steel siphon.[16]

The siphon blowout at Sand Canyon was the single largest failure on the aqueduct, and Mulholland had had his doubts about its construction from the beginning. Because rock siphons of this type had been used on the New York Aqueduct and because of technical literature extolling them, the original consulting engineers tended to favor them over steel siphons. Mulholland, with his knowledge of seismic activity in California, had been dubious, but the eastern experts had overridden him. He had agreed to this one because the span was to be short and because the rock seemed to be solid. Now sadly vindicated by this costly failure, he announced that he was through with experiments, had wired orders for the necessary pipe, and would install a steel siphon. As the work camp at Sand Canyon was intact and the necessary equipment at hand, sixty men were immediately deployed under Van Norman to build a new, all-steel, aboveground siphon in another location across the canyon. The added cost was under $40,000, which Mulholland defended as representing only ⅛ of 1 percent of the total cost of the project. He also expressed the belief that the people of the city would not feel sorry for themselves because of this failed experiment. "We were all desirous of turning over this project to the city without a single accident, of course, but when we wished for that, we wished for a miracle." Optimists and boomers such as Frank Wiggins of the Chamber of Commerce used the delay as an opportunity to expand and embellish plans for an aqueduct celebration, while opponents such as the *Record* made dire predictions that the loss would come to $80,000. Setbacks notwithstanding, work on the aqueduct was coming to an end. On May 10, the board of public works announced that it would transfer all affairs of the aqueduct bureau to the control of the public service commission; Mulholland was to remain as head of the water department, while Lippincott would simply be paid $20 a day for time actually employed in helping Mulholland complete the report on the aqueduct.[17]

NEW FACES IN CITY POLITICS

The spring mayoral campaign kicked off with Job Harriman avowing "to lay bare the Aqueduct frame-up." Because he was no longer in contention as a candidate, Mulholland for the first time in his life campaigned for a friend, John W. Shenk, whose plurality had forced Harriman out of the race in the primary. Shenk finally lost by 8,000 votes after Harriman backers, organized labor, and Hearst's pro-labor *Examiner* threw their support to the primary candidate who had come in second, Henry Howard Rose, a somewhat unpredictable Republican. The new mayor was also an Episcopalian, a Mason, and an Elk who had come from Wisconsin to Los Angeles in 1888 and served in various legal capacities for the city since 1903. A police judge since 1905, he promised to fight vice and prostitution, strongly appealing to women who had only begun to vote and at a time when police corruption was still rife in a wide open city. Los Angeles had just witnessed a sensational morals trial involving a deputy district attorney accused of contributing to the delinquency of a sixteen-year-old girl. Further indicating this election's blurred political divisions and party lines is that while Socialists had supported Rose as an alternative to Shenk, whom they saw as representing conservative forces, non-Socialists helped elect to city council Fred Wheeler, who thereby became the first Socialist in Los Angeles history to win an elective position in city government.[18]

Because he had a busy schedule and also had been offended by the new mayor's labeling Shenk a puppet of conservative Progressives, Mulholland did not meet with Rose until two months after his election. Before that, however, a new set of charges forced the Chief to appear before the city council to defend himself against possible censure for having barred certain "people's representatives" from a trip to the aqueduct. After the election, while Mulholland and Lippincott were preparing the final annual aqueduct report, the Socialist members of the former AIB pursued their goals of wresting the Owens River project from its present managers and reclaiming from Fred Eaton certain of his Owens Valley lands. Working with an organization devised for these purposes, the Independent Civic League, former AIB investigator Henry A. Hart and his allies began to file nuisance suits against the city, beginning with one claiming that city residents were being cheated with "used water" from Owens Valley. When that had failed to generate much political heat, they turned to Fred Eaton and his Long Valley lands. Deciding to inspect the lands, they went before the city council to announce their need for funds to make the journey. Receiving the money, they next accused Mulholland of barring them from taking the trip and called for his censure. When he appeared in his own defense, he spoke at length; praised the aqueduct and the men who built it; called it "the big thing in my life," and vouched for its integrity, knowing that the project was "clean, straight, honest." Yet he also acknowledged that the continued attacks by innuendo and unsubstantiated charges had hurt the enterprise as well as himself. "I have not lost caste with my profession nor with the part of the community that knows," he declared, but he foresaw that "if you repeat a lie often enough those who do not know begin to accept it as truth."[19]

Of the suggested suit against Fred Eaton, he said, "I want to see the suit brought against Fred Eaton for which the enemies of the aqueduct have been clamoring, attacking on behalf of the city his right to the 4200 acres of Owens Valley lands which he retained when he turned the option for lands and water rights over to the city." He found it "a heartbreaking thing to have these charges scattered broadcast. They say Fred Eaton made a million dollars out of the deal. He is really a comparatively poor man, with his 4200 acres of grazing land of small value, while the city got 34,000 acres of valley land."

As for denying transportation to the investigators, Mulholland wryly acknowledged that if it had been possible and had they given him enough time, he would have hired a hearse, if it had been necessary, to take them along. As it was, he had received late notice on the afternoon of his and attorney Stephens's departure for Mojave. He had been in a water board meeting at the time and had no idea he was supposed to make travel arrangements for them. As for affronting the council, he wondered if the council had not affronted him in asking him "to act as nurse-maid to these men who have been persistent enemies of the Aqueduct."

He ended by praising progress on the aqueduct, which had just come through an epic desert cloudburst and flood that piled gravel and boulders in places over the line with only a few ribs of pipeline showing signs of cracking. Assigning September 12 as the projected completion date for the Sand Canyon siphon, he explained, "I have some sentiment on that score, as I left for my first trip over the route of the proposed aqueduct on that date, my birthday, and I told the boys on the job that I wanted the new steel siphon done by that time." After his peroration, even the lone councilman who had first voted to censure Mulholland abandoned his attempt as the entire council rejected sending the investigating party to the aqueduct and declared the incident closed. Eaton later filed a denial that he had taken aqueduct cement to make improvements on his ranch in Long Valley, and the city council formally exonerated him of this charge on December 18, 1913. The Independent Civic League waited to spring its next ambush in the weeks preceding the celebration of the aqueduct opening.[20]

A TIMELY COMPLETION

A week after his defense before the city council, Mulholland met Mayor Rose in an encounter described as "brief and cordial." Since taking office, Rose had honored his pledge to support the city's water and power projects, nor could his overhaul of the board of public works have displeased the Chief. He had replaced high-line defenders Graham and Henderson and two other Alexander appointees with longtime water loyalists and Democrats: banker Boyle Workman and former mayor Meredith "Pinkie" Snyder. Reginaldo del Valle, the only survivor from the old board, was at last elected president of the commission.[21]

On June 23, Mulholland submitted the report on the completion of the aqueduct, whose $24.6 million cost had met the original estimate. The city auditor later reported that after examining the books he gave high marks to the accounting on the aqueduct project although he had found certain discrepancies largely attributable to the inefficiency of some of the clerical force and some negligence on the part of division engineers to account properly for all the material used. His other cavil was that further savings could have been effected had other railroads than the Southern Pacific been given a chance to compete for the transcontinental freight. One item of mystery was $15,000 in unclaimed laborers' checks; about 5,000 checks had accumulated since 1907 and still awaited distribution in 1913.[22]

On the eve of the aqueduct's completion, questions of water distribution, annexation, and rate schedules continued to perplex the citizenry. Areas served by private companies were anxious to have aqueduct water, but not all wished to annex to Los Angeles. In the San Fernando Valley meetings were held amid sharp debate. Ranchers who had developed wells and used limited irrigation opposed annexation. Others, who wanted more irrigated agriculture and larger towns, favored it.[23]

On Friday, June 13, the city broke its record for water consumption when it used 69.4 million gallons, over 10 million more than the previous ten days' average. At this rate, worried the Chief, the supply would be exhausted in a year, even though by then aqueduct water would have arrived and the city's troubles would be over. By late September, however, a dry hot spell, a large downtown fire, and an outbreak of fires in the hills and mountains north of La Cañada and Tujunga made draws on the water supply that almost emptied Buena Vista Reservoir. Mulholland asked the people of the city to curtail watering gardens and to use water frugally. "I am not an alarmist. I am not in the habit of crying wolf. But in this case I want to say to the water users of the city that prodigality in the use of water for the next day or so may cost us dearly. The reservoirs are low and the consumption is higher than it has ever been in the history of the city water department." He reported that although the supply would be replenished in a few days, it would be drawing from underground basins in the San Fernando Valley that were being conserved for use a year hence. In short, as time drew near for the completion of the aqueduct, the city found itself dipping deep into its existing water capital.[24]

AQUEDUCT EUPHORIA

On September 1, a group of city fathers traveled to the north end of the San Fernando Valley to stand at the terminus of the aqueduct and witness the first flow of water down the spillway that Mulholland had named the Cascade. Days later, he left on the night train to Mojave for his last end-to-end inspection before the project's completion. Accompanying him were city councilman Martin F. Betkouski, city building inspector J. J. Backus, and journalist Alan Kelly, who had just completed an official history of the aqueduct. At Independence they were to meet Fred Eaton, who was then to guide Betkouski on a tour of Long Valley. Mayor Rose, planning to meet the group in Owens Valley, had set out earlier in the day with his chauffeur to travel alone by automobile. Ten days later, when Rose returned from his inspection tour, he commented that as far as he could determine, "criticism of the aqueduct is captious." He had seen an astonishing supply of pure sweet water, found Haiwee Reservoir filling up, and not, as had been rumored in the city, afloat with dead cattle and drowned varmints. Betkouski reaffirmed the mayor's findings and also spoke of the great surplus of water ("twice as much as the aqueduct will carry") and the need in future for a storage reservoir at Long Valley. A satisfied Mulholland reported that the rumored leak at Haiwee was water percolating through a lava formation that had holes in it like a Swiss cheese. When asked if he were worried about the "leak," he replied, "About as much as I am that the sun won't come up tomorrow. We'll get in there when we get ready and stop the percolation. But there's no hurry." (The stoppage was not accomplished until 1919.)[25]

Ten days later, on September 24, the Chief traveled along the line to see if the Sand Canyon siphon were ready to begin receiving water. After it had withstood its test and water flowed on its way to Fairmont Reservoir, he exulted that only an act of God could stop it now. For the next five days, with engineers McKay and Van Norman, he oversaw the 135-mile stretch of ditch and tunnel between Haiwee and Fairmont. Asked if there had been any ceremony when the gates were opened at Haiwee, he replied there was none. He had been thirty miles south of the reservoir and, after phoning the dam keeper to open the gates, simply waited overnight for the water's first appearance. "Perhaps we did start the water going without much hurrah," he amplified, "but there never has been much sentiment about the aqueduct—it has been a plain business proposition from start to finish, but a mighty big proposition." Reflecting that everything that could be said about the immensity of the work had been said a hundred times before, he asked that one fact be considered. "There are fifty-three miles of tunnel in the 217 miles of aqueduct's length. Just imagine riding at a good smart clip in an automobile for two or two and a half hours in total darkness through them, if it could be done, and you will have some idea of the mountainous character of the country traversed by the project."[26]

Excitement heightened all through October as the public was informed of the Owens River water's progress. On October 1, Mayor Rose opened the gates at Fairmont Reservoir along with Councilman Betkouski and the Chief. They made so many toasts to the city with water samples that Mulholland remarked that he was gratified for the sake of Los Angeles's reputation that it was water they were imbibing. The general spirit and expansiveness of celebration were enhanced by the mayor's proclamation to celebrate on October 10 the completion of the Culebra Cut on the Panama Canal, which would create the meeting of the waters of the Atlantic and Pacific Oceans and herald the promise of an unimaginable expansion of trade and traffic on the Pacific Coast. Flags were to be flown, bells rung, and schoolchildren told of this important day in the world's history.[27]

Civic spirits rose as each increment of the aqueduct line proved sound, but elsewhere voices of doom tolled their plaints of failure and wrongdoing. From Owens Valley came predictions that the project would prove to be a blunder; that the intake was in the wrong place and to receive pure water it would have to be relocated higher in the valley; and that city officials recently seen in Owens Valley with Fred Eaton may well have had more than mere sociability on their minds. Days after he had opened the gates at Fairmont and prepared to celebrate the blowing-out of the Culebra Cut, Mayor Rose was presented with a long document from the Independent Civic League requesting detailed information about the alleged secret conferences between city officials and Owens Valley representatives concerning water rights in the valley. The mayor replied that there had been only one meeting with Fred Eaton, on September 4 in the office of the public service commission. Accompanying Eaton, now chairman of an Owens Valley committee of water users of Big Pine Creek, was his fellow member, S. E. Vermilyea. The aim of the meeting had been "to bring about a better and clearer understanding of the water rights of the city and the owners in the Owens River Valley, thereby making it possible to better protect the city from encroachment by outside power companies and other interests." Rose also explained that neither Eaton's holdings on the Rickey lands in Long Valley nor any monetary amounts had been discussed.[28]

The sour notes were muted as the city prepared to receive its long-awaited water with an opening-day ceremony of cannon booms, fireworks, steam whistles, car horns, and a great banquet in the evening. The second day of festivity was to begin with a mammoth parade celebrating the city's industrial might, followed in the afternoon with ceremonies for the official opening of the County Museum of History, Science and Art at Exposition Park. As invitations went out, letters of congratulations came in from all over North America. By mid-October, Mulholland, water officials, and members of the celebration committee readied the spectacle to take place on November 5. They had turned on a head of between 8,000 and 9,000 inches of water to test the effect of the tumbling liquid, which at full capacity would roar down the spillway in a 20,000-inch cataract. "The big job is finished," Mulholland declared, "thanks to the faith of the people of Los Angeles, the loyalty and intelligence of the aqueduct workers, and to the cooperation and wise advisory course pursued by city officials. Nothing remains now but to shoot off a few firecrackers, turn on the water and tackle the next big job."[29]

As he knew, water issues never took a holiday, and the eve of the celebrations found Lippincott presenting a brief to the Colorado River Commission then in Los Angeles to hear Southwest arguments against four upper-Colorado diversion schemes, a topic that would increasingly dominate engineering interests once the aqueduct was complete. Meanwhile, Scattergood, head of the power bureau, was active in the current debate over whether to approve a $6.5 million power-bond election in mid-November. Most immediate, however, were the unresolved complexities of the city's relationships with parties in Owens Valley, especially those who had pending litigations over water and power rights in Inyo County. On October 19, a delegation from Inyo County met with Mayor Rose to seek ways to cooperate and set mutual goals. The mayor suggested that improved rail and highway connections would bring the two areas closer, but the Owens Valley Defense Association, which included large Inyo landholders, sought permanent stipulation of rights to the waters of the Owens River Valley. Still others attempted to adjudicate their differences over power development at the Owens River gorge. The ground for future battles was also being laid at this time, as the city began to consider claiming the water that fed the creeks at Mono Lake, a move that would bring increased conflict with private power companies such as Silver Lake Power Company.[30]

A few days before the official aqueduct opening, Mulholland and Mathews hastened to Independence for a day in court as the Natural Soda Products Company's suit got under way. With top western legal talent appearing for each side, the case generated a good deal of interest, some considering it the greatest water rights case ever tried in the West. The soda company contended that Owens Lake possessed at least

70 million tons of soda (some said the largest deposit anywhere in the world) and that removing the river's water would dry up and ruin the deposit (and the soda industry). On Saturday, November 1, after hearing the soda company's affidavits concerning its operations at Owens Lake, Mathews asked for, and was denied, a continuance so the city might better prepare its case. Mulholland once again testified as to the aqueduct's conception and history, while Mathews, who was later asked if it were not true that at least 80 percent of Owens River water would be used for irrigation in Southern California, refused to answer.[31]

"THERE IT IS. TAKE IT."

As Los Angeles geared up for its big day, the daily newspapers provided schedules and details of the coming ceremonials, as well as human interest items such as Mulholland's discovery while rooting in his closet for his formal wear that the family cat had lodged her new litter in his top hat; that moths had perforated his dress suit; and that his long-unused dress shirt had turned the shade of tufa cement. He thought the suit could be salvaged and a new shirt was not out of the question, but the hat he decided to leave to the cat and her kittens, declaring that in all the years he had owned the thing, he had worn it only twice—both times to funerals, and this occasion was to be no funeral. Mingling with the levity and jubilation, however, was the uncertainty of his wife's well-being. Only days before the crowning moment of his professional life, Lillie Mulholland had been forced to undergo critical surgery for uterine cancer. With her fate in doubt, daughters Rose and Lucile took her place at the opening ceremonies, during which they received word that she had "passed the danger line." A measure of the day's giddiness may be read in the story's headline: WATER CURES SICK WOMAN.[32]

Fred Eaton did not attend the ceremonies because he claimed the water tumbling down the Cascade that day would not be truly from Owens River but simply stored rainwater. This rather lame explanation, however, must have masked a tumult of warring emotions. Even though Mulholland publicly continued to champion and defend his old friend and certainly Eaton was everywhere credited with conceiving the idea of bringing Owens River water to Los Angeles, the two men's conflicting goals were driving them apart. Still determined to profit from his land deals in Owens Valley, Eaton had just consummated a sale of 6,000 acres in Long Valley to the Symon brothers, local landowners, for a reputed

$60,000 As chairman of a ditch-owners group, he also had produced an engineering report for water use on Big Pine Creek. Both activities were prelude to events that would explode in the 1920s.[33]

The city had never seen anything like the celebration of the aqueduct's completion. The intricate logistics of the two-day carnival had fallen largely to the Chamber of Commerce, which could later congratulate itself on a job well done. Crews from ships of the United States fleet that were in harbor were granted leave to join in the merriment; the Shriners were in town for a convention; and two nights before the big event, the San Fernando Valley received its first night illumination when the developers of the new towns of Van Nuys, Owensmouth (Canoga Park), and Marian (Reseda) turned on street lights along the recently completed Sherman Way. On Wednesday, November 5, at least 30,000 people (some said 50,000) converged at the site near present-day Sylmar in the San Fernando Valley to watch the water come down. They had traveled from the city and surrounding territories by car, buckboard, buggy, and special trains. Some made it a family outing with picnic lunches. One valley old-timer remembered in 1977 how "Dad put us all in that old Ford and we went up there and watched that water come down."

The weather was perfect: fair and sunny. The popular Catalina Island band played for the first hour as the crowd settled in around the open area below the Cascade and along the channel through which the released water would make its way across the San Fernando Valley towards the city. In the prevailing festive mood, cheers went up as dignitaries took their places on a grandstand erected for the occasion just below the Cascade. First to speak was Congressman William Stephens, followed by General Otis, resplendent in full dress as he paid tribute to his favorite hometown singer, Ellen Beach Yaw, who had composed an anthem for the occasion. Undaunted by gusting canyon breezes that blew the ostrich plumes of her elegant chapeau across her face and threatened to muffle her voice as well, "Lark Ellen" sang "California—Hail the Waters!"— "Lift your voices in gratitude/A river now is here."

Former governor George C. Pardee next delivered a classic oration with allusions to the ancient Romans and their aqueducts. History, he declared, tended to remember those who had destroyed human life—the conquerors—but the aqueduct that day, bringing pure water to the inhabitants of a great city, "ranks higher than the bloody accomplishments of all the Caesars; sets high among the great men of the world those whose genius has made it possible, and records among the great people of the earth the Californians who commanded that it should be built."

After the band played "I Love You, California," Mulholland was introduced—"the man who built the aqueduct." Amid the cheers, as one reporter described, a "slow, silent, tired man" came forward. Without notes and apparently unprepared, he made a brief, heartfelt speech. He thanked all those who had worked in partnership with him in the great enterprise and acknowledged the importance of the celebration not only to those present but to the entire municipality. As a steward of the people, he wished to render his account. He then sketched the reasons for building the aqueduct and paid homage to Fred Eaton, the pioneer of the project. "I am sorry that the man whom I consider the father of the aqueduct is not here, former Mayor Eaton. To him all the honor is due. He planned it—we simply put together the bricks and the mortar." Then, reverting to the imagery and language of the faith he had long ago abandoned, he concluded, "This rude platform is an altar, and on it we are consecrating this water supply and dedicating this aqueduct to you and your children and your children's children—for all time." He stopped then, as if pausing to collect his thoughts for another utterance, but instead brusquely said, "That's all," and went back to his seat.

The Chamber of Commerce then made a "surprise" presentation of handsome silver loving cups to Mulholland and Lippincott, the latter speaking in tribute to colleagues and workers, singling out for praise the work of General Chaffee. Chaffee, with four of the aqueduct engineers (Roderick McKay, D. L. Reaburn, A. C. Hansen, and H. A. Van Norman), stood above, manning the wheels that would open the gates. At the grand climax, Mulholland, the central figure in the scene, unfurled the Stars and Stripes as a signal to release the water.

> A stream of water began to trickle from beneath the big iron gates set in the concrete frame on the hillside. The gates ascended with painful slowness. The man at the flagpole stood inert, hearing nothing, noticing nothing, seeing nothing of the jubilant confusion about him.
> The stream grew into a flood, the flood into a torrent, the water boiled and seethed down the steep incline laid for it. It topped the rise immediately above the grandstand and came rushing over, pell-mell.
> Then, as he watched this miracle, the grizzled man sat down with a sigh that had a sob in it. For just a moment he closed his eyes. A smile replaced his drawn look, his shoulders straightened, his head was thrown back and he laughed—laughed like a boy.
> "Well, it's finished!" he said simply.[34]

In the happy confusion of aerial bombs and gun salutes that followed, the crowd moved forward to see and sample their new water. The program called for Mulholland to make a formal presentation of the project to the city, but amid the noisy, festive stampede and after his daughters had thrown their arms around him with expressions of love and pride, all he could manage to call out to Mayor Rose was, "There it is. Take it." Praised later as the greatest short speech ever made, it also became the best remembered moment of the occasion. The mayor could only reply, "Thank you," as he assured those around him that his prepared acceptance would be printed in the afternoon newspapers.

As Mulholland mingled afterwards and prepared to attend a celebratory luncheon party in nearby San Fernando, he found himself standing by a man watching the swiftly rushing aqueduct waters. "I wonder," mused the man, "how fast that water travels." Suddenly his hat—a Tyrolean felt adorned with a peacock feather—dropped off his head into the water and as he watched it sail away, Mulholland answered, "You'll find it at the dam in seven minutes."[35]

Two hundred dignitaries attended the lunch at Fred L. Boruff's San Fernando ranch. Boruff, who had married Ben Porter's widow, had been one of the valley's chief boosters for the aqueduct. After another round of tributes to Mulholland, Boruff presented him with a set of nested silver cups, each engraved with a scene from the aqueduct: the intake, Owens River, Haiwee Reservoir, and others. Again Mulholland praised those he had worked with, this time singling out for special commendation the mayors and General Chaffee. Even a bad city administration (Mayor Harper's), he declared, had produced the appointment of Chaffee, of whom he said, "Failure cannot come to anything that Southern California undertakes with such citizens. We are undoubtedly a people doomed to success."[36]

The banquet that night at the Alexandria Hotel was crowded with dignitaries and awash with oratory and more gifts as Chaffee acted as toastmaster. Like ancient Danes in their mead-hall celebrating and presenting gifts to a hero returned from a successful voyage, they feted and gifted Mulholland the Chief again at the end of the long exhausting day. Lippincott in his address, "He Who Goes to the Mountain Goes to His Mother," predicted that other communities of Southern California would again go to the eastern Sierra for water. The Engineers and Architects Association presented a scroll with a depiction of a Roman aqueduct, while a large bronze medallion came from the engineers of the Spring Valley Water Company ("From San Francisco Friends in Token of their appreciation of his worth as a man and his ability as an engineer"). Inscribed below a handsome bas relief of a crouching Native American holding a bowl up to a freshet of water flowing from a cleft stone were the words "He hath compassed the waters, with Bounds, until the day and night comes to an end."

By the time Mulholland rose to give the last speech, he must have been pixilated by the long day's overwhelming events, for he whimsically referred to his heritage with an account of an old Irish mate who had once advised him when he was debating whether to leave his life at sea. The mate had warned him that the reason the Irish did not succeed was that they lacked frugality and prudence. So, Mulholland explained, "I sort of figured that I would have to grow whiskers and wait for the restoration of the Democratic party to power, and then I would get a job as a policeman." Instead, he visited an uncle in Pittsburgh who was in the dry goods business and where he "tore off calico by the yard for about three months." His uncle (given the fictitious name of Duffy) lived where the coal trains went by and soon he learned, after hearing a thundering clatter above, that "Uncle Duffy" kept a goat tied on the tin roof of the house. Each time a train came by, the fireman on the train threw a lump of coal at the goat, which as his uncle explained, was how he laid in his winter supply of fuel. And so from that, Mulholland concluded his apocryphal tale, "I learned that even an Irishman may turn things to his account in unexpected ways and being more encouraged I came West."

Having delivered this curious preamble, he talked about the aqueduct, describing how in 1902 and 1903, the city had found itself in dire straits ("we were at our wits' end for water"). He spoke of Eaton; how he had proposed that they get water from the Sierras; how he had been up there on his own account, "with the purpose of exploiting that great water supply and had succeeded in getting options on a great deal of land." He admitted that he knew from the first they would have to buy Eaton out and praised the old water board that had been willing to gamble on the scheme ("it had red blood in its veins"). He applauded Mathews and his adroit management of aqueduct affairs ("there has never been a sacrifice of the city's interests") and admitted that although the criticism of the project was annoying, he kept much too busy to become nervous over it, knowing that when the water was finally delivered, all would bless its coming.[37]

What was so momentous in Los Angeles rated only a mention in San Francisco, then battling to create its own controversial Hetch Hetchy water project. Buried on the fifth page of the *San Francisco Chronicle* was a brief item headlined OWENS WATER IN HUGE AQUEDUCT. The front page of the *New York Times* heralded its own city's latest expansion of the Catskill Water Project by proclaiming its importance as an engineering feat second only to the Panama Canal—a claim Los Angeles was also making for its aqueduct. Back on page six was the Los Angeles story, headed PIPES WATER 250 MILES. The few lines devoted to the subject mentioned only General Chaffee by name. The *Boston Globe,* however, acknowledged editorially that the aqueduct was "one of the monumental engineering achievements of all ages, and of all lands." It had, moreover, been built without graft and for the benefit of the people and the municipality.[38]

CHAPTER 20

After the Aqueduct

1914–1919

IN THE WAKE: CRITICS AND ADMIRERS

Mulholland's pace did not slacken after the aqueduct hoopla. Five days later he was back in Independence for the soda works case. Shortly after he testified that Fred Eaton's water appropriations were on behalf of the City of Los Angeles and that work on the surveys and preliminary construction had begun one year before the city had voted its first bonds for the project, a writ of prohibition stopped the hearings. A change of venue had been requested, claiming conflict of interest as presiding Judge William D. Dehy was a riparian owner of Owens River property, and now an appellate court had enjoined Dehy from proceeding. Days later, Mulholland confronted the board of public works over its recent purchase of electrical machinery with aqueduct funds needed for tunnel building in San Francisquito Canyon. The resulting delay, he told them, would hinder the ultimate completion of the aqueduct. The next day, after receiving the silk flag he had unfurled at the opening ceremonies (purchased by a subscription of the office force) and expressing his pleasure and appreciation for the gift, he left on a night train to San Francisco, where he was scheduled to appear November 24 as an expert in a lawsuit between the fledgling East Bay Water Company and the City of Oakland. When asked during the deposition what difficulties he had encountered in the construction of the aqueduct, he replied, "The real difficulties of the Aqueduct were not the physical difficulties. They were human difficulties."[1]

Celebrations aside, the aqueduct would not be pronounced finished until the end of June 1914, when the trunk line across the San Fernando Valley and through Franklin Canyon began to deliver Owens River water to Los Angeles. As construction work continued through the winter, naysayers kept up their attacks, establishing a theme that would be heard in the years ahead as the city attempted to establish its municipal power system. Only three days after the civic celebration at the Cascade, Frederick Finkle published a long letter in the *Examiner* calling the celebration premature, the project incomplete, and the aqueduct's construction flawed. Predicting cost overruns and expressing doubts that the system would ever be able to deliver 20,000 inches of water as promised, he concluded the city would never receive more from Owens River than its leavings or wastewater because of prior claims to the upper reaches of the stream. "History," he prophesied, "will no doubt record that no one was benefitted by the celebration, except those having real estate for sale in the San Fernando Valley." The *Record* chimed in to report that "the monster Haiwee Reservoir" was leaking and insisted that Mulholland's $15,000 salary should be slashed by $5,000.[2]

Finkle was correct on one score: the great work could not be considered completed until both water and electric power had been brought to Los Angeles under municipal control, and this proved a long and difficult task. Whereas the city's business interests had fairly unanimously supported a municipal water system, opinion divided sharply on the power question, especially in the manner of its distribution, which had been under the control of private power companies now wanting to buy at wholesale the coming city system's power. The power companies delayed a decision to lease and/or sell their private distributing systems to the city as it pushed to resubmit to the voters the lately defeated $6.5 million power bond issue. Without funds to continue the project, aqueduct water would go unused for the production of power, and some warned that the aqueduct could prove to be a white elephant, or as one headline put it, AQUEDUCT WATERS AT REST GATHER NO REVENUES. After a long and stormy session on March 1, the city council agreed to call a bond election in May.[3]

Mathews at this point announced his retirement as water bureau counsel to make his transition to the public service commission, where he began his long fight for city power. At the banquet in his honor, he was presented with a silver loving cup, and among the praises from his associates was Mulholland's. "I don't know how good a lawyer Mathews is, but I know he was always valuable in extricating us from difficulties into which we were continually falling. We would go to him and tell him we were in trouble again about something and he would get down Jones on torts and Smith on polygamy and go off there to the City Hall and fix it up somehow." He also used the occasion to take a swipe at the old city charter. "I don't know who was the author of the city charter we used to have, but I think I discerned from its literary style that it was written by the man who invented reinforced concrete. We used to be violating something that the charter prohibited all the time, but I may say that Mathews never failed to get us out of our scrapes." (In after years, Mulholland sometimes joked, "I did the work, but Mathews kept me out of jail.")[4]

A week after Mathews's "retirement" banquet, Charles "Charlie" Dwight Willard lost his long battle with tuberculosis. His funeral, held under the auspices of the Sunset Club, of which he had been a founder, lasted all afternoon. While an army of friends paid their final respects to one of the city's most ardent boosters, a driving rain developed into the fiercest storm Southern California had experienced since the aqueduct project began. (The season proved wet—23.31 inches—and its damage to Southern California led later in the year to the famous Reagan Report on flood control.) When word came from those who patrolled the aqueduct line that sand and debris had washed into the open conduit in Owens Valley and that boulders and trees had broken some concrete slabs and caused minor damage to a temporary dam near San Francisquito Creek, Mulholland left to inspect and oversee the repairs. Although damage proved slight, continued rainfall was to test the system further.[5]

The rains' most dramatic and publicized result was the collapse of about two hundred feet of siphon in the Antelope Valley when two concrete piers supporting it washed out. This gave Finkle new ammunition with which to attack Mulholland's competence, and in a trade journal, *The Contractor,* he wrote on March 7 that the mishap had been far more serious than the earlier failure at Sand Canyon and that these breakdowns stood in stark contrast to the excellence of the Edison plants, which had withstood the storm's onslaughts. Mulholland ignored the bad-mouthing and proceeded to repair the pipe just as he said he would. Introducing water at full pressure restored the siphon's original shape—as good as if it had never been damaged. The negative reports spurred Mayor Rose to an inspection tour of the aqueduct, but upon return in early April, he pronounced the horror stories of faulty construction "all bosh and invented by people who want to hurt the aqueduct." Earlier in March, J. Waldo Smith, of the Catskill Aqueduct, had also toured the system and pronounced it one of the greatest municipal accomplishments of modern history, giving high praise to its chief engineer who had achieved the work "without suspicion of graft."[6]

With the spring campaign for power bonds came oddly assorted opposition from Finkle; the Independent Civic League; the *Record;* the Socialist journal *The Gopher;* the Building Trades Council; and the conservative *Los Angeles Times.* Not only did *The Gopher* ("Goes to the roots" was its motto) accuse Mulholland of being in league with private water and power companies; it also concocted a fiction that he was an engineer of dubious, even sinister, character who took a huge salary from the city while also receiving money for acting on behalf of a private water company as well as for a power corporation owned by E. T. Earl that had power rights on the Feather River. He was also later accused of ill-treating labor on the aqueduct, while the Building Trades Council headlined him as a "Corporation Hireling on the City Payroll." The Chamber of Commerce remained divided on the power question, but even some of its conservative leaders deplored Otis's "brazen aspersions" against municipal power and, under the spirited influence of Dr. John Randolph Haynes and his Progressive allies, finally gave its approval for the bonds. Organized labor was split: the Central Labor Council approved passage of the bonds; the Building Trades Council did not and was suspected of receiving secret financing from the private power companies. In a vigorous and noisy campaign that again sent Scattergood and Mulholland to the hustings, municipal power triumphed on May 8 when voters gave a generous excess (56,183 for; 23,164 against) over the two-thirds vote required for the bonds' passage.[7]

In a triumphant mood, Mulholland left the city to participate in a happy event when, on May 12, the University of California at Berkeley awarded him an honorary doctorate during its commencement exercises. Two years earlier, Meyer Lissner had recommended the honor to Governor Johnson ("upon suggestion of one of Mulholland's most ardent admirers in the engineering profession"). "The University would not [only] honor the man but would honor itself by showing that it appreciated true achievements, whether coming from a college man or from a man who has attained prominence through self-education, and it would be thoroughly appreciated I assure you by the people in this end of the state." Also honored were George Washington Goethals, chief engineer of the Panama Canal, and David Starr Jordan, educator and president of Stanford University. For a man who had never studied a day at any university, it was a rare and deeply satisfying moment to march in academic procession to the Greek Theatre and receive this prize from the hands of the university's president, Benjamin Ide Wheeler. As a prelude (and probably also to validate him professionally as he had no academic degrees), he was also granted membership into the largest engineering society in America, Tau Beta Pi.[8]

Five days later, Mulholland was back guiding a group of city officials and the new public service commission along the system, many of whom had never seen it. Shortly after, on May 27, the city council heard the Independent Civic League's demand to reduce Mulholland's salary from $15,000 to $7,000 and to dismiss Scattergood. The council denied both items, while one member declared, "I believe that if we paid Mulholland ten times his present salary, and he lived to draw it 150 years, we would still owe him a great deal." During this busy spring, the Chief wedged in an agreeable if somewhat quirky encounter with the builder of Egypt's Aswan Dam, Sir William Willcocks. The federal government had retained Willcocks, a world authority on irrigation and water systems, to inspect and report on reclamation projects in the West and Southwest. When the two Williams met, Sir William said, "I take my hat off to you," to which plain Bill replied, "Mine is already off to you." A tiny but vigorous octogenarian who insisted on taking a morning constitutional before embarking on a day of touring the southern end of the aqueduct, Willcocks must have impressed Mulholland favorably, for the Chief prevailed upon his ailing wife to make a rare appearance in his office that he might introduce her to the distinguished visitor. Both men spoke that night at a banquet in Willcocks's honor. Some attendees left disappointed when neither addressed serious questions of engineering and instead told stories of experiences in their work. Mulholland set the informal tone for the evening when he announced, "In England they have a custom of knighting men who distinguish themselves in their professions. In America it is the custom to roast them."[9]

THE CHIEF DEFENDS HIS WORK

With honors and distinguished visitors behind him, Mulholland began a project he had wished to see undertaken for the past ten years: the laying of a filtration bed to purify the water drawn from the Los Angeles River. Located at the Narrows on the old Hooker-Pomeroy land, the installation would free the surface water of impurities and also wash out the clay particles that discolored and muddied the present water supply. The system was to be used until aqueduct water was completely connected with the city water system, a process that would take several years.

A week later, Mulholland announced that the first delivery of aqueduct water to city mains from the Franklin Canyon pipeline had been completed. The system could now deliver 40 million gallons of water a day, yielding to the city a revenue of $200,000 a year. By the end of July, residents west of Western Avenue who had long complained of poor water service now reported that the water from Owens River was proving "softer and purer" than that to which they had been accustomed.[10]

Ironically, at this moment of success, a particularly malicious attack on the aqueduct began and would result in a long trial the following year. The familiar Socialist participants of the Aqueduct Investigation Board, H. A. Hart and attorney Ingle Carpenter, led the onslaught with a court appearance before Judge John D. Works in mid-August, at which they filed a petition for an injunction against the further use of aqueduct water on the grounds that it was a menace to public health. They produced depositions from city health officers and chemists questioning the sanitary conditions along the aqueduct's route. The *Record,* which had never ceased its anti-Otis attacks and accusations against San Fernando Valley millionaire profiteers with their links to Owens River water, jumped into the fray by printing sections of one report with the scare front-page headline AQUEDUCT WATER IS POISON. The subheadline, "Owens River Unfit For Humans Says Bacteriologist," was followed by a description of the filth and unsanitary conditions along the aqueduct. Three days later the second report was headlined AQUEDUCT WATER IS LIQUID MANURE.[11]

Mulholland protested, "The claim that Owens River water is not fit for human consumption is too preposterous to talk about—it is too outrageously ridiculous to even consider. I have had thousands of men working on the aqueduct, all drinking the water, and not a single instance of ill effect. Since the aqueduct water has been turned into the city mains I have had hundreds of letters congratulating me on its excellent quality." He branded the attempt "one of the most mendacious outrages that has been perpetrated on this city," an effort "to create public hysteria to promote private ends." He clinched his response with two hard questions. "Where are you going to get pure water if we haven't it in the Owens River Valley? If it isn't pure in the Sierras, where is it pure? There is not a water supply to any city of any size in the country that is as pure and free from contamination. The city of London draws its supply from a watershed where the inhabitation is 400 to the square mile, as against 1¼ per square mile in the Owens River Valley."[12]

The author of this alarmist report was Dr. Ethel Leonard, who, although currently residing in Chicago, had a long history of activity in the medical and health affairs of Los Angeles. Of remarkable accomplishment, Ethel Langdon Leonard, a native of Chicago, had graduated from medical school at the University of Southern California and done postgraduate work at Johns Hopkins, as well as further studies in England, Germany, and Canada. In 1903, under the city health officer, Dr. L. M. Powers, she became city bacteriologist and, in an age newly aware of the need for better hygiene and sanitation, seems to have been a zealous microbe hunter.[13]

Leonard's motives in lending her talents to attacking the aqueduct remain obscure. She later testified in court that she did not know her report would be published, although a posed newspaper photograph of her at work in her laboratory suggests she could not have been altogether innocent of the *Record*'s interest in her. Moreover, while working on a project in Chicago, she had been highly vocal to reporters there about the abominable condition of Owens River water, and in her report she wrote a pious self-justification. "Poisoning or polluting the wells is one of the most outrageous crimes known to history . . . and yet in Los Angeles we have the spectacle of a city government itself deliberately poisoning the entire water supply of the whole population. They are committing one of the worst offenses in all the category of crimes known to man. And the facts in my report prove it." In spite of these dire utterances, however, when she was requested to appear at the first court hearing in the fall, she declared she was too busy in Chicago to come west, although she indicated that she would be available for a payment of $1,000 and a round-trip railway ticket. Her terms denied and the hearing delayed, she did not appear in court until she was subpoenaed to the trial at the beginning of the following year.[14]

The city fathers closed ranks to defend the safety of the water while several leading bacteriologists and chemical engineers of impeccable credentials also vouched for its purity. At a preliminary hearing in September Mathews wondered who was financing this costly attack, and although guesses included the private power companies, bottled water suppliers, and the private Hollywood Union Water Company, denials arose from all quarters and the matter remained undetermined. Mulholland began to hear from engineers around the country who had received in the mail a small booklet containing Hart's and Carpenter's charges against the aqueduct water. Deploring the attempt to blacken his work and the city's reputation ("a most treasonable thing," he raged), the Chief continued to insist that it was the work of the power interests.[15]

Whatever the complexities of his life, Mulholland remained focused on engineering matters. While sitting home one evening "with nothing to do" during this post-aqueduct period he thought of a new (and better) method of concreting tunnels. Instead of the usual way of mixing concrete outside the tunnel and loading it onto cars and shoveling it out, he devised a system of forcing cement through pipes against the walls of the tunnel. When it was tried in the power tunnels at San Francisquito Canyon, it not only proved successful but reduced the expense by half.[16]

IS THE WATER PURE?

The trial to restrain Owens River water from Los Angeles took forty days in court during the first three months of 1915. While his wife was dying at home, Mulholland sat in court as Mathews defended the aqueduct. Among the early deponents and witnesses for the plaintiff were Owens Valley men who testified to the polluting presence of dead cattle and corral drainages into the creeks in the Owens River Valley. (One of these was George Watterson of the Watterson clan, later to play a prominent role in the valley's opposition to Mulholland and Los Angeles.) After Mathews attempted early on to discover who was behind the suit, the court ruled that the only issue to be considered was the purity of the water. Leonard reported her bacteriological findings but under cross-examination admitted that they were "of no value." At the end of January, Mulholland spent a day testifying and refuting the statements of a San Francisco bacteriologist who claimed that the canyon winds in Owens Valley moved the water too rapidly to allow for the devitalization of bacteria. When Mulholland set out to explain how water became purified in Haiwee Reservoir, he was challenged about his fitness to testify as an expert witness on geological matters, to which he replied, "I have been a student of geology for the last thirty years. I at first took it up as a sort of fad because I liked it, but soon found that it was useful to me in my profession as an engineer. Since then I have become familiar with the works of practically all the well-known authorities on the subject of geology, and on one occasion I qualified as an expert witness on geology." With the objection overruled, Mulholland spent the rest of the day on the stand explaining the principles of purification at work in a storage reservoir, explaining also that Haiwee is not properly a storage reservoir, as the water rushes through it from ingress to egress. He declared sanitary conditions along the Owens River and the aqueduct superior to those along the streams and watersheds of San Francisco, Oakland, Cincinnati, and many other cities. His testimony also provided a seminar on the winds of that area based on his years of observation. When he next appeared a few days later, he produced some moments of mirth as his patience wore thin with attorney Ingle Carpenter's unremittingly hostile objections and questions. When Carpenter asked, "Mr. Mulholland, how fast does water flow through a reservoir?" he shot back, "What's the use of answering a question like that? That's about as silly as how big is a piece of chalk? How do I know?"

When next goaded to comment on the "grossly polluted condition of the water as it enters Haiwee reservoir," Mulholland roared, "What do you mean by grossly? None of that water's polluted—let alone being grossly." He then proceeded to explain that it would take a drop of water from three to four years to flow from the intake at Owens River to the city's water mains. From Haiwee it would take sixty to seventy days, not the two or three contended by the plaintiff. The Haiwee itself is the purifier, he explained, and in comparing the amount of organic matter lying in its depth to that in the Catskill Reservoir supplying the City of New York, he declared, "The Haiwee is as a painted lily compared to that." He explained that on the site of the Catskill Reservoir had once stood four towns whose organic matter existed below to a depth of between thirty and forty feet.[17]

The heaviest blows to the plaintiff's case came when subsequent testimony by distinguished scientists corroborated Mulholland's claims. One of the world's leading bacteriologists, Dr. Edwin O. Jordan of the University of Chicago, whom the plaintiffs had frequently cited as an authority, undermined their contentions when he inspected the aqueduct and concluded that the "water at the effluent of the Haiwee reservoir is potable and safe for human consumption." The next powerful endorsement of the water's purity came with the testimony of Professor Charles Gilman Hyde, engineer for the state board of health and engineering professor at the University of California, Berkeley. He declared that if the waters of the Mississippi or Missouri Rivers in their most polluted state should be emptied into the upper reaches of the Los Angeles Aqueduct, Haiwee Reservoir would render the water wholesome and pure, so great was its capacity as a purifying agent. Del Valle of the water board remarked at the time that he wished the city's schoolchildren could have attended the hearings, for they would have received a liberal education in several of the sciences from leading authorities in their field.[18]

Finally, in the late afternoon of March 19, 1915, Judge Works announced his decision to deny the injunction and allow the city judgment for its costs in defending its water system. Mulholland stood with Mathews and upon hearing that they had prevailed, jubilantly exclaimed, "It's all said, you old tar heel, and I knew it ten years ago. Let's go drink some of that 'polluted stuff' they say comes from up the valley, just to show them how good it is." Mathews agreed that the aqueduct had just been put to the severest possible test and not been found wanting. The decision was appealed, however, and not until 1919 did the state supreme court make a final decision for the city. By then, it was academic, for as the president of the public service commission remarked at the time, "The aqueduct water has long ago been proved to be healthful and pure, and the fact that the city has the aqueduct supply to fall back on proves the wisdom of the project." In fact, in a ten-year period, cases of typhoid in Los Angeles had decreased from 20 per 100,000 in 1909 to 3 per 100,000 in 1919.[19]

Throughout the trial, Mulholland kept busy with other urgent water matters for the city. One weekend in late February, he traveled to Alameda to work out a sale of steam shovels as part of the aqueduct salvage program. As the San Fernando Reservoir, completed on January 22, began to fill with Owens River water and water lines were rapidly being extended to expand water service in the city, two vexing issues remained unresolved: annexation and buying up the remaining private water companies. After months of negotiation and debate, the Hollywood Union Company at last sold to the city, and on March 20, eligible voters of the sparsely settled San Fernando Valley chose almost unanimously to annex: 681 for and 25 against. As the next step was an election on May 4 to secure the city's approval, opposition to annexation arose from certain groups advocating the building of S. C. Graham's high line. When Graham argued his case in the city council, Mulholland rebutted by citing statistics showing that Graham, despite all his efforts, had not signed up as many users for water along the high line as were already prepared and anxious for aqueduct water in the San Fernando Valley.[20]

A DEATH AND NEW CHALLENGES

In early April 1915, with councilmen Betkouski and Wheeler, Mulholland escorted a party of Socialist office seekers along the aqueduct line in the valley in an attempt to win them to the cause of valley annexation. He had also planned to escort the same group to San Francisquito Canyon at the end of April, but instead remained with his wife, who was to die of cancer on April 28 at the age of forty-seven. The day of her funeral, the executive offices of the water department remained closed. (Even the collection offices were briefly shut.) All of the pallbearers were the Chief's close friends and water associates so that in death as in life, Lillie Mulholland was overshadowed by the events and men surrounding her husband.[21]

Now a widower with five grown but unmarried children, Mulholland increasingly allowed work and public life to dominate his existence. Two days after the funeral, he was back in his office, where, on April 30, he issued a public statement to the citizens of Los Angeles, recommending that they vote yes on annexation in the May 4 election. After a fiercely argued campaign, the annexation measures prevailed but were eclipsed by the amazing mayoral victory of the currently suspended chief of police, C. E. Sebastian, whose chief recommendation for office seems to have been his good looks. At the time of the election, Sebastian faced a felony charge of sexual misconduct; although acquitted of the immorality charges, he was forced to resign a year later in the wake of accusations of municipal corruption.[22]

For the next four or five years, Mulholland constantly improved and refined the city's water system. The long-awaited filtration gallery for purifying Los Angeles River water, for instance, went into operation in 1915. He occasionally acted as a troubleshooter as well. When he heard that ranchers and residents in the Zelzah area (today, Northridge) were stealing water from the Zelzah Ditch by secretly diverting it at night from the land to which it was being ditched, he went immediately to straighten the matter out in a powwow with valley ranchers. He sometimes found time for lesser projects as when, for the Panama-Pacific Exposition (1915–1916) and an annual meeting of the American Society of Civil Engineers where he was to read a paper on the aqueduct, he devised a scale relief map of the Owens River Aqueduct with a process he invented using layered vulcanized pasteboard to reproduce topographical surveys. (Subsequently the United States government adopted the method for making relief maps.) Because he understood that the average city-dweller had little idea of the magnitude of the project, he urged them to come and see an accurate replica at the department offices in the Knickerbocker Building at Olive near Seventh. "There is nothing like it in the whole world," he assured them.[23]

He continued to act as guide and diplomat along the aqueduct to a passing parade of politicians, officials, dignitaries, and visitors, many out west from Washington, D.C., to view reclamation projects, flood control plans, and aqueduct construction. Above all in the post-aqueduct years, he jousted with councilmen and mayors. Mayor Sebastian, who was supported (and possibly coerced) by the Municipal League, which had become stridently opposed to public power, tried to put through a cost-cutting budget by insisting upon the city's need for $500,000 from the water department. He succeeded in strong-arming the public service commission into conceding that it could spare $225,000 without injuring the progress of its expansion plans for water and power, but the power bureau, desperate for funds, requested and on August 29 received from the council $38,000 from its reserve fund for development work in the Owens River Gorge and Long Valley region. With this amount, work could continue until April 1917, when, the bureau hoped, the power bonds would be voted and approved. Part of the urgency was to hold off incursions from the private power companies: "The city of Los Angeles has some valuable holdings in the Long Valley region and the Owens River Gorge. . . . Certain private power interests are trying to get a foothold in the Owens River Gorge, but the city so far has been winning the fight."[24]

Scandal-ridden Mayor Sebastian retired in 1916 "for reasons of health," and the council replaced him with Frederic Thomas Woodman, a New England attorney who had come to California in 1908 because of his wife's delicate health and who, as a member of the harbor commission, had worked to quiet title and recover all the tide lands at the harbor. A civic booster and student of the administration of police affairs (an area of city government sorely in need of reform), Woodman, a staid conservative and somewhat colorless Republican and Mason, epitomized the white, Protestant male who now dominated the city's politics. The new mayor immediately announced that he could make no decisions on the power matter until he had toured the aqueduct. When he told Mulholland to go with him, he received a curt response. "Is that your order?"

To which the mayor replied, "That is my order."

"Then I will go," rejoined Mulholland.[25]

After four days along the line, Mayor Woodman returned to the city declaring his commitment to developing municipal power and a willingness to mediate the disputes with the private power companies. During his administration, however, the water and power men suffered defeat when voters trounced the important 1917 bond measure. It was to have funded the completion of generating facilities at what would become Power House No. 2 in San Francisquito Canyon and to have paid for land and rights for future development along the Owens River Gorge. The combined opposition of the *Times* and *Record,* of various business groups (including the revived Committee of 1000, largely the creature of the Edison Company), of parties that hinted the city was secretly in league with private power and intended ultimately to sell to the power trust—all these foes of varying persuasions, as well as general resistance to an increased tax load, handed the water and power establishment one of its worst defeats. A 40 percent turnout delivered a vote of 33,370 for and 51,267 against the power bonds. Labor, which had supported municipal power, also found itself a heavy loser, as bond passage would have resulted in jobs for members of its local unions. The defeat at the polls also reflected the waning of progressivism and the ascendancy of conservatism in an increasingly business-minded and open-shop city. The bonds did not succeed until after World War I, when in June 1919, they passed with 4,000 more votes than needed for a two-thirds majority, 46,656 for and 21,248 against. At that time, voters also swept Woodman out of office and replaced him with former mayor Meredith "Pinky" Snyder.[26]

During the successful campaign against municipal power in 1917, while the *Times* decried public power as a Socialist plot, the *Record* expressed its opposition to the water-power establishment with a series of clever, albeit vicious, cartoons portraying Mulholland and Scattergood as a pair of broken-down vaudeville comedians, Mul and Skat, constantly harried in their attempts to nurse back to health a strange-looking creature known as Acqua-Duck, or Bill's Ducky. Ducky resembled the Tik-Tok man of Oz, a spherical duck-billed creature of iron-plated patchwork possessed of an insatiable appetite for taxpayer dollars, which its desperate caretakers attempted to satisfy by bilking taxpayers of their hard-earned money. A more serious note was struck when warnings of a dynamiting plot at Haiwee forced the city to place extra guards along the aqueduct. At this same time, the Owens Valley newspaper, the *Inyo Register*, began to reprint the *Record*'s attacks amid reports of increasing resistance in the north to the city's plans for municipal power.[27]

BLOWOUTS AND RUMORS OF RETIREMENT

On July 11, shortly after the disastrous bond election and a heat wave that produced record-breaking drains on the water supply, an Owens Valley earthquake cracked a piece of the aqueduct in the Alabama hills. At the time, Mulholland was overseeing the installation of filtration galleries to purify irrigation water for domestic use in the Boyle Heights district and preparing to begin work on the Chatsworth Reservoir. Hastening to the scene, Mulholland promised immediate repair, but later, on Sunday, July 15, at one o'clock in the afternoon, he received word at home that two new blowouts had occurred along the aqueduct: one near Neenach in the Antelope Valley, the other near Little Lake south of Haiwee. He set out immediately for Neenach, while Van Norman hurried down from Haiwee to Little Lake. Mayor Woodman blurted that he suspected dynamitings, which produced headlines along with his declaration that he would place added guards along the aqueduct and near reservoirs with orders of "Shoot to Kill." Mulholland deplored disseminating such alarmist information without verification and, after an inspection of the break near Neenach, phoned a more cautious statement to his secretary, Burt Heinly. "Two widely separated and serious breaks occurred in the Los Angeles Aqueduct early this morning. I have investigated one of them and can say that there are circumstances which make me suspicious as to the agency responsible. I do not want to charge that some outside agency is responsible for what has happened. A most thorough inquiry will be made to learn just what happened and just why the breaks occurred."[28] What Mulholland had discovered near Neenach was a sixty-foot break in the line, which he estimated would require three days to repair. Van Norman reported more extensive destruction near Little Lake, where the damaged tunnel had blocked water flow and caused flooding that washed out two hundred feet of rail track and weakened the supports of a bridge so that a southbound freight train partially derailed when it crossed the weakened structure. The water engineers at first observed that both breaks had in common a proximity to manholes that, although securely covered, could have been easily opened so that an explosive could be dropped into the conduit. After a week of inspection, however, Mulholland concluded that the break near Little Lake resulted from earthquake. He remained suspicious of the Neenach break, however, and extra surveillance along that stretch of the line produced the arrest of one man after he had been observed loitering for four days in the vicinity of Fairmont Dam. Suspicions increased when he turned out to be an employee of the city's foe, the Los Angeles Gas and Electric Corporation, especially after he could not account for his presence there. Although taken into custody, he was later released.[29]

Mulholland and Van Norman spent the remainder of July examining and overseeing repairs, while down in the city, the *Record* used the blowouts as a pretext to renew its attack on Mulholland's competence. These attacks against the water and power establishment sufficiently swayed Mayor Woodman that at the end of summer he requested a complete audit of the public service commission by a disinterested accountant, with the results to be made public. Woodman also defended his public statements about dynamitings, saying he thought the public should be informed and that Mulholland's silence on the matter presented an appearance of secrecy. After accusing him and Scattergood of "too much of the star chamber idea in their methods," the mayor declared his intention to make changes on the water board, adding that although good engineers, the two leaders were not successes as executives.[30]

With gossip about Woodman's possible shake-up of the public service commission rife in City Hall, four members handed in their resignations, while the *Record* crowed that it alone was responsible for defeating "Invisible Government," "Earlism," and "the schemes of Bill Mulholland." Through all these flaps, Mulholland remained silent. He had seen mayors and administrations come and go while he remained a fixture on the civic landscape. At sixty-two, he had learned to control his temper most of the time, and he remained clear about one of his missions: to keep whoever was mayor on the path of supporting municipal water and power. Private concerns took much of his time and energy in 1918, which led to rumors of his retirement, but the hopes of those who wished to see him disappear were dashed in January 1919, when he announced that he had no thought of retiring.[31]

A GROWING CITY DURING WORLD WAR I

In spite of crises and interruptions, by the end of the decade, Los Angeles had created a reliable water supply for its population of 533,535 (which now outstripped its northern rival, San Francisco, with 471,023). Growth, however, meant the need to convince citizens to vote funds for a continued expansion of water and power services and to familiarize them with issues often complex, unclear, and usually to a layman, matters of indifference. As World War I ended with its lifting of domestic restrictions, plans and hopes for municipal power quickened. When construction began on cottages and facilities in San Francisquito Canyon, even the unfriendly *Los Angeles Times* printed a Sunday feature piece on construction there of Power Plant No. 2 with the headline CITY REARS NEW TEMPLE OF THOR. With unabated growth and bustle in the city, as well as continued annexation (Sawtelle came in, and the Dominguez and Palos Verdes Ranchos planned to join in the near future), concern for increased demands on water supplies continued. By March 1919, only 6.07 inches of rain had fallen (the season's total would be 8.62 inches), so that by midsummer, when San Fernando Valley ranchers were at the peak of their irrigation season and Mulholland expected them to use one-third more than they had the year before, he cautioned them to organize, to learn to take their turns, and in some cases, to rely on night irrigation. Planning ahead for a possible drought, he directed Van Norman to begin drilling 100 wells in Owens Valley as a precautionary measure, while in August, work began on the large reservoir known as San Fernando No. 1, north of No. 2. Repairs to the leak that had long plagued Haiwee Dam finally became possible when its lowered water level revealed the problem to be a crevasse in the side of the canyon near the dam.[32]

Shortly before Christmas 1919, as a harbinger to the turbulent decade ahead, word came from Washington, D.C., that the all-important power right-of-way bill was in trouble. Nine large power companies, along with Inyo-Kern power and irrigation project advocates, had blocked this legislation that would have cleared up titles to the aqueduct's power line rights-of-way. Mathews, just back from the capital, was forced to turn around and return, while Mulholland was alerted that he would probably be needed to testify in the Senate early in the new year.[33]

CHAPTER 21

A Stormy Decade Begins

1920–1923

THOUGHTS OF BOULDER DAM

The fight for municipal power in Los Angeles and the later campaign to build the federal project of Boulder Dam occurred during the politically reactionary years of the Harding, Coolidge, and Hoover administrations and produced some of the ugliest political hate campaigns in the history of the West. Permanent scars yet remain on the reputations of those who battled in those wars, for the private interests proved almost insuperable adversaries against the advocates of public ownership. Not until 1936, a year after Mulholland's death, would the municipalization of power in Los Angeles be fully realized, nor did the Chief live to see the completion of Boulder Dam and the Colorado River Aqueduct. In those years of struggle when hopes rose only to be dashed, skillfully crafted propaganda campaigns against the city's aims so artfully manipulated public sentiment and made such deep inroads into the popular psyche that many of the spurious charges not only were believed but have long since grown entrenched. As Tom Sitton has written in his biography of municipal power champion John Randolph Haynes, "The legacy of this struggle is a never-ending parade of historical accounts, some expounding conspiracy theories and others staunchly defending Los Angeles in its quest for Owens Valley water."[1]

In early April 1920, Mulholland left for Washington, D.C., with Scattergood, Mathews, and the president of city council, Ralph Criswell, to appeal to the Senate for passage of the aqueduct right-of-way bill. At the time, Mulholland and his family were in the throes of settling into a new home at 426 South Saint Andrews Place in the recently opened Windsor Square Tract after leaving Boyle Heights, where they had lived for twenty-five years. Daughter Rose recalled that after "Papa" had assured her he was all packed for the trip, she investigated the Gladstone bag he always carried and discovered its entire contents to consist of two clean collars and a bottle of whiskey. The passage of the important amendment was to insure the city against encroachments from private power companies in Inyo County, but within two weeks of their arrival in Washington, the attorney for the Southern Sierra and Nevada-California Power Companies made a surprise attack, challenging the city's power right-of-way for the Owens River Gorge below the Long Valley Reservoir. The city, he argued, had water rights but not power rights in the land it had acquired. If upheld, the claim would have thrown the city into years of litigation. Mathews and Mulholland argued otherwise and ultimately prevailed when the bill was approved June 5, but similar land mines threatened each step on the long tortuous path.[2]

SOME PENALTIES OF RAPID GROWTH

By 1920, Los Angeles had in part fallen victim to its own success, which in many quarters excited hostility, not to say envy and its counterpart, derision. It was now the tenth most populous city in the United States (estimated at 730,000); its aqueduct was a triumph, as was its harbor; agriculture in the San Fernando Valley had earned $13 million in 1919; and a thriving movie industry was gaining worldwide fame and popularity. When Mulholland participated in a panel at the Sunset Club in 1921 to discuss "Some of the Penalties of Rapid Growth in Los Angeles," he must have cited as one penalty the increasing need for resources that others were loath to share or part with. As the statewide competition for water supplies grew through the decade, so would animosities.

The city's success was predicated on an efficient municipal water organization's providing an adequate supply at low rates, along with a growing power system able to produce low-priced electricity in competition with existing private systems. In the spring of 1920, for example, when the state railroad commission granted Edison Electric Company a 27 percent rate increase, the city's power bureau announced that it would not raise light rates. Later in the year, when Mulholland announced the need to increase water rates, he countered protests by pointing out that Los Angeles's metered rates were lower than the average

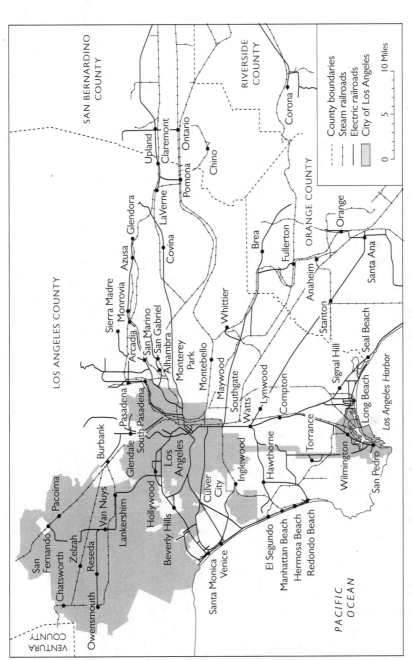

Map 5. Greater Los Angeles, 1925 (adapted from Lester S. Ready, J. O. Marsh, and Richard Sachse, *Joint Report on Street Railway Survey, City of Los Angeles to the Railroad Commission of the State of California* [Los Angeles, 1925], Los Angeles Department of Public Utilities).

maximum and minimum rates for the forty-nine largest cities in the United States.[3]

As the city pressed its cause in Washington for additional water rights to ensure a greater production of hydroelectric power, a statewide flurry of protests arose. The previous winter (1919–1920) had been dry. Much of California suffered from drought, and by late summer, such acute power shortages occurred in the north that San Francisco had to curtail commercial sign and window lighting. Yet with Haiwee Dam full and other storage areas in good supply, Los Angeles was not severely affected. Neighboring communities, however, did not applaud this success. Bakersfield was suffering, and one of its editors, remarking on Los Angeles's recent victory in Congress allowing it to purchase water rights in Mono Basin, warned that "Los Angeles has its eyes on Mono lake waters and if she can freeze out a few homesteaders she will be without just that much opposition in the final grab." When San Francisco city officials learned that Los Angeles had made preliminary filings for possible power plants on both the Tuolumne and Merced Rivers as well as Yosemite Creek, they threatened action along with the Sierra Club. Mathews hastened to assure all parties that Los Angeles would undertake no project that would conflict with any San Francisco plan, but headlines in Bakersfield and Owens Valley papers quickly protested the city's "mad grab of all water and hydro-electric rights in Southern and Central California." The *Bakersfield Californian* condemned Los Angeles as a "water hog" and described its public service commission as "a group of radicals and public ownership faddists," while an Owens Valley paper declared BISHOP WILL ASSIST IN CURBING L. A. At a town meeting held in Bishop in July 1920, one lone dissenter dared to say he thought the local hysteria was a movement "favored by the Southern Sierras Power Company."[4]

The Bakersfield editor also acknowledged that his information about Los Angeles and Owens Valley came largely from the Los Angeles *Record,* which, acting as the exchange editor, was supplying material about "the outrage of smaller communities over L. A.'s water-grabbing." The *Record* also resumed its old vendetta against Mulholland, now referring to him as "Aqueduct Bill" and portraying him as an intractable curmudgeon. According to the *Record,* when Aqueduct Bill offered an opinion, he never "spoke" or "uttered"; instead, he "grunted" or "wrathfully charged." Scare headlines warned of possible water famine and polluted aqueduct water under Aqueduct Bill's mismanagement, while cartoons of "Bill's Acqua-Duck" ridiculed both his engineering and business ability.[5]

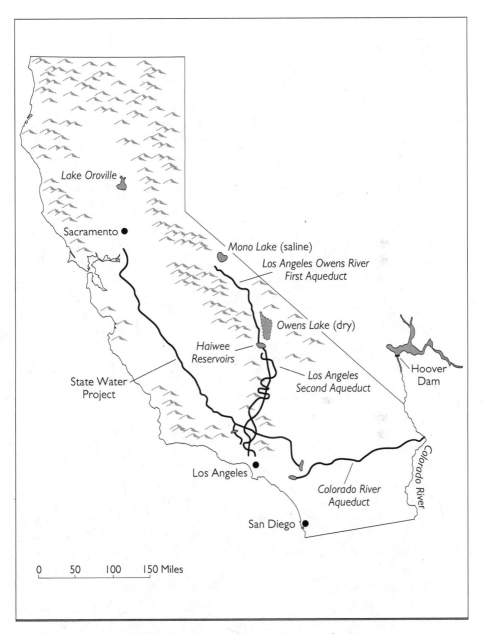

Map 6. Southern California water supply, 1925 (Los Angeles Department of Water and Power).

Against this backdrop of negative comment appeared an increasing number of articles couching the city's behavior in terms of theft, rape, and exploitation. An August 3, 1921, editorial in the conservative *Bakersfield Californian* forcefully struck the theme. "Los Angeles, preoccupied in the task of working out its splendid destiny, has long failed to realize that there are penalties attached to ruthless aggression and disregard of the rights of others." As this campaign expanded through the state, a story evolved to resonate with the sentimental fiction of the Old West and wring the hearts of all who champion the underdog. Written and rewritten in many places throughout the decade, it became an enduring tale of the sad fate of decent, modest pioneer folk betrayed and skinned by highbinders and money boys from the city. Other than an occasional grumbling comment throughout the war years, Owens Valley newspapers had said little about Los Angeles. The aqueduct builders' and workers' presence in Owens Valley seemed no longer noteworthy, and although certain locals harbored animosity, relationships overall had been peaceful. Then abruptly, in 1920, seven years after the aqueduct had been completed and fifteen since the whole enterprise began, many valley residents and land owners, as if long in deep slumber, awakened and began to describe themselves as victims of a great oppressor, Mulholland, and those who did his bidding, the public service commission of Los Angeles. A harsh new tone arose as local journalists heightened their rhetoric and flailed out with reckless and malicious accusations of the city's wicked destruction of Owens Valley.

This outpouring of exposé stories—a veritable renaissance of muckraking journalism—appears, in retrospect, orchestrated rather than spontaneous. Between 1920 and 1924, the number of articles attacking Los Angeles quadrupled in the three Owens Valley newspapers, two of which were in part underwritten (or at least in debt to) the two major factions of opposing landowners in Owens Valley. Devoted to unmasking the city's villainy, the *Owens Valley Herald* was edited by Harry A. Glasscock, nephew of one of the paper's founders, and copublished by a Watterson in-law, newspaperman Court E. Kunze. Its accusations against the city became so virulent and false that at one point the public service commission debated suing for slander. The second journal, the *Bishop Index,* edited by local attorney Leicester C. Hall, was sponsored by a rival group who were considered pro–Los Angeles. The *Bishop Index* seemed dedicated to opposing the *Owens Valley Herald* and denouncing Fred Eaton. The third (most respectable, independent, and almost certainly, least subsidized) was the venerable journalistic voice of the *Inyo Register,* owned

and edited by an honorable descendant of Owens Valley journalist-print-
ers, William A. Chalfant. Chalfant had always been anti–Los Angeles,
but in the 1920s as the verbal abuse against the city and its representatives intensified, even he sometimes was a voice of moderation. During
some of the most abusive attacks, he pointed out that the city did after
all pay county taxes on all the land it had acquired in Owens Valley and
thus provided needed revenues to Inyo County.[6]

Mulholland had long been accused of an unfeeling disregard for the
people of Owens Valley, and by the 1920s, this may well have appeared
true as Owens Valley affairs by then drew only a fraction of his professional attention. Unlike Goethals, who after completing the Panama
Canal, left Panama and never returned, Mulholland, a man who rarely
took a day off, remained devoted to his adopted city, became ever more
deeply involved in civic affairs, and with Scattergood, began to consider
the Colorado River as a source of hydroelectric power. In early 1921,
they made an exploratory trip to study possible dam sites there, which
resulted in a later decision to send survey parties to continue the work.
Since his wife's death, Mulholland seemed to find it difficult to turn down
requests, so that when his old associate, G. E. Elliott, chief engineer of
the Spring Valley Water Company, asked him to take on the additional
task of serving on an advisory committee on storage and distribution of
water for the state department of public works, he found himself unable
to refuse. (Also serving were George Goethals and Arthur P. Davis.) Thus,
during many of the major negotiations and confrontations in Owens Valley during the 1920s, longtime coworkers Ed Leahey and Harvey Van
Norman served as the city's representatives, both having worked, lived,
and established good relationships with many people in the valley.[7]

To imagine that Mulholland was unaware and uncaring of the people
of Owens Valley is to misread the man. Of course, he knew that irrevo-
cable change would occur with the removal of Owens River water and
the purchase of lands. Years before he had acknowledged Mary Austin's
Cassandra-like prophecies, but as an engineer, he was allied to those who
believed their technical skills contributed to civilization's advance. He
also understood that Roosevelt's Benthamite utilitarian principle of "the
greatest good for the greatest number" would not necessarily lead to the
"greatest good for *all*"; that the contradiction in this philosophy that
could logically lead to either complete bureaucracy or complete anarchy
would inevitably injure some in this region of seven thousand souls. As
a pragmatist, he did not believe that the interests of the valley people had
been stinted. The city had paid fair prices to those who willingly sold

their land, while those who remained had enough water to serve their needs. The Owens Valley, after all, had not been vacated and drowned as upstate villages had been in the New York Aqueduct project, where even the dead had been removed from their burial sites. Nor was this so-called ruthlessness directed against small landowners and townspeople but against those few who wished to profit at the expense of the city, the private interests that he believed thwarted "the greatest good" by blocking its intentions. Here he could be fierce. Even such a city partisan as public service commissioner William Paul Whitsett once commented that when it came to the city's interest, Mulholland drove a hard bargain, and no one in Owens Valley knew this better than his old friend and associate Fred Eaton.[8]

THE LONG VALLEY QUESTION

The issue of the Long Valley dam site had never gone away, and in the 1920s Eaton and certain Owens Valley landowners were to use it as a lever in their attempt to wrest concessions from Los Angeles and get top prices for their land. Mulholland's frugality with the expenditure of public moneys was one of his virtues as a public administrator, so that when Eaton years before had asked a price for his Long Valley lands that Mulholland judged too high, the Chief set aside the original plan to build a 140-foot dam on the site and declared it only "possibly necessary" at some future date. Since that standoff, Eaton no longer dealt directly with Mulholland on city matters. Mathews, for example, sought Scattergood's help when he wished Eaton to adjudicate among the protesting parties in Mono County during the contention over the power rights-of-way legislation in Washington, D.C., in 1919.[9]

Eaton and his wife divided their time between Los Angeles and Owens Valley, where his older son, Harold, now also with a second wife, lived and managed many of their land and ranching operations. Although Eaton continued to use the California Club as his city address and spend time in Santa Monica, his principal interests centered on his Long Valley ranch (the former Rickey Ranch was now the Eaton Land and Cattle Company, with an area devoted to chicken growing called the Owens River Poultry Corporation). By 1923, when Eaton was encountering financial difficulties and arranging for a mortgage loan, the holding was thus described: "May 16—Eaton Land & Cattle Co. Fred Eaton, Pres. Report from THE MERCANTILE AGENCY, Bishop, Inyo County. Incorporated under Calif. law with a capital of $300,000 and has between

2,000 and 3,000 head of cattle. Well managed, has good holdings, pays bills promptly, and 'no one is found who is familiar with the details of the company.'"[10]

Eaton and his son had joined a group of leading Owens Valley owners and businessmen to form an irrigation district after the city's success in Congress over the right-of-way matter not only promised that it could take water from the Mono Basin but indicated that it would probably have to build the Long Valley Reservoir to impound the flows from above. By pooling their holdings, this group intended to be better able to drive a hard bargain with the city when it came to selling. Called the Owens Valley Property Owners Protective Association, it was dominated by two brothers of the prolific pioneering Watterson family, Wilfred W. and the younger Mark Q. Another member of their large clan was brother-in-law J. C. "Jake" Clausen, who had long ago written the report recommending building the Long Valley Reservoir as a Reclamation Bureau project. By 1922, the Watterson brothers had created a banking monopoly with their ownership of all five valley banks, which, along with their many local interests and business connections, assured their financial dominance in Owens Valley.[11]

The Protective Association comprised major owners of irrigation ditches at the northern end of Owens Valley above the aqueduct intake. Claiming that the city's piecemeal buying amounted to a divide-and-conquer acquisition of water-bearing valley lands, they intended to press the city into buying land en bloc. The city answered this charge through its land agents, John Martin and George Shuey (the latter having been on the Owens Valley scene since 1903). The city, they acknowledged, had always bargained for the lowest prices it could get, a practice Chalfant scornfully characterized as "peaceful assimilation."[12]

Of the other three most important ditch companies expressing opposition to any diversion of waters in the upper valley, one, the Owens River Canal Company, was considered friendlier to the city than the Eaton-Watterson group, which feared that the former's selling to the city would almost certainly undermine their goal. After the Canal Company had negotiated with the city in the spring of 1921 and gained assurances that its members would continue to receive adequate irrigation water during the growing season, the Eaton Land and Cattle Company brought suit against the Canal Company in July to establish riparian claims along certain creek tributaries to Owens River. This infighting between two ditch-owning groups was complicated by the presence in the rival group of Wilfred and Mark Watterson's uncle, George Watterson, secretary of the

Bishop Creek Ditch. Assisting him was Bishop attorney Leicester C. Hall, also editor of the *Bishop Index* and treasurer of the Owens River Canal Company. The third participant consisted of McNally Ditch owners (known as the Associated group) whose president was William Symons. Attorney-editor Hall editorialized for his group while Harry Glasscock, owner-editor of the *Owens Valley Herald*, did the same for the Watterson-Eaton group.[13]

Six months after Eaton had filed his action against the Owens River Canal Company, on January 20, 1922, Ed Leahey, the city's chief representative in Owens Valley since 1919, wrote Van Norman concerning Eaton's activities. He included clippings from the *Owens Valley Herald* that, he had been told, were the work of Fred Eaton and in which he was sure Van Norman would recognize Eaton's "fine Italian hand." The articles proclaimed that "the Owens Valley is standing together" against the depredations of Los Angeles, and to this end, Eaton had gone to San Francisco to retain some of the top legal talent of California. Throughout the year, attack pieces appeared featuring horror stories of the city's egregious misuse of water. "We suppose you are aware that waters of Owens River flowing down the aqueduct for municipal purposes are used in irrigating lands in the San Fernando Valley owned by Mulholland, Van Norman, McKay—then flowing through Beverly Hills and Benedict Canyon to the ocean and lost." The reality of the 130,000 acres the city had already purchased at the southern end of Owens Valley provoked wrenching descriptions of ruined farmlands, dead orchards, and alfalfa fields reverting to sagebrush. These accounts helped fuel local passions against the city so that they approved the creation of an irrigation district in a December 1922 election, followed on August 7, 1923, by the passage of over a million dollars in bonds for the acquisition of its waters and for new facilities and improvements. Although touted as a measure to save Owens Valley, this new irrigation district ultimately created nothing other than a convenient governmental instrument for bargaining with the city. All future contentions with the city centered on top prices for land sales, demands for reparations for past injuries, and the question of whether a dam would be built in Long Valley.[14]

On June 1, 1923, as Los Angeles focused on an election that, among other items, would determine the passage of a $35 million bond measure for Boulder Dam (it was defeated by 11,790 votes), a small notice in the Los Angeles *Express* announced that the city had just paid a million dollars for almost 12,000 acres of rich farmlands in the Owens Valley. The purchases had been made over a long time by land agent John T.

Martin and had been done in secrecy "for the purpose of protecting the city's water rights in the valley." It would add 10,000 miner's inches to the present supply and be adequate for the needs of 3 million persons. The city now owned 80 percent of the McNally Ditch interests, and this purchase confirmed to the Watterson-Eaton Protective Association that the rival Watterson-Hall-Symon Associated group were sellouts to the city. The *Inyo Register* accused the city of getting its land at bargain prices and claimed owners "had been panicked into selling all the rewards that should have been theirs for the years of work they have put in." A month later, in early July, Mathews and Mulholland met with the rival Protective Association (Watterson, Clausen, and others) at a public service commission meeting in Los Angeles to hammer out a tentative agreement over water and pumping rights, but nothing definitive was decided.[15]

Mulholland spent a busy July in the city. A magazine article about him that month claimed, "Even now, at more than 67, he is still a tremendous worker." He attended meetings on flood control plans for the Los Angeles River, which under the Reagan Plan was about to be riprapped; discussed with Goethals what type of dam would best withstand earthquakes at Boulder Canyon (both favored a rock-filled dam); and after a big earthquake shook the southland on Sunday night, July 22, spoke publicly with a geologist about the phenomenon of seismic movement and the need for further study in order to guard against serious results and loss of life. He also noted the continuing attacks of the *Los Angeles Times* against the power bureau over its so-called wanton expenditures in the recent election and refuted the false charges that he had created an artificial water famine in the San Fernando Valley. By the end of the month, he also learned that Fred Eaton, on behalf of the Eaton Land and Cattle Company, had filed a temporary injunction against Los Angeles to prohibit the construction of a dam 150 feet high in Long Valley. Two weeks later, on August 17, after city workers had cleared brush and begun to dig a diversion ditch on its recently acquired property along Big Pine Ditch, a troop of armed ranchers mounted guard over the headgate of Big Pine Ditch and halted the work. Four days later, a Bridgeport court began hearing a suit brought by the Eaton Land and Cattle Company against the City of Los Angeles for damages inflicted by its agents on the claimant's dams and ditches. Harold Eaton testified in protest of their actions, while Ed Leahey, representing the city, said the action had been taken at the directive of Mulholland and Scattergood. These events set the stage for what came to be known as the Owens Valley Water War.[16]

LOS ANGELES, THE WATER HOG

Opposition to Los Angeles was not confined to Owens Valley. At the end of 1920, during a League of Municipalities banquet in Bakersfield, that town's mayor had remarked in a backhanded jesting compliment to the mayor of Los Angeles, "You stole our water, gas and power while our eyes were shut to our own opportunities." Amid laughter, he added, "Next thing you know, they will want to use the Vernal Falls at Yosemite." Mayor Snyder of Los Angeles gave a wan smile and jested back that in spite of his city's glories, its city hall and jail were nothing to be proud of. While Mayor Snyder caught flak from fellow mayors in Bakersfield over the city's greediness, Mulholland, seeking new solutions embracing a broader vision of water and power regulation for California, attended a banquet in Los Angeles with Elwood Mead and other water gurus to discuss Colonel Robert Marshall's irrigation plan for the San Joaquin Valley. In September, he already had attended a similar meeting at Sacramento to consider Marshall's plan to use California's rivers to irrigate 12 million acres of San Joaquin Valley land, and at that time, both he and Colonel M. M. O'Shaughnessy, engineer of the Hetch Hetchy project, viewed it with favor. Some of this plan later merged into the Water and Power Act, a proposed constitutional amendment created in 1921 by Progressive forces for state regulation of water and electrical power. Mulholland threw the weight of his not inconsiderable prestige behind the measure. (In April 1921, the American Association of Engineers had just named him one of the top engineers in the world, placing him in company with Goethals, Steinmetz, and Orville Wright.) He served on the executive board of the Water and Power Act campaign along with its two chief financial supporters, Dr. John R. Haynes, of Los Angeles, and Rudolph Spreckels, of San Francisco; and leading Progressives, William Kent, of Kentfield, and Louis Bartlett, mayor of Berkeley. The proposal, opposed by the private power companies (it was later said they had spent $500,000 to defeat it) and the conservative press, went down to defeat in the reactionary flood of 1922 that swept Warren G. ("Back to Normalcy") Harding into the White House.[17]

Among those rejoicing in the Water and Power Act's defeat was Harry Chandler, whose *Times* had predictably deplored the proposed amendment and afterward insulted Mulholland's motives and intelligence by apologizing for him with the suggestion that "demagogues and socialists" had duped him. The proponents of the defeated amendment, determined to continue the fight, warned of the propaganda being used against Los Angeles in its municipal ownership projects. Spreckels accused the *Times* of making people believe that its municipal power project was a failure, while local public service commissioner John Kemp declared, "Nearly every day some article attacking the Public Service Commission appears in an opposition paper [the *Record* or the *Times*]."[18]

The election of 1922 also brought to Sacramento one of the dreariest, most backward-looking governors the state has ever had, Friend Richardson, who proved to be mostly a friend to vested interests. Of his term from 1922 to 1926, Mowry has written that the "new California conservatism was mainly interested in lower taxes for corporations and in legislation granting long term franchises to electric power companies and other public utility corporations." An early example of Richardson's bias was his unsuccessful attempt to remove one of the city's leading Progressives and champions of public power ownership, Dr. John R. Haynes, from the board of regents of the University of California. Thus, in this political climate and amid waning Progressive influence, the battle was waged for the creation of Boulder Dam and the Colorado River Aqueduct, projects on which Mulholland pinned his hopes as the answer to the city's ever-growing needs for water and power.[19]

In his annual report for 1922, Mulholland noted that the population of Los Angeles had more than tripled since 1905 and, foreseeing increased water problems, warned the city to curtail its wholesale annexation of territory and expressed concern that the San Fernando Valley was fast becoming a residential center rather than an agricultural one. Elsewhere he began to urge the development of all possible hydroelectric power as he raised the specter of the depletion of the nation's oil reserves in the foreseeable future. He admonished that "what nature took millions and millions of years to store and conserve, man would use up in less than one century." So persuaded was he by the truth of this idea that at a San Joaquin League of Municipalities dinner, he warned that the United States had already used one-quarter of its oil supplies in twenty-five years, and that at the present rate, it could not be sentimental about turning to hydroelectric power, even if it meant using water in the national parks. Eventually, he declared, the power of the Yellowstone Falls would have to be utilized just as that of Niagara Falls was about to be. Later critics of Mulholland have taken such statements to demonstrate that he was an antienvironmentalist, which in itself is an anachronism, as the environment had not emerged as a powerful issue in his day. Such opinions on oil and hydroelectric power were current among men of science. Thomas Edison expounded them, and when Charles Steinmetz, the electrical wizard of

General Electric, spoke at the Los Angeles Electric Club the following year, he also urged harnessing rivers for electric power.[20]

Much of Harry Chandler's reputation as the "boss" of Los Angeles dates from this period, yet as one Progressive Republican congressman of the 1920s later observed (citing items in which Chandler had an interest such as ship subsidies, airmail contracts, national parks, and protection from governmental interference in the formation of power monopolies), when it came to "Big Business in Politics" Chandler was "no more than a field general in a far-off province who must take orders from the titanic dinosaurs and who must deliver the goods in the form of subservient Congressmen from his province if he desired to share in the profits of invisible government." Making this assessment was Joe Crail, who had begun his political career in 1916 as Hiram Johnson's campaign manager in Southern California during the latter's initial run for the Senate and who, by the early 1920s, after becoming active in supporting Boulder Dam and public power, announced his intention to run for Congress. Seeking support from the *Times,* he was granted an interview with Chandler soon after his announcement. Led before the presence (accompanied by the chairman of the Republican Congressional Committee), Crail was quickly told that the city's plans for the Colorado River were not correct from either an engineering or an economic standpoint. Then, according to Crail, Chandler imparted startling information. "There is a secret agreement between the city on the one hand and the Southern California Edison Company on the other, by which they will jointly file application to the Federal Power Board for authority to develop power from the Colorado River. The city will get all of the water it needs, or wants, through long trenches in the sand which will filter out the silt." Whether Chandler believed this fantasy is moot, but after Crail answered that he supported the Colorado plans as well as the All-American Canal, an angered Chandler declared that if his judgment was that poor, then he would not support him for Congress. In the end, however, party loyalty prevailed, and the *Times* recommended Crail, who won by a large margin and went on to Washington, where he worked on behalf of the Boulder Dam bill.[21]

Political tensions and hostilities sometimes took a toll on the water and power warriors. In March 1923, Scattergood, while in an elevator with Mulholland and Van Norman, had crumpled to the floor in a state of collapse. His "nervous breakdown," as it was called, came two months before the bitterly contested and crucial $35 million power bond election, which was narrowly defeated. The *Times* subsequently gloated and accused the power bureau of having spent $50,000 on campaign posters, letters, and (horrors!) "JAZZ BANDS." Yet the vote was sufficiently close that success seemed possible at a future election, and two months later a recovered Scattergood was back in the fray as he reported that Power Plant No. 1 at San Francisquito had begun to generate power. At the same time he informed the public that the city was still forced to purchase 30 percent of its power for consumers at more than twice the cost per kilowatt hour as the city's own production.[22]

Continued drought prompted Mulholland to warn people to be frugal with water, and when the leading Los Angeles golf clubs complained of high water rates and brought suit against the city to secure lower costs, Mulholland suggested in the ensuing hearing that "If the golfers threaten to leave town, let 'em. We don't want 'em." He continued the ban against reservoir fishing and criticized the big mess a film crew left around Chatsworth while shooting Mary Pickford's *Tess of the Storm Country*. Even though four more dams were in various stages of planning and construction in Weid (Hollywood) Canyon, Stone Canyon, Encino, and San Francisquito, worry remained constant over how to provide the ever-growing city with water and power.[23]

THE FLOURISHING OF THE CHIEF

Amid these contentious public issues in the early 1920s, Mulholland's reputation as a successful leader in a dynamic city flourished, his opinions sought and valued in many quarters. Perhaps to reassert his Irish origins, he assumed the presidency of the Celtic Club in 1922, continued his participation in the Sunset Club, where he spoke that year on the Boulder Canyon Dam project, and served on the executive committee of the Southwest Museum under the leadership of Charles Lummis. He even had a brief moment as a movie actor when he performed in a municipal film production, *Into the Future*, to boost Los Angeles's water and power establishment. This venture led to a suit by private power interests accusing the city of having wasted public funds for political purposes. At the hearing, Mulholland testified that he had played "a sort of Bill Hart of the aqueduct," and testified that he had found the life of a film star hard. With Scattergood and a delegation of Los Angeles leaders he spoke at a major conference in Phoenix at which Herbert Hoover presided. Given an ovation, he addressed the flood threat to Imperial Valley and urged the dam project, exhorting, "Let's build now and settle the quibbles later."[24]

In early 1923, Mulholland and Scattergood attended an important irrigation conference in Fresno. The two engineers had endorsed the Pine Flat project to provide water and power for the Fresno area and assured the thirty-seven districts present that Los Angeles wanted harmony with the San Joaquin Valley and not one ounce of their irrigation water. Days after returning home, Mulholland received a singular distinction, the naming of a highway in his honor. On February 9, he stood with the mayor to watch the first turning of earth for a ridge route that he had long ago proposed to run from Hollywood to the sea. To inaugurate the future Mulholland Scenic Highway, William Gibbs McAdoo (soon to be a Democratic contender for the presidency and later a United States senator) ceremonially buried a casket with the three flags that had flown over California: Spanish, Mexican, and United States.[25]

Mulholland and Scattergood's efforts to create a municipal power system drew increasing recognition. One article from the *Dearborn Independent* (later reprinted in the *Rochester, New York Times-Union*) applauded the city's willingness to fight its powerful foes, while nearer home the *Sacramento Bee* cited Los Angeles as a model of the wisdom of public ownership of hydroelectric service. In all comparisons of consumer rates with those of Edison, it asserted, the city's had proven lower, and at less cost. Further accolades came from Senator George N. Norris of Nebraska, then fighting Henry Ford's attempt to take over Muscle Shoals as well as seeking governmental support for Boulder Dam, while Carl Hayden of Arizona declared that Los Angeles was now the best lighted city in the world, with the cheapest manufacturing power. Locally, P. D. Noel of the Sierra Club and the Central Labor Council warned that "a desperate effort is being made by selfish private power companies, their financial allies and their Los Angeles morning newspaper mouthpiece to wreck and discredit this city's notably successful Municipal Bureau of Power and Light."[26]

A TOUR ON THE COLORADO RIVER

After sailing down the Colorado in November on a five-day observation tour with Van Norman and a group of engineers, Mulholland announced that the trip had confirmed his studies and observations of the past ten years; that the project of bringing Colorado River water to Los Angeles was feasible; and that the dam site should be in Boulder Canyon. He hoped shortly to resume the voyage from Parker, Arizona, but important business had brought him home. He was to be a chief speaker at a major Boulder Dam Association conference in Santa Ana as well as a witness in a suit brought against the city by one Volney Craig on behalf of a few disgruntled irrigators in the San Fernando Valley who claimed they were being deprived of water. The judge subsequently denied the injunction (in 1924), declaring the principle that the Los Angeles Aqueduct should be used primarily to satisfy the needs of water consumers and only secondarily to generate hydroelectric energy.[27]

Days after Mulholland's return from the Colorado came news that San Franciscans had voted for the Hetch Hetchy project, which represented yet another triumph over private interests. As the boring of the Hetch Hetchy Tunnel began in the north, Mulholland began construction on the dam in Weid Canyon that he promised would be completed in two years and should be called Hollywood Reservoir. In 1924, however, the public service commission voted to call it Mulholland Dam.[28]

CHAPTER 22

Boulder Dam and Dynamite

1924

THE SWING-JOHNSON BILL AND TROUBLING RUMORS

Controversy over Boulder Dam and the second Swing-Johnson bill (a bill to provide for the protection and development of the lower Colorado River Basin) dominated the news in Los Angeles during the fifteen months after armed ranchers had mounted the Big Pine Ditch and stopped work on the city's proposed diversion ditch in the summer of 1923. At the beginning of 1924, the discontents in Owens Valley were somewhat muted, and with a continued drought in the state, Mulholland's most critical concern was planning future water and power supplies in his burgeoning city. To maintain the power system, he felt it urgent to complete the dams in Weid and San Francisquito Canyons and to continue the campaign for the Boulder Dam project. Owens Valley water could supply current needs, but because he was responsible for future supplies and forced to look ten years ahead, he deemed that with the city's present rate of growth, only the Colorado River could supply those needs, especially for hydroelectric power. Concerned about the present supply's limits, however, he deplored some of the annexations and distant subdivisions being developed far in advance of need while land lay idle well within the existing city limits.[1]

Joining in the Boulder Dam promotion was Arthur P. Davis, who in a political play had been relieved of his Reclamation post as chief engineer of the Boulder project and replaced by Frank Weymouth. Secretary of the Interior Hubert Work claimed the project needed an administrator rather than an engineer, but Davis believed his support of public power had led to his removal. Quickly hired as a consultant for the city, Davis claimed that a dam in Boulder Canyon could be built for less than $50 million and that electricity could be generated three to four years after work started. He found Mulholland's plans for getting Colorado water to the city physically possible but questioned their magnitude and cost. As the campaign for public water and power continued, former senator James Phelan of San Francisco attended a public service commission meeting in Los Angeles with Mulholland and Scattergood, at which he declared that San Francisco's fight with private power interests was exactly similar to Los Angeles's. The two cities were bound together by a common enemy and should join forces to protect the rights of consumers. At the end of January, Mulholland and a delegation of Southern Californians that included Mathews, Scattergood, electrical engineer W. F. Durand, and several mayors of Southern California cities set out for Washington, D.C., to throw their support behind the second Swing-Johnson bill for Boulder Dam.[2]

After two weeks of conferences with members of the secretary of the interior's staff and members of the arid lands committee, during which, according to columnist Joseph Timmons, Mulholland's eloquence opened their eyes to the undercover opposition and falsehoods being disseminated by "a Los Angeles morning paper" (the *Times*), the aging Chief stood up in Congress on February 15 and dropped the bombshell that Congressman Phil Swing, coauthor of the bill, had feared would further complicate the already tangled fight over Colorado River waters but that he later decided had helped the cause along. "I am here," Mulholland declared, "in the interest of a domestic water supply for the City of Los Angeles, and that injects a new phase into this whole matter."[3]

Mulholland testified for two days, insisting that Boulder Dam would fit well with the city's plan to build an aqueduct connecting the Colorado River to Los Angeles. He predicted that the Boulder project would produce more power than all the oil fields in California and argued against creating the Topoc Dam being touted by private interests. Calling it the Poppycock Dam, he joked that its chief virtue was that, although it would hold water, it would produce no power. When probed to name the power companies and other organizations fighting the Swing-Johnson bill, he sidestepped by saying most of the activity was covert but that everybody recognized it. "It is a good deal like a mole," he described. "You know the mole is there; you see where he has made the hole and the hump in the ground where he has crawled; but if you try to jab a snickersnee into

him he may not be there. We had the same sort of opposition to building the Aqueduct." He concluded with the observation that there are
"some men whose religion it is to be against public ownership of every
kind," but when pressed to identify corporations active in this fight, he
named only the Southern California Edison Company, which, he claimed,
had filings for power on the entire river. He added that he had heard one
of its vice presidents, R. H. Ballard, declare their intention to develop it
all—to create, in short, a monopoly. He admitted that he had thought
the Owens Valley Aqueduct would supply Los Angeles for forty or fifty
years, but the city's surprising population increase had proven him wrong.
Drought had forced that project, he recalled, just as the current drought
forced this one. "You must understand," he told the House Committee
on Irrigation and Reclamation, "that the very salubrity of our climate
brings about aridity."[4]

After an afternoon of cross-examination by Representative Carl Hayden of Arizona and others over the Colorado project's flood control aspects, Mulholland concluded his testimony and left for the West Coast,
leaving behind a hearing that was to drag on into spring. After months
of stalling, Harry Chandler finally made a bland appearance, imparting
the impression that he had never in his life heard of such a thing as a
power grab by private interests. Hiram Johnson, one of the bill's authors,
was so infuriated by the performance that he called Harry Chandler a
greater enemy to California than the Southern Pacific railroad octopus
had ever been. The bill failed to get out of committee before the session
adjourned, and a disappointed Phil Swing returned to California to face
a hard fight for reelection.[5]

When Mulholland arrived home on February 19, he brought optimistic words that the Teapot Dome scandal's eruption had created an
atmosphere of support for the people's cause and one of embarrassment
for the opposing private interests. Adding that the people of Los Angeles should thank Providence for the aqueduct ("It is such a protection in
this enormously destructive drought"), he cautioned that even with that
blessing they must look ahead and go to the Colorado River for a future
water supply.[6]

Meanwhile, with the snowpack in the Sierras only 10 inches deep
against a 65-inch average, the drought showed no sign of abating. Other
disturbing reports also came to the returning Mulholland as the ditch
owners in Owens Valley pursued their plans to press the city. One ominous note was the repetition of a September 1923 warning by Catholic

priest John J. Crowley, who, on February 12, in an open letter to the citizens of Inyo County, again deplored the presence in their midst of a Ku Klux Klan organizer, one M. B. Haver, who, he avowed, had arrived not for religious reasons but rather to make "a misguided attempt to solve our water situation." The priest, whose later efforts to reconcile Owens Valley with Los Angeles were honored by the naming of Lake Crowley, also noted that although the *Inyo Register* had printed his first warning against this organization of "bigotry and ignorance," the *Owens Valley Herald* had refused.[7]

Another more immediate mischief afoot in Owens Valley prompted Mulholland on February 27 to wire Mathews, who was still at the Boulder hearings:

> Longyear group of banker owners Owens Valley lands are trying to stir up rebellion amongst farmers San Fernando Valley representing that they have plenty of water that city must buy STOP Streams are now so low quite satisfied they will see contrary in month or two STOP Hope you may return and press Eaton matter otherwise we will be completely deprived of all benefit of our efforts of past year to obtain water STOP Condition our reservoirs and review of our prospects for year indicate safe margin for domestic use and permanent tree growth in Fernando Valley This of course implies complete exhaustion of stores of water by first of November STOP Come soon[8]

William Douglas Longyear was a prominent member of the Los Angeles banking-investor fraternity as well as an associate of the San Fernando land syndicate headed by General Otis, Harry Chandler, Otto F. Brant, and H. J. Whitley, which had acquired in 1909–1910 the southern half of the San Fernando Valley. Longyear's holdings centered around present-day Sherman Oaks. In 1917, Longyear and his son, David, obtained land southwest of Bishop, where the latter now lived and purportedly ranched. The Longyears, active members of the ditch owners' Owens Valley Protective Association, were not only involved with the small group of irrigators in the San Fernando Valley who in the spring of 1924 went to Owens Valley in a scheme to buy irrigation water direct from the ditch owners; they also played a hand in the later land-selling controversy in which the Watterson-Eaton faction attempted to sell their holdings at what the city considered exorbitant rates. (Although much has been written about the Eaton-Mulholland feud as the chief impediment to the city's purchasing of land at high prices, absentee owners and sellers trying to gouge the city were equally salient.) A month after receiving Mulholland's admonitory wire, Mathews managed an apparent coup by securing the services of William Symons, head of the rival McNally's Ditch group, to take on commission all of the options he could arrange with that ditch's property owners. Some observers later believed this development triggered the subsequent water war.[9]

By spring, with an impending primary election on May 6, fierce debate arose over two issues: power bonds for the city and approving the Boulder Dam project. Power issues were intensely fought, with both labor and Progressive forces in favor while conservatives (with powerful backing from the *Los Angeles Times*) opposed. In retrospect, several marvelous coincidences militated against passage of a pro-public power bond issue. First, under protest from public power interests, a $35 million bond issue for flood control in the San Gabriel Mountains was suddenly forced on the ballot to compete with other costly municipal items. Not surprisingly, the *Times* piously touted the need for flood control over the need for public power and urged a no vote on the latter. When all the dust had settled, the voters had passed the flood control measure and approved the Boulder Dam power project but resoundingly defeated the city power bonds. On the eve of the election, councilman Wheeler declared, "For twenty years I have been active on behalf of municipal ownership and I will say in the present campaign we have had more lies per square inch than in all the rest of the campaigns put together." Feelings were so inflamed that when a camp of water department workers from the Encino Reservoir came to vote in Encino, a woman on the election board announced, "I'm not going to let that riffraff vote. They're all employed by the water department and are going to vote for the bonds." It took a call to the registrar of voters before they were allowed to cast their ballots.[10]

OWENS VALLEY FIGHTS BACK

The second apparently coincidental preelection event was the appearance, beginning in late March and concluding one week before the primary election, of a series of twelve articles in the *San Francisco Call* by staff writer Court E. Kunze, Watterson brother-in-law and coeditor of the *Owens Valley Herald*. Kunze's sketches of Los Angeles's nefarious behavior against the poor, embattled Owens Valley dwellers were artful contrivances and effective propaganda, as they oversimplified complex issues and reduced the players to villain and victim. Kunze compared "the tragedy of Owens Valley" to *Evangeline* and declared that because Los Angeles was deaf to all pleas, it had created "a valley of broken hearts."

Much praised in Owens Valley and reprinted throughout the state, this series, by shading the truth, went far to confirm the increasing impression of a victimized people under the foot of an uncaring tyrant, namely, Mulholland. Implied was the proposition that if only the city were to build a dam at Long Valley, many hearts in Owens Valley would be healed. Whatever else may be said, these pieces without a doubt helped whip up the outrage that led on May 21, 1924, at 1:30 A.M., to the first dynamiting of the aqueduct.[11]

The explosion occurred twenty-two miles north of Haiwee and blasted away a section of concrete canal and part of the hill slope where the dynamite had been placed. From Independence, engineer Roderick McKay called Mulholland, who proceeded immediately to City Hall to announce the news. "We had heard of threats from disgruntled persons," he told the council, "but going on the theory that barking dogs do not bite, we did not pay any attention to them. Last night they bit."[12]

After the council voted to appropriate a $10,000 reward for the capture of the perpetrators, Mulholland left to investigate the damage and to personally superintend the repairs. He was asked before leaving about a possible motivation. Considering that his masterpiece had been seriously tampered with, his remarks seem moderate, although in the frenzied spirit of hatred and resentment now loose in Owens Valley, even they were construed malevolent. "Dissatisfaction in the valley?" he asked rhetorically. "Yes, a lot of it. Dissatisfaction is a sort of condition that prevails there, like the hoof-and-mouth disease. You can't tell where the infection is until it breaks out, and it keeps breaking out in new spots." As if that were not enough to incite fury in Owens Valley, he added, "There are those in the valley like Tam O'Shanter's wife who nursed her wrath to keep it warm."[13]

Everybody had a theory. The *Times* accused the Kunze articles of fanning the flames of dissension; city detectives in the police department's radical bureau suspected the IWW and set out to look for Wobblies. When the fragment of a love letter on the back of a movie theater program from Bishop was discovered near the scene, hopes rose that it would provide a lead. In fact, the malefactors were apparently well known to most of the valley, and it was generally acknowledged that in the Klan-like fashion of nightriders, at least forty men had set out from Bishop on the night of the deed in a caravan of cars that had been observed by the inhabitants of the little towns along their southerly route. Throughout the ensuing investigation, the valleyites were unrepentant, even gleeful, at the stir. Ed Leahey received veiled threats on his life when he appeared in Bishop, and Fred Eaton made a pallid defense of valley people's being "law-abiding citizens" who did not countenance violence. At last, ran local sentiment, we have gotten the attention we have been looking for. In the midst of this hullabaloo, Los Angeles mayor George Cryer (who had replaced Snyder in June 1921) left town with his wife for a three-week vacation in the East while a Los Angeles businessman announced he was going to build a new $80,000 hotel in Bishop. Reginaldo del Valle, the longest serving member of the public service commission, stated that in the past eighteen months, the city had expended $3,684,969 to purchase water lands in Owens Valley. "Greed," he concluded, "prompting its possessors to attempt to wring exorbitant prices from Los Angeles for water lands in Owens Valley, is at the root of all the trouble which led up to and follows the dynamiting of the Aqueduct near Lone Pine."[14]

Because of the aroused passions in Owens Valley, the hearings on the dynamiting eventually were moved to remote northern Alpine County. As negotiations between city officials and Owens Valley men began, the incident might have been minimized if not for certain of the press. The debate over Boulder Dam continued to dominate the news in Los Angeles, but in Owens Valley, all other issues were suppressed in order to keep anger over the city's villainy alive. Mulholland was excoriated ("King of Home Destroyers") and compared to Albert Fall, the corrupt secretary of the interior who was about to be indicted for giving away federal oil lands to private oil men led by Edward Doheny. As summer wore on, a Los Angeles dry goods merchant showed up in Bishop and told a complete fabrication to the *Inyo Register:* Mulholland was interested in Owens Valley land deals to enrich some privileged few just as he had done in the San Fernando Valley. Even two local suicides were blamed on the city's heartlessness toward the benighted settlers.[15]

DYNAMITE AND "PEACE" MEETINGS

A month after the explosion, the publisher of the *Record,* B. H. Canfield, arrived in Owens Valley with four of his staff to ascertain the "truth." The locals hailed him as the only man to publish the truth in Los Angeles since Sam Clover had once dared to oppose "the controlling ring and political interests." (Unmentioned, however, was Sam Clover's current editorship of a Los Angeles periodical, *Saturday Night,* for which he composed laudatory profiles of such former enemies as Henry Huntington,

Harry Chandler, and William Mulholland, collected and published as *Constructive Californians* in 1926.)[16]

The *Record* began a series of exposés recounting Los Angeles's perfidy to Owens Valley. So wanton were some press attacks against Los Angeles and its water establishment that by the end of summer the *Fresno Republican* published an editorial warning the city's enemies to exercise restraint. Unheeded at the time, it proved shrewdly prophetic as the final drama played itself out in the following years. To the city's attackers, the Fresno editor offered a parable from the Old Testament story of Ahab, the king of Israel, who desired the vineyard of Naboth. When Naboth denied Ahab, he found himself at the mercy of Jezebel and was slain. (Here, by the editor's own admission, the analogy became a bit strained as he asked, "Is there a Jezebel?") Likening the Owens Valley dwellers to Naboth, he described the current scene:

> Naboth is in revolt. And he is doing some very irregular things. He is blowing up the property of Ahab. And he is going out "nightriding" to the discomfort of Ahab's plants. In due time Naboth will be sorry for these things. He will be arrested and indicted, and shown the error of his ways. While he is in jail, his crops will perish for want of attention as well as for water. And he will sell his depreciated acres for the cost of hiring an attorney in a vain attempt to show that he had a right to take a sideswipe at Ahab. The sale will turn out to be one more good turn for Ahab.
>
> Naboth was stoned to death. We do it differently these days.[17]

A month before this editorial appeared, Mulholland had begun construction of the dam in Weid Canyon, even as he announced that water supplies were holding but that conservation should be continued in this driest spell in fifty years. When Lippincott and two other engineers who had been exploring Los Angeles's water resources reported to the Chief that all sources were exhausted, he stepped up his argument that the city must look to the Colorado River for a solution. Then a crisis flared that caused him to threaten his resignation. Home from his vacation, Mayor Cryer had gone to Owens Valley with his secretary at the end of July. After two days of being shown around and listening to local ranchers and businessmen, he returned home persuaded that the city should meet the landowners' demands to buy them out and, moreover, to pay their prices. When Cryer referred to antagonism in the valley towards "certain Aqueduct officials," Mulholland erupted at what he considered a public undercutting of his policies. "I would resign right now rather than have such charges left unanswered," he flared. "I have no defense to make and I don't intend, after forty-odd years in the work of this department, to have my service assailed in this way without meeting it in the most emphatic manner possible." With that, he spent the next day writing a statement rebutting each of Cryer's charges as del Valle and councilman Criswell echoed equal outrage. Cryer responded to this barrage by fleeing to San Bernardino on the excuse that he had to fetch his children home from summer camp. The city council next attacked him, while banker J. A. Graves took time out from his vacation in Bohemian Grove to send a wire calling the mayor "spineless" and asserting of Mulholland, "No man has ever charged him with a dishonest act." Only the *Record* applauded the mayor and questioned both Mulholland's competence and integrity.[18]

In the next two weeks, the public service commission announced Owens Valley purchases of the Manzanar Tract (4,958 acres) and the McNally Ditch (2,031 acres). To further protect the city's water supply, Mulholland also initiated irrigation restraints against the San Fernando Valley bean growers. He continued to defend his land acquisition policy, which was to buy Owens Valley land only as needed. "I will not stand for any wholesale purchases," he declared, "especially at figures ranging from $4,000,000 to $8,000,000."[19]

Two weeks after the uproar, on August 14, Cryer and Mulholland met at a luncheon for city employees and shook hands, thus disappointing those who expected fireworks. As a Progressive who supported public power and the Boulder project, and in view of the all-important city power bond issue coming up on August 26, Cryer's lapse could be overlooked, especially as it had been so generally disapproved. Although only 25 percent of voters turned out, they approved the city power bonds this time by a ratio of eight to one, while Phil Swing, by retaining his congressional seat, also insured that the Boulder project would retain its California supporter.[20]

In Owens Valley, however, news of the city's latest land purchases spurred new responses, and on the heels of the primary election came word that a gang of Bishop men had snatched from a local restaurant attorney-editor L. C. Hall (one of the Watterson-Symons group), whom they had roughed up and later released on condition that he leave Owens Valley. They suspected Hall of having bought up water rights for the city behind the backs of the group that had pooled its holdings. Also threatened were the lives of George Watterson, Symons, and others accused of being in league with Los Angeles. Mulholland, about to leave on a "peace tour" to Owens Valley, remarked that Hall had not been engaged in any capacity for Los Angeles in several months and that the legal services he had rendered in the past were not of sufficient importance to warrant the Bishop crowd's drastic measures. Ed Leahey also had been threatened as word went out for Mulholland to stay out of the valley. Revealing then that he had received at least a dozen anonymous letters from Owens Valley threatening his life, Mulholland left undeterred on September 2, in a car with Van Norman, while other city dignitaries followed by rail. Valley nerves had become so edgy that when two strange men on motorcycles accosted and beat up a foreman on the Eaton Ranch, instant suspicion fell on Los Angeles agents. As ranchers fanned out into the hills in search of the enemy, the attackers were apprehended, one of whom proved to be an ex-pugilist from San Francisco, evidently pursuing some grudge against the foreman.[21]

The peace meetings at Haiwee, which included W. W. Watterson, resulted in guarded optimism about a future harmony between the city and Owens Valley. The Big Pine Chamber of Commerce hosted a luncheon at which Mulholland received a generous ovation when he rose to speak. Soon after, however, local businessmen asked the city to reimburse them for the losses and depreciations of their property resulting from the loss of water on the city-owned ranch lands. The Los Angeles men acknowledged the merit of their requests and indicated the city's willingness to pay for such damage. Mulholland said, "The people are entitled to justice, and justice they shall have." Some felt, however, that while the city had kept strictly within its legal rights, it had also incurred a moral obligation that it had not met. When Mulholland urged them to back the Swing-Johnson bill and stated his belief that the ultimate solution would come with the development of Colorado River water, their response was emotional. "You have ruined our community. We are bankrupt. Something must be done for us now, and not at some future date." Out of this session, agreement was reached that the Big Pine Committee should come to Los Angeles to present its case to city representatives. A bit of public relations was also arranged at Big Pine with a reunion of Mathews, Mulholland, and their old Lone Pine landlady of aqueduct days, "Mother" Green, whose company and hospitality the two men had always enjoyed as well as her memorable line, "Us akeyducks has got to stick together." In comparing the newspaper photo in 1924 with one taken almost twenty years earlier that showed Mathews and a jaunty Mulholland with his arm around Mrs. Green (then jocularly referred to as "the Bride of the Aqueduct"), one notes that although time had taken its toll, they all looked to be even yet three tough old birds.[22]

As the delegation moved up the valley, one of the newest members of the public service commission, William Paul Whitsett, chief founder and developer of Van Nuys in the San Fernando Valley and long an enthusiast of the beauty and grandeur of the Sierras, extolled the area's possibilities as an American Alps. He had been to Switzerland and studied its tourist resources after being struck by the similarities he had found between the two magnificent mountain regions. Now he proposed Owens Valley as a great mountain playground and park. "All you need is publicity," he declared. "When tourists learn what you have here there will not be enough hotels to contain them." Whitsett, a new and younger voice who did not prevail against Mulholland and his older colleagues, recalled in later years how he had argued on the commission for the purchase and annexation of the Owens Valley towns to the city in order to create a park not unlike the Rocky Mountain park of Denver. The plan, he reasoned, would have been not unlike the shoestring annexation employed by the city for the creation of its harbor, but Mulholland and del Valle, he remembered, had disagreed.[23]

The entire town of Bishop turned out to meet with its city visitors at the high school auditorium on September 5. Chairing the event, W. W. Watterson announced that this was to be a business meeting and that there should be no hisses or applause, then read a position paper from the Bishop landowners to the members of the public service commission seated at a table in front with him. In the front row, Mathews and Mulholland, who did not speak, listened to those on the stage. Earlier in the day, however, a rough patch had arisen that augured ill for future peace. In the morning, on a tour of an area near Big Pine where earlier city construction work had been halted, Watterson and Fred Eaton urged the need to construct the Long Valley Dam. After hearing them out, Mulholland, with Van Norman's backing , rejected outright any notion of doing so, citing the porous volcanic formation that would cause leakage problems were such a structure to be placed there. His refusal provoked an ominous statement from Fred Eaton about city water officials endangering water sources for the aqueduct and warning that unless there were a change in attitude, its entire water supply might find itself in jeopardy. Then he resorted to an ad hominem rebuke. "The main difficulty, as far as I can determine, is Bill Mulholland's animosity towards me. Petty personalities should not be permitted to enter into a matter like this that vitally affects the life of two communities."[24]

This remark, delivered at a moment when all sides were attempting to remain civil, was gratuitous. What was not then public knowledge was that an increasingly bitter Eaton was falling into serious financial difficulties. By the time of the peace conference, he and another ditch owner, Frank Butler, had begun to receive duns from the public service commission in Los Angeles for unpaid rentals on cattle grazing lands on the city's Crooked Creek property. Moreover, Eaton had been unable to get his price for the Long Valley lands in ongoing behind-the-scenes negotiations with Ed Leahey. His old friend may have made a convenient scapegoat, but Mulholland was in no way the author of all of Fred Eaton's woes.[25]

An unresponding Mulholland returned to the city with Van Norman and commissioners Clarence Dykstra and Haynes, saying simply of the conference, "There is unquestionably, an economic, or if you prefer, a sociological side to the question, an equity difficult to appraise, but nevertheless existent, of which the board will undoubtedly take cognizance." If that statement was a bit murky, there was nothing vague about the land-buying policy from which he refused to retreat, concluding that "there is no sense in buying land to acquire water that can't be delivered." Much has been made of the Eaton-Mulholland feud, almost all of it emanating from Fred Eaton and Owens Valley defenders. Mulholland never made a public remark about it in his life, and certain of his family members believed that Mulholland, although silent, had been deeply hurt by Eaton's remarks.[26]

If not exactly a love feast, the conference did seem to move towards conciliation, as the public service commission promised to begin a study to ameliorate conditions and make good on a pledge to expedite building a good highway from Mojave to Bishop. Yet almost before Mulholland and company had left the valley, cries of dissatisfaction sounded in its local newspapers. The only creature in California larger than the Oakland Mole, mocked the *Owens Valley Herald,* was the Los Angeles Bull. Mulholland was a "cruel heartless destructionist," and "the Czar of L. A." A cartoon portrayed him in the guise of the sleepy little boy in pajamas from a famous automobile tire advertisement whose legend was "Time to Retire." New fuel for the fire arrived with the start of the grand jury hearing on the May aqueduct bombing and the L. C. Hall kidnapping. Fortunately it fizzled. Although everyone in Owens Valley apparently knew who was responsible, no one was inclined to speak, while Hall had been allowed to flee to Mexico after promising not to identify his kidnappers. Two weeks later, back from Baja California, he was es-

tablished at a Glendale address and gave Mulholland as a credit reference in applying for a charge account at the May Company. Mulholland
recommended him by stating that from what he knew of Hall as an employee, "he is steady and reliable and it would be my personal opinion
that he would be fully able to take care of his obligations up to a reasonable amount."[27]

THE TAKING OF THE ALABAMA GATES

Mulholland was honored on his sixty-ninth birthday with an observance
of the twentieth anniversary of the 1904 aqueduct survey when he and
a nameless Scottish cook had spent forty days in the desert surveying the
route for an aqueduct that now served a city of almost a million people
and whose accomplishment had brought to its builder much satisfaction
but little rest. At the end of September, he also received a gold service
badge for thirty-eight years as chief engineer of the municipal waterworks. Then, after preparing a speech for a large Boulder Dam conference in Pasadena that his assistant, W. W. Hurlbut, read in his absence
and which Van Norman reinforced with more material, Mulholland left
for the East Bay area to report on his recent survey of the water resources
of Oakland, Alameda, and Berkeley, where his friend and associate,
Arthur P. Davis, was about to become head of the East Bay Municipal
Utility District (EBMUD).[28]

Trouble stirred again in October in Owens Valley. Although the public service commission had followed through with a petition to the state
for a highway from Mojave to Bishop, it also decided to comply with
Mulholland's policy and announced it would make no blanket land purchases. Amid valley charges of "insincere" and "unfair," Mathews declared that those crying loudest were the members of an irrigation district association "which does not own an inch of water or an acre of land
in the valley." The board further announced at this time that it would
lease land for orchards in Owens Valley.[29]

With Owens Valley matters unresolved, Mulholland left town November 6 to escort a group of officials from a number of Southern California towns on a five-day inspection trip to the Colorado River region,
while Mathews and Van Norman began a series of conferences with
Owens Valley ranchers. Although the Colorado junket went well and secured the enthusiastic support of Mayor Cryer, who accompanied them,
the Chief must have been feeling the weight of the year's tumultuous
events. As he stood above the river in Boulder Canyon on an autumn

day, he dropped his usual confident front and before an assemblage of dignitaries "mused his thoughts aloud," as one reporter described it. After reflecting that he believed the Boulder project to be historic, he added, "For myself, I should prefer to see Los Angeles get its water elsewhere. I'm growing to be an old man; in a few months I shall pass three score and ten, the allotted span. Before I slip into the wooden overcoat I should prefer for myself a few years of rest and peace. For me, this enterprise means only more strife and fatigue in a life that has been filled with both. I can hardly hope to see it accomplished—but my desire is not for myself."[30] He returned home to more bad news. The conference in Owens Valley had not gone well. Nothing had been settled. Certain ranchers now accused one of their own, George B. Warren, of treason for selling what was called "a worthless piece of property" for $46,000 in exchange for becoming a city partisan. Warren had also reported favorably on the city's plan to set aside 30,000 acres for agricultural development around the greater Bishop area, based on the recommendation of Mathews, Van Norman, Lee, and Louis G. Hill, a member of the special Owens Valley committee. After listening to Warren, who was their president, the Associated Chambers of Commerce in Owens Valley framed a resolution to remove him from the presidency. An *Owens Valley Herald* column ridiculed the city's proposal to plant orchards as "a utopian dream of making the country bloom again, but everyone knows it is the bunk, coming from the City's agents as it does." Watterson's group, now calling itself the Big Pine Property Owners' Association, rejected the city's proposal, which provoked Van Norman to declare, "Although I have been in close touch with Owens Valley for more than fifteen years, I never knew until this morning that there existed an organization known as the 'Big Pine Property Owners' Association.'"[31]

Then, on Sunday, November 16, all hell broke loose up in Owens Valley. Over a hundred residents of Inyo County, led by Mark Q. Watterson, seized a part of the aqueduct, opened the Alabama gates about four miles north of Lone Pine, and let the water flood out on the land. The leaders proclaimed their intention to remain until the city met their demands. Mulholland refused to deal, declaring that the seventy-five or one hundred men responsible for the deed "were not representative of the people of Owens Valley." The incident became a media event, a high-profile act that seized everyone's attention and brought to a climax the drama that had been building throughout recent years. With local feeling against Los Angeles at fever pitch, a crowd of more than one hundred local ranchers in a spirit combining the features of an outdoor frolic and a lynching bee, seized, opened, and held for five days the headgates as precious water intended for Los Angeles flowed instead out onto desert lands. It became a community spree as housewives arrived with food for the rebels and newsmen swarmed to photograph and interview them. Tom Mix, the cowboy film star who happened to be shooting a western in the Alabama hills, provided a Hollywood touch with incidental western music. Mix's presence cannot be reckoned as a political statement, however, for a month later, he starred in a rodeo at Calabasas as part of the entertainment he and Cecil B. DeMille planned and produced for the festivities to celebrate the Mulholland Highway's December opening.[32]

Governor Richardson denied the local sheriff's request for help by refusing to call in the militia, saying he found it strange that the aggressors should be asking for troops while the injured parties asked for nothing. The presence of troops, he believed, would only create another opportunity for more "yellow journalism." The whole matter, he declared, should be settled in the courts. City officials, apparently in agreement, announced they would bring suits against Inyo County for the loss of their water, estimated at $15,000 a day. When the sheriff served injunction papers on the rebels, they greeted him with merriment and told him they would love to keep them as souvenirs. The governor sent state engineer W. S. McClure as his emissary to investigate the Inyo County matter, but McClure's report in 1925 was to result only in further obfuscation. The *Fresno Bee* rationally called the Inyo action a tempest in a teapot, while Los Angeles papers understandably covered the event at length, expressing outrage over its lawlessness. Certain human interest pieces, however, recognized that injuries had been sustained in the valley, while the *Record* predictably issued warnings of possible bloodshed and civil war and urged Mulholland's removal.[33]

When W. W. Watterson appeared before the Los Angeles Clearing House Association to urge appointing a commission of disinterested men to adjust the differences over water rights between the Owens Valley ranchers and the city, J. A. Graves, president of Farmers' and Merchants' Bank and chairman of the association, agreed to undertake the commission, but only if the mob would retire from the headgates and allow the courts to decide. Graves also stipulated that all Owens Valley claims must be presented to the clearing house in writing. This agreed to, the crowd surrendered the gates but before going home held a final barbecue to finish off all the food they had accumulated against the long siege they were prepared to maintain against the city. One worldly Los Angeles reporter saw overtones of a Wild West drama and, as he watched the rebels pack up and depart, remarked that the "producers of the 'Battle of Lone Pine' have not yet announced when the next installment of their serial will be released."[34]

By December 3, Watterson had handed the clearing house committee a document demanding that the city pay the valley's ranchers $5.3 million in reparations for the Owens River's diversion into the aqueduct and offering to sell their land en bloc to the city for $12 million. Graves responded to this wish list with some hard questions. First, what damages, if any, had the farmers of Owens Valley suffered by reason of any acts of the city? Evidence would be needed, as a mere unsupported statement could not be the basis for such a claim. Second, if damages had been incurred, was the city liable, either in law or in equity? Graves further asked,

> Another question which would have great weight with me is this: Whether any moneys which the city would agree to pay are to be divided among the farmers of the valley, or whether the lion's share thereof would go to a junta of Los Angeles and Bishop capitalists who do their farming through the newspapers, who are reported to have bought both lands and water rights at a low figure, and for which they now want from the city millions?
>
> It would appear that all the propaganda going on and, I imagine, much of the trouble and dissatisfaction created in the minds of the people of the Owens River Valley, has been fomented by this junta.[35]

MULHOLLAND HIGHWAY

As the turbulent year came to an end, Los Angeles celebrated the Mulholland Highway's opening. Private land developers had underwritten a million-dollar bond issue for its construction, calling it a gift to the city from the owners of 10,000 acres of land along the route. Its engineer, DeWitt L. Reaburn, had been an associate of Mulholland on the aqueduct, and the gala opening, months in planning, extended all the way from Hollywood Boulevard to Calabasas, as its promoters promised the new roadway would create yet another link between isolated parts of the expanding metropolis. On the morning of December 27, standing at a floral gate with a golden key, Mulholland dedicated the roadway with a bottle of aqueduct water. (This was Prohibition; no champagne!) With the symbolic gate to the highway unlocked, the crowd next moved on to a rodeo in the fields of Calabasas with the omnipresent Tom Mix and his cowboys, a depiction of a wild and woolly forty-niners' mining camp staged by Universal Studios, and an exhibition of daredevil stunt flying. An automotive caravan then advanced to the Hollywood Bowl for a second program produced by Cecil B. DeMille, where Mayor Cryer and Mulholland were principal speakers followed by dignitaries and film stars introduced for the occasion. A parade through Hollywood was followed by a street carnival and open-air dance on Vine Street with thousands of participants and strolling bands. When rumors of renewed attacks on the aqueduct and threats against Mulholland spread during the celebration, the unfailingly hostile *Record* reported that they had emanated solely from Mulholland himself.[36]

CHAPTER 23

More Dynamite

1925–1927

WHY NOT BUY ALL OF OWENS VALLEY?

Although no further acts of violence against the aqueduct occurred in 1925, the war of words persisted, especially after state engineer W. F. Mc-Clure in January released his report on the Owens Valley–Los Angeles controversy to the state legislature in Sacramento. McClure, who had once lived in Owens Valley and was friendly to its people, produced a wildly one-sided document, almost as if he were an attorney preparing a brief for his client. Freighted with reprints of editorials from the Owens Valley–San Joaquin Valley newspapers and reports from the major ditch companies, the "letter of transmittal" offered little for the Los Angeles side other than selected snippets from the first annual aqueduct report to prove that Mulholland had once approved building Long Valley Dam, along with an editorial from the *Los Angeles Times* urging peace and moderation among all parties after the Alabama Gates incident. The city was indignant, citing a bias against Los Angeles in Sacramento. On the basis of the report, the senate nonetheless formed a committee to investigate the matter. After they had chosen four members, however, sentiments became so divided that the legislators could not agree on a fifth member and the probe stalled.[1]

The public service commission denounced the McClure Report, rebutted with its own pamphlet, and rejected the proposal to pay reparations and buy the ranchers' lands en bloc. The Clearing House Association now announced its withdrawal from the controversy, citing as impediments to an adequate investigation a lack of facts and "too many cooks." Its chairman, banker Jackson A. Graves, would also later cite financial irregularities he had noted in the Watterson records. The Wattersons remained indefatigable, however, and next appeared in Sacramento with a committee of ranchers to ask the legislature "to right the grievous wrong which is being done to the business interests of this valley." The legislature answered that it had no power to prevent the purchase of as much land as owners wished to sell, "particularly as in this case, when such purchase is done solely from a desire to peacefully settle a controversy." Thwarted, the group turned its efforts to combat a bill from Los Angeles that would make it a felony to injure water systems owned by a municipality. By the end of the legislative session, it had also successfully lobbied for the passage of a reparations act that would make municipal corporations such as Los Angeles liable for damages caused by the "acquisition of a water supply, or taking, diverting and transporting of water from a watershed." In response to valley demands for reparations, the public service commission demurred, replying that it wished to have the courts test the bill's legality before making any payments.[2]

Some writers have criticized Mulholland for intransigence in his dealings with the Owens Valley ditch owners. Why not buy up Owens Valley, as Mayor Cryer had been willing to consider, pay the high prices, and be done with it? Such a policy might have avoided trouble, but Mulholland, schooled in an older, sterner system, believed he had pledged his word to the taxpayers of Los Angeles to deliver their waterworks at the amounts they had agreed to pay for through their bond elections. Having already been falsely accused of conspiring with vested interests in the San Fernando Valley in building the aqueduct, he was gun-shy when it came to making overly generous arrangements with apparently wealthy landholders who were using images of embattled pioneers and victimized smallholders as their ammunition against Los Angeles. He was privately convinced, too, that some in the Owens Valley group simply saw Los Angeles as a gold mine. He knew that some of the city's bankers and moneyed men held interests in Owens Valley, and, moreover, as he had pointed out in his report to Mayor Cryer, the city's land purchases of 1923 had brought the city very little additional water, "as the remaining owners in the valley contest the right of the city to take the water she purchased with that land out of the valley." His attitude toward profiteering is best expressed in an anecdote he liked to tell his sons about a man he admired and often saw downtown—a hauler of fat and renderings. Passing him one hot day, with his wagon stinking and dripping with the greasy leavings from restaurants and markets, Mulholland had called out, "That's a dirty job you've got there, Sal." Sal called back, "Yes, Bill. But the money's clean."

His behavior fits Ortega y Gasset's description of the man with a clear head "who can perceive under the chaos presented by every vital situation the hidden anatomy of the movement"; the man, in a word, who does not lose himself in life is "the man with the really clear head." This clarity, perceived by some as ruthlessness, accompanies "the inevitable sternness with which anyone who has his life fixed on some undertaking must bear himself. When we are really going to do something and have dedicated ourselves to a purpose, we cannot be expected to be ready at hand to look after every passer-by and to lend ourselves to every chance display of altruism." If Mulholland sometimes failed in "displays of altruism," he also avoided the pitfalls of corruption, cheating, favoritism, and failure. The man with a clear head is not always lovable.[3]

In an effort to satisfy grievances, the city undertook more land purchases in 1925 and by August had acquired about 16,000 more acres, bringing the total of city-owned acres in Owens Valley to 189,000. This left approximately 11,000 acres of remaining arable land to be purchased. These constituted a compact parcel in the general contour of a half-moon west of Bishop along the west bank of the Owens River. This acreage led to the next phase of the water war.

WATER EXPANSIONS

The Owens Valley controversy rode tandem with the ongoing struggle for the Colorado River project. The boom years of the 1920s had produced similar controversies throughout the nation. Because of its rapid growth, Chicago was currently in conflict with Canada over the amounts of water the Chicago Drainage Canal was taking from the Great Lakes. Other water and power struggles in California included San Francisco's with Hetch Hetchy; Fresno's with Pine Flat Dam; and the Edison Company's water fight with owners along the San Joaquin River. Greatest of all and involving all the states along the Colorado River was the Boulder Dam proposal. When the McClure Report on Owens Valley was issued, Mulholland was preoccupied with a bill in Sacramento providing for a huge water district in Southern California that would allow the formation of a Colorado River domestic water district. It would comprise thirty or more cities and towns in the southern part of the state supplied by a giant aqueduct. The legislature defeated the bill in the first round, amid strong opposition from Harry Chandler's *Times* and the Los Angeles Chamber of Commerce, but it finally passed a second bill organizing the Metropolitan Water District at the beginning of 1927.[4]

On Saint Patrick's Day 1925, in homage to Mulholland's Irish origins, the board of the public service commission declared a day of celebration for the dedication of Mulholland Dam in Weid Canyon. Standing by the most romantic and scenic of all his dams, the Chief praised his codesigner and engineer, H. L. Jacques, for his work with the department since 1910. Self-deprecating, he said that his associates often twitted him on the appearance of his work. "They say it looks like an old woman's apron—an object of utility, but not of beauty." Then he made a rare smile as he pointed towards the graceful curve of the concrete wall. "But in this job," he added, "I think I may take a little pardonable pride." He recalled the man for whom the canyon had been named, Ivar Weid, a wine gauger who had lived in the canyon at the present site of the dam and whom he remembered from 1882. At the time, Mulholland had been quarrying rock in the canyon for the city jail. He jested that he was happy to have outlived the ignominy of that and to have his name now identified with a structure more in keeping with the spirit of Los Angeles. He also took the occasion to encourage support for the upcoming water bond issue with a bit of blarney and fatherly instruction. "I am glad there is such a large and intelligent audience here because the people have been greatly misinformed concerning their water supply. For your telephone talks you are paying two and one-half the times the cost of your water supply, or a little more than a third of what it costs other cities of similar size."[5]

Mayor Cryer, in the midst of a hot mayoral campaign, limited his remarks to a gracious appreciation of Mulholland's service to the city. "Long may he live and prosper!" Six weeks later, the mayor prevailed over his opponent, Judge Benjamin F. Bledsoe, an ally of Harry Chandler in the fight against municipal ownership of power. The removal of three of the five assemblymen who had voted against the Metropolitan Water District Act further manifested favorable public attitudes toward municipal water and power. After actively campaigning throughout May for Boulder Dam and water bonds mostly to fund the land purchases in Owens Valley, Mulholland and Scattergood were gratified by the wide margins favoring both issues.[6]

THOUGHTS ON MORTALITY
AND THE DEATH OF A FRIEND

At the end of June, torrential rains in the Tehachapis and high desert (the worst in fifteen years) washed out rail communication north of Mojave and shattered 400 feet of the aqueduct at locations near Jawbone, Sand Canyon, and Dove Springs, south of Little Lake. Tons of debris and silt clogged the damaged sections and stopped the flow from Haiwee. Mulholland went immediately to consult with Roderick McKay, who was desperately working with crews to open the line. For the next ten days, he remained to help supervise repairs before he set out on an unusual expedition with his associate and fellow engineer E. A. Bayley. They journeyed to the Gros Ventre country north of Jackson, Wyoming, to study a giant landslide that had removed part of Sheep Mountain into the path of a river and thus created a lake behind it. Bayley took photographs while Mulholland pondered the work of nature to see what hints it might provide for a man-made lake. Could the towering canyon walls at Boulder perhaps be toppled into the abyss at their base with a titanic dynamite blast? Mulholland cheerfully reported that Mother Nature had done a bang-up job. "Never saw a better job in my life. The dam is a typical earth and rock fill structure and when I saw it, it was tight as a trivet. Of course, it won't stand. Nature made no provisions for a spillway and, in time, the water will cut a new channel to its old level." Back in town, he immediately set out again with Van Norman to inspect the repair work on the aqueduct.[7]

Two weeks later, just as fears of brewing trouble and possible violence in Owens Valley had led the city to increase its police guard along the aqueduct, Roderick McKay, one of the Chief's closest associates since joining the water bureau in 1907, collapsed and died while rushing repairs on the line. The stress and urgency of the demanding work had proven too much for the sixty-two-year-old Scotsman, whom del Valle eulogized by saying that he had given his life in service to his city.[8]

Days after McKay's death, Mulholland requested that Van Norman return to the water bureau to serve as the Chief's assistant. For the past two years, he had been loaned out to the department of public works to oversee the completion of the outfall sewer and then had been named city engineer. As Van Norman would take over the active detailed work of the department, the board directed Mulholland to take the vacation that he had earned, but he demurred by repeating his old story of spending an afternoon at Long Beach once and becoming so bored that he showed up for work next morning. To reporter Joseph Timmons, who reminded him that he would soon be seventy, Mulholland spoke bluntly. "I may die some day. Nothing is more certain than that. I may go as suddenly as McKay. But I am not thinking of retiring." The truth emerged; he loved his work. "If I knew of anything that would afford me as much amusement and entertainment as the constructive work in this job, I would retire and do it." He did not intend to quit unless God called him or "some of those who wish I would retire can induce the Water and Power Commission to get rid of the old codger."[9]

He had decisions to make, he told Timmons, about the tunnel that would carry Colorado River water through San Gorgonio Pass. Should it be dug through sandstone or granite? Should it be swung towards the Yucaipa side through sandstone or toward the San Jacinto side and be granite-walled? He sometimes rode across the desert in his limousine—which he referred to as his hearse—simply to contemplate the work ahead. He was awed by it, he said, but not scared. Then he spoke of an early experience at sea.

> Soon after I went to sea at 14, I had a task to do on the quarterdeck. An old sailor named Jack, for whom I had formed a liking, was at the wheel. I had often edged up to him and let my hand rest on the wheel, while I watched the sails with him, getting the instinct for steering by the wind. This day as I stood there he remarked that he wished he had his sou'wester, as spray was wetting him. I said, "Why don't you go get it? I'll take the wheel." He did it, without stopping for second thought and, as I stood there with the rolling ship responding to my touch as I held her to the right course, with wind abeam, I felt an elation, an exultation that cannot be described. I felt like Jove.

He concluded, "That is the way one feels at 70 at the wheel of an organization like this, and a task like the building of the Colorado aqueduct ahead. I am awed, as I was then by the majestic harmony of ship and sea and sail and wind, but I wasn't afraid then, and I'm not now."[10]

For his seventieth birthday on September 11, he took a week off but not for recreation. Instead, he headed for Oakland and Berkeley to consult over plans for a new $35 million East Bay water project, after which he proceeded to Sacramento for more consultations and inspection tours. Before he left, he also moved his office into new quarters at the end of August when the water and power bureaus moved into a thirteen-story building with a seven-story annex on the south side of Second Street between Broadway and Hill Streets. The move produced another burst of reminiscence as he recalled the early days of the water company when he and Tom Brooks had lived over the office at Alameda and Marchessault Streets.[11]

TESTIFYING FOR BOULDER DAM

By October, two large work camps along the Colorado River were doing preliminary surveys and road building near San Gorgonio. The end of the month found the Chief at the top of his form, doing battle with an Arizona senator who wanted to abandon plans for a high dam at Boulder Canyon and substitute a low dam proposed by a rival engineer, C. A. LaRue. Mulholland laid into the plan, called it "an atrociously preposterous pipe dream." As the interchanges grew hot, some of Mulholland's answers evoked merriment among the crowd of three hundred in the ballroom of the Biltmore Hotel, where the hearing was held. "Do you mind me asking these questions?" Senator Ashurst asked at one point. "No," countered Mulholland. "Pitch right in. They give me a rest."[12]

The hearings continued at Las Vegas with an inspection of Boulder Dam, during which Arthur P. Davis, Frank E. Weymouth, and Mulholland all spoke to the project's engineering feasibility. State engineer McClure, who had condemned Los Angeles's water activities in his report, now accompanied the Los Angeles engineers (who included Mulholland, Lippincott, Van Norman, and E. A. Bayley) on an eight-day inspection tour along Mulholland's proposed route of the Colorado River Aqueduct. Unfortunately, no reports of their conversations seem to have survived.[13]

THE PLOT THICKENS IN OWENS VALLEY

Owens Valley dwellers had done a lot of sniping through their local newspapers in 1925. They described the guards at Haiwee Reservoir, for instance, as an "armed invasion of Los Angeles hirelings." But the area remained peaceful until the announcement of the city's August purchase of the Longyear holdings for $300,000. With credit given to William Lacy, president of the Los Angeles Chamber of Commerce, and Harvey Van Norman for their services in resolving the negotiation, Longyear declared that he had sold low because he wanted an amicable settlement between Owens Valley and the city. The sale meant that the city now owned all of the improved water-bearing land in that portion of northern Owens Valley except the so-called Keough pool (4,482 acres), which was under the sway of Carl Keough and W. W. Watterson. The city had offered them

$1.25 million (or 4.6 times the assessed value), but the owners turned it down, demanding $2.1 million.[14]

Some of this group saw in the Longyear sale evidence of George Watterson's influence, so in mid-September, when the only recent violence in Owens Valley had been rifle shots during deer season, and while W. W. Watterson was recuperating from an appendectomy in Glendale (in the same hospital with his wife, who months earlier had suffered a general breakdown and been hospitalized), three of his rancher allies visited Uncle George and told him to get out of Bishop until the land and water matters with the city had been resolved. The threatening men claimed they represented 80 percent of northern Inyo County ranchers who wanted him out because they thought he was the cause of lower land prices. An indignant Watterson declared he had no intention of leaving the place where he had lived for thirty-five years and complained to the justice of the peace, who fined the men fifty dollars apiece for offensive conduct and disturbing the peace.[15]

Other Owens Valley owners were suing the city, claiming their ranches had been rendered arid by nearby wells that the city had drilled during the drought. Geologists shot down these claims in court, demonstrating that the rock strata precluded the wells, which had been drilled at some distance away, from affecting the ranches. Amid these contentions, the city announced that since the valley had refused to accept the public service commission's plan to leave 30,000 acres of the best land in the district under private ownership and permanent cultivation, it now intended to maintain the best sections of the city-owned land for agriculture and grazing and began to encourage bids for their use. Since 1923, the city had expended $8 million on land purchases in Owens Valley, and the current acquisitions amounted to $4 million more, which satisfied many in Los Angeles that the water and power commission had dealt generously and expeditiously with Owens Valley residents while also protecting the city's interests.[16]

Throughout 1925, various city representatives, mainly Mathews and Van Norman, had dealt with Fred Eaton as attorneys and associates plugged along, trying to reach an agreement on the Long Valley matter. (Duns for Eaton's unpaid grazing rentals piled up in the water department's files until, after four years, attempts at collecting seem to have been abandoned.) At one point in May, Eaton, with his associates and attorneys, indicated a willingness "to play ball" with the city, but the Eaton Land and Cattle Company now had a number of shareholders who were apparently not of one mind, so that time ran out for an agreement.[17]

At the beginning of 1926, Eaton suffered a stroke. Van Norman wired the news to Mathews, then in Washington, where he would remain for the next six months to attend the congressional hearings for the third Swing-Johnson bill. Eaton's son, Harold, and an associate of Eaton now requested that the Eaton properties in Long Valley be appraised the same as those lands "of same character lately purchased in Owens Valley." According to Van Norman, Mulholland was agreeable, and Leahey had been instructed to get the appraisal committee right on it. He also informed Mathews in the same wire that Longyear had sold his cattle to Hearst and was ready to close the deal and that the "water situation looks good with prospect of above deals and other deals pending on Owens River Canal."[18]

Two weeks later, Mathews wired Mulholland via the Chief's private secretary, Eve H. Shoemaker. "My home advises Fred Eaton seriously ill and anxious about my return Please get from him or those caring for him any message he may wish sent me Also convey to him my affectionate regard and earnest hope for early recovery." A week later, on March 11, when Van Norman wired Mathews for advice on matters before the public service commission, he added that Harold Eaton was pressing for the sale of the Eaton property. Van Norman suggested a deal for 12,000 acres at $40 an acre ($480,000) might be possible. Harold, however, had "intimated that the deal could be closed for sixty-six per acre" ($792,000). The younger Eaton also reported that his father's associate, banker John E. Fishburn, was forming a syndicate "to tie up property for five years with option to purchase at end of this time." After Van Norman and Mulholland decided the latter development was probably a bluff, Mulholland indicated he was reluctant to have anything to do with it. Van Norman then consulted with Mathews over a proper price, also informing him that he was heading for Owens Valley to investigate and concluded with the good news that forty feet of water was now in the "new St. Francis."[19]

With the city's refusal to pay their price, the Eatons arranged a mortgage with Watterson Bros., Inc., for $200,000, to consist of forty promissory notes of $5,000 each, payable on or before five years after date, with interest of 8 percent per annum, payable semiannually. By year's end, Wilfred Watterson was deeply involved in Eaton's holdings, as he requested abstracts of the Long Valley property and clarification of documents regarding lands near Haiwee that Eaton had previously sold to the city. Because Eaton and his wife were living in Los Angeles-Santa Monica during his recovery, and because Eaton's right side had been partially paralyzed so that he now had to use his left hand to sign his name, his wife, Alice, acted as his amanuensis for his business correspondence.[20]

In the spring of 1926, while the dealings with Fred Eaton remained unresolved, a well was mysteriously dynamited on property that W. W. Watterson had sold to the city a year before. Dynamite caps were found in the automobile of Carl Keough, president of the Owens River Canal Company, that was still holding out on a sale to the city and in which Watterson also had an interest. Leahey traveled down to Los Angeles to report the incident, but it was not a matter of grave concern. More newsworthy were the water and power board's threat to sue the editor of the *Owens Valley Herald,* Harry Glasscock, for libel, and plans to celebrate the opening in early May of a new highway between Los Angeles and Bishop. (The first 104 miles to Mojave were all concrete, while the next stretch to Bishop was a graded dirt roadway.) Weeks later, however, another blast ripped a ten-foot hole in the aqueduct about four miles from Lone Pine, near the Alabama Hills. Again, the blast was linked to the Keough group but Mulholland declared it "simply a gesture to get our attention. . . . They do it now and then up that way," he explained. "Then they make reparation claims. The dynamite is set off one night and we get a boxful of reparations claims the next morning. . . . That," he concluded, "tells the whole story." Again, repairs on the line were quickly made.[21]

On July 1, a third blast ushered in the Fourth of July by blowing up a construction shack northeast of Bishop, but in Los Angeles it scarcely rated a notice amid the celebration of Mathews's return from Washington, D.C., after six months of work on behalf of the Boulder Dam Act. Mulholland paid his old friend high tribute, saying that without him the aqueduct could not have been built and that now he was equally invaluable in the Boulder fight. Politicking took up much of the summer until the primary election on August 31 approved the much-needed water and power bonds. Voters also selected candidates for the November election who would usher out Richardson and bring to office a strong proBoulder candidate, former lieutenant-governor C. C. Young.[22]

WATTERSON TAKES CHARGE

On December 31, 1926, W. W. Watterson wrote a less than jolly New Year's letter to Fred Eaton as he slowly recovered from his stroke. After speaking of certain problems finding accurate records for the Long Valley property, he indicated that if Eaton's deal for a sale to the city did not materialize, he believed they could work something out for him "in connection with other plans we have." The same day, Watterson wrote with great candor to his brother-in-law, J. C. "Jake" Clausen, then living in Los Angeles and in almost daily contact with Eaton. Acknowledging that he was glad "we have the mortgage and have it duly recorded and under our control since you have told us of his [Eaton's] mental attitude towards the situation. Reminds me of old Charlie Summers for whom we have done more than almost any other man in the country and he is one of our nastiest enemies." (Summers, hard-boiled and cantankerous, was one of the old-time Owens Valley cattlemen and, probably because of depressed market prices during this period, must have been encumbered with mortgages at the Watterson banks.)[23]

Watterson outlined to Clausen various strategies for successful land deals in Owens Valley. One was to put the squeeze on Eaton for an option on his Long Valley land; the other was "to get a big lot of property under pool—this of course quite confidentially—and then make an effort to sell it to the City. I can't give you in this letter the details of our plan but I am satisfied it will work out just as successfull [sic] as our efforts to sell Round Valley and West Bishop did," that is, their earlier campaign that involved forming the Big Pine Property Owners Association and ousting George Warren from the presidency of the Associated Chambers of Commerce in Owens Valley.

What Watterson also saw fit to include in this letter were instructions on wangling an option on Eaton's Long Valley land, as "I am satisfied that if we had that we would accomplish more for Eaton than anything he will be able to do for himself." He cautioned about Eaton's lack of trust in anybody else's ability to achieve successful dealings with the city but argued that he could point out to him their success in Round Valley and West Bishop, "where the sales amounted to over a million dollars" and "we sold every piece of property placed in our hands at the price the farmer named and did not in any instance have to reduce the price a single dollar."

EATON HOLDS OUT

With the beginning of 1927, Los Angeles continued its fight for Boulder Dam, sending off a team headed by veteran attorney Mathews to Washington, D.C. At home the stalemate on Long Valley continued as Harold Eaton asked for $800,000 while the city agreed to $600,000. Mulholland's response to the stalemate was to authorize a dam at the Tinemaha site and secure agreements with the railway to begin moving its rail sites to the west side of the valley from Owenyo to Laws.[24]

In precarious health and with no good economic news, Eaton held out for his price of $2.1 million. He next received a blockbuster letter from W. W. Watterson. Written February 6, 1927, it announced without preamble that none of Eaton's strategies for selling had succeeded nor ever would; that none of his city friends had been of help to him; that they (the Wattersons) had carried him along as a friend, but "after three years of fruitless effort" on the Long Valley property, it was time to yield and follow their advice. Soon, Watterson continued, the city would have acquired "all of the properties in this watershed except those belonging to two or three men to whom they feel antagonistic like yourself, Longyear, and the Crowell Zombro interests." (J. Crowell and Sumter F. Zombro were Los Angeles financiers.)[25]

After detailing his plans for cleaning up land sales in Owens Valley, Watterson informed Eaton of their dealings with the city:

> Senator Joe Inman, our attorney in Sacramento, has been active lately in making arrangements to sell to the City the remaining lands here. We are encouraging the movement because it seems to be the most feasible channel through which to get all the remaining interests consolidated. Inman is working with Jess Hession [district attorney of Inyo County], and if they get enough property under option so that it will be worthwhile to carry on a proper campaign to make a sale to the City of the same, and also that there will be enough of the property to insure proper compensation to Inman and his group, it will go through. We are giving Inman an option on our ranch holdings and town property along with many other people who are doing the same, and we feel that you should join us in this movement and do so immediately. The sooner it is done, the sooner something can be accomplished in the way of working out our program.

Watterson instructed Eaton to put his price as "the net amount that you are to get out of it, leaving it so that Hession and Inman will have to depend on the raise in price above your option for their compensation." He also advised Eaton not to think of what the property is worth to the city but rather "what a given amount of money is worth to you now and to your families after you are gone. . . . You should not," he warned, "under any circumstances gamble with the property at this time. A reasonable amount now, and safety, is the only path you should follow in arriving at a price to set on the property." Reminding him that for several years the Wattersons had been providing funds to carry him along but now seeing no hope of future improvement ("the indebtedness is growing steadily"), he warned that Eaton could not expect future help unless he accepted a one-year option.

Silence followed this hard-nosed letter until ten days later, when Clausen reported to Watterson that he surmised Eaton had been "put out," having heard nothing from the man who customarily called him almost every day. Eaton's daughter-in-law, Mrs. Burdick Eaton, had told Clausen that he felt "very badly" and warned him to stay away for a while. Eaton's brother-in-law also informed Clausen that "Mr. Eaton was much peeved," declared he did not know who Inman was and was sure he could not do anything anyway, and wondered if "Wilfred was trying to make some money out of the situation." Clausen confided that in his opinion, "Fred is mentally impossible to deal with—He is suspicious of everybody—and you will surely get into difficulties with him if you attempt to carry out any cooperation plan—no matter how advantageous to him."[26]

While Watterson worked on Eaton, Van Norman was writing his concerns to Mathews. On February 3, he included the annual report of the Owens Valley Irrigation District (dominated by the Wattersons) and noted that its costs and salaries came to $12,000, of which the city paid 80 percent. "This money is being used by the officers of the district in promoting law suits and propaganda against the city." Was there no way to stop it, he wondered. He also spoke of problems dealing with the Inyo County banks, all Watterson-owned: "like pulling teeth to get the documents out" (mortgages, land titles, and such). In some cases, Van Norman complained, "the City's money has been in the bank as long as six months for the satisfaction of a mortgage before the bank would complete transactions; there being no reason other than that the bank has held the money to use as long as possible." Citing other difficulties, he concluded, "We do not feel safe in depositing large sums of money there under the present conditions and if another bank is opened in the Valley, it will go a long ways towards solving our problem." More positively, he reported that the Lone Pine Chamber of Commerce had written a letter of thanks to the public service commission for its attitude toward the valley, "especially in the matter of advertising last year; the movement . . . to get the railroad broad-gauged; and its assistance in building roads into the mountains." He also indicated that similar letters of appreciation would be forthcoming from other chambers in the valley.[27]

THE LAST ROUND OF "SHOOTING THE DUCK"

Fighting words preceded the dynamitings in the second phase of the water war. After the Big Pine Property Owners Association met in February, the *Owens Valley Herald* heightened the event by likening it to the well-known statue of a defeated Indian warrior on his horse, *The End of the Trail*. As Senator Inman began his fight for the reparations act in Sacramento, a powerful propaganda barrage against Los Angeles began. Various legislators were invited to view the havoc wrought in Owens Valley. Frederick Faulkner, editor of the *Sacramento Union,* arrived and subsequently wrote a series entitled *Owens Valley: Where the Trail of the Wrecker Runs* (March 28 to April 2). The columns coincided with the attempt to push through the reparations act. Los Angeles rebutted with Don Kinsey's pamphlet, *The Owens Valley Dispute.* Then, on April 6, the *Owens Valley Herald* announced that a fistfight between a Los Angeles deputy sheriff and an Owens Valley Property Owners Protective Association officer had drawn first blood. Magnifying this scuffle outside a pool hall into a portent of the Los Angeles Aqueduct's running red with human blood, the paper began to report each dead creature found in a local creek (a deer, a mountain lion) as victims of the aqueduct and a reminder to the people of the south that the water they drank and imagined to be pure was, because of the dead bodies it sometimes contained, "a kind of a cannibal soup, flavored with the carcasses of the lower animals."[28]

Journalist C. E. Kunze and his wife next arrived in Bishop to rewrite and reprint in pamphlet form his successful series, *The Valley of Broken Hearts,* which was now to be distributed throughout the United States along with 10,000 mailers of Faulkner's pieces. (Watterson's later claim that he had spent $30,000 on these efforts seems to confirm Van Norman's accusation that Los Angeles was subsidizing attacks against itself.) After two months of widely disseminated assaults against the city and mounting anger in Owens Valley as the reparations bill neared a vote, the senate tabled the reparations resolution on April 27. A pleased Mulholland branded the Owens Valley charges false and was further elated a week later when Governor Young signed the Metropolitan Water District Act. Ten days hence, however, the disappointed Owens Valleyites renewed their sport of "shooting the duck." Between May and July seven dynamitings shook the aqueduct.[29]

The first two explosions occurred only days apart on May 20 and 28, destroying the No Name Siphon and 475 feet of aqueduct as well as the penstock of the Big Pine powerhouse. As guards and police rushed to the scene from Los Angeles to protect against further depredations, the board of water and power commissioners condemned the deeds, as did the city council. Mulholland, with Van Norman, hastened north to meet with Leahey and W. J. Clark, a former deputy district attorney of Los Angeles now delegated to investigate the sabotage. After viewing the damage, Mulholland expressed his outrage but also, as he had done so many times before when the water supply appeared threatened, reassured the city that the destruction would not cause a water shortage. Both he and Scattergood cited the recent completion of the Saint Francis Dam as providential in the crisis because its current capacity would help the city to avoid serious power shortages.[30]

Having done what he could, Mulholland left in a chauffeured car and returned safely to Los Angeles. His colleagues, however, following later in a large and speeding touring sedan, missed a sharp turn on a mountain road in Mint Canyon about twenty miles north of Saugus. The back brakes locked and the car plunged down an embankment, turning over several times. Although all fortunately escaped death, at this moment of crisis two of Mulholland's most valuable coworkers, Van Norman and Leahey, lay in the hospital with severe injuries.[31]

Five days after the car accident, a June 6 dynamiting crippled a section of the aqueduct near the Cottonwood powerhouse; two more damaging blasts followed two weeks later. Amid growing consternation and the city's demands to bring in state troops, Governor Young refused, speaking vaguely of the need for arbitration, a proposal promptly shot down by Owens Valleyites. On July 6, Mulholland made an urgent request to the Federal Radio Commission for permits and licenses for shortwave radio transmitters between Owens Valley and Los Angeles. "Due to extreme dangers and threats to life and property along Los Angeles Aqueduct System, it is vitally necessary to establish an emergency means of communication between Headquarters of the Department of Water and Power in Los Angeles and its Lone Pine, California, maintenance branch at the source of its water supply." Citing "recent depredations" that had destroyed both telephone and telegraph lines, the message declared it "imperative to have an emergency source of intelligence that Radio alone can supply."[32]

A week after Mulholland sent that wire, another section of the aqueduct north of Independence was blown out July 15. A blast that followed the next day proved to be the last. The city's efforts to quell the destruction and round up the culprits had met with some success, but the violence finally ended because Owens Valley events and plots unraveled on their own. First, an ex-major, C. Percy Watson, was found with a cache of dynamite and arrested as a principal in the dynamitings. (Later, to the surprise of many, he was exonerated.) Then amid this atmosphere of increasing lawlessness that threatened a serious disruption of water and power supplies, a turn worthy of Greek tragedy produced a reversal of fortunes. Bank examiners, discovering irregularities in the five Watterson banks, ordered their closure and charged the brothers with embezzlement and fraud. One million dollars could not be accounted for, and by the end of August, the Wattersons had been arraigned.[33]

What ensued was a sorry saga of local betrayals and a further deepening of hatreds, as what had been portrayed as the Valley of Broken Hearts due to predatory water men from the big city truly became a place of heartbreak and loss at the hands of its own. As costly and demoralizing as the dynamitings had been to the city—damage to the aqueduct was estimated at $250,000, to say nothing of the lost water and interrupted power service in Los Angeles—they paled beside Owens Valley's emotional and financial losses as it grew clear that Los Angeles had prevailed and loomed now as a permanent overlord. In the propaganda war, however, Owens Valley triumphed, for its charges and insinuations have long since been woven into the tapestry of myths depicting Los Angeles as a water stealer and exploiter. Just as later writers have credulously used the many undocumented charges of that time, so today do some Owens Valleyites remain as intransigent towards the city as unreconstructed Southerners towards the Yankee North. Fifty years after the dynamitings, a woman who had been a young mother at the time of the Alabama Gates incident remained unyielding in her opinion. "Had the men who owned the bank had a chance they could have made every dime good. The two men went to prison. The Water & Power was behind it all. My father lost what money he had and so did my father-in-law." As the Fresno editor had prophesied, Naboth had met his doom.[34]

THE PLAYING OUT OF A SAD SAGA

With attention focused on the upcoming and highly emotional Watterson trial, Mulholland observed his seventy-second birthday. By then, Leahey and Van Norman were sufficiently recovered from their injuries to return to work and oversee the continuing aqueduct repairs while Los Angeles and Owens Valley civic leaders attempted to find grounds for reconciliation. The public service commission announced it would buy Longyear's and Zombro's lands at prices the Los Angeles bankers had earlier refused. Other appeals for the city to buy lands now flooded in with the vain hope that it might save the ailing banks, but as Mulholland pointed out, "If we should proceed to buy the remaining ranches, mighty little of the money we paid would be thrown into the pot by the ranch owners to save the banks. The Wattersons long ago sold us their ranches and turned their attention to trying to force us to pay millions in reparations to the townspeople. The banks have mortgages on some of the ranches we have not bought and a part of the money, if we bought them now, would go to the banks, but not enough to re-establish the banks."[35]

Amid the valley's misfortunes, Harry Glasscock of the *Owens Valley Herald* maintained an unrepentant bravado and continued to blame the valley's woes on the city. With uncertainty, anger, and the threat of violence palpable throughout the valley, and after more explosives were discovered near the aqueduct around Lone Pine, the city purchased sixteen Thompson machine guns to beef up security along the line. To compound the confusion, cloudbursts and an earthquake clogged a portion of the aqueduct with debris, so that crews rushed in to clear away the rocks and dirt.[36]

The unremitting strain and worry of the strife between Los Angeles and Owens Valley had taken an unimaginable toll on all the players in this saga. On September 11, Mulholland's birthday, Ben Leete, president of the Owens Valley Protective Association, a close associate of the Wattersons and one of the leaders in the fight against Los Angeles, dropped dead of a heart attack. Later, editor Glasscock would commit suicide. With the approach of the explosive Watterson trial and continued anonymous threats against Mulholland's life, his family and friends insisted that he absent himself from the city and take a genuine vacation. Even though his extraordinary vigor had allowed him to maintain a pace arduous for a man of any age, intimations of mortality had begun to encroach. Increasingly his name appeared as an honorary pallbearer at the funerals of old associates, while McKay's sudden death, old friend and contemporary Eaton's afflictions, and the recent auto accident that had almost cost the lives of two of his most valued (and younger) friends and coworkers crowded in to demonstrate life's uncertainties. The Chief continued to dismiss threats against him as pure bluff but at last succumbed to the wishes of his concerned family.[37]

The day the Watterson trial began in Owens Valley, October 31, 1927, Mulholland, with his son and daughter-in-law, Perry and Addie Mulholland, sailed on the SS *Mongolia* of the Panama Pacific Line for a cruise to New York via the Panama Canal. He was about to see firsthand the engineering marvel that rivaled his own. Fifty years had passed since he last saw what was then the precanal Isthmus of Panama, hiking across it with his brother. Now he sailed out of San Pedro as a world-renowned engineer on a swift modern steamer under the command of one Captain H. A. T. Candy. Quartered in a first-class cabin and seated at the captain's table, Mulholland enjoyed the status of an honored guest. "They made a big fuss over Dad," Addie later recalled. One week out and on the eve of their November 8 arrival at Balboa, she wrote her sister-in-law, Rose Mulholland, that the honor of the captain's table was proving a dubious pleasure, for Captain Candy was "inclined to be rather obstinate." She explained, "He and Dad have had several very heated discussions but I hope they are through for the trip." She thought, however, that he was enjoying the cruise, for he "generally finds some one interesting to talk to and if he doesn't he sleeps." The day before, he had spent the afternoon with "an *Examiner* man named Talbert." On other days, he and Perry had spent "a great deal of time looking at the scenery which consists *principally* of salt water." He had not, she reported, opened a book on the trip.[38]

Mulholland returned from vacation a month later with renewed hope that matters might be resolved in Owens Valley. During his absence, the Wattersons had been found guilty and sentenced to ten years in San Quentin. Negotiations between the city and Owens Valley inched along, and after five months of work, Tinemaha Dam was half finished under the supervision of engineer Stanley Dunham, who had built the Saint Francis Dam in 1926. An earth-fill structure south of Big Pine, Tinemaha was intended as a holding basin in the event of trouble between itself and Haiwee.[39]

With the focus once more on the Boulder Dam proposal that was about to be argued yet again in Congress, Mulholland left for Washington, D.C., in early January 1928, with Van Norman and Mathews, to testify on behalf of the third Swing-Johnson bill. Upon returning from his Panama trip, he had made a strong public statement in favor of the upcoming bill and expressed his impatience with the years of foot-dragging since 1923–24. Even Senators Swing and Johnson were beginning to feel discouraged about its chances of passage.[40]

Hearings were to have begun January 6, 1928, but by the tenth, Mulholland wrote to Rose from his hotel in Washington, D.C., "I imagined that by this time I could give you some idea of the time of my return but it still is uncertain. . . . I had a bad attack of neuritis for two days but am all right now." He never testified, and as congressmen, engineers, and lobbyists for the Colorado River states continued to tilt over the bill, he and Van Norman departed on January 16, leaving Representative Evans of Glendale to enter into the *Congressional Record* Mulholland's report arguing Los Angeles's need for Boulder Dam and asserting that at the current rate of growth, its present water supply would be inadequate by 1947. Back in Los Angeles, Mulholland announced his belief that the long-contested Swing-Johnson bill would ultimately pass, but by the time it had, on December 28, 1928, Mulholland's world had irrevocably broken.[41]

MULHOLLAND VISITS EATON

Soon after his return from Washington, Mulholland visited Fred Eaton. Van Norman in turn reported by wire to Mathews on February 13: "Fred is in about same frame of mind respecting property as he has always been." Since the Watterson debacle, the Eaton Land and Cattle Company had gone into receivership. Van Norman, hoping to persuade him to sell to the city, asked Eaton's old friend and associate, G. J. Kuhrts, former city engineer and now general manager of the Los Angeles Railway Company, to intercede. Mulholland reported the results of that mission in a long letter to Mathews:

> Burdick Eaton's wife called me last Friday to come and see Fred. I was somewhat alarmed by the urgency of her call and responded at once, but found when I got there that he was merely in a talkative mood, due to a recent visit of George Kuhrts. He wanted to prod me up about his affairs. He doesn't seem to me to be ailing any more than he did a couple of months ago when he called here at my office, but seems to realize that the time is getting short to urge his case in the land matter on the Board.
> This morning George Kuhrts called on me, and having accomplished nothing with Fred,—as he refrained from telling me anything about what he expected to get from the land, in spite of my inquiry,—Van and I put it directly up to Kuhrts. He seemed shy about revealing to us anything in regard to what Eaton expected, but started in with a million dollars, and finally worked down to the point where he said he understood we would give $800,000. I thought I would let you know this so that you might be informed of what took place here.
> Kuhrts is quite sure that Eaton won't accept this figure, but Van was in a mood to test him out anyway and find out really what was in the back of his head. We have not had the matter up with anyone since we left you in Washington. In fact, as you know, I am keeping clear of it altogether myself, except when urged to talk about it, as I was on my visit to Eaton, but I avoided discussion of the matter as much as I could. I told him he would have to take it up with the proper committee. The Board has not approached the subject in my presence at any time within the last three or four months, or at any

time since you left here. My purpose in writing you this is, as I stated, so as to let you know how things stand as far as anything we have done here is concerned.

In closing, Mulholland said that nothing new was going on, but that the winter was dry. "We are now twenty per cent shy of the normal, and snow falls so far have been very light." Expressing a hope for rain, he also gave thanks that the storage supply was better than it had ever been because of the "excessive precipitation of the last two years." He closed by saying that he hoped to hear good news soon about the Boulder bill. A month later, his career was in ruins.[42]

CHAPTER 24

The Saint Francis Dam
Disaster and After

1928–1935

AN ILL-STARRED DAM

Great human defeats are never forgotten. They pass into the annals of
history and myth, even enter our racial memory as the Achilles' heels of
human aspirations: the sinking of the *Titanic*, the explosion of the *Graf*
zeppelin, the failure of the space ship *Challenger*, and the collapse of the
Saint Francis Dam. Rose Mulholland remembered how the horrible news
came to their home in the middle of the night. When the upstairs telephone rang sometime after midnight in the hallway just outside her father's bedroom door, she took the call. It was Van Norman, who told
her the dam had gone out. She went to her father's bed and awakened
him with the news. As he rose and stumbled toward the phone, she heard
him repeat over and over, "Please, God. Don't let people be killed."

The day before, on March 12, he and Van Norman had inspected the
dam and declared it sound, although there had been talk and concern
for some time about leakage at its west abutment. Mulholland remained
unworried, said such leakage was typical of concrete dams and not
significant. But less than twelve hours later, sometime after midnight, the
dam had given way and released an ocean of impounded water to cut a
destructive swath to the sea. In those roiling waters, more than four hundred people lost their lives in what became the greatest man-made disaster in the history of California and the greatest American civil engineering failure in the twentieth century.[1]

Construction of the Saint Francis Dam grew out of the California drought of the 1920s, the apparently unending growth of Los Angeles, and the need to store additional water acquired since the city's most recent purchases in Owens Valley. The specter of a water dearth always haunted the city's water men. To forestall that possibility and provide storage for a year's supply of water for Los Angeles, they built nine new reservoirs during that decade, the largest of which was the Saint Francis Dam.[2] Its site in the picturesque San Francisquito Canyon was a second choice for Mulholland, whose first had been nearer the city in Tujunga Canyon. When landowners in that area began to inflate their prices, however, he decided that rather than meet their expensive demands or wait for lengthy condemnation proceedings, he would turn to the canyon site where the city already generated its electric energy at two power plants. Under the supervision of Stanley Dunham, who would later supervise construction of Tinemaha Dam, the Saint Francis was begun in August 1924. The work proceeded without incident except for nearby ranchers and growers who expressed concern over the city's designs on their water from San Francisquito Creek. The city assured them that it did not intend to impound the San Francisquito Creek's waters. On March 12, 1926, as the attention of the city's water men focused on the fight for Boulder Dam and passage of the Swing-Johnson bill, the Saint Francis Dam began to fill with water. Then, two years later to the day, it failed.[3]

The story of this ill-starred dam has been told in many places and the causes of its failure remain controversial. Geologists had long recognized the site's problematic nature because of potentially unstable mica schist on its southeastern canyon wall, but its topography also offered an ideal location for a dam. Caught by the urgency to impound waters and maintain hydroelectric power generation, Mulholland recognized geological difficulties in San Francisquito Canyon yet still believed it to be safe and decided to build there. Instead of the usual hydraulic fill dam such as the South Haiwee and Fairmont, the Saint Francis was modeled after the city's first concrete gravity arch dam structure, the Hollywood Reservoir. Because of the increasing annual use of water in Los Angeles and the desire to achieve maximum storage capacity, the Saint Francis was built 20 vertical feet higher than planned without substantially widening its base. These elements, along with the state of engineering at that time, which did not yet appreciate certain technical knowledge available today such as the destabilizing effects of uplift pressures, may all have contributed to the dam's failure.[4]

Even as water rose for the first time in the reservoir, cracks had appeared on the face of the main structure. They were filled, cemented, and sealed to prevent further seepage. Then, during spring runoff in January 1928, with the dam at full capacity (32,000 acre feet), new leaks appeared on both abutments. For these Mulholland ordered corrective measures. By March, however, the leaking water had turned muddy, suggesting that the ground beneath the west abutment was giving way. Locals, especially those who lived below the dam and had long entertained anxieties about the amount of seepage and leakage they had observed, began to jest in a kind of gallows humor about the imminent collapse of the dam. One, in leaving a companion, had joshed, "Well, good-bye, Ed, I will see you again if the dam don't break." A rancher who survived the disaster would later not forget the last words he had heard from the assistant dam keeper, Jack Ely, two days before the dam went out. As they stood observing the leaks on the west abutment, the rancher twitted him, "Ely, what are you sons-of-guns going to do here, going to flood us out down below?" to which Ely joked back, "We expect this dam to break any minute!"[5]

Minutes before midnight, on March 12, ground gave way on the east side, and the force of the onrushing water collapsed the abutment. Moments later the west side fell, as an overwhelming mountain of water roared down the canyon to run its annihilating course along the bed of the Santa Clara River to the Pacific Ocean. As the monster cataract made its crushing way, it overwhelmed Castaic Junction in a sixty-foot tide. Eleven miles further on, it inundated a construction camp of Southern California Edison Company workers, killing 84 of the 140 people then sleeping there. Next, it began its destructive path across the Santa Clara Valley, as those in the little towns of Piru, Fillmore, and Santa Paula were alerted to the impending juggernaut.[6]

"AFTER THE FIRST DEATH THERE IS NO OTHER"

The horror of any catastrophe has many faces. How can one tell all the stories of that terrible time? Tales of heroism and courage (the young telephone operator in Santa Paula who risked her life by remaining at her post in the path of the coming waters in order to warn people) and tales of shame (looters in the flood-torn little towns). A profusion of records and testimony exists in official papers, engineering reports, and especially, the transcription of the Los Angeles County's coroner's report at the inquest over victims of the Saint Francis Dam disaster. For those with the stomach to look, there are morgue photographs of corpses recovered from the mud, rock, and sand in which the flooding waters churned and mauled their victims. There is the stark dead look of Mulholland, photographed with Van Norman as they stood in the nightmare of every engineer: to have been responsible for a structure that not only failed but killed. There is the progression of his words as at first he said some terrific earth movement (not an earthquake) must have caused the collapse. Then in testimony at the coroner's inquest, after hinting at the possibility of sabotage, with tears coursing down his face and at the point of breaking down, he said he envied the dead.[7]

Endless stories are told of that terrible time, but as Dylan Thomas wrote in "A Refusal to Mourn," his elegy to a child killed in a London fire raid early in World War II, "After the first death there is no other." So let here stand one letter for the many lost on that appalling night. Its author, Daisy Shaw Orton, lived with her family in Fillmore. Her husband, Lucius R. "Luce" (pronounced *Loosh*) Orton, a former undersheriff of Ventura County, was managing the Ventura Distributing Company, which sold and delivered the Ventura Refining Company's gasoline and oil. Anxious to let family in the San Fernando Valley know that they had survived, Daisy wrote the following day:

FILLMORE
MARCH 14, 1928

Dear Folks.

Ever since yesterday morning we have had calls into all our relations to tell that "all is well" with us—and the only call I have succeeded in getting thru was to my folks and as we were limited to three minutes I didn't have brains enough to ask them to relay messages for me to all of you.

For us right here in Fillmore there haven't been so many missing. With very few exceptions all are safe. The bodies that are being found here some 50 in number are from further up toward Castaic.

I don't believe I will ever forget that terrible night we went thru. The fire bell at 2-o'cl. woke us & we could keep hearing an awful roar. Luce dressed and started out and when he got out the door the neighbor man was just going out and told him what had happened. He came back and told us—the children were all awakened by the bell ringing—and then he went to the river to see just where the water was. In just a few minutes more the phone rang—calling more men out—and that the water was at Ventura St. Just the block below us. We then all dressed. 2 A.M.—no lights but my lovely red ornamental candles. I put some clothes for the children in a suitcase and when Luce got back he said the water was going down. We didn't go back to bed but built a fire in the fireplace and stayed up. It was sure a terrible night and I don't believe I will ever forget that awful roar of the water. Who would ever have thot that such a calamity could have overtaken us here.

The Bridge at Bardsdale is completely gone, taken by the water and debris. The river is absolutely clean of trees. Not a willow in sight. All of the houses on the Bardsdale side just off the Bridge are moved—some gone. This side what few were near the river are moved onto the street.

Luce has been gone all day yesterday and into the night and again today. The men here have organized searching parties and have recovered some 50 bodies. Luce says they were not drowned—but battered and bruized [sic]—but don't show anguish—so that probably they were taken in their sleep and didn't know what had happened.

Santa Paula's lower street—River St—had houses moved and twisted. Their lovely new school filled with water—many people left homeless. There is lots of outside aid coming in and as far as we can hear—everything is being done that can possibly be done. There are hundreds of your high powered—blue uniformed—Los Angeles police up here.

I understand from our truck drivers today that they are stopping everyone at the Saticoy crossing—The only way at present that you could get over here would be that way—But I imagine in a couple of days everything will be normal. All companies concerned are clearing roads—building bridges—putting up light and telephone lines. The only ones who they let thru must have *urgent* business. There were hundreds of sight-seeers yesterday—and Luce says that they have hindered men that were working trying to get things in shape. Will Bland was here from Lompoc. Got thru by knowing one of the cops on duty. He said that John was coming down but don't suppose they can get thru.

Gragg was here today. Had gotten *pinched* and had to come to court. Since I have started this your bookkeeper has phoned. So glad. Understand the mail was going out today. No trains—only from Ventura here. No further as yet, but think you will get this all right.

Daisy[8]

WHAT WENT WRONG?

Everyone had an explanation or surmise. Official response was immediate, sometimes surprisingly so. Within three days of the failure, Governor Young ordered a state investigation after the state engineer made the rapid and facile judgment that foundation weaknesses in the dam's abutments were responsible for the collapse and therefore declared "the responsibility rests with the Los Angeles city engineering authorities who built the dam." Mulholland had already asserted that if there were human error, it was his and his alone, which earned him praise and respect in many quarters as he went on to say, "We must have overlooked something." Newspapers throughout America headlined the story and editorially praised the old engineer's courage and honesty in assuming responsibility.

The city was quick to acknowledge its responsibility for the disaster, and within days, a committee under the leadership of George Eastman, president of the Los Angeles Chamber of Commerce, met with Ventura County leaders not only to take care of emergency relief but also to provide for permanent reconstruction. This arbitration committee would work for the next two years to achieve rehabilitation and restitution. Money from the city's general fund was quickly forthcoming after Eastman called on the city council to approve $1 million to begin reconstruction, while engineers from the Los Angeles Department of Water and Power supervised cleaning up the devastation, an enormous job that took three months and involved thousands of laborers, hundreds of tractors, and other heavy equipment. Ultimately, the city paid all claims established by the various committees—a total of $15 million. Charles Collins Teague, the Santa Paula area's leading citrus and walnut grower and owner of the immense Limoneira Ranch, was later to write, "Never before in the history of the world, as far as I am able to learn, was complete and equitable restitution and rehabilitation made by a great metropolitan people to a rural people, where damage had been done and where large sums of money were involved, without recourse to court action. In fact, these settlements were made on the broad ground of moral responsibility without the legal responsibility having been previously determined by the courts."[9]

Investigations followed swiftly upon the dam failure. First, on March 14, engineers for the state arrived, and within a day, one had declared that the dam had been built on a faulty site. Their later report to Governor C. C. Young, today regarded by most engineers as cursory and inadequate, concluded that "the manner in which the dam failed" had not been determined but that there were foundation weaknesses at the abutments, and, finally, that "the responsibility rests with the Los Angeles city engineering authorities who built the dam." Thus, the state washed its hands although the state board of inquiry's recommendation that plans for all future dams should be subject to outside consultants led to pioneer legislation afterward adopted by other states. All but federally sponsored dams and reservoirs would subsequently be subject to state review.[10]

Various city agencies now called for investigations and reports: district attorney Asa Keys called a group; the Los Angeles County Board of Supervisors retained J. B. Lippincott to write a report; and the city council appointed a committee of engineers headed by Elwood Mead (later, chief engineer of Boulder Dam), which reported on April 10 that a defective foundation had failed on the west wall. Most powerful of all the hearings, however, was the inquest of the Los Angeles coroner that began on

March 21 in the Hall of Justice, ten days after the disaster. Technically, the inquest would be for the sixty-five flood victims found in Los Angeles County, while a later inquest was to be held for those found in Ventura County. In a room crammed with spectators, Mulholland took the witness stand, where he testified at length concerning the details of building the Saint Francis Dam. He declared that he had personally supervised the building of the dam, had inspected it often, and had not regarded the leaks as serious: "All dams have leaks." When asked if he knew what caused the dam to go, he replied, "I have a suspicion but I do not want to say." When asked to clarify, he would only state that he would not build there again, that "there is a hoodoo on it." Asked to explain, he would only allow, "Well, it was vulnerable." To what, he would not say, but because of the recent Owens Valley dynamitings, suspicions had inevitably turned to the possibility of sabotage. (Today, most scholars believe that the failure resulted from geological problems rather than human wrongdoing.) Later, in his testimony, he accepted the responsibility for what had happened when, almost breaking down, he declared, "Fasten it on me if there was any error of judgment—human judgment!"[11]

Because the dam failed on the eve of the passage of the Swing-Johnson bill in Washington, opponents of Boulder Dam swooped like vultures to indict the break. To express his sorrow, Mathews hurried back from Washington, where he had been working as a member of California's Colorado River Commission. "Our hearts have been broken by this awful loss of life," he declared. The *Wall Street Journal,* however, editorially viewed the catastrophe not only as a refutation of the value of municipal ownership but as a warning to curtail the Boulder project. The *Los Angeles Examiner* damned the editorial, saying, "it is hard to remember a more ghoulish and contemptible use of public calamity to serve private interests." The bill did finally pass on December 14, 1928.[12]

Other political fallout included renewed questions about the safety of every dam and reservoir in the city's system. The Mulholland Dam especially, although nestled in the Hollywood hills and aesthetically the loveliest of Mulholland's dams, nevertheless shared its design with the Saint Francis, so that, understandably after the disaster, people living nearby were apprehensive. As one of his last acts as chief, Mulholland prudently ordered the water lowered in the Hollywood Reservoir, which, according to engineer Rogers, likely saved the dam, for subsequent studies found its base also lacked sufficient width to "withstand uplift and earthquake loading, or against basal sliding," elements that may have contributed to the failure of the Saint Francis. After engineering recommendations in 1931, the dam was closed down in 1932 for two years of massive retrofitting. Today the structure stands as a peaceful oasis in the Hollywood hills.[13]

Engineers have long studied and debated the causes of the dam's failure without arriving at agreement. Recently the widely published consulting geological engineer J. David Rogers, after years of research, has created renewed interest in the subject with his findings. His investigation, which began with a low regard for Mulholland's character and engineering skills, ultimately led to a reconsideration. "I am of the opinion that we should be so lucky as to have any men with just half his character, integrity, imagination and leadership today."

THE AFTERMATH

Had I but died an hour before this chance
I had lived a blessed time; for, from this instant,
There's nothing serious in mortality,
All is but toys; renown and grace is dead,
The wine of life is drawn, and the mere lees
Is left this vault to brag of.

                                    Macbeth

Lillian Darrow, a native of Newark, New Jersey, had come to California in 1921 and as a young woman in her early twenties worked for the Department of Water and Power in the right-of-way and land department. At the time of the dam failure, she was in the legal department dealing with belongings of the victims. Her memory years later of sorting out clothes and other possessions evoked the remark, "Some of the things I saw were pitiful." She also recalled that Mulholland before the tragedy had been "such a sweet man," who had always greeted her pleasantly whenever they met, but afterward "He went down. His face aged twenty years."[14]

Those who hated Mulholland (or just the idea of him) now had reason to hate him even more. Threats were made against his life, and he lived with an armed guard around his home. He requested a leave of absence, not wishing to embarrass the water board with his presence during the investigation, and although the commission refused to grant it, he knew he could no longer be effective. Even as he accepted responsibility, he remained puzzled. "This expert testimony is all very good," he was heard to say during the coroner's inquest. "But I wish I knew why the St. Francis Dam went out." One reporter noted that "the testimony of the numerous experts did not seem to satisfy him. He shook his head occasionally and a puzzled look came over his face." Fifty years later, his nephew and namesake, William Bodine Mulholland, said his uncle had never been satisfied. "With the knowledge that was available—and he had as much knowledge of those kinds of things as anybody in the world, and he used every bit of the knowledge that was available, and it [the dam] didn't stay there."[15]

Be that as it may, Mulholland's time was over, and in March 1929, Van Norman became chief engineer and general manager of a newly unified organization to be known henceforth as the Department of Water and Power (Scattergood, head of the formerly separate power bureau, became the chief electrical engineer, while Frank E. Weymouth, the hydraulic engineer formerly with the United States Reclamation Service, became assistant to Van Norman in the water bureau). Somewhat in the manner of a professor emeritus, the old Chief was retained as a consultant with an office in the department at a salary of five hundred dollars a month. Even this stipend after a lifetime of service to his city provoked the relentless *Record* to print a letter declaring it preposterous for "a man who had practically acknowledged his responsibility in connection with the Saint Francis tragedy and its sacrifice of over 400 lives, to continue to hold a position of such prestige."[16]

Public opprobrium was one thing; Mulholland had had a lifetime of it mingled with praise and adulation. But certain private hurts cut deep. One mechanical engineer who had worked with him since the days of the old private water company in the 1890s; who had traveled with him on business trips to San Francisco and Owens Valley; had lunched with him almost daily when the two were at the department—now, whether out of disapproval or from an inability to face the Chief—quit speaking to him. One of Mulholland's nephews still puzzled over it years later. "After having been that close to him all that time, he *shunned* him. It was the craziest thing I ever heard of."[17]

A month after the shutdown of the Mulholland Dam for retrofit in December 1931, the Chief suffered another hurtful loss with the sudden and unexpected death after abdominal surgery of his old "partner in crime," attorney W. B. Mathews. No law man in the history of Los Angeles had fought more legal battles for the public good. Eight months after the Saint Francis disaster, he had witnessed the White House signing of the Swing-Johnson bill, and almost to the time of his death, he continued to combat the ongoing threats against the Boulder project. He also lived to see the final approval of the Metropolitan Water District Act, for whose passage he had worked so long and hard. Lake Mathews in Riverside County remains a fitting memorial for the man whose intelligence and imagination are in part responsible for its very existence.

LAST YEARS

It has become a cliché to say that Mulholland was broken by the failure of the dam, and it is true that not unlike the American poet Ezra Pound, incarcerated in a madhouse for treason after World War II, Mulholland sought ever greater refuge in silence. Yet even after all the investigations and studies and speculations about the failure of the Saint Francis Dam, he remained unconvinced that an ultimate explanation had been reached. In accepting responsibility, he did not thereby consider himself to blame for something that had occurred beyond his power. Still, his cup was bitter as he and his family, having endured years of public controversy over water issues, drew further inward. He visited more frequently at the ranch in the San Fernando Valley, where, between 1910 and 1916, he had eventually acquired 640 acres on which his son, Perry, developed and managed the Mulholland Orchard Company, a family partnership. On the old Chief's seventy-fifth birthday in 1930, friends, family, and associates gathered for a private banquet at the ranch, but there were no public announcements or observances. He accompanied his children and grandchildren more frequently on outings and excursions: a day riding the cable car up Mount Lowe, a weekend cruise to Ensenada.[18]

One vivid recollection is of a trip to El Centro and Palm Springs in either 1930 or 1931, part of whose purpose was doubtless to view waterworks in connection with Imperial Valley and the Colorado River. (Among the men of our family, viewing waterworks was considered recreational in the way that museums, amusement parks, or zoos might be to others.) The family car was a dark green 1927 LaSalle touring sedan with a commodious interior. We stayed one night at the Barbara Worth Hotel in El Centro, where the lobby mural of Barbara Worth in the desert captured my imagination. (Years later I discovered in my grandfather's library a copy of *The Winning of Barbara Worth* [1911] by Harold Bell Wright. A best-selling romance celebrating engineers, water, the desert, and an orphan heroine, it upheld the virtues of westerners over materialistic easterners. Pasted in the book was a letter from Wright thanking Mulholland for the tour of the aqueduct and "his kindness in the days when I was collecting material for this story.")

As we motored towards Palm Springs at the end of the next day, discussion arose as to where we would stay the night. (In those days, one could make such impromptu arrangements for lodgings.) Approaching the elegant and newly opened Desert Inn, someone suggested that we ask about accommodations there. My father went in and returned to the car with the information that rooms were available, but rates began at $10.00 a night. Rates at the Barbara Worth Hotel the night before had ranged from $3.50 to $5.00. Grandpa, who had been semidozing up to then, came suddenly to life. "Did you tell them we didn't want to buy the place?" he protested.

We motored on, and instead of the Desert Inn, ended up in decidedly downscale tourist cabins. Next morning, some now long-forgotten exchange arose between my father and grandfather, one of those tense moments which the enforced intimacy of car travel seems to stimulate; perhaps it concerned how best to arrange the luggage in the car. Whatever it was, my agitated father backed over a water hydrant outside the cabin. From the broken pipe spouted a geyser of water, and as both men clambered out of the car, the rest of us emerged from our cabins ready to depart. Water spewed everywhere, and as my father went for help at the front office, I saw my grandfather alone beside the jetting stream. Only the excitement and confusion of the scene registered on me then, but now, years later, the memory of that old man who had been one of the world's leading hydraulic engineers standing helpless by a broken water pipe outside a tourist cabin in the desert strikes me as one of those consummately ironic moments when the gods play their Olympian jokes and laugh in heartless derision at us mere mortals.

GOING OUT

In his iconoclastic study of Los Angeles, *City of Quartz*, Mike Davis has with some justice called Mulholland a Promethean figure. Certainly he was not granted an easy end. He kept his old habits, went to the office where he was no longer in charge and could be of no further public use in the Boulder fight. His name vanished from the newspapers and except for family, close friends and associates, he receded from view. He attended some public events and received small honors from well-wishers. In 1931, on National Hospital Day (to honor the birth of Florence Nightingale, mother of nursing from the time of the Crimean War), old friends and associates of the Chief gathered in the boardroom of the Water and Power Commission, where once he had been the power on the throne and watched as dignitaries from the Florence Nightingale Institute of Honorables awarded him a certificate of honor for public service as "an individual whose forward-looking vision contributed infinitely to enhance the happiness, prosperity and progress of multitudes of human beings by enabling you to conceive and execute methods for producing a supply of water in the City of Los Angeles adequate for the uses of a population calculated on an unprecedentedly rapid basis of increase." He responded graciously, remembered that he had been born at the time of the Crimean War and that some of his people had fought in it. Florence Nightingale, he said, had been a household word in his family, and he had never dreamed that any of her humanitarian work would ever be associated with any honor that might come to him. He held up the plaque for a photograph, and although his expression was kindly, the eyes looking towards the camera seem to be staring into the void.[19]

Yet even with a blasted life, he kept his equanimity. When the powerful and destructive 1933 Long Beach earthquake shook his home at five o'clock in the afternoon, he was reading the evening paper in the den. Daughter Rose rushed to him from the kitchen, calling, "Get under a door, Dad. It's an earthquake!"

"Oh! Is that what it is," he replied without looking up from his paper. "I thought that physic I took this morning had begun to work."

Fred Eaton died March 11, 1934, and not long after, Mulholland told Rose that he had dreamed of Fred. They were walking together—young and virile as both had once been—but he recognized in the dream that they both were dead. During August of that year, Rose often drove him to visit the ramshackle beach house in Santa Monica that my family had rented for the month to escape the valley heat. By a bay window in a chintz-covered overstuffed chair, he sat muffled in his dark suit and gazed out to sea. When we children waved to him from the surf, he did not wave back. In October, he fell and broke his arm, a harbinger of the major stroke in December that paralyzed not only his body but his throat, so that he could neither speak nor take solid food. Although the death certificate later stated cause of death as arteriosclerosis and apoplexy, his nurses agreed that he had simply starved to death. Stretched like an old hulk on a hospital bed in his own bedroom and ministered to by a doughty day nurse with rust-colored hair and an apt name—Miss Ironsides—the tough old man's durable body resisted death for six months. The end came on July 22, 1935, at 9:45 A.M. Flags in the city hung at half-staff. On July 24, his body lay in state in the rotunda of Los Angeles City Hall as mourners passed and civic leaders eulogized. During later private services at Forest Lawn, all work on the Colorado River Aqueduct ceased for a minute of silence in tribute to his memory while the waters at Haiwee Dam were also stopped in their flow to the city. Robert V. Phillips, then a teenaged lad, happened to be with his father, J. E. Phillips, head of the aqueduct division. Amid the noise and clangor of men, engines, and equipment, he remembered when the silence began. It went on and on, he said—that silence on the desert—tribute to the man who had meant so much to all of them and also to Southern California. No more fitting tribute could have been paid to the man who long ago had said, "I want it written on my monument that I helped to build the Aqueduct."

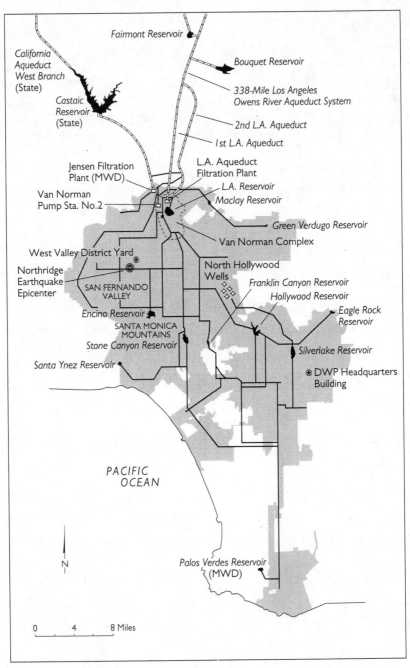

Map 7. Major water distribution facilities, City of Los Angeles (Los Angeles Department of Water and Power).

Afterword

In 1989, a filmmaking group for public television asked me to participate in a documentary video film, *Mulholland: The Dream-Builder* (part
of the Los Angeles History Project series for KCET). One of the shoots
took place April 28 in San Francisquito Canyon, where I had not been
since I was five years old when my shaken father had taken me the day
after the disaster to view the wreckage. Sixty years later, although trepid
about visiting what still seemed haunted and forbidden grounds, I hiked
with the crew on a warm sunny day to the former dam site where few
traces of the tragedy remain. (The standing portion of dam wall had been
blasted away in 1929.) Perched on a boulder in the riverbed of the canyon,
I spoke before camera of the devastation that overtook so many in this
place, including my grandfather.

Afterwards, Richard Callison, one of the young Department of Water
and Power engineers who had escorted us, drove me up to Power House
One and beyond to see the employees' quarters, which, being above the
dam, had been untouched by its failure. In this idyllic spot in the quiet
of the canyon where ancient native sycamores shade the ground stood
vintage wooden bungalows recalling the Southern California of my childhood. Callison told me the department engineers enjoyed duty there because of the beauty and quiet of the place, and then he said he would
like to give me something. We proceeded to his garage, where after rum-
maging about in a carton, he brought forth a small water glass of lavender tint.

"We explore down there where the dam went out," he explained, "and sometimes we find things. This glass came from the area where the old cookhouse was washed away." He held it out to me. "Would you like it?" he asked.

Moved, I expressed my appreciation and taking the small tumbler, remarked on its opalescent hue and said I had seen glass that had turned this shade in old houses.

"The action of the sun and weather on old glass," he went on to explain. It had lain in the riverbed for over half a century.

As we headed back to join the others, he turned and spoke. "You know what you said about the dam. That was a terrible thing, I know, but it was only one part of a whole. The only part which failed. The rest has held." Then to make his meaning clear, he repeated, "The whole system has held. Because it has integrity."

I thought then, and I think today, that those words could very well stand as an epitaph for William Mulholland. On a shelf in my home, that little water glass stands beside another memento from a thoughtful acquaintance, a small vial containing Owens River water, a souvenir handed out by the San Fernando Chamber of Commerce on the opening day of the Owens River Aqueduct in 1913. The whole story abides for me in those two objects: water as blessing, water as curse; water as life giver and destroyer. The clear little bottle holds the life-giving water that enabled a great city to grow, while the lavender glass speaks of the darker consequences of man's efforts to master a world he ultimately never fully comprehends or controls.

Notes

The titles of Los Angeles newspapers will appear in abbreviated form—for example, *Times* for *Los Angeles Times*. All out-of-town papers are cited with full title, such as *San Francisco Chronicle*.

The following works will be cited by author's last name only:

Hoffman, Abraham, *Vision or Villainy*

Kahrl, William, *Water and Power*

Nadeau, Remi, *The Water Seekers*

Ostrom, Vincent, *Water and Politics*

Many of Mulholland's office files came to light in the late 1980s. The chance circumstances of one discovery are best described by Elizabeth Wimmer, retired Department of Water and Power special projects officer. "William Mulholland's office file material was received from Russell A. Majors of Valley Generating Station, who said he received it from a painter who bought an old file from salvage and found the papers inside it." Wimmer to C. Mulholland, January 1991.

Not so fortunate is the fate of the wonderful collection of clippings books kept by the Department of Water and Power since 1903. In the course of microfilming them in the late 1990s, a foolish decision was made to destroy some of the originals, thus degrading the possibility of making good-quality reproductions for future publication from the many interesting cartoons contained there.

CHAPTER 1: THE LONG JOURNEY
FROM DUBLIN TO LOS ANGELES, 1855–1876

1. John Omicinski, "Modern Times," September 13, 1990, Gannett News Service, Washington.

2. John Russell McCarthy, "Water: The Saga of Bill Mulholland," *Pacific Saturday Night,* March 26, 1938, p. 5; Phil L.Snyder, ed., *Detachment and the Writing of History* (Ithaca, New York: Cornell University Press, 1958), p. 19.

3. "Mulholland is almost exclusive to Ulster, where it is most common in Counties Antrim, Down, and Derry. The name is in Gaelic ó Maolchalann, 'son of the devotee of St. Calann.' Although there was a sept of Mulhollands in Co. Donegall, most of the name descend from the Mulhollands of Loughinsholin in Co. Derry. They are famous for having been, with the Mallons, the hereditary keepers of St. Patrick's bell, the Bell of the Testament. From the fourteenth century the family spread into the western and southern part of Massereene in Co. Antrim, in which barony the name is seventh most numerous" (Bell, *The Book of Ulster Surnames,* p.198).

4. F. S. L. Lyons, *Ireland Since the Famine* (London: Fontana Press, 1971), p. 87.

5. Edmund Valel, *The Mail Coach Men of the Late Eighteenth Century* (London: Cassell, 1960), p. 49.

6. Lyons, op. cit., p. 47.

7. Classification of Studies, School Registry No. 4, O'Connell School, Dublin.

8. John deCourcy Ireland, *Ireland and the Irish in Maritime History* (Dublin: The Glendale Press, 1986), pp. 237–77.

9. Lloyd's Register of Shipping, 1869. The *Gleniffer* was rated as "a vessel well and sufficiently found." Built in 1866 in Glascow, she was typical of many small ships of the era that carried small cargoes great distances. Her destination on Mulholland's first voyage was Montreal, and her shipmaster was S. J. Coffey, who left his command the same year that Mulholland came ashore.

10. Bancroft, "History of California," vol. 7, p. 704.

CHAPTER 2: THE CITY OF ANGELS, 1877

1. H. Raitt and C. Wayne, *We Three Came West: A True Chronicle* (San Diego: Tofua Press, 1974), pp. 30–31.

2. *Evening Express,* January 8, 11, 1877; *Star,* February 3, 6, 9, 25, 1877; March 2; April 14; May 2, 1877. The four daily newspapers of the 1870s were the *Los Angeles Express,* the *Los Angeles Star,* the *Evening Express,* and the *Daily Herald.* A weekly, the *Los Angeles Mirror,* became the *Times* after Harrison Gray Otis purchased it from his partner, H. H. Boyce, in 1886.

3. Bell, *On the Old West Coast,* pp. 164–65.

4. *Star,* January 8; August 9, 23, 1878.

5. *Herald,* August 31, 1878; September 17, 26; October 6, 1878.

6. Spriggs, *History of Domestic Water Supply,* p. 67; *Times,* July 7, 1907; undated clipping, Mulholland scrapbook, probably 1911–12.

7. *First Annual Report of the Los Angeles Aqueduct,* p. 3. Layne, *Water and*

Power for a Great City (1957), presents a detailed account as do Hoffman and Stern's undated paper, "The Zanjas" (DWP). Background information may also be found in the writings of Horace Bell, J. M. Guinn, Harris Newmark, and William A. Spalding, as well as those of Fogelson, Ostrom, and Starr.

8. The term *zanja* originated in Cuba, according to F. de Santamaria, *Diccionario de Mejicanismos* (1959), to denote a person who digs *zanjas* (ditches, canals or drains) or *acequias,* a synonym deriving from the Arabic. As late as the 1960s, ranchers in Southern California used the anglicized term *sanky* for the district water manager to whom they addressed their orders for irrigation water.

9. Bell, op. cit., p. 251. Turner was mayor in 1869–70.

10. Layne, op. cit., p. 41.

11. Mulholland, "Municipal Ownership of Public Utilities," speech to the Sunset Club, 1905. Mulholland, office files, WP04-22:24 . Much about the old water company is unverifiable, as its records and books have been either lost or destroyed.

12. The promise must have been poorly kept, for when city chronicler W. A. Spalding got his reporting job at the *Los Angeles Herald* in 1874, his first piece addressed the dilapidated appearance of the plaza and its fountain "reminiscent of Hood's 'The fountain was a-dry—neglect and time/Has marred the work of artisan and mason.'" (*History and Reminiscences,* pp. 15–16). Nor had matters improved by the 1880s when Helen Hunt Jackson visited the city, for she found the plaza "a dusty and dismal little place with a parsimonious fountain in the centre . . ." (*Glimpses of Three Coasts* [1886], p. 111).

13. Layne, op. cit., p. 47, and Spalding, *History of Los Angeles,* vol. 1, p. 203.

14. Layne, op. cit., p. 48.

CHAPTER 3: THE PRIVATE WATER COMPANY AND ITS OWNERS, 1878–1879

1. Spriggs, pp. 70–71.

2. *Times,* March 3, 1898.

3. *Herald,* July 12, 1878; July 9, August 16, October 31, 1879. Attorney Frank H. Howard, who argued for the city in 1878, was later greatly admired by Mulholland. The *Herald* commented then that no member of the bar was more knowledgeable about water rights than he, and that because he was an accomplished linguist, he had "all the good concerning irrigation that is contained in the laws of the Romans, the French, of Spain, Italy and Mexico."

4. Brooks, "Notes"; Layne, pp. 51–52; *Times,* January 15, 1882.

5. Bell, op. cit., pp. 75, 80–81; *Herald,* Sept. 28, 1881; Brooks, "Notes."

6. *Evening Express,* July 23–27, 1877.

7. Mulholland, Speech, Sunset Club, 1905, p. 5; Brooks, "Notes."

8. W. A. Spalding, *History of Los Angeles City and County,* vol. 1, p. 171.

9. Hayes, *Pioneer Notes,* p. 167; *Illustrated History of Los Angeles County,* pp. 462–63; John Steven McGroarty, vol. 3, p. 482.

10. In consultation with Miles, Fred Eaton's father undertook a similar project in Pasadena to bring water from Devil's Gate in the Arroyo Seco to a reservoir site at the present intersection of Colorado Street and Orange Grove Avenue.

Miles also organized and became the chief engineer of the first volunteer fire brigade, created when the Los Angeles Water Company, in 1872–73, installed a few fire hydrants about the town (young Eaton being one of the first volunteers). In the 1880s, Miles also served as county recorder. Once described as "popular and sometimes festive," his festiveness ended in 1885, when he was arrested for embezzling $12,000. Charges were dismissed when he paid back the money, but he was still ousted from office. Fellow employees, however, continued to hold him in esteem as he had been an effective worker. McGroarty, *History of Los Angeles County,* vol. 3, p. 482; Layne, p. 39; Page, *Pasadena: Its Early Years,* p. 39; Hine, *Spalding,* p. 20.

CHAPTER 4: ADVANCING IN THE WATER BUSINESS, 1880–1886

1. Spriggs, pp. 68–69; *Intake,* Dept. of Water and Power, January 1933.

2. Layne, *Water and Power,* p. 99. Layne interviewed J. B. Campbell on December 10, 1947.

3. *Evening Express,* June 20, 1884; *Porcupine,* October 8, 1892.

4. *Express,* August 4, 1884.

5. Mary Foy, member of the pioneer Macy-Foy clan, attended Los Angeles High School and got her library post in 1880 by simply going to the mayor and each member of the city council and telling them that she could do a good job. *Herald,* October 7, 1881; *Times,* November 16, 1947.

6. *Herald,* January 7, 1881; *Times,* March 18, 1882. Also assuming office in the IOOF with Eaton and Mulholland was Moses L. Wicks, prominent land boomer and water developer. For his activities, see Dumke, *The Boom of the Eighties,* pp. 210–211.

7. In 1883 the Water Works Company consisted of S. B. Caswell, collector and bookkeeper; Fred Eaton, superintendent and engineer; Tom Burns, assistant; Thomas Brooks, assistant to Burns; four laborers plus two ditch and reservoir keepers. The directors were W. H. Perry, president of the board; S. H. Mott, secretary and treasurer; William Ferguson; Solomon Lazard; Charles Ducommon; and W. J. Broderick (Brooks, "Notes").

8. *Herald,* May 16, 1879; *Evening Express,* March 15, 1884.

9. *Times,* February 10, 1882.

10. *Times,* November 18, 1882; Brooks, "Notes."

11. Reagan Report, vol. 2, pp. 536, 553.

12. City Council Proceedings, V.XIV, pp. 729–30; V.XVIII, pp. 341, 353, September 29, 1883. Eaton and Mulholland bid for construction of a sewer line on Seventh Street. Rejected. Bids were M. S. Baker & Co., "to make fire hydrants at $45 each; S. M. Perry, ten at $75 each; William Mulholland, five or ten at $92 each. Referred to Committee on Fire and Water." The *Evening Express,* August 9, 1884. Also Council Proceedings, December 2, 1884, Los Angeles Water Company Time Book (1884–85), Public Affairs Division, Dept. of Water and Power.

13. William Perry participated in the founding of Fillmore, California, in 1887. The year before, during the height of the boom, he and a group of Los Angeles businessmen purchased 3,400 acres of Rancho Sespe. Then, for $25,000, they

secured water rights on Sespe Creek from a man named Dye, and in April 1886, they incorporated as the Sespe Land and Water Company (Freeman, pp. 24–25); *Express,* January 17, 1917.

14. *Times,* December 16, 1886.

15. Mulholland, Eaton, et al., pamphlet, "Wooden Pipes a Failure"(1905), Huntington Library.

CHAPTER 5: THE NEW SUPERINTENDENT, 1887–1892

1. Spalding, vol. 1, p. 263; *Evening Express,* January, February, 1887.

2. *Times,* April 15, 26, 1887.

3. *Times,* November 9; December 13, 1887.

4. *Times,* December 21, 1887.

5. Reagan Report, II, p. 545; Schuyler, Papers, Nos. 30, 31; *Times,* October 8, 1888. Eaton's dam was probably near Twin Lakes. Engineer James D. Schuyler measured water flows for this project in May 1888. The development coincided with a proposed railroad linking Ventura to Los Angeles via the Simi and Santa Susana Pass. Tradition has it that Chatsworth was named by someone with ties to (or knowledge of) the estate of the duke of Devonshire in England. As the overseer of the water project was a man named Forbes, who had built many dams in England, he likely named it. Much about the enterprise is murky. In the original plat, one of the streets was named Ben Porter Avenue, and probably Porter still held title to much of the land in question, for after the failure, a great deal of the tract reverted to the Porter Estate, and no further development occurred until 1893. The Porter Land and Water Company, with a firm hold on the north half of the San Fernando Valley, also had begun to create a water system west of San Fernando in conjunction with opening tracts for sale in the Mission area for citrus growing. The company boasted that it was spending fifty thousand dollars for a waterworks and offered land at $150 an acre, "with plenty of pure free water piped to each tract."

6. *Times,* May 11, 1888.

7. *Times,* March 8; May 12, 27, 1888.

8. *Times,* May 27, 1888.

9. Thomas Brooks, "Notes." Mulholland's later friend and associate, Joseph B. Lippincott, once described G. F. Fanning's treatise on water supply engineering as the hydraulic engineer's bible. *Herald,* January 31, 1892.

10. *Times,* July 16, 18, 1890. The gold watch remains in the Mulholland family.

11. Crystal Springs could supply daily 15,000,000 gallons of clear pure water, the amount needed to fill Buena Vista Reservoir. Steam dredgers were brought in to dig trenches down to ten and fifteen feet until they reached a layer of gravel "in which innumerable springs have their source." Large pipes from 14 to 24 inches in diameter were then laid to receive the water percolating through the gravel. To prevent damage and washouts such as had been previously experienced, a tunnel three-quarters of a mile was dug into one of the western hills and pipe was run through it to connect ultimately with Buena Vista Reservoir. In addition, a wooden flume was constructed around the hill as a backup system in

the event that trouble arose in the tunnel. It was a major undertaking, estimated at $200,000, but it would assure water without sediment or sand. *Evening Express,* August 19, 1890.

12. Spalding, vol. 1, p. 266. "Ivanhoe was situated on the Los Feliz Rancho, comprising the eatern portion of the Lick Tract; it was recorded June 2, 1887, and consisted of 700 acres divided into 1,300 lots, ranging in size from one-hundred-foot frontages to five acres and in price from $150 to $750. A free carriage went to the tract daily" (Dumke, *The Boom of the Eighties,* p. 188).

13. McGroarty, vol. 3, pp. 482–85; Spalding, vol. 1, pp. 167, 198, 402; *Herald,* June 22, 1890. Inquiries to the Eaton family have been met with silence. In 1988 during the official celebration of the seventy-fifth anniversary of the completion of the Owens River Aqueduct, descendants of both Eaton and Mulholland attended, but the *Los Angeles Times* (November 18, 1988) reported only the words of an Eaton, who in response to a question about her ancestor, replied, "They were all crooks."

14. *Herald,* June 7, 1890; *Evening Express,* July 23, 1890.

15. *Evening Express,* "Review of the City," December 31, 1889.

16. *Illustrated History of Los Angeles County,* pp. 462–63.

17. After designers had completed a new dado in the entry halls of the Perry residence, the following description appeared in the *Times,* March 5, 1892: "In the old Empire style, the walls had been finished in marron flake, highlighted in gold, copper and green bronze. The newel in the lower hall was carved in the shape of a Moor holding in his hand a three-light candelabra, which Mr. Perry had imported from Italy at a cost of $380. The 'aerial blue' ceilings of the upper halls were graced with painted cupids."

CHAPTER 6: WATER PLOTS AND POLITICS, 1893–1895

1. *Times,* October 5, 1898; Mulholland, *First Annual Report,* Board of Water Commissioners, 1902, p.13. Material for this chapter chiefly derives from newspaper reports, which often gave fuller accounts than city council records. For more generalized accounts (although not always accurate in details), see Fogelson, pp. 94–96; Ostrom, pp. 44–46; Kahrl, pp. 12–13.

2. *Times,* July 30, October 12, December 16, 1886. Ostrom (p. 45) and Kahrl (p. 11) both describe this work as surreptitious, yet reports of its progress appeared in the daily press.

3. Layne, pp. 53–46; Ostrom, p. 96.

4. *Herald,* April 11, 1890; *Times,* August 22, 26, 28; September 6, 8, 1890; *Evening Express,* December 29, 30, 1891.

5. *Herald,* February 2, 16, 17, 21, 25, 26, 1892; *Times,* February 2, 1892.

6. *Herald,* January 11, 1892; *Times,* January 1, 11, 13, 1892.

7. *Herald, Times,* February 21, 22, 1892.

8. *Times,* January 1, 1892; April 21, 1892; *Herald,* April 21, 1892. The *Herald* was partially subsidized by the water company, although its editor, W. A. Spalding, who was in favor of public ownership, wrote that no one ever interfered with his editorial stands. "Had the *Herald* . . . , known to be the property

of the water magnates, urged some settlement unfair to the city . . . , it would have raised such a storm as to more than negative [sic] all our efforts, and would have been fatal to the paper besides" (Hine, *Spalding,* pp. 141–142).

9. *Times,* June 22, 1893.

10. *Times,* September 30, October 10, November 14, 1893.

11. *Times,* November 14, 21, 1893.

12. Layne, p. 67; Ostrom, p. 34.

13. *Times,* May 27, 1893; *The Porcupine,* October 29, 1892. A small notice appeared in the latter over the name "Wm. Mulholland" for proposals from pump manufacturers for "one four-million gallon high duty pumping engine." The engine was "to pump water for domestic use to the hill portions of the city of Los Angeles."

14. *Times,* May 30, 1893.

15. See Ostrom, chapter 6. As a result of the court decision, Garvanza and Highland Park voted to annex to the City of Los Angeles, while Vernon rejected annexation. According to Ostrom, "this wave of annexation added 14.05 square miles to the area of the city giving it a total area of 43.26 square miles at the turn of the century"(p. 146).

16. Spalding, vol. 1, p. 315; Mulholland, *Owensmouth Baby,* pp. 19, 67; *Who's Who in the Pacific Southwest,* p. 295.

17. *Times,* June 9, 1893. The newspaper printed the opinion verbatim.

18. *Times,* September 15, 1896.

19. *Times,* September 15, 17; November 10, 1896; Ostrom, p. 147.

20. *Times,* November 3, 1894.

21. Brooks, "Notes"; *Times,* November 8, 1894.

22. *Times,* August 18, 1895; Mulholland, "Municipal Ownership of Public Utilities," speech to Sunset Club, 1905. The photographs of *El Almuerzo* always hung in Mulholland's home, and his children often mentioned the occasion as memorable to their father.

23. Mulholland, "Municipal Ownership of Public Utilities," op. cit.; *Times,* February 18, 1896; June 2, 1898.

24. Mulholland, "Municipal Ownership of Public Utilities," op. cit.

25. Steffens, *Autobiography,* pp. 572–574; Sitton, *Haynes,* pp. 79–80.

CHAPTER 7: THE YEARS OF MAYOR EATON, 1898–1900

1. *Times,* January 1, 1898; Layne, p. 65; Spalding, vol. 1, pp. 319–320; Spriggs, pp. 50–52. Mulholland's children remembered their father's discussions of the conflict he underwent during those years. For an analysis of the political climate of 1890s Los Angeles and the rise of Progressivism, see Fogelson, pp. 210–12.

2. Spriggs, p. 53; *Times,* March 1, 17, 1898; Hine, *Spalding,* p. 145. W. A. Spalding, editor of the respected *Herald,* then owned by certain members of the water company, wrote of the trial, "I got through the ordeal without taking partizan ground for the water company, and there was no complaint or remonstrance from our backers."

3. Hine, op. cit., p. 133; Gottlieb and Wolt, *Thinking Big,* p. 123. On June 5,

1894, Chandler, a widower and then circulation manager of the *Times*, had married Otis's second daughter, Marion Otis. She was, according to Spalding, a much respected member of her father's business staff.

4. *Times*, May 24, June 1, 1898; Layne, p. 66; Spriggs, pp. 54–56.

5. *Times*, June 22, 25, 1898.

6. *Times*, September 29, 1898.

7. *Times*, November 26, 27, 1898.

8. Lippincott, pp. 161–62; *Times*, November 23, 24, 26, 27; December 1, 8, 1898.

9. O'Melveny, Journals, December 25, 1898.

10. Election returns suggest the tenuous nature of Eaton's victory, which the *Times* had whooped up as a great triumph for the Republicans ("Democratic City Ticket Goes Down Like a Spanish Fleet in a Fight"). Eaton's plurality over Snyder was only 580 votes (8,273 to 7,693), while Socialist candidate Henning Hansen received 510 votes. In the next mayoral election, Snyder overwhelmed his Republican opponent, Herman Silver, with a plurality of 3,131 votes. *Times*, December 6, 1898; *Herald*, December 6, 1900.

11. L. M. Powers, M.D., born 1853 in North Carolina, came to Los Angeles in 1887 and entered private practice. He received his M.D. at Washington University and trained at Bellevue and College of Physicians and Surgeons in New York (1877–1885). In Los Angeles, he introduced new systems of quarantining persons with certain contagious diseases and improved sanitation in waste disposal, slaughterhouse practices, and water usage. He also introduced the new diphtheria antitoxin and inaugurated milk testing and meat inspection. In the Municipal Reform organization of 1900 he was also a member of the Committee of One Hundred (*Who's Who In the Pacific Southwest*, p. 302; *Times*, November 8, 1890).

12. *Times*, January 5, 18, 1899.

13. Layne, p. 66; Mulholland, address to Sunset Club, 1904.

14. *Times*, April 3, June 1, 1899.

15. *Times*, May 6, 1899.

16. *Times*, July 3, 18, 20, 1899.

17. O'Melveny, July 22, 1899; *Times*, August 4, 5, 6, 10, 26, 1899. Was the threat of a disruption in water supply during the neediest time of the year and only two weeks before a bond election to fund a municipally owned system an accident or a contrived coincidence? No one raised a public doubt at the time, but similar suggestions of collusion by later weavers of conspiracy theories would become a stock element in future accusations that the city's water men created artificial water famines to frighten citizens into voting for proposed waterworks.

18. *Times*, August 5, 1899.

19. *Times*, August 5, 6, 7, 1899.

20. Layne, p. 57; *Times*, August 22, 29, 1899.

21. *Times*, November 16, 1899; December 16, 1900.

22. *Times*, January 24, 27, 1900; Stimson, *Rise of Labor Movement in Los Angeles*, p. 203.

23. *Times*, February 20, 21, 1900.

24. *Times*, February 7, 1900.

25. *Times,* March 23, 1900.

26. *Herald,* May 23, 29, 1900; *Times,* April 17, May 26, June 15, 1900.

27. The United States had recently appropriated $25,000 for such a study. Further indication of how the dry years and increased population had heightened interest in water projects was a recently completed report by Professor Frank Soulé, University of California, Berkeley, regarding water rights and litigations along the San Joaquin River. At the end of July, Soulé planned to conduct further studies north of Fresno. *Times,* July 10, 1900.

28. *Times,* September 29; November 25, 1900.

29. *Times,* November 23, 29, 1900.

30. *Times,* December 4, 1900; January 6, 1901. Eaton may have been scheming to lay the ground for his plan of an Owens River project, as Kahrl suggests in *Water and Power* (p. 47), but certainly nothing of a concrete nature occurred during his mayoralty. Whatever his private designs, his dislike of the water company seems to have been powerful and personal, and there is no proof that his belief in municipal ownership of water was insincere.

31. *Times,* October 7, 1900; January 6, 7, 1901; September 18, 1993.

CHAPTER 8: THE CITY'S VICTORY OVER
THE "GRAND MONOPOLY," 1901–1902

1. *Times,* May 18, July 19, 1901. Two months later, a chief stockholder in the Mountain Water Company sought an injunction against the directors, charging that they had conspired to defraud him.

2. *Times,* May 20, 21, 1901.

3. *Times,* April 19, 1901.

4. Spriggs, p. 58; Mulholland, Office Files, WP04–22:13. Speech prepared for the Board of Trade, City of Pasadena, April 6, 1904; "Municipal Ownership of Public Utilities," speech to the Sunset Club, April 1905.

5. *Times,* August 2, 1901.

6. *Times,* August 11, 15, 1901.

7. *Times,* August 23, 25, 27, 1901; Workman, pp. 297, 462–63. The senior Waldron owned thirty-five acres on the southwest corner of Main and Washington Streets that he had developed into a popular pleasure resort, Washington (later, Chutes) Park. By using zanja water, he kept his water bill low. Other opposition leaders were John R. Newberry, successful merchant whose Newberry variety stores were widespread in Southern California (Newmark, p. 551); Joseph Mesmer, businessman and philanthropist, whose father had come to Los Angeles in 1858 (Newmark, p. 644); Sherman Page, attorney, whose family had come to Los Angeles when he was seven. He apprenticed under C. C. Wright, expert on water law who created the Wright Irrigation Act, and was also the son-in-law of Judge R. H. F. Variel (*Who's Who in the Pacific Southwest,* p. 283).

8. *Times,* August 27, 28, 29, 1901.

9. *Times,* August 29, 30, 1901.

10. *Times,* October 22, 1901. Elliott provided the public a lengthy and rational explanation of bond market conditions in the East.

11. Workman, p. 297.

12. *Times,* February 5, 26, 1902. Workman, who had forgone a planned visit to his birthplace in Booneville, Missouri, in order to return to Los Angeles to celebrate, later received a bill from the city council for $1,100 for his expenses during his two-month stay in New York and Washington. Accused of extravagance, Workman defended his expenditures by explaining that on the advice of eastern attorneys, he had been forced to move about lest the defaulting company attempt to serve papers on him that could involve the water bonds in litigation. Such moving had proved expensive, as had his time in Washington, D.C., where he had lobbied members of Congress for appropriations for the harbor and a new post office. "Why, sir, my God! I had to keep up the reputation of the town," expostulated Uncle Billy." I couldn't go around with those men and be entertained and not reciprocate." Upon the advice of attorney Mathews, who had feared such criticism, he had unhappily stayed at "a second-rate hotel" (the Hoffman House instead of the Waldorf-Astoria), and moveover, had spent $400 of his own money on cigars, treats, and the like, so as not to appear cheap before those with whom he was dealing (*Times,* May 10, 1902).

13. Layne, *Water and Power for a Great City,* pp. 69–70. The day before this event, Mayor Snyder had presented an ordinance to the council, which it then voted to accept. Layne's account derives from an interview with L. M. Anderson, who was present that day and who, shortly after, became auditor of the new water department, a position he held his entire working life.

The new civil service requirement was waived because of the men's known qualifications. Anderson's list of the thirty-one men then employed with the old water company on a monthly salary in 1902 named William Mulholland, A. W. Ryan, Niles Knickerbocker, L. M. Anderson, Edward Leake, T. G. Haines, George H. Kimball, C. L. Brimhall, H. H. Gibbs, George T. Gilmore, J. W. Bullas, Charles E. Brown, John Horner, F. W. Parker, W. S. Reavis, Charles W. Clark, F. R. Cady, J. W. Gillette, J. O. Bradbury, W. H. Carter, John Herlihy, W. M. Hughes, E. Ihm, A. P. Stevenson, J. A. Osgood, J. P. Vroman, F. W. Cook, Thomas Brooks, F. J. Fischer, and George Read.

14. *Times,* March 18, 1902. Ostrom, p. 69; Annual Report, Board of Water Commissioners, 1902, p. 5. Members of the first water commission were Herman Silver, president; Henry T. Lee; James M. Elliott; Charles H. Toll; F. W. King; L. A. Grant; and J. C. Drake.

15. *Times,* February 7, 1902.

16. Mulholland, Speech to Sunset Club, 1905; *Times,* February 14, 1902; Brooks, "Notes on Los Angeles Water Supply."

Also on the agenda were completion of work at the Angeleno Heights Reservoir, construction of several new water lines along Alameda Street and Central Avenue as far south as Ninth Street, and the purchase of 1,000 tons of four- and six-inch pipe for replacements and extensions. As the new policy required that no water main of a diameter less than four inches was to be laid, many old two-inch mains were about to be replaced. As Mulholland noted, with 337 miles of water pipe in the city streets, the system was "a marvel of attenuation alongside of which Barnum's living skeleton would be considered the very embodiment of unwieldy corpulence" (Annual Report of Water Commissioners, 1902, p. 30).

17. *Times,* February 16, 1902.

18. *Times,* April 25, 1902; McGroarty, *History of Los Angeles County,* vol. 3, p. 483.

19. O'Melveny, Journals, April 5, 1902. The Sunset Club was organized in 1895.

20. *Times,* May 18, 1902; Annual Report of Water Commissioners, 1902, pp. 6–9. Brooks, "Notes." Tom Brooks had installed the first meter in Los Angeles's domestic water system on August 16, 1889, at Charles Stern's Winery on Macy Street west of Mission Road. It was a two-inch Worthington piston type. Other meters were later installed at various business and manufacturing organizations. Slightly over 1 percent of water-users were metered in Los Angeles in 1902.

21. *Times,* May 13, 14, 1902; Robinson, *Lawyers of Los Angeles,* p. 315. For analyses of the Wright Act and its mixed consequences, see Cooper, *Aqueduct Empire,* pp. 94–97; Hundley, *The Great Thirst,* pp. 98–100; Reisner, *Cadillac Desert,* pp. 113–14; Starr, *Material Dreams,* p. 14.

22. *Los Angeles Times,* June 17, August 18, 1903. Mulholland could also be brutal with the humorless and self-important. His daughter, Rose, remembered her mingled embarrassment and amusement when shopping once with her father at Barker Brothers (a leading furniture store). An officious young salesman insisted that a library table they were examining was solid mahogany. Mulholland, who prided himself on his knowledge of woods, said it was veneer. When contradicted, Mulholland took out his penknife and scratched a side to reveal the veneer, saying as he did so, "I knew about woods before your head was the size of a cranberry."

23. *Los Angeles Times,* May 18, 1902.

24. *Times,* June 3, 1902. When W. T. Spilman became a leading propagandist for the antiaqueduct forces, he charged that the people of the city had been hornswoggled by Mulholland's lies about daily water consumption and that "it is difficult for the average mind to understand how meters could make any material saving when the people were already restricted as to the amount of water they used." Out of this spurious argument, he evolved the conclusion that the water department was secretly disposing of the water in order to create a water shortage for "a designing purpose" (Spilman, *The Conspiracy,* pp. 20–21).

25. *Times,* May 18, 1902.

26. Mulholland, Office Files, WP04–22:5, Mulholland to Willard, August 30, 1902. *Times,* May 18; September 6, 18; October 21; November 30, 1902. Mulholland's semiannual summary of local water conditions in May 1902: present water available, 25,000,000 gallons daily; present water consumption, 23,000,000; probable supply from present sources in July, 23,500,000; highest demand in 1901, 24,100,000; probable highest demand in 1902, based on increase in population, 26,765,000; shortage to be supplied, 3,264,000. Of this shortage, 2,000,000 was expected to be filled from the new work and the balance from the main supply ditch. The estimated per capita daily consumption: 267 gallons.

CHAPTER 9: NEW REGIME FOR A BOOMING TOWN, 1903–1904

1. *Times,* February 3, 4, 6, 1903; Layne, p. 69; Ostrom, pp. 52–53; Workman, p. 298. In September 1995, Robert V. Phillips, a former general manager of the Department of Water and Power, commented to me, "Although technically the DWP is still an independent department the fact is that over the years the council has increasingly destroyed its independence until now it is almost completely politicized. The people who first established the DWP as an independent agency, free of political misuse (and they tried desperately to accomplish this) were absolutely right in their intent."

2. *Times,* February 4, 6, 1903; Layne, p. 74; McGroarty, vol. 2, p. 159; *Who's Who in the Pacific Southwest,* p. 252.

3. *Times,* February 3, 11; March 8, 1903. Willard was among those committed to cleansing government of corruption and corporate control. He believed that democracy should be a positive moral force and challenged Theodore Roosevelt's characterization of democracy as merely a means to an end. "It is a soul-satisfying thing," he wrote the president (Mowry, *The California Progressives,* p. 99).

4. *Times,* March 17, 1903.

5. Annual Report of the Board of Water Commissioners, 1902, p. 28; *Times,* January 20; April 14, 1903.

6. *Times,* June 28, 1903. One fan letter to Mulholland came from East Los Angeles from one William Holgate, proprietor of a furniture store on Downey Avenue. Along with other Eastside neighbors, Downey wrote their thanks "for your success in giting [*sic*] us water so that we do not have to stay up nights this summer to get even a drink of water." He added, "You have done what *you promised you would do—years ago* if they would only give you a show . . . LA has got the Right man in the Right place" (Mulholland, Office Files, WP04–21:22, May 4, 1903).

7. Mulholland, Office Files, WP04–22:15.

8. *Times,* July 18, 1903; Mulholland, Office Files, WP04–21:7, Mulholland to City Council, July 29, 1903.

9. *Los Angeles Times,* September 18, 1903.

10. McGroarty, *History of Los Angeles County,* p. 483. The first annual report of the aqueduct by the chief engineer in 1907 gives the date as 1893.

An intriguing item in Mulholland Office Files is a letter dated July 15, 1903, from Mulholland to J. D. Fredericks, district attorney of Los Angeles County. Responding to Frederick's request for road conditions from Mojave to Bishop, Mulholland supplies careful details of mileage and conditions. For example, "Haiwee Meadows to Olancha, 9 miles, road is slow and for 3 miles midway between the two points is exceedingly heavy. This part of the trip will fully test the power of any machine of less gauge than 59 inches (standard gauge of auto is 55" to 56")." The letter gives no indication of why Fredericks desired this information, and as Mulholland supposedly had never been to Owens Valley, experienced travelers to the area such as Eaton or Lippincott would have been the logical choices to consult (Mulholland, Office Files, WP04–21:19).

11. *Times,* September 20, 1903.

12. *Times,* October 2, 1903.

13. *Times,* July 26; August 24, 1903.

14. *Times,* December 1, 1903.

15. *Times,* December 1, 1903; *Herald,* December 15, 1903.

16. *Herald,* December 15, 1903.

17. Writers who either espouse or lend credence to the "San Fernando Valley land grab" story include Bonelli, Caughey, Gottlieb and Wolt, Kahrl, McWilliams, and Walton.

18. *Herald,* December 13, 1903; April 3, 1904. Mulholland, *Owensmouth Baby,* pp. 7–8. Hendricks, *M. H. Sherman,* provides a good account of Sherman's early life.

19. Spalding, *History,* vol. 1, p. 303.

20. This case (44 Cal. 16) was cited as an authority in another water suit in 1895, *Santa Ana Water Company v. the Town of San Buenaventura* (56 Fed. Rep. 339), an action involving the rights of an incorporated town to establish water rates. Judge Ross of the United States Circuit Court had found that a trustee for the city was also treasurer of the water company. He quoted from the prior case in which Sherman's role had been questioned: "We do not doubt that a majority of the trustees might execute the power, but the question is, whether Sherman, who was a stockholder and director of the railroad company, could be one of that majority. When he entered upon the duties of trustee, his relations to the city became those of an agent to his principal, or of a trustee to his cestui que trust, and while holding the office he could do nothing inconsistent with those relations. This is clear upon principle, and rests upon abundant authority" (*Times,* January 15, 1895).

21. *Times,* May 10, 11, 1894. The story was first carried in the *San Francisco Examiner* and later picked up by the *Times.*

22. *Times,* December 14, 1895; January 25, 1899.

23. *Times,* April 25, 1903.

24. Stimson, *Rise of Labor,* pp. 205–15; *Times,* April 26, 1903.

25. *Times,* October 23, 1903; Hoffman, p. 126.

26. O'Melveny, Journals, December 25, 1903; *Herald,* December 15, 27, 30, 1903; *Times,* December 6, 29, 1903. City Attorney Mathews, who took a hard line against the transit companies, prevailed in bringing suit for their failure to perform their contracted duties. Among those cited was M. H. Sherman's partner, E. P. Clark, president of the Pacific Electric Line.

CHAPTER 10: DESPERATE REMEDIES IN A DRY SEASON, 1904

1. *Herald,* January 17, 27; February 3, 1904; *Times,* January 22, 24; February 27; March 11, 1904; National Weather Service, WeatherData, Inc. With great pains and dubious evidence, Kahrl accuses Mulholland of having created a mythical drought and cites what he calls "the perfectly average" rainfall of 11.88 inches in 1903–1904 to confirm that the dearth was fabricated as a scare tactic to stampede voters later to support the aqueduct bonds (Kahrl, pp. 83–86).

Contemporary accounts of arid conditions run counter to Kahrl's conspiracy charges, as do those of modern researchers. See Freeman, *People-Land-Water,* pp.

168–69. Engineer-hydrologist Robert V. Phillips has rebutted Kahrl by pointing out that the "mean annual rainfall in Los Angeles was 15 inches a year. . . . If it drops to a 'perfectly average' 11.88," he has written, "we are in deep trouble."

Using the hydrologic measurement of years from October 1 to September 30, Phillips establishes the following annual rainfall average from 1898 to 1904:

1898–1899—5.5"

1899–1900—7.5"

1900–1901—16.5"

1901–1902—11.0"

1902–1903—19.0"

1903–1904—8.0"

Average—11.25"

2. *Herald,* January 12, 17, 23, 27, 28; February 4, 1904; *Times,* January 14, 1904.

3. *Herald,* March 10, April 8, 1904; *Times,* March 10, 1904.

4. *Herald,* January 5, 1904.

5. *Herald,* June 5, 1904; *Times,* May 23; June 3, 14, 1904.

6. Layne, pp. 76–77; *Herald,* June 6, 1904; *Times,* June 12, 1904.

7. Layne, p. 77; Brooks, "Notes."

8. Mulholland, Office Files, WP04-22:2, Mulholland to Lee and Scott, July 25, 1904; *Herald,* July 28, 1904.

9. Mulholland, Office Files, WP04-22:3; *Herald,* July 28; August 2, 1904; *Times,* August 4, 1904.

10. *Herald,* August 16, 1904.

11. *Times,* August 16, 1904.

12. *Herald,* September 17, 18, 1904; Nadeau, pp. 22–23; Sitton, p. 49.

13. Hoffman, p. 60; Kahrl, p. 49; McGroarty, vol. 2, pp. 483–84; Nadeau, pp. 21–24. The Progressive editor (and strong temperance man), E. T. Earl, testified in 1912 before the Aqueduct Investigation Board (p. 46 of their report) that aqueduct workers joked about the trail of liquor bottles they followed to mark their way. Mulholland always told his children that he and Fred made the trip with "a mule team, a buckboard, and a demijohn of whiskey." In view of the ultimate productive outcome of the trip, the idea of two sots on a spree is improbable, but the story has been happily retold by many antagonists who seem unaware that beans and whiskey had been stock trail fare since the days of the forty-niners.

14. McGroarty, vol. 2, pp. 483–84; Nadeau, p. 23.

15. McGroarty, vol. 2, pp. 483–84; *Herald,* October 4, 1904.

16. Hoffman, pp. 19–24, gives a good summary of Lippincott's first years in the Southwest. *Who's Who in the Pacific Southwest,* pp. 228–29.

17. Hoffman, pp. 51–59. Hoffman gives the best and clearest account of Lippincott's tangled relations with the federal government and the City of Los Angeles. Kahrl's is detailed but less lucid. Both consulted primary documents from Bureau of Reclamation files, and I am indebted to their research.

18. McGroarty, vol. 2, pp. 483–84. U.S. Congress, Senate Report 928, Part 3, Vol. 2. The use of the Owens River to irrigate the Antelope Valley had been proposed to the Senate Committee hearing on Arid Lands by M. A. Knapp.

19. Freeman, *People-Land-Water*, p. 42; Smythe, *The Conquest of the Arid West*, p. 297. Arthur P. Davis was the nephew of John Wesley Powell, leader of the National Geological Survey, surveyor of the Colorado River, and powerful critic of national land policies.

20. Hoffman, pp. 50–51.

21. *Times*, November 7, 1897.

22. *Times*, August 18, 1899.

23. *Times*, November 22, 25; December 24, 1899.

24. Hoffman, p. 51.

25. *Herald*, April 3; May 18, 1904; Kahrl, p. 48; O'Melveny, Journals, March 7, 22, 1904. Eaton may have been telling the truth, because he maintained a busy schedule in Los Angeles in the spring of 1904. In March Henry O'Melveny retained him as a referee in setting land valuations in *City of Los Angeles v. Rowland and Van Nuys,* and in April, he served with Charles D. Willard on a special committee with the board of supervisors for harbor improvements at San Pedro. None of this precludes his presence in Owens Valley, but neither does any hard evidence prove it.

26. Hoffman, op. cit., pp. 56–58; Kahrl, op. cit., pp. 47–48. Kahrl ascribes the most cynical motives to Eaton based mostly on a letter from Arthur Davis in 1905. I would want more evidence than that before indicting the man.

27. *Herald*, April 20, July 27, 1904.

28. Hoffman, pp. 58–59.

29. Hoffman, p. 60; *First Annual Report of the Los Angeles Aqueduct*, p. 18; Layne, p. 99.

30. *First Annual Report*, p. 18; Mulholland, Office Files, WP04-24, "Water Supply of Southern California," speech to the Sunset Club, Dec. 1904. Mulholland joined the Sunset Club in 1904, served as its president in 1919, and remained a member for the rest of his life, saying that it had been for him "a sanctum of peaceful communion," as he likened it to the biblical "Shadow of a Great Rock in a Weary Land." The Sunset Club, patterned after the original in Chicago, was founded in 1895 by Charles D. Willard, W. C. Patterson, Charles F. Lummis, Burt Estes Howard, and Fred L. Alles. Meetings were held on the last Friday of each month at sunset in a popular restaurant for two hours of dining and conversation; then, at eight, after the topic for discussion was announced, a principal paper was read, followed by two shorter ones and a discussion. Its members played an important role in the intellectual and political life of the city at the turn of the century.

CHAPTER 11: A PLAN REVEALED, 1905

1. *Examiner*, December 4, 16, 17, 1904. A few days after these articles appeared, the Los Angeles Chamber of Commerce met on December 21 and named a committee of Mulholland, Lippincott, and H. Hawgood to take up the question of a water supply for Los Angeles "outside of the present one." Mulholland

responded December 28 with a preliminary report with statistics indicating that current consumption, if unabated, would continue to exceed the city's supply. Of this report, Mulholland wrote shortly afterward to Lippincott, who was in Washington, D.C., "I wrote the document myself and as you will notice from its tenor it is somewhat of a standoff as I did not altogether approve of taking up the investigation in your absence, especially with Hawgood, as I understand from outside sources he is back of a project to promote the sale of some alleged rights to the Mojave River to the City of Los Angeles" (Mulholland, Office Files, WP04–21:16 and 22:4). For a good discussion of this period, see Hoffman, pp. 79–86.

2. Mulholland, Office Files, WP04–21:6, January, March–June, 1905.

3. *Herald,* April 23, August 30, 1905.

4. *Imperial Valley News,* February 10, 1905. A syndicate of capitalists headed by H. G. Otis, Harry Chandler, and O. F. Brant of the Title Insurance and Trust Company had acquired the Colorado River Land Company, consisting of about 800,000 acres in the Mexicali Valley and, on the American side, another 1,000 acres in the Imperial Valley. The enormous holding along part of the Colorado Delta aroused the suspicions and enmities of locals, who also suspected that the Reclamation Service, with its Yuma project under way, might be in cahoots with the syndicate. The editorial that questioned Lippincott's allegiances concluded with a rallying cry of "Let's defeat Otis!" For a full account, see Stowe, "Pioneering Land Development," *California Historical Society Quarterly* 47, No. 1 (1968), pp. 16–39. Also, Gottlieb and Wolt, *Thinking Big,* pp. 165–68.

5. Mulholland, Office Files, WP04–22:4, Lippincott to Mulholland, February 20, 1905. The conflict of interest problem was brewing in January 1905, when Lippincott's chief at Reclamation in Washington, D.C., Arthur P. Davis, denied Mulholland's request to allow Lippincott and government geologist W. C. Mendenhall to appear as witnesses for Los Angeles in a case attempting to establish water rights in the San Fernando Valley. Davis later gave provisional consent because of the men's previous studies of the Los Angeles River and "because we wish to be of service to the City of Los Angeles" (Mulholland, Office Files, WP04–21:17, Davis to Mulholland, January 25, 1905).

6. *Herald,* March 10–15, 1905.

7. *Herald,* March 16, 17, 1905.

8. *Herald,* May 3, July 22, 1905; *Times,* May 3, 1905. During this period Mulholland was also enduring with his family the anguish of losing their youngest child to spinal meningitis. Born in 1903, Richard James Mulholland died on May 15, 1905. Weeks later, Mulholland wrote his friend J. Henry Dockweiler, former Los Angeles engineer-attorney but now a consulting engineer and city attorney in San Francisco, to explain why he would not be able to testify in the valuation hearings of the Spring Valley Water Company. "I confess I am still as much in the dark as ever as things are developing very rapidly here on the scheme for increased water supply for the City of Los Angeles and my presence in consequence is required about constantly. I have had to give up the idea of a Portland trip I had promised to take with my wife who is much worn out since the death of our little boy about six or seven weeks ago" (Mulholland, Office Files, WP04–21:17, Mulholland to Dockweiler, June 26, 1905).

9. *Herald,* July 22, 1905. In "The Straight of the Owens River Deal," Mulholland wrote, "All through the period with which our investigations proceeded, the Commission was beseiged by schemers with all kinds of propositions to furnish water to the city, until one would think that the whole country was crisscrossed with roaring torrents of water. It is from these parties, some of whom are simply deluded individuals while others are arrant schemers, that we expect our greatest opposition to the Owens River scheme" (*Graphic,* September 1905).

10. Mulholland, Office Files, WP04–22:4, Mulholland to Lippincott, August 15, 1905. Nadeau, pp.32–33; Kahrl, pp. 91 ff. Both Nadeau and Kahrl discuss the newspapers' rivalry without emphasizing the fierce circulation war or the chronically inflamed rhetoric then characteristic of the *Times,* when the mildest dissent from its opinions became a pretext for outrage. A careful reading of the six dailies in the six weeks after the Owens Valley announcement demonstrates that they all gave extensive and largely supportive coverage to the plan. Although the *Examiner* later wrote hard-hitting and hostile editorials, its news coverage remained comprehensive, and its editorial of July 31, 1905, had given enthusiastic support, pointing out its earlier "agitation for an adequate and unfailing supply of water for the needs of Los Angeles." For a good account of the *Examiner*'s entry into Los Angeles, see Stimson, *Rise of the Labor Movement in Los Angeles,* pp. 270–80. Begun as a pro-labor voice against the *Times*'s open shop policy, the *Examiner* failed to buck the power of the *Times*'s moneyed interests and by 1906 had begun to back off from its pro-labor stance.

The short-lived *Evening News* (October 2, 1905, to April 18, 1908) would have been only a transient curiosity in the history of Los Angeles journalism had it not been produced by the talented newspaperman Samuel "Alkali Sammy" Clover. All denials to the contrary, the paper was almost certainly bankrolled by special interests: local old-guard opponents and private electric power companies. An attractive small paper, it is chiefly remembered for having become an *omnium gatherum* of aqueduct opponents, ranging from Progressives such as John R. Haynes and Councilman Arthur D. Houghton to dissenting engineers, private water and electric interests, and certain pipe manufacturers.

11. *Examiner,* August 2, 3, and 6, 1905; *Times,* August 1–6, 1905; *Herald,* August 1–6, 1905.

12. Mulholland, Office Files, WP04–22:4, Mulholland to Lippincott, August 11 and 15, 1905.

13. Stimson, pp. 284–85; *Herald,* September 1, November 29, 1904; *Times,* October 30, 1904; August 10, 1905.

14. *Herald,* August 15, 1905. Two days earlier, when Mulholland learned that Dr. Houghton intended to visit Owens Valley with culture tubes to test the purity of the water, he had scoffed, "It is all nonsense in my opinion. At this time of the year cattle will be found wading in the water. The water has been analyzed and found to be purer in some respects than our present city water" (*Examiner,* August 13, 1905).

15. *Examiner,* August 15, 1905.

16. Mulholland, Office Files, WP04–22:4, August 15, 1905. Frederick Cecil Finkle came to Los Angeles from his native Wisconsin in 1887 and was associated with irrigation and water developments in San Bernardino and Riverside

Counties. In 1897, he became the chief hydraulic engineer for Southern California Edison Company and from 1906 was a consultant for a number of western hydroelectric companies. He had extensive commercial landholdings in Southern California and, according to *Who's Who in the Pacific Southwest* (1913), claimed interest in "reforms which will benefit the working classes." Finkle remained a bugbear in Mulholland's life and was unceasing in his disparagement of Mulholland's engineering abilities.

17. *Examiner,* August 15, 1905.

18. *Examiner,* August 16, 1905. Major Henry T. Lee, attorney and special counsel in water litigation for Los Angeles (1895–1907), was chairman of the evening and described Mulholland as "Bill Mulholland, water superintendent, true as steel, straight as a string, and saturated with knowledge of the needs of the city" (*Times,* August 16, 1905).

19. Elliott did not mention that the group, as reported in the *Times,* had posed as a party interested in inspecting Mount Whitney with a view to developing a summer resort area. (Other versions claimed that they represented themselves as cattlemen to avoid local suspicions.) Nor did he reveal that the journey's rigors had almost undone him, for he fell ill before they reached Independence and had to be taken out of the valley by J. J. Fay, president of the water commission, on the little narrow-gauge Reno and Carson Railway into Nevada and thence into San Francisco, where he spent the next three weeks in the hospital (*Times,* July 29, August 16, 1905).

20. *Times,* August 23, 1905.

21. My father, Perry Mulholland, used to cite to me as a parallel case Franklin Roosevelt's decision in 1940—when America was officially neutral—to aid England in its fight against Germany by slipping old World War I destroyers to the British Navy. To do so, he had to circumvent a suspicious Congress by an exchange of boats for leases of naval bases on British territory. Because the bases could be regarded as strengthening America's defense, Roosevelt, as commander in chief, could act without Congress. When the transfer became public, isolationists claimed the deed bordered on treason, but the public at large was sufficiently pro-British and anti-Nazi to find the matter of minor import. In like manner, the Los Angeles waterseekers' activities would have been viewed more critically had there not been powerful public sentiment favoring their goals.

22. *Times,* July 29, 1905; *Herald,* August 1, 1905. The "trickster" observation is by magician James Randi ("Secrets of the Psychic," *Nova,* PBS,1993).

23. *Examiner,* July 30, 1905; *Times,* August 3, 5, 1905; Mulholland, Office Files, WP04-2:11, August 3, 1905.

24. Mulholland, Office Files, WP04–22:4, Mulholland to Lippincott, August 15, 1905.

25. *Examiner,* August 3, 1905.

26. *Times,* September 8, 1905; *Herald,* September 2, 9, 1905. The *Times* boasted that this lopsided vote was the greatest majority ever given at a bond election in Los Angeles. Kahrl discredits the returns as a scanty vote reflecting voter indifference and cites returns double that size in a previous municipal election in 1904 and one on an antisaloon proposal in 1905 (p. 103). What he omits are comparisons to analogous water bond elections. The returns on the acquisi-

tion of the West Side Water Company in April 1904 had yielded a total of only 1,121 votes, while even the crucial and long-debated decision to acquire the private water company in 1901 produced a mere 7,551 votes. Voter turnout was historically light for water and sewer bonds, perhaps because, as it was said in 1901, when it came to those issues, there was "no dough out there to hustle the vote." When voters made the big decision to approve the $23 million bond issue to build the aqueduct the following year, however, more than 24,000 cast votes, a ratio of over ten to one in favor of the aqueduct. The accusation by historians such as Carey McWilliams (*Southern California Country,* p. 189) and John Caughey (*California,* p. 369) that capitalistic interests bilked the voters into bankrolling a water project for the former's interest is not only a slur on voter intelligence but also a failure to concede the average consumer's realistic desire for good and abundant water.

CHAPTER 12: PREPARATIONS FOR AN AQUEDUCT AND A TRIP TO WASHINGTON, D.C., 1906

1. *San Francisco Chronicle,* September 13, 1905; Hoffman, p. 123; Kahrl, pp. 134–35.

2. Mulholland, Office Files, WP04–21:16, 17, January 6, 1905; January 13, 15, 1906. *Times,* December 27, 1905. See also note 8, chapter 11.

3. Mulholland, Office Files, WP04–22:4, Jan. 9, 1906; Hoffman, pp. 104–5.

4. *Times,* February 7, 1906. Houghton also objected to John J. Fay's reappointment to the water board. So obstreperous did he become during this period that by March he and Mayor McAleer almost came to blows after the mayor accused Houghton of graft in granting favors to the Santa Fe Railway. When Houghton in turn accused the mayor of having formed a company to make pipe for the Owens River conduit, McAleer lunged at him, shouting, "You have lied about me as no man ever dared lie before." Thinking better of it, however, he struck no blow (*Times,* March 16, 1906).

5. Mulholland, Office Files, WP04–22:6, Mulholland to Young, March 9, 1906.

6. *Times,* March 30, 1906. The following account derives from an unsigned article, most likely by Allen Kelly (see note 19). Of local sentiment in Owens Valley, the column opined, "The kickers don't like Eaton a little bit, but their animosity is mild compared to their hostility to Engineer Lippincott. They say something serious would happen to Lippincott if he should venture to visit Bishop, and they say it in a way that can be interpreted only as a threat of personal violence."

7. Mulholland, Office Files, WP04–23:6, Mulholland to Young, April 20, 1906.

8. Mulholland, Office Files, WP04–21:7, Mulholland to Brooks, April 20, 1906. A similar correspondence occurred between Mulholland and the editor of the Pasadena *Evening Star,* WP04–22:8, May 15, 1906.

9. Mulholland, Office Files, WP04–21:12, Mulholland to Duryea, March 30 to July 14, 1906. *First Annual Report,* p. 55.

10. According to Cannon's biographer, President Theodore Roosevelt's great-

est concern about California at the time was its Japanese population. After Japan's victory at Mukden in the Russo-Japanese War the year before, Roosevelt's fears of a Japanese threat resulted in increased expenditures for the defense of Pearl Harbor in what were then called the Sandwich Islands; a large appropriation for battleships and torpedo boats; and in 1907, the barring of Japanese immigrants into the United States (Busbey, *Uncle Joe Cannon,* pp. 224–228).

11. For a full discussion, see Hoffman, *Vision or Villainy?* pp. 128–35. *San Francisco Chronicle,* June 16, 22, 1906; *Times,* June 23, 1906. *Times* columnist Harry Carr castigated Hitchcock's behavior in the Owens River matter, but acknowledged that from Mulholland Hitchcock had received "some of the plainest, most dynamic English ever hurled at the head of a Cabinet officer" and that some of the California delegates had feared lest Mulholland's "vigorous talk" should alienate him. (Carr elsewhere claimed that Mulholland's tongue "could scrape barnacles off a ship bottom.") Eight months later, however, when Roosevelt requested Hitchcock's "retirement," Carr allowed that the secretary was an honest man even though "irascible, obstinate and domineering," and that he could be unbearably insulting to those with whom he did business (*Times,* July 29, 1906; March 10, 1907).

12. Mulholland, *First Annual Report of the Los Angeles Aqueduct,* pp. 26–27. Members of the committee chosen by the Los Angeles Chamber of Commerce were W. J. Washburn and J. O. Koepfli, of the chamber; Wm. Mulholland, department of water; and W. B. Mathews, city attorney. Also attending were Chas. D. Walcott, director of the Geological Survey; F. H. Newell, chief engineer of the Reclamation Service; Gifford Pinchot, chief forester; and Senator F. Flint.

13. *Times,* June 24, 27; October 12, 1906; Mulholland, Office Files, WP04–21:19, Mulholland to Eaton, July 14, 1906.

14. *Times,* July 30 and 31, 1906. Some writers (notably Kahrl) have portrayed George Chaffey as a wronged victim of grasping, water-greedy Los Angeles while maligning Eaton for his secret manipulations on behalf of the city. Yet the two men shared striking similarities. Both were pioneer developers of water systems in Southern California in the 1880s and '90s; both were land promoters and equally well connected in financial circles, as well as in rail and transportation. Each was a clever strategist, and to imagine that Chaffey's motives were higher than Eaton's is, at the least, ingenuous. Many private money interests were active in Owens Valley at this time, and Chaffey aimed not merely to create an idyllic community (Manzanar) but also to secure water rights for private electric companies (see Burdette, *American Biography,* vol. 1, pp. 74–81; Cooper, *Aqueduct Empire,* pp. 70–71; Robert Glass Cleland and Osgood Hardy, "The March of Industry," *California,* pp. 213, 353–54; Jackson Graves, *My Seventy Years in California,* pp. 247–48; Clipping Book, Department of Water and Power, vol. 3, 1906; Mulholland, Office Files, WP04–22, Mulholland to Lippincott, June 29, 1909).

15. Copies of the chamber's proclamation were given to Senator Frank Flint, Representative James MacLachlan, William Mulholland, William B. Mathews, and chamber members W. J. Washburn and J. O. Koepfli. Among various other expressions of gratitude, the document states, "You indignantly rejected all the invidious conditions and trammels which if accepted would have prevented the

City from using its own waters as it may see fit in every lawful ways [*sic*] for the benefit of this municipality and surrounding territory." It continued, "You accomplished these great things for us during the last days of the session of Congress in the face of most determined opposition both from private and official sources, which to men of a lesser loyalty and pluck would have seemed and would have been insurmountable." Mulholland's copy of this tribute, executed in graceful calligraphy, hung in his home for the rest of his life. Mulholland, Office Files, WP04-22:17, Schuyler to Mulholland, August 31, 1906. James D. Schuyler's engineering skills were further vindicated in 1908, when an English syndicate appointed him to a commission to report on the construction of a plant that would power street railways in Tokyo and Yokohama as well as supply current for electric lighting and various industrial enterprises in Japan. The first installation would cost $5 million and would be the greatest of its kind ever attempted in Japan (*Times*, March 13, 1908).

16. *Fifth Annual Report of the Board of Water Commissioners*, p.7.

17. *San Francisco Chronicle*, August 29, 1906.

18. *Examiner*, October 29, 1906.

19. Details here derive from a long account by Allen Kelly, *Times*, December 2, 1902. Kelly's accounts of these early trips to Owens Valley are sharply observed. On this trip, he noted a "remarkable change in the attitude of Bishop towards the city's project . . . none of the wild talk I heard a year ago." He also attacked speculators buying up property, claiming they followed Eaton around to discover his movements and then rushed in with options to buy. He singled out A. H. Koebig, water system engineer and entrepreneur with ties to power corporations. "He wants nothing until the city needs it. And behind Koebig, the jackal engineer, is a power company using the money it makes out of Los Angeles to prevent the city from obtaining Owens Valley water. . . ." He also named Frederick Finkle and the Edison Company. Doubtless, Kelly reflected the opinions of Mulholland and Lippincott, but at the same time, the *Record*, a prolabor Scripps' newspaper with little sympathy for either the *Times* or the *Examiner*, also editorialized against men such as Chaffey and Koebig, calling them moneygrubbers with no civic pride (*Record*, December 13, 1906).

Writers who dismiss Kelly as no more than an apologist for the *Times* and the aqueduct forces seem unaware of his earlier journalistic career. A veteran reporter who had observed and written of New York politics under Boss Tweed, he had a reputation for being a social reformer with a knack for sizing up people. Ten years earlier, while with the *San Francisco Examiner*, he was described as "a small, slight, dark, nervous-looking chap who affects good clothes and large canes" and whose only mark of unconventionality was a black slouch hat. A crack shot who was known as "the man who is looking for something to be afraid of," he was sent by the *Examiner* in 1889 to capture a grizzly bear and write about it. He went missing in the wilds for five months, and just as the newspaper was about to give up on him, he returned with a bear (Arthur McEwen, "Allen Kelly, the Journalist and Grizzly Catcher," *Los Angeles Evening Express*, July 19, 1890).

20. *Evening News*, November 27, 1906. The *News* suggested that Mulholland had demonstrated his incompetence by indicating a route later altered by

experts, but others, including reporter Kelly, argued that the route was deliberately fudged to some degree to keep speculators from buying.

21. Mulholland's use of an oil lining on Ivanhoe Reservoir prompted a query about its success from the distinguished professor of irrigation at the University of California, Berkeley, B. A. Etcheverry. Mulholland replied that it had proved out except for a southern embankment "on which the work was but very poorly and hastily done." Strong north winds had raised waves high enough to spray over the bank, and after twenty-four hours unabated, cut holes in the slopes. Still, Mulholland maintained that with proper application the method would prove "a complete success" (Mulholland, Office Files, WP04–21:19, Mulholland to Etcheverry, December 11, 20, 1906). The Ivanhoe, completed in 1906, was subsequently plagued with algae and "larva and mulluscan growths," so that in 1907, both it and Bellevue Reservoir had to be roofed with timber supported by reinforced concrete girders and posts. The wooden posts erected in 1896 to support the Bellevue's previous roof had rotted and collapsed. Mulholland, ever alert to possible charges of extravagance, reported that the greater portion of the lumber had been saved and was being used again in reconstruction (*Sixth Annual Report of the Board of Water Commissioners,* pp. 6–7).

22. Mulholland, Office Files, WP04–21:7, May 9, 1906; Spriggs, pp. 40–41; Layne, p. 85; *Times,* November 26, 1906; July 31, 1907. Anthony Chabot's construction of Lake Temescal and Lake Chabot in the Oakland area during the 1870s had already used sluicing techniques derived from California mining practices (Burgess, *The Water King,* pp. 126–130).

23. Mulholland, Office Files, WP04–21:7, Mulholland to C. D. Brown, July 9, 1906.

24. *Evening News, Times,* December 20, 1906.

25. *First Annual Report of the Los Angeles Aqueduct,* Appendix E, pp. 117–132; J. D. Schuyler et al., "Report of the Consulting Engineers on the Project of the Los Angeles Aqueduct from Owens River to San Fernando Valley," December 22, 1906; *Examiner,* December 23, 1906; *News,* December 22, 1906.

26. *Express,* December 26, 27, 1906.

27. *Evening News,* December 25, 1906; *Examiner,* December 26, 1906; *Record,* December 31, 1906. Earlier in the year a scandal had occurred over undone work recommended by Mulholland on the outfall sewer. When City Engineer Harry Stafford was found dead by gas asphyxiation in August with his records hopelessly disordered, suspicions arose that shady deals with outside contractors had been made out of his office. Stafford had been appointed by previous City Engineer Frank Olmstead, who was now with the San Gabriel Electric Company. With this recent scandal in mind, the *Record* feared that the new mayor's possible connections to some of the suspects, especially the Southern Pacific "Nofziger-Stansbury & Powell crowd," could taint the Owens River works and turn the people against it.

CHAPTER 13: THE BIG JOB BEGINS, 1907

1. Spalding, *History of Los Angeles City and County,* vol. 1, p. 348. For a fuller discussion, see Mowry, *The California Progressives,* pp. 40–45.

2. *Herald,* January 13, 1907; *Times,* January 30, 1907.

3. On January 3, 1907, the board of public works, and later the city council, voted to approve Mathews as special legal adviser to the Los Angeles Aqueduct. His salary jumped from $3,000 a year as city attorney to $6,000 a year, and his office was moved to the Union Trust Building, closer to Mulholland. The precedent for such acts stemmed from the earlier litigations with private water companies when the city employed a special attorney. Under the special contract, either Mathews or the city could terminate the appointment by giving sixty days' notice. *Herald,* January 4, 5, 31, 1907; *Examiner,* January 4, 1907; *Evening News,* January 5, 1907; *Times,* January 31, 1907.

4. Mulholland, Office Files, WP04-22:13, "Chaffee Appropriations," September 21, 1906; WP04-21:21, Gray-Mulholland correspondence, 1907–1908; WP04-22:20, Shuey-Mulholland correspondence, 1907.

5. *Intake,* September, 1944, pp. 5–9.

6. Ibid.; *Saga of Inyo,* p. 216.

7. *Examiner,* March 25, 27, 31, 1907; *Record,* March 25, 1907; *Times,* March 28, 1907.

8. *Herald,* May 26, 1907. The auditor, W. M. Nelson, had been a traveling auditor with the Southern Pacific. When he joined the aqueduct staff, he introduced the railroad's system of accounting and financial management—a system that the Interstate Commerce Commission had mandated for all railways. Already in use for work on the Panama Canal, the system included a voucher system of payment, timekeepers placed under bond to guard against irregularities and overpayments, and competitive bidding for all purchases.

9. Mulholland, Office Files, WP04-21:19, April 2, 1907; *News,* April 1, 1907; *Examiner,* April 3, 1907.

10. Mulholland, Office Files, WP04-21:22, April 12, 1907; *News,* April 18, 19, 1907; *Times,* April 23, 27, 1907.

11. *Evening News,* April 22, 1907. The fourteen "Veritas" letters appeared on April 18, 20, 22, 23, 24, 25, 29; May 10, 22, 27, 29, 30, 31; and June 1, 1907. Entries in city directories suggest that W. T. Spilman's affairs had not prospered since his business and domestic failures in the 1890s. The 1905 directory listed him as a contractor living in rooms at 315 West Sixth; those from 1907 to 1911, as a machinist at 343 North Main.

12. *Times,* June 7, 1907.

13. *Times,* May 23, 1907.

14. Mulholland, Office Files, WP04-21:7, Mulholland to Brooks, May 17, 1907.

15. *Evening News,* June 8, 1907; *Herald,* June 4, 1907.

16. *Express,* June 10, 1907; *Times,* July 28, 1907. Clipping Book, DWP, May–June 1907.

17. *Express,* June 7, 10, 1907.

18. Clipping Book, DWP, "Owens River: Questions Answered"; *Evening News,* June 8, 1907.

19. *Times,* May 22, 1907; *Examiner,* June 12, 1907. Herriman lived much of his life in Los Angeles and at one time was a neighbor of Mary Mulholland (a niece of William) on the Arroyo Seco. One of Mary's brothers remembered stand-

ing with Herriman after a winter flood had taken out thirteen houses along the wash. While "99 percent of the people were out having a Roman holiday . . . the cartoonist soberly remarked, 'Nature can be terrible'" (William "Bill" Mulholland, interview by author, 1978).

20. *Express,* June 8, 1907.

21. *Express,* June 8, 11, 1907; *Times,* June 11, 1907.

22. *Herald,* June 23, 1907; Mulholland, Office Files, WP04–22:13, Mulholland to Shuey, June 12, 1907.

23. *Examiner, Herald, News, Times,* June 13, 1907.

24. *Record,* June 20, 1907; *Express,* June 20, 1907.

25. *Evening News,* June 13, 1907; Mulholland, Office Files, WP04–22:11, July 1, 1907.

26. *Times,* July 7,28, 1907.

27. *Times,* July 28, 1907.

28. *Times,* July 28, 31, 1907.

29. Mulholland, Office Files, WP04–22:20, Shuey-Lippincott-Mulholland correspondence, August 3, 6, 7, 1907; WP04–21:6, Mulholland to Bailey, August 15, 1907. *Times,* July 31, 1907.

30. Stimson, *Rise of Labor Movement in Los Angeles,* p. 318; Mulholland, Office Files, WP04–22:2, Mulholland to Editor, *Denver Post,* September 12, 1907.

31. *Times,* November 1, 1907.

32. *Times,* December 14, 1907. Hamlin had already supplied the Smithsonian Institution with fossils found while building the new outfall sewer, some of which the institution believed might be a new variety of camel from the Pleistocene. Of these finds, Hamlin had commented, "Looks as though we drove the outfall through a zoölogical garden."

33. *Times,* October 1; November 1, 1907.

34. Mulholland, Office Files, WP04–22:4, Gray to Mulholland, December 21, 1907; 22:26, Van Norman to Mulholland, December 26, 1907. Stimson, *Rise of the Labor Movement in Los Angeles,* p. 318; *Los Angeles Times,* November 27; December 1, 27, 1907.

CHAPTER 14: THE CHIEF AND THE GENERAL, 1908

1. Mulholland, Office Files, WP04–21:23, Harper; *Los Angeles Times,* July 7 and 31, 1907.

2. *Who's Who in the Pacific Southwest,* p. 81; Layne, pp. 111–112; *Times,* February 11, 1908. In 1906, Chaffee had refused the police commissionership of New York (*San Francisco Chronicle,* April 6, 1906).

3. Rumors about Otis's pressuring Mayor Harper to name Chaffee persisted, however, and a year later, as the campaign to recall Harper was under way, Otis published in the *Times* a letter of denial to Major Henry T. Lee, in which he claimed to have spoken only twice to Harper on the matter. Harper in turn told Otis he felt undue pressure was being put upon him to reappoint Anderson, and Otis charged the Municipal League with insincerity and trouble-making in driving Harper out of office (*Times,* October 10, 1908; February 19, 28, 1909; see also Ostrom, pp. 93–94, and Sitton, *Haynes,* p. 82).

4. Spalding, *History of Los Angeles City and County,* vol. 3, pp. 428–29; *Record,* March 25, 1908; Mulholland, Office Files, WP04–22:2, July 28, 1908; Mulholland Scrapbook, undated clipping.

5. Layne, pp. 108–9; *Times,* February 21, 26, and March 19, 1908. A year later, shortly after the inauguration of President William Howard Taft, Mulholland wrote W. C. Mendenhall of the United States Geological Survey expressing his concern over an Interior Department appointment proposed for Koebig's attorney, Oscar Lawler. "Lawler has been the attorney of the Koebig Silver Lake crowd and in his capacity as U.S. District Attorney for this District gave us considerable annoyance here. His appointment, no doubt, was dictated by machine influences opposed to us and I believe that our good friend [Representative] Smith had some intimation of what was coming as in our interview with him in [Representative] McLachlan's office he hinted very broadly of changed conditions under the incoming administration." (Mulholland, Office Files, WP04–22:5, Mulholland to Mendenhall, March 26, 1909; see also note 19, chapter 12.) Lawler had been appointed United States attorney to the Southern California District; in 1909, he was appointed assistant to the attorney general of the United States (Spalding, vol. 1, pp. 348, 358).

6. *Times,* February 26, March 10, 1908.

7. *Times,* March 10, 1908.

8. Taylor, *Men, Medicine and Water: The Building of the Los Aqueduct,* p. 22.

9. Taylor, *Men, Medicine and Water,* p. 23; *Times,* May 15, 1908.

10. The engineer in question was W. C. Aston, who, according to Dr. Taylor's aforementioned memoir (p. 25), was never "very friendly; in fact, he was rather belligerent in all his dealings with us." Although Taylor eventually found a way to get along with the difficult engineer, apparently the civil service examiner did not. Aston was, in fact, a graduate mining engineer from Ohio State University with thirteen years' experience in the mines of Colorado. He had gained a certain fame there for having driven what was then known as the Joker Tunnel, which drained for seven miles (*Times,* May 29, June 3, 1908; March 12, 1911).

11. *Times,* January 13, 1909; Sitton, *Haynes,* pp. 78–79.

12. Mulholland, Office Files, WP04–22:2, July 28, 1908; *Complete Report—Aqueduct Construction,* pp. 267–68; *Los Angeles Times,* June 23, July 9, 10, 11, 1908.

13. *Complete Report—Aqueduct Construction,* pp. 194–97; Layne, pp. 135–137.

14. *Times,* July 21, 1908; September 12, 1909. Mulholland maintained an Argus-like alertness at his work. His sons remembered that while others might drowse during monotonous stretches along the aqueduct, their father remained observant. After one inspection tour, he wrote to one of his chief surveyors stationed near Freeman, Kern County, "On my way home, in looking up at the mountain side running southerly from your work, I think if you have a laborer to take pick and shovel and blaze marks in the hill where the grade line runs, say every two or three hundred feet, the line will show up perfectly from the road . . . and will be a great aid in finding the stakes while traversing that rough country" (Mulholland, Office Files, WP04–21:6, July 12, 1906).

15. Mulholland, Office Files, WP04–22:10, October 3, 1908. Subsequent events seemed to vindicate Mulholland's suspicions about the Haiwee postmaster, for in 1911, the same "Doctor" Merritt was convicted and sentenced in San Francisco for fraudulent use of the mails in an oil scam called the Haiwee–Pacific Oil Company (*Express,* April 13, 1911).

16. Mulholland, Office Files, WP04–22:2, July 28, 1908; *Complete Report— Aqueduct Construction,* p. 259.

17. Taylor, p. 22; *Times,* December 13, 1908; *Engineering-Contracting: A Weekly "Methods and Costs" Journal for Civil Engineers and Contractors,* October 20, 1909, p. 325. The editor of this Chicago journal conceded that for the first time in his long editorial life, he was acknowledging that economical tunnel work had been done by the day labor method on the Los Angeles Aqueduct. He also credited the bonus system: "*Make sub-contractors out of all your foremen and workmen by paying them a bonus for work performed in excess of a stipulated minimum daily output.*" He questioned, however, the practicality of such a method in municipalities because of graft: "Imagine a Tammany applying a bonus system to streetcleaning!" he mused. Yet he also conceded that the bonus system stimulated achievement. This debate flourished in technical engineering and contracting publications of the time and remains unresolved. The bonus system prevailed in 1994 after the Northridge Earthquake in Los Angeles, when the severely damaged Santa Monica Freeway was repaired ahead of schedule and its contractor given a bonus of $4 million. The day labor method on public works received an added boost in 1908 when, after local private contractors sought injunctions against the city on both the aqueduct and sewer projects, a court upheld the city's right. The court did, however, question whether in an age of keen competition, public works could be built to the best advantage on these terms (*Pacific Outlook,* December 11, 1909).

18. Stimson, *Rise of Labor Movement in Los Angeles,* pp. 95, 147, 203, and 324; *Times,* June 12, 1908.

19. Mulholland, Office Files, WP04–21:17, June 30–September 8, 1908.

20. *Times,* December 1, 1908.

21. Mulholland, Office Files, WP04–21:19; O'Melveny, Journals, November 4, 17, 1908. Harold Eaton was having marital difficulties and in the following year separated from his wife, who charged him with nonsupport (*Times,* November 23, 1909).

22. Mulholland, Office Files, WP04–21:9, November, 1908; *Third Annual Report; Times,* December 3, 1908.

23. Mulholland, Office Files, WP04–21:7, Mulholland to Brooks, December 26 and 29, 1908.

CHAPTER 15: BUILDING THE AQUEDUCT: THE BEST YEAR, 1909

1. Mulholland, Office Files, WP04–21:17, Dockweiler-Mulholland correspondence, January 30, February 3 and 9, 1909; WP04–22:7, March 4, 1909.

2. Mulholland, Office Files, WP04–23:6, Mulholland-Young correspondence, October 7 and 12, 1905.

3. Widney, "We Build a Railroad," *Touring Topics*, March 1931, p. 36. See also Taylor, *Men, Medicine and Water*, pp. 28–29.

4. Hoffman, *Vision or Villainy*, pp. 150–151; *Times*, January 19, 20, 23; February 2, 1909.

5. Mulholland, Office Files, WP04-21:17, February 6 and May 3, 1909; *Times*, February 4 and 10, 1909.

6. *Times*, February 19; April 17, 20, 1909.

7. *Complete Report—Aqueduct Construction*, p. 219.

8. Layne, *Water and Power for a Great City*, p. 136; Nadeau, pp. 37–38; personal recollections of Van Norman and my father, Perry Mulholland, reminiscing about aqueduct days and "Whistling Dick."

9. *Times*, April 4, 1909.

10. In August 1909, Flanigan's crew drove 1,061.6 feet, a world record for fast tunnel driving for one month's run. The Swiss at Loetchberg Tunnel, working in limestone, had held the record with 1,013 feet. They had used compressed-air-driven machine drills, however, while the Americans used only hand drills. *Complete Report—Aqueduct Construction*, p. 156. *Express*, September 3, 1909; *Herald*, September 12, 1909; *Times*, September 2, 1909.

11. *Times*, September 12, 1909.

12. *Complete Report—Aqueduct Construction*, p. 151; *Times*, April 5, June 5, 1909.

13. For a good account of the mayoral campaign, see Sitton, *Haynes*, pp. 81–83. Upon his election, Alexander was reported to want all the city's commissioners ousted to fulfill the Democratic League's recommendations. He especially singled out a man on the water board "inimical to the interests of the city" (*Times*, April 23, 1909).

14. Mulholland, Office Files, WP04-21:1, undated and unlabeled news clipping, "Yoakum's Bombshell Failed to Explode," April 1909; *Times*, May 1, 1909.

15. Mulholland, Office Files, WP04-21:8, April 19, 1909.

16. Mulholland, Office Files, WP04-21:20, November 1, 1909; *Examiner*, September 21, 1909.

17. Mulholland, Office Files, WP04-22:26, Mulholland-Willard correspondence, June 5; July 17, 18, 1909; *Times*, May 2, June 11, 1909; *Times*, December 2, 1909.

18. *Times*, June 29, July 1, 1909.

19. Taylor, pp. 165–66; *San Francisco Chronicle*, September 28, 1906; *Examiner*, December 26, 1909. Members of the Desmond family had been passengers aboard the ship on which Mulholland and his brother had stowed away from New York to Panama in 1876 and had befriended their aunt, Catherine Deakers, during her trials on that voyage.

20. Taylor, pp. 112–13; *Times*, July 1, 3, 13, 1909.

21. *Times*, November 16, 1909.

22. Mulholland, Office Files, WP04-21:6, October 20, 1909. *Times*, December 2, 1909.

23. *Times*, November 30, December 14, 1909.

24. *Times*, October 27, November 16, December 17, 1909.

CHAPTER 16: TROUBLES AND INTERRUPTIONS, 1910

1. Hoffman, p. 149; *Times,* January 1, 11, 1910.

2. *Graphic,* January 24, 1910; *Pacific Outlook,* January 29, 1910; *Times,* January 20, 1910; Kahrl, pp. 172–73. Kahrl denigrates the differences between the Progressives and the old guard (and dismisses Mayor Alexander as a fumbler) in his assertion that an oligarchy of business interests controlled the city. For a more even-handed and accurate estimate of the Progressive efforts to modernize city government and restructure political power in Los Angeles, see Sitton, pp. 106–8.

3. *Graphic,* January 29, 1910; *Pacific Outlook,* January 29, 1910; *Examiner,* February 16, 1910; *Express,* February 15, 1910; *Herald,* February 15, 16, 1910; *Times,* January 11, 17, 20, 1910; February 15, 1910.

4. *Fifth Annual Report,* pp. 14–15; *Examiner,* February 11, 1910.

5. Mulholland, Office Files, WP04-21:19, March 3, 1910; *Examiner,* April 28, 1910; *Inyo Register,* January 13, 20, 27, 1910; June 9, 1910. The editor of the *Inyo Register,* W. A. Chalfont, had earlier alerted Owens Valley people to gather their forces for the land hearing (Sept. 9, 1909).

6. *Express,* March 20, 1910; *Examiner,* March 20, 1910; *Herald,* March 22, 1910.

7. Mulholland, Office Files, WP04-21:17, March 17, 1910; *Fifth Annual Report,* pp. 27–8; *Los Angeles Times,* March 5, 1910; *Los Angeles Examiner,* April 11, 1910; Clipping Book, Department of Water and Power, vol. 4, April 1910.

8. *Tenth Annual Report,* p. 21.

9. *Examiner,* May 9, 27, 1910.

10. For a full account of this enterprise, see Grenier, *California Legacy: The Watson Family,* pp. 326–332. O'Melveny, Journals, April 9, 21; October 15, 31; November 30; December 14, 1910.

11. *Final Report—Aqueduct,* pp. 268–69; Mulholland, Office Files, WP04-21:19, June 17, 19, 1910. The bond syndicate was Kountze Bros. and A. B. Leach and Company of New York.

12. Mulholland, Office Files, WP04-22:17, Mulholland to Smith, June 1, 1910; *Examiner,* May 9, 25, 27; June 3, 1910; *Herald,* May 23, 1910.

13. *Examiner,* June 25, 26; July 5, 9, 10, 11, 12, 1910; *Express,* July 9, 11, 12, 13, 1910; *Herald,* July 12, 13, 15, 16, 1910; *Record,* July 11, 13, 1910; *Spectator,* July 13, 16, 1910; *Times,* June 26, 1910; All above clippings from Scrapbook, Department of Water and Power, vol. 4, 1910. For a negative interpretation, see Kahrl, pp. 165–67. He writes, "Precipitate haste had been a hallmark of the city's handling of water bonds ever since the first issue to pay the costs of buying up the works of the Los Angeles Water Company." He rejects the possibility that the private electric power companies could have had a hand in the matter, although every newspaper in the city suspected as much.

14. *Examiner,* July 20, 21, 1910; *Express,* July 20, 1910; *Herald,* July 20, 1910; *Times,* July 21, 1910.

15. *Examiner,* July 29, 30; August 8, 1910; O'Melveny, Journals, July 1910. Mulholland spoke of his sons (then eighteen and sixteen) to a reporter. "They are good boys, right good boys, but they can't take their father as anything but

a huge joke. They read what the papers publish about me like they read about Buster Brown [a popular comic strip character]" (*Record*, July 21, 1910).

16. *Times*, June 1, 1910; Stimson, pp. 340–344. Many historians and journalists have written of the *Times* bombing, the most remembered event of labor conflict in Los Angeles. Notable among them are Louis Adamic, "The McNamara Affair," *Dynamite* (1931); Grace Stimson, "Crime of the Century," *Rise of the Labor Movement in Los Angeles* (1955); and Gottlieb and Wolt, "The Bombing of the Times' Building," *Thinking Big* (1972).

17. *Examiner*, November 21, 1910; *Express*, November 2, 21, 1910; *Herald*, November 4, 1910; *Inyo Register*, November 24, 1910; *Record*, November 11, 1910. Stimson, p. 351.

J. Desmond had threatened the city with a suit to reclaim his alleged losses on the aqueduct concession and received the increase after insuring that the quality of the food would improve. Years later, Dr. Taylor recalled that General Chaffee asked how much he and Desmond had made on the aqueduct job. After Taylor, who had headed the aqueduct medical department, said he had made about $6,000 a year for the five years, or $30,000, Desmond said, "I made about a quarter of a million," at which Chaffee exploded. "Damn it, Joe, you made too much and the doctor didn't make enough" (Taylor, *Men, Medicine and Water*, p. 157).

18. *Record*, November 22, 1910. The *Inyo Register* had reported earlier in March that "improper mixing of cement" had caused cave-ins, and that scores of aqueduct workers were leaving for the Bakersfield oil fields (March 24, 1910).

19. *Fifth Annual Report*, p. 7; *Times*, November 16, 1910; *Herald*, November 4, 1910; *Record*, November 7, 11, 21, and 22, 1910; *Examiner*, November 21, 1910. At the end of 1911, Rinehart left the *Record* to become a press association's state correspondent in Sacramento; he returned to Los Angeles in 1912 to manage and edit the new but short-lived Progressive experiment, the *Municipal News*. A Woodrow Wilson Democrat, he believed in municipal ownership and felt Mayor Alexander to be "a better Socialist than Harriman" (*Times*, February 14, 1912).

20. Chalfant, *Story of Inyo*, p. 213; *Inyo Register*, October 20, 1910. The impact of expanded transportation facilities during the years of aqueduct construction upon Owens Valley has been inadequately remarked. A month before the silver spike ceremony, a California governor had visited Inyo County for the first time in its history. Under the auspices of the Good Roads Committee, Governor James Norris Gillett visited the valley towns with speeches extolling the beauties of the area, which, he predicted, with better roads and increased access, would be visited and admired as were the Alps in Europe. Hopes for a bright future stirred in Owens Valley, for which some credited the influence of Los Angeles and the aqueduct, which might prove a blessing in disguise. Others, like Chalfant, doubted—although conceding that the railroad would improve their lives (*Inyo Register*, September 1, 15, 1910; *Times*, September 7, 1910).

21. *Express*, November 4, 1910; *Herald*, November 4, 1910; *Pacific Outlook*, November 5, 1910; *Times*, October 30, November 3, 5, 1910.

22. *Times*, October 21, 23; November 5, 1910.

23. *Express*, November 4, 1910; *Times*, November 5, 1910.

24. *Express,* November 4, 1910; *Herald,* November 4, 1910.

25. Mulholland, Office Files, WP04–21:16, December 2, 1910; *Examiner,* November 18, 1910; *Express,* November 25, 1910; *Herald,* November 22, 1910; *Times,* November 28, 1910.

26. Mulholland, Office Files, WP04–22:17, Mulholland-Stearns correspondence, November 23; December 6, 1910. *Express,* September 29, 1910; *Examiner,* September 24, 28, 29, 1910; *Herald,* September 28, 30, 1910; *Times,* September 23, 28, 1910.

CHAPTER 17: AQUEDUCT PROGRESS
.AND POLITICAL FIREWORKS, 1911

1. *Herald,* March 7, 8, 1911. Years later, Scattergood recalled that Mayor Alexander had buttonholed him after the election to exhort, "Get ready to manufacture, distribute and sell to the people of Los Angeles, the power you say you can develop from the aqueduct." He also credited the mayor with instilling in him his idealism about municipal ownership (*Herald-Express,* July 10, 1940). On the other hand, Progressive Lissner and three other members of the public utilities commission resigned after the election in disapproval of the mayor's power policies. Calling the post "a thankless task," Lissner refused further public support of Alexander although he kept "hands off" the subsequent mayoral campaign (Meyer L. Lissner Papers, Box 3, Folders 42, 43, June 30 and July 17, 1911). For discussion of the municipal ownership movement, see Fogelson, *Fragmented Metropolis,* Chapter 11; and Sitton, *Haynes,* Chapter 5.

2. Mulholland, Office Files, WP04–21:11, Alexander to Mulholland, January 5, 6, 1911; *Herald,* February 10, 1911; *Record,* February 16, 1911.

3. *Examiner,* February 26, 27, 28, 1910; *Express,* February 25, 1910.

4. *Sixth Annual Report of the Aqueduct, 1911,* pp. 38–41; *Christian Science Monitor,* March 1, 1911; *Examiner,* March 21, 1911; *Times,* March 12, 1911.

5. Ostrom, p. 96; *Los Angeles Record,* January 30, 31, 1911.

6. Ostrom, pp. 95–96; *Express,* April 7, 1911; *Examiner,* March 26, 28; April 16, 1911; *Herald,* March 23, 26, 1911; *Times,* March 26; April 7, 16, 1911.

7. Ostrom, pp. 96–97; *Herald,* May 3, 1911; *Times,* April 19, 1911.

8. Ostrom, pp. 148–50; *Herald,* March 16, 1911; *Examiner,* March 16, July 4, 1911; *Times,* March 26, 1911.

9. Hoffman, pp. 156–58; Kahrl, pp. 182–83; Ostrom, pp. 150–52; *Times,* August 4, 10, 1911; *Tribune,* August 23, 1911. Earl was then under grand jury investigation for stealing a wireless message relating to the *Times* bombing and publishing it in his papers. Otis in turn attacked Earl in the harshest terms as a "friend of dynamiters." By 1914, Earl had a court case pending against Otis for libel.

10. *Sixth Annual Report—Aqueduct,* pp. 7–8; *Examiner,* July 16, 18, 1911; *Herald,* July 16, 1911.

11. Stimson, *Rise of the Labor Movement in Los Angeles,* pp. 331 ff.

12. Mulholland, Office Files, WP04–22:23, Statement by Public Service Commission, November 17, 1911; *The Citizen,* December 3, 1911; *Times,* September 29, 1911; *Tribune,* October, 23, 25, 1911. The unnamed district Harriman

intended the city should buy for water storage was probably near Redondo Beach, according to Mellie A. Calvert, who once worked as Harriman's secretary. The daughter of Midwestern Socialists, she had settled with her family in the utopian Socialist colony of Llano, later married, and taught biology and physiology at Canoga Park High School from 1932 until her retirement in the 1950s. Regrettably, she was never interviewed for an oral history; but she was my teacher, and I had several conversations with her in the late 1970s about Socialist attitudes towards the Owens River project.

13. For a more detailed account of this group's activities in the San Fernando Valley, see my *Owensmouth Baby*, Chapter 1, pp. 3 ff. Also, Fogelson, pp. 104–5; Hundley, *The Great Thirst*, pp. 158–60.

14. Fogelson, pp. 214–15; Mowry, pp. 50–52; Sitton, pp. 110–12; *Examiner,* October 24, 1911; *Tribune,* October 23, 25, 1911.

15. Burdette, *American Biography,* pp. 274–76; *Times,* October 15, 1911; *Tribune,* October 25, 1911. In his memoirs, *Sixty Years in Southern California,* Harris Newmark, expressing the most conservative view of the time, held Alexander responsible for the success of the Progressive Party whose "Socialistic policies" he deplored (p. 639).

16. *The Citizen,* December 3, 1911; *California Outlook,* December 2, 1911; *Express,* December 1, 2, 3, 1911; *Times,* November 19, 25, 26, 28, 1911; *Tribune,* November 28, 1911.

17. Steffens, *Autobiography,* pp. 670–89; *Pacific Outlook,* December 2, 1911. C. D. Willard, editor of the *Outlook,* published Steffens's November 25 speech to the City Club, "How to Beat the Socialists." "By facing the social problem," said Steffens, one then secures the participation of "bad" men (that is, Otis, Chandler, and the others) in the experiment.

18. *Express,* November 4, 1911; *The Citizen,* December 2, 3, 1911; Mulholland, Office Files, WP04–22:24, Statements and Speeches of William Mulholland, City Club, December 2, 1911. The twenty-seven-page, double-spaced, unpaginated typescript includes Meyer Lissner's introduction and the questions and answers after the speech. Following paragraphs in this text derive from that document (also, *Times,* December 2, 1911). Lissner, although silent about Mayor Alexander, was an important backer of Hiram Johnson in Southern California and during this period had sought Mulholland's recommendations for candidates to the state engineer's office. In forwarding one such recommendation to the governor, Lissner wrote, "I know of no man in the state of California whose opinion I would rather have on a question of this sort than Mulholland" (Lissner Papers, Box 3, Folder 45, Lissner to H. Johnson, October 18, 1911).

19. *Examiner,* December 23, 1911; *Tribune,* December 18, 23, 1911.

CHAPTER 18: THE INVESTIGATION, 1912

1. *Express, Herald,* March 25, 26, 1912. Ostrom, pp. 56–59. For a detailed chronological account of the formation of the AIB, see Abraham Hoffman, "The Los Angeles Aqueduct Investigation Board of 1912: A Reappraisal," *Southern California Quarterly,* vol. 62, No. 4, (1980), pp. 329–60.

2. *Sixth Annual Report of Los Angeles Aqueduct, 1911,* pp. 34–36; *Herald,*

January 6, 16, 1912; *Record,* February 16, 1912; *Times,* February 20, 1912; *Tribune,* February 15, 1912.

3. *Times,* January 13, March 3, 1912.

4. *Record,* March 11, 1912; *Examiner,* March 22, 1912.

5. Mulholland, Office Files, WP04-22:18, Mulholland to John Wilson, March 12, 1912; *Record,* March 22, 1912; Hoffman, *Vision or Villainy,* pp. 125–128; Mulholland, *Owensmouth Baby,* pp. 73–74.

6. *Complete Report—Aqueduct Construction,* pp. 208–9; *Examiner,* January 25, 1912; *Times,* February 3, 1912.

7. *Examiner, Express, Tribune,* March 20, 21, 22, 1912; *Record,* March 21, 22, 1912; *Times,* March 21, 24, 1912.

8. *Express, Record,* and *Times,* March 29, 1912; *Examiner,* March 30, 31, 1912; *Tribune,* March 31, 1912.

9. *Examiner,* March 30, 31; April 1, 1912; *Tribune,* March 31, April 1, 1912.

10. *Record,* April 1, 4, 12, 1912; *Times,* April 3, 1912.

11. *Express,* April 4, 1912; *Times,* April 4, 1912; *Record,* April 5, 6, 1912.

12. Spilman, *The Conspiracy,* p. 71.

13. Mulholland, Office Files, WP04-21:5, Mulholland to Board of Investigation, April 16, 1912.

14. *Times,* April 27, 1912; *Tribune,* May 2, 1912.

15. *Tribune,* April 18 and May 14, 1912; *Municipal News,* May 5, 1912.

16. *Express,* April 17, 24, 1912; *Municipal News,* January 22, 1913; *Record,* April 25, 1912; *Times,* April 26, 1912.

17. *Examiner,* May 21, 1912; *Record,* May 21, 1912.

18. *Express* and *Record,* April 12, 1912; *Examiner,* May 2, 21, and 22, 1912; *Herald,* May 22, 1912; *Municipal News,* May 22, 1912.

19. *Examiner,* May 22, 1912; *Record,* June 4, 1912; *San Fernando Democrat,* May 30, 1912.

20. *Record,* May 25, 31; June 1, 1912.

21. *Seventh Annual Report—Aqueduct,* 1912, p. 8; *Los Angeles Times,* May 29, 1912.

22. *Express,* June 17, 1912; *Herald,* June 14, 1912; *Record,* June 5, 1912; *Tribune,* June 7, 1912.

23. *Express,* June 14, 17, 1912; *Times,* June 17, 1912; *Examiner,* June 20, 1912; *Herald,* July 5, 1912.

24. *Examiner, Express, Tribune,* June 19, 1912; *Record,* June 20, 21, 1912.

25. *Times,* June 22, 1912.

26. *Times,* June 22, 1912. Family letters in author's possession: Perry Mulholland to Lillie and Rose Mulholland, June 25 and July 1, 1912. *Tribune,* July 6, 1912. In February 1912, Mulholland and Lippincott had written for the Spring Valley Water Company a groundwater study for a proposed catchment on Alameda Creek. On this trip they consulted with both F. C. Herrman, chief engineer, and S. P. Eastman, vice president and manager of Spring Valley Water. Between 1910 and 1913, Mulholland was also a consultant on Calaveras Creek Dam along with engineers John R. Freeman and Samuel Storrow and geologists Andrew Lawson of the University of California, Berkeley, and John Caspar Brauner of Stanford. In his report, Mulholland reverted to sea imagery in de-

scribing how water surrounding the outlet tower for the dam would "dampen the effect of an earthquake on the tower," just as, he wrote, "in a ship the vibrations from the machinery may be plainly felt when the hand is placed against the side above the water line, but not below the water line." He recommended the sluicing method used on Silver Lake, Dry Canyon, and Haiwee Dams. The Calaveras Dam failed during construction (March 24, 1918) when the soft core mud flowed out at the footing. Investigating engineers found that the "fine core material over the extended interior of the dam had remained mobile as near-liquid," yet concluded that the sluicing method was acceptable if properly controlled. Some later critics have cited the dam's failure as evidence that Mulholland was not a good engineer. Derleth Papers, Reports on the Calaveras Dam.

27. Mulholland, Office Files, WP04–21:19, Mulholland to Flint, July 5, 1912.

28. *Examiner,* July 6, 10, 1912; *Express,* July 10, 1912; *Municipal News,* July 10, 1912; *Record,* July 3, 8, 10, 1912; *Tribune,* July 10, 1912.

29. *Express, Herald, Record, Tribune,* July 16, 17, 1912.

30. *Examiner,* July 11, 1912; *Express,* July 16, 1912; *Herald,* July 11, 1912; *Record,* July 11, 12, 1912. Warner's zeal to demonstrate Mulholland's incompetence included writing to the British admiralty to verify a statement the chief had made to answer the criticism of "certain engineers" that the steel siphons had not been painted until rust had accumulated. He was alleged to have said that it was a practice in Britain to send vessels to sea in order that the hulls might become rusty before being painted. Warner was happy to learn from the admiralty that such was not the case, and the *Record* headlined the finding BRITISH ADMIRALTY FAILS TO SUPPORT MULHOLLAND THEORY (*Record,* August 27, 1912).

31. *Express,* July 25, 26, 1912; *Times,* July 26, 1912.

32. *Examiner,* July 18, 19, 1912; *Express,* July 23, 24, 25, 1912; *Record,* July 20, 23, 24, 25, 1912; *Times,* April 24; July 17, 23, 24, 25, 1912; *Tribune,* July 23, 24, 25, 1912. E. T. Earl's *Express,* in its apparent glee over Otis's discomfiture, reported only Mulholland's denial of friction on the board and omitted his opposition to Graham's plan. The trial ended with a verdict of not guilty (*Times,* July 31, 1912).

33. *Record,* August 1, 8, 15, 16, 19, 1912; *Times,* August 25, 1912.

34. *Municipal News,* August 28, 1912; *Record,* August 22, 29, 1912; September 3, 1912. See also Hoffman, pp. 352–56.

35. *Examiner,* September 2, 3, 1912; *Record,* September 3, 1912; *Times,* August 27, 1912.

36. *Examiner,* October 27; November 6, 13, 1912; *Express,* October 8, 1912; *Times,* September 26; October 27, 31, 1912.

37. *Express,* December 6, 7, 1912; *Tribune,* December 11, 12, 1912.

38. *Express,* December 26, 1912; *Record,* December 11, 1912; *Tribune,* December 31, 1912.

39. *Tribune,* October 26, December 31, 1912; *Express,* December 7, 1912; Los Angeles Aqueduct and Water Company, Press Clippings, vol. 7, 1912.

40. *Tribune,* December 31, 1912. A year before, Mulholland had recommended Johnson for the office of state engineer (Lissner Papers, Box 3, Folder 45, Meyer Lissner to Hiram Johnson, October 18, 1911).

CHAPTER 19: THE COMPLETION OF THE AQUEDUCT, 1913

1. *Municipal News,* January 8, 1913; Mulholland, *Owensmouth Baby,* pp. 58–60; O'Melveny, Journals, January 4, 5, 6, 1913.

2. *Examiner,* January 19, 1912; *Express, Tribune,* January 18, 1912; *Municipal News,* February 5, 1913.

3. Department of Water and Power, Clipping Book, vol. 8, 1913, No.1; *Examiner,* January 1, 1913; *Inyo Register,* January 7, 1913; *Record,* January 1, 1913.

4. *Herald,* January 10, 1913; *Tribune,* January 5, 1913.

5. *Express, Tribune,* January 22, 23, 27, 1913; *Examiner, Times,* January 23, 1913; Meyer Lissner Papers, Box 15, Folder 314, Mulholland to M. Lissner, January 30, 1913; E. T. Earl to M. Lissner, January 31, 1913. In the letter to Lissner, Mulholland also expressed his regret for his differences with the new public service commissioners ("I found myself outside the pale of concert of action"), but he also insisted that his opinions had been long held, and, he concluded, "consistency is a jewel."

6. C. D. Willard Papers, Mulholland to Willard, January 24, 1913.

7. *Examiner,* February 9, 16, 1913; *Express,* February 13, 1918; *Herald,* February 13, 1913; *Inyo Register,* February 20, 1913; *Municipal News,* February 26, 1913; *Times,* February 14, 1912; *Final Report—Aqueduct Construction,* p. 111.

8. O'Melveny, Journals, January 30, 1913; February 28, 1913.

9. *Inyo Register,* February 20, 27, 1913; *Times,* March 11, 1913; *Tribune,* February 23, 1913.

10. Department of Water and Power, Clipping Book, vol. 8, 1913, No. 1; *Pasadena Record,* March 9, 1913; *Times,* March 2, 13, 1913; *Final Report,* pp. 270–271.

11. *Tribune,* March 14, 1913; undated clipping, Mulholland Scrapbook.

12. *Examiner,* November 5, 1913.

13. *Express,* April 1, 1913; *Times,* March 31, 1913; *Municipal News,* April 2, 1912; *Tribune,* March 29, 1913; Mowry, *The California Progressives,* pp. 196–97. For a recent evaluation of the 1913 municipal election, see Sitton, *Haynes,* pp. 118–19. Mowry is inaccurate when he states that Earl's choice of Mulholland reflected the former's rift with the other leading Progressive, Meyer Lissner. In fact, Lissner's papers reveal that both Earl and Lissner sought Mulholland and only after his unequivocal refusal to run did they chose the nonpartisan candidate John W. Shenk (E. T. Earl to M. Lissner, January 31, 1913, Meyer Lissner Papers, Stanford). Mowry also errs in dismissing Shenk (misspelled "Schenk," pp. 206 ff.) as an "honest but otherwise undistinguished conservative." Unmentioned is Shenk's able service as assistant, and later, city attorney (elected in 1911 with a majority of 34,663), when he successfully led the city's fight against the Pacific Electric and the Southern Pacific for valuable tide and submerged lands around San Pedro. A political independent who had worked with Mathews on a number of water cases and also helped to create an early roadblock for Graham's high line, Shenk was well liked by Mulholland, who at the time was working with him and Mathews on arriving at amicable settlements

with private water companies in Owens Valley (*Inyo Register,* April 10, 1913). Shenk, in his failed run for mayor, was the only political candidate Mulholland ever openly campaigned for in his entire public career (*Who's Who in the Pacific Southwest,* p.337; Robinson, *Lawyers of Los Angeles,* pp. 124–25).

14. Mulholland Scrapbook, Otis to Mulholland, April 17, 1913; *Examiner,* April 16, 1913; *Times,* April 10, 14, 15, 1913.

15. *Examiner,* April 15, 16, 1913; *Tribune,* April 22, 1913.

16. *Final Report—Aqueduct Construction,* pp. 227–34; *Examiner,* April 21, 1913.

17. *Final Report—Aqueduct Construction,* pp. 227–235; *Examiner,* May 1, 1913; *Herald, Times,* May 21, 1913; *Tribune,* April 21, May 22, 1913; *Record,* May 26, 1913.

18. *Examiner, Times,* May 1, 5, 1913; Department of Water and Power, Clipping Book, vol. 8, No. 2; Fogelson, pp. 216–17. Shenk resumed his duties as city attorney and soon left for Sacramento to fight the Inman Bill, legislation designed to prevent municipalities from disposing of surplus water to outside districts and thus thwart the city's present plans for water distribution. Soon after, Shenk became a superior court judge where he served until 1924, at which time he was advanced to the Supreme Court of California, where he served until his death in 1959 (Robinson, pp. 320, 341).

19. Department of Water and Power, Clipping Book, vol. 8, No. 2, 1913; *Examiner,* August 7, 8, 9 ,11, 12, 1913; *Express,* July 8; August 6, 1913; *Record,* August 6, 7, 1913; *Times,* August 9, 1913. The following paragraphs derive from the above sources.

20. *Times,* December 19, 1913.

21. *Examiner,* July 16, 1912; *Express,* July 8, 1913; *Tribune,* July 8, 27, 1913; *Times,* August 6, 1913. Sitton points out that although Rose unseated Progressives, he still retained some reformers on city commissions, so that he did not put the quietus on Progressivism (p. 119).

22. *Final Report—Aqueduct Construction,* p. 270; *Examiner,* July 4, 1913; *Times,* June 19, 1913; *Tribune,* June 22, 1913. City auditor Myers had initiated legal action against the Southern Pacific when the Santa Fe had made a bid that would have saved $40,000 on the total cost of hauling aqueduct steel. The Southern Pacific had originally offered to meet any bid that was made, but after the Santa Fe withdrew its offer, the Southern Pacific refused to equal it. Myers then withheld the difference until the city attorney held they did not have sufficient grounds for a legal action, even though a moral obligation was implied (*Times,* September 18, 1913).

23. Mulholland, *Owensmouth Baby,* pp. 64–68; *Examiner,* June 21, 1913; *Express,* August 19, 20, 1913; *Times,* August 20, 1913.

24. *Examiner,* July 11, September 12, 1913; *Express,* July 11, 1913.

25. Los Angeles Aqueduct and Water Department, Clipping Book, vol. 9, 1913–14. *Examiner,* August 17, 1913; *Tribune,* July 9; August 1, 17, 1913; *Express,* October 11, 1919.

26. *Times,* September 26, 1913; *Tribune,* September 28, 29, 1913.

27. Department of Water and Power, Clipping Book, vol. 9, 1913–1914; *Times,* October 2, 1913.

28. *Record,* October 7, 1913; *Express,* October 7, 1913; *Inyo Register,* September 26, October 30, 1913; *Times,* October 8, 1913.

29. *Examiner,* October 17, November 5, 1913; *Express,* October 14, 1913; *Tribune,* October 15, 1913.

30. *Times,* October 3, 19, 21, 1913; *Examiner,* October 19, 1913; *Express,* October 13, 1913; *Inyo Register,* October 30, 31, 1913.

31. *Examiner,* October 31, November 1, 1913; *Inyo Register,* November 6, 1913; *San Francisco Chronicle,* November 1, 2, 1913.

32. Department of Water and Power, Clipping Book, vol. 9, 1913–14; *Examiner,* November 4, 1913; *Times,* November 4, 5, 6, 1913.

33. Hoffman, p. 172; Nadeau, pp. 66–67; *Inyo Register,* October 13, 30, 1913. The rift between Eaton and Mulholland has been oft-told and oversimplified. In 1913, the Eaton and Mulholland men remained on good terms. Perry Mulholland, William's oldest son, worked that year with the United States Geological Survey on its first survey of the White Mountains. In July he wrote from Bishop that at the hotel he had met Fred Eaton's son, Harold, who reported that he was "running the chicken ranch and says he is doing well" (Mulholland Family Papers).

34. *Tribune,* November 6, 1913. The preceding description of opening ceremonies is derived from the Los Angeles newspapers' many accounts.

35. *Examiner,* November 6, 1913.

36. *Examiner,* November 6, 1913.

37. *Examiner,* November 6, 1913.

38. Department of Water and Power, Clipping Book, vol. 9, 1913; *San Francisco Chronicle,* November 6, 1913; *New York Times,* November 6, 1913; *Boston Globe,* November 7, 1913.

CHAPTER 20: AFTER THE AQUEDUCT, 1914–1919

1. *Examiner,* November 19, 1913; *Herald,* November 11, 1913; *Inyo Register,* November 13, 1913; *San Francisco Chronicle,* December 9, 1913; *Tribune,* November 12, 19, 29, 1913. Mulholland, Testimony, November 24, 1913. I am indebted to J. David Rogers for having lately provided me with a partial copy of the deposition in which Mulholland's sworn testimony happily corroborates my own account.

2. *Examiner,* November 9, 1913; *Municipal News,* January 16, 1914; *Times* and *Record,* January 17, 1914. Finkle was also embroiled in a row over Mayor Rose's removal of a public utilities commissioner. During the ensuing controversy, Finkle was accused of "having grown rich in the employ of public service corporations as expert" (*Times,* November 26, 1913).

3. *Examiner,* February 6, 1914; *Tribune,* February 13, 14, 17, 1914.

4. Mulholland, Office Files, WP04-22:6, B. Heinley to John R. Mathews, January 14, 1914; *Examiner,* January 18, June 12, 1914.

5. O'Melveny, Journals, January 24, February 18, 1914; *Express,* January 29, 1914.

6. Department of Water and Power, Clipping Book, vol. 9, 1913–14; *Exam-*

iner, March 30, 1914; *Express,* March 24, 1914; *Herald,* March 24, 26, 1914; *Record,* March 26, 1914; *Times,* March 25, 1914.

7. Department of Water and Power, Clipping Book, vol. 10, April–May 1914; *Examiner,* April 8; May 2, 4, 5, 1914; *Municipal News,* May 18, 25, 1914; *Record,* April 8, 1914. For a discussion of the Progressives in the campaign, see Sitton, *Haynes,* pp. 120–121. A split between the Socialist Party and organized labor came as labor perceived the Socialists as more interested in political goals than in economic objectives. Even Fred Wheeler, the first Socialist elected to the city council, fell afoul of his own party when he sided with the labor cause (Perry and Perry, *History of the Los Angeles Labor Movement,* pp. 118–119).

8. Meyer Lissner Papers, Stanford University, Box 3, Folders 56, 57, M. Lissner to H. Johnson, March 13, 1912; M. Lissner to J. B. Lippincott, March 29, 1912; Box 43, Folder 744. *Examiner,* May 1, 1914. Apparently Lippincott was responsible for having suggested Mulholland to Lissner for such an honor. Henry O'Melveny also recommended it. Both diplomas remain with Mulholland's family.

9. *Examiner,* May 24, 1914; *Express,* May 27, 5, 1914; *Tribune,* May 14, June, 6, 1914.

10. *Examiner,* July 15, 28, 1914; *Herald,* June 18, 1914; *Record,* July 7, 1914. One of the long-standing canards against the water establishment has been that when it wanted to influence the public to achieve its selfish ends, it wasted water by allowing it to run to the sea. (This alleged practice was one of the evils portrayed in the motion picture *Chinatown.*) The opening of the Franklin Canyon conduit demonstrates that engineers had more rational and practical motives for letting water run. Before the conduit was activated, a wastegate allowed water from Owens River to run for two days down through Ballona to the ocean in order to clear the Franklin Canyon pipes of mud.

11. *Record,* August 1, 15, 17, 18, 19, 1914; *Examiner,* August 18, 1914.

12. *Express,* August 22, 1914; *Examiner,* August 16, 1914; *Record,* August 20, 1914.

13. *Who's Who in the Pacific Southwest,* p. 224; *Times,* September 7, 21, 25, 1904; *Herald,* January 19, 1905; January 19, 1907. Leonard is mentioned in passing in an essay detailing the development of clinical laboratories in Los Angeles in the early twentieth century (James Howard Cremin, "The Los Angeles Clinical Laboratory Medical Group," *Southern California Quarterly* 67, No. 4 [1985], pp. 395–96).

14. *Examiner,* August 21, 1913; *Herald,* August 20, 1914; *Record,* August 18, 19, 1914. Kahrl, pp. 217–18. Kahrl ascribes Leonard's behavior simply to her gullibility in accepting horror stories about bad water from Owens Valley locals, but this seems much too simplistic in view of her training and background. There is some hint of her socialist sympathies but nothing well documented.

15. *Examiner,* August 25, 26, 30, 1914; *Express,* August 25, 1914; *Inyo Register,* August 20, 1914; *Record,* August 22, 1914.

16. *Examiner,* December 16, 1914.

17. The paragraphs above derive from Department of Water and Power, Clipping Book, vol. 10, 1914–15, especially the following: *Examiner,* January 6,

28, 29; February 3, 19, 1914; *Express,* January 5, 28, 1914; *Express,* January 5, 1914; *Tribune,* January 8, 29, 30; February 3, 1914; *Times,* January 6, 8, 23, 29, 1914. Engineer Robert V. Phillips has criticized Kahrl's flawed knowledge concerning the aqueduct, citing as one flagrant example his dismissal of Haiwee Reservoir as "a small settling reservoir the city proposed to build at Haiwee Point" (*Water and Power,* pp. 156, 200). The Haiwee (there is no Haiwee Point, Phillips points out) was from the beginning "a major and keystone element of the Aqueduct," constructed "in order to equate the variable flow from the north to the constant flow south." Built in a long narrow gorge, the reservoir stretches seven miles and when built had a capacity of 63,000 acre feet, "by far the largest reservoir in the Los Angeles water system until Long Valley Dam was finished in 1940." Phillips adds that although the Haiwee does provide a clarification function, that is "the icing on the cake—not the cake," so that Kahrl's misapprehension leads him to "attack Mulholland for failing to provide the very function Haiwee Reservoir was designed to—and does—provide" (Phillips, "Water and Power—Wm. Kahrl").

18. *Examiner,* February 17, 19, 24, 1914; *Express,* February 20, 24, 1914; *Times,* February 24; March 6, 1914; *Tribune,* February 11, 24, 1914.

19. *Examiner,* September 15, 1919; *Express,* August 12, 1919. Mulholland was to remain ever after touchy on the subject of the purity of aqueduct water. The daughter-in-law of Haiwee engineer Phil Wintz recalled that one hot day when she and her husband, Homer Wintz, were ranching in the San Fernando Valley in the 1930s she had spied from her house "Mr. Mulholland sitting in a car while [his son] Perry and [Wintz's son] Homer stood on the road discussing farm matters." Thinking that the old fellow looked warm and uncomfortable, she carried a glass of water out to him from her olla in the kitchen. One sip, however, and he spit it out, gave her one of his famous glares, and said, "This is bottled water!" (Lucy Wintz Allen, interview by author, Woodland Hills, California, April 15, 1983).

20. Fogelson, pp. 221–28; Ostrom, pp. 156–58; *Examiner,* February 28; March 20, 22, 1915; *Times,* March 3; April 1, 1915; *Tribune,* February 21; March 21, 1915.

21. *Examiner,* April 20, 29, 1915; *Times,* April 25, 1915; *Tribune,* April 24, 29, 1914.

22. Sitton, *Haynes,* pp. 124–25; Department of Water and Power, Clipping Book, vol. 11, May 1915. For an entertaining, albeit unreliable, account of Sebastian as mayor, see Adela Rogers St. Johns, *Final Verdict* (New York: Doubleday, 1962), pp. 487 ff.

23. *Examiner,* July 17, 1915; *Herald,* June 1, 1915; *Times,* May 6, June 10, July 17, 1915; *Tribune,* June 2, 9; July 17, 26, 1915. For the eighty-fifth anniversary of the aqueduct in 1998, Linda Colton, civil engineer with the Department of Water and Power, located the map in storage, cleaned it, and supervised its installation beneath a portrait of Mulholland on the executive floor of department headquarters.

24. *Examiner,* August 29, 1916.

25. Spalding, *History of Los Angeles,* vol. 3, pp. 177–78; *Times,* September 3, 5, 22, 1916; *Examiner,* September 21, 1916.

26. Department of Water and Power, Clipping Book, vol. 12, 1916–17; Ostrom, pp. 59–60; Perry and Perry, *History of the Los Angeles Labor Movement*, pp. 119–20; *Examiner*, September 21, 1916; *Express, Herald*, June 4, 1919.

27. Kahrl, pp. 234–36. Kahrl outlines a not altogether accurate version of the struggle for municipal power. His statement that "Mulholland's lack of expertise in the field of hydroelectric generation" was "politically convenient for him" (p. 235), while Scattergood was left to take the flak, is simply not borne out by the literature of the period. For a more accurate account, see Ostrom, pp. 63–64. *Record*, January 13, 30; February 1; March 30, 1917; *Times*, January 8, April 2, 1917; *Inyo Register*, February 1, 22, 1917; *Tribune*, March 30, 1917. Space limitations prevent a more detailed account of the struggle for municipal power, but it should be noted that a subtext to the controversy was the animus among various owners of city newspapers which resulted in varying treatments of the same story. Hearst's *Examiner* remained a champion of municipal ownership, while Otis-Chandler's *Times* favored only municipal water and opposed power. The *Record* (suspected at this time of being subsidized by the Los Angeles Gas and Electric Corporation, a leader of opposition to municipal water and power) constantly attacked an "invisible government" that seemed to consist mostly of those connected with the Progressives, especially E. T. Earl and his allies. The other dailies supported municipal ownership.

28. Department of Water and Power, Clipping Book, Box PR-56–886, June 2, 1917 to November 18, 1917; *Examiner*, June 17; July 8, 16, 1917; *Herald*, July 16, 1917; *Inyo Register*, July 16, 1917; *Record*, June 16, 18; July 16, 1917; *Times*, June 16, July 11, 1917; *Tribune*, July 15, 1917.

Wartime jitters doubtless played a role in the summer tensions of 1917, as a rash of violent events punctuated the season. At the same time as the aqueduct blowouts, a fire in Mojave at dawn on Sunday, July 15, wiped out a good part of the town, destroying the press office (where the fire began), the Miners' Union Hall, a general store, a dance hall, and the Postal Telegraph Building. Suspicions fell on the International Workers of the World ("Wobblies"), whose activities in Southern California had turned them into the easiest scapegoat when violence occurred. (They were at this time also suspected in two recent mysterious emptyings of Santa Monica's high-line reservoir.) Added anxiety about possible sabotage by the German enemy was heightened in mid-August when an unidentified airplane was discovered on a field in Lancaster (*Examiner*, August 11, 1917).

29. *Examiner*, July 17, 1917; *Tribune*, July 17, 1917. The proximity of the breaks to manholes raises an interesting speculation over a small squib in the *Record* (May 29, 1917) that reported Mulholland had ordered manholes with removable covers installed along the route so that desert dwellers and passersby could drop down a bucket on a rope and get a drink, but the pull of the stream was such that it could also pull in the bucket and the holder of the rope. After hearing a desert rancher say that when one tried to get water from the aqueduct it was "good bye, bucket," Mulholland had locked the manholes and installed hand pumps on top of them—perhaps also to forestall exactly the kind of violence that was to come.

30. *Record*, July 19, 24; August 11, 1917; *Express*, September 8, 1917. The *Record's* intemperate rhetoric subsided slightly the following year, after its edi-

tor of the previous two years, Dana Sleeth, had the misfortune of driving under the influence on Main Street the night of December 7 and colliding with the automobile of an attorney whose wife was injured in the accident. A suit against Sleeth resulted in his resignation from the *Record* in mid-December (*Record,* December 17, 1917; *Tribune,* January 24, 1918).

31. *Examiner,* January 8, 1919. Details of Mulholland's private life have been largely omitted here. It should be remarked, however, that between 1915 (the year of his wife's death) and 1921, his family underwent many turmoils and changes. His daughter Lucile made two rash and fleeting marriages, marrying her third (and last) husband in 1921. Her only child, Mulholland's first grandchild, was Lillian Sloan (born 1917), over whom a brief custody battle was settled amicably in 1920–21. Also in 1917 William's beloved brother, Hugh Mulholland, died after a long struggle with cancer. Oldest son, Perry, began to farm his father's San Fernando Valley acreage in 1916 and married Addie Haas, a descendant of valley pioneers, in 1921. William's second son, Thomas, fought on the front with the American Expeditionary Force in 1918, was gassed during the Battle of Argonne, and returned home at the end of 1919. Youngest daughter, Ruth, had a failed marriage in 1922 and eventually lived most of her adult life in New York. Rose, the oldest, remained at home and kept house for her father and brother, Tom. For brief vignettes of the domestic Mulholland, see my "Recollections of a Valley Past," in *California Childhood* (Berkeley: Creative Arts Book Company, 1988), pp. 179 ff., and *Owensmouth Baby,* pp.170–71.

32. *Public Service,* DWP, vol. 1, Nos. 4, 5, 6, 1917; *Examiner,* February 14, 1919; *Express,* July 25, 26, 1919; *Herald,* July 26, 1919; *Times,* March 2; July 24, 26, October 11, 1919; *Record,* July 26, 1919.

33. *Times,* December 21, 1919.

CHAPTER 21: A STORMY DECADE BEGINS, 1920–1923

1. Sitton, *Haynes,* p. 170.

2. *Examiner,* May 13, 1920; *Express,* April 26, May 4, June 2, 1920; *Herald,* April 6, 20, 1920; *Times,* April 6, 22, 1920.

3. *Examiner,* May 9, 12, 1920; *Herald,* April 1, 1920.

4. *Examiner,* August 10, 1920; *Bishop Index,* July 24, 29, 1920; *Bakersfield Californian,* August 3, 5, 1920.

5. Chief author of these articles was R. W. "Rube" Borough, whose managing editor, Bruce Knisely, along with B. H. Canfield (head of the board of directors of the Record Publishing Company), were later revealed to have heavy involvements in financial dealings with leading Owens Valley banker-businessmen (the Wattersons) in their fight against the city (See *Municipal League of Los Angeles Bulletin,* vol. 5, no. 3, October 31, 1927; Haynes Papers, Box 124, Folder 30, Knisely to Haynes, July 31, 1926). This connection helps to explain the sometimes baffling and contradictory positions the newspaper took on water and power issues; for instance, while attacking the city's alleged depredations against Owens Valley, it remained in favor of public power. Recognized as an advocacy paper that provided a countervoice to the major dailies in offering different perspectives on timely issues, the *Record* sometimes found itself in anomalous

stances, as when it supported the state Water and Power Act in 1922–23 but never mentioned that Mulholland was actively campaigning for it. As an exchange editorial, the *Record* also disseminated slanderous material that sometimes took circuitous routes. A charge that Mulholland planned to steal water from Owens Valley ranchers simply to supply Japanese gardeners in the south first appeared in the Tonopah *Daily News,* June 21, 1921, followed by its next appearance in the Bishop *Index,* July 8, 1921.

6. *Saga of Inyo,* p. 21; Chalfant, *Story of Inyo,* p. 373. One former Owens Valley landowner, George B. Warren, later stated his belief that the city had paid liberal prices and that many had been eager to sell. In 1933, now a resident of Los Angeles, he complained, "The city owns about 90% or better, of all town and ranch property in Valley, and I do not believe it has 2% influence politically. This is bad. The people of the [Owens] Valley vote for county purposes, and the City pays the taxes" (Haynes Papers, Box 124, Folder 1–24, G. B. Warren to Haynes, August 20, 1933).

7. Mulholland, Office Files, No. 1-File "E"—Elliott to Mulholland, May 2, 1922; Mulholland to Elliott, May 9, 1922; *Herald, Times,* February 26, 1921.

8. Even San Fernando land developers who were supposed to be benefiting from aqueduct water confirmed Mulholland's toughmindedness on the city's behalf. When H. J. Whitley, head of the L. A. Suburban Land Development Co., tried to get the city to bear some of the cost of connecting water lines to new services for recent land purchases in the southern half of the San Fernando Valley, he was refused and wrote in his journal of Mulholland and Scattergood, "The Scotchman Mulholland was sometimes mistaken for a Scotsman because of a slight trace of burr then remaining in his speech] and the man from Mr. Chandler's state, where they sell wooden nutmegs, are certainly the limit. They want someone else to pay the bills" (H. J. Whitley Papers, Box 16, Minutes of the Board Meeting, March 6, 1914). Whitley erred again; Scattergood was born in New Jersey; Harry Chandler in New Hampshire.

9. *Examiner,* January 9, 15, 1919; *Times,* February 13, 1919. Leading the rival groups were George Watterson and Edson F. Adams, attorney for private power companies. Mathews had wired, "If Eaton available and would not feel embarrassed in relations with friends neighbors in valley think his presence here advisable to secure harmonious adjustment hearing next Friday morning ten o' clock" (Mathews, WP01–70:13, W. B. Mathews to E. F. Scattergood, Feb. 1, 1919).

10. Mulholland, Office Files, WP06–1:8, May 15, 1923.

11. Hoffman, pp. 178–79; Kahrl, pp. 274–75; Layne, pp. 153–54.

12. *Inyo Register,* August 1, 18, 1923; *Owens Valley Herald,* August 1, 1923.

13. Owens Valley Historical Records, WP06–2:11, *Eaton Land and Cattle Co. vs. Owens River Canal Co.,* Mono Cty. *Bishop Index,* June 17, July 8, December 9, 1921; *Inyo Register,* July 19, 1922; *Owens Valley Herald,* September 21, November 30, December 7, 1921.

14. Mulholland, Office Files, WP06–2:11, January 20, 1922; *Owens Valley Herald,* March 29, 1922; *Inyo Register,* August 1, 18, 1923. For various versions and interpretations of these three groups, see Hoffman, pp. 178–80; Kahrl, pp. 278–81; Layne, pp. 158–59.

15. *Express,* June 1, 1923; *Inyo Enterprise,* July 26, 1923; *Owens Valley Herald,* July 12, 1923.

16. Mulholland Office Files, WP06–2:11; Lloyd Hampton, "An Irishman Moves West," *Success Magazine,* August 1923; *Owens Valley Herald,* July 12, 1923; *Examiner,* July 17, 22, 1923; *Herald,* July 23, 1923; *Inyo Register,* July 26, 1923. The issue of the dam site at Long Valley remains a bone of contention among various commentators (Hoffman, pp. 178, 193; Kahrl, pp. 245–52; Layne, pp. 212–13). R. V. Phillips has commented, ". . . the Long Valley reservoir was never an essential part of Mulholland's aqueduct plan. He recognized it was a good reservoir site and might be useful in the future and he would have liked to tie up the land for it at the beginning. Negotiations with Eaton, owner of the site, failed, so that when the Long Valley Reservoir and dam [Crowley Lake] were completed, both men were dead." Harvey Van Norman later oversaw construction of the 100-foot contour dam originally planned by Mulholland. It was dedicated to Fr. John J. Crowley, who had served as a peacemaker and advocate for the people of Owens Velley (Karl, pp. 361–66; Hoffman, pp. 261–62; Nadeau, pp. 132–33).

17. Bakersfield *Morning Echo,* March 5; December 16, 20, 1920; *Bakersfield Californian,* September 15; December 4, 16, 1920; *Herald,* December 21, 1920. For a good account of the Water and Power Act campaign, see Sitton, *Haynes,* pp. 164–65.

18. *Examiner,* December 12, 1922. For a discussion of Hearst's support of the Progressives' efforts for municipal ownership, see Sitton, *Haynes,* p. 167.

19. Mowry, pp. 289–90; Sitton, pp. 152–53.

20. *Examiner,* December 16, 1922; *Express,* December 20, 1922; September, 17, 1923; *Herald,* July 21, 1920; *Times,* February 25, 1921; Bakersfield *Morning Echo,* February 23, 1921. In 1924, Thomas Edison prophesied that "when man has exhausted the possibilities of oil as a fuel, and of water power as a source of energy, he will learn how to harness the sun, the winds, tides and growing vegetables, and to generate from them energy sufficient for all his needs" (*Record,* February 19, 1924).

21. Crail, *My Twin Joe,* pp. 354–56. In articles decrying the building of Boulder Dam, the *Times* skirted Mulholland's support of the project by directing its chief barbs at Mathews and Scattergood. The *Examiner,* enthusiastic about Boulder Dam and municipal power, ran frequent informative interviews with Mulholland by veteran journalist Joseph Timmons.

22. *Examiner,* June 12, 1923; *Herald,* June 11, 1923; *Times,* June 7, 1923.

23. *Examiner,* March 11, 1923; *Times,* March 23, April 10, 1923.

24. Mulholland, Office Files, 1–1923; *Examiner,* March 13, July 9, August 17, 1922; *Express,* January 30, 1922; *Herald,* March 15, 17, 25, 1922.

25. *Fresno Herald,* February 5, 1923; *Herald,* January 3, 13, 1923; *Times,* February 9, 1923. Actual construction on Mulholland Highway began in December, after voters approved a $1 million bond four to one in a tiny vote of 398 for, 89 against (*Examiner,* October 9, 1923).

26. *Examiner,* March 12, October 21, 1923; *Rochester, N.Y. Times-Union,* January 27, 1922; *Sacramento Bee,* October 18, 1923.

27. *History and First Annual Report,* Metropolitan Water District of Southern California, pp. 35–36. The Volney Craig case seems to have been yet another

attempt to stifle the development of municipal hydroelectric power. Representing himself as the head of a taxpayers' association, Craig had published a series of twelve letters in 1923 charging Mulholland with various incompetencies, among them the creation of a water famine, which also included the old chestnut about wasting good water into the ocean. These ran variously in the *Owens Valley Herald, Record,* and *Los Angeles Times.* In denying Craig's charges, Mulholland wondered aloud, ". . . as his only taxable property is a house and lot in Pasadena, it is hard to understand what his interest is." For two days, Mulholland testified that most valley ranchers were satisfied with the city's handling of irrigation water, and that so much aqueduct water had been used in the San Fernando Valley that the water plane had been raised to the point that the soil was saturated in many places. One reporter observed that although Mulholland raised a few smiles with his spirited replies, interest in the trial was minor, as one lone spectator observed besides the newsmen (*Express,* November 21, 22, 1923; *Times,* January 11, 1924).

28. *Examiner,* November 6, 1923; *Times,* January 11, 1924.

CHAPTER 22: BOULDER DAM AND DYNAMITE, 1924

1. Moeller, *Phil Swing and Boulder Dam,* p. 30; *Daily News,* January 5, 1924; *Examiner,* January 5, 11, 1924; *Herald,* January 5, 1924.

2. Department of Water and Power, Clipping Book, 1923–24; Hoffman, p. 245; *Daily News,* January 3, 11, 1924; *Examiner,* December 13, 21, 23, 27, 28, 1923; January 5, 11, 1924; *Herald,* December 20, 1923; January 8, 24, 25, 1924; *Record,* January 4, 1924.

3. Moeller, pp. 48–54, 154; *Examiner,* February 15, 1924; *Record,* February 15, 1924; *Daily News,* February 19, 1924.

4. Moeller, pp. 50–51; *Daily News,* February 19, 1924; *Examiner, Herald, Times,* February 16, 1914. For a good review of the Boulder Dam controversy, see Hundley, *The Great Thirst,* pp. 203–20.

5. Moeller, pp. 48–54, 157; Los Angeles Board of Public Service Commission, Clipping Scrap Book, February 18 to August 2, 1924, especially, *Daily News,* May 8, 1924; *Examiner,* February 16, 21; May 10, 1924; *Herald,* February 16, 21, 1924; *Times,* May 8, 1924.

6. *Examiner, Herald, Record,* February 21, 1924.

7. Los Angeles Department of Water and Power, Scrap Book, File No. PR 56–883: Crowley, "Open Letter to Citizens of Inyo," February 12, 1924; Layne, pp. 159–60. In expressing his sorrow that the Klan had come to Inyo, Father Crowley wrote, "No one knows better than the writer that the real reason for the coming of the Klan to this county was not religious, but rather a misguided attempt to solve the water situation, yet no one knows better than the writer either that many have joined the local Klan with full approval of its anti-Catholic platform." Some latter-day Owens Valley proponents have denied any Klan activity in the valley, but if there were none, why would the only Catholic priest in the area have bothered to sound such an alarm?

8. Mulholland, Office Files, WP06–3:12, 1922–1930. Mulholland to Mathews, February 27, 1924.

9. Layne, pp. 158–59; Mulholland, *Owensmouth Baby,* pp. 20, 175; *Inyo Register,* June 28, 1917; *Owens Valley Herald,* December 7, 1921; August 1, 1923; April 4, 1924. The Longyear property four miles southwest of Bishop consisted of 2,110 acres of land with 1,550 shares of stock in Bishop Creek and Rawson Ditches. A basin area, the land was heavily saturated with water. Longyear was asking $250 an acre, or $527,000. He sold to the city in August 1925, for $300,000 (J. R. Haynes Collection, Box 124, especially Folder 2–22).

10. *Record,* May 5, 1924; *Examiner,* May 7, 1924. The director of publicity for the public service commission had warned that the election would be bitter, even suggesting that it might be necessary "to directly charge a conspiracy of Power Barons against Los Angeles" (Haynes Papers, MacGillivray to Public Service Commission, March 7, 1924, Box 113, Folder 45).

11. *San Francisco Call,* March 20; April 1, 2, 19, 20, 22, 24, 26, 27, 29; May 1, 3, 1924. Kunze was evidently long active in public affairs in Owens Valley, for in December 1911, he had written Meyer Lissner in Los Angeles requesting his help in appointing "a progressive Postmaster in Bishop." Lissner had replied that he did not interfere in matters of this kind and suggested that Kunze seek help from Senator Works (M. Lissner Papers, Box 3, Folder 48, M. Lissner to C.E. Kunze, December 11, 1911).

12. *Express, Herald, Record,* May 21, 1923.

13. *Express,* May 22, 1923; *Times,* May 22, 1923.

14. Los Angeles Board of Public Service Commission, Newspaper Clippings, May 2 to August 19, 1924. *Daily News,* May 30, 1924; *Examiner,* May 25, 30, 1924.

15. Department of Water and Power, Clipping Book, PR-56–884. "Re. Owens Valley Settlers' Controversy," 1921–1928. *Inyo Register,* June 5, 19, 1924; *Owens Valley Herald,* June 5, 18, 1924.

16. *Inyo Register,* June 5, 1924; *Owens Valley Herald,* June 4, 18, 21, 1924.

17. *Fresno Republican,* September 1, 1924. The editorial was most probably the work of Progressive editor Chester Rowell.

18. *Examiner,* July 23 and August 1, 2, 1924; *Owens Valley Herald,* July 30, 1924; *Express,* July 30 and August 2, 1924; *Record,* August 4, 1924.

19. *Daily Journal,* August 7, 1924; *Examiner,* August 7, 13, 1924; *Times,* August 6, 13, 1924; *Record,* August 13, 15, 1924.

20. *Examiner, Herald, Times,* August 27, 1924.

21. *Examiner,* August 29, September 2, 1924; *Fresno Bee, Fresno Republican, Bakersfield Echo,* August 28, 1924; *Times,* September 2, 1924; *Record* and *Herald,* September 1, 2, 1924; *Herald,* September 2, 1924.

22. *Examiner,* September 2, 1924; *Fresno Republican,* September 6, 1924; *Herald,* September 8, 1924; *Inyo Register,* September 11, 1924; *Owens Valley Herald,* September 3, 10, 1924; *Record,* September 6, 1924.

23. *Times,* September 4, 1924; *Examiner,* September 7, 1924; Whitsett, *Success Is No Accident,* pp. 130–31.

24. *Examiner, Record,* September 5, 6, 7, 1924; *Herald,* September 6, 1924; *Owens Valley Herald,* September 10, 1924.

25. Mulholland, Office Files, WP06-1:8, February 23, 1924; March 3, 1925; *Times,* September 9, 1924; *Herald,* September 8, 1924.

26. *Herald,* September 8, 1924; *Times,* September 11, 1924.

27. Mulholland, Office Files, No. 1, September 25, 1924; *Owens Valley Herald,* September 10, 17, 1924; *Inyo Register,* September 11, 1924.

28. Mulholland, Office Files, No. 1, Mulholland to W. Mayo Newhall, September 27, 1924. *Express,* September 24, 1924; *Herald,* September 10, 1924.

29. *Examiner,* October 18, 1924; *Herald,* October 18, 23, 1924; *Times,* October 5, 1924.

30. *Times,* November 16, 1924.

31. *Owens Valley Herald,* November 12, 1924; *Times, Record, Herald, Examiner, Herald,* December 10, 12, 1924.

32. Hoffman, p. 185; Kahrl, pp. 292–93; Nadeau, pp. 85–90. *Owens Valley Herald,* November 19, 20, 1924; *Record,* November 18, 20, 1924. This oft-told episode may be found in many writings, of which the above are only a sample.

33. *Fresno Bee,* November 22, 1914; *Record, Examiner, Times,* November 19, 1924.

34. *Express,* November 20, 1924; *Record,* December 3, 1924.

35. Kahrl, p. 294; *Herald,* December 3, 1924; *Examiner,* December 4, 1924.

36. *Daily News,* December 28, 1924; *Examiner,* December 28, 1924; *Express,* December 26, 1924; *Record,* December 28, 1924; *Times,* December 27, 1924.

CHAPTER 23: MORE DYNAMITE, 1925–1927

1. McClure, "Letter of Transmittal," January 9, 1925; *Daily News,* January 21, 1925; *Examiner,* January 13, 1925; *Express,* February 3, 1925; *Fresno Californian,* January 19, 23, 24, 1925; *Inyo Register,* January 22, 1925; *Herald,* January 30, 1925; *Times,* February 3, 1925.

2. Department of Water and Power, "Facts Concerning the Owens Valley Reparations Claims," undated pamphlet; *Examiner,* January 11, March 26, 1924; *Express,* January 10, February 3, 1925; *Herald,* January 9, 1925; *Daily News,* January 10, 1925; *Fresno Californian,* January 19, 1925; *Inyo Register,* January 9, 1925; *Owens Valley Herald,* January 9, 1925; *Times,* January 9, 11, 20, 1925.

3. Ortega y Gasset, *The Revolt of the Masses,* authorized translation (New York: W. W. Norton, 1932), pp. 105, 115.

4. Hundley, *The Great Thirst,* pp. 214–15; *Examiner,* January 30, 1925; *Express,* February 3, 1925.

5. *Examiner, Herald, Times,* March 18, 1925.

6. Gottlieb and Wolt, *Thinking Big,* pp. 198–99; *Examiner,* June 2, 1925; *Record,* March 8, April 9, 1925; *Times,* May 5, 6, 1925.

7. *Herald,* July 20, 25, 1925; *Times,* June 30, 1925. E. A. Bayley had been a locating engineer for the Salt Lake Railroad and the aqueduct. In recommending him for the job of state engineer in 1911, Mulholland had described him as "a mathematical genius" (M. Lissner Papers, Box 3, Folder 45, Lissner to Hiram Johnson, October 14, 1911).

8. *Herald, Times, Record,* August 6, 1925; *Daily News,* August 7, 1925; *Examiner,* August 6, 9, 1925.

9. *Examiner,* August 12, 14, 1925; *Record,* August 14, 1925; *Times,* August 12, 1925.

10. *Examiner*, August 14, 1925.

11. *Express*, August 26, 1925; *Herald, Times*, September 15, 1925.

12. *Examiner*, October 25, 1925; *Herald*, October 27, 1925.

13. *Times*, December 6, 1925.

14. See note 9, chapter 22; *Express, Herald, Owens Valley Herald, Record*, August 5, 1925; *Examiner, Record, Times*, August 12, 1925. The *Owens Valley Herald* described the Longyear sale as "another chapter to the disgraceful story of how the City of Los Angeles is forcing the ruination of Owens Valley . . ."

15. *Daily News, Examiner, Herald, Record, Times*, September 1, 5, 18, 1925.

16. *Daily News*, August 23, 1925; *Examiner*, August 22, 1925; *Times*, August 16, 1925.

17. Mulholland, Office Files, WP06–1:8, Jas. Vroman to Van Norman, October 23, 29, 1924; Chas. H. Lee to Van Norman, October 30, 1925; Geo. Young to Mathews, December 15, 1925.

18. Mulholland, Office Files, WP06–1:8, Van Norman to Mathews, January 15, 1926.

19. Mulholland, Office Files, WP06–1:8, Van Norman to Mathews, January 15, 1926; Mathews to Shoemaker, March 3, 1926; Van Norman to Mathews, March 11, 1926.

20. Owens Valley Historical Records, WP06–2:11, April 6, 1926. Mortgage recorded May 8, 1926.

21. *Examiner*, April 6, May 13, 1926; *Express*, May 10, 13, 1926; *Daily News*, May 13, 1926.

22. *Daily News*, July 1, 1926; *Examiner*, July 1, 2, 1926; *Herald*, July 1, 1926; *Record*, July 1, 1926. In its continuing attack against the city's water men, the *Record* was the only local paper to report the relatively inconsequential blasting of the construction shed. An interesting letter in the Haynes papers further reveals that the connections between the *Record* and Owens Valley property owners were more than casual. In what is apparently a transcript of a conversation between Haynes and B. Knisely (editor and close associate of the *Record*'s publisher, B. H. Canfield), Knisely outlines the *Record*'s willingness to support the bonds in the upcoming city election if the board would agree to use the money ($600,000) to clear up "the purchase of remaining ranch land." Haynes Papers, Box 124, Folder 30, July 31, 1926.

23. Owens Valley Historical Records, DWP, WP06–5:9, Watterson to Eaton, December 31, 1926; *Saga of Inyo*, p. 124.

24. Owens Valley Historical Records, WP06–1:8, Van Norman to Mathews, January 10, 1927.

25. Owens Valley Historical Records, DWP, Watterson to Eaton, February 6, 1927.

26. Owens Valley Historical Records, DWP, Clausen to Watterson, February 16, 1927.

27. Owens Valley Historical Records, DWP, WP06–2:12, Van Norman to Mathews, February 3, 1927.

28. *Owens Valley Herald*, April 6, 1927.

29. Don J. Kinsey, *The Owens Valley Dispute* (Los Angeles: Department of Water and Power, 1927); *Big Pine Citizen*, March 12, 1927; *Examiner*, April 27,

1927; *Inyo Register*, March 31, April 7, 1927; *Owens Valley Herald*, March 9, 16, 23; April 6; May 4, 11, 1927; *Sacramento Union*, March 23–April 2, 1927. By year's end, an exchange of letters between Burton Knisely, editor of the *Record*, and W. W. Watterson came to light, further substantiating the connection between the newspaper and Owens Valley interests. Those implicated were not only B. H. Canfield, president of the board of directors of the Record Publishing Company, but stockholders W. D. Longyear and Andrae Nordskog, later a vociferous attacker of the city's water establishment (*Municipal League Bulletin*, vol. 5, no. 3, October 1927).

30. Department of Water and Power, Clippings Scrap Book, "Owens Valley Dynamitings," 1927; Department of Water and Power, Clippings Scrap Book, DWP, PR, 56–884, Out of Town Articles, 1927. For samples of the increasingly intemperate language emanating from Owens Valley, see the *Owens Valley Herald*, May and June 1927; the *Record* often reprinted these inflamed attacks.

31. *Daily News, Examiner, Express, Times*, June 1, 1927.

32. DWP, File No. 450–55, Mulholland to Federal Radio Commission, July 6, 1927.

33. Department of Water and Power, Clippings Scrapbook, DWP, July–August, 1927; *Examiner*, July 17; August 5, 13, 24; September 28, 1927; *Spartan News*, August 18, 1927.

34. *The Saga of Inyo*, p. 66.

35. *Daily News, Herald*, August 6, 1927; *Examiner*, August 13, 1927.

36. *Times*, September 2, 1927; *Examiner*, September 17, 18, 1927; Office Files, DWP, telegram from Haiwee to Hurlbut, September 22, 1927. The wire gives the sixteen machine guns' serial numbers.

37. *Examiner*, September 11, 1927. The most visible evidences of Mulholland's advancing age were hand tremors and a shuffled gait. Described in other writings as Parkinson's disease, it was never so diagnosed by his personal physicians. His maternal uncle, Richard Deakers, as well as his sons, Perry and Tom, suffered the same involuntary hand tremor, which our family unmedically referred to as "the Deakers Shake." Stress aggravated the trembling, yet my father recalled that his own dad could so control his unsteady hand that in executing a sketch, he was able, painstakingly and with tiny strokes, to draw a straight line that showed no sign of interruption. His later handwriting, however, with its wavering lines, betrays the condition, and I remember from childhood observing him shakily—yet deftly—carving a joint or roast fowl at family dinners. Until he suffered his first stroke in 1934, he always stood with his snickersnee in hand, ready, as a true Victorian paterfamilias, to do the honors of the table.

38. Addie Mulholland to Rose Mulholland, November 8, 1927. Letter in author's possession.

39. According to Robert V. Phillips, at 16,500 acre feet, Tinemaha Dam and Reservoir was less than one-tenth the proposed Long Valley Reservoir's capacity and was never intended as an alternative to Long Valley. As its purpose is operational, its normal condition is empty or near-empty (conversation, September 13, 1995).

40. Moeller, p.105; *Times*, December 9, 1927.

41. Mulholland to Rose Mulholland, January 10, 1928. Letter in author's possession.

42. Owens Valley Historical File, WP06-1:8, Mulholland to Mathews, February 13, 1928. The Long Valley matter was not resolved until 1933, when the city authorized the purchase of the Eaton property in Long Valley for $650,000 (see above file, November 7, 1932, January 13, 1933).

CHAPTER 24: THE SAINT FRANCIS DAM
DISASTER AND AFTER, 1928–1935

1. Parts of this chapter appeared in different form in my essay, "Mulholland and the St. Francis Dam," from Nunis, *The St. Francis Dam Disaster Revisited*, pp. 111–37.

2. The other reservoirs were Lower Franklin, Stone Canyon, Upper and Lower San Fernando, Encino, Sawtelle, Ascot, and Hollywood.

3. Layne, p. 186; Nadeau, p. 116; Rogers, "A Man, a Dam, and a Disaster: Mulholland and the St. Francis Dam," *The St. Francis Dam Disaster Revisited*, pp. 20–21.

4. Rogers, pp. 26–28. Rogers's discussion of geology and dam construction and his analysis of uplift theory and advanced methods of dam building since Mulholland's day are not detailed here, not only because of space limitations but because he has already covered them masterfully in his own writings. When recently challenged for his apparent vindication of Mulholland in an article by journalist Kermit Patterson ("Why Did the Dam Burst?" *American Heritage of Invention & Technology,* Summer 1998, pp. 23–31), Rogers commented, "That non-scientifically-trained historians can pass judgment on historic standard-of-care in civil engineering seems incredulous [*sic*] to me, but that's the world we live in" (Rogers to C. Mulholland, February 24, 1998).

Also invaluable to this subject is Charles Outland's pioneer study *Manmade Disaster*. Charles Outland was a Santa Paula native who as a youth had lived through the experience and devoted years to his study. See also Abraham Hoffman's critique of Outland's work in *The St. Francis Dam Disaster Revisited*, pp. 165–76. Of additional interest is the long narrative poem, "The Death of the Dam," by Charles H. Lawrance (privately printed, Santa Barbara, 1971, 1995). Lawrance, a consulting engineer, wrote this ambitious literary work before Rogers's work had been published. Since reading Rogers, he has remarked,"Someday I might even add 5 or 6 verses to the poem to recognize this aspect" (Lawrance to C. Mulholland, April 24, 1998).

An effective video recording on famous American floods (the Johnstown, the Saint Francis, and the inundations on the upper Mississippi in 1993) is "The Wrath of God: Torrents of Death" (Tower Productions, 1997.)

5. Nadeau, pp. 116–17; Outland, pp. 52–53.

6. For excellent and vivid accounts, see Nadeau, pp. 117–22 and Outland, chapters 6 to 10, pp. 79–139.

7. Clippings Scrapbook, DWP, "St. Francis Dam, 1928." Los Angeles County Coroner, Transcript and Verdict of the Coroner's Jury in the Inquest over Victims of the St. Franics Dam Disaster: Book 26902.

8. I am indebted to an old family friend, Raymond Orton, for having provided me with this eyewitness document. Orton, at this writing in his nineties and living in Upland, California, explained, "When the San Francisquito Dam failed . . . Daisy Shaw Orton sent a letter to my parents in Owensmouth [pioneer settlers in what is now Canoga Park in the San Fernando Valley] telling them of the tragic event. Mother sent the letter on to me and I have kept it in my files ever since." Raymond, a recent graduate of UC Berkeley, was living and working in San Francisco at the time. Orton to C. Mulholland, August 8, 1993.

9. Layne, pp.199–200; Nadeau, p. 122; Outland, pp. 178–79; Teague, *Fifty Years a Rancher*, pp. 182–85; *Times,* March 17; April 5, 1928; April 18, 1929. The city paid for the flood damages through a tax increase to its property owners (*Daily News,* August 29, 1928).

10. Rogers, *A Man, a Dam, and a Disaster,* pp. 83–84.

11. *Examiner,* April 20, 21, 22, 1928.

12. Moeller, *Phil Swing and Boulder Dam,* p. 111. *Examiner,* March 23, 1928.

13. Rogers, pp. 85–86. In September 1928, a motion picture director, David Horsely, fueled flood fears when he began to issue a weekly sheet, *Hollyood Dam News,* that called into question Mulholland's work and featured horror stories about cracks in concrete, other dam failures, and anti–Boulder Dam propaganda.

14. Telephone conversation with Lillian Darrow, 1988.

15. Plainfield, New Jersey, *Courier,* April 7, 1928; interview, William B. Mulholland, March 7, 1978.

16. *Examiner,* March 13, 20, 1929; *Record,* March 20, 1929.

17. William B. Mulholland, interview, March 7, 1978.

18. Mulholland, "Recollections of a Valley Past," *California Childhood,* pp. 179 ff; *Owensmouth Baby,* pp. 73–75. Such were the passions aroused by the Mulholland name that on the rare occasions when my mother and father traveled into Owens Valley and the high desert area they registered under my mother's maiden name in hotels or tourist accommodations. We children were never taken there, and my first visit was shortly after my marriage in 1949, when I was in my mid-twenties and had the protection of a new surname.

19. *Daily News,* May 12, 1931.

Bibliography

The following includes chief sources and influences. Further bibliographic material and commentary are to be found in the back notes.

BOOKS

Adamic, Louis. *Dynamite: The Story of Class Violence in America.* New York: Viking Press, 1931.

Annals of the Sunset Club of Los Angeles. Vols. 2 and 3. Privately printed, Los Angeles, 1927.

Armitage, Merle. *Success Is No Accident: The Biography of William Paul Whitsett.* Yucca Valley, California: The Manzanita Press, 1959.

Austin, Mary. *Earth Horizon: Autobiography.* New York: The Literary Guild, 1932.

Bancroft, Hubert Howe. *Works.* San Francisco: The History Company Publishers, 1890.

Baur, John E. *The Health Seekers of Southern California.* San Marino, California: The Huntington Library, 1959.

Bell, Horace. *On the Old West Coast.* New York: Wm. Morrow & Co., 1930.

Bell, Robert. *The Book of Ulster Surnames.* Belfast and St. Paul, Minnesota: The Blackstaff Press, 1988.

Bixby, Sarah. *Adobe Days.* Cedar Rapids, Iowa: The Torch Press, 1926.

Bonelli, William G. *Billion Dollar Blackjack.* Beverly Hills: Civic Research Press, 1954.

Brewer, William H. *Up and Down California in 1860–1864.* Ed. Francis P. Farquhar. New edition. Berkeley and Los Angeles: University of California Press, 1966.

Burdette, Robert J. *American Biography and Genealogy.* 2 vols. Chicago: The Lewis Publishing Company, [1907–1908?].

Burgess, Sherwood D. *The Water King: Anthony Chabot, His Life and Times.* Davis, California: Panorama West Publishing, 1992.

Busbey, L. White. *Uncle Joe Cannon.* New York: Henry Holt and Company, 1927.

Carr, Harry. *Los Angeles: City of Dreams.* New York: Grosset and Dunlap Publishers, 1935.

Caughey, John W. *California: A Remarkable State's Life History.* Englewood Cliffs, N.J.: Prentice Hall, 1970.

Chalfant, W. A. *The Story of Inyo.* Rev. ed. Privately printed, Bishop, California, 1933.

Chatterton, E. Keble. *Seamen All.* Boston: Little, Brown and Co., 1924.

Cleland, Robert Graves, and Osgood Hardy. *March of Industry.* Los Angeles: Powell, 1929.

Cooper, Erwin. *Aqueduct Empire: A Guide to Water in California: Its Turbulent History, Its Management Today.* Glendale, California: Arthur Clark Company, 1968.

Crail, Charles S. *My Twin Joe: A Romantic Biography.* Garden City, New York: Country Life Press, 1932.

Dumke, Glenn S. *The Boom of the Eighties in Southern California.* San Marino, California: Huntington Library, 1970.

Dunbar, Robert G. *Forging New Rights in Western Waters.* Lincoln: University of Nebraska Press, 1983.

Engh, Michael E., S.J. *Frontier Faiths: Church, Temple, and Synagogue in Los Angeles, 1846–1888.* Albuquerque: University of New Mexico Press, 1992.

First Annual Report of the Chief Engineer of the Los Angeles Aqueduct to the Board of Public Works, March 15, 1907. Los Angeles, California, 1907.

Fogelson, Robert M. *The Fragmented Metropolis: Los Angeles 1850–1930.* Cambridge, Massachusetts: Harvard University Press, 1967.

Freeman, Vernon M. *People-Land-Water: Santa Clara Valley and Oxnard Plain, Ventura County, California.* Los Angeles: Lorrin L. Morrison, 1968.

Gottlieb, Robert, and Irene Wolt. *Thinking Big: The Story of the Los Angeles Times, Its Publishers and Their Influence on Southern California.* New York: G. P. Putnam's Son, 1977.

Graves, Jackson A. *My Seventy Years in California, 1857–1927.* Los Angeles: Times-Mirror Press, 1927.

Grenier, Judson A., with Robert C. Gillingham. *California Legacy: The Watson Family.* N.P.: Watson Land Company, 1987.

Guinn, J. M. *A History of California and an Extended History of Its Southern Coast Counties.* Vols. 1 and 2. Los Angeles: Historic Record Company, 1907.

Hancock, Ralph. *Fabulous Boulevard.* New York: Funk and Wagnalls Company, 1949.

Hayes, Benjamin. *Pioneer Notes from the Diaries of Benjamin Hayes, 1849–1875.* Privately printed, Los Angeles, 1929.

Hine, Robert V., ed. *William Andrew Spalding: Los Angeles Newspaper Man.* San Marino, California: The Huntington Library, 1961.

Historical Record and Souvenir of the Los Angeles County Pioneer Society. Los Angeles: Times-Mirror Press, 1923.

Hoffman, Abraham. *Vision or Villainy: Origins of the Owens Valley-Los Angeles Water Controversy.* College Station: Texas A&M University Press, 1981.

Hundley, Norris, Jr. *Water and the West: The Colorado River Compact and the Politics of Water in the American West.* Berkeley and Los Angeles: University of California Press, 1975.

———. *The Great Thirst: Californians and Water, 1770s-1990s.* Berkeley and Los Angeles: University of California Press, 1992.

An Illustrated History of Los Angeles County. Chicago: The Lewis Publishing Company, 1889.

Kahrl, William L. *Water and Power.* Berkeley and Los Angeles: University of California Press, 1982.

King, Clarence. *Mountaineering in the Sierra Nevada.* New York: Charles Scribner's Sons, 1905.

Lavender, David. *California: Land of New Beginnings.* New York: Harper & Row, 1972.

Lloyd's Register of Shipping, 1870–1876.

Los Angeles Board of Public Service Commissioners. *Complete Report on Construction of the Los Angeles Aqueduct.* Los Angeles: Department of Public Service, 1916.

McGroarty, John Steven. *History of Los Angeles County.* 3 vols. Chicago: The American Historical Society, 1923.

McWilliams, Carey. *Southern California Country: An Island on the Land.* New York: Duell, Sloan and Pearce, 1946.

Matson, Robert Mayson. *William Mulholland: A Forgotten Forefather.* Stockton, California: Pacific Center for Western Studies, University of the Pacific, 1976.

Moeller, Beverley Bowen. *Phil Swing and Boulder Dam.* Berkeley and Los Angeles: University of California Press, 1971.

Mowry, George E. *The California Progressives.* Berkeley and Los Angeles: University of California Press, 1951.

Mulholland, Catherine. *Owensmouth Baby: The Making of a San Fernando Valley Town.* Northridge, Calif.: Santa Susana Press, 1987.

Myers, William A., and Ira L. Swett. *Trolleys to the Surf: The Story of the Los Angeles Pacific Railway.* Glendale, California: Interurban Publications, 1976.

Nadeau, Remi. *The Water Seekers.* Garden City, New York: Doubleday and Company, 1950.

Newmark, Harris. *Sixty Years in Southern California, 1853–1913.* New York: The Knickerbocker Press, 1916.

Nunis, Doyce B., Jr., ed. *The St. Francis Dam Disaster Revisited.* Los Angeles: Historical Society of Southern California; Ventura: Ventura County Museum of History of Art, 1995.

Ostrom, Vincent. *Water and Politics: A Study of Water Policies and Administration in the Development of Los Angeles.* Los Angeles: The Haynes Foundation, 1953.

Outland, Charles. *Man-Made Disaster: The Story of St. Francis Dam.* Glendale, Calif.: Arthur H. Clark, 1977.

Page, Henry Markham. *Pasadena: Its Early Years*. Los Angeles: Lorrin L. Morrison, 1964.

Perry, Richard B., and Louis S. Perry. *A History of the Los Angeles Labor Movement, 1911–1941*. Berkeley and Los Angeles: University of California Press, 1963.

Reagan, James W. *Report of J. W. Reagan, upon the Control of Flood Waters in the Los Angeles Flood Control District*. Los Angeles: Los Angeles County Flood Control District, 1917.

Robinson, W. W. *Lawyers of Los Angeles: A History of the Los Angeles Bar Association and of the Bar of Los Angeles County*. Los Angeles: Los Angeles Bar Association, 1959.

Sauder, Robert A. *The Lost Frontier: Water Diversion in the Growth and Destruction of Owens Valley Agriculture:* Tucson: University of Arizona Press, 1994.

Sitton, Tom. *John Randolph Haynes: California Progressive*. Stanford, California: Stanford University Press, 1992.

Smith, Henry Nash. *Virgin Land: The American West as Symbol and Myth*. Cambridge, Massachusetts: Harvard University Press, 1950.

Smythe, William E. *The Conquest of Arid America*. Rev. ed. Seattle: The University of Washington Press, 1969.

Somerville-Large, Peter. *Dublin*. London: Hamish Hamilton, 1979; London: Granada, 1981.

Southern Inyo American Association of Retired Persons, Chapter 183. *Saga of Inyo County*. Covina, Calif.: Taylor Publishing Co., 1977.

Spalding, William A. *History and Reminiscences: Los Angeles City and County California*. 3 vols. Los Angeles: J. R. Finnell & Sons Publishing Company, 1929.

Starr, Kevin. *Material Dreams: Southern California Through the 1920s*. New York: Oxford University Press, 1990.

Steffens, Lincoln. *The Autobiography of Lincoln Steffens*. New York: Harcourt, Brace and Co., 1931.

Stimson, Grace Heilman. *Rise of the Labor Movement in Los Angeles*. Berkeley and Los Angeles: University of California Press, 1955.

Taylor, Raymond G. *Men, Medicine and Water: The Building of the Los Angeles Aqueduct, 1908–1913, a Physician's Recollections*. Edited, with a prologue and epilogue by Doyce B. Nunis, Jr. Los Angeles: Friends of the LACMA Library with the assistance of Los Angeles Department of Water and Power, 1982.

Teague, Charles Collins. *Fifty Years a Rancher: The Recollections of Half a Century Devoted to the Citrus and Walnut Industries of California and to Furthering the Cooperative Movement in Agriculture*. Los Angeles: The Ward Ritchie Press, 1944.

U.S. Congress. Senate Report 928, Part 3 of the Special Committee of the United States Senate on the Irrigation and Reclamation of Arid Lands. Vol. 2, The Great Basin Region and California. Washington, D.C., 1900.

United States Patent Office Records, 1891.

Walton, John. *Western Times and Water Wars: State, Culture, and Rebellion in California*. Berkeley and Los Angeles: University of California Press, 1992.

Who's Who in the Pacific Southwest. Los Angeles: The Times-Mirror Printing & Binding House, 1913.

Wood, J. W. *Pasadena, California: Historical and Personal, a Complete History of the Organization of the Indiana Colony*. Privately printed, 1917.

Wood, Richard Coke. *The Owens Valley and the Los Angeles Water Controversy: Owens Valley as I Knew It*. Stockton, California: Pacific Center for Western Historical Studies, University of the Pacific, 1973.

Workman, Boyle. *The City That Grew, 1840–1936*. Los Angeles: Southland Publishing Co., 1936.

PAMPHLETS, THESES, ARTICLES, AND UNPUBLISHED MATERIALS

Blake, Donal S. "The Christian Brothers and Education in Nineteenth-Century Ireland." Unpublished master's thesis, University College, Cork; National University of Ireland, 1977. Program Library.

Brooks, Thomas. "Notes on Los Angeles Water Supply," 1938, typescript, Los Angeles Department of Water and Power Historical Records, Program Library, Ephemera Collection, Box II:8.

Davenport, Robert W. "Weird Note for the Vox Populi: The Los Angeles *Municipal News.*" *California Historical Society Quarterly* 44 (March 1965), pp. 3–15.

Derleth, Charles. Calaveras Creek Dam. Reports, Water Resources Center Archives. University of California, Berkeley.

Eaton, Mulholland, et al. "Wood Pipes a Failure." Pamphlet for Oakland Bond Election, 1905. Huntington Library, San Marino, California.

"Facts Concerning the Owens Valley Reparations Claims for the Information of the People of California." Los Angeles Department of Water and Power, 1926.

Hendricks, William O. *M. H. Sherman, a Pioneer of the Southwest*. Corona del Mar, California: The Sherman Foundation, 1973.

Hoffman, Abraham. "Joseph Barlow Lippincott and the Owens Valley Controversy: Time for Revision." *Southern California Quarterly* 54, No. 3 (Fall 1972), pp. 239–54.

———. "The Los Angeles Aqueduct Investigation Board of 1912: A Reappraisal." *Southern California Quarterly* 62, no. 4 (1980): 329–60.

Hoffman, Abraham, and Teena Stern. "The Zanjas: Pioneer Water System," undated, typescript, Los Angeles Department of Water and Power.

Layne, J. Gregg. "Water and Power for a Great City," 1957, typescript, Los Angeles Department of Water and Power.

———. "William Mulholland—Engineer, Pioneer, Raconteur," parts 1 and 2, *Civil Engineering* 2 (February and March 1941).

Los Angeles City Council Minutes. Los Angeles Archives.

McCarthy, John Russell. "Water: The Story of Bill Mulholland." *Los Angeles Saturday Night*, October 30, 1938.

McClure, W. F. "Letter of Transmittal Concerning the Owens Valley–Los Angeles Controversy." Senate, California Legislature, Sacramento, California, 1925.

McCorkle, Julia Norton. "A History of Los Angeles Journalism." *Annual Pub-*

lications: *Historical Society of Southern California, 1915–16,* vol. 10. Los Angeles, 1916, pp. 24–43.

Mulholland, William. "The Water Supply of Southern California." *Proceedings of the Engineers and Architects Association of Southern California.* Vol. 2. Los Angeles: Engineers and Architects Association of Southern California, 1907.

Phillips, Robert V. "Water and Power—Wm. Kahrl," typescript, November 18, 1997.

Pratt, Lowell Clark. "Theodore Roosevelt 'Discovers' California." *Journal of the West* 3, no. 1 (January 1964), pp. 40–46.

Rodriguez, Mary Louise Bine. *The Earthquake of 1906.* Privately printed, San Francisco, 1951.

Spilman, W. T. *The Conspiracy: An Exposure of the Owens River Water and San Fernando Land Frauds.* Los Angeles: The Alembic Club, 1912.

Spriggs, Elizabeth Mathieu. "The History of the Domestic Water Supply of Los Angeles." Master's thesis, University of Southern California, 1931.

Stowe, Noel J. "Pioneering Land Development in the Californias: An Interview with David Otto Brant." *California Historical Society Quarterly* 47 (1968), pp. 15–39, 141–55, 237–50.

Van Norman, H. A. "Memoir of William Mulholland." *Transactions of the American Society of Civil Engineers* 62, No. 8 (1936).

Wayte, Beverly. "Linda Vista Revisited." *Southern California Quarterly* 73 (Summer 1991), pp. 125–56.

Widney, Erwin W. "We Build a Railroad." *Touring Topics,* March 1931, pp. 36–41, 52–53.

MANUSCRIPT COLLECTIONS

Haynes, John Randolph. Papers. University of California, Los Angeles.

Lippincott, Joseph B. Papers. Water Resources Center Archives. University of California, Berkeley.

Lissner, Meyer. Papers. Stanford University.

Means, Thomas H. Papers. Water Resources Center Archives. University of California, Berkeley.

Mulholland, William. Office Files. 1902–1914. Also, Owens Valley Historical Documents. Los Angeles Department of Water and Power.

O'Melveny, Henry W. Journals. Huntington Library. San Marino, California.

Schuyler, James Dix. Papers. Water Resources Center Archives. University of California, Berkeley.

Sherman, Moses Hazeltine. Papers. Sherman Foundation Library. Corona del Mar, California.

Whitley, Hobart Johnstone. Papers. University of California, Los Angeles.

Willard, Charles Dwight. Papers. Huntington Library. San Marino, California.

NEWSPAPERS

Press Clipping Books, 1902–1942. Los Angeles Department of Water and Power.
Inyo Independent
Inyo Register
Los Angeles Evening Express
Los Angeles Examiner
Los Angeles Herald
Los Angeles Record
Los Angeles Times
San Francisco Chronicle
San Francisco Examiner

INTERVIEWS

(CASSETTES IN AUTHOR'S POSSESSION)

Mitchell, Frances. June 16, 1976, Berkeley, California; April 17, 1981, Fairhope, Alabama.
Mulholland, Joseph. April 16, 1978, Thousand Oaks, California.
Mulholland, William Bodine. March 7, 1978, Van Nuys, California.
Waith, Margaret Deakers. February 23, 1978, Los Angeles, California.

Index

AFL. *See* American Federation of Labor

Agricultural Park (*now* University of Southern California campus), 25, 220

Aguilar, Don Cristobal, 20–21, 26

AIB (aqueduct investigation board), 229; creation of, 207–8, 209; findings of, 210, 212–13, 225; Mulholland's testimony before, 222–23, 367n30; witnesses before, 224–25

Alabama Gates incident, 295–96, 314

Alembic Club, 213

Alexander, George, 178; aqueduct tour of, 192, 194; in bond sales negotiations, 188, 194; Harriman's loss to, 207; municipal appointments by, 164, 183, 184; on water and power issues, 197, 203–4, 361n13, 364n1, 365n15

Alhambra, 200

Allen, Lucy Wintz, 372n19

Alles, Fred L., 349n30

El Almuerzo de la Cabeza Tatemada (The Lunch of the Roasted Head), 58, 341n22

American Federation of Labor (AFL), 78–79

American Forestry Service conference (1899), 68

The American Magazine, 212

American Society of Civil Engineers, 136, 138, 145, 221

Anderson, James A., 51–52, 157, 159, 160

Anderson, L. M., 90, 149, 344n13

Andrews, Harry, 223–24, 367n32

Angeleno Heights Reservoir, 94, 344–45n16

Annexations: Eaton on, 101; map of, 217 fig.; Mulholland on, 94; Owens Valley proposed as, 292; of San Fernando Valley, 239, 258, 259; for use of water, 55, 200, 216, 263, 341n15

Antelope Division, 167

Antelope Valley, 107, 349n18

Antipicketing ordinance (1910), 189

Aqueduct. *See* Los Angeles Acqueduct; Owens River Project

Aqueduct bonds: and bond-selling difficulties, 164, 187, 188–89, 204, 211, 362n13; disbursements from, 147; election campaigns for, 118–19, 121, 122, 141, 150–52; voter approval of, 125, 152–53, 352–53n26

Aqueduct distribution system: compromise proposal for, 218–19; experts' recommendations for, 200; Harriman on, 202–3, 364n12; high line issue of, 200–201, 216, 222, 229–30, 258; Mulholland on, 194–95, 206, 224, 234; municipal power issue of, 250; Otis on, 234; voter's decision on, 226

Aqueduct investigation board. *See* AIB

Aqueduct right-of-way bill. *See* Power right-of-way bill

Ashurst (senator), 305
Aston, William C., 176, 185, 198, 232, 359n10
Austin, Frank, 106–7
Austin, Mary Hunter, 107, 271
Austin, Stafford, 107
Ayers, J. J., xv, 58
Azusa, 200

Backus, J. J., 240
Baker, Fred, 190
Baker Iron Works, 150, 190
Bakersfield, 268, 276
Bakersfield Californian, 268, 270
Baldwin, Leon, 25
Ballard, R. H., 284
Bancroft, Hubert Howe, 12
Bandini, Juan, 58
Barbara Worth Hotel (El Centro), 328, 329
Barker Brothers (furniture store), 345n22
Barnard brothers, 20
Bartlett, Louis, 276
Bayley, E. A., 165, 232, 303, 305, 379n7
Beaudry, Prudent, 54–55; private water venture of, 19–22
Beaudry, Victor, 19
Beaudry's High Reservoir (Reservoir No. 4), 20, 22, 25, 38, 101
Becker, Carl, 5
Bell, Horace, xv, 15, 19, 26, 31, 46, 49, 58
Bellevue Reservoir, 57, 356n21
Bellevue Terrace, 19–20
Belvedere, 101
Betkousky, Martin, 225, 240, 258
"Big Bill" dredger, 168
Big Freeze (1913), 228
Big Pine Creek, 241, 244
Big Pine Ditch, 282
Big Pine Property Owners' Association, 295, 309, 311–12
Big Red Cars (trolley cars), 45, 96
Big Rock Creek scheme, 146, 147
Big Tujunga Wash, 38, 56–57, 77–78, 116–17
Bishop: highway from Mojave to, 293, 294; Longyear's property in, 378n9; Mulholland's peace tour to, 292–93; reaction to Eaton in, 122–24, 129, 353n6
Bishop Index, 270, 274, 374–75n5
Bledsoe, Benjamin F., 302
Board of Public Works: Chaffee's appointment to, 160, 358n3; engineering appointments by, 135; Mulholland's relations with, 157; Owens Valley tour of, 128–30; and

Silver Lake's water rights, 160–61, 359n5
Boddy, Manchester, xv
Bonds. See Aqueduct bonds; Power bond elections; Water bonds
Bonus system, 166–67, 177, 190, 198, 360n17
Borough, R. W., 374–75n5
Boruff, Fred L., 246
Boston Globe, 248
Boulder Dam project, xvi, 274; Crail's support of, 278; Davis's support of, 282–83; inspection tour of, 294–95, 305; Mulholland's campaign for, 279, 280–81, 282, 283–84, 301–2, 308, 316–17; newspapers' positions on, 376n21; Swing-Johnson bill on, 282, 283, 291, 316–17, 325; type of construction for, 275; voter approval of, 286
Boyce, H. H., 336n2
Boyle Heights, 5, 38, 73, 91, 103
Bradbury, J. O., 344n13
Brady, Handsome, 37, 86
Brand, L. C., 99, 178, 207, 211
Brant, O. F., 350n4
Brauner, John Caspar, 366–67n26
Brimhall, C. L., 344n13
Broderick, William J., 27, 338n7
Brooks, Harry, 130, 131, 149, 170
Brooks, Thomas, 305, 344n13; Jenkins's clash with, 26–27; meter installation by, 345n20; on Mulholland, 42, 46–47; on Water Company, 28, 33; Water Company position of, 37, 338n7
Brown, Charles E., 344n13
Browne, J. Ross, 15
Brown's Canyon, 40
Bryan, William Jennings, 73, 168, 169
Buena Vista Pumping Station, 54, 87; infiltration gallery at, 82, 86, 91, 102–3
Buena Vista Reservoir, 22, 24, 25; capacity of, 67, 339–40n11; improvement projects at, 29, 31–32, 34–35, 40, 43, 339–40n11; 1913 draws on, 239
Building Trades Council, 252
Bullas, J. W., 344n13
Bunker Hill, 101
Burdick, Horace, 51
Burdick Block (commerical building), 45
Burns, Tom, 26, 338n7
Butler, Frank, 293

Cadillac Desert (Reisner), xiv
Cady, F. R., 344n13
Cahuenga Mining and Water Company, 56

Cahuenga Valley, 16, 56–57, 101
Calaveras Creek Dam, 221, 366–67n26
California Edison. *See* Edison Electric Company
California Hospital (Los Angeles), 162
California League of Municipalities, 144
California River Convention (1904, San Francisco), 109–10
California Supreme Court: on Pomeroy and Hooker case, 67; on river water rights, 55–56; on Water Company's contract, 67–68
California Water and Power Act (1921), 276–77, 374–75n5
Callison, Richard, 333–34
Calvert, Mellie A., 364n12
Campbell, J. H., 31
Camp tours. *See* Construction camp tours
Candy, H. A. T., 316
Canfield, B. H., 288, 374–75n5, 380–81n29
Cannon, Joseph, 132, 133
Carpenter, Ingle, 254, 257
Carr, Harry, 354n11
Carter, W. H., 344n13
Cast iron pipeline, 29, 337–38n10
Caswell, S. B., 41, 338n7
Caterpillar tractors, 168, 210
Catskill Water Project, xv, 136, 188, 248, 257
Caughey, John, 352–53n26
Celtic Club, 279
Cement: city's plant for, 157; Duryea's expertise in, 131–32; and faulty construction, 191, 363n18; Finkle on, 215; for substructural pipeline, 130–31; theft of, at Monolith, 229
Central Labor Council, 252
Chabot, Anthony, 356n22
Chaffee, Adna Romanza, 224, 248; on aqueduct completion date, 219; at aqueduct opening, 245, 246; aqueduct tour of, 192, 193; background of, 159–60, 358n2; on civil service requirements, 163; on contracts system, 166–67; on Desmond's earnings, 363n17; on food quality, 180, 181; on medical care, 162; municipal board positions of, 160, 358n3; retirement of, 227; and Warner, 212
Chaffey, George, 134, 144, 354n14, 355n19
Chalfant, William A., 192, 271, 273, 362n5, 363n20
Chamber of Commerce: and dam

disaster, 324; on Metropolitan Water District, 302; on municipal power, 252; opening festivities by, 244–47; tribute to aqueduct delegation from, 134, 354–55n15; water supply report to, 349–50n1
Chandler, Harry, xv, xvi, 166; on Boulder Dam issue, 278, 284; Henderson's suit against, 223–24, 367n32; land syndicates of, 97, 285, 350n4; marriage to Marion Otis, 341–42n3; on state regulation bill, 276–77; in Steffens's experiment, 204
Chandler, Marion Otis, 341–42n3
Charles Stern's Winery, 345n20
Charley's Butte (Owens Valley), 128
Chatsworth reservoirs, 40, 98–99, 261, 339n5
Chatsworth Tunnel, 99
Chinatown (film), 4
Chinese Massacre in Nigger Alley (1871), 15
Christian Brothers Schools, 8–9
Christian Science Monitor, 198
The Citizen (labor newspaper), 202, 204
Citizens' Water Company, 49, 54
City council: on commissioner appointees, 88–90; Mulholland's hearing before, 237–38; municipal waterworks proposals of, 51–52, 53–54; and Owens River project, 118, 119, 134–35, 146–48, 181; on Pirtle Cut, 56–57; purchase offers to Water Company by, 75–77; recalled member of, 104–5; Water Company investigation by, 27–28; Water Company's ties to, 21, 46; water lease agreement of, 19, 20–22, 61, 337n11; in water rates battles, 34, 59, 63, 70–71
City of Los Angeles v. Rowland and Van Nuys, 349n25
City of Los Angeles v. the Los Angeles Water Company, 48
City of Quartz (Davis), 329
Civil Service Commission, 89–90, 110
Civil Service Examination, 138–39, 156, 162–64
Civil War, 26
Clark, Charles W., 344n13
Clark, Eli P., 45, 96, 97
Clark, W. J., 312–13
Clausen, Jacob C., 106, 110, 111, 120; and Eaton's land deal, 273, 309, 311
Clearwater Tunnel accident, 220, 229
Clover, Samuel Travers, 117, 148, 153, 288–89, 351n10
C&M Company, 203

Code, William H., 200
Coffey, S. J., 336n9
Colorado River, 17, 242; domestic water
  district of, 302; exploratory trips to,
  271, 280–81; for hydroelectric power,
  282–83. See also Boulder Dam project
Colorado River Commission, 242
Colorado River Land Company, 350n4
Colton, Linda, 372n23
"The Coming Victory" (Socialist Party
  pamphlet), 202, 206
Committee of One Hundred, 69, 342n11
The Conspiracy: An Exposure of the
  Owens River Water and San Fernando
  Valley Land Frauds (Spilman), 214–15
Construction camp tours, 161–62,
  180–81, 185–86. See also Workers,
  aqueduct
Constructive Californians (Clover), 289
Contract labor, 70, 166–67
The Contractor (journal), 251
Cook, F. W., 344n13
Coolgardie Aqueduct (New South
  Wales), 116
Corcoran (Kings County), 202
Coronel, Antonio, 55
Cottonwood Creek (Inyo County), 129,
  219; Chaffey's appropriations on,
  134, 144; dynamiting incident at, 313;
  power plant site at, 127–28, 157, 165,
  193
Covina, 200
Crags, the (mountain retreat), 82
Craig, Volney, 281, 376n27
Crail, Joe, 278
Crescent City of Liverpool (ship), 12
Criswell, Ralph, 265, 290
Croton Aqueduct (New York), 31, 214
Crow, George F., 40
Crowell, J., 310
Crowley, Father John J., 285, 376n16,
  377n7
Cryer, George, 288, 289–90, 294, 298,
  300, 302
Crystal Springs, 23; bacteria count
  in, 93; collapsed tunnel at, 68–69,
  342n17; conduit system for, 36–37,
  49, 179, 340n2; legal controversy
  over, 24, 48–49, 61–62, 63, 71–72,
  341n2; percolation pipes project at,
  43, 339–40n11; Water Company's
  claims to, 24, 49
Crystal Springs Land and Water
  Company, 62, 63, 68, 71, 108;
  formation of, 24, 49
Culebra Cut of Panama Canal, 138, 241
Culver, J. P., 36–37

Dalton, E. H., 55
Darrow, Clarence, 204
Darrow, Lillian, 326
Davis, Arthur P., 152, 271, 294, 349n19;
  in Boulder Dam campaign, 282–83,
  305; and Lippincott, 106, 107, 108,
  350n5; on Owens River project, 151,
  210–11
Davis, Margaret Leslie, xvi–xvii
Davis, Mike, 329
Day labor system, 166–67, 360n17
Deakers, Catherine (née Thorpe), 12–13,
  361n19
Deakers, Ella (Mulholland's cousin), 13
Deakers, Richard, Jr. (Mulholland's
  uncle), 7–8, 12, 381n37
Dearborn Independent, 280
Dehy, William D., 249
Del Valle, Reginaldo, 58, 184, 213, 219,
  238, 257, 288, 290, 303
DeMille, Cecil B., 296, 298
Democratic League, 178, 361n13
Denver Post, 156–57
Desmond, Daniel Joseph, 180–81, 189,
  191, 197, 212, 361n19, 363n17
Dewey, George, 62
Dickson, Edward, xv, 160, 234
Dillon and Hubbard (New York law
  firm), 105
Diptheria epidemic (1903), 99
Dockweiler, J. Henry: Mulholland's
  correspondence with, 127, 186, 194,
  350n8; and Owens River project, 147–
  48; on San Francisco waterworks,
  171–72; on Water Company's value,
  53, 67
Doheny, Edward, 85, 91–92, 288
Domestic water: citizen complaints about,
  27–28, 31, 39, 54; city council's lease
  of, 20–22; controversial source of,
  24, 49, 61–62; metering of, 83–86,
  345nn20,24; oil refineries' threat to,
  91–92; private ownership schemes
  for, 19–20; water pressure demands
  on, 90–91, 346n6
Dominguez, Manuel, 17, 187
Dominguez Rancho, 187, 231
Dorward, David, 91, 166
Downey, John, 22
Drake, J. C., 344n14
Dredger invention, 168
Drought: of 1870s, 15, 16, 30–31; as
  mythical, 214, 347–48n1; and night
  sprinkling, 15; of 1903–1904, 99, 100
Dublin (Ireland), 8, 10
Ducommon, Charles, 338n7
Dunham, Stanley, 186, 316, 320

Durand, W. F., 283
Duryea, Edwin, Jr., 131–32
Dykstra, Clarence, 293

Earl, Edwin T., xv, 207; AIB testimony
of, 348n13; land syndicate of, 98, 224;
and Mulholland's mayoral prospects,
230, 234, 368–69n13; and municipal
power, 252; and Otis, 201, 364n9
Earthquakes, 261–62, 275, 330; safety
of pipes in, 130–31
East Bay Water Company (Oakland),
249, 370n1
Eastman, George, 324
Eastman, S. P., 366–67n26
East Side Springs Water Company, 49
Eaton, Alice (née Slosson), 134, 307
Eaton, Benjamin S., 24, 29, 30–31, 152
Eaton, Frederick, 32, 34, 77, 240;
and AIB investigation, 224, 225;
on annexations, 101; aqueduct tour
of, 192; background of, 29; Chaffey
compared to, 354n14; character traits
of, 44, 73–74; Chatsworth Park reservoirs of, 40, 98–99, 339n5; as city
surveyor, 38–39; civic/political activities of, 44–45; condemned profiteering
of, 122–24, 129, 353n6; critical of
Water Company, 35, 37, 61, 64, 71;
death of, 330; divorce of, 74, 92; on
dynamiting incident, 288; and Independent Civic League, 237, 238, 241;
and Lippincott, 108, 109, 110; Long
Valley land deals of, 169, 243–44, 272,
293, 306–7, 308–9, 310–11, 317–18,
382n42; marriage to Alice Slosson,
134; as mayor, 63–66, 342n10; Mulholland on, 223, 237, 245, 247; Mulholland's rift with, 169, 243–44, 292–
93, 370n33; at Municipal League
banquet, 120–21; municipal waterworks goal of, 51, 66, 69–70, 71–72,
73, 108, 343n30; Owens Valley interests of, 30–31, 82, 92, 105, 106–7,
113, 115, 348n13, 349n25; at Owens
Valley peace conference, 292–93;
in power right-of-way battles, 272,
273–75, 375n9; real estate commissions to, 147; San Joaquin Valley
expedition of, 72, 343n27; Water
Company role of, 26, 38–39, 338n7;
Water Department role of, 81
Eaton, George, 31
Eaton, Harold, 169, 272, 307, 360n21,
370n33
Eaton, Helena (née Hayes), 29, 92
Eaton, Mrs. Burdick, 311

Eaton Land and Cattle Company (formerly Rickey Ranch), 272–73, 275,
306, 317
Edison, Thomas, 277–78, 376n20
Edison Electric Company, 140, 161,
196, 355n19; city's rates versus,
266, 280; Colorado River interests
of, 284; McCartney bill of, 142, 144
Egan, Richard, 44
Elizabeth Lake Tunnel, 163, 168, 196;
completion of, 198; drilling records at,
176, 185; inspection tour of, 161–62;
miners strike at, 189
Elliott, G. E., 271
Elliott, John M., 82–83; Owens Valley
trip of, 121, 352n19; on Waldron
litigation, 79–80, 343n10; on water
commission, 89, 90, 344n14
Ely, Jack, 321
Elysian Park: reservoir project in, 90,
101; waterworks structures in, 50 fig.
Engineers: recruitment of, 127, 131–32,
135, 136, 138–39, 145; relocation of,
232–33. See also Workers, aqueduct
Engineers' and Architects' Society of
Southern California (1902), 82
Etcheverry, B. A., 356n21
Eucalyptus trees, 179
Evans (Glendale congressman), 317
Exposition Park, County Museum at, 242

Fairmount Reservoir, 157, 240, 241
Fall, Albert, 288
Fanning, G. F., 339n9
Faulkner, Frederick, 312
Fay, John J., 89, 90, 184, 352n19, 353n4
Federal Radio Commission, 313
Feliz Ditch, 20, 24
Feliz Rancho, 20, 24
Ferguson, James, 43
Ferguson, Lillie. See Mulholland, Lillie
Ferguson, William, 338n7
Feynes, Adelbert, 117
Fillmore, 36, 338–39n13
Finkle, Frederick C.: critical of aqueduct,
118, 119, 215, 250, 251, 355n19,
370n2; and Hooker-Pomeroy suit,
152; on municipal power, 250, 252;
professional background of, 351–
52n16; on surplus water issue, 216,
218–19
Fire hydrants, 34, 58–59, 67, 337–38n10
Fischer, Fred. J., 91, 344n13
Fishburn, John E., 307
Flanigan, T. F., 176, 232–33, 361n10
Flint, Frank, 128, 133, 134, 221,
354–55n15

Flint-MacLachlan Bill, 132–34, 354n12
Florence Nightingale Institute of Honor-
    ables, 330
Food concessions: concessionaire of, 180;
    food quality from, 185–86, 191, 212,
    213; prices of meals at, 180–81, 189,
    190, 197; total earnings of, 363n17
Forbes (engineer), 339n5
Ford, Henry, 280
Forster, Don Marco, 44, 45
Fountains: in Los Angeles plaza, 21–22,
    337n12; Mulholland's Memorial, 23
Foy, Mary, 32, 338n5
Franklin Canyon, 216, 219, 226, 254,
    371n10
Fredericks, J. D., 346n10
Freeman, John R., 135, 136–37, 139–40,
    164, 366–67n26
Frémont, John Charles, 16
Fresno Bee, 296
Fresno Republican, 289, 378n17

Garvanza (Arroyo Seco), 49, 84–85,
    341n15
Gasset, Ortega y, 301
Geronimo (Apache chief), 17
Gibbs, H. H., 344n13
Gillett, James Norris, 363n20
Gillette, J. W., 344n13
Gilmore, George T., 344n13
Glasnevin cemetery (Dublin), 7
Glasscock, Harry A., 270, 274, 308, 315
Glendale, 216
Glendora, 200
Gleniffer (ship), 10, 336n9
Goethals, George Washington, 252, 271,
    275
Gompers, Samuel, 203
Good Government. See Progressives
The Gopher (journal), 252
Graham, Margaret Collier, 14
Graham, S. C., 200, 216, 218, 224, 226,
    238, 258
Grant, Lewis A., 89, 344n14
Graves, J. A., 290, 296, 297
Gray, John, 144, 158, 176, 185, 198,
    220, 232
Gray, Louis, 220
The Great Thirst (Hundley), xiv
Greeley, Horace, 28
Green, "Mother," 291
Griffin, John S., 19–22, 24, 26, 29
Griffin, Louise (née Hayes), 29
Griffith, Griffith J., 92
Griffith Park, 36–37, 92, 110, 179
Grunsky, C. E., 126–27
Guaranty Trust Company (New York), 80

Haines, T. G., 344n13
Haiwee postmaster, 166, 360n15
Haiwee Reservoir, 130, 191; in Big
    Freeze, 228; leakage at, 240, 250, 264;
    Mulholland tribute at, 331; water
    purification in, 256, 257, 371n17
Hall, Leicester C., 270, 274, 290–91,
    293–94
Hamlin, Homer, 108, 157, 200, 358n32
Hammond, A. B., 98
Hanna, George, 55–57
Hanna, Phil Townsend, 46
Hansen, A. C., 176, 245
Hansen, George, 19, 20
Hansen, Henning, 342n10
Harding, Warren G., 276
Harkins, Pat, 37, 86
Harper, Arthur G., 140, 152, 158;
    appointment of Chaffee by, 159–60,
    358n3; aqueduct schemes of, 146;
    at Elizabeth Tunnel site, 161–62;
    mayoral election of, 141–42; Owens
    River trip of, 147–48; resignation of,
    163–64, 178
Harper's Weekly, 15
Harriman, E. H., 98
Harriman, Job, 150, 151, 201, 233;
    in mayoral race, 236; Mulholland's
    refutation of, 205–7; Socialist Party
    platform of, 202, 203, 364n12
Harrison, Benjamin, 44
Hart, Henry A., 237, 254
Harvey House (Mojave), 173
Hasker, Thomas, 7
Hatfield, Charles, 114
Hawgood, Harry, 57, 67, 349–50n1
Hayden, Carl, 280, 284
Hayes, Benjamin J., 29
Hayes, Helena, 29
Hayes, Louisa, 29
Haynes, John R., 213, 265, 293, 351n10,
    380n22; on civil service commission,
    110, 163, 164, 183; on municipal
    power, 252, 276, 277; and recall
    election, 104–5
Hazard, Henry T., 49, 94, 192
Hearst, William Randolph, xv, 116
Heinly, Burt, 174, 180, 187, 262
Hellman, H. W., 58
Hellman, I. W., 52, 58, 76
Hellman, Marco H., 188
Helsey, C. F., 122
Henderson, Frank, 218, 223, 238
Henry, S. T., 185–86, 187
Herlihy, John, 344n13
Herriman, George, 151, 357–58n19
Herrman, F. C., 366–67n26

Hession, Jess, 310
Hetch Hetchy project (San Francisco), 247, 281
Hewitt, Leslie, 144, 186
Hicknell, F. T., 72, 343n27
Highland Park, 341n15
Highland Water Company, 49
High line distribution, 216, 258; contract plan for, 218–19; Mulholland's opposition to, 218, 221–22, 224, 229–30, 234; voter approval of, 226
Hill, Louis G., 295
Hitchcock, Ethan A., 126–27, 128, 132, 354n11
Hittell, John S., 18
Hobson, Uncle (relative of Deakers family), 12
Hoffman, Abraham, xiv, 348n17
Holgate, William, 346n6
Hollenbeck Park (Boyle Heights), 73
Hollister, William Welles, 28
Hollywood, 94, 97–98
Hollywood Dam News (weekly sheet), 383n13
Hollywood Reservoir, 320, 325
Hollywood Union Water Company, 255, 258
Holt, Benjamin, 168
Holt, L. M., 16
Hooker, J. D., 53, 152
Hooker and Pomeroy case, 53–54, 67, 80, 108, 148, 152
Hoover, Herbert, 279
Horner, John, 344n13
Horsely, David, 383n13
Houghton, Arthur D., 125, 153, 351n10; and McAleer, 353n4; on Owens River project, 118–20, 128, 351n14
Howard, Burt Estes, 349n30
Howard, Frank H., 337n3
"How to Beat the Socialists" (Steffens), 365n17
Hubbard, A. A., 157
Hughes, W. M., 344n13
Humphreys, William, 189
Hundley, Norris, xiv
Hunt, George C., 98
Huntington, Henry E., 45, 96, 98, 113
Hurlbut, W. W., 294
Hyde, Charles Gilman, 257
Hydraulic sluicing innovation, 138, 156, 356n22, 366–67n26
Hydroelectric power: from Colorado River, 271, 282–83; at Cottonwood site, 127–28, 157, 165, 193; debate on ownership of, 196–97, 252, 260, 364n1, 371n7; Mulholland's support

of, 277–78; from Owens River project, 139, 140, 186, 196–97. See also Municipal power
Hygiene practices. See Public health

Ihm, E., 344n13
Imperial Valley, 113, 350n4
Imperial Valley News, 114
Imperial Valley Press, 166
"The Impounding of Flood Waters" (Schuyler), 114
Independence (Inyo County), 123, 193–94, 231
Independent Civic League, 237–38, 241, 252, 253
Indianapolis Journal, 53
Infiltration gallery, 82, 86, 91–92, 102–3
Inman, Joe, 310, 311, 312
International Order of Odd Fellows (IOOF), 32, 338n6
International Workers of the World (IWW), 287, 373n28
"Into the Future" (municipal film), 279
Inyo County taxes, 271, 375n6
Inyo Register, 185, 190, 192, 261, 270–71, 275, 285
IOOF (International Order of Odd Fellows), 32, 338n6
Ireland: Mulholland's ancestors in, 6–8, 336n3; Mulholland's boyhood in, 8–10
Irrigation water: extra-municipal petitions for, 55–56, 93–94; municipal control of, 24, 55–57; Owens River as source of, 132–34; theft of, 24–25, 56–57; Water Company's depletion of, 76
Isthmian Canal Commission, 138
Ivanhoe (real estate tract), 43, 340n12; reservoir project of, 137–38, 201, 356n21
IWW (International Workers of the World), 287, 373n28

Jackson, Helen Hunt, 337n12
Jacques, H. L., 302
Japanese immigrants, 353–54n10
Jawbone Division, 219; cost of, 164; day labor system of, 166–67; fatal accident on, 229; mule teams of, 175–76; 1909 progress on, 171; obstacles to, 164–66; tunnel drilling on, 176, 181–82
Jenkins, Charles, 26–27
Jenkins, William, 27
Jenner vaccine, 14
Johnson, Edward, 227, 367n40

Johnson, Hiram, 184, 201, 278, 284
Jordan, David Starr, 252
Jordan, Edwin O., 257
Joyce, James, 7, 9, 10
Joyce, John, 9

Kahrl, William, xiv, 340n2, 348n17,
  351n10; on Eaton's post-mayoral
  plans, 343n30; on Haiwee Reservoir,
  371n17; on municipal power, 373n27;
  on mythical drought, 347–48n1; on
  1905 bond election, 352–53n26; on
  1910 bond sales, 362n13; on role of
  Progressives, 352n2
Kays, James C., 88
Kelley, W. J., 35, 37
Kelly, Allen, 160, 240, 353n6; on Mul-
  holland's abilities, 177; on Owens
  River project, 154, 176–77, 355n19,
  355–56n20; professional background
  of, 355n19
Kemp, John, 277
Kenealy, John, 58
Kenilworth (real estate tract), 43
Kent, William, 276
Keough, Carl, 305, 308
Kerckhoff, W. G., 98
Kern, Edward, 116
Kester Ranch fire (1878), 16
Keys, Asa, 324
Killian, J. A., 123
Kimball, George H., 344n13
King, A. J., 21
King, F. W., 344n14
Kings River Valley, 72, 343n27
Kinsey, Don, 312
Knapp, M. A., 349n18
Knickerbocker, Niles, 90, 344n13
Knisely, Bruce, 374–75n5, 380nn22,29
Knox, George C., 39
Koebig, A. H., 108, 161, 355n19
Koepfli, J. O., 354nn12,15
Kountze Brothers (New York), 164
Kuhrts, G. J., 317
Kuhrts Street Bridge, 39
Ku Klux Klan, 285, 377n7
Kunze, Court E., 270, 286–87, 312,
  378n11

Labor, organized, 126; on aqueduct
  bonds, 150; and miners' strike, 189,
  190–91, 197–98; on municipal power,
  252, 261; on municipal water, 78–79;
  and railway strike, 98; Socialist Party's
  ties to, 201–2, 371n7; Times versus
  Examiner on, 118, 351n10
Lacy, William, 190, 305

Lacy Manufacturing Company, 190
LaRue, C. A., 305
Lawler, Oscar, 116, 117, 359n5
Lawrance, Charles H., 382n4
Lawson, Andrew, 366–67n26
Lazard, Solomon, 19–22, 338n7
Leach and Company (New York), 164
Leahey, Ed, 312; in car accident, 313; as
  emissary to Owens Valley, 271, 274,
  275; threats against, 287–88, 291
Leake, Edward, 344n13
LeConte, Joseph, 17
Lee, Henry T., 184, 189, 213, 295,
  352n18, 358n3
Leete, Ben, 315
Leonard, Ethel Langdon, 93, 254–55,
  256, 371nn13,14
Life (magazine), 4
Limoneira Ranch (Santa Paula), 323
Lincoln, Abraham, 9
Lippincott, J. A., 142
Lippincott, Joseph B., xvi, 77, 120,
  221, 224, 236, 339n9, 366–67n26;
  at aqueduct opening, 245, 246;
  aqueduct tour of, 192; Bishop's
  condemnation of, 129, 353n6; civil
  service examination of, 163–64; and
  Colorado River project, 242, 305;
  commissioner appointment of, 183;
  conflicting allegiances of, 113–14,
  117, 127–28, 183, 350n5; and dam
  disaster, 324; and federal reclamation
  prospects, 106, 109, 110, 126;
  Mulholland's correspondence with,
  119, 124, 127–28, 349–50n1; and
  Mulholland's honorary award, 371n8;
  on municipal water, 69; and Owens
  River project, 134, 136–37, 142,
  147–48, 150, 232; professional background of, 105–6, 107–8; San Fernando Valley surveys by, 67, 71; San
  Joaquin Valley expedition of, 72,
  343n27; at silver spike ceremony, 192;
  at Simpson Auditorium rally, 152; on
  timber laws, 68
Lippincott, Josephine (née Cook), 107
Lippincott, Joseph Reading, 110
Lippincott, Rose, 107
Lissner, Meyer: and Kunze, 378n11; on
  municipal power, 151–52, 197, 364n1;
  and Sherman's removal, 183–84; supportive of Mulholland, 205, 230, 252,
  365n18, 368nn5,13, 371n8; and
  Warner, 210, 212
Little Lake break (1917), 262, 373n29
Llewellyn, John, 190
Llewellyn, William, 58

Llewellyn Iron Works, 190
Lodging House Association, 70
Loetchberg Tunnel (Switzerland), 361n10
Loewenthal, Henry A., 116, 119, 224–25
Lone Pine earthquake (1872), 131
Long Beach, 216
Long Valley (Owens Valley), 105; Eaton's
   land deals in, 243–44, 272, 293, 306–
   7, 308–9, 310–11, 317–18, 382n42;
   federal government's interest in, 109,
   110, 114; reservoir construction issue
   in, 123, 240, 272, 273–74, 275, 287,
   292, 376n16
Longyear, David, 285
Longyear, William D., 285, 380–81n29;
   land sale of, 305–6, 314, 378n9,
   380n14
Lopez, Don Antonio, 77
Los Angeles: annexations to, map of, 217
   fig.; Big Freeze of 1913 in, 228; Con-
   federate sentiments of, 26; drought
   problems of, 15, 16, 30–31, 99, 100;
   dust in, 34; Eaton's suit against, 275;
   first land boom in, 38; first metered
   water of, 345n20; heterogenous cul-
   tures of, 16, 32–33; Inyo County taxes
   on, 271, 375n6; in land purchase controversy, 243–44, 274–75, 285–86,
   290, 299–300, 305–6, 305–9, 310–
   11, 317–18, 380n14, 382n42; and
   Long Valley dam issue, 240, 272,
   273–74, 275, 287, 292, 376n16; Los
   Angeles River water rights of, 24,
   55–57, 104, 206; map of Greater, 267
   fig.; Mulholland's journey to, 12–13;
   Owens Valley media attacks on, 268,
   270–71, 274, 286–87; Panic of 1907
   in, 156, 158; plaza fountain of, 21–22,
   337n12; San Fernando Valley water
   rights of, 182; surplus water rights
   of, 194–95, 200–201, 206, 215–16,
   218–19; Tujunga Wash stragegy of,
   77–78; Water Company purchased
   by, 76–80; Water Company sued by,
   48, 49, 75, 108; water consumption
   record in, 239; water distribution
   facilities in, 332 fig.; Watterssons's suit
   against, 229. See also Annexations
Los Angeles Aqueduct: Alabama Gates
   incident at, 295–97; construction
   inventory from, 232; and demand for
   reparations, 297, 300, 312; dynamite
   attacks on, 287–88, 289, 308, 312–
   13, 314, 380n22; Finkle's criticism of,
   250, 251; maps of, 143 fig., 155 fig.;
   Mulholland's relief map of, 259,
   372n23; newspaper coverage of,

247–48; 1917 blowouts on, 261–63,
   373n28; opening ceremonies of, 231,
   241–42, 243–47; rains' damage to,
   251, 303; security directives for, 313,
   315; seventy-fifth anniversary of,
   340n13; terminus of, 206, 207. See
   also Aqueduct bonds; Aqueduct
   distribution system; Owens River
   project; Workers, aqueduct
Los Angeles Canal and Reservoir
   Company, 20, 24
Los Angeles City Water Company. See
   Water Company
Los Angeles City Water Department. See
   Water Department
Los Angeles Clearing House Association,
   296–97, 299–300
Los Angeles Consolidated Electric
   Railway, 97
Los Angeles Daily Herald, 336n2
Los Angeles Daily Star, 14
Los Angeles Department of Water
   and Power, xvii, 327. See also Water
   Department
Los Angeles Evening Express, 34, 85–86,
   336n2, 338n12
Los Angeles Evening News, 203; anti-
   aqueduct stance of, 117, 127, 134,
   136, 140, 153; attacks on Mulholland
   in, 135, 148–49, 150, 355–56n20,
   357n11; financial backers of, 351n10;
   on Schuyler's appointment, 135; on
   Simpson Auditorium debate, 151
Los Angeles Examiner: on Boulder Dam
   project, 325, 376n21; on Eaton, 124;
   eucalyptus article in, 179; Finkle's
   letter in, 250; on Harper, 146; on
   Harriman, 204; on Houghton, 118;
   on miners' strike, 190–91; on municipal ownership, 373n27; in newspaper
   rivalries, 116; on 1910 bond sales,
   188; on Owens River project, 112,
   117, 119, 140, 351n10
Los Angeles Express, 160, 222, 226,
   234, 274, 336n2
Los Angeles Gas and Electric Company,
   199, 262
Los Angeles Herald: on Buena Vista
   leaks, 103; on Houghton, 118; on
   Howard, 337n3; on Jenkins, 27; on
   Mulholland's vacation, 104–5; in
   newspaper rivalries, 116; on 1910
   bond sales, 188; on Pendleton bill,
   115; on sale of Water Company, 52,
   340–41n8; on Moses Sherman, 97;
   on water commission, 95
Los Angeles Mirror, 336n2

Los Angeles–Pacific Railway Company,
    89, 97, 103
Los Angeles Record: on Alabama Gates
    incident, 296; on aqueduct investiga-
    tion, 219, 367n30; contradictory
    positions of, 374–75n5; critical of
    aqueduct, 236, 262–63, 289, 370n2,
    373–74n30; critical of Mulholland,
    160, 261, 268, 327, 367n30; on
    Harper, 140, 146, 356n27; on land
    speculators, 355n19; on miners' strike,
    190, 191; on municipal power, 140,
    197, 252, 260–61, 373n27; on Owens
    River water, 232, 254; Owens Valley
    ties of, 380nn22,29; on water com-
    mission, 199
Los Angeles River, 275; bacteria count in,
    93; city's legal rights to, 24, 55–57,
    104, 206; Crystal Springs waters of,
    24, 48–49, 61–62; origin and water-
    shed of, 24; salt content explorations
    of, 71; theft of water from, 24–25,
    56–57; zanja system of, 18. *See also*
    Zanja system
Los Angeles Star, 336n2
Los Angeles Times, 51; on Beaudry,
    55; bombed building of, 189, 201,
    363n16, 364n9; on Boulder Dam
    project, 278, 376n21; on Clover,
    149; on dynamiting incident, 287;
    on Eaton, 63, 64, 74, 342n10; on
    Eaton family, 340n13; Henderson's
    suit against, 223–24, 367n32; on
    Houghton, 118; on Metropolitan
    Water District, 302; on miners' strike,
    190; *Mirror* becomes, 336n2; on Mul-
    holland as mayor, 234; on municipal
    power, 252, 260–61, 276–77, 278–
    79, 286, 373n27; in newspaper
    rivalries, 116, 351n10; on Owens
    River project, 115, 116, 152–53,
    352–53n26, 354n11; on Perry resi-
    dence, 340n17; on railway strikers,
    98; on Sherman's removal, 184; on
    Waldron litigation, 79; on Water
    Department, 87
Los Angeles Tribune, 212, 234
Los Feliz Ditch, 20, 24
Los Feliz Point, 102
Los Feliz Rancho, 20, 24
The Lost Frontier (Sauder), xiv
Lummis, Charles F., 279, 349n30
Lungren, Fernand, 110
Lynch, J. D., xv

Macedo, Lillian Sloan (Mulholland's
    granddaughter), 32, 374n31

MacLachlan, James, 132, 133, 354–
    55n15
Maclay, Charles, 98
Maclay waterworks, 113
Mail service, 165–66
Mammoth (Mono County), 154
Manhole covers, 262, 373n29
Manzanar Tract, 290
Markham, Edwin C., 58
Marshall, Robert, 276
Martin, John T., 273, 274–75
Massarene, viscount, 6
Mathews, John R., 184
Mathews, William B., 153, 224, 294,
    295, 354n12, 368–69n13; as aque-
    duct's legal adviser, 134, 357n3; bond-
    selling missions of, 80, 187, 211; in
    Boulder Dam campaign, 283, 309,
    316, 380; death of, 327–28; and
    Eaton's land deal, 306, 307, 317–18;
    on Eaton's land profit, 124; lawsuits
    by, as city attorney, 86–87, 104,
    347n26; Mulholland on, 247, 250–
    51; and municipal ownership, 75, 76,
    186, 265–66, 268; and Owens River
    project, 105, 115, 121, 128, 134, 142,
    144; Owens Valley peace tour of, 291,
    292; on Pendleton Eminent Domain
    Bill, 115; and right-of-way bill, 272,
    375n9; at Soda Company's trial,
    242–43; and Water Department's
    administration, 87; at water purity
    trial, 256, 258
Matson, Robert, xvi
McAdoo, William Gibbs, 280
McAleer, Owen, 115, 128–30, 353n4
McCarthy, John Russell, 4–5
McCartney bill, 142, 144
McClure, W. S., 296, 299, 305
McClure Report (1925), 296, 299, 301,
    305
McGregor, D., 35
McKay, Roderick, 232, 240, 245, 287,
    303, 315
McKinley, William, 62, 73, 79
McNally Ditch, 274–75, 286, 290
McNamara trial, 201, 202, 204–5
McWilliams, Carey, 352–53n26
Mead, Elwood, 108, 276, 324
Mead, William, 89
Means, Thomas H., 71, 109, 110, 111
Medical department, 162, 167, 363n17
Mendenhall, Walter C., 114, 135, 350n5,
    359n5
Merchants and Manufacturers' Associa-
    tion, 78, 189
Mesmer, Joseph, 343n7

Meters: on Buena Vista sewer lines, 103; first installation of, 345n20; Mulholland's proposal of, 82, 83–85; opposition to, 85–86, 345n24; "Water Waste" paper on, 114
Metropolitan Life Insurance Company, 188
Metropolitan Water District Act, 302, 312
Miles, Charles E., 29, 337–38n10
Miners' strike, 189, 190–91, 197–98
Mission Land Company, 178
Mix, Tom, 296, 297–98
Mojave: climate of, 172; disreputable establishments of, 172–74; highway from, to Bishop, 293, 294; livestock needs of, 144; 1917 fire in, 373n28
Mojave River, 136, 161, 349–50n1
Mono County, right-of-way battle in, 242, 268, 272, 375n9
Morse, H. C., 117
Mosher, Ed, 31
Mott, S. H., 53, 80, 338n7
Mountain Water Company, 49, 75
Mowry, George E., 277, 368–69n13
Muir, John, 121, 150–51
Mules, 168, 174–76, 219, 228–29
Mulholland, Addie (née Haas), 315–16, 374n31
Mulholland, Ellen (née Deakers, Mulholland's mother), 6, 7, 8
Mulholland, Hugh (Mulholland's father), 6–7, 8
Mulholland, Hugh Patrick (Mulholland's brother), 6, 10, 11–13, 17, 31–32, 374n31
Mulholland, Irving (newspaper editor), 129
Mulholland, Jane (née Smith, Mulholland's stepmother), 9
Mulholland, Joseph (Mulholland's stepbrother), 9
Mulholland, Lillie (née Ferguson, Mulholland's wife), 5, 42–43, 234, 243, 258–59
Mulholland, Lucile (Mulholland's daughter), 5, 243, 374n31
Mulholland, Mary (Mulholland's niece), 357–58n19
Mulholland, Mary (Mulholland's stepsister), 9
Mulholland, Michael (Mulholland's stepbrother), 9
Mulholland, Patrick (Mulholland's grandfather), 6
Mulholland, Richard James (Mulholland's son), 350n8

Mulholland, Rose Ellen (Mulholland's daughter), 11, 234, 266, 316, 374n31; at aqueduct ceremonies, 243; birth of, 43; on dam disaster, 319; in Mulholland's last years, 5, 330; on Mulholland's traits, 266, 345n22
Mulholland, Ruth (Mulholland's daughter), 374n31
Mulholland: The Dream-Builder (documentary film), 333
Mulholland, Thomas (Mulholland's brother), 6, 8–9
Mulholland, Thomas Ferguson (Mulholland's son), 43, 154, 374n31, 381n37
Mulholland, William: ancestry/origins of, 6–8, 44, 336n6; awards/recognitions of, 4, 23, 42, 134–35, 144–45, 245, 246–47, 252–53, 276, 280, 294, 302, 330, 354–55n15, 371n8, 376n25; boyhood of, 8–10; in British Merchant Marine, 10–11; with Deakers family, 11–12; death of, 330–31; and death of son, 350n8; and death of wife, 258–59; Eaton's rift with, 169, 243–44, 292–93, 370n33; family dwellings of, 5, 266; family members of, 1915–1921, 374n31; geology interest of, 17, 256; at Highway opening, 297–98; in human interest stories, 226–27, 243; as independent contractor, 35, 37, 338n12; insomnia of, 211; inventions/innovations of, 45, 138, 168, 256; lasting notoriety of, 383n18; in last years, 328–30; in logging accident, 11; marriage to Lillie Ferguson, 5, 42–43; and mayoral prospects, 230–31, 233–34; Memorial Fountain to, 23; as movie actor, 279; naturalization of, 37; odd jobs of, 11, 17; on Otis, 206–7; papers of, 111, 114, 266; Parkinson's disease of, 381n37; Perry's influence on, 28, 46–47; Pittsburgh to Los Angeles trip of, 12–13; in professional associations, 83, 279, 349n30; reading choices of, 17, 42, 339n9; at Rowland's breakfast, 58, 341n22; Sespe Creek project of, 36; vacations of, 154, 189, 315–16
Mulholland, William, character traits of, 5; alertness, 41, 359n14; autocratic/domineering, 230–31; avid reader, 32, 42, 339n9; bluntness, 84–85, 120, 211, 345n22, 352n18, 354n11; clarity of purpose, 301; discretion, 33; fairmindedness, 64–65; frugality, 272; hygiene notions, 66; prodigious memory, 64, 177; public speaking disinclination, 150

Mulholland, William, as Chief of Owens
River project: at Agricultural Park
festivities, 220–21; at AIB hearing,
222–23, 367n30; annual reports of,
146–47, 158, 169–70, 191, 197, 201,
219; aqueduct map of, 259, 372n23;
at aqueduct opening, 231, 243, 245–
46, 247; aqueduct tours of, 161–62,
192–94, 199–200, 239–40; and board
of public works, 157–58; in bond campaign, 150, 152–53; on civil service
requirements, 162–63; on completion
date, 179–80, 182, 187, 189, 197,
201, 235; confirmed appointment of,
134–35; on earthquake safety, 130–
31; on Eaton's land purchases, 123–
24, 169, 352n21; enemies' attacks on,
202–3, 205–7, 237–38, 368n18; grand
jury's endorsement of, 139–40; and
Harper's subversion, 146, 147–48; on
high line, 218, 221–22, 224, 229–30,
234; investigatory trips of, 105, 110–
11, 115, 136–37, 348n13, 355n19;
on Jawbone digging, 164–65; on labor
recruitment schemes, 156; labor system
of, 166–67, 177, 360n17; Long Valley
dam plans of, 272, 292, 376n16; on
Mathews, 247, 250–51; military
analogy of, 159; at Municipal League
banquet, 120–22, 352n18; at Owens
Valley land hearing, 185–86, 362n5;
pipeline route of, 137, 139, 355–
56n20; on post office locations, 165–
66, 360n15; in preliminary construction phase, 144; recruitment of
engineers by, 127, 131–32, 135, 136,
138–39; salary of, 181, 250, 253;
on San Fernando Valley land grab,
178, 211; on Spilman's *Conspiracy*,
214–15; on surplus water distribution,
194–95, 200–201, 206, 218, 224,
226; at *Times* libel trial, 223–24,
367n32; at U.S. Congressional hearing, 132–33, 354nn11,12; on water
quality, 118, 149–50, 254, 256–58,
351n14, 372n19
Mulholland, William, as city water
superintendent: abandonment of zanja
system by, 18, 93; on annexations, 94;
appointment of, 80, 90; Boulder Dam
campaign of, 279, 280–81, 282, 283–
84, 294–95, 301–2, 305, 308, 316–17;
city focus of, 271–72, 375n8; and
Cryer incident, 289–90; and dynamiting incidents, 261–63, 287, 288,
308, 312–13; on hydroelectric power,
277–78; improvement projects of, 82,

86, 90, 101, 102–3, 137–38, 138, 179,
259, 344–45n16, 356n21; irrigation
patrols of, 102; land purchase policy
of, 169, 290, 300–301, 314–15, 317–
18; meter system of, 82, 83–85, 103;
and municipal power issue, 186, 261,
264, 265–66, 276–77, 373n27; at new
Water and Power Department, 327;
1902 water condition summary of,
345n26; on oil refinery threat, 91–92;
Owens Valley peace tour of, 290–93;
on Saint Francis Dam collapse, 319,
322, 323, 325, 326–27, 328; salary of,
81; Spilman's attack on, 148–49, 150,
214–15; on water pressure demands,
90–91; on water shortages, 83, 84,
87, 101–2, 112, 135, 349–50n1
Mulholland, William, at Water Company: as deputy zanjero, 23–24, 25;
gold watch for, 42; and main tunnel
crisis, 68–69, 342n17; promotions
of, 30, 32, 37–38; in purchase offer
negotiations, 76–77; on rate increase,
70–71; San Joaquin Valley trip of,
72, 343n27; tunnel/pipeline projects
of, 35, 37, 39–40, 43, 49, 54, 57; at
water arbitration hearings, 62, 64–65,
67; on Water Company policies,
58–59, 62
Mulholland, William Bodine (Mulholland's nephew), 33, 327
Mulholland, William Perry (Mulholland's son), 234, 352n21, 361n8;
birth of, 43; on Eaton, 370n33; hand
tremors of, 381n37; high school gradu-
ation of, 221; marriage to Addie Haas,
374n31; at Panama Canal, 315–16;
ranch of, 328; on trips with Mulholland, 91, 154
Mulholland Dam (*formerly* Weid Canyon
Dam), 281, 282, 289, 302, 325–26,
383n13
Mulholland Highway, 280, 296, 297–98,
376n25
Municipal Affairs (magazine), 180
Municipal League: and Harper's election,
141–42; on municipal power, 260; and
Owens River project, 120–22, 352n18
The Municipal News, 213–14
Municipal power: bond campaigns for,
186, 234–35, 252, 260–61, 278–79,
286, 290, 378n10; Craig lawsuit and,
281, 376–77n27; distribution issue of,
250; divisive stands on, 196–97, 252,
260, 265, 364n1, 371n7; newspapers'
treatment of, 234–35, 276–77, 280,
373n27; 1936 realization of, 265; and

Water and Power Act campaign, 276.
  See also Hydroelectric power
Municipal waterworks: city's proposals
  for, in 1890s, 51–52, 53–54; Eaton's
  support of, 51, 66, 69–70, 71–72, 73,
  108, 343n30; Lippincott on, 108; and
  McCartney bill, 142, 144; Mulholland's support of, 59–60; 1901 bond
  election on, 77, 78–79; opposition to,
  78, 113, 115–16, 117, 343n7, 351n9.
  See also Water Department
Mushet, W. C., 144, 147, 179, 203
Myers (city auditor), 369n22

Nadeau, Remi, xiii, 351n10
Narrows, the, 82, 215, 253
National Bank of California (Los
  Angeles), 44
National Geological Survey, 107, 108,
  349n19
National Reclamation Service. *See* U.S.
  Reclamation Service
Natural Soda Products Company, 229,
  242–43
Neenach break (1917), 262, 373n29
Nelson, W. M., 357n8
Nevada-California Power Company, 266
Newberry, John R., 343n7
Newell, Frederick H., 108, 120, 131,
  354n12; at American Forestry Service
  conference, 68; and Otis, 114; and
  Owens Valley project, 106, 108, 109,
  110–11, 127, 128, 136; San Joaquin
  Valley expedition of, 72, 343n27
Newmark, Harris, 365n15
New York Life Insurance Company, 188
New York Times, 4, 247–48
Noel, P. D., 280
Nofziger, Frank, 89
Nordskog, Andrae, 380–81n29
Norris, George N., 280
Northridge (*formerly* Zelzah), 259
Norton, John, 184

O'Connell, Daniel, 7
O'Connell School (Dublin), 8–9
Oil, 91–92, 277, 376n20
Olmstead, Frank L., 67, 70, 73, 108,
  127, 129
Olvera Street plaza, 18
O'Melveny, Henry, xvi, 65, 90, 371n8;
  and Dominguez Rancho, 187, 231;
  and Eaton, 169, 349n25; and Lippin-
  cott, 110; Mulholland's social ties to,
  82–83, 189; rainfall records of, 73, 99
Orr, Mira E., 129, 136
Orton, Daisy Shaw, 322–23, 383n8

Orton, Lucius R., 322–23
Orton, Raymond, 383n8
Osgood, J. A., 344n13
O'Shaughnessy, M. M., 276
Ostrom, Vincent, xiii–xiv, 340n2,
  341n15
Otis, Harrison Gray, xv, 88, 225; at
  aqueduct opening, 244; and Chaffee's
  appointment, 159–60, 358n3; and
  Earl, 201, 364n9; Henderson's suit
  against, 223–24, 367n32; on high line,
  234; home of, 98; land syndicates of,
  97, 98, 285, 350n4; Mulholland on,
  206–7; on municipal power, 234,
  252; in newspaper rivalries, 116; at
  Rowland's breakfast, 58; in Spanish-
  American War, 62; in Steffens's
  experiment, 204
Outland, Charles, 382n4
Owens Lake, soda content of, 242–43
Owens River Canal Company, 273, 274
Owens River project: accounting system
  for, 147, 357n8; AIB's investigation of,
  207–8, 209–10, 212, 222–23, 224–25,
  367n30; announcement of, 116–17,
  351n10, 355n19; annual reports on,
  146–47, 158, 169–70, 191, 197, 201,
  219; cement needs of, 131–32, 144,
  157; city auditor's report on, 238–
  39, 369n22; city council's role in,
  119, 134–35, 146–48; civil service
  employees on, 156, 162–63; cost
  estimates of, 127, 139, 238; earthquake safety of, 130–31; equipment/
  machinery for, 168; failed rock siphon
  of, 235–36; fatal accidents on, 220,
  221, 229; and faulty construction
  rumors, 191, 363n18; funding difficulties of, 158, 164, 187, 188–89,
  204, 211, 362n13; grand jury's
  approval of, 139–40; Harriman's
  attacks on, 202–3, 205–6, 207; hydroelectric power from, 139, 140, 186,
  196–97; inspection tours of, 192–94,
  239–40; Interior's decision on, 126–
  27; as irrigation resource, 132–34;
  Jawbone Division of, 164–66; labor
  problems on, 189, 190–91, 197–98;
  labor system of, 166–67, 177, 190,
  198, 360n17; and McCartney bill,
  142, 144; medical department for,
  162, 167, 363n17; mules for, 168,
  174–76, 219, 228–29; Municipal
  League banquet for, 120–22, 352n18;
  1909 progress on, 171, 179–80, 181–
  82; preliminary construction of, 144;
  private opposition to, 117–20, 148–

Owens River project (*continued*)
49, 150, 214–15, 351nn14,16;
recruitment of engineers for, 127,
131–32, 135, 136, 138–39, 145;
route of pipeline for, 137, 355–56n20;
rumors of, in *Examiner,* 112, 349–
50n1; tunnel drilling in, 161–62, 176,
181–82. *See also* Aqueduct bonds;
Aqueduct distribution system; Los
Angeles Aqueduct; Workers, aqueduct
Owens River water: alarmist report on,
254–55, 371n14; Muir on, 121, 150–
51; Mulholland on, 118, 149–50, 254,
258, 351n14, 372n19; trial on purity
of, 256–58
Owens Valley: and Alabama Gates incident, 295–97; California governor
in, 363n20; city's inspection tour of,
128–30; Cryer's response to, 289–90;
and dynamiting incidents, 287–88,
289, 308, 312–13, 380n22; earthquake in, 261–62; Eaton's interest in,
30–31, 82, 92, 105, 106–7, 113, 115,
122–25, 169, 348n13, 349n25; federal
government's interest in, 106, 107,
109, 110–11, 349n18; Ku Klux Klan
in, 285, 377n7; land purchase controversy in, 243–44, 274–75, 285–86,
290, 299–301, 305–9, 310–11, 317–
18, 380n14, 382n42; Long Valley dam
issue of, 240, 272, 273–74, 275, 287,
292, 376n16; McClure report on, 296,
299, 301; Mulholland's investigations
in, 105, 110–11, 115, 136–37, 348n13,
355n19; Mulholland's peace tour to,
290–93; orchards proposal for, 294,
295; proposed annexation of, 292;
reaction of, to aqueduct, 122–24, 185,
362n5; reparation demands by, 297,
300, 312; road conditions in, 346n10;
water rights issue in, 241, 242–43,
268, 270–71, 274; well drilling in,
264, 306
Owens Valley: *Where the Trail of the
Wrecker Runs* (Faulkner), 312
Owens Valley Defense Association, 242
The Owens Valley Dispute (Kinsey), 312
Owens Valley Herald, 270, 274, 285,
293, 295, 311–12, 315
Owens Valley Irrigation District, 92,
106–7; costs of, to city, 311; formation of, 273, 274
Owens Valley Property Owners
Protective Association, 273, 275, 285,
312
Owenyo, silver spike ceremony at, 191–
92, 363n20

Pacific Bank, 96–97
Pacific Electric Railway, 45
Pacific Outlook (magazine), 180
Page, Sherman, 343n7
Panama Canal, 138, 241, 315–16
Panama-Pacific Exposition (1915–1916),
259
Panic of 1907, 156, 158, 164
Pardee, George C., 109, 115, 144, 244
Parker, F. W., 344n13
Parker, O. K., 67, 109
Pasadena, 29, 76–77, 182, 195, 216,
337–38n10
Patterson, Kermit, 382n4
Patterson, W. C., 349n30
Peekskill Aqueduct (New York City),
153
Pendleton Eminent Domain Bill, 115
People's Party, 167
Perry, Florence, 47
Perry, Mamie, 47
Perry, William Hayes, 80; background
of, 28; and Eaton, 35; and Mulhol-
land, 28, 42, 46–47; Sespe Creek
project of, 36, 338–39n13; sewer line
bid of, 338n12; social status of, 47,
340n17, 349n17; Water Company
position of, 21, 46, 338n7; on Water
Company's value, 51, 78
Perry, Woodworth & Co., 28
Pessell, George D., 90
Phelan, James, 283
Phillips, J. E., 331
Phillips, Robert V., 331, 346n1, 347–
48n1, 371n17, 376n16
Phoenix Water Company, 96
Pico, Pio, 62
Pinchot, Gifford, 68, 110, 133, 179,
354n12
Pipeline, cast iron, 29, 337–38n10
Pirtle, John A., 55–57
Pirtle Cut, 56–57
Piru Creek, 117
Pomeroy, A. E., 53, 54, 152. *See also*
Hooker and Pomeroy case
Porcupine (weekly newspaper), 15, 31,
46, 54, 341n13
Porter, Benjamin F., 40, 98–99, 339n5
Porter, George K., 98–99
Porter Land and Water Company, 339n5
Potts, J. W., 55
Powell, John Wesley, 349n19
Power bond elections: of 1910, 186; of
1913, 234–35; of 1914, 252; of 1917,
260–61; of 1919, 261; of 1923, 278–
79; of 1924, 286, 290, 378n10. *See
also* Municipal power

Power right-of-way bill, 264, 265–66, 272, 273–74, 375n9

Powers, Luther Milton, 101, 211; on bacteria count, 93; and Ethel Leonard, 255; and oil refinery investigation, 91–92; on Owens River project, 179; public health contributions of, 66, 342n11

Progressives (Good Government), 126; on antipicketing ordinance, 189; on Chaffee's appointment, 160; on Mojave perils, 173; and Mulholland's mayoral prospects, 230–31, 233–34, 368–69n13; on municipal power, 196–97; political allies of, 210; and Governor Richardson, 277; and Mayor Rose, 369n21; on surplus waters issue, 213; victorious candidates of, 184, 201; and water commission upheaval, 183–84, 362n2

Providencia Rancho Company, 53

Public health, 14, 66, 93, 100, 342n11

Public service commission (formerly water commission): aqueduct bureau under, 236; establishment of, 199; on McClure Report, 299; 1912 turnover in, 213, 219; Owens Valley peace tour of, 291–93; Owens Valley policy decisions of, 294; Rose's overhaul of, 238, 369n21; suit against Times by, 223–24; on surplus water issue, 200–201, 216, 218–19; Woodman's audit of, 263. See also Water commission

Quinton, John H., 200

Railways: civilizing impact of, 15; Eaton's ventures in, 45, 89; from Los Angeles to Hollywood, 97–98; Sherman's ventures in, 45, 96–98; water sprinkling duty of, 99, 347n26. See also Southern Pacific Railroad

Rainfall: damage to aqueduct from, 251, 303; in 1883–1884, 35; in 1887, 38; in 1898–1904, 347–48n1; in 1903–1904, 99, 100; in 1919, 263–64; O'Melveny's records of, 73, 99

Ramirez, Juan R., 58

Rancho Bartolo Water Company, 115

Rancho El Tejon, 203

Reaburn, DeWitt L., 232, 245, 297–98

Read, George, 154, 344n13

Reagan Report, 251, 275

Reavis, W. S., 344n13

Red Rock Canyon, 165, 176

Reisner, Marc, xiv

Republican Party, 63, 88

Reservoir No. 4. See Beaudry's High Reservoir

The Resources of California (Hittell), 18

Ricardo settlement, 165–66

Richardson, Friend, 277, 296

Ricken Tunnel (Switzerland), 176

Rickey, Thomas B., 109, 123, 124

Rickey Ranch (later Eaton Land and Cattle Company), 109, 123, 124, 272. See also Eaton Land and Cattle Company

Rindge, Frederick, 99, 113

Rinehart, Robert E., 191, 363n19

Riparian rights, doctrine of, 52

Risdon Iron and Locomotive Works (San Francisco), 91, 102

Rivers in the Desert (Davis), xvi–xvii

Rochester, New York Times-Union, 280

Rogers, Earl, 92

Rogers, J. David, 325, 326, 370n1, 382n4

Rogers, Ralph, 49

Roosevelt, Franklin D., 352n21

Roosevelt, Theodore, 79, 98, 133, 353–54n10

Root, Erastus, 152

Rose, Henry Howard, 251; at aqueduct opening, 241, 246; final inspection tour of, 240; 1913 mayoral election of, 236; overhaul of city commissions by, 238, 369n21, 370n2; and Owens Valley project, 241, 242

Ross (U.S. Circuit Court judge), 347n20

Rowell, Chester, 378n17

Rowena Reservoir, 43

Rowland, William, 58, 192–93

Royal British Mail, 6–7

Royal British Navy, 10

Ryan, A. W., 344n13

Sacramento Bee, 280

Sacramento Union, 312

Saint Francis Dam, 313; collapse of, 319, 320–21; construction methods for, 320, 382n4; geology of site for, 320

Saint Francis Dam disaster, 4; city's response to, 323–24; Coroner's inquest into, 324–25; lives lost from, 319, 321; Mulholland's reaction to, 319, 322, 323, 325, 326–27, 328; possible causes of, 320, 324, 325, 326, 382n4; survivor's letter on, 322–23, 383n8

Salaries/wages: of aqueduct workers, 174, 197–98; and bonuses, 166, 177, 190, 198, 360n17; of city zanjero, 26; of Lippincott, 183, 236; of Matthews,

Salaries/wages (*continued*)
357n3; of Mulholland, 35, 37, 81,
181, 250, 253, 327; of water commissioners, 87; of Water Company
workers, 26, 35, 37
Saloons, 65–66, 216
Sand Canyon siphon, 235–36, 238, 240
*San Diego v. the San Diego and Los
Angeles Railroad Company*, 96,
347n20
San Fernando (city), 98
San Fernando Dam, 201, 211
San Fernando Mission Land Company,
211
San Fernando Tunnel, 98
San Fernando Valley: annexation of, 239,
258, 259; aqueduct's terminus in, 206,
207; city's suit against, 104; city's
water rights in, 182; Craig lawsuit for,
281, 376n27; first nighttime illumination in, 244; land grab issue in, 98–99,
178, 211; Lippincott's surveys of, 67,
71; Longyear's role in, 285; 1919
agricultural earnings in, 266; 1906
water usage in, 135; and surplus water
issue, 200–201, 202, 203, 206, 216;
watershed of, 214–15
San Fernando Valley Water Company, 40
San Francisco: municipal power issue in,
283; 1906 earthquake in, 126, 130–
31; soup kitchens of, 180–81; in water
rights dispute, 268; waterworks
project in, 171–72
San Francisco Call, 286–87
San Francisco Chronicle, 135, 247
San Francisco Examiner, 97, 116,
355n19
San Francisquito Canyon, 282; power
plant site at, 157, 186, 212, 260, 263,
279; Saint Francis Dam site at, 320,
333; tunnel building in, 249
San Francisquito Creek, 320
San Gabriel Valley, 16, 216, 226
San Joaquin Valley, 72, 276, 280,
343n27
San Juan-by-the-Sea, 44–45
Sanky (term), 337n8
San Pedro, 216
*Santa Ana Water Company v. the Town
of San Buenaventura*, 347n20
Santa Clara River, 113
Santa Fe Railroad, 89, 369n22
Santa Monica, 216
Santa Paula, 321, 324
Sartori, J. F., 98
Saturday Night (periodical), 288
Sauder, John, xiv

Sawyer, R. H., 144
Scattergood, Ezra F., 145, 165, 181, 186,
253; collapse of, 278; and Colorado
River project, 271, 283; criticism of,
263, 375n8; on dynamiting incident,
313; and municipal power issue, 196,
279, 280, 364n11, 373n27; power
bureau role of, 199, 242; *Record*'s
cartoon of, 261; at Water and Power
Department, 327
Schuyler, James D., 108, 114, 339n5;
engineering skills of, 135, 354–55n15;
and Owens River project, 136–37,
139–40
Sebastian, C. E., 259, 260
Seely, Joseph, 107
Sepulveda, Ygnacio, 58
Sespe Land and Water Company, 36,
338–39n13
Shattuck, E. S., 180–81
Shaw, George Bernard, 8
Shaw, Lucien, 55
Sheep Mountain (Wyoming), 303
Shenk, John W., 226, 236, 368–69n13,
369n18
Sherman, Moses Hazeltine, 45, 89;
business background of, 95–97,
347n20; and Porter Ranch deal, 98–
99; removed from water board, 178,
183–84
Sherman, William Tecumseh, 16, 96
Shoemaker, Eve H., 307
Shuey, George, 144, 273
Sierra Club, 268, 280
Silver, Herman, 72, 83–84, 85, 138,
342n10, 344n14
Silver Lake Power and Irrigation Com-
pany, 160–61, 242, 359n5
Silver Lake Reservoir, 20, 138, 156
Simpson Auditorium rally, 151–52
Siphons, rock versus steel, 235–36
Sisters of Charity, 14
Sitton, Tom, 265, 369n21
Slauson, James, 43
Sleeth, Dana, 373–74n30
Smallpox epidemic, 14
Smith, J. Waldo, 177, 188, 251–52
Smith, Sylvester C., 132
Smythe, William E., 107
Snow Steam Pump Company (Buffalo,
New York), 102
Snyder, Meredith P., 65, 72, 238, 261,
342n10; at Bakersfield banquet, 276;
on Lippincott, 110; on Los Angeles-
to-Hollywood railway, 98; municipal
appointments by, 88–89, 95; and mu-
nicipal waterworks, 79, 80

Socialist Party, 79; AIB role of, 208, 209, 222, 237; anti-aqueduct stance of, 202–3, 364–65n12; on municipal power, 252; political allies of, 201–2, 210, 371n7
"Some of the Penalties of Rapid Growth in Los Angeles" (Mulholland), 266
Southern California Edison Company. See Edison Electric Company
Southern California Irrigation Congress (1905), 114
Southern California water supply, 269 fig.
Southern Pacific Railroad, 96; aqueduct's contract with, 165, 239, 369n22; civilizing impact of, 15; freight rates of, 156, 157, 161; silver spike ceremony of, 191–92, 363n20; wages on, 174; Water Company's ties to, 61
Southern Sierra Power Company, 266
South Pasadena, 200
Spalding, W. A., 337n12, 340–41n8, 341n2
Spanish-American War (1898), 62
Spectator (journal), 188
Spilman, William T., 203; on meter system, 345n24; Mulholland's response to, 149–50, 214–15; on Owens River project, 148–49, 214, 357n11
Spilman Suburban Water Company, 148
Spreckels, Rudolph, 276, 277
Spring Valley Water Company (San Francisco), 64, 271, 350n8, 366–67n26
Stafford, Harry, 82, 356n27
Standard Oil Company, 81
Steadman, J. J., 221
Stearns, Frederick P., 135, 136–37, 138, 139–40, 195
Steffens, Lincoln, 60, 204, 365n17
Stegner, Wallace, xiv
Steinmetz, Charles, 277–78
Stephens, William D., 184, 185, 244
Stevenson, A. P., 344n13
Storrow, Samuel, 366–67n26
"Stream Characteristics of Southern California" (Lippincott), 114
Strikes, 201; miners', 189, 190–91, 197–98; railway, 98
Sullivan, Mark, xv–xvi
Summers, Charlie, 309
Sunset Club, 83, 170, 266, 349n30
Surplus waters. See Aqueduct distribution system

Sweetwater Dam (Oregon), 136
Swing, Phil, 283, 284, 290
Swing-Johnson bill, 282, 283, 291, 307, 316–17, 325
Symon brothers, 243–44
Symons, William, 274, 286, 290

Taft, William Howard, 168, 169, 205
Taney, J. S., 232
Taylor, Raymond G., 167, 359n10, 363n17
Teague, Charles Collins, 323
Teddy's Terrors (marching group), 98
Tehachapi, 165; cement plant at, 157, 170, 215
Terminal Island Water Company, 216
Tess of the Storm Country (film), 279
Third Street Tunnel, 70
Timmons, Joseph, 283, 304, 376n21
Tinemaha Dam, 309, 316, 320, 381n39
Toll, Charles H., 71, 82, 344n14
Tonopah Daily News, 374–75n5
Topoc Dam project, 283
Transit companies. See Railways
Trolley cars, 45, 96
Tropico land scheme, 148
Truman, Benjamin, xv, 58
Tujunga Wash. See Big Tujunga Wash
Tunnel drilling: broken records in, 176, 361n10; at Buena Vista infiltration gallery, 86; at Elizabeth Lake, 161–62, 163, 168, 176; at Jawbone, 176, 181–82
Tunnel 17-M (Red Rock Canyon), 176
Turner, Joel H., 19
Typhoid fever, 93, 117

Union Consolidated Refining Company, 91–92
Union Hollywood Water Company, 94
Union Labor News, 78
Union League Club, 44
Unions. See Labor, organized
University of California at Berkeley, 4, 252
U.S. Congress: and Boulder Dam testimony, 283–84; and Flint-McLachlan Bill, 132–34, 354n12
U.S. Department of Agriculture, 99
U.S. Geological Survey, 107, 108, 349n19
U.S. Land Office hearing (1910), 185, 362n5
U.S. Reclamation Service: Duryea with, 131–32; financial difficulties of, 111; Lippincott with, 105–6, 113–14, 127–28, 350n5; and Otis, 350n4;

U.S. Reclamation Service (*continued*)
Owens Valley interests of, 92, 106,
107, 109, 110–11, 349n18
U.S. Supreme Court decision, 71–72

The Valley of Broken Hearts (Kunze),
286–87, 312
Van Norman, Bessie, 145–46, 231
Van Norman, Harvey, xvi, 173, 189,
224, 264, 303; at aqueduct's opening,
245; background of, 145; and Boulder
Dam project, 305, 316; in car accident,
313; and dam disaster, 319; final
inspection tour of, 240; and Little
Lake blowout, 262; mule teams of,
175, 228, 361n8; in Owens Valley
negotiations, 274, 291, 292, 294, 295,
307, 311, 317–18; steel siphon project
of, 236; at Water and Power Depart-
ment, 327
Van Nuys, 201
Variel, R. H. F., 343n7
Vasquez, Tiburcio, 16, 58, 192
Veritas letters (Spilman), 148, 149, 214,
357n11; Mulholland's response to,
149–50
Vermilyea, S. E., 241
Vernon, 55–56, 341n15
*Vernon Irrigation Company v. City of
Los Angeles,* 55–56
Victorio (Apache chief), 17
*Vision or Villainy: Origins of the Owens
Valley–Los Angeles Water Controversy*
(Hoffman), xiv
Vollmer, B. A., 147
Vroman, J. P., 90, 344n13

Wages. *See* Salaries/wages
Walcott, Charles D., 133, 354n12
Waldron, David V., 78, 79–80, 343n7
Waldron, S. A., 78
Wallace, A. J., 220
Wall Street Journal, 325
Walton, John, xiv
Warner, Charles W., 210; aqueduct
investigation by, 212, 213, 222, 223,
225, 367n30
Warren, George B., 295, 309, 375n6
Washburn, W. J., 354nn12,15
Washington Park (*later* Chutes Park),
343n7
*Water and Politics: A Study of Water
Policies and Administration in the
Development of Los Angeles*
(Ostrom), xiii–xiv
Water and Power (Kahrl), xiv
Water and the West (Hundley), xiv

Water bonds: Eaton's campaign for,
69–70; funding payments on, 101;
1901 election on, 77, 78–79; ruled
invalid, 76; sale of, 80; Waldron's
litigation against, 79–80, 343n10.
See also Municipal waterworks
Water Canyon, 165
Water commission (*later* public service
commission): announcement of
aqueduct by, 116; financial record
of, 199; *Herald* on, 95; membership
of, 81, 88–89, 344n14, 346n1; 1910
upheaval in, 183–84; 1911 reorganization of, 199; Owens Valley tour of,
128–30; salaries of, 87, 89; on serving
outlying areas, 93–94; Water Department appointments by, 90. *See also*
Public service commission
Water Company: asking price of, 76, 77;
city council's ties to, 21, 46; city's
lawsuits against, 48, 49, 75, 108;
city's purchase of, 76–80; and Crystal
Springs controversy, 24, 49, 61–62,
63, 64–65, 67–68, 341n2; directors
of, 28, 338n7; Eaton's criticism of, 35,
37, 61, 64, 71; estimated revenues of,
78; estimated value of, 67; fire hydrants
of, 34, 58–59, 67, 337–38n10; leased
water rights of, 20–22, 61, 337n11;
Mulholland on, 58–59, 76–77; new
headquarters for, 41; personnel of,
26, 338n7; primitive equipment of,
26, 33; quality of water from, 27–28,
31, 39, 54; reservoir projects of, 22,
57; retained employees from, 344n13;
salaries at, 26, 35, 37; sale of, to Indianapolis syndicate, 51, 52–53; in water
rates battles, 34, 59, 63, 70–71, 72;
zanjero's clashes with, 26–27, 76
Water Department: first commissioners
of, 81, 88–89, 344n14, 346n1; funds
from, for aqueduct, 158; headquarters
of, 81; improvements/reforms by, 82,
344n16; private schemes against, 113,
115–16, 117, 351n9; rates of, 87, 95,
266, 268; revenues of, 87, 95. *See
also* Municipal waterworks; Water
commission
Water pressure demands, 90–91, 101,
346n6
Water rates: Water Company's battles
over, 34, 59, 63, 70–71, 72; of Water
Department, 87, 95, 266, 268
The Water Seekers (Nadeau), xiii
"The Water Steal" (flier), 78
"The Water Supply of Southern
California" (Mulholland), 111

"Water Waste" (Mulholland), 114
Watson, C. Percy, 313
Watt, R. S., 152
Watterson, George, 256, 273–74, 290, 306, 314, 316
Watterson, Mark Q., 256, 314, 316
Watterson, Wilfred W., 291; and Eaton's land deal, 307, 308–9, 310–11; fraud trial of, 314, 316; and Longyear sale, 305–6; in water rights dispute, 229, 256, 292, 296–97
Weid, Ivar, 302
Weid Canyon Dam. See Mulholland Dam
Wellborn, Charles, 216, 218
Western Federation of Miners, 190, 197
Western Times and Water Wars (Walton), xiv
West Los Angeles Water Company, 56–57
West Side Water Company, 67, 78, 110, 352–53n26
Weymouth, Frank, 282, 305, 327
Wheeler, Fred, 236–37, 258, 286, 371n7
"Whistling Dick" (mule skinner), 175–76, 361n8
White, Stephen M., 58, 65
White Steamer automobiles, 129–30, 136
Whitley, H. J., 285, 375n8
Whitley Heights (Hollywood), 97–98
Whitsett, William Paul, 272, 292
Wicks, Moses L., 49, 338n6
Widney, Erwin W., 173
Widney, R. M., 151–52
Wiggins, Frank, 112, 236
Wilde, Oscar, 8
Willard, Charles Dwight, xvi, 346n3, 349nn25,30; death of, 251; Mulholland to, on completion date, 180; Mulholland to, on mayoralty, 230–31; as water commissioner, 89–90
Willcocks, Sir William, 253
William Mulholland: A Forgotten Forefather (Matson), xvi
William Mulholland Memorial Fountain, 23
Wilson (mule skinner), 175
Wilson, Ben C., 183

Wilson, John, 211
Wilson, Stanley, 202
Wilson, Woodrow, 226
Wintz, Homer, 372n19
Wintz, Philip, 36, 191, 233
Woodard, J. H., 51, 52, 53
Woodman, Frederic Thomas, 260, 262–63
Woolen Ditch Dam. See Beaudry's High Reservoir
Work, Hubert, 282–83
Workers, aqueduct: bonus system of, 166–67, 177, 190, 198, 360n17; civil service requirements of, 162–63; with families, 167–68; labor unrest of, 186–87, 189–91; mail service for, 165–66; meals for, 180–81, 185–86, 189, 190, 212, 363n17; medical care for, 162; Mojave's lure for, 172–74; number of, 171, 174, 181, 219; potable water for, 165; recruitment of, 156; relocation of, 232–33; wages of, 174, 197–98. See also Engineers
Workman, Boyle, 78, 238
Workman, William, 39, 40, 58, 80, 343n12
Works, John D., 254, 257–58, 378n11
Wright, C. C., 83–84, 343n7
Wright, Harold Bell, 328
Wright Irrigation Act, 83

Yaw, Ellen Beach, 244
Yoakum, M. G., 178
Young, C. C., 312, 313, 323, 324
Young, T. W., 128, 129, 130, 172
Yuma reclamation project, 109, 111

Zanja (term), 337n8; anglicization of, 31
Zanja Madre (Mother Ditch), 18, 69
Zanja Madre Tunnel, 35
Zanja system: abandonment of, 18, 93; described, 18; equipment of, 26; headed by Jenkins, 26–27; low-cost water from, 78, 86, 343n7; management of, 19
Zanjero (water steward), 19, 26–27, 31, 76
Zelzah (now Northridge), 259
Zombro, Sumter F., 310, 314

Compositor: Integrated Composition Systems
Text: 10/13 Sabon
Display: Bodoni